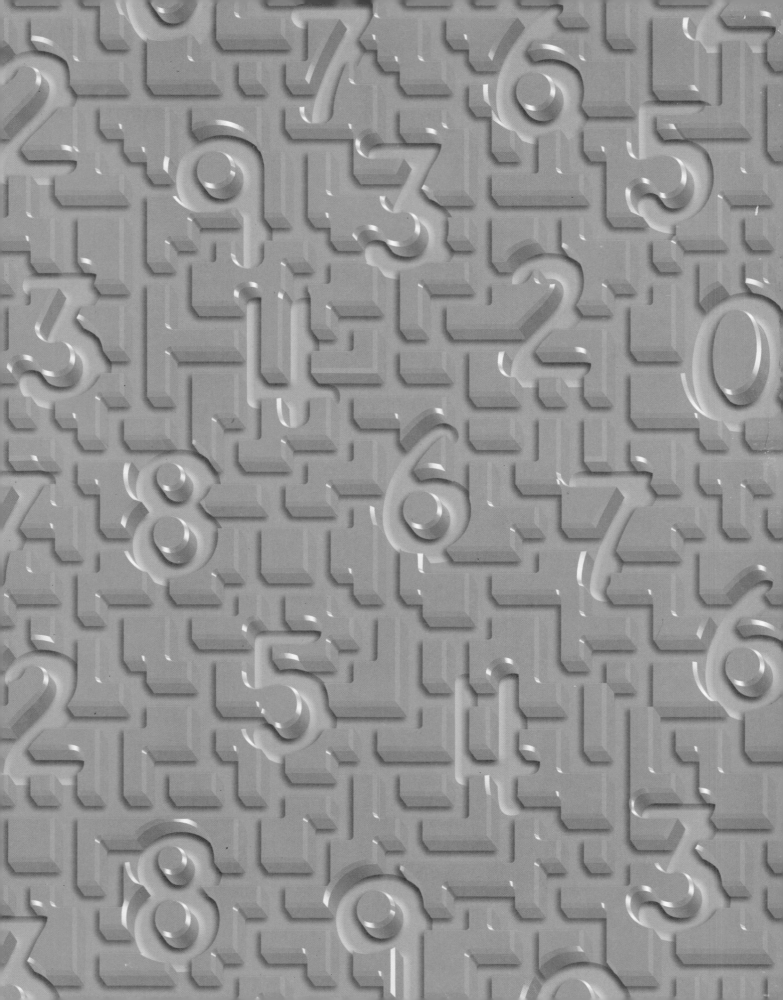

# HARCOURT

# Math

## FLORIDA EDITION

 **Harcourt**

Orlando   Austin   Chicago   New York   Toronto   London   San Diego

Visit *The Learning Site!*
**www.harcourtschool.com**

Grateful acknowledgment is made to National Audubon Society for permission to reprint the map from *Great Backyard Bird Count 2002* by BirdSource (http://www.birdsource.org). Copyright 2002.

Printed in the United States of America

ISBN 0-15-336697-4

1 2 3 4 5 6 7 8 9 10 048 10 09 08 07 06 05 04 03

## Senior Author
**Evan M. Maletsky**
*Professor of Mathematics*
Montclair State University
Upper Montclair, New Jersey

## Mathematics Advisor
**Richard Askey**
*Professor of Mathematics*
University of Wisconsin
Madison, Wisconsin

## Authors

**Angela Giglio Andrews**
*Math Teacher, Scott School*
Naperville District #203
Naperville, Illinois

**Jennie M. Bennett**
*Instructional Mathematics Supervisor*
Houston Independent School District
Houston, Texas

**Grace M. Burton**
*Professor, Watson School of Education*
University of North Carolina
 at Wilmington
Wilmington, North Carolina

**Lynda A. Luckie**
*Administrator/Math Specialist*
Gwinnett County Public Schools
Lawrenceville, Georgia

**Joyce C. McLeod**
*Visiting Professor*
Rollins College
Winter Park, Florida

**Vicki Newman**
*Classroom Teacher*
McGaugh Elementary School
Los Alamitos Unified School District
Seal Beach, California

**Tom Roby**
*Associate Professor of Mathematics*
California State University
Hayward, California

**Janet K. Scheer**
*Executive Director*
Create A Vision
Foster City, California

## Program Consultants and Specialists

**Janet S. Abbott**
*Mathematics Consultant*
California

**Elsie Babcock**
*Director, Mathematics and
 Science Center
Mathematics Consultant*
Wayne Regional
 Educational Service
 Agency
Wayne, Michigan

**William J. Driscoll**
*Professor of Mathematics*
Department of
 Mathematical Sciences
Central Connecticut State
 University
New Britain, Connecticut

**Lois Harrison-Jones**
*Education and
 Management Consultant*
Dallas, Texas

**Rebecca Valbuena**
*Language Development
 Specialist*
Stanton Elementary School
Glendora, California

# UNIT 1
## CHAPTERS 1-4

# Use Whole Numbers and Decimals

## 1 PLACE VALUE OF WHOLE NUMBERS

## 2 PLACE VALUE OF DECIMALS . . . . . . . . . . . . . . . 20

### 💻 Technology Link

**Harcourt Mega Math:** *Chapter 1, p. 2;*
*Chapter 2, p. 26; Chapter 3, pp. 46, 48;*
*Chapter 4, pp. 67, 72*

**The Harcourt Learning Site:**
www.harcourtschool.com

**Multimedia Math Glossary:**
www.harcourtschool.com/mathglossary

# UNIT 2  Data and Graphing

**Technology Link**

**Harcourt Mega Math:**
*Chapter 5, p. 102*
*Chapter 6, p. 120*

**The Harcourt Learning Site:**
www.harcourtschool.com

**Multimedia Math Glossary:**
www.harcourtschool.com/mathglossary

# UNIT 3
CHAPTERS 7-8

# Multiply Whole Numbers and Decimals

### Technology Link

**Harcourt Mega Math:**
*Chapter 7, p. 153*
*Chapter 8, p. 171*

**The Harcourt Learning Site:**
www.harcourtschool.com

**Multimedia Math Glossary:**
www.harcourtschool.com/mathglossary

# UNIT 4
## CHAPTERS 9-12
# Divide Whole Numbers and Decimals

### Technology Link

**Harcourt Mega Math:**
*Chapter 9, p. 199*
*Chapter 10, p. 213*
*Chapter 11, p. 231*
*Chapter 12, pp. 248, 251, 255*

**The Harcourt Learning Site:**
www.harcourtschool.com

**Multimedia Math Glossary:**
www.harcourtschool.com/mathglossary

# UNIT 5
**CHAPTERS 13-15**

# Number Theory and Fractions

### Technology Link

**Harcourt Mega Math:**
*Chapter 13, p. 277; Chapter 14, p. 303;
Chapter 15, p. 321*

**The Harcourt Learning Site:**
www.harcourtschool.com

**Multimedia Math Glossary:**
www.harcourtschool.com/mathglossary

# 15 FRACTION CONCEPTS ................... 312

## UNIT WRAPUP

# UNIT 6
### CHAPTERS 16-19

# Operations with Fractions

**Technology Link**

**Harcourt Mega Math:**
*Chapter 16, p. 346; Chapter 17, p. 373;*
*Chapter 18, p. 387; Chapter 19, p. 403*

**The Harcourt Learning Site:**
www.harcourtschool.com

**Multimedia Math Glossary:**
www.harcourtschool.com/mathglossary

# UNIT 7    Geometry and Algebra

**Technology Link**

**Harcourt Mega Math:**
*Chapter 20, pp. 443, 447; Chapter 21, pp. 457, 462, 471;
Chapter 22, pp. 481, 484; Chapter 23, pp. 503, 505*

**The Harcourt Learning Site:** www.harcourtschool.com

**Multimedia Math Glossary:**
www.harcourtschool.com/mathglossary

# UNIT 8 Measurement

CHAPTERS 24-27

### Technology Link

**Harcourt Mega Math:**
*Chapter 24, pp. 533, 535*
*Chapter 26, p. 564*
*Chapter 27, p. 593*

**The Harcourt Learning Site:**
www.harcourtschool.com

**Multimedia Math Glossary:**
www.harcourtschool.com/mathglossary

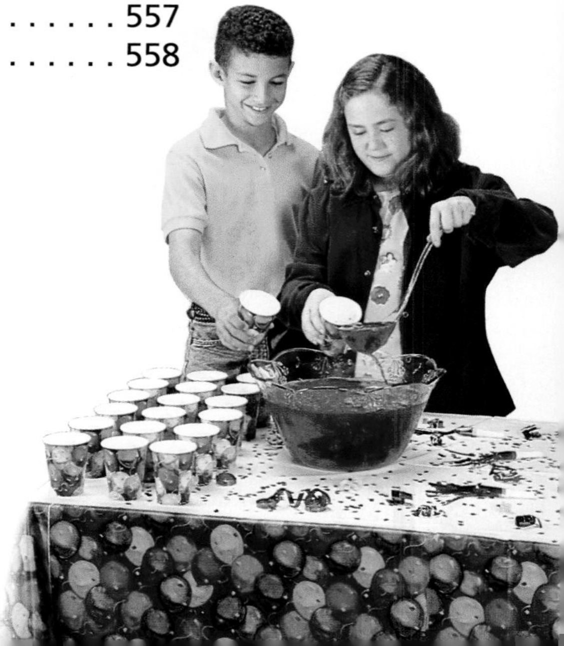

# UNIT 9 Ratio, Percent, and Probability

CHAPTERS 28-30

**Technology Link**

**Harcourt Mega Math:**
*Chapter 29, p. 642*
*Chapter 30, pp. 655, 658*

**The Harcourt Learning Site:**
www.harcourtschool.com

**Multimedia Math Glossary:**
www.harcourtschool.com/mathglossary

# Using Math In
# Florida

▶ ## Building Success Now

◀ You use addition and multiplication to keep score when you play games.

You use computation skills when you earn, save, and spend money. ▼

▲ You use mean, median, mode, and range when you track individual and team sports data.

You will use the mathematics that you learn in **Harcourt Math** every day. The skills you learn will help you **build success** both now and in the future.

# ▶ Building Success for the Future

◀ If you become a computer animator, like these in Orlando, algebra and geometry skills will help you create complex images for animated films.

▲ The space shuttle transports materials to the International Space Station. If you become a scientist, you might use measurement and geometry to help prepare the shuttle for launch at Cape Kennedy.

▲ If you become a building contractor, you will use measurement skills and spatial visualization concepts to construct a house.

**Have a great year and enjoy learning Math!**

# PRACTICE WHAT YOU LEARN

## It's in the Bag

**PROJECT** In each unit of this book, you'll do a project that will help you practice the math skills you've learned. Make the Math Pockets Plus below to hold some of these projects.

### Materials

- 9 paper lunch bags (size 12)
- Clear, wide packaging tape
- Scissors
- Markers, crayons, and color pencils

### Directions

1. Cut off the bottom of each bag. Then open each bag by unfolding the pleats, and lay the bag flat. Tape the bottom of each bag closed to make a pocket. (*Picture A*)

2. Turn down the top of each bag. Cut along each end of the turned-down part, and cut off the bottom flap. Cut off the corners of the top flap, making an envelope-like closing. (*Picture B*)

3. Lay the bags next to each other, and tape them together at the edges. Then fold them accordion-style to make an organizer. (*Picture C*)

4. Decorate and label each bag with the unit number on the flap and the unit title on the pocket. Apply a hook-and-loop fastener to the opening of each bag, if desired.

# SHOW WHAT YOU LEARN

Taking a test is one way to show what you've learned. Being a good test taker is like being a good problem solver. When you answer test questions, you are solving problems.

Each time you take a test, remember to:

- Listen carefully to your teacher's instructions.
- Read all the directions.
- Pay attention to where and how to mark the test.
- Read the problems carefully.
- If you don't understand a problem, read it again.
- Mark or write your answers clearly.
- Answer questions you are sure about first.
- Work quickly but carefully.
- If you finish early, go back and check your work.
- Relax and do the best that you can.

# GETTING READY!
## Practice Addition and Subtraction

You can use mental math strategies and regrouping to find sums and differences.

### *BREAK APART* STRATEGY

Find the sum.
79 + 37

**Think:** 79 = 70 + 9
37 = 30 + 7

70 + 30 = 100    Add the tens.
9 + 7 = 16    Add the ones.
100 + 16 = 116    Add the sums.

So, 79 + 37 = 116.

### *MAKE A TEN* STRATEGY

Find the difference.
285 − 38

**Think:** Add 2 to 38 to get 40.

38 + 2 = 40    Add 2 to 285 to
285 + 2 = 287    adjust the difference.
287 − 40 = 247    Subtract 287 − 40.

So, 285 − 38 = 247.

### REGROUPING IN ADDITION

$$\begin{array}{r} 1\phantom{00} \\ 643 \\ + 95 \\ \hline 738 \end{array}$$

**Think:** Regroup tens as 1 hundred 3 tens.

### REGROUPING IN SUBTRACTION

$$\begin{array}{r} 9\phantom{0} \\ 3\,10\,10 \\ \cancel{400} \\ - 176 \\ \hline 224 \end{array}$$

**Think:** Regroup 4 hundreds as 3 hundreds 9 tens 10 ones.

## ▶ Practice

Find the sum or difference.

**1.**
$$\begin{array}{r} 62 \\ + 18 \\ \hline \end{array}$$

**2.**
$$\begin{array}{r} 75 \\ - 49 \\ \hline \end{array}$$

**3.**
$$\begin{array}{r} 80 \\ - 36 \\ \hline \end{array}$$

**4.**
$$\begin{array}{r} 93 \\ + 25 \\ \hline \end{array}$$

**5.**
$$\begin{array}{r} 73 \\ - 24 \\ \hline \end{array}$$

**6.**
$$\begin{array}{r} 138 \\ + 57 \\ \hline \end{array}$$

**7.**
$$\begin{array}{r} 300 \\ - 124 \\ \hline \end{array}$$

**8.**
$$\begin{array}{r} 419 \\ + 68 \\ \hline \end{array}$$

**9.**
$$\begin{array}{r} 503 \\ - 146 \\ \hline \end{array}$$

**10.**
$$\begin{array}{r} 783 \\ + 544 \\ \hline \end{array}$$

**11.**
$$\begin{array}{r} 250 \\ - 193 \\ \hline \end{array}$$

**12.**
$$\begin{array}{r} 639 \\ + 754 \\ \hline \end{array}$$

**13.**
$$\begin{array}{r} 32 \\ 57 \\ + 28 \\ \hline \end{array}$$

**14.**
$$\begin{array}{r} 42 \\ 68 \\ + 59 \\ \hline \end{array}$$

# Practice Multiplication and Division

You can use multiplication fact families, place value, and regrouping to review multiplication and division.

## EXAMPLES

Use place value and regrouping to find products.

$$
\begin{array}{r}
1 \phantom{0} \\
62 \\
\times\ 47 \\
\hline
434 \\
+\ 2480 \\
\hline
2{,}914
\end{array}
$$

**Think:** Multiply by 7 ones, then by 4 tens, or 40.

$7 \times 62$

$40 \times 62$

Use place value to place the first digit in the quotient.
Then, use the order of division.

$$
\begin{array}{r}
56 \text{ r}3 \\
7)\overline{395} \\
-35 \\
\hline
45 \\
-42 \\
\hline
3
\end{array}
$$

$3 < 7$, so look at the tens.
$39 > 7$, so use 39 tens.
Place the first digit in the tens place.

Divide.
Multiply.
Subtract.
Compare.

## ▶ Practice

Multiply or divide.

| | | |
|---|---|---|
| **1.** $\begin{array}{r}17\\ \times\ 49\end{array}$ | **2.** $\begin{array}{r}67\\ \times\ 15\end{array}$ | **3.** $\begin{array}{r}40\\ \times\ 38\end{array}$ |
| **4.** $\begin{array}{r}66\\ \times\ 24\end{array}$ | **5.** $\begin{array}{r}307\\ \times\ 65\end{array}$ | **6.** $\begin{array}{r}514\\ \times\ 87\end{array}$ |
| **7.** $\begin{array}{r}148\\ \times\ 52\end{array}$ | **8.** $\begin{array}{r}760\\ \times\ 19\end{array}$ | **9.** $\begin{array}{r}114\\ \times\ 23\end{array}$ |

**10.** $5)\overline{79}$  **11.** $4)\overline{83}$  **12.** $6)\overline{78}$

**13.** $7)\overline{294}$  **14.** $9)\overline{470}$  **15.** $8)\overline{809}$

# Place Value of Whole Numbers

Satellite image of North America at night

**FAST FACT** • SOCIAL STUDIES

One person is added to the United States population every 17 seconds. Much of the population lives in just a few areas.

PROBLEM SOLVING Look at the graph. Which two states have about the same populations? List the states in order from the greatest population to the least population.

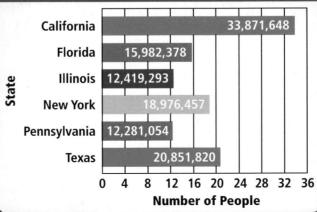

**MOST-POPULATED STATES**

| State | Number of People |
|---|---|
| California | 33,871,648 |
| Florida | 15,982,378 |
| Illinois | 12,419,293 |
| New York | 18,976,457 |
| Pennsylvania | 12,281,054 |
| Texas | 20,851,820 |

0 4 8 12 16 20 24 28 32 36
**Number of People**

# CHECK WHAT YOU KNOW

Use this page to help you review and remember important skills needed for Chapter 1.

## PLACE VALUE

Write the value of the digit 6 in each number.

**1.** 62,980      **2.** 368      **3.** 56,709      **4.** 906

Write the value of the blue digit.

**5.** 560      **6.** 3,072      **7.** 47,092      **8.** 30,561

**9.** 6,257      **10.** 13,348      **11.** 97,812      **12.** 20,465

## READ AND WRITE WHOLE NUMBERS

Write each number in two other forms.

**13.** sixteen thousand, forty      **14.** 50,000 + 4,000 + 200 + 4

**15.** eighty-seven thousand, forty-two      **16.** 20,000 + 3,000 + 50 + 6

Write the number in expanded form.

**17.** 387      **18.** 2,412      **19.** 43,671      **20.** 35,902

**21.** 60,234      **22.** 12,084      **23.** 13,087      **24.** 92,530

Write the number in word form.

**25.** 409      **26.** 2,010      **27.** 5,102      **28.** 73,249

**29.** 14,013      **30.** 89,738      **31.** 30,952      **32.** 16,870

# VOCABULARY POWER

## REVIEW

**digit** [di′jit] *noun*

*Digit* is one of the oldest mathematical words. In addition to meaning "a numeral," *digit* can also mean "a finger or a toe." Name two ways the word *digital* is used today.

## PREVIEW

billion

benchmark

www.harcourtschool.com/mathglossary

# Understand Place Value

## ▶ Learn

**BUSY BEES**   Mr. Howard is a beekeeper. He raises bees for the honey they produce. His two colonies have about 128,000 bees. To understand how many bees this is, you need to understand the place value of each digit in 128,000.

 **MATH IDEA**   Each digit in a number has a place value. The value of a digit depends on its place, or position, in the number.

The place value of the digit 8 in 12**8**,000 is thousands. The value of 8 in 12**8**,000 is $8 \times 1,000 = 8,000$.

**Remember**

Starting from the right, each group of three digits forms a period. Commas separate the periods.

PERIOD

| THOUSANDS | | | ONES | | |
|---|---|---|---|---|---|
| Hundreds | Tens | Ones | Hundreds | Tens | Ones |
| 1 | 2 | 8, | 0 | 0 | 0 |
| $1 \times 100,000$ | $2 \times 10,000$ | $8 \times 1,000$ | $0 \times 100$ | $0 \times 10$ | $0 \times 1$ |
| 100,000 | 20,000 | 8,000 | 0 | 0 | 0 |

 **Technology Link**

More Practice: Harcourt Mega Math The Number Games, *Tiny's Think Tank,* Level A

**Standard Form:** 128,000

**Expanded Form:** $100,000 + 20,000 + 8,000$

**Word Form:** one hundred twenty-eight thousand

## Examples

**Ⓐ**

**Standard Form:** 2,641

**Expanded Form:** $2,000 + 600 + 40 + 1$

**Word Form:** two thousand, six hundred forty-one

**Ⓑ**

**Standard Form:** 97,508

**Expanded Form:** $90,000 + 7,000 + 500 + 8$

**Word Form:** ninety-seven thousand, five hundred eight

**1. Explain** how to find the value of the digit 4 in the number 2,467.

**Write the value of the blue digit.**

**2.** 567      **3.** 38      **4.** 6,459      **5.** 45,088      **6.** 123,047

**Write each number in expanded form and in word form.**

**7.** 430      **8.** 36,025      **9.** 8,922      **10.** 12,608      **11.** 690,000

▶ **Practice and Problem Solving**    ( Extra Practice, page 16, Set A )

**Write the value of the blue digit.**

**12.** 979      **13.** 345,671      **14.** 23,874      **15.** 861,113      **16.** 909,904

**Write each number in expanded form and in word form.**

**17.** 653      **18.** 44,703      **19.** 1,922      **20.** 723,651      **21.** 400,230

**Write each number in standard form.**

**22.** 70,000 + 6,000 + 400 + 10 + 8      **23.** 600,000 + 20,000 + 1,000 + 70 + 3

**24.** twenty-five thousand, seventy-five      **25.** four hundred sixteen thousand, three hundred twelve

**26.** A truck driver delivers 20,000 honey jars to 3 grocery stores. If 10,200 jars are delivered to the first grocery store, 1,600 to the second, and the remaining jars to the third store, how many jars are delivered to the third store?

**27.** A butterfly migrated four thousand, eight hundred twenty-eight kilometers! Write this number in standard form.

**28. Vocabulary Power** In some sports, *periods* are the equal portions of time into which a game is divided. How does this relate to the *periods* of a number?

**Getting Ready for ★FCAT**

**29.** Mount McKinley, located in Alaska, is the highest peak in the United States. It is 20,320 feet high. How is its height written in word form?

    **A.** two thousand, three hundred twenty

    **B.** twenty thousand, three hundred two

    **C.** two hundred thousand, three hundred two

    **D.** twenty thousand, three hundred twenty

# Millions and Billions

## Quick Review

Write in expanded form.

1. 309,421   2. 821,938
3. 710,090   4. 195,265
5. 252,603

**VOCABULARY**

billion

▶ **Learn**

**MOONWALK** An estimated 1 million people crowded Florida roads and beaches to see the launch of *Apollo 11*. You can use a grid to understand the size of 1 million.

**HANDS ON**

## Activity

**MATERIALS:** grid paper, crayons, tape

**STEP 1**

Use a 10 × 10 sheet of grid paper. Draw a dot in each box on the grid paper. Let each dot represent 1 person. How many people are shown on this grid?

**STEP 2**

How many people does the grid paper show when it is filled? Write the total at the bottom of the grid paper.

**STEP 3**

Tape your grid paper to another student's grid paper. Write the total number of people shown by the 2 sheets of grid paper.

▲ The *Apollo 11* mission was the first to land astronauts on the moon. *Apollo 11* blasted off from Earth on July 16, 1969.

• Will you need more than or fewer than 100 sheets to show 1 million people? Explain.

An estimated 726,300,000 people watched Neil Armstrong take the first step on the moon. You can show this number on a place-value chart.

| MILLIONS | | | THOUSANDS | | | ONES | | |
|---|---|---|---|---|---|---|---|---|
| Hundreds | Tens | Ones | Hundreds | Tens | Ones | Hundreds | Tens | Ones |
| 7 | 2 | 6, | 3 | 0 | 0, | 0 | 0 | 0 |

**Standard Form:** 726,300,000

**Expanded Form:** 700,000,000 + 20,000,000 + 6,000,000 + 300,000

**Word Form:** seven hundred twenty-six million, three hundred thousand

# Billions

The National Aeronautics and Space Administration (NASA) funding for Project Apollo's human spaceflights was $19,407,134,000.

A billion has one more period than a million. One **billion** is 1,000 million.

| BILLIONS | | | MILLIONS | | | THOUSANDS | | | ONES | | |
|---|---|---|---|---|---|---|---|---|---|---|---|
| Hundreds | Tens | Ones | Hundreds | Tens | Ones | Hundreds | Tens | Ones | Hundreds | Tens | Ones |
| | 1 | 9, | 4 | 0 | 7, | 1 | 3 | 4, | 0 | 0 | 0 |

**Standard Form:** 19,407,134,000

**Expanded Form:** 10,000,000,000 + 9,000,000,000 + 400,000,000 + 7,000,000 + 100,000 + 30,000 + 4,000

**Word Form:** nineteen billion, four hundred seven million, one hundred thirty-four thousand

• How do periods help you read a number?

**REASONING** There are 1,000 millions in 1 billion. How many 10 millions are in 10 billion?

**MATH IDEA** Place value and periods help you read and write greater numbers.

▲ Neil Armstrong snapped this picture of Buzz Aldrin as Aldrin stepped onto the moon.

## ▶ Check

1. **Explain** how the word form and the expanded form for 3,450,632 are alike. How are they different?

**Write each number in standard form.**

2. five million, three hundred fourteen

3. two billion, six hundred eleven thousand, one hundred seven

4. thirty-three million, two hundred seven thousand, twelve

5. eighty million, three hundred eight thousand, four

**Use the number 4,302,698,051.**

6. Write the name of the period that has the digits 698.

7. Write the name of the period that has the digits 302.

8. Write the digit in the ten-millions place.

9. Write the place value of the digit 4.

**LESSON CONTINUES**

FCAT TESTED  SSS/GLEs MA.A.2.2.1.5.2 Expresses numbers to millions or more in expanded form using powers of ten, with or without exponential notation. *also* MA.A.2.2.1.5.1

**Write each number in standard form.**

**10.** twenty-one million, eleven thousand, two hundred twelve

**11.** fifty-three billion, two million, one hundred sixteen thousand, seven

**Write the value of the blue digit.**

**12.** 35,4**2**7,231

**13.** **7**80,904,652

**14.** 413,9**1**6,102

**15.** 19,413,5**7**2

**16.** 8,102,67**3**,124

**17.** 1**4**,956,630,210

**18.** **9**,124,432,212

**19.** 42**4**,984,127

**In which number does the digit 7 have the greater value?**
**Explain.**

**20. a.** 17,854
  **b.** 105,079

**21. a.** 7,089,000,000
  **b.** 7,089,000

**22. a.** 760
  **b.** 750,000

**For 23–24, copy and complete.**

**23.** The number 2,984,052,681 represents two billion,
  __?__ hundred eighty-four million, fifty-two thousand,
  __?__ hundred eighty-one.

**24.** 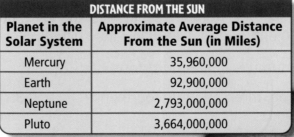**ALGEBRA**
  5,000,000 + ■ + 10,000 + 6,000 + ■ + 50 + 1 = 5,716,651

**Write each number in two other forms.**

**25.** two million, three hundred six thousand, fifteen

**26.** 1,000,000,000 + 10,000,000 + 10,000 + 100 + 1

**27.** 65,200,108

**28.** 207,111,006

**29.** 1,480,200,965

**USE DATA** For 30–31, use the table.

**30.** Which planet is about ninety-two million, nine hundred thousand miles from the sun?

**31.** About how many billion miles is Neptune from the sun?

**32.** **? What's the Error?** Mary wrote the number 5,67,890. Explain her error. Write the number correctly in standard form.

**33.** **REASONING** If your printer could print a number every second, how many hours would it take for it to print all the numbers from 1 to 1,000,000?

| DISTANCE FROM THE SUN | |
|---|---|
| **Planet in the Solar System** | **Approximate Average Distance From the Sun (in Miles)** |
| Mercury | 35,960,000 |
| Earth | 92,900,000 |
| Neptune | 2,793,000,000 |
| Pluto | 3,664,000,000 |

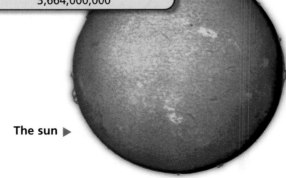

The sun ▶

**34.** ≡**FAST FACT** • SCIENCE The distance between Earth and the moon is about 240,250 miles. Write this number in expanded form.

**35.** **REASONING** Write the least 9-digit number possible without repeating a digit. What is the value of the digit 2?

## Getting Ready for FCAT

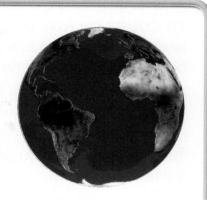

**36.** The Atlantic Ocean covers an area of 31,814,640 square miles. How is this written in expanded form?

   **A.** 30,000,000 + 1,000,000 + 800,000 + 10,000 + 4,000 + 60 + 4

   **B.** 30,000,000 + 1,000,000 + 800,000 + 10,000 + 4,000 + 600 + 40

   **C.** 30,000,000 + 10,000,000 + 800,000 + 10,000 + 600 + 40

   **D.** 30,000,000 + 1,000,000 + 800,000 + 10,000 + 4,000 + 600 + 4

## Problem Solving  Thinker's Corner

**WHAT'S THE NUMBER'S SIZE?** The students at Forest Lake Elementary School collected pennies for one year to pay for new band uniforms. At the end of the year, they had collected one million pennies.

Is the value of one million pennies greater than or less than $1,000,000?

Since it takes 100 pennies to make one dollar, then 1,000,000 pennies has to be less than $1,000,000.

**Use these questions to help you see how 1,000,000 relates to other numbers.**

 **1.** Is 1,000,000 greater than or less than 100,000?

 **2.** Does your school library have more than or fewer than 1,000,000 books?

 **3.** Is 1,000,000 books more than or fewer than 850,000 books?

 **4.** Is 1,000,000 closer to 900,000 or closer to 1,500,000?

**For 5–7, use the numbers 680,000; 850,000; and 2,450,000.**

 **5.** Which two numbers are closest to each other?

 **6.** Name a number that is less than all 3 numbers.

 **7.** Name a number between 680,000 and 850,000.

# Benchmark Numbers

**Quick Review**

Write the value of the digit 8.

**1.** 108      **2.** 4,801
**3.** 38,234    **4.** 56,980
**5.** 89,095

**VOCABULARY**

benchmark

▷ **Learn**

**TO COUNT OR NOT TO COUNT!** A benchmark is a familiar number used as a point of reference. You can use a benchmark to determine a reasonable estimate.

Notre Dame Stadium is in South Bend, Indiana. In the top photo each outlined section seats about 1,000 people. About how many people can sit in the 3 outlined sections?

The benchmark is 1,000 people. The larger section is about 3 times as great.

So, about 3,000 people could sit in the in the 3 outlined sections.

## Examples

**A**
Which estimate of the number of trading cards is more reasonable, 500 or 1,500?

**Benchmark:**
100 cards

The taller stack of cards is about 5 times the benchmark amount.
5 × 100 = 500

**B**
What is a reasonable estimate of the number of pieces of macaroni in the full jar?

**Benchmark:**
500 pieces

The full jar of macaroni holds about 4 times the benchmark amount.
4 × 500 = 2,000

So, the more reasonable estimate of the number of trading cards in the taller stack is 500.

So, a reasonable estimate of the number of pieces of macaroni in the full jar is 2,000.

• In Example A, why is 1,500 not a reasonable estimate?

▲ Notre Dame Stadium

▷ **Check**

1. **Explain** how a benchmark of 20 people in one row could help you estimate the number of people in a movie theater.

**Use the benchmark to find a reasonable estimate.**

**2.** dog food in a full jar

100 pieces      __?__

**3.** baseballs in a full carton

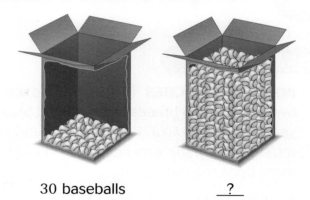

30 baseballs      __?__

## ▶ Practice and Problem Solving    Extra Practice, page 16, Set C

**Use the benchmark to find a reasonable estimate.**

**4.** bricks in a wall

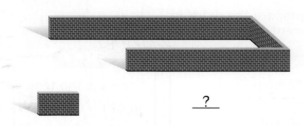

100 bricks      __?__

**5.** CDs in a stack

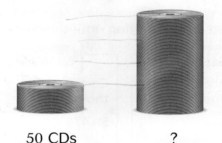

50 CDs      __?__

**6. ESTIMATION** In every major league baseball game, about 6 dozen baseballs are used. If 5 games are played in a week, how many baseballs will be used?

**7.**  **Write About It** Explain how you can use a benchmark of 50 bike riders per grade to estimate the number of bicycles at your school.

## Getting Ready for FCAT   THINK SOLVE EXPLAIN

**8.** The section marked on the picture of the necklace has about 50 beads. Use this benchmark to find a reasonable estimate for the total number of beads in the necklace. Explain how you made your estimate.

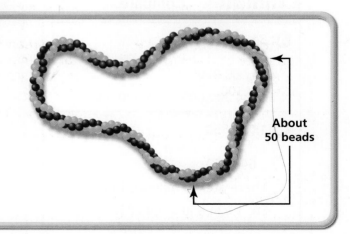

About 50 beads

FCAT TESTED   SSS/GLEs MA.A.4.2.1.5.2 Estimates quantities of objects to 1,000 or more and justifies and explains the reasoning for the estimate (for example, using benchmark numbers, unitizing).

Chapter 1   **9**

# Compare and Order

▶ **Learn**

**POPULAR POOCHES** The dachshund and the beagle are two popular dog breeds in the United States. In a recent year, there were 50,478 dachshunds and 50,419 beagles registered with the American Kennel Club. Which breed had more dogs registered?

**One Way** Use a number line to compare 50,478 and 50,419.

50,419    50,478    **Think:** 50,478 is to the right of 50,419, so 50,478 > 50,419.

50,000  50,100  50,200  50,300  50,400  50,500  50,600  50,700  50,800  50,900  51,000

**Another Way** Use place value. Start at the left. Compare the digits in each place-value position until the digits are different.

| **STEP 1** | **STEP 2** | **STEP 3** | **STEP 4** |
|---|---|---|---|
| Compare the ten thousands. | Compare the thousands. | Compare the hundreds. | Compare the tens. |
| 50,478 | 50,478 | 50,478 | 50,478 |
| ↓      same | ↓      same | ↓      same | ↓    7 > 1 |
| 50,419 | 50,419 | 50,419 | 50,419 |
| | | | So, 50,478 > 50,419. |

Since 50,478 > 50,419, there were more dachshunds registered than beagles.

• How does aligning the digits by place value help you compare numbers?

**Examples** Compare.

Ⓐ 84,200,000
     ↓      2 < 9
84,900,000

So, 84,200,000 < 84,900,000.

Ⓑ 1,024,850
   ↓      1 > 0
   643,850

There are no millions in 643,850.

So, 1,024,850 > 643,850.

# Order Whole Numbers

In that same year, there were 40,005 poodles, 42,025 Yorkshire terriers, and 37,035 boxers registered. Order these breeds from the least number of dogs registered to the greatest.

**One Way** Use a number line to order numbers.

> **Think:** 37,035 is to the left of 40,005, and 40,005 is to the left of 42,025.
> 37,035 < 40,005 < 42,025

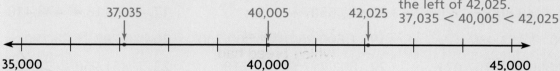

**Another Way** Use place value.

**STEP 1**

Compare the ten thousands.

40,005
↓
42,025
↓
37,035        3 < 4

So, 37,035 is the least of the three numbers.

**STEP 2**

Compare the other two numbers using thousands.

40,005
↓            0 < 2
42,025
So, 40,005 < 42,025

So, 37,035 < 40,005 < 42,025

From the least number of dogs registered to the greatest, the breeds are boxer, poodle, and Yorkshire terrier.

**MATH IDEA** To compare and order numbers, place the numbers in order on a number line or use place value to compare the digits from left to right.

## Check

1. **Explain** how you can show that 7,609,000 is greater than 7,600,009.

2. **Describe** two different ways you can order these numbers: 10,435; 9,590; 10,299.

**Start at the left. Name the first place-value position where the digits differ. Name the greater number.**

3. 8,007; 87,000

4. 205,768; 205,796

5. 35,090; 35,909

**Compare. Write <, >, or = for each ●.**

6. 180,551 ● 180,451

7. 3,154,270 ● 3,154,830

8. 4,902,677 ● 4,902,830

9. 198,335 ● 198,335

10. 314,308 ● 304,004

11. 996,035 ● 986,350

**LESSON CONTINUES** ▶

FCAT TESTED    SSS/GLEs MA.A.I.2.2.5.2 Compares and orders whole numbers using concrete materials, number lines, drawings, and numerals. *also* MA.E.I.2.I.5.6

Chapter 1    **11**

**Start at the left. Name the first place-value position where the digits differ. Name the greater number.**

**12.** 6,712; 61,365

**13.** 680,742; 680,789

**14.** 351,604; 351,408

**Compare. Write <, >, or = for each ●.**

**15.** 48,922 ● 49,800

**16.** 15,650 ● 5,650

**17.** 187,418 ● 178,418

**18.** 451,300 ● 452,030

**19.** 1,800,250 ● 1,800,250

**20.** 28,792 ● 28,790

**21.** 20,767,300 ● 2,767,071

**22.** 602,717 ● 602,718

**23.** 7,451,950 ● 7,045,950

**24.** 509,782,650 ● 509,562,710

**25.** 1,098,254,701 ● 1,082,276,535

**Find the missing digit.**

**26.** 1,988,678 < 1,98■,678

**27.** 192,717,568 > 19■,717,568

**28.** 5,323,134 > 5,323,■34

**29.** 537,691,432 > 537,69■,432

**Order from greatest to least.**

**30.** 26,295; 216,925; 219,625

**31.** 235,289; 236,287; 236,178

**32.** 78,935; 77,590; 178,286

**33.** 234,650,200; 234,850,100; 38,950,500

**Order from least to greatest.**

**34.** 895,000; 8,595,000; 859,000

**35.** 4,210,632; 2,410,781; 4,120,681

**36.** 49,086; 49,680; 48,690

**37.** 335,219; 336,007; 336,278

**USE DATA For 38–40, use the graph.**

**38.** Order from greatest to least the number of terriers registered.

**39.** How much greater is the number of Yorkshire terriers than the total number of silky, Boston, Scottish, cairn, and Airedale terriers?

**40.** When comparing the number of Scottish terriers to Airedale terriers, in which place value do the digits differ?

**41.** ✎ Write About It Explain how to compare 1,879,987 and 1,979,987.

**42.** ? What's the Question? There are 3 numbers: 345,789; 355,984; and 355,798. The answer is 355,984.

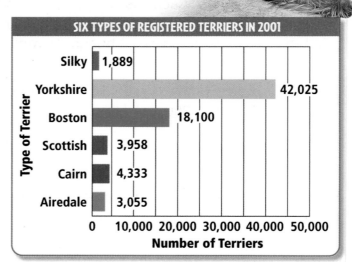

**SIX TYPES OF REGISTERED TERRIERS IN 2001**

| Type of Terrier | Number of Terriers |
|---|---|
| Silky | 1,889 |
| Yorkshire | 42,025 |
| Boston | 18,100 |
| Scottish | 3,958 |
| Cairn | 4,333 |
| Airedale | 3,055 |

0  10,000  20,000  30,000  40,000  50,000
**Number of Terriers**

**REASONING** Kim, Juan, and Karen went to the annual dog show. Kim drove 455 miles to get there. Juan drove 110 miles farther than Kim. Karen drove 150 miles less than Juan. Use this information for 43–44.

**43.** How far did each person drive to the dog show?

**44.** Who drove the least distance? Who drove the greatest distance?

565

**45.** The table shows the populations of 6 Florida counties in the year 2000. Which counties had greater populations than Clay County?

   **A.** Osceola and Santa Rosa

   **B.** Okaloosa and Indian River

   **C.** Okaloosa and Osceola

   **D.** Osceola and Citrus

| POPULATION OF 6 FLORIDA COUNTIES (in 2000) | |
|---|---|
| **County** | **Population** |
| Clay | 140,814 |
| Citrus | 118,085 |
| Indian River | 112,947 |
| Okaloosa | 170,498 |
| Osceola | 172,493 |
| Santa Rosa | 117,743 |

# Problem Solving    Thinker's Corner

**VISUAL THINKING** Rachel is using base-ten blocks to help her compare 1,380 and 1,365. She uses cubes to represent thousands, squares to represent hundreds, rods to represent tens, and units to represent ones.

**1.** Look at the photo. Which number is represented by the base-ten blocks, 1,380 or 1,365?

**2.** Use base-ten blocks to show 1,380 and 1,365.

**3.** Draw your models.

**4.** Explain how you can use the blocks or drawings to help you decide which number is greater.

**Use base-ten blocks to model. Draw your models. Write <, >, or = for each ●.**

**5.** 432 ● 408

**6.** 1,521 ● 1,512

**7.** 1,055 ● 1,505

**8.** 290 ● 209

# Problem Solving Skill
## Use a Table

UNDERSTAND ▶ PLAN ▶ SOLVE ▶ CHECK

**SIZE IT UP** Rhode Island is the smallest state in the United States. Delaware is the second smallest state. What is the difference between the areas of Delaware and Rhode Island?

| AREA AND POPULATION OF STATES | | |
|---|---|---|
| **Name** | **Area (sq mi)** | **Population** |
| Delaware | 2,396 | 783,600 |
| Florida | 65,755 | 15,982,378 |
| Indiana | 36,418 | 6,080,485 |
| Michigan | 58,527 | 9,938,444 |
| New Jersey | 8,215 | 8,414,350 |
| Rhode Island | 1,231 | 1,048,319 |

Find the areas of Delaware and Rhode Island. Then subtract to find the difference.

```
Area of Delaware        2,396  square miles
Area of Rhode Island   -1,231  square miles
                        1,165  square miles
```

So, the difference in areas is 1,165 square miles.

## Talk About It

• How are the states ordered in the table? How would you change the table to show the state populations in order from greatest to least?

• Explain how reading the data from a table helps you solve problems.

USE DATA   For 1–4, use the table.

| CAPITAL CITIES | |
|---|---|
| **City and State** | **Population** |
| Baton Rouge, LA | 227,818 |
| Indianapolis, IN | 791,926 |
| Nashville, TN | 569,891 |
| Oklahoma City, OK | 506,132 |
| Richmond, VA | 197,790 |

1. Which city has the greatest population? the least?

2. How much greater is the population of Nashville than the population of Oklahoma City?

3. **ALGEBRA**   Which equation shows the combined populations of Nashville and Richmond if *n* represents the total population?

   A  $569{,}891 + 197{,}790 = n$
   B  $n + 197{,}790 = 569{,}891$
   C  $n = 197{,}790 - 569{,}891$
   D  $569{,}891 + n = 197{,}790$

4. Which states' capital cities have populations of 1 million when rounded to the nearest million?

   F  VA, IN, OK       H  IN, TN, OK
   G  IN, TN, VA       J  LA, TN, OK

## Mixed Applications

5. The clock shows the time Mike's 1-hour flight landed in Richmond. It took him 30 minutes to drive to the airport, and he was 45 minutes early for his flight. At what time did he leave his house?

6. Sasha's family is planning a trip. They can go to either Orlando or New York. They can drive, fly, or take the train to their destination. Make a list of their choices.

7. Bill said, "The greater the state's area, the greater the population." How can you use the table on page 14 to decide whether Bill's statement is correct?

8. **ALGEBRA**   The Smiths drove a total of 540 miles in 2 days. They drove twice as far on Tuesday as they did on Monday. How many miles did they drive on Monday? on Tuesday?

9. **Write a problem** using the "Capital Cities" table above. Then solve the problem.

FCAT TESTED   SSS/GLEs MA.A.3.2.2.5.1 Uses problem-solving strategies to determine the operation(s) needed to solve one- and two-step problems involving addition, subtraction, multiplication, and division of whole numbers, and addition, subtraction, and multiplication of decimals and fractions. *also* MA.A.1.2.2.5.2

**Chapter 1** **15**

# Extra Practice

## Set A (pp. 2–3)

**Write the value of the blue digit.**

**1.** 14,350      **2.** 54,079      **3.** 635,017      **4.** 3,980

**Write each number in expanded form and in word form.**

**5.** 34      **6.** 6,080      **7.** 123,689      **8.** 991

**Write each number in word form.**

**9.** 642,007      **10.** 2,311      **11.** 1,078      **12.** 601

## Set B (pp. 4–7)

**Write each number in standard form.**

**1.** 3,000,000 + 40,000 + 9,000 + 200 + 7

**2.** 50,000,000 + 1,000,000 + 400,000 + 10,000 + 300 + 20 + 5

**3.** forty-three million, three hundred ten thousand, five hundred seven

**4.** six billion, five hundred six million, thirteen thousand, four hundred twenty

**Write the value of the blue digit.**

**5.** 9,450,180      **6.** 47,329,052      **7.** 8,506,332,189

## Set C (pp. 8–9)

**Use the benchmark to find a reasonable estimate.**

**1.** nails in a bucket

50 nails      _?_

**2.** buttons in a box

200 buttons      _?_

## Set D (pp. 10–13)

**Compare. Write <, >, or = for each ●.**

**1.** 18,276 ● 18,287      **2.** 845,418 ● 845,418      **3.** 50,967,300 ● 5,967,021

**Order from greatest to least.**

**4.** 12,945; 12,693; 12,990

**5.** 10,235,561; 1,235,561; 10,253,561

**Order from least to greatest.**

**6.** 436,042,303; 463,054,119; 64,332,989

**7.** 1,525,202; 1,252,202; 1,522,202

# Review/Test

 **CHECK VOCABULARY AND CONCEPTS**

**Choose the best term from the box.**

1. A thousand thousands is equal to one __?__. (p. 4)

2. A familiar number used as a point of reference is called a __?__. (p. 8)

> million
> billion
> benchmark
> period

 **CHECK SKILLS**

**Write the value of the blue digit.** (pp. 2–7)

3. 162,408

4. 27,140,652

**Write each number in two other forms.** (pp. 2–7)

5. 2,030,909

6. three billion, two hundred three million, forty-two thousand, five

**Use the benchmark to find a reasonable estimate.** (pp. 8–9)

7. peanuts in a jar

100 peanuts          __?__

**Compare. Write < , > , or = for each ●.** (pp. 10–13)

8. 104,690 ● 140,690     9. 3,250 ● 13,250     10. 9,782,650 ● 9,782,650

**Order from least to greatest.** (pp. 10–13)

11. 9,519; 10,003; 9,195

12. 1,502,369; 1,501,369; 1,507,369

✓ **CHECK PROBLEM SOLVING**

**USE DATA   For 13–14, use the table.** (pp. 14–15)

13. Order the lakes from the least area to the greatest area.

14. List the lakes in order from the greatest maximum depth to the least maximum depth.

15. In the future, a spaceship might be built that could travel 100,000 miles a second. How long would it take to travel 1 million miles? 10 million miles? (pp. 4–7)

| AREAS OF THE GREAT LAKES | | |
|---|---|---|
| Lake | Area (sq mi) | Maximum Depth (ft) |
| Michigan | 22,300 | 923 |
| Erie | 9,910 | 210 |
| Ontario | 7,550 | 802 |
| Superior | 31,700 | 1,330 |
| Huron | 23,000 | 750 |

# Getting Ready for FCAT

 **NUMBER SENSE, CONCEPTS, AND OPERATIONS**

| SOME LANGUAGES IN THE U.S. | |
| --- | --- |
| **Language** | **Number of Speakers** |
| French | 1,702,000 |
| Greek | 388,000 |
| Chinese | 1,249,000 |
| Spanish | 17,339,000 |

1. This table shows languages other than English that are spoken in the United States. Which language is spoken by the **greatest** number of people?

   A. French

   B. Greek

   C. Chinese

   D. Spanish

2. Randi read about the heights of mountains in the United States. Mt. Bear is 14,831 feet tall; Mt. Elbert is 14,433 feet; Mt. Ranier is 14,410 feet, and Mt. Whitney is 14,494 feet. Which shows the heights in order from **greatest** to **least**?

   F. 14,831; 14,494; 14,433; 14,410

   G. 14,494; 14,433; 14,831; 14,410

   H. 14,410; 14,433; 14,494; 14,831

   I. 14,831; 14,410; 14,433; 14,494

3. **Explain It** A bookstore sold 249 books on Friday and 475 books on Saturday. ESTIMATE the number of books sold during the two days. Explain your estimate.

 **MEASUREMENT**

4. Which weighs about 3 kilograms?

   A. a balloon

   B. a watermelon

   C. a pencil

   D. a notebook

> **TIP** **Decide on a plan.** See item 5. Using the strategy *draw a diagram* may help you find the perimeter of the park. Draw a square and label the sides 115 m.

5. Timothy jogs around the park every morning. The park is a square with sides 115 meters long. What is the perimeter of the park?

   F. 460 meters

   G. 450 meters

   H. 345 meters

   I. 330 meters

6. Which of these units is the most reasonable unit to use when measuring the distance between Atlanta and Miami?

   A. inch

   B. foot

   C. yard

   D. mile

7. **Explain It** A juice bottle holds 4 pints. Is this enough to serve one cup each to 4 people? Explain how you know.

## DATA ANALYSIS AND PROBABILITY

8. Lara tossed a coin a number of times and drew this bar graph of the results. How many times did the coin land on tails?

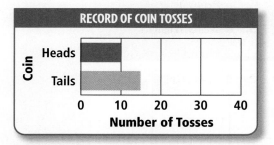

**F.** 5    **G.** 10    **H.** 15    **I.** 25

9. Suppose you have the following cards in a bag.

How does the probability of drawing a red card compare with the probability of drawing a yellow card?

**A.** The probability of drawing a red card is less.

**B.** The probability of drawing a red card or a yellow card is the same.

**C.** The probability of drawing a red card is greater.

**D.** There is no probability of drawing either a red card or a yellow card.

10. **Explain It** Carlos can choose from 2 kinds of pizza crusts and 6 toppings. How many different choices of crust and one topping does he have? Explain how you found your answer.

 ## GEOMETRY AND SPATIAL SENSE

11. Which of the following is an obtuse angle?

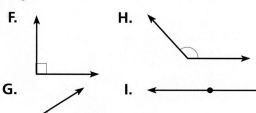

12. Which **best** describes the lines in the figure?

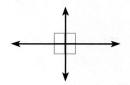

**A.** intersecting and parallel

**B.** parallel and perpendicular

**C.** intersecting and perpendicular

**D.** intersecting and NOT perpendicular

13. Which ordered pair shows the location of the pool?

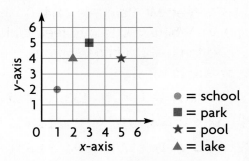

**F.** (5,4)    **H.** (4,4)

**G.** (3,2)    **I.** (2,1)

14. **Explain It** Look at the figure below. Describe how the figure was moved.

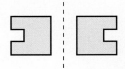

### CHAPTER 2

# Place Value of Decimals

**FAST FACT** • SCIENCE

Pollen grains produced by plants are microscopic. Wind, water, and animals can carry pollen grains to new locations. Pollen can drift in from 400 miles out at sea and 2 miles high in the air.

PROBLEM SOLVING The main features that make one type of pollen different from another are size, shape, and the surface of the grain. Look at the graph. Order the sizes of the pollen grains from greatest to least.

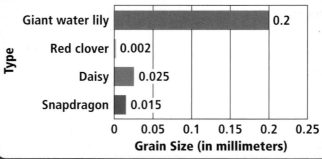

POLLEN GRAINS

| Type | Grain Size (in millimeters) |
|---|---|
| Giant water lily | 0.2 |
| Red clover | 0.002 |
| Daisy | 0.025 |
| Snapdragon | 0.015 |

Pollen of giant water lilies

Red clover and pollen

Daisies and pollen

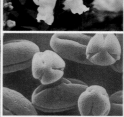

Snapdragon and pollen

Use this page to help you review and remember
important skills needed for Chapter 2.

## ✔ ORDER WHOLE NUMBERS

**Write the numbers in order from least to greatest.**

**1.** 8,945; 8,962; 8,974

**2.** 890,104; 809,192; 899,110

**3.** 45,325; 44,254; 42,124

**4.** 3,004; 3,040; 3,404

**Write the numbers in order from greatest to least.**

**5.** 3,257; 3,268; 3,284

**6.** 743,125; 734,216; 763,326

**7.** 23,322; 23,321; 23,335

**8.** 302,233; 326,799; 328,232

## ✔ READ AND WRITE DECIMALS

**Write as a decimal.**

**9.**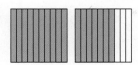

**10.**

**11.**

**Write the number in two other forms.**

**12.** fourteen and three tenths

**13.** 7,000 + 4 + 0.1

**14.** 3,000 + 20 + 7 + 0.2

**15.** 16.4

# VOCABULARY POWER

### REVIEW

**equivalent** [i•kwiv´ə•lənt] *adjective*

Equivalent is the combination of two Latin
roots, *aequus* and *valere*. The word *aequus*
means "equal" and *valere* means "value."
Explain how this information helps you find
the number that is equivalent to 72 ÷ 9.

### PREVIEW

decimal
tenth
hundredth
thousandth
ten-thousandth
equivalent decimals

**GO ON-LINE**   www.harcourtschool.com/mathglossary

# Decimal Place Value

▶ **Learn**

**TINY GRAINS!** **Decimals** name wholes and parts of a whole. Scientists use decimals to measure pollen.

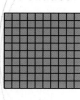

**One whole is shaded.**

1
1.0
one

**One tenth is shaded.**

$\frac{1}{10}$
0.1
one tenth

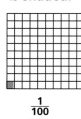

**One hundredth is shaded.**

$\frac{1}{100}$
0.01
one hundredth

**VOCABULARY**

decimal
tenth
hundredth
thousandth
ten-thousandth

**Example 1** Use a place-value chart to find the value of each digit in the number 1.75. Then write the decimal in standard form, in expanded form, and in word form.

| Ones | Tenths | Hundredths |
|------|--------|------------|
| 1 | 7 | 5 |
| $1 \times 1 = 1.0$ | $7 \times 0.1 = 0.7$ | $5 \times 0.01 = 0.05$ |

**Standard Form:** 1.75      **Expanded Form:** $1 + 0.7 + 0.05$

**Word Form:** one and seventy-five hundredths

▲ The marrow pollen grain is one of the largest pollen grains. Its size is 0.2 mm.

• How are $1\frac{75}{100}$ and 1.75 related?

 **MATH IDEA** As you move from left to right on the place-value chart, the value of each place is one-tenth of the value of the place to its left.

You can locate decimals on a number line.

**Remember**

A *mixed number* is made up of a whole number and a fraction.

$1\frac{75}{100}$ is a mixed number.

## Example 2

Locate 1.75, 0.35, and 0.8 on a number line.

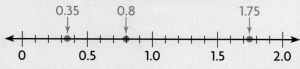

• What if you were to locate 1.23 on the number line above? Would it be closer to 1.2 or closer to 1.3?

# Thousandths and Ten-Thousandths

If you divide one whole by 1,000, you get one **thousandth**. If one square of a hundredth decimal model were magnified and one column of it were shaded, you could see one thousandth.

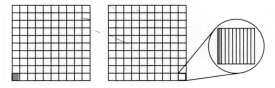

one hundredth · one thousandth

If you divide one whole by 10,000, you get one **ten-thousandth**.

$$1 \div 10{,}000 = \frac{1}{10{,}000} = 0.0001 = \text{one ten-thousandth}$$

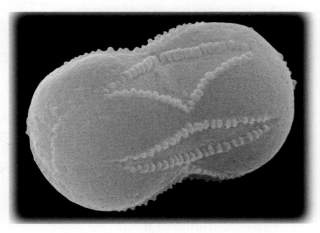

▲ The forget-me-not pollen grain is the smallest pollen grain. Its size is 0.006 mm.

You can also use a place-value chart to find the value of each digit in decimals to ten-thousandths. The chart below shows 2.7835.

| Ones | Tenths | Hundredths | Thousandths | Ten-thousandths |
|------|--------|------------|-------------|-----------------|
| 2 | 7 | 8 | 3 | 5 |
| 2 × 1 | 7 × 0.1 | 8 × 0.01 | 3 × 0.001 | 5 × 0.0001 |
| 2.0 | 0.7 | 0.08 | 0.003 | 0.0005 |

**Standard Form:** 2.7835
**Expanded Form:** 2 + 0.7 + 0.08 + 0.003 + 0.0005
**Word Form:** two and seven thousand, eight hundred thirty-five ten-thousandths

- How many thousandths are in one hundredth? in one tenth? in one?

## Check

1. **Explain** a rule for the pattern: 10, 1, $\frac{1}{10}$, $\frac{1}{100}$. Write the next number.

**Write as a decimal and as a fraction or mixed number.**

2.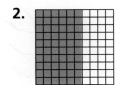

3.

4.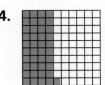

5. 3 + 0.57

6. eight and two tenths

7. thirty-two thousandths

LESSON CONTINUES ▶

**Write as a decimal and as a fraction or mixed number.**

**8.** 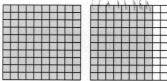  **9.** 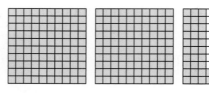  **10.**

**11.** 4 + 0.7

**12.** 10 + 7 + 0.7 + 0.01

**13.** 0.3 + 0.04

**14.** nine and six tenths

**15.** eighteen hundredths

**16.** one and six hundredths

**Write each decimal in expanded form and in word form.**

**17.** 1.067    **18.** 11.03    **19.** 1.045    **20.** 0.1234    **21.** 2.9

**Write in standard form.**

**22.** eight thousandths

**23.** fifty-four ten-thousandths

**24.** five hundredths

**25.** one and sixty-two thousandths

**For 26–29, copy the number line below. Then locate each decimal.**

**26.** 0.45    **27.** 1.8    **28.** 0.07    **29.** 1.65

**USE DATA For 30–33, use the circle graph.**

**30.** How many people voted?

**31.** Mary says more than half of the voters chose daisies or sunflowers. Is Mary correct? Explain.

**32.** What fraction of the people voted for daisies?

**33.** ✎ Write a problem that can be solved by using the circle graph.

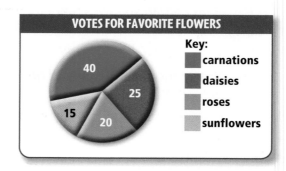

**REASONING In 34–37, the decimal point in some of the numbers has been placed incorrectly. Write the correct decimal number for each.**

**34.** A car usually travels on the highway at 5.05 miles per hour.

**35.** When Wanda was sick, her temperature was 10.15 degrees.

**36.** In the fishing tournament, only fish 9 inches or longer can be kept. Joe threw back his fish because it measured 85 inches.

**37.** The long jump was won by Jake, whose jump measured 0.99 feet.

**24**

**38.** **≡FAST FACT • SCIENCE** One of the greatest producers of pollen is the ragweed. A plant can release 8,000,000 pollen grains in just 5 hours. How many grains can one plant release in 10 hours?

**39.** **Vocabulary Power** When you write a number in expanded form, you actually "unfold" the place values and show the number in more detail. Write the expanded form of 0.327.

**40.** Liam was doing a project on Florida's precipitation. He wrote Jacksonville's average rainfall in inches on the board in expanded form.

$$50 + 1 + 0.3 + 0.02$$

What is this number in standard form?

**A.** 5.132  **C.** 513.2

**B.** 51.32  **D.** 5,132

**41.** Rebecca is buying a package of chicken that weighs 4.58 pounds. How would Rebecca read this number?

**F.** four hundred fifty-eight

**G.** four hundred fifty-eight hundredths

**H.** four and fifty-eight hundredths

**I.** four and fifty-eight thousandths

## Problem Solving  LiNKUP... to Science

**BOTANIST** Botanists are scientists who study plants and trees. Sequoias are the tallest trees in the world. The tallest sequoias are as tall as 26-story buildings. The heaviest sequoias can be 10 times the weight of the world's largest animal, the blue whale.

Giant sequoias begin life as tiny seeds. When botanists measure the very small parts of sequoias, they use decimals.

**Use the Sequoia Fact Box to solve.**

1. Use expanded form to write the width of a sequoia cone.

2. Write the length of a sequoia cone in word form.

3. Write the length of a sequoia seed as a fraction.

4. Use standard form to write the weight of a sequoia seed.

| SEQUOIA FACT BOX | |
|---|---|
| **Average length of cone** | 2.75 in. |
| **Average width of cone** | 1.875 in. |
| **Average weight of seed** | three ten-thousandths oz |
| **Average length of seed** | 0.1875 in. |

# Equivalent Decimals

## Quick Review

Write in expanded form.

**1.** 3.7        **2.** 0.72

**3.** 4.908      **4.** 8.365

**5.** 13.004

**VOCABULARY**

**equivalent decimals**

## ► Learn

**SAME BUT DIFFERENT** Newborn red kangaroos, called joeys, are just 2.5 cm long. Adult red kangaroos can grow to a height of 1.6 m. Write an equivalent decimal for 1.6.

**Equivalent decimals** are different names for the same number or amount. These are some different ways to express the decimal 1.6 or its equivalent.

one and six tenths     1 + 0.6     1.60     1.600

To determine if two decimals are equivalent, draw models or line up the decimal points and compare the digits in the same place-value positions.

### Examples

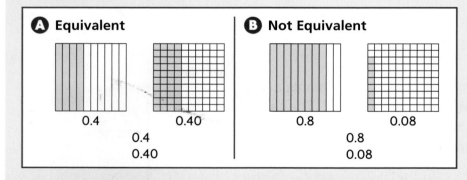

**A** Equivalent

0.4          0.40

0.4
0.40

**B** Not Equivalent

0.8          0.08

0.8
0.08

▲ The red kangaroo is Australia's largest kangaroo.

 **MATH IDEA** Placing a zero to the right of the last digit of a decimal does not change the value of the decimal.

## ► Check

**Technology Link**

More Practice: Harcourt Mega Math Fraction Action, *Number Line Mine,* Level M

**1. Explain** how to determine if 0.046 is equivalent to 0.0406.

Write *equivalent* or *not equivalent* to describe each pair of decimals.

**2.** 0.09 and 0.009        **3.** 3.8 and 3.80        **4.** 4 and 4.0        **5.** 7.2 and 7.02

Write an equivalent decimal for each number.

**6.** 5.3          **7.** 0.034          **8.** 0.1230          **9.** 9.030

**Write *equivalent* or *not equivalent* to describe each pair of decimals.**

**10.** 1.02 and 1.20          **11.** 6 and 6.0          **12.** 3.007 and 3.07

**13.** 7.02 and 7.020          **14.** 4.09 and 4.099          **15.** 4.008 and 4.08

**Write an equivalent decimal for each number.**

**16.** 0.03          **17.** 4.630          **18.** 0.2          **19.** 5.600          **20.** 0.83

**21.** 5.550          **22.** 7.10          **23.** 0.900          **24.** 0.103          **25.** 2.4

**Write the two decimals that are equivalent.**

**26.** 0.0502          **27.** 0.017          **28.** 1.00050          **29.** 8.01
    0.00502              0.01700              1.0050              8.0010
    0.05020              0.00170              1.005              8.01000

**USE DATA** For 30–31, use the table.

**30.** Which two animals have tails which are equivalent in length?

**31.** Write an equivalent decimal for the length of a leopard's tail.

**32.** A 0.5-pound block of cheddar cheese costs $1.89. The Swiss cheese costs $2.98 per pound. Which cheese is less expensive per pound? Explain.

**33.** The cash register showed change of $2.50. Miko said this is two and one half dollars. Is Miko correct? Explain.

**34.** **? What's the Error?** Jeb's batting average is .309, and Tom's is .390. Tom says they have the same average. Describe Tom's error.

| MAMMALS WITH THE LONGEST TAILS ||
| Mammal | Tail Length (in meters) |
| --- | --- |
| African buffalo | 1.1 |
| African elephant | 1.3 |
| Asian elephant | 1.5 |
| Giraffe | 1.1 |
| Leopard | 1.4 |

**35.** **REASONING** Explain how to use a number line to show that 0.4 is not equivalent to 0.04.

**Getting Ready for FCAT**

**36.** The table shows the 110-meter hurdles for five Olympic athletes. Which decimal in the table is equivalent to 13.2?

**A.** 13.38
**B.** 13.26
**C.** 13.20
**D.** 13.00

| 110-METER HURDLES |||
| 1984 | Roger Kingdom | 13.20 sec |
| 1988 | Anthony Campbell | 13.38 sec |
| 1992 | Jack Pierce | 13.26 sec |
| 1996 | Mark Crear | 13.09 sec |
| 2000 | Anier Garcia | 13.00 sec |

# Compare and Order Decimals

**Quick Review**

Compare.
1. 34 ● 43
2. 250 ● 205
3. 600 ● 600
4. 450 ● 4,500
5. 26,983 ● 29,683

▶ **Learn**

**FIRST PLACE!** The cardinal is the most popular state bird. The seven states which have adopted the cardinal are Indiana, North Carolina, Virginia, West Virginia, Illinois, Kentucky, and Ohio. Suppose two cardinal eggs weigh 0.28 oz and 0.32 oz. Which egg is heavier?

You can use decimal models or a number line to compare decimals.

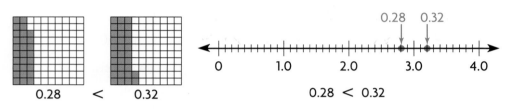

0.28 < 0.32

0.28 < 0.32

So, the egg weighing 0.32 oz is heavier.

You can also use place value to compare decimals.

**Example 1** Compare 1.42 and 1.46. First, line up the decimal points. Then, compare the digits from left to right until they are different.

**STEP 1**
Begin at the left. Compare the ones.
1.42
↓     same
1.46

**STEP 2**
Compare the tenths.
1.42
↓     same
1.46

**STEP 3**
Compare the hundredths.
1.42
↓   6 > 2, or 2 < 6
1.46

So, 1.46 > 1.42, or 1.42 < 1.46.

- Show how you could use decimal models or a number line to compare 1.42 and 1.46.

**Example 2** Order 2.853, 2.844, and 2.862 from least to greatest.

**STEP 1**
Begin at the left.
Compare the ones and tenths.
2.853
↓ ↓
2.844   same
↓ ↓
2.862

**STEP 2**
Compare the hundredths.
2.853
↓      different
2.844   4 < 5 < 6
↓
2.862

**STEP 3**
Order the numbers.

2.844 < 2.853 < 2.862

So, 2.844 < 2.853 < 2.862.

1. **Explain** how you can use a number line to order 1.468, 1.452, and 1.469 from least to greatest.

Write <, >, or = for each ⬤. Use the number line.

6.10   6.11   6.12   6.13   6.14   6.15   6.16   6.17   6.18   6.19   6.20

2. 6.152 ⬤ 6.125

3. 6.14 ⬤ 6.140

4. 6.114 ⬤ 6.118

5. 6.3 ⬤ 6.589

6. 6.170 ⬤ 6.175

7. 6.176 ⬤ 6.167

▶ **Practice and Problem Solving**    ( Extra Practice, page 32, Set C )

Write <, >, or = for each ⬤. You may wish to use a number line.

8. 0.65 ⬤ 0.63

9. 0.307 ⬤ 0.037

10. 0.759 ⬤ 0.769

11. 132.94 ⬤ 132.48

12. 156.93 ⬤ 156.98

13. 99.989 ⬤ 99.998

14. 0.905 ⬤ 0.905

15. 63.938 ⬤ 63.939

16. 476.069 ⬤ 476.096

**Order from least to greatest.**

17. 6.58, 6.38, 6.29, 7.08

18. 13.393, 13.309, 13.339, 13.039

19. 4.102, 4.105, 4.118, 4.110

20. 15.259, 15.389, 15.291, 15.301

**USE DATA**   For 21–23, use the menu.

21. Write the salads in order from the least expensive to the most expensive.

22. Name two items that cost more than yogurt but less than onion soup.

23. **NUMBER SENSE** Lisa has $5 in her wallet. Which two soups can she buy?

24. ✎ **Write About It** Explain how to compare 1.23 and 1.27.

**Power Lunch Menu**

| Bean Soup | $2.25 |
| Onion Soup | $2.95 |
| Tomato Soup | $2.75 |
| Taco Salad | $1.89 |
| Garden Salad | $1.80 |
| Fruit Salad | $1.85 |
| Yogurt | $1.95 |

⌐ **Getting Ready for** ⭐**FCAT**

25. An electrician uses wires that are color-coded by the lengths of their diameters. Which color of wire has the **least** diameter?

 A. red          C. yellow
 B. green        D. black

| SIZES OF WIRES | |
|---|---|
| **Color** | **Diameter (in.)** |
| red | 0.060 |
| green | 0.085 |
| yellow | 0.009 |
| black | 0.125 |

FCAT
TESTED ▶  SSS/GLEs MA.A.1.2.2.5.3 Compares and orders commonly used fractions, percents, and decimals
to thousandths using concrete materials, number lines, drawings, and numerals. *also* MA.A.1.2.1.5.2          Chapter 2   **29**

# Problem Solving Skill
## Draw Conclusions

UNDERSTAND ⟩ PLAN ⟩ SOLVE ⟩ CHECK ⟩

**Quick Review**

1. $7 \times 4$
2. $18 \div 6$
3. $25 \div 5$
4. $120 \div 12$
5. $24.08 \div 10$

**THINK FOR YOURSELF** Sometimes you will need to analyze data to draw conclusions.

The table and the bar graph below display data about an experiment involving five plants all of the same type. You can use the data to draw conclusions.

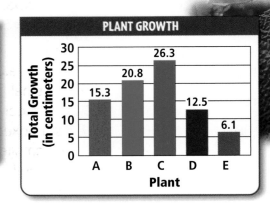

| PLANT FOOD DROPS USED | |
|---|---|
| **Plant** | **Number of Plant Food Drops** |
| A | 1 |
| B | 5 |
| C | 9 |
| D | 13 |
| E | 17 |

▲ This Pacific giant kelp can grow 18 inches in one day.

| ANALYZE | CONCLUSION |
|---|---|
| • Look at the graph. Which plant grew the tallest? | Plant C grew the tallest. |
| • Look at the table. How many drops of plant food did the tallest plant receive? | Plant C received 9 drops. |
| • What relationship do you notice between the number of drops of plant food and the plant's growth? | Up to 9 drops, more plant food helped the plants grow taller. With 13 and 17 drops, growth decreased. |

• What conclusion can you draw about Plants A, B, and C? about Plants D and E?

• **What if** the total growth for Plant D had been 35.89 cm and for Plant E, 38 cm? What conclusion could you draw about all five plants?

## ▶ Problem Solving Practice

**For 1–4, can the conclusion be drawn from the information given? Write *yes* or *no*. Explain your choice.**

**Mrs. Carson measured the heights of her fifth graders. The shortest student is 50 inches tall, and the tallest student is 64 inches tall. There are 25 students in Mrs. Carson's class.**

**1.** All of the students are taller than 5 feet.

**2.** The tallest student in the class is taller than 5 feet.

**3.** All of the students are shorter than Mrs. Carson.

**4.** The difference between the tallest student and the shortest student in the class is 14 inches.

**Lena thinks that the smaller box of cereal is a better buy than the larger box. The larger box has 10 servings, and the smaller box has 8 servings. The smaller box costs $3.20, and the larger box costs $3.90.**

**5.** Which expression describes the price per serving for the smaller box?
 **A** $3.20 × 8
 **B** $3.20 ÷ 20
 **C** $3.20 ÷ 8
 **D** $3.20 × 20

**6.** What conclusion can you draw from the data?
 **F** The smaller box costs less per serving.
 **G** The larger box costs less per serving.
 **H** Both boxes cost the same per serving.
 **J** The smaller box costs twice as much per serving.

## Mixed Applications

**USE DATA** For 7–11, use the table.

**7.** Does the weight of the animal determine its speed? Explain.

**8.** 💥 **What's the Error?** Don says that the more an animal eats, the more it sleeps. Explain the error in Don's conclusion.

**9.** Which animal eats the greatest amount of fruits and vegetables?

**10.** How many hours longer does the bear sleep than the elephant? than the giraffe?

**11.** 💥 **What's the Question?** Use the data from the table. The answer is 2 times as many kilograms.

| ANIMALS | | | |
|---|---|---|---|
| | **Elephant** | **Bear** | **Giraffe** |
| **Weight** | 5,450 kg | 725 kg | 1,180 kg |
| **Speed** | 51 kph | 48 kph | 51 kph |
| **Sleep per day** | 180 min | 8 hours | 240 min |
| **Fruits and vegetables eaten per day** | 1.8 kg | 0.9 kg | 0.1 kg |

1 hour = 60 minutes (min)
kph = kilometers per hour

**FCAT TESTED** 🟠 SSS/GLEs MA.A.3.2.2.5.1 Uses problem-solving strategies to determine the operation(s) needed to solve one- and two-step problems involving addition, subtraction, multiplication, and division of whole numbers, and addition, subtraction, and multiplication of decimals and fractions. *also* MA.A.1.2.2.5.2, MA.A.1.2.2.5.3

**Chapter 2** **31**

# Extra Practice

## Set A (pp. 22–25)

**Write in expanded form and in standard form.**

**1.** two hundred sixteen ten-thousandths

**2.** five and five hundredths

**3.** two and seven hundred two thousandths

**Write in word form.**

**4.** 44.009　　　　**5.** 2.0189　　　　**6.** 0.8　　　　**7.** 0.505

**Write as a decimal and as a fraction or mixed number.**

**8.** $4 + 0.07$

**9.** $10 + 0.3 + 0.09$

**10.** $8 + 0.8 + 0.01$

**11.** thirteen and four hundredths

**12.** fifty-seven hundredths

**13.** Mike rode his bike three and four hundredths of a mile. Write this number in standard form.

## Set B (pp. 26–27)

**Write *equivalent* or *not equivalent* to describe each pair of decimals.**

**1.** 3.45 and 3.450

**2.** 0.097 and 0.970

**3.** 23.504 and 23.50

**Write an equivalent decimal for each number.**

**4.** 5.2　　　　**5.** 9.320　　　　**6.** 87.0800　　　　**7.** 2.02

## Set C (pp. 28–29)

**Order from greatest to least.**

**1.** 54.453, 54.59, 54.811

**2.** 7.564, 17.4, 11.94

**Order from least to greatest.**

**3.** 31.104, 31.05, 31.94

**4.** 6.309, 6.42, 6.341

**5.** Leslie has $4.68 in her pocket. Which of the following items can she buy?

| Notebook | $2.30 | Box of Pencils | $4.67 |
| Binder | $8.53 | Markers | $4.69 |

# Review/Test

## ✓ CHECK VOCABULARY AND CONCEPTS

**Choose the best term from the box.**

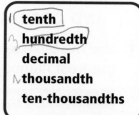

tenth
hundredth
decimal
thousandth
ten-thousandths

1. A decimal or fraction that names one part of ten equal parts is one __?__. (p. 22)

2. If you divide one whole by 1,000, you get one __?__. (p. 22)

3. A decimal or fraction that names one part of 100 equal parts is one __?__. (p. 22)

4. The decimal 0.0016 is sixteen __?__. (p. 22)

## ✓ CHECK SKILLS

**Write as a decimal and as a fraction or mixed number.** (pp. 22–25)

5. twenty-one and one hundredth

6. seven and six tenths

7. three hundred forty-nine thousandths

**Write each decimal in expanded form and in word form.** (pp. 22–25)

8. 17.0002     9. 1.002     10. 13.201     11. 4.076

**Write *equivalent* or *not equivalent* to describe each pair of decimals.** (pp. 26–27)

12. 0.650 and 0.65

13. 9.502 and 9.52

14. 3.0040 and 3.040

15. 10.01 and 10.010

**Order from least to greatest.** (pp. 28–29)

16. 0.057; 0.56; 0.05     17. 5.98; 5.908; 5.809     18. 6.969; 9.696; 6.696

## ✓ CHECK PROBLEM SOLVING

**Solve.** (pp. 30–31)

19. Jim worked 5 hours last week and earned $31.25. Sara earned $43.75 and worked 7 hours. Latasha earned $56.25 and worked 9 hours. Draw a conclusion about this information.

20. Kerry, Stu, Beth, and Julio are in line. Kerry is first in line. Julio is between Kerry and Stu. Beth is after Stu. Beth is last in line. Draw a conclusion about where Julio stands in line.

# Getting Ready for FCAT

## ★ NUMBER SENSE, CONCEPTS, AND OPERATIONS

**1.** Use the table to order the meats from **greatest** number of calories to **least**.

| CALORIES IN MEATS | |
|---|---|
| **Type (3 oz)** | **Calories** |
| Ham | 205 |
| Liver | 185 |
| Ground Beef | 245 |
| Steak | 240 |

- **A.** liver, ham, steak, ground beef
- **B.** ham, steak, ground beef, liver
- **C.** steak, ham, liver, ground beef
- **D.** ground beef, steak, ham, liver

**2.** The average annual precipitation in Miami is fifty-five and ninety-one hundredths inches. How is this number written in standard form?

- **F.** 5.91
- **G.** 50.91
- **H.** 55.90
- **I.** 55.91

> **TIP** **Look for important words.** See item 3. *Estimate* is an important word. It tells you to round the addends to estimate rather than find the exact answer.

**3. Explain It** The table shows the results of a survey. ESTIMATE to find the total number of people who have pets. Explain your estimate.

| SURVEY RESULTS | |
|---|---|
| **Pet** | **Number of People** |
| Cat | 30,482 |
| Dog | 27,407 |

## ★ DATA ANALYSIS AND PROBABILITY

**4.** The bar graph shows the average airport departure delays. Which airport had the shortest average departure delays in 2000?

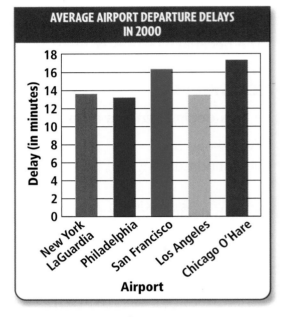

- **A.** New York LaGuardia
- **B.** Philadelphia
- **C.** Los Angeles
- **D.** Chicago O'Hare

**5.** Jodi has 3 dimes, 1 quarter, and 2 pennies in her wallet. She takes one coin out. What is the probability that it is a quarter?

- **F.** one out of six
- **G.** two out of six
- **H.** three out of five
- **I.** three out of three

**6. Explain It** A spinner has 6 sections, 2 red, 2 blue, and 2 yellow. Explain how you can determine the probability of spinning red, blue, or yellow.

**ALGEBRAIC THINKING**

**7.** Rafael drew this geometric pattern.

Which figure did he draw next in the pattern?

**A.**

**B.**

**C.**

**D.**

**8.** Which is the missing number in the pattern below?

3, 7, 11, 15, ■, 23, 27

**F.** 15

**G.** 17

**H.** 19

**I.** 21

**9. Explain It** Describe the relationship between x and y in this table.

| INPUT | OUTPUT |
| --- | --- |
| x | y |
| 1 | 4 |
| 2 | 5 |
| 3 | 6 |
| 4 | 7 |
| 5 | 8 |

 **GEOMETRY AND SPATIAL SENSE**

**10.** Suppose four bright stars are located at A, B, C, and D. Which is the correct location of star C?

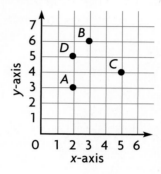

**A.** (2,5)

**B.** (5,4)

**C.** (3,6)

**D.** (2,3)

**11.** Which two lines are perpendicular?

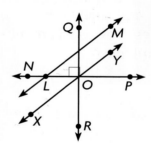

**F.** $\overleftrightarrow{NP}$ and $\overleftrightarrow{QR}$

**G.** $\overleftrightarrow{LM}$ and $\overleftrightarrow{NP}$

**H.** $\overleftrightarrow{QR}$ and $\overleftrightarrow{XY}$

**I.** $\overleftrightarrow{QR}$ and $\overleftrightarrow{LM}$

**12. Explain It** A polygon has sides of 4 feet, 5 feet, 4 feet, 5 feet, and 6 feet. Draw and name the polygon.

### CHAPTER 3

# Add and Subtract Whole Numbers and Decimals

**≡FAST FACT • SCIENCE**

The rarest of all sea turtles is the Kemp's ridley turtle. It weighs between 80 and 100 pounds.

**PROBLEM SOLVING**   The heaviest sea turtle is the leatherback turtle. It can weigh 1,000 pounds more than the heaviest turtle shown in the graph. What is the maximum weight of a leatherback?

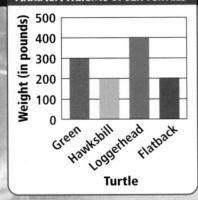

**MAXIMUM WEIGHTS OF SEA TURTLES**

Weight (in pounds): 0, 100, 200, 300, 400, 500

Turtle: Green, Hawksbill, Loggerhead, Flatback

The hawksbill turtle was so named because it has a beaklike mouth.

# CHECK WHAT YOU KNOW

Use this page to help you review and remember important skills needed for Chapter 3.

## ROUND WHOLE NUMBERS AND DECIMALS

Round each number to the nearest thousand.

1. 17,922
2. 308,389
3. 3,278,623
4. 45,325

5. 82,390
6. 3,569,203
7. 20,344
8. 23,056

9. 12,005
10. 4,035,654
11. 28,138
12. 456,979

Round each number to the nearest hundredth.

13. 4.108
14. 0.598
15. 12.835
16. 3.652

17. 9.305
18. 0.133
19. 2.846
20. 9.673

## ADD AND SUBTRACT MONEY

Find the sum or difference. Estimate to check.

21. $5,789
   +$4,569

22. $9,468
   −$4,263

23. $2,635
   +$3,508

24. $7,545
   −$5,023

25. $6,390
   +$4,743

26. $8,092
   −$1,953

27. $7,597
   +$8,146

28. $6,204
   −$2,132

29. $6.87 + $3.87
30. $8.75 − $6.43
31. $4.99 + $12.64
32. $2.03 + $27.89

33. $56.78 − $6.89
34. $76.02 + $34.85
35. $25.83 + $20.40
36. $65.47 − $31.23

# VOCABULARY POWER

**REVIEW**

**sum** [sum] *noun*

*Sum* is originally from the Latin root word *summus,* which means "highest." The Greeks and Romans added numbers from the bottom and wrote the answer or sum at the top. What word for the top of a mountain comes from *summus*?

**PREVIEW**

estimate

front-end estimation

www.harcourtschool.com/mathglossary

# Round Whole Numbers

Quick Review

**What is the value of each 5?**

1. 582,017
2. 3,456
3. 5,034,768
4. 57,316
5. 17,063,521

## ▶ Learn

**CROWD PLEASERS** The programs for this year's women's college basketball championships need to be ordered. The programs come in boxes of 10,000 each. Last year, 29,619 people attended the championships. How many boxes of programs should be ordered?

To be sure enough programs are ordered, round 29,619 up to the next ten thousand. You can use a number line to round.

29,619 rounded to the next ten thousand is 30,000.

So, 3 boxes of 10,000 programs should be ordered.

Another way to round is to use the rounding rules.

## Example

Round 149,987 to the nearest hundred thousand.

**STEP 1**

| | |
|---|---|
| Decide the place to which you want to round. | ↓<br>1 49,987 |

**STEP 2**

| | |
|---|---|
| If the digit to the right is less than 5, round down. If the digit to the right is 5 or greater, round up. | 149,987<br>↓　　　4 < 5<br>100,000　Round down. |

▲ 1982 was the first year the NCAA held championships for women's basketball. About 10,000 people attended.

## More Examples

Round 1,265,483 to the place of the blue digit.

**Ⓐ**

1,265,483
↓　　　2 < 5
1,000,000　Round down.

1,265,483 rounded to the nearest million is 1,000,000.

**Ⓑ**

1,265,483
↓　　　6 > 5
1,300,000　Round up.

1,265,483 rounded to the nearest hundred thousand is 1,300,000.

**Ⓒ**

1,265,483
↓　　　5 = 5
1,270,000　Round up.

1,265,483 rounded to the nearest ten thousand is 1,270,000.

1. **Explain** why 735,489 rounded to the nearest ten thousand is 740,000.

**Round each number to the place of the blue digit.**

2. 2,681    3. 178,365    4. 1,532,300    5. 33,689    6. 6,023,490

**Round 1,654,508 to the place named.**

7. thousands    8. ten thousands    9. hundred thousands

10. hundreds    11. tens    12. millions

▷ **Practice and Problem Solving**    ( Extra Practice, page 58, Set A )

**Round each number to the place of the blue digit.**

13. 78,210    14. 350,962    15. 5,811,326    16. 606,310    17. 890,352

**Round 2,908,365 to the place named.**

18. thousands    19. ten thousands    20. hundred thousands

21. hundreds    22. tens    23. millions

**Name the place to which each number was rounded.**

24. 191,562 to 190,000    25. 4,236,810 to 4,000,000    26. 80,154 to 80,200

**USE DATA For 27–29, use the table.**

27. Which 2 years had the same attendance, rounded to the nearest thousand?

28. How many people in all attended the NCAA Women's Championships in 1999, 2000, and 2001?

29.  **What's the Error?** Sean says that, rounded to the nearest thousand, the attendance in 1997 was the same as in 1998. Describe Sean's error.

**NCAA Women's Basketball Championship Game Attendance**

| Year | Attendance |
|------|-----------|
| 1996 | 23,291 |
| 1997 | 16,714 |
| 1998 | 17,976 |
| 1999 | 17,733 |
| 2000 | 20,060 |
| 2001 | 20,551 |

**Getting Ready for** FCAT **THINK SOLVE EXPLAIN**

30. In 2000, Rob saw this sign at the Florida state border. To the nearest million, what was the population of Florida in 2000?

Explain how you found your answer.

**Welcome to Florida**
The Sunshine State
Population 15,982,378

FCAT TESTED    SSS/GLEs MA.A.4.2.1.5.1 Chooses, describes, and explains estimation strategies used to determine the reasonableness of solutions to real-world problems.

**Chapter 3    39**

# Round Decimals

## ▷ Learn

**WINGING IT** The Pygmy Blue is the smallest butterfly in the United States. Its average width is 0.563 inch. What is the width rounded to the nearest hundredth of an inch?

You can use a number line to round 0.563 to the nearest hundredth.

0.563

```
  ←+——+——+——+——+——+——+——+——+——+——+→
  0.56                            0.57
```

0.563 is closer to 0.56 than to 0.57. So, 0.563 inch rounded to the nearest hundredth of an inch is 0.56 inch.

**Remember**

Rounding rules:
- Find the place to which you want to round.
- If the digit to the right is less than 5, round down.
- If the digit to the right is 5 or greater, round up.

### Examples

Round 0.4537 to the place of the blue digit. Use the rounding rules.

**A**
0.45**3**7   7 > 5
↓
0.45**4**   Round up.

**B**
0.453**7**   3 < 5
↓
0.45   Round down.

**C**
0.4**5**37   5 = 5
↓
0.5   Round up.

## ▷ Check

**1. Explain** how you can use the rounding rules to round $8.49 to the nearest dollar and to the nearest tenth of a dollar.

**Round each number to the place of the blue digit.**

**2.** 0.7**8**3      **3.** 0.2**5**6      **4.** 0.17**3**2

**5.** 0.6**8**5      **6.** 0.6**6**

**Round 0.6285 to the place named.**

**7.** tenths          **8.** hundredths

**9.** thousandths     **10.** ones

**Round each number to the place of the blue digit.**

**11.** 3.193      **12.** 29.423      **13.** 2.0475      **14.** 0.86      **15.** 1.234

**Round 2.5438 to the place named.**

**16.** tenths      **17.** hundredths      **18.** thousandths      **19.** ones

**Name the place to which each number was rounded.**

**20.** 0.562 to 0.56      **21.** 6.8354 to 6.835      **22.** 80.154 to 80.2

**23.** 1.7592 to 1.759      **24.** 5.9273 to 6      **25.** 2.3625 to 2.36

**Round to the nearest tenth of a dollar and to the nearest dollar.**

**26.** $10.56      **27.** $0.42      **28.** $0.98      **29.** $5.45

**30.** $4.02      **31.** $32.36      **32.** $9.49      **33.** $10.91

**Round each number to the nearest hundredth.**

**34.** nine hundred thirty-four thousandths

**35.** $10 + 5 + 0.2 + 0.06 + 0.002$

**36.** seven and eighty-three thousandths

**37.** $2 + 0.8 + 0.09 + 0.005 + 0.0003$

**USE DATA For 38–40, use the graph.**

**38.** Round the width of the Dwarf Blue to the nearest tenth of an inch.

**39.** Which two butterflies are the same width when each width is rounded to the nearest hundredth of an inch?

**40.** Which butterfly is 0.88 inch wide when its width is rounded to the nearest hundredth of an inch?

**41.** **Vocabulary Power** *Round* means "to increase or decrease to the nearest unit." What is another math definition for *round*?

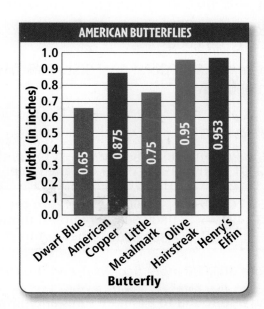

**Getting Ready for FCAT** [THINK SOLVE EXPLAIN]

**42.** Rachel weighed a bunch of grapes at the store. The scale shows the weight of the grapes in pounds. What is the weight to the nearest tenth of a pound? Explain how you got your answer.

2.54

FCAT TESTED ► SSS/GLEs MA.A.4.2.1.5.1 Chooses, describes, and explains estimation strategies used to determine the reasonableness of solutions to real-world problems.

Chapter 3   **41**

# Estimate Sums and Differences

### Quick Review

Round to the nearest thousand.

**1.** 457,986 **2.** 2,057,516
**3.** 2,954 **4.** 9,051,687
**5.** 326,198

**VOCABULARY**

estimate
front-end estimation

**UNDERWATER FLORIDA** John Pennekamp Coral Reef State Park, located on Key Largo, off the coast of southern Florida, was the first undersea park in the United States. The park consists of 60,124 underwater acres and includes the famous coral reef. It also has 2,960 acres of coastal land. About how many total acres does the park have?

You can round to estimate sums and differences of whole numbers. When you **estimate**, you find a number that is close to an exact amount.

$$
\begin{array}{rcl}
60,124 & \to & 60,000 \\
+\ 2,960 & \to & +\ 3,000 \\
\hline
 & & 63,000
\end{array}
$$
Round to the nearest thousand. Then add.

So, John Pennekamp Coral Reef State Park has about 63,000 acres.

## Example 1

About how many more people visited the park in 2000–2001 than in 1991–1992? Use the table.

$$
\begin{array}{rcl}
1,050,749 & \to & 1,100,000 \\
-\ \ 782,421 & \to & -\ \ 800,000 \\
\hline
 & & 300,000
\end{array}
$$
Round to the nearest hundred thousand. Then subtract.

| JOHN PENNEKAMP STATE PARK ATTENDANCE | |
|---|---|
| **Year** | **Number of Visitors** |
| 1991–1992 | 782,421 |
| 2000–2001 | 1,050,749 |

So, about 300,000 more people visited the park in 2000–2001.

You can also round to estimate sums and differences of decimals.

## More Examples

**A** Round to the nearest whole number. Then subtract.

$$
\begin{array}{rcl}
89.5 & \to & 90 \\
-\ 1.83 & \to & -\ 2 \\
\hline
 & & 88
\end{array}
$$

**B** Round to the nearest tenth. Then add.

$$
\begin{array}{rcl}
3.675 & \to & 3.7 \\
2.502 & \to & 2.5 \\
+0.32 & \to & +0.3 \\
\hline
 & & 6.5
\end{array}
$$

**C** Round to the nearest dollar. Then add.

$$
\begin{array}{rcl}
\$10.00 & \to & \$10 \\
+\$\ 8.19 & \to & +\$\ 8 \\
\hline
 & & \$18
\end{array}
$$

## Front-End Estimation

Another way to estimate a sum or difference is to use **front-end estimation**. When you use front-end estimation, you add or subtract the values of the front digits of each number.

Jacksonville

FLORIDA

Orlando

420.9 miles

289.5 miles

John Pennekamp
State Park

### Example 2

About how much farther is the park from Jacksonville than from Orlando?

| | | |
|---|---|---|
| 420.9 → | 400 | Subtract the values of the |
| −289.5 → | −200 | front digits of each number. |
| | 200 | |

So, the park is about 200 miles farther from Jacksonville than from Orlando.

### More Examples

| **Ⓐ** 3,287 + 4,501 | **Ⓑ** 587 − 435 | **Ⓒ** 13.6 + 22.9 |
|---|---|---|
| 3,287 → 3,000 | 587 → 500 | 13.6 → 10 |
| +4,501 → +4,000 | −435 → −400 | +22.9 → +20 |
| 7,000 | 100 | 30 |

- In Example A, how would a rounded estimate differ from the front-end estimate?

- When you use front-end estimation to estimate a sum, is your estimate greater than or less than the actual sum? Explain.

### ▶ Check

1. **Explain** how you use front-end estimation to estimate the sum 73.25 + 91.02.

2. How is estimating sums and differences of decimals like estimating sums and differences of whole numbers?

**Estimate by rounding.**

| 3. | 85,476 | 4. | 845,008 | 5. | 1.22 | 6. | $1.78 | 7. | 4.87 |
|---|---|---|---|---|---|---|---|---|---|
| | −41,131 | | +124,895 | | +3.51 | | −$1.04 | | +2.94 |

LESSON CONTINUES

FCAT
TESTED   SSS/GLEs MA.A.4.2.1.5.1 *Chooses, describes, and explains estimation strategies used to determine the reasonableness of solutions to real-world problems.*

**Estimate by using front-end estimation.**

**8.**  752,401
   −491,922

**9.**  21,421
   +32,970

**10.**  $52.89
   −$18.78

**11.**  5.681
   +3.025

**12.**  4.35
   −0.78

## ▶ Practice and Problem Solving    Extra Practice, page 58, Set B

**Estimate by rounding.**

**13.**  93,582
   +82,785

**14.**  82,631
   −22,965

**15.**  $7.92
   +$5.39

**16.**  30.23
   +13.65

**17.**  $7.36
   −$6.41

**18.** 397,352 + 187,590

**19.** 512,824 − 495,008

**20.** 1,289,405 + 3,321,945

**21.** 2.39 + 8.06

**22.** 0.702 − 0.397

**23.** 14.782 + 8.110

**Estimate by using front-end estimation.**

**24.**  502,963
   −132,631

**25.**  42,110
   +16,850

**26.**  2.704
   +1.818

**27.**  $500.00
   −$279.65

**28.**  7.153
   +4.099

**29.** 5,278 + 3,621

**30.** 13,500 − 11,693

**31.** 6,345,672 − 1,254,789

**32.** 24.89 − 17.34

**33.** 33.872 + 12.946

**34.** 37.054 + 27.922

**Estimate to compare. Write < or > for each ●.**

**35.** 69,210 + 24,391 ● 68,258 + 45,924

**36.** 74,361 + 24,391 ● 91,308 − 25,924

**37.** 82,356 − 14,638 ● 86,551 − 13,725

**38.** 8.14 − 4.89 ● 7.45 − 2.37

**39.** 2.8 + 9.1 ● 11 + 5

**40.** 7.925 + 5.392 ● 15.431 − 4.974

**USE DATA For 41–42, use the table.**

**41.** About how much farther is it to John Pennekamp State Park from Chattanooga, TN, than from Montgomery, AL?

**42.** Josh drove from his home in Greensboro, NC, to John Pennekamp State Park, and then he drove to visit his cousin in Tallahassee, FL. About how many miles did he drive?

**43.** ✏ **Write a problem** in which front-end estimation gives an estimate closer to the exact answer than rounding.

| DISTANCE TO JOHN PENNEKAMP STATE PARK (in miles) | |
|---|---|
| Chattanooga, TN | 836.22 |
| Greensboro, NC | 850.34 |
| Montgomery, AL | 746.49 |
| Tallahassee, FL | 539.02 |

**44.** Three duffel bags weigh 49.49 pounds, 53.73 pounds, and 77.89 pounds. Estimate the total weight to the nearest pound.

**45.**  **What's the Question?** Ally and three friends are in line to buy tickets for a snorkeling trip. Ally is right behind Eric and in front of Lynn. Lee is last. Eric is the answer.

**46.** **REASONING** There are 1.609344 kilometers in 1 mile. Estimate to the nearest tenth the number of kilometers in 3 miles.

## Getting Ready for FCAT [THINK SOLVE EXPLAIN]

**47.** The furniture store has the items shown on sale. Mrs. Wilson wants to buy the sofa, the lamp table, and the rug for her living room. ESTIMATE how much Mrs. Wilson will spend. Explain.

 **$698**   **$429**   **$269**

**48.** Mrs. Wilson also wants to buy a chair that costs $263.95 and a lamp that costs $126.50. ESTIMATE how much she will spend on these two items.

## Problem Solving  Thinker's Corner

Another way to estimate is called clustering. **Clustering** is a method used when all addends are close to, or clustered around, a number.

Estimate: 24.8 + 26.82 + 24.3 + 25.7

Look at the number line. These four numbers all cluster around 25.

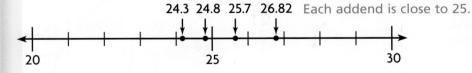

24.3  24.8  25.7  26.82   Each addend is close to 25.

20        25        30

Use 25 + 25 + 25 + 25   or   4 × 25 = 100.

So, the estimated sum is 100.

**Use clustering to estimate each sum.**

**1.** 445 + 463 + 455

**2.** 891 + 904 + 912 + 885

**3.** 10.51 + 11.2 + 9.9 + 9.65

**4.** 1,891 + 1,975 + 2,004

# Add and Subtract Whole Numbers

▶ **Learn**

**MAKE A DIFFERENCE!** At the Wildlife Center, volunteers are helping scientists place black-footed ferrets back into their natural habitats. This year's volunteers have logged 12,385 hours of service. Last year they logged 10,098 hours. How many hours did they log for both years?

## Example 1

Add. 12,385 + 10,098

Estimate. 12,000 + 10,000 = 22,000

```
  1 1
 12,385     Start with the ones.
+10,098     Regroup as needed.
 22,483
```

So, the volunteers logged 22,483 hours for both years. This is close to the estimate, so the answer is reasonable.

## Example 2

How many more hours were logged this year than last year?

Subtract. 12,385 − 10,098

Estimate. 12,000 − 10,000 = 2,000

```
      17
    2 7 15
 12,385     Start with the ones.
−10,098     Regroup as needed.
  2,287
```

So, the volunteers logged 2,287 more hours this year than last year. This is close to the estimate, so the answer is reasonable.

- How do you use place value when you add and subtract?

▲ A black-footed ferret

**Technology Link**

More Practice: Harcourt Mega Math The Number Games, *Tiny's Think Tank*, Levels B, C

**1. Explain** how you know which place values to regroup when adding.

**Find the sum or difference. Estimate to check.**

| 2. | 3. | 4. | 5. | 6. |
|---|---|---|---|---|
| 6,317 <br> +8,903 | 12,911 <br> −10,260 | 11,004 <br> + 8,986 | 607,411 <br> −249,897 | 998,623 <br> −771,128 |

▶ **Practice and Problem Solving**  ( Extra Practice, page 58, Set C )

**Find the sum or difference. Estimate to check.**

| 7. | 8. | 9. | 10. | 11. |
|---|---|---|---|---|
| 5,752 <br> −1,842 | 8,875 <br> +4,908 | 327,032 <br> −109,986 | 17,620 <br> − 9,003 | 675,531 <br> +318,746 |

**12.** 234 + 125 + 681

**13.** 6,010 − 498

**14.** 2,943 + 7,894

**15.** 1,298 + 786 + 412

**16.** 511,832 + 238,778

**17.** 61,933 − 12,040

**18.** 208 + 816 + 7,049

**19.** 17,001 − 8,542

**20.** 209,123 − 146,897

**USE DATA** For 21–23, use the circle graphs.

**21.** How many species of birds are *not* threatened and *not* extinct? How many species of reptiles? How many species of mammals?

**22.** How many threatened and extinct species are there in all three classes of animals?

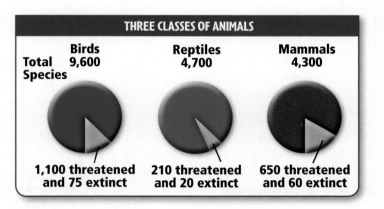

**THREE CLASSES OF ANIMALS**

| | Birds | Reptiles | Mammals |
|---|---|---|---|
| Total Species | 9,600 | 4,700 | 4,300 |

1,100 threatened and 75 extinct      210 threatened and 20 extinct      650 threatened and 60 extinct

**23.** ✏ **Write About It** How many more bird species are threatened than reptile species? Explain.

**24.** During track practice, four runners ran the $\frac{1}{4}$-mile run. Greg finished after Sean. Alex finished before Sean but after Louis. Who finished first?

**Getting Ready for FCAT**

**25.** At the carnival, what was the total amount raised by the two booths that collected the most money?

   **A.** $910
   **B.** $1,206
   **C.** $1,342
   **D.** $1,729

| SPRING CARNIVAL | |
|---|---|
| **Booth** | **Amount Raised** |
| Bean Bag Toss | $387 |
| Basketball Shoot | $523 |
| Balloon Break | $819 |

FCAT TESTED  SSS/GLEs MA.A.1.2.3.5.1 Translates problem situations into diagrams, models, and numerals using whole numbers, fractions, mixed numbers, decimals, and percents. *also* MA.A.3.2.1.5.3, MA.A.3.2.2.5.1

Chapter 3  **47**

## LESSON
# 5 Add and Subtract Decimals

### Quick Review

1. 321 + 40
2. 64 − 17
3. 1,643 + 2,309
4. 969 − 333
5. 1,075 + 762 + 956

▶ **Learn**

**SPLISH SPLASH** Tyler's science class recorded the weather for the first week in March. Tyler's job was to measure the rainfall. It rained 2 days during that week. On Tuesday, Tyler recorded 1.95 inches of rain, and on Friday another 0.85 inch fell. How much rain did Tyler record during the first week in March?

**Technology Link**

More Practice: Harcourt Mega Math The Number Games, *Tiny's Think Tank*, Level L *Buggy Bargains*, Level I

## Example 1 Add. 1.95 + 0.85

Estimate. 2 + 1 = 3

**STEP 1**

Line up the decimal points to align place-value positions. Add the hundredths.

$$\begin{array}{r} {}^{1}\phantom{0} \\ 1.95 \\ +0.85 \\ \hline 0 \end{array}$$

**STEP 2**

Add the tenths.

$$\begin{array}{r} {}^{1}\ {}^{1} \\ 1.95 \\ +0.85 \\ \hline 80 \end{array}$$

**STEP 3**

Add the ones. Place the decimal point in the sum.

$$\begin{array}{r} {}^{1}\ {}^{1} \\ 1.95 \\ +0.85 \\ \hline 2.80 \end{array}$$

So, Tyler recorded 2.80 inches of rain during the first week of March. This is close to the estimate, so the answer is reasonable.

## More Examples

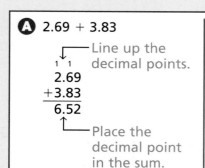

**A** 2.69 + 3.83

Line up the decimal points.

$$\begin{array}{r} {}^{1}\ {}^{1} \\ 2.69 \\ +3.83 \\ \hline 6.52 \end{array}$$

Place the decimal point in the sum.

**B** 13.76 + 8.5

$$\begin{array}{r} {}^{1}\ {}^{1} \\ 13.76 \\ +\ 8.50 \\ \hline 22.26 \end{array}$$ ← Place a zero for an equivalent decimal.

• When is it helpful to show an equivalent decimal in addition?

## Subtract Decimals

Tyler recorded 2.75 inches of rain during the first week in April, and then he measured 4.92 inches of rain for the entire month of April. How much rain fell in April after the first week?

### Example 2 Subtract. 4.92 − 2.75

Estimate. 5 − 3 = 2

| **STEP 1** | **STEP 2** | **STEP 3** |
|---|---|---|
| Line up the decimal points to align place-value positions. Subtract the hundredths. Regroup if needed. | Subtract the tenths. Regroup if needed. | Subtract the ones. |
| $$\begin{array}{r} {}^{8\,12} \\ 4.9\not{2} \\ -\ 2.75 \\ \hline 7 \end{array}$$ | $$\begin{array}{r} {}^{8\,12} \\ 4.9\not{2} \\ -\ 2.75 \\ \hline 17 \end{array}$$ | $$\begin{array}{r} {}^{8\,12} \\ 4.9\not{2} \\ -\ 2.75 \\ \hline 2.17 \end{array}$$ Place the decimal point. |

So, 2.17 inches of rain fell in April after the first week.
This is close to the estimate, so the answer is reasonable.

## More Examples

**A** 5.12 − 1.08

$$\begin{array}{r} {}^{0\,12} \\ 5.\not{1}2 \\ -\ 1.08 \\ \hline 4.04 \end{array}$$

**B** 24.23 − 11.6

$$\begin{array}{r} {}^{3\,12} \\ 24.\not{2}3 \\ -\ 11.60 \\ \hline 12.63 \end{array}$$ Place a zero to show an ←equivalent decimal.

**C** 1.6 − 0.342

$$\begin{array}{r} {}^{9} \\ {}^{5\,10\,10} \\ 1.6\not{0}\not{0} \\ -\ 0.342 \\ \hline 1.258 \end{array}$$ Place zeros ← to show an equivalent decimal.

- Where do you place the decimal point in the answer?

**MATH IDEA** You can add and subtract decimals the same way you add and subtract whole numbers if you line up the decimal points first.

## ▶ Check

1. **Explain** why you can place zeros to the right of the last digit in a decimal without changing its value.

**Find the sum. Estimate to check.**

| **2.** | **3.** | **4.** | **5.** | **6.** |
|---|---|---|---|---|
| 0.3 | 2.7 | 11.74 | 5.08 | 12.1 |
| +0.9 | 1.15 | 5.12 | +4.18 | + 9.01 |
| | +0.62 | 6.3 | | |
| | | + 1.54 | | |

**LESSON CONTINUES** ▶

**Find the difference. Estimate to check.**

**7.** 0.8
−0.3

**8.** 1.23
−0.47

**9.** 4.06
−2.85

**10.** 10.2
− 8.67

**11.** 23.05
−12.8

**12.** 4.3 − 3.6

**13.** 1.6 − 0.8

**14.** 7.2 − 5.69

**15.** 17.13 − 10.9

---

## ▶ Practice and Problem Solving    Extra Practice, page 58, Set C

**Find the sum or difference. Estimate to check.**

**16.** 5.6
7.8
+1.7

**17.** 40.8
25.17
+16.3

**18.** 6.008
+1.883

**19.** 45.903
9.374
+51.28

**20.** 13.046
+ 0.298

**21.** 1.5
−0.7

**22.** 4.12
−1.852

**23.** 7.095
−5.64

**24.** 16.1
− 7.34

**25.** 43.18
−29.9

**26.** 20.1
− 8.652

**27.** 3.15
− 1.99

**28.** 5.07
−0.68

**29.** 22.6
− 9.45

**30.** 21.064
− 9.33

**31.** 1.84 + 1.92

**32.** 1.34 + 4.61

**33.** 2.05 + 0.97

**34.** 3.1 + 0.42 + 8.3

**ALGEBRA** **Find a pattern. Write a rule. Use your rule to find the missing numbers in the pattern.**

**35.** 2.3, 2.5, 2.4, 2.6, 2.5, ■, 2.6, 2.8, ■

**36.** 0.45, 0.55, 0.65, ■, ■, 0.95, 1.05, 1.15

**37.** 3.96, 3.98, ■, 4.02, 4.04, ■, 4.08, 4.10

**38.** 1.25, 1.50, 1.75, 2.00, 2.25, 2.50, ■, ■

**USE DATA For 39–40, use the graph.**

**39.** Between which two months does the average monthly precipitation have the greatest increase? How many inches?

**40.** The record in Indianapolis for the most precipitation in one month occurred in July 1875, when 13.12 inches of rain fell. How much greater was this than the average precipitation for July?

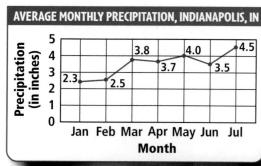

**41.** **GEOMETRY** Bob is enclosing a rectangular field with fencing. The field is 120 feet long and 50 feet wide. How much fencing does he need?

**42.** **REASONING** Without adding, how do you know that the sum of 36.179 and 8.63 will have a 9 in the thousandths place?

**43.** ▤**FAST FACT** • **SCIENCE** In August 1992, during Hurricane Andrew, 57.68 inches of rain fell in Florida. The average amount of rainfall for an entire year in Florida is 53.52 inches. How much greater was the hurricane's rainfall than Florida's annual rainfall?

**44.** Steve spent $9.45 on a ticket to the game and $3.75 for snacks. He had $7.35 left at the end of the day. How much did he have at the beginning of the day?

## Getting Ready for ⭐FCAT

**45.** Brian's father helped him draw this map of his neighborhood. Following the roads shown, what is the shortest distance from Brian's house to the library?

**A.** 9.7 miles
**B.** 6.1 miles
**C.** 3.35 miles
**D.** 3 miles

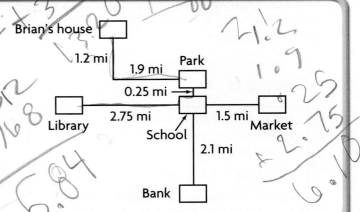

Brian's house
1.2 mi
1.9 mi
Park
0.25 mi →
Library
2.75 mi
School
1.5 mi
Market
2.1 mi
Bank

# Problem Solving  LiNKÜP... to Science

Scientists use weather instruments to collect data about rainfall. The graph below shows the average annual precipitation for five cities in the United States.

**USE DATA** For 1–3, use the graph.

**1.** How much less was the precipitation in Roanoke, VA, than in Memphis, TN?

**2.** How much greater was the precipitation in Miami, FL, than in Asheville, NC?

**3.** How much greater was the precipitation in the city with the greatest precipitation than in the city with the least precipitation?

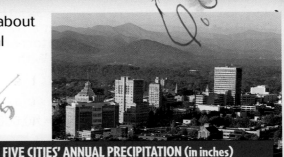

| FIVE CITIES' ANNUAL PRECIPITATION (in inches) | | |
|---|---|---|
| Asheville, North Carolina | ☁☁☁☁☁ | 47.59 |
| Roanoke, Virginia | ☁☁☁☁☁ | 41.13 |
| Gary, Indiana | ☁☁☁☁ | 34.66 |
| Memphis, Tennessee | ☁☁☁☁☁ | 52.10 |
| Miami, Florida | ☁☁☁☁☁☁ | 55.91 |

Key: Each ☁ = 10 inches of rain.

# Choose a Method

▶ **Learn**

**AD TIME ADDS UP!** During Super Bowl XXXVI, the average cost for a 30-second commercial was $1,900,000. A 1-minute commercial cost $3,800,000. If a company bought a 1-minute commercial and a 30-second commercial, how much was the combined cost?

## Example 1

**Use Mental Math** Find the combined cost of a 30-second and a 1-minute commercial.

$1,900,000 + 3,800,000 = 5,700,000$

So, the combined cost was $5,700,000.

## Example 2 
A survey showed that 42,663,850 households watched Super Bowl XXXVI. Of those, 3,041,660 said they watched just to see the commercials. How many households tuned in to see the game?

**Use a Calculator** To find the exact answer, subtract using a calculator. Calculators are especially useful when computing with greater numbers.

Subtract. $42,663,850 - 3,041,660$

Estimate. $43,000,000 - 3,000,000 = 40,000,000$

**Use Paper and Pencil** The answer can also be computed using paper and pencil.

$\begin{array}{r} {\scriptstyle 3\,12} \quad\ {\scriptstyle 7\,15} \\ 42,663,8\cancel{5}0 \\ -\ 3,041,660 \\ \hline 39,622,190 \end{array}$  Start with the ones.
Regroup as needed.

So, 39,622,190 households tuned in to see the game. This is close to the estimate, so the answer is reasonable.

# Decimals

At the Super Bowl, Kasey had $40.00 to spend. She bought a sandwich for $8.25 and a soda for $2.75. How much money did Kasey have left?

## Example 3

**Use Mental Math**

| | | |
|---|---|---|
| $8.00 + $2.00 | = $10.00 | **Think:** Add the dollar amounts first. |
| $0.25 + $0.75 | = $1.00 | Add the cents. |
| $10.00 + $1.00 | = $11.00 | Find the sum. |

So, $8.25 + $2.75 = $11.00

$40.00 − $11.00 = $29.00    Subtract the sum from $40.00.

So, Kasey had $29.00 left.

## Example 4

**Use a Calculator** At the end of the game, Kasey wanted to buy a Super Bowl cap for $18.95 and a key chain for $4.85. Did Kasey have enough money to buy both?

Since $23.80 < $29.00, Kasey had enough money to buy both.

**Use Paper and Pencil** You can also use paper and pencil.

| | |
|---|---|
| $18.95 | Align place-value positions. |
| + 4.85 | Add. |
| $23.80 | Place the decimal point in the sum. |

Since $23.80 < $29.00, Kasey had enough money to buy both.

## Check

1. **Explain** which method you could choose to find $7.08 + $73.92.

**Choose a method. Find the sum or difference.**

| 2. | 56,219 | 3. | 5,462,000 | 4. | 4,234.85 | 5. | $40.50 |
|---|---|---|---|---|---|---|---|
| | +62,793 | | −3,450,000 | | +2,567.76 | | − $20.75 |

**LESSON CONTINUES** ▶

FCAT
TESTED  SSS/GLEs MA.A.1.2.3.5.1 Translates problem situations into diagrams, models, and
numerals using whole numbers, fractions, mixed numbers, decimals, and percents.
also MA.A.3.2.3.5.1

Chapter 3  **53**

**Choose a method. Find the sum or difference.**

6.  3,432,213
    +3,513,568

7.  743,041
    −244,130

8.  45,000
    +35,000

9.  2,001,005
    +7,011,300

10. 990,000
    −840,000

11. 49,672
    −18,770

12. 873,450
    +234,684

13. 87,654
    +12,345

14. $9.15
    − $8.85

15. 145.000
    −125.000

16. $87.96
    + $13.13

17. 143.097
    − 29.798

18. 10.357
    + 4.321

19. 4.000
    −0.832

20. $87.00
    + $23.00

21. 2,480.50
    −1,240.25

22. 47,205 − 32,000

23. 3,556,014 + 879,843

24. 7,800,000 − 4,200,000

25. 38.00 + 21.5

26. 1,234.5 − 927.68

27. 450.34 + 387.56

### ALGEBRA  Find the missing digits.

28. 7,2■5
    +6,■72
    1■,357

29. 8,47■
    −4,3■8
    ■,145

30. 1,369,36■
    − 526,■23
    84■,239

31. 4,382,1■7
    + 4■8,287
    4,■20,404

**USE DATA For 32–34, use the table.**

32. How many more households watched Super Bowl XX compared to Super Bowl XVI?

33. What is the order of the Super Bowls from the one with the highest ratings to the one with the lowest ratings?

34. ✏ **Write a problem** that can be solved by using mental math. Use the information in the table.

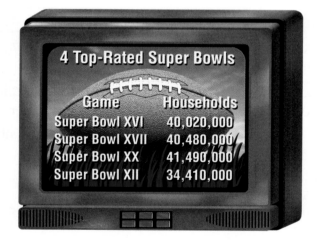

**4 Top-Rated Super Bowls**

| Game | Households |
| --- | --- |
| Super Bowl XVI | 40,020,000 |
| Super Bowl XVII | 40,480,000 |
| Super Bowl XX | 41,490,000 |
| Super Bowl XII | 34,410,000 |

35. **ESTIMATION** Angie estimates that 234,678 + 785,000 is about 100,000. Is she correct? Explain.

36. **NUMBER SENSE** Write a decimal that is less than 10.55 + 12.45 but greater than 31.75 − 19.25.

37. The computer club has raised $119.25 for new software. The club wants to buy 3 programs that cost $34.95, $24.99, and $69.99. About how much more money does the club need to raise to buy the 3 programs?

38. India, Ukraine, and the United States combined have more than 40,000 movie theaters. India has 8,975 theaters. Ukraine has 8,702 fewer than the U.S. and 5,985 more than India. How many theaters are in the U.S.?

**39.** The cost of a 30-second commercial in the 1967 Super Bowl was $42,500. In 2001, the cost of a 30-second commercial was $2,157,500 more than in 1967. What was the cost of a 30-second commercial in 2001?

**40.** After the game, Colleen spent $3.50 for a snack, $2.25 for a drink, and $10.95 for a shirt. She then had $8.30 left in her wallet. How much money did she have in her wallet before she went shopping?

## Getting Ready for FCAT

**41.** The table at the right shows the votes for the governor of Florida in 1998. What was the total number of votes for Florida's governor in 1998?

| FLORIDA, 1998 GUBERNATORIAL ELECTION | |
|---|---|
| **Candidate** | **Number of Votes** |
| Jeb Bush | 2,192,105 |
| Buddy MacKay | 1,773,054 |

**A.** 3,965,159

**B.** 3,865,159

**C.** 1,621,151

**D.** 419,051

## Problem Solving  Thinker's Corner

**MENTAL MATH** **Compatible numbers** are numbers that are easy to compute mentally. Two decimals which have a whole-number sum are compatible numbers.

$3.2 + 4.8 = 8$   3.2 and 4.8 are compatible numbers.

*3.9 and 2.1 are compatible numbers*

*2.5 and 7.5 are compatible numbers*

Using the Commutative and Associative Properties, along with mental math strategies, can help you solve problems.

**Find the sum.**  $3.9 + 2.5 + 2.1 + 7.5$

$$3.9 + 2.5 + 2.1 + 7.5 = 3.9 + 2.1 + 2.5 + 7.5 \quad \text{Commutative Property}$$
$$= (3.9 + 2.1) + (2.5 + 7.5) \quad \text{Associative Property}$$
$$= 6 + 10$$
$$= 16$$

So, the sum is 16.

**Use compatible numbers and the Commutative and Associative Properties to find each sum.**

**1.** $2.6 + 3.0 + 1.4 + 4.0$

**2.** $0.25 + 3.7 + 2.3 + 0.75$

**3.** $2.3 + 8.2 + 3.8 + 5.7$

**4.** $1.5 + 2.5 + 8.5 + 2.5$

# Problem Solving Strategy
## Use Logical Reasoning

**PROBLEM** Paco, Rob, Shawna, and Milly each won an award at Field Day. Rob's total score was less than 5,000 points. Shawna scored the fewest points. Paco scored 355 more points than Shawna. How many points did they each score?

### UNDERSTAND

- What do you need to find out?

- What information will you use?

### PLAN

- What strategy can you use?

  You can *use logical reasoning* to organize the information in a table.

FIELD DAY
Points Scored
1ˢᵗ Award 6,050 pts.
2ᴺᴰ Award 4,230 pts.
3ᴿᴰ Award 1,820 pts.
4ᵀᴴ Award 1,465 pts.

### SOLVE

- How can you solve the problem?

  Make a table to show the information you know. Since each person won an award, there can be only one *yes* in each row of the table.

  *Shawna* scored the fewest points. Put *yes* in the 1,465 column for Shawna and *no* in the remaining columns.

  *Paco* scored 355 + 1,465 points. Put *yes* in the 1,820 column for Paco.

  *Rob* must have scored 4,230 points, since his total score was less than 5,000 points.

  So, *Milly* won the remaining award, with 6,050 points.

| FIELD DAY SCORES | | | | |
|---|---|---|---|---|
| | **6,050** | **4,230** | **1,820** | **1,465** |
| **Paco** | No | No | Yes | No |
| **Rob** | No | Yes | No | No |
| **Shawna** | No | No | No | Yes |
| **Milly** | Yes | No | No | No |

### CHECK

- Look back at the problem. Does the answer make sense for the problem? Explain.

## Problem Solving Practice

### Strategies

Draw a Diagram or Picture
Make a Model or Act It Out
Make an Organized List
Find a Pattern
Make a Table or Graph
Predict and Test
Work Backward
Solve a Simpler Problem
Write an Equation
▶ **Use Logical Reasoning**

**Problem Solving**

**Use logical reasoning to solve.**

1. **What if** the problem did not say that Shawna scored the fewest points? Could you still solve the problem? Explain.

2. Tom, Andy, and Neil mixed up their clothes at the beach. Each one had someone else's hat and sandals. Andy had Tom's hat and Neil's sandals. Whose hat and sandals did each person have?

**Ari, Sue, and Jack are hauling truckloads of fruit. The loads weigh 87,500; 76,750; and 91,250 pounds. Ari's load weighs more than Sue's, but their loads weigh the same when rounded to the nearest ten thousand. Jack's load is lighter than Ari's.**

3. If you listed the weights of Ari's, Sue's, and Jack's truckloads in order from greatest to least, which list is correct?

   **A** Jill, Jack, Ari
   **B** Ari, Sue, Jack
   **C** Sue, Jack, Ari
   **D** Jack, Ari, Sue

4. Which information is *not* necessary to solve problem 3?

   **F** Ari's load weighs more than Sue's.
   **G** Ari's and Sue's weights rounded to the nearest ten thousand are equal.
   **H** Jack's load is lighter than Ari's.
   **J** Weights: 87,500; 76,750; 91,250

## Mixed Strategy Practice

5. Decimals A, B, C, D, and E are shown at the right. C is the least of the decimals. D is greater than A. C and E have the same thousandths digit. D is less than B. Which decimal goes with which letter?

6. **REASONING** You have two sand-filled egg timers, one for 9 minutes and one for 2 minutes. How can you use them to time a 5-minute egg?

7. Lightning can be as hot as 50,000°F. The surface of the sun is about 11,000°F. How much hotter can lightning be than the surface of the sun?

8. Last year, the West Plant of the Citrus Company processed 809,309 lemons. The East Plant processed 978,503 grapefruits. If the Citrus Company processed 689,444 more oranges than grapefruits and lemons, how many oranges were processed?

FCAT TESTED  SSS/GLEs MA.A.1.2.2.5.2 Compares and orders whole numbers using concrete materials, number lines, drawings, and numerals. *also* MA.A.3.2.2.5.1

Chapter 3  **57**

# Extra Practice

## Set A (pp. 38–39, 40–41)

**Round each number to the place of the blue digit.**

**1.** 2,517     **2.** 450,339     **3.** 724,950     **4.** 3,620,740     **5.** 7,852,060

**6.** 2.0647     **7.** 1.3686     **8.** 34.0685     **9.** 7.3168     **10.** 79.5063

## Set B (pp. 42–45)

**Estimate by rounding.**

| | | | |
|---|---|---|---|
| **1.**    48,502 <br> $+37,154$ | **2.**    518,273 <br> $-284,043$ | **3.**    3.85 <br> $+7.07$ | **4.**    7.948 <br> $-2.034$ |

**Estimate by using front-end estimation.**

| | | | |
|---|---|---|---|
| **5.**    35,704 <br> $+40,355$ | **6.**    547,041 <br> $-231,454$ | **7.**    32.75 <br> $+50.15$ | **8.**    9.68 <br> $-3.50$ |

## Set C (pp. 46–47, 48–51)

**Find the sum or difference. Estimate to check.**

| | | | |
|---|---|---|---|
| **1.**    9,002 <br> $-7,784$ | **2.**    16,456 <br> $+\ 9,023$ | **3.**    31,216 <br> $-18,927$ | **4.**    48,898 <br> $+61,124$ |
| **5.**    $5.83 <br> $+\$3.74$ | **6.**    6.57 <br> $-3.45$ | **7.**    15.04 <br> $-\ 4.835$ | **8.**    $367.09 <br> $+\$\ \ 14.52$ |

**9.** 80.54 + 29.06     **10.** 482.37 − 129.693     **11.** 83.6 + 154.73

**12.** There were 11,561 fans at Game 1 and 15,907 fans at Game 2. How many more fans attended Game 2?

## Set D (pp. 52–55)

**Choose a method. Find the sum or difference.**

| | | | |
|---|---|---|---|
| **1.**    78,000 <br> $+23,000$ | **2.**    89,504 <br> $-43,750$ | **3.**    8,400,000 <br> $-\ \ 600,000$ | **4.**    2,600,898 <br> $+\ \ \ 452,917$ |
| **5.**    $6.18 <br> $-\$4.79$ | **6.**    $89.36 <br> $+\$14.89$ | **7.**    132.65 <br> $+\ 58.936$ | **8.**    5,104.8 <br> $-1,987.36$ |

**9.** 403,687 + 280,321     **10.** 8,311,298 − 6,901,283     **11.** 6,352.839 + 4,972.42

# Review/Test

 **CHECK VOCABULARY AND CONCEPTS**

**Choose the best term from the box.**

| front-end estimation |
| round |
| estimate |

1. To find an answer that is close to an exact amount, you can __?__ a sum or difference first. (p. 42)

2. When you estimate by using the values of the front digits of numbers, it is called __?__. (p. 42)

 **CHECK SKILLS**

**Round 4,508,684 to the place named.** (pp. 38–39)

3. ten thousands
4. hundred thousands
5. millions

**Name the place to which each number was rounded.** (pp. 40–41)

6. 0.784 to 0.78
7. 0.11 to 0.1
8. 7.5748 to 7.575

**Estimate by rounding.** (pp. 42–45)

| 9. | 10. | 11. | 12. |
|---|---|---|---|
| 507,294 | 0.404 | 129,054 | 4.807 |
| + 45,602 | −0.231 | +562,081 | −3.746 |

**Estimate by using front-end estimation.**

| 13. | 14. | 15. | 16. |
|---|---|---|---|
| 604,485 | 32,153 | $55.84 | 6.954 |
| +735,327 | −15,407 | +$34.06 | −4.013 |

**Choose a method. Find the sum or difference.** (pp. 46–47, 48–51, 52–55)

| 17. | 18. | 19. | 20. |
|---|---|---|---|
| 5,000 | 950,729 | 6,074,851 | 8,382,900 |
| +2,000 | −563,072 | +5,733,509 | −3,985,631 |

21. 6.062 + 17.581
22. 23.009 − 5.3
23. 840,000 + 670,000

 **CHECK PROBLEM SOLVING**

**Solve.** (pp. 56–57)

24. José, Mary, and Rick played cards. The scores were 725, 510, and 225 points. Rick was *not* third. Mary scored about 300 points more than José. Who earned which score?

25. Ann, Linda, and Hugh have pets. One of them has a turtle, one has a cat, and the other has a goldfish. Ann's pet has 4 feet, but it cannot climb trees. Hugh is allergic to fur. Who has which pet?

# Getting Ready for FCAT

 **NUMBER SENSE, CONCEPTS, AND OPERATIONS**

**1.** What is the difference between the longest jump and the shortest jump listed in the table below?

| LONGEST LONG JUMPS | | |
|---|---|---|
| Year | Distance (in meters) | Athlete |
| 1991 | 8.87 | Lewis |
| 1991 | 8.95 | Powell |
| 1987 | 8.86 | Emmiyan |
| 1968 | 8.90 | Beamon |

**A.** 0.03 meter     **C.** 0.30 meter

**B.** 0.09 meter     **D.** 0.90 meter

**2.** Carl Lewis won the gold medal for the long jump in four of the Olympic Games.

| CARL LEWIS'S LONG JUMPS | |
|---|---|
| Year | Distance (in meters) |
| 1984 | 8.54 |
| 1988 | 8.72 |
| 1992 | 8.67 |
| 1996 | 8.50 |

Which shows Carl Lewis's jumps listed from shortest to longest?

**F.** 8.72, 8.54, 8.50, 8.67

**G.** 8.54, 8.50, 8.67, 8.72

**H.** 8.50, 8.54, 8.67, 8.72

**I.** 8.54, 8.67, 8.72, 8.50

**3. Explain It** Darla bought a 395-page book. If she reads 15 pages each evening, will she finish the book in one month? Explain how you know.

 **DATA ANALYSIS AND PROBABILITY**

**4.** At the school carnival's Win-a-Stamp booth, students spin a wheel to win animal stamps. What is the probability of winning a shark stamp if you spin the wheel once?

**A.** $\frac{1}{8}$     **C.** $\frac{3}{8}$

**B.** $\frac{1}{4}$     **D.** $\frac{5}{8}$

**5.** April recorded her math quiz scores on a stem-and-leaf plot.

| Stem | Leaves |
|---|---|
| 7 | 6 9 9 9 |
| 8 | 3 5 8 |
| 9 | 0 0 1 3 |

What is the mode of her scores?

**F.** 17     **H.** 85

**G.** 79     **I.** 90

**6. Explain It** Serena is designing a board game that will have 16 squares all the same size. She wants the probability of landing on a green square to be $\frac{1}{2}$. How many squares should she color green? Explain your answer.

**GEOMETRY AND SPATIAL SENSE**

**7.** Beth is sewing a patchwork quilt that will be 10 feet wide and 8 feet long. The quilt will be made from squares that are 1 foot on each side. How many squares does Beth need for the quilt?

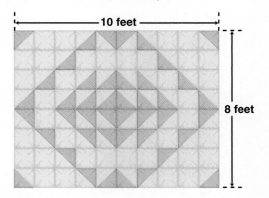

**A.** 10      **C.** 36

**B.** 18      **D.** 80

**8.** Brad covered his math book with a paper book cover. He drew a plane figure on the cover. The figure had 3 angles and 3 sides. None of the sides was congruent. Which term **best** describes the figure Brad drew?

  **F.** equilateral triangle

  **G.** isosceles triangle

  **H.** scalene triangle

  **I.** trapezoid

**9. Explain It** How many lines of symmetry does a square have? Draw a square and show all the lines of symmetry. Explain how you know that the lines you drew are lines of symmetry.

 **MEASUREMENT**

> **TIP**   **Decide on a plan.** See item 10.
> Find the elapsed time for each movie.

**10.** Katie wants to see the longest movie. Which movie should she choose?

  **A.** *Space Exploration*

  **B.** *Happy-Go-Lucky*

  **C.** *The World Around Us*

  **D.** *Clowning Around*

**11.** A large egg weighs about 2.5 ounces. About how much will a dozen large eggs weigh?

  **F.** about 1 pound

  **G.** about 2 pounds

  **H.** about 2.5 pounds

  **I.** about 12 pounds

**12. Explain It** Daniel's goal is to jog 6 kilometers each week. He jogged 2,350 meters on Monday and 1,900 meters on Tuesday. If he jogs 2,000 meters on Wednesday, will he meet his goal? Explain how you know.

# Algebra: Use Addition and Subtraction

**≡FAST FACT** • SCIENCE During the Great Backyard Bird Count, bird enthusiasts across North America count birds for four days. In 2002, a total of 4,727,536 individual birds were counted.

**PROBLEM SOLVING** During the count, a total of 201 belted kingfishers were sighted across Florida. The greatest count in one location was 29 kingfishers in Merritt Island, Florida. Write an equation to find how many were counted in the rest of Florida.

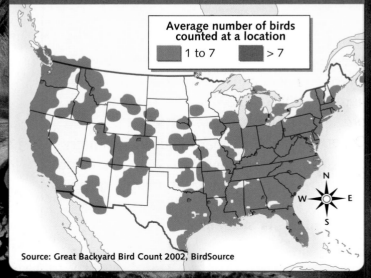

**GREAT BACKYARD BIRD COUNT RESULTS**
(Belted Kingfisher Group Size Map)

Average number of birds counted at a location

■ 1 to 7    ■ > 7

Source: Great Backyard Bird Count 2002, BirdSource

# CHECK WHAT YOU KNOW

Use this page to help you review and remember
important skills needed for Chapter 4.

## MISSING ADDENDS

Find the missing addend.

**1.** $9 + \blacksquare = 15$   **2.** $13 + \blacksquare = 17$   **3.** $8 + \blacksquare = 14$
**4.** $\blacksquare + 6 = 20$   **5.** $\blacksquare + 3 = 15$   **6.** $9 + \blacksquare = 18$
**7.** $\blacksquare + 7 = 15$   **8.** $\blacksquare + 6 = 13$   **9.** $\blacksquare + 8 = 21$

## ADDITION PROPERTIES

Write the letter of the addition property used in
each equation.

**A. Order Property**          **B. Grouping Property**          **C. Identity Property**

**10.** $9 + 8 = 8 + 9$        **11.** $24 + 0 = 24$             **12.** $(5 + 6) + 3 = 5 + (6 + 3)$
**13.** $0 + 12 = 12$          **14.** $23 + 9 = 9 + 23$         **15.** $7 + (1 + 4) = (7 + 1) + 4$

## EXPRESSIONS

Find the value.

**16.** $(8 + 12) - 6$         **17.** $8 + (15 - 5)$            **18.** $17 + (21 - 5)$
**19.** $(21 + 60) - 30$       **20.** $(12 + 9) - 11$           **21.** $50 - (14 + 6)$

# VOCABULARY POWER

**REVIEW**

**Order Property** [ôr′dər prä′ pər•te] *noun*

The word *order* can be used to mean an
arrangement such as alphabetical or
numerical order. Explain what the word
*order* means in this example of the
Order Property.

$6 + 10 + 5 = 10 + 5 + 6$

**PREVIEW**

| | |
|---|---|
| expression | inequality |
| variable | Commutative Property |
| equation | Associative Property |
| solution | compensation |

 www.harcourtschool.com/mathglossary

# Expressions and Variables

▶ **Learn**

**GO FISH**  An **expression** is a mathematical phrase that combines numbers, operation signs, and sometimes variables. It does *not* have an equal sign. These are some expressions:

$$15 + 4 \qquad 9 - 7 \qquad (4 + 6) - 11 \qquad 3 \times 2$$

You can write an expression and find its value.

## Quick Review

**Write the words for each.**

1. $3 + 5$
2. $6 - 2$
3. $10 + 2 + 8$
4. $(2 + 7) - 4$
5. $9 - (5 + 1)$

**VOCABULARY**

**expression**

**variable**

### Example 1

> Matt had 12 fish in his tank. Then he added 3 more fish. How many fish are in his tank now?
>
> | **12 fish in tank** | **plus** | **3 more fish** |
> |:---:|:---:|:---:|
> | ↓ | ↓ | ↓ |
> | 12 | + | 3 |
>
> 15
>
> So, Matt has 15 fish in the tank now.

An expression *may* have a variable. A **variable** is a letter or symbol that stands for one or more numbers. These are some expressions with a variable:

$$4 + n \qquad f - 5 \qquad 6 \times a \qquad 3 + x - 2$$

You can use a variable in an expression to model a situation.

### Example 2

> Julie had 16 fish in her tank. She gave some fish to her sister. Write an expression to show this.
>
> | **16 fish in tank** | **minus** | **some fish** |
> |:---:|:---:|:---:|
> | ↓ | ↓ | ↓ |
> | 16 | − | $f$ |

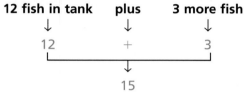

- What can you use to represent a number that you do not know in an expression?

# Find the Value

**MATH IDEA** You can find a value of an expression by replacing the variable with a number and using that number to compute the result.

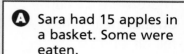

## More Examples

**A** Sara had 15 apples in a basket. Some were eaten.

Let $a$ = the number of apples eaten.

| apples in a basket ↓ | | apples eaten ↓ |
|:---:|:---:|:---:|
| 15 | − | $a$ |

Expression: $15 - a$

---

If 10 apples were eaten, how many were left?

Let $a$ = 10.

$$15 - a$$
$$\downarrow \quad \downarrow$$
$$15 - 10 = 5$$

So, 5 apples were left.

**B** There are 11 people joining the swim team.

Let $p$ = people already on the swim team.

| on swim team ↓ | | joining swim team ↓ |
|:---:|:---:|:---:|
| $p$ | + | 11 |

Expression: $p + 11$

---

If 23 people were already on the team, how many people are on the swim team now?

Let $p$ = 23.

$$p + 11$$
$$\downarrow \quad \downarrow$$
$$23 + 11 = 34$$

So, there are 34 people on the swim team now.

**C** Tom had 18 baseball cards. He traded some of his cards for 3 of Tammy's cards.

Let $c$ = number of cards Tom traded.

| cards Tom had ↓ | | cards Tom traded ↓ | | cards Tom received ↓ |
|:---:|:---:|:---:|:---:|:---:|
| 18 | − | $c$ | + | 3 |

Expression: $18 - c + 3$

---

If Tom traded 6 cards, how many cards does Tom have now?

Let $c$ = 6.

$$18 - c + 3$$
$$\downarrow \quad \downarrow \quad \downarrow$$
$$18 - 6 + 3 = 15$$

So, Tom has 15 baseball cards.

## Check

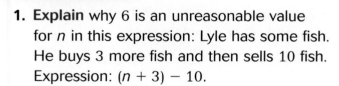

1. **Explain** why 6 is an unreasonable value for $n$ in this expression: Lyle has some fish. He buys 3 more fish and then sells 10 fish. Expression: $(n + 3) - 10$.

**Write an expression. Find the value.**

2. Sam had 10 dimes. He gave Gary 4.

3. eleven added to five

4. Kim had 24 cookies, ate 6, and then baked 12 more.

**Write an expression with a variable. Explain what the variable represents.**

5. Rona had 96 pencils and then sold some.

6. Tim had 17 cards. Joe gave him more.

7. Lee gave me 12 cookies. I ate 6 and then baked more.

**LESSON CONTINUES**

FCAT TESTED SSS/GLEs MA.D.2.2.1.5.2 Uses a variable to represent a given verbal expression (for example, 5 more than a number is $n + 5$). *also* MA.D.2.2.1.5.1

Chapter 4 **65**

**Write an expression. Find the value.**

**8.** Eleven cars were in the race. Seven more cars joined the race.

**9.** Len had 17 shells. He gave 5 shells to Joan.

**10.** The gardener grew 10 rosebushes. Then he sold 2 of them.

**11.** Sam had 23 books. Ann gave him 7 more books, and he gave 13 to Ellen.

**12.** There were 21 cups on the shelf. Three fell off, and six were added.

**Write an expression with a variable. Explain what the variable represents.**

**13.** Don had 37 toys but lost some.

**14.** Holly bought several books. Jon gave her 9 more.

**15.** I had 14 pretzels. I ate some and gave 3 to Mia.

**16.** Julio had some CDs. He gave 2 to Eric and bought 6 new CDs.

**17.** Dina had 73 pens. She sold several.

**18.** Allie had 26 beanbag toys. She gave 9 away and got more for her birthday.

**Find the value of the expression.**

**19.** $50 + n$ if $n$ is $20

**20.** $n + 3,600$ if $n$ is 400

**21.** $n - 3.5$ if $n$ is 18.9

**22.** $2,000 - n$ if $n$ is 1,000

**23.** $120 + ($41 - n)$ if $n$ is $2

**24.** $(2.2 + n) - 4.6$ if $n$ is 8

**For 25–26, choose the expression for each situation.**

**25.** The temperature dropped 10 degrees and then went up 4 degrees.

  **A** $(n + 10) + 4$    **C** $(10 - n) + 4$

  **B** $(n - 10) + 4$    **D** $(n + 10) - 4$

**26.** At the bus stop, 5 of the 23 passengers got off the bus and other people got on.

  **F** $(n + 23) + 5$    **H** $(23 - n) + 5$

  **G** $(n - 23) + 5$    **J** $(23 - 5) + n$

**Use the expression to complete each table.**

**27.**

| n | n + 6 |
|---|-------|
| 4 | 10 |
| 5 | 11 |
| 6 | ■ |
| 7 | ■ |
| 8 | ■ |

**28.**

| n | n − 28 |
|----|--------|
| 46 | 18 |
| 53 | ■ |
| 60 | ■ |
| 67 | 39 |
| 74 | ■ |

**29.**

| n | 20 − n |
|----|--------|
| 5 | ■ |
| 8 | 12 |
| 10 | ■ |
| 15 | ■ |
| 18 | ■ |

**30.** Mary has tuna salad, lemonade, and yogurt for lunch. The lemonade costs $1.29, and the tuna salad is twice the cost of the lemonade. Mary paid $5.76 for lunch. How much did the yogurt cost?

**Technology Link**

More Practice: Harcourt Mega Math Ice Station Exploration, *Arctic Algebra*, Level G

**31.** **?** **What's the Error?** Pedro says the next expression in the following pattern is $n + 17$: $n + 18$, $n + 15$, $n + 16$, $n + 13$, $n + 14$, ■. Explain his error and write the correct expression.

**32.** **MEASUREMENT** In 1932, the Indy 500 auto race was won at a speed of 104.144 mph. The following year, the winning speed was 0.018 mph faster. In 1934, the winning speed was 0.701 mph faster than in 1933. What was the winning speed in 1934?

**33.** **Write About It** Describe a situation that can be written as an expression with a variable and explain what the variable represents.

---

## Getting Ready for FCAT

**34.** At the first floor, a group of people got on the elevator. The elevator only stopped at the third, fifth, and eighth floors. At the third floor, 3 people got off, and then 2 people got on at the fifth floor. Which expression could be used to represent the number of people who rode the elevator to the eighth floor?

**A.** $3 + n + 2$

**B.** $n + 3 - 2$

**C.** $n - 3 + 2$

**D.** $3 + 2 - n$

---

## Problem Solving **Thinker's Corner**

**LET'S MODEL** You can use models to represent expressions and find their values. Use square and hexagon pattern blocks to represent the expression $p + 5$.

$p$  $\quad$  5

To find the value of $p + 5$ if $p = 3$, replace the hexagon with 3 squares. Place the squares in one group to show the value of the expression. So, the value of $p + 5$ when $p = 3$ is 8.

$3 \quad + \quad 5 \quad = \quad 8$

**1.** Use a model to represent $7 + c$. Find its value if $c = 11$.

**2.** Explain how to use a model to represent $4 + c + 2$. Find its value if $c = 8$.

# Write Equations

## Learn

**HISSSS!** The reticulated python is the longest snake in the world. At birth it is 2 feet long, and some adult pythons are 29 feet long. How much do these pythons grow to reach adult length? Write an equation with a variable to model the problem.

An **equation** is a number sentence that shows that two quantities are equal. Use the variable $f$ for the number of feet the python grows.

| number of feet at birth | + | number of feet of growth | = | number of feet as an adult |
|:---:|:---:|:---:|:---:|:---:|
| ↓ | | ↓ | | ↓ |
| 2 | + | $f$ | = | 29 |

So, the equation is $2 + f = 29$.

▲ The largest python is the reticulated python. One found in Indonesia in 1912 was 33 feet long.

### Examples

**A**

Write an equation for the problem.

Tate had 12 CDs and got more for her birthday. Now she has 21 CDs. How many CDs did Tate get?

| 12 CDs | + | birthday CDs | = | 21 CDs |
|:---:|:---:|:---:|:---:|:---:|
| ↓ | | ↓ | | ↓ |
| 12 | + | $c$ | = | 21 |

**B**

Write a problem for the equation $m − 7 = 5$.

| $m$ | − | 7 | = | 5 |
|:---:|:---:|:---:|:---:|:---:|
| ↓ | | ↓ | | ↓ |
| money to start with | − | $7 | = | $5 |

After Paolo paid $7 for a movie, he had $5. How much money did Paolo have to start with?

## Check

**1. Explain** how to write a problem for the equation $n + 8 = 15$.

**Write an equation for each. Explain what the variable represents.**

**2.** Erica had 24 crayons. After she put some on the table, she had 12 left in the box. How many crayons did she put on the table?

**3.** Jim had some pencils. After Lee gave him 5 new pencils, he had 12. How many pencils did Jim have to start with?

**Write an equation for each. Explain what the variable represents.**

**4.** Ashley has 16 beads. She needs 24 beads to make a bracelet. How many more beads does she need?

**5.** A cheetah runs 70 mph, and a lion runs 50 mph. What is the difference in their speeds?

**6.** Bob paid $3 for breakfast and $5 for lunch and then bought dinner. He spent $20 in all. How much did he pay for dinner?

**7.** After a number is subtracted from 22 and 5 is added, the result is 10. What number is subtracted?

**8.** After the temperature rose 15 degrees, it was 95 degrees outside. What was the temperature to start with?

**9.** After 7 people quit the tennis team, there were 30 players. How many players were on the team to start with?

**Write a problem for the equation. State what the variable $n$ represents.**

**10.** $31 - n = 20$

**11.** $n + 5 = 13$

**12.** $(6 + n) - 4 = 17$

**USE DATA** For 13–15, use the bar graph to write an equation with a variable.

**13.** What is the difference between the length of an anaconda and the length of a cobra?

**14.** When a rattlesnake and another snake are laid end to end, their total length is 17 feet. How long is the other snake?

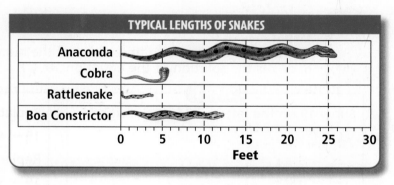

**TYPICAL LENGTHS OF SNAKES**

Anaconda
Cobra
Rattlesnake
Boa Constrictor

0   5   10   15   20   25   30
Feet

**15.** If an anaconda grows 25 feet from birth to adult length, how long are anacondas at birth?

**16. Geometry** A square's side is $n$ feet long, and its perimeter is 20 feet. Write an equation for the perimeter of this square.

**17.** Tran arrived at the mall at 1:15. She spent 45 minutes in the gift shop, 35 minutes in the shoe store, and 1 hour and 10 minutes in the music store. When did she leave the mall?

**Getting Ready for FCAT**

**18.** The zookeeper weighs the animals at the zoo once a month. Use the information in the table to write a problem for the equation $950 - w = 500$. State what the variable $w$ represents.

| TYPICAL WEIGHTS OF ANIMALS | |
| --- | --- |
| **Animal** | **Weight** |
| Chimpanzee | 150 lb |
| Gorilla | 450 lb |
| Polar bear | 715 lb |
| Horse | 950 lb |

# Solve Equations

▶ **Learn**

**ZZZZZ . . .** Koalas sleep most of the day because of their low-energy diet of leaves. In fact, of the 24 hours in a day, koalas sleep 19 hours. How many hours a day are koalas awake?

**VOCABULARY**

**solution**

Write an equation to model this situation.

| **hours asleep** | + | **hours awake** | = | **hours in a day** |
|:---:|:---:|:---:|:---:|:---:|
| ↓ | | ↓ | | ↓ |
| 19 | + | *h* | = | 24 |

If an equation contains a variable, you solve the equation by finding a value for the variable that makes the equation true. That value is the **solution**.

## Activity

**MATERIALS:** balance and weights

You can use a balance to find which of the numbers 4, 5, or 7 is the solution of the equation $19 + n = 24$.

**STEP 1**

Show 19 on the left and 24 on the right.

**STEP 2**

Replace *n* with 4.    Place 4 on the left side.

$19 + 4 \overset{?}{=} 24$    →    $23 = 24$   false

Replace *n* with 5.    Place 5 on the left side.

$19 + 5 \overset{?}{=} 24$    →    $24 = 24$   true

Replace *n* with 7.    Place 7 on the left side.

$19 + 7 \overset{?}{=} 24$    →    $26 = 24$   false

The solution is 5 because the values on both sides of the balance are equal. So, Koalas are awake 5 hours a day.

## Example

Is 10, 11, or 13 the solution of $n - 6 = 7$?

| $10 - 6 \overset{?}{=} 7$ Replace *n* with 10. | $11 - 6 \overset{?}{=} 7$ Replace *n* with 11. | $13 - 6 \overset{?}{=} 7$ Replace *n* with 13. |
|:---|:---|:---|
| $4 = 7$ false | $5 = 7$ false | $7 = 7$ true |

## Mental Math

Jason and his family traveled in Australia for 2 weeks. In his journal, Jason kept a count of all the koalas he saw. In the first week, he saw 13 koalas. During the entire trip, he counted 22 koalas. How many koalas did Jason see in the second week of the trip?

Write an equation to solve the problem.

| koalas seen first week | + | koalas seen second week | = | total koalas seen |
|:---:|:---:|:---:|:---:|:---:|
| ↓ | | ↓ | | ↓ |
| 13 | + | $k$ | = | 22 |

You can solve the equation using mental math.

$13 + k = 22$     **Think:** 13 plus what number equals 22?
$k = 9$

**Check:** $13 + 9 = 22$     Replace $k$ with 9.
$22 = 22$ √ The equation checks. The value of $k$ is 9.

### Examples

**Ⓐ**

$5 + n = 12$     **Think:** 5 plus what
$n = 7$          number equals 12?

**Check:** $5 + 7 = 12$
$12 = 12$ √

**Ⓑ**

$7 = 17 - n$     **Think:** 17 minus what
$10 = n$         number equals 7?

**Check:** $7 = 17 - 10$
$7 = 7$ √

 **MATH IDEA** The value of the variable that makes the equation true is the solution of the equation.

### ▷ Check

1. **Explain** how you know when the value of a variable in an equation is correct.

**Which of the numbers 6, 8, or 11 is the solution of the equation?**

**2.** $9 + n = 17$     **3.** $n - 2 = 9$     **4.** $n + 7 = 13$     **5.** $11 - n = 3$

**Which of the numbers 3, 5, or 15 is the solution of the equation?**

**6.** $n + 10 = 15$     **7.** $4 + n = 19$     **8.** $21 = n + 18$     **9.** $16 - n = 11$

**Use mental math to solve each equation. Check your solution.**

**10.** $8 + n = 15$     **11.** $25 - n = 5$     **12.** $\$60 - n = \$52$     **13.** $n + 10 = 72$

**14.** $8 = n + 4$     **15.** $n - \$7 = \$30$     **16.** $36 = n - 10$     **17.** $n + 6 = 13$

LESSON CONTINUES ⏵

FCAT TESTED   SSS/GLEs MA.D.2.2.2.5.1 Uses concrete or pictorial models and graphs (for example, drawings, number lines) to solve equations or inequalities. *also* MA.D.2.2.1.5.1, MA.A.3.2.3.5.1

Chapter 4   **71**

**Write which of the numbers 5, 7, or 12 is the solution of the equation.**

**18.** $4 + n = 11$

**19.** $n + 6 = 18$

**20.** $53 - n = 48$

**21.** $2 = n - 10$

**22.** $n = 2 + 5$

**23.** $45 - 38 = n$

**24.** $16 = a + 9$

**25.** $b = 23 - 18$

**26.** $37 - 25 = c$

**Technology Link**

More Practice: Harcourt Mega Math Ice Station Exploration, *Arctic Algebra*, Level S

**Use mental math to solve each equation. Check your solution.**

**27.** $11 = n - 5$

**28.** $n - 3 = 20$

**29.** $n + 9 = 26$

**30.** $32 = 10 + n$

**31.** $n + 8 = 14$

**32.** $15 = n - 9$

**33.** $n + 35 = 48$

**34.** $(n - 24) + 3 = 7$

**Solve the equation. Check your solution.**

**35.** $25 + n = 31$

**36.** $n - 17 = 8$

**37.** $26 - n = 13$

**38.** $7 + (2 + n) = 18$

**39.** $30 = 17 + a$

**40.** $b = 12 - 9$

**41.** $51 - 18 = c$

**42.** $d = 10 + 43$

**43.** $x + 9 = 26$

**44.** $29 - y = 7$

**45.** $72 + 54 = z$

**46.** $44 = 52 - n$

**REASONING** For 47–50, each symbol represents one number. Find the value of each symbol.

**47.** $\heartsuit + 3 = 9$

$4 + \star = \heartsuit$

**48.** $\triangle + 6 = 10$

$\triangle - \clubsuit = 1$

**49.** $12 - \blacklozenge = 7$

$\blacklozenge + \blacksquare = 6$

**50.** $5 = 12 - \bullet$

$\bullet + \blacktriangleright = 15$

**USE DATA** For 51–54, use the bar graph to write the equation. Then solve.

**51.** How many hours a day is a cat awake?

**52.** Which animal sleeps 4 times as many hours as the horse?

**53.** How many more hours a day does a lion sleep than a cow?

**54.** Which animal sleeps 5 hours more per day than a horse?

**55.** ⭐ **? What's the Question?** Bob has 9 pets: 2 dogs, 4 cats, and some birds. Tim uses the equation $6 + n = 9$. The answer is 3 birds.

**56.** ≡**FAST FACT** • SCIENCE Koalas eat about 2 pounds of eucalyptus leaves each day, which is almost one tenth of the total body weight. About how many pounds of eucalyptus leaves will a koala eat if it lives 15 years?

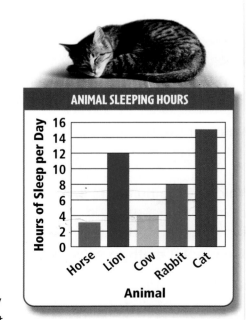

**ANIMAL SLEEPING HOURS**

*Hours of Sleep per Day* — Horse, Lion, Cow, Rabbit, Cat — **Animal**

**57.** Jane drove from Orlando to Tampa and still had 53 miles to go to reach Sarasota. The distance from Tallahassee to Sarasota is 289 miles and from Orlando to Sarasota is 132 miles. How many miles has Jane already driven?

**A.** 79 miles     **C.** 153 miles

**B.** 98 miles     **D.** 236 miles

# Problem Solving   LINKUP . . . to History

Math symbols have been used for hundreds of years. The symbols $>$ and $<$ were first used by the English mathematician Thomas Harriot in a book published in 1631. The symbols for *greater than or equal to* ($\geq$) and for *less than or equal to* ($\leq$), are credited to the French mathematician Pierre Bouguer who first used them in 1734.

You can use the symbols $\geq$ and $\leq$ to show relationships.

$5 \leq 5$   Read: "5 is less than or equal to 5".

$7 \geq 2$   Read: "7 is greater than or equal to 2".

$x \leq 9$   Read: "$x$ is less than or equal to 9".

In $x \leq 9$, the value of $x$ is any number less than or equal to 9. If $x$ is a whole number, its value can be 0, 1, 2, 3, 4, 5, 6, 7, 8, or 9.

**Write the whole numbers that can be values of the variable.**

▲ It has been said that while helping survey North America, Thomas Harriot got the idea for the $<$ and $>$ symbols when he saw this design shown on the pottery on the arm of a Native American.

**1.** $x \leq 5$     **2.** $a \leq 2$     **3.** $b \geq 8$     **4.** $x \leq 10$     **5.** $c \geq 0$

**Use the variable and $\leq$ or $\geq$ to write a mathematical sentence for each word sentence.**

**6.** All numbers $x$ are less than or equal to 7.

**7.** All numbers $y$ are greater than or equal to 12.

# Inequalities

▶ **Learn**

**MORE OR LESS** An **inequality** is a number sentence that shows that two amounts are not equal.

$x < 7$ is an inequality.

A solution of an inequality with a variable is a value for the variable that makes it true.

5 is a solution of the inequality $x < 7$ because $5 < 7$.

You can use a number line to show solutions of an inequality.

Locate points to show whole numbers from 0 to 7 that are solutions.

**VOCABULARY**

inequality

**Remember**

< "is less than"
> "is greater than"
≤ "is less than or equal to"
≥ "is greater than or equal to"

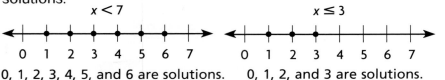

$x < 7$

0 1 2 3 4 5 6 7
0, 1, 2, 3, 4, 5, and 6 are solutions.

$x \le 3$

0 1 2 3 4 5 6 7
0, 1, 2, and 3 are solutions.

0 1 2 3 4 5 6 7
5, 6, and 7 are solutions.

**Activity** MATERIALS: balance and weights

Find solutions of the inequality $n + 6 > 7 + 5$.

- Put weights on the 7 and 5 on the right side to represent $7 + 5$. What happens to the balance?

- Put a weight on the 6 on the left side. Then, for one number at a time, put additional weights on the left side from 1 to 10. For which numbers does the balance tilt to the left?

- What values of $n$ from 1 to 10 are solutions for the inequality $n + 6 > 7 + 5$?

**MATH IDEA** An inequality may have many solutions.

## Examples

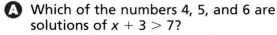

**A** Which of the numbers 4, 5, and 6 are solutions of $x + 3 > 7$?

| | |
|---|---|
| $4 + 3 > 7$ | Replace $x$ with 4. |
| $7 > 7$ | false |
| $5 + 3 > 7$ | Replace $x$ with 5. |
| $8 > 7$ | true |
| $6 + 3 > 7$ | Replace $x$ with 6. |
| $9 > 7$ | true |

So, $x = 5$ and $x = 6$ are solutions.

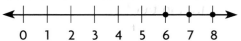

**B** For $m \ge 6$, show the whole-number solutions from 0 to 8 on a number line.

0 1 2 3 4 5 6 7 8

$m \ge 6$

6 is a solution because $6 \ge 6$.
7 is a solution because $7 \ge 6$.
8 is a solution because $8 \ge 6$.

## ▶ Check

1. **Explain** why $x = 3$ is a solution of the inequality $x + 2 \leq 5$, but $x = 4$ is not a solution.

**Which of the numbers 3, 4, and 5 are solutions of each inequality?**

2. $x < 5$ 　　　　3. $x \geq 4$ 　　　　4. $x - 3 > 1$ 　　　　5. $x \leq 4 - 1$

**Copy the number line. Locate points to show the whole-number solutions from 0 to 8 for each inequality.**

6. $x > 2$ 　　　　7. $x \leq 5$ 　　　　8. $x + 5 \leq 6$

## ▶ Practice and Problem Solving 　Extra Practice, page 82, Set D

**Which of the numbers 6, 7, 8, and 9 are solutions of each inequality?**

9. $x > 5$ 　　　　10. $x + 4 \geq 12$ 　　　11. $x - 5 < 4$ 　　　　12. $x < 7$

**Which of the numbers 8, 9, 10, 11, and 12 are solutions of each inequality?**

13. $x \geq 8$ 　　　　14. $x + 4 < 13$ 　　　15. $x - 5 \geq 5$ 　　　　16. $x \leq 6 + 2$

**Copy the number line. Locate points to show the whole-number solutions from 0 to 8 for each inequality.**

17. $x < 6$ 　　　　18. $x + 4 \leq 4$ 　　　19. $x - 3 > 2$

20. **REASONING** An inequality has $x = 4$ as a solution, but $x = 5$ is not a solution. What is the inequality?

21. ✎ **Write About It** Describe the whole-number solutions of the inequality $m + 3 > 7$.

22. The borzoi is a large dog also known as a Russian wolfhound. Males can weigh from 75 pounds to 104 pounds. Write two inequalities that together show $w$, the weight of a borzoi.

23. The product of the factors is 91. The sum of the factors is 20. The difference is 6. What are the factors?

## Getting Ready for FCAT ▢THINK ▢SOLVE ▢EXPLAIN

24. Look at the inequality shown below.

　　　　$n \leq 6$

Copy the number line. Then draw dots to show all the whole numbers greater than 0 that $n$ could represent to make the inequality true.

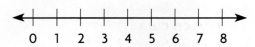

FCAT TESTED 🌴 SSS/GLEs MA.D.2.2.1.5.1 Solves problems involving equations or simple inequalities using manipulatives, diagrams, or models, symbolic expressions, or written phrases. *also* MA.D.2.2.1.5.1

Chapter 4 **75**

# Mental Math: Use the Properties

## Quick Review

1. 6.3 + 3.6
2. 1.05 − 0.01
3. 950 + 2,050
4. (23 + 5) − 14
5. (6 + 8) + (4 − 1)

 **Learn**

**FAIR PRICE?** Claire and her brother Tom went to the fair. Claire paid $5 for a hat. For lunch she bought a drink for $1 and a sandwich for $4. Tom bought a drink for $1 and a salad. He also paid $4 for a video game. They both spent the same amount of money. How much was Tom's salad?

You can write an equation to model this problem.
Let $s$ = the amount Tom spent on a salad.

hat + lunch = lunch + game
↓ ↓ ↓ ↓
5 + (1 + 4) = (s + 1) + 4

Solve for $s$.

$5 + (1 + 4) = (s + 1) + 4$    Think about the Grouping Property.
$5 + (1 + 4) = (5 + 1) + 4$    $s$ must equal 5.

So, Tom spent $5 for his salad.

The Order Property is also called the **Commutative Property**.
The Grouping Property is also called the **Associative Property**.

**MATH IDEA** You can use the properties of addition to help you solve problems.

## VOCABULARY

**Commutative Property**
**Associative Property**
**compensation**

**Remember**

You can use mental math and the properties of addition to solve problems.

**Order Property**
12 + 8 = 8 + 12

**Grouping Property**
(5 + 6) + 7 = 5 + (6 + 7)

**Identity Property**
37 + 0 = 37

---

**Examples** Find the value of $n$.

**Ⓐ** $(12 + 8) + 3 = 12 + (n + 3)$

Using the Associative Property, $n$ must be 8.

---

**Ⓑ** $17 + 4 = n + 17$

Using the Commutative Property, $n$ must be 4.

---

**Ⓒ** $n + 0 = 6$

Using the Zero Property, $n$ must be 6.

---

• How are the Commutative and the Associative Properties different?

• Does the Commutative Property work for subtraction? Explain.

## Use Mental Math Strategies

You can use mental math with the Commutative and Associative Properties to help you solve an addition problem.

### Examples

At the fair, Sid went on 8 rides, Todd went on 9 rides, and Vickie went on 2 rides. How many rides did they go on in all?

| **A** Use the Commutative Property. | **B** Use the Associative Property. |
|---|---|
| $8 + 9 + 2 = 8 + 2 + 9$ | $(8 + 9) + 2 = 8 + (9 + 2)$ |
| $\quad\quad\quad = 10 + 9$ | $\quad\quad\quad = 8 + 11$ |
| $\quad\quad\quad = 19$ | $\quad\quad\quad = 19$ |

So, they went on 19 rides.

For some addition and subtraction problems, you can use a mental math strategy called **compensation**. For addition, you change one addend to a multiple of ten and then adjust the other addend to keep the balance.

### More Examples

| **C** $37 + 25 = (37 + 3) + (25 - 3)$ | **D** $27 + 49 = (27 - 1) + (49 + 1)$ |
|---|---|
| $\quad\quad\quad = 40 + 22$ | $\quad\quad\quad = 26 + 50$ |
| $\quad\quad\quad = 62$ | $\quad\quad\quad = 76$ |

When you use compensation to subtract, you have to do the same thing to each number. Try to make the second number a multiple of 10.

| **E** $37 - 29 = (37 + 1) - (29 + 1)$ | **F** $71 - 42 = (71 - 2) - (42 - 2)$ |
|---|---|
| $\quad\quad\quad = 38 - 30$ | $\quad\quad\quad = 69 - 40$ |
| $\quad\quad\quad = 8$ | $\quad\quad\quad = 29$ |

• In Example D, show how you can find the value of the expression by changing the first addend to a multiple of 10.

 **MATH IDEA** Using the properties and other mental math strategies will help you add and subtract mentally.

LESSON CONTINUES

FCAT TESTED SSS/GLEs MA.A.3.2.3.5.1 Solves real-world problems involving addition, subtraction, multiplication, and division of whole numbers, and addition, subtraction, and multiplication of decimals, fractions, and mixed numbers using an appropriate method (for example, mental math, pencil and paper, calculator).

Chapter 4 **77**

1. **Explain** how using the Commutative and Associative Properties can make finding the sum $(25 + 48) + 25$ easier.

2. **Explain** how to use compensation to find $127 + 59$ mentally.

**Find the value of $n$. Identify the property used.**

3. $n + 15 = 15 + 3$

4. $(16 + 5) + 4 = 16 + (n + 4)$

5. $n + 1.5 = 1.5$

**Use mental math strategies to find the value.**

6. $17 + 28$

7. $(4 + 9) + 11$

8. $31 + 19$

▷ **Practice and Problem Solving** ( Extra Practice, page 82, Set E )

**Find the value of $n$. Identify the property used.**

9. $7 + 18 = n + 7$

10. $256 + (15 + n) = (256 + 15) + 2$

11. $0 + n = 5,681$

12. $4.7 + n = 2 + 4.7$

**Use mental math strategies to find the value.**

13. $17 + 24$

14. $17 + (23 + 3)$

15. $48 + 32$

16. $28 + 35 + 12$

17. $(25 + 21) + 19$

18. $88 + (19 + 2)$

19. $43 - 17$

20. $5 + 25 + 40$

21. $51 - 28$

22. $67 + (3 + 20)$

23. $35 + 7 + 15$

24. $(12 + 23) + 8$

**ALGEBRA** **Name the property used in each equation.**

25. $(a + b) + c = a + (b + c)$

26. $a + 0 = a$

27. $a + b = b + a$

28. $\blacktriangle + (\bigcirc + \star) = (\blacktriangle + \bigcirc) + \star$

29. At the fair, Tanya bought a hamburger and roast corn for lunch. Then she had popcorn. John had a fruit bar before lunch and then bought a hamburger and a drink. They spent the same amount of money. Write an equation to model the problem. What drink did John buy? Explain how you know.

30. ✎ **Write a problem** using the information in the table. Then solve the problem.

**FAIR FOOD**

| | |
|---|---|
| Hamburger | $3.50 |
| Pizza Slice | $4.00 |
| Fresh-squeezed | |
| Lemonade | $2.50 |
| Orange Juice | $3.00 |
| Roast Corn | $2.50 |
| Popcorn | $3.00 |
| Fruit Bar | $2.50 |

**31.** Sam and Joe went to the fair. Sam bought 9 ride tickets for $1.50 each and peanuts for $1.29. Joe paid $3 for popcorn and bought 8 ride tickets. Who spent more money at the fair?

**32. Vocabulary Power** When you *group* things, you separate them according to some criteria. You may put them into separate piles or into boxes. What do you use to *group* numbers in an expression?

## Getting Ready for FCAT

**33.** The bar graph shows the number of points scored by four friends at the fair. Marla joined the girls at the Midway Games. Altogether, the five girls scored 50 points. How many points did Marla score?

**A.** 8      **C.** 10

**B.** 9      **D.** 12

**34.** Look at the graph. How many more points did Ashley and Clarissa score than Becca and Diana?

**F.** 1      **H.** 2

**G.** 3      **I.** 4

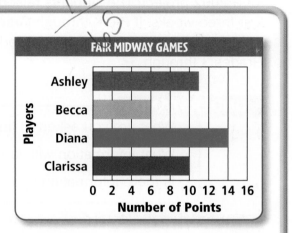

FAIR MIDWAY GAMES

---

# Problem Solving  THiNKer'S CorNer

Copy the magic square. In a magic square, the sums of the numbers in each row, each column, and each diagonal are the same. Find the value of the variable in each equation below. Place the values in the magic square. Check the sums of each row, column, and diagonal to see if each sum is a magic sum of 15.

**1.** $6 + 1 = a + 6$

**2.** $8 + 0 = b$

**3.** $45 + (c + 9) = (45 + 5) + 9$

**4.** $2.8 + d = 2 + 2.8$

**5.** $(482 + 9) + 21 = 482 + (e + 21)$

**6.** $7 = f + 0$

**7.** $(458 + 6) + 2 = (458 + 2) + g$

**8.** $0 + 4 = h$

**9.** $7 + (3 + 59.2) = (7 + j) + 59.2$

| b | a | g |
|---|---|---|
| j | c | f |
| h | e | d |

# Problem Solving Strategy
## Write an Equation

**PROBLEM** J.T. Barber Elementary School in New Bern, North Carolina, collected pennies to buy plants and trees for a 2002 project. The students raised $362.30 during the first three weeks. If Pre-K through Grade 2 students raised $151.65, how much money was raised by the students in Grades 3 through 5?

**Remember**

In an *equation*, the values on both sides of the equal sign are the same.
Example:
$$10 + 5 = 15$$
$$\downarrow \qquad \downarrow$$
$$15 \quad = 15$$

### UNDERSTAND

- What are you asked to find?
- What information will you use?
- Is there information you will not use? If so, what?

### PLAN

- What strategy can you use to solve the problem?

  You can write and solve an equation to find the amount of money raised by students in Grades 3 through 5.

### SOLVE

- How can you use the strategy to solve the problem?

  Write an equation using the total amount raised and the amount raised by Pre-K through Grade 2. Let $n$ represent the amount raised by Grades 3 through 5.

| Pre-K–Grade 2 amount raised | | Grades 3–5 amount raised | | total amount raised |
|:---:|:---:|:---:|:---:|:---:|
| $\downarrow$ | | $\downarrow$ | | $\downarrow$ |
| $151.65 | + | $n$ | = | $362.30 |
| **Think:** $151.65 plus what number equals $362.30? | | $n$ | = | $210.65 |

So, students in Grades 3 through 5 raised $210.65.

### CHECK

- How can you decide if your answer is correct?

**Write and solve an equation for each problem. Explain what the variable represents.**

1. **What if** Pre-K through Grade 2 students raised $146.20? How much money would students in Grades 3 through 5 have raised?

2. Pre-K through Grade 2 planted 168 more plants than Grades 3 through 5. If Grades 3 through 5 planted 138 plants. How many plants were planted in all?

### Strategies

Draw a Diagram or Picture
Make a Model or Act It Out
Make an Organized List
Find a Pattern
Make a Table or Graph
Predict and Test
Work Backward
Solve a Simpler Problem
▶ **Write an Equation**
Use Logical Reasoning

**Problem Solving**

**USE DATA** For 3–4, use the table. The table indicates the number of words each student spelled correctly on a spelling test.

| SPELLING TEST | | | |
|---|---|---|---|
| Erin | Jacob | Theresa | Tom |
| 19 | 18 | 15 | 16 |

3. If there were 20 words on the spelling test, which students missed fewer than 3 words each?

   **A** Jacob and Erin    **C** Tom and Theresa
   **B** Tom and Jacob    **D** Tom, Theresa, and Jacob

4. Which equation uses $n$ to represent how many more words Erin spelled correctly than Theresa?

   **F** $n = 19 + 15$     **H** $15 = 19 + n$
   **G** $15 + n = 19$     **J** $19 = n - 15$

## Mixed Strategy Practice

5. Goro arrived at Kennedy Space Center at 1:15 P.M. He spent 25 minutes in The Space Shop, 20 minutes in the Launch Status Center, and 35 minutes in the Rocket Garden before he left. What time did he leave the Kennedy Space Center?

6. Bob's car gets 20 miles to the gallon. He has about 4 gallons left in the tank. Does he have enough gas to drive 125 more miles? Explain.

7. **REASONING** Two numbers have a difference of 4 and a sum of 34. What are the two numbers?

8. The astronaut received 23 fan letters on Monday, 54 on Tuesday, and more on Wednesday. If she got 127 letters in all, how many did she get on Wednesday? Write and solve an equation. Explain what the variable represents.

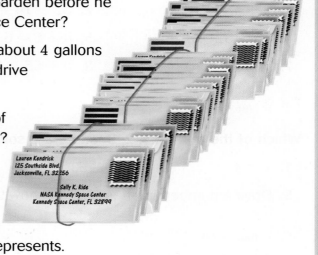

9. Write a problem that can be solved with the equation $42 - n = 18$.

FCAT TESTED ❧ SSS/GLEs MA.A.3.2.2.5.1 Uses problem-solving strategies to determine the operation(s) needed to solve one- and two-step problems involving addition, subtraction, multiplication, and division of whole numbers, and addition, subtraction, and multiplication of decimals and fractions. *also:* MA.D.2.2.1.5.1

**Chapter 4** **81**

# Extra Practice

## Set A (pp. 64–67)

**Write an expression. Explain what the variable represents.**

1. Eric had some baseball cards. Tracy gave him 5 more.

2. Rebecca gathered 18 pinecones. On the way home, she dropped some.

**Find the value of the expression.**

3. $7 + n$ if $n$ is 9

4. $(n - 4) + 6$ if $n$ is 12

5. $19 - (n + 3)$ if $n$ is 6

## Set B (pp. 68–69)

**Write an equation for each. Explain what the variable represents.**

1. Jesse had 5 goldfish, and his friend gave him some more. Now Jesse has 12 goldfish. How many did his friend give him?

2. A store had 83 lawn mowers for sale. The store sold some on Monday and had 60 left. How many did the store sell?

**Write a problem for the equation. State what the variable $n$ represents.**

3. $n + 17 = 25$

4. $(n - 2) + 7 = 16$

## Set C (pp. 70–73)

**Solve the equation. Check your solution.**

1. $9 + n = 19$

2. $52 - 14 = n$

3. $12 + 2 = n - 8$

4. $18 + 32 = n$

5. $n + 6 = 6$

6. $15 + n = 11 + 8$

7. $n - 12 = 40$

8. $n + 55 = 123$

9. $16 + n = 38$

## Set D (pp. 74-75)

**Which of the numbers, 2, 3, and 4 are solutions of each inequality?**

1. $x < 4$

2. $x \geq 3$

3. $x \leq 3$

4. $x + 3 > 6$

5. Draw a number line from 0–8 to show the solutions for the inequality $n - 2 \geq 4$.

## Set E (pp. 76–79)

**Use mental math strategies to find the value.**

1. $(6 + 40) + 14$

2. $127 - 52$

3. $146 + 126$

4. $295 - 43$

5. $87 - 47$

6. $9 + (25 + 10) = (9 + 25) + 10$

# Review/Test

## ✓ CHECK VOCABULARY AND CONCEPTS

**Choose the best term from the box.**

| |
|---|
| equation |
| equal sign |
| expression |
| variable |

1. A mathematical phrase that combines numbers, operation signs, and sometimes variables is a(n) __?__. (p. 64)

2. A number sentence that uses the equal sign to show that two quantities are equal is a(n) __?__. (p. 68)

3. A letter or a symbol that stands for one or more numbers is called a(n) __?__. (p. 64)

## ✓ CHECK SKILLS

**Write an expression and explain what the variable represents.** (pp. 64–67)

4. The school has 16 computers. More will be added next year.

5. There were 53 passengers on the train. Then some got off.

**Find the value of the expression.** (pp. 64–67)

6. $17 - n$ if $n$ is 5

7. $n + 92$ if $n$ is 0

8. $13 + n + 4$ if $n$ is 10

**Write an equation. Explain what the variable represents.** (pp. 68–69)

9. Tony had 17 pencils. After he gave some to Marla, he had 9. How many pencils did he give to Marla?

10. Julie had 12 CDs. After buying new ones, she had 18 CDs. How many did she buy?

**Solve the equation. Check your solution.** (pp. 70–73)

11. $4 = n - 18$

12. $(n - 13) + 4 = 5$

13. $18 - n = 9 + 3$

**Which of the numbers 4, 5, 6, and 7 are solutions of each inequality?** (pp. 74–75)

14. $x < 6$

15. $x \geq 5$

16. $x - 2 > 3$

**Use mental math strategies to find the value.** (pp. 76–79)

17. $123 + 62$

18. $14 + (6 + 3)$

## ✓ CHECK PROBLEM SOLVING

**Solve.** (pp. 78–79)

19. Peter used a coupon to help pay for a pack of trading cards. The original price of the cards was $10.00. The coupon reduced the price to $6.50. What was the value of the coupon?

20. There were 80,409 people at the football game on Saturday and 110,986 people on Sunday. How many people were at both games?

# Getting Ready for FCAT

##  ALGEBRAIC THINKING

1. Which statement can be modeled by the equation $9 - y = 4$?

   **A.** Some number minus nine is four.

   **B.** Nine minus four is some number.

   **C.** Nine minus some number is four.

   **D.** Four minus some number is nine.

   > **TIP** **Understand the problem.** See item 2. The equation states that $n - 5$ equals $7 + 12$, which is 19. Since 5 is subtracted from $n$, you need to find a number that is 5 more than 19.

2. What is the value of $n$ for $n - 5 = 7 + 12$?

   **F.** 24

   **G.** 19

   **H.** 14

   **I.** 10

3. Which is an expression for this situation?

   The temperature dropped 5 degrees and then went up 7 degrees.

   **A.** $(t + 5) - 7$

   **B.** $(t - 5) + 7$

   **C.** $(5 - t) + 7$

   **D.** $(5 - t) - 7$

4. **Explain It** At the station, 86 people got off the train and 35 stayed on. Write an equation that can be used to find the number of people on the train before some got off. Tell what the variable represents. Solve the equation.

##  DATA ANALYSIS AND PROBABILITY

5. Which equation can be used to find $w$, the difference between the wingspan of the albatross and the wingspan of the trumpeter swan?

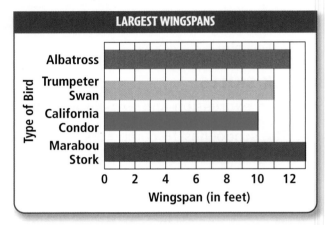

   **F.** $w - 12 = 11$

   **G.** $12 - 11 = w$

   **H.** $12 + w = 11$

   **I.** $11 - w = 12$

6. Use the bar graph in Problem 5. Which bird's wingspan is 3 feet longer than the wingspan of the California condor?

   **A.** marabou stork

   **B.** trumpeter swan

   **C.** albatross

   **D.** both albatross and marabou stork

7. **Explain It** You and a friend are playing a game. You each flip a coin. If both coins land heads up, you win. If both coins land tails up, your friend wins. Is this a fair game? Explain how you know.

**MEASUREMENT**

**8.** Kaitlin took these measurements to help her decide how much wallpaper to buy for her bedroom.

| KAITLIN'S BEDROOM MEASUREMENTS | |
| --- | --- |
| **Dimensions** | **Measurement (in feet)** |
| bedroom length | 12 |
| bedroom width | 10 |
| bedroom height | 8 |
| door height | $6\frac{1}{2}$ |

Which measurement is equal to 96 inches?

**F.** bedroom length

**G.** bedroom width

**H.** bedroom height

**I.** door height

**9.** Use the table in Problem 8. Which measurement is equal to 4 yards?

**A.** bedroom length

**B.** bedroom width

**C.** bedroom height

**D.** door height

**10. Explain It** Chris will buy these grocery items for his mother.

| | |
| --- | --- |
| cereal | $3.95 |
| bag of apples | $3.69 |
| cookies | $2.79 |
| orange juice | $1.95 |

She will give him one bill to pay for the items. ESTIMATE to determine the smallest bill she can give him. Explain.

 **NUMBER SENSE, CONCEPTS, AND OPERATIONS**

**11.** Which numbers are in order from **least** to **greatest**?

**F.** 5,387; 5,373; 5,874; 5,840

**G.** 5,373; 5,387; 5,840; 5,874

**H.** 5,840; 5,874; 5,387; 5,373

**I.** 5,373; 5,387; 5,874; 5,840

**12.** Shana bought 4 packs of beads.

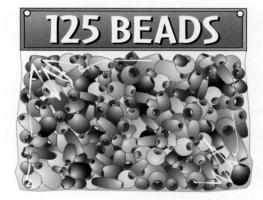

How many beads did Shana buy?

**A.** 400

**B.** 425

**C.** 500

**D.** 600

**13. Explain It** ESTIMATE to solve.

about 25 flowers

The section marked in the field has about 25 flowers. Based on this information, ESTIMATE the total number of flowers in the field. Explain how you made your estimate.

# IT'S IN THE BAG

## Scavenger Hunt Tote

**PROJECT** Make a tote bag to carry numbers from the newspaper scavenger hunt.

### Materials

- **Scavenger Hunt worksheet**
- **Brown bag, size 12**
- **Construction paper**
- **Glue**
- **Markers, pencils, highlighter**
- **Scissors**
- **Newspapers, magazines**

### Directions

1. Cut off a strip from the brown bag, about 6 inches from the top. Open the strip wide, and cut it at one end. Fold the strip to form the handle of the tote. *(Picture A)*

2. Glue the folded handle to the outside of the bag. *(Picture B)*

3. Cut a piece of construction paper smaller than the size of the front of the bag. Cut out the Scavenger Hunt list from the worksheet. Glue it to the construction paper. Decorate the border. Then glue the construction paper to the front of the bag. *(Picture C)*

4. Use newspapers and magazines to find each number on the Scavenger Hunt list. As you find each number, cut it out, label it with its corresponding letter from the list, check it off the list, and place it in your tote.

5. Compare your numbers with those of a classmate.

# Challenge

## Roman Numerals

About 2,500 years ago, the Romans used letters to represent numbers. Today we call these letters *Roman numerals*. The numbers we use are called *decimal numbers*.

| I | V | X | L | C | D | M | V̄ |
|---|---|---|---|---|---|---|---|
| ↓ | ↓ | ↓ | ↓ | ↓ | ↓ | ↓ | ↓ |
| 1 | 5 | 10 | 50 | 100 | 500 | 1,000 | 5,000 |

To change Roman numerals to decimal numbers, follow these rules:

When a letter is repeated, add the value of each letter.

When a letter with a lesser value follows a letter with a greater value, add the values of the letters.

When a letter with a greater value follows a letter with a lesser value, subtract the lesser value from the greater value.

### Examples   Change each Roman numeral to a decimal number.

**A** Roman numeral: XXVI

| X | X | V | I |
|---|---|---|---|
| ↓ | ↓ | ↓ | ↓ |

10 + 10 + 5 + 1 = 26

Decimal number: 26

**B** Roman numeral: CCLXIV
**Think:** 1 < 5, so subtract.

| C | C | L | X | IV |
|---|---|---|---|----|
| ↓ | ↓ | ↓ | ↓ | ↓ |

100 + 100 + 50 + 10 + (5 − 1) = 264

Decimal number: 264

## Talk About It

• How do you know whether to add or subtract when changing a Roman numeral to a decimal number?

## Try It

**Write each Roman numeral as a decimal number.**

**1.** III **2.** DCIV **3.** CXLV **4.** DCCIII **5.** V̄MMIV **6.** MCCXII

**Write each decimal number as a Roman numeral.**

**7.** 11 **8.** 79 **9.** 452 **10.** 341 **11.** 1,927 **12.** 6,205

# Study Guide and Review

## VOCABULARY

**Choose the best term from the box.**

1. A decimal or fraction that names one part of ten equal parts is one __?__. (p. 22)

2. The number 12,865,105 is 13,000,000 when rounded to the nearest __?__. (p. 38)

> million
> tenth
> billion

## STUDY AND SOLVE

### Chapter 1

**Identify place value of whole numbers.**

> Write the value of the blue digit.
>
> 395,752,023 — The 9 is in the ten millions place.
>
> 90,000,000

**Write the value of the blue digit.**
(pp. 2–7)

3. 34,902
4. 12,045,748
5. 8,157,993,030
6. 13,987,456
7. 501,653
8. 7,961,614

**Compare and order whole numbers.**

> Compare 7,932,654 and 7,805,308.
>
> 7,932,654 — • Start at the left.
> ↓ — • Compare digits.
> 7,805,308 — 7 = 7, 9 > 8
>
> So, 7,932,654 > 7,805,308.

**Compare. Write <, >, or = for each ●.** (pp. 10–13)

9. 256,087 ● 256,807
10. 4,083,147 ● 4,803,610
11. Order 39,325; 38,865; and 39,789 from greatest to least.

### Chapter 2

**Identify, read, and write decimals.**

> Write in word form.
>
> 4.012 — The 2 is in the thousandths place.
>
> four and twelve thousandths

**Write each decimal in expanded form, in word form, and as a fraction.**
(pp. 22–25)

12. 1.25
13. 0.357
14. 11.04
15. 0.268
16. 1.07
17. 4.203

**Compare and order decimals.**

> Compare 5.627 and 5.683.
>
> 5.627 — • Line up the decimal points.
> ↓ — • Compare digits from the
> 5.683 — left. 5 = 5, 6 = 6, 2 < 8
> So, 5.627 < 5.683.

**Write <, >, or = for each ●.**
(pp. 28–29)

18. 2.041 ● 2.410
19. 4.110 ● 4.11
20. 0.043 ● 0.034
21. 1.543 ● 1.532
22. Order 11.897, 11.987, and 11.917 from least to greatest.

## Chapter 3

**Estimate sums and differences of whole numbers and decimals.**

Estimate by rounding.

| 514,752 | → | 500,000 | to the nearest |
| +173,091 | → | +200,000 | hundred |
| | | 700,000 | thousand |

**Estimate by rounding.** (pp. 38–45)

**23.** 2,389,241
+8,542,334

**24.** 687,511
−325,874

**25.** $1.84 + $1.08

**Add and subtract whole numbers and decimals.**

| 3,648 | | 25.7 |
| −1,724 | | + 0.48 |
| 1,924 | | 26.18 |

**Find the sum or difference.** (pp. 46–51)

**26.** 10,225
− 8,541

**27.** 19.074
+ 4.96

**28.** 7.84
−3.75

**29.** 592,707
+ 28,033

## Chapter 4

**Write an expression with a variable.**

Chris had 12 eggs. He cooked some of them for breakfast. Let $b$ = number of eggs cooked.

| 12 eggs | minus | some eggs |
| ↓ | ↓ | ↓ |
| 12 | − | $b$ |

Expression: $12 - b$

**Write an expression with a variable.**
(pp. 64–67)

**30.** Susan had collected 20 rocks. Then she found some more.

**31.** Michael had 20 pencils. He bought 7 more and gave some to Pauline.

**Solve addition and subtraction equations.**

Solve the equation.

$17 + m = 30$  **Think:** 17 plus what number equals 30?

$m = 13$

**Solve the equation.** (pp. 70–73)

**32.** $52 = n + 6$

**33.** $n + 9 = 13$

**34.** $n - 14 = 39$

**35.** $48 = 60 - n$

## PROBLEM SOLVING PRACTICE

**Solve.** (pp. 56–57; 80–81)

**36.** Yesterday was not Tuesday or Thursday. Tomorrow will not be Tuesday or Friday. Today is a weekday. What day is it?

**37.** Latifah scored a total of 271 points on three tests. She scored 94 on the first test and 85 on the second test. Write an equation to find Latifah's score on the third test.

# PERFORMANCE ASSESSMENT

## TASK A • LUNCH AND A MOVIE

Rachel has $10.25 to spend on lunch and a movie. The movie ticket costs $5.00.

**a.** Rachel wants to buy a sandwich and a dessert for lunch. Estimate to find the cost of lunch. Make sure Rachel will have enough money left to buy a movie ticket. Then find the actual cost of these items and compare it with your estimate.

**b.** List two possible lunches Rachel could buy and still have enough money left to buy a box of popcorn for $1.50 after she pays for the movie ticket.

**c.** Rachel wants to save enough money so that next time she can buy the most expensive sandwich and the most expensive dessert on the menu and still have money left for a movie ticket. How much money will she need?

**MOVIE CAFÉ MENU**

| SANDWICHES | | DESSERTS | |
|---|---|---|---|
| TUNA SALAD | $2.25 | COOKIE | $0.89 |
| FISH | $3.79 | FRUIT CUP | $2.65 |
| HAMBURGER | $3.19 | YOGURT CONE | $1.79 |
| VEGGIE | $1.89 | | |

## TASK B • MATH GAME

Carla and Sandy are playing a math game. They take turns choosing an equation card and writing a word problem for the equation. Then they exchange problems.

$14 + n = 25$    $m - 8 = 3$    $0 + y = 37$    $15 - b + 2 = 12$

$9 = 14 - t$    $24 = s + 18$    $28 + d = 28$    $4 + 12 = k + 4$

**a.** The equation on Carla's card has a subtraction sign. Choose an equation that could be Carla's, and write a word problem for that equation. Explain how you would solve that equation.

**b.** The equation on Sandy's card illustrates an addition property. Choose an equation that could be Sandy's. Tell which property the equation illustrates. Explain how you know.

# Technology Linkup

## Order and Add Numbers on a Spreadsheet

The table shows the amounts Susan earned babysitting last year. Susan can use a spreadsheet to order the amounts and to find the total amount she earned.

| Month | Amount | Month | Amount | Month | Amount |
|-------|--------|-------|--------|-------|--------|
| January | $72.25 | May | $61.75 | September | $61.00 |
| February | $87.75 | June | $71.00 | October | $56.00 |
| March | $65.50 | July | $89.75 | November | $66.25 |
| April | $54.75 | August | $79.25 | December | $71.50 |

| ◇ | A | B |
|---|---|---|
| 1 | January | $72.25 |
| 2 | February | $87.75 |
| 3 | March | $65.50 |
| 4 | April | $54.75 |
| 5 | May | $61.75 |
| 6 | June | $71.00 |
| 7 | July | $89.75 |
| 8 | August | $79.25 |
| 9 | September | $61.00 |
| 10 | October | $56.00 |
| 11 | November | $66.25 |
| 12 | December | $71.50 |

- Open the spreadsheet. Enter the months into Column A and the amounts into Column B.
- Click in cell B1 and highlight the data in Columns A and B. Click ⬇ to order the data from greatest to least.
- Click in cell B13. Click $f_x$. Select *SUM* and click *OK*.
- Type B1:B12 to add the cells from B1 to B12. The formula may already be there as the default choice on the spreadsheet.
- Click *OK*.

| ◇ | A | B |
|---|---|---|
| 1 | July | $89.75 |
| 2 | February | $87.75 |
| 3 | August | $79.25 |
| 4 | January | $72.25 |
| 5 | December | $71.50 |
| 6 | June | $71.00 |
| 7 | November | $66.25 |
| 8 | March | $65.50 |
| 9 | May | $61.75 |
| 10 | September | $61.00 |
| 11 | October | $56.00 |
| 12 | April | $54.75 |
| 13 | | $836.75 |

## Practice and Problem Solving

Use a spreadsheet to order the amounts from greatest to least and to find each total.

1. Chuck earned $55.25 last winter, $72.50 last spring, $95.25 last summer, and $62.50 last fall.

2. The Snake River is 1,038 miles long, the Colorado River is 1,450 miles long, the Red River is 1,290 miles long, and the Ohio-Allegheny River is 1,310 miles long.

**GO ON-LINE**

**Multimedia Math Glossary** www.harcourtschool.com/mathglossary

**Vocabulary Power** Locate four words from this unit in the Multimedia Math Glossary. Write a story to help you remember them.

# PROBLEM SOLVING IN FLORIDA

## A SHINING BEACON

Located near Daytona Beach, the Ponce de Leon Lighthouse is one of Florida's most interesting, historical treasures. It is 175 feet tall and is the second-tallest lighthouse in the nation. The lighthouse and seven of its original buildings provide a unique look at Florida's history. The Ponce de Leon Lighthouse is a National Historic Landmark.

Ponce de Leon Lighthouse

◁ The Ponce de Leon Lighthouse gets about 87,000 visitors a year.

Ponce Inlet
LIGHTHOUSE
Museum

MUSEUM & SHIPSTORE HOURS
OPEN 10:00am until 9:00pm
Last Lighthouse Admission - 8:00pm

1. In 2002, thousands of people visited the lighthouse. Of those visitors, 78,000 climbed the steps to the gallery at the top. Suppose that in 2003, 800 more people climbed the steps than climbed in 2002. Write an equation to find the total for 2003.

2. The tower has 9 outside steps, 194 inside steps, and 10 steps to the lantern. How many steps do you climb if you go from ground level to the lantern and back down? Write this number in word form.

3. About one million, two hundred fifty thousand bricks were used to build the lighthouse. Write this number in standard form and in expanded form.

4. The lighthouse is wider at the base than it is at the top. Near the top of the lighthouse, the walls are 1.5 feet thick. At the base, the walls are 6.5 feet thicker than they are near the top. How thick are the walls at the base of the lighthouse?

# TOWERS OF LIGHT

All along the Florida coastline, are many lighthouses. The design of a lighthouse can vary depending on its location. Lighthouses must be strong enough to resist harsh ocean storms so the beams of light can help ships navigate safely into the harbor.

**USE DATA** For 1–4, use the table.

| FLORIDA LIGHTHOUSES | | |
|---|---|---|
| Lighthouse | Height (in feet) | Number of Visitors 2001 |
| Ponce de Leon | 175 | 87,000 |
| St. Augustine | 165 | 180,000 |
| Key West | 86 | 65,300 |
| Gasparilla Island | 44 | 23,000 |

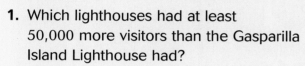

1. Which lighthouses had at least 50,000 more visitors than the Gasparilla Island Lighthouse had?

2. Which lighthouses had fewer than seventy thousand visitors?

3. The height of one of the lighthouses rounded to the nearest ten is 170 feet. Which lighthouse is this?

4. Suppose you were to make a graph showing the heights of these lighthouses. What type of graph would you choose to display these data? Why?

5. Hannah and her family drove from the St. Augustine Lighthouse to the Ponce de Leon Lighthouse. They drove 28.4 miles before lunch and 24.3 miles after lunch. About how many miles is the distance between the two lighthouses?

Florida lighthouses can be constructed of brick, iron, or wood. ▼

# Analyze Data and Graphs

**FAST FACT • SPORTS**

Dr. James Naismith invented basketball in 1891. The first official college basketball game took place in 1897, when Yale University defeated the University of Pennsylvania, 32–10. The graph shows the average points per game scored by college basketball's top scorers for 1997 through 2001.

**PROBLEM SOLVING**
How much greater was Ronnie McCollum's average than Courtney Alexander's? Can you tell from the graph how many total points Charles Jones scored during the 1997 season? Explain.

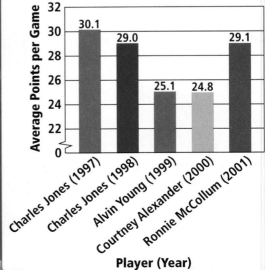

**NCAA MEN'S BASKETBALL LEADING SCORERS**

Player (Year)

# CHECK WHAT YOU KNOW

Use this page to help you review and remember
important skills needed for Chapter 5.

## FREQUENCY TABLES

For 1–4, use the frequency table.

1. How many students scored 90 on the test?

2. How many students scored either 90 or 100?

3. How many students took the test?

4. How many students scored less than 90?

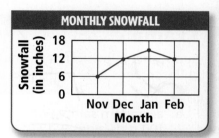

| TEST SCORES | |
|---|---|
| Score | Frequency |
| 70 | 12 |
| 80 | 15 |
| 90 | 17 |
| 100 | 12 |

## READ GRAPHS

For 5–8, use the line graph.

5. Which two months had equal amounts of snowfall?

6. Which month had the greatest amount of snow?

7. Which month had the least amount of snow?

8. What was the total snowfall for November
and December?

MONTHLY SNOWFALL

For 9–11, use the circle graph.

9. What flavor received the most votes?

10. How many people chose vanilla?

11. How many people voted?

FAVORITE ICE CREAM FLAVORS

Strawberry 3
Mint Chip 6
Vanilla 9
Chocolate 12

# VOCABULARY POWER

## REVIEW

**data** [dā′tə] *noun*

Data are information collected about
people or things. Data can be numbers,
words, pictures, photos, or videos. List
three ways to collect data.

## PREVIEW

| | |
|---|---|
| survey | outlier |
| sample | mean |
| population | median |
| random sample | mode |

www.harcourtschool.com/mathglo

# Collect and Organize Data

▶ **Learn**

**WHAT'S THE QUESTION?** A survey can be used to gather information about a group. Often, a part of the group, called a sample, is chosen to represent the whole group, or population.

A sample must represent the population fairly. In a random sample each person in the population has an equal chance of being chosen.

### VOCABULARY

survey
sample
population
random sample
cumulative frequency
outlier

## Example

Suppose a television network wants to find the time of day that most children ages 9–12 watch TV. Which sample represents the population?

**a.** a random sample of 100 girls, ages 9–12

**b.** a random sample of 100 children, ages 9–12

**c.** a random sample of 100 children

**d.** a random sample of 100 adults

Choice **a** leaves out boys. Choice **c** could include children who are younger than 9 or older than 12, and choice **d** does not include children. Only choice **b** represents the population.

## Activity

Design your own survey and collect data.

- Select one of the topics listed below.
  - a. Hours spent studying each week
  - b. Favorite type of movie
  - c. Favorite breakfast food

- Decide what population you want to survey. Do you want to include all students at your school, or just fifth graders?

- Write a question for your survey.

  The question should be clear and simple, use words that have the same meaning to everyone, and have only one response, or answer, per person.

- Survey a random sample of at least 30 students.

- Make a recording sheet for your data.

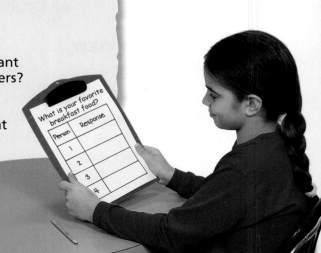

# Frequency Tables and Line Plots

A frequency table shows the total for each category or group. The **cumulative frequency** column is a running total of the frequencies.

**Remember**

The range is the difference between the greatest and least numbers in a set of data.

## Examples

May Elementary had a pet fair. The student council surveyed students by asking, "How many pets do you have at home?"

**A** Read from the frequency column to find how many students have just 3 pets at home.

Five students have 3 pets at home.

---

**B** Read from the cumulative frequency column to find how many students have 3 or fewer pets at home.

Twenty-seven students have 3 or fewer pets at home.

---

**C** Read the last entry in the cumulative frequency column to find how many students were surveyed.

Thirty students were surveyed.

### Pet Survey

| Pets | Tally |
|------|-------|
| 0 | ⊬⊬ II |
| 1 | ⊬⊬ I |
| 2 | ⊬⊬ IIII |
| 3 | ⊬⊬ |
| 4 | II |
| 7 | I |

### PET SURVEY

| Number of Pets | Frequency | Cumulative Frequency | |
|----------------|-----------|---------------------|---|
| 0 | 7 | 7 | |
| 1 | 6 | 13 | ← 7 + 6 = 13 |
| 2 | 9 | 22 | ← 13 + 9 = 22 |
| 3 | 5 | 27 | ← 22 + 5 = 27 |
| 4 | 2 | 29 | ← 27 + 2 = 29 |
| 5 | 0 | 29 | ← 29 + 0 = 29 |
| 6 | 0 | 29 | ← 29 + 0 = 29 |
| 7 | 1 | 30 | ← 29 + 1 = 30 |

You can graph these data by using a line plot.

The line plot gives a visual picture of the data. You can quickly see that the most common number of pets is 2.

Some students have no pets, and one student has 7 pets. So, the range for these data is 7 − 0, or 7.

• Organize your data from the Activity on page 96 in a frequency table. Draw a line plot or other graph to display the data.

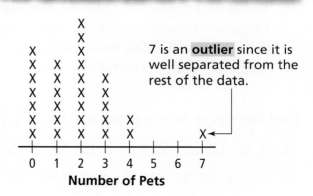

7 is an **outlier** since it is well separated from the rest of the data.

**LESSON CONTINU**

FCAT TESTED · SSS/GLEs MA.E.3.2.1.5.2 As a class project, discusses ways to choose a sample representative of a large group such as a sample representative of the entire school. *also* MA.E.3.2.1.5.1, MA.E.1.2.1.5.4

**Chapte**

96

1. **Explain** one way to select a random sample of the fifth-grade students at your school.

**A toy company surveyed children ages 8–12. Tell whether the sample represents the population. If it does not, explain.**

2. a random sample of 250 boys, ages 8–12

3. a random sample of 250 children, ages 8–12

▷ **Practice and Problem Solving**  ( Extra Practice, page 110, Set A )

**Nelton Elementary wants to name the new school mascot. Tell whether the sample represents the population. If it does not, explain.**

4. a random sample of 100 students from a list of all students in school

5. a random sample of 100 fifth-grade students

**Write *yes* or *no* to tell whether the question would be a good survey question. If it would not, explain.**

6. Is your favorite sport soccer or tennis?

7. Which state would you most like to visit?

**For 8–11, use the tally table.**

8. Make a cumulative frequency table for the data.

9. Which time was selected by the greatest number of students?

10. If each student took part in only one event, how many students participated in Field Day?

11. **Vocabulary Power** In physics, the word *frequency* means "rate of repetition," as in a vibration. Explain what *frequency* means in a frequency table.

| SIGN-UP FOR FIELD EVENT TIMES | |
| --- | --- |
| **Event Times** | **Number of Students** |
| 9:30 A.M. | 卌 卌 卌 I |
| 10:30 A.M. | 卌 卌 III |
| 1:30 P.M. | 卌 卌 卌 II |
| 2:30 P.M. | 卌 卌 卌 III |

12. ✎ **Write About It** Explain why a sample is often used rather than a population when conducting a survey.

**Find the range for each set of data.**

13. 8, 12, 17, 15, 20, 9

14. 34, 26, 37, 31, 37, 22

15. 100, 110, 105, 103

16. 96, 74, 83, 81, 64

17. 156, 147, 145, 168, 155

18. 38, 45, 59, 32, 47, 51

19. Survey 20 people to find the number of servings of fruit they eat each week. Make a frequency table and a line plot. Find the range, and describe the results.

20. Find survey results from a newspaper or magazine. Identify the sample size and the question. Describe the results of the survey.

**21.** John made a tally table to show the hair colors of the students in his class.

| Color | Number of Students |
|-------|-------------------|
| Brown | ЖЖ ЖЖ ЖЖ I |
| Blonde | ЖЖ II |
| Red | ЖЖ IIII |
| Black | IIII |

How many more students have brown hair than blonde hair?

**A.** 7   **B.** 9   **C.** 13   **D.** 16

**22.** Suppose you plan to take a survey at your school to find the favorite sport of all students in your school. Which sample would represent the population?

**F.** a random sample of the teachers

**G.** a random sample of 100 athletes

**H.** a random sample of 100 fifth-grade students

**I.** a random sample of 100 students

# Problem Solving   LiNKUP... to Reading

**STRATEGY • USE GRAPHIC AIDS**   Examining each part of a table can help you understand the data presented. The title tells you what data are represented. The labels on the columns and rows give you more details about the data. As you read a problem about data in a table, match what you read with what you see.

**For 1–6, use the frequency table.**

1. What does the title tell you?

2. What does the frequency column tell you?

3. Where would you look in the table to find the total number of students represented by the data?

4. How many students read for 60 minutes during the week?

5. How many more students read for 40 minutes or more than read for less than 40 minutes?

6. **Explain** how using a graphic aid, such as a table or graph, can help you analyze data.

| MINUTES STUDENTS SPENT READING MAGAZINES (1 WEEK) | | |
|---------|-----------|----------------------|
| Minutes | Frequency | Cumulative Frequency |
| 20 | 5 | 5 |
| 30 | 9 | 14 |
| 40 | 10 | 24 |
| 50 | 14 | 38 |
| 60 | 11 | |

# LESSON 2

# Find the Mean

## ▶ Learn

**"WE THE PEOPLE . . ."**  The table shows the ages of some of the youngest signers of the Declaration of Independence. What is the mean age of these signers?

The **mean**, or average, is one number that is representative of the data. You can find the mean by dividing the sum of a set of numbers by the number of addends.

### SIGNERS OF DECLARATION OF INDEPENDENCE

| Signer | Age |
| --- | --- |
| Edward Rutledge | 26 |
| Benjamin Rush | 30 |
| Elbridge Gerry | 31 |
| Thomas Jefferson | 33 |

### Example

**STEP 1**

Add all the data.

```
  26
  30
  31
+ 33
─────
 120
```

**STEP 2**

Divide the sum by the number of addends.

```
    30
 4)120
```

So, the mean age is 30.

▲ Edward Rutledge

▲ Starting on August 2, 1776, 56 members of Congress signed the Declaration of Independence.

- **What if** the table included the oldest signer, Benjamin Franklin, who was 70 years old? How would that affect the mean?

### More Examples   Find the mean for each set of data.

**A**   74, 91, 63, 92, 85

```
  74              81
  91   number of → 5)405
  63   addends     40
  92                05
+ 85                 5
─────                0
 405
```

**B**   357, 562, 411, 584, 294, 372

```
  357              430
  562   number of → 6)2580
  411   addends      24
  584                18
  294                18
+ 372                00
─────                 0
2,580                 0
```

▲ Benjamin Franklin

You can also use a calculator to find the mean.

  ( 357  562  411  584  294  372  )  ÷ 6  =   =    430

## ▶ Check

1. **Look** at this set of data: 5, 16, 17, 17, 17, 18. Do you think the mean will be closer to 5 or to 16? Explain.

**Find the mean for each set of data.**

2. 18, 22, 14

3. 58, 105, 172, 45

4. 33, 36, 35, 37, 39

## ▶ Practice and Problem Solving · Extra Practice, page 110, Set B

**Find the mean for each set of data.**

5. 9, 6, 5, 9, 11

6. $6, $7, $9, $10

7. 19, 25, 28, 32

8. 1,250; 980; 350

9. 110, 75, 135, 160

10. 147, 116, 148, 128, 116

11. 95, 84, 72, 73, 76

12. 124, 130, 100, 122, 124

13. 202, 213, 315, 285, 285

14. 100, 150, 200, 170, 250, 300

15. 1,200; 2,400; 1,320; 2,560

**ALGEBRA** Use the given mean to find the missing number in each data set.

16. $1, $3, $5, ■; mean: $4

17. 5, 7, 10, 13, ■; mean: 10

18. 12, 15, 18, 10, ■; mean: 13

19. 20, 25, 30, ■, 32, 18; mean: 25

**For 20–24, use the table.**

20. What is the average of Andrew's test scores?

21. How can you tell what Lin's test average is without calculating it?

22. Who had the highest test mean, or average, Ally, Andrew, or Lin?

23. **REASONING** What score does Karen need to get on Test 4 to raise her average to 85?

24. ✎ **Write a problem** using the information in the table. Then solve the problem.

| HISTORY TEST SCORES | | | | |
|---|---|---|---|---|
| **Name** | **Test 1** | **Test 2** | **Test 3** | **Test 4** |
| Ally | 87 | 93 | 100 | 80 |
| Andrew | 95 | 92 | 89 | 76 |
| Karen | 81 | 86 | 82 | absent |
| Lin | 85 | 85 | 85 | 85 |

25. Ally, Andrew, Karen, and Lin sit in the same row. Ally sits in front of Karen and behind Lin. Andrew sits in the front seat. Who sits right behind Andrew?

## Getting Ready for FCAT

26. The table shows the amount of money saved for four weeks by four friends. Who had a mean savings of $16?

   **A.** Amy

   **B.** Edna

   **C.** Carl

   **D.** Dave

| WEEKLY SAVINGS | | | | |
|---|---|---|---|---|
| **Name** | **Week 1** | **Week 2** | **Week 3** | **Week 4** |
| Amy | $12 | $19 | $14 | $15 |
| Edna | $14 | $16 | $19 | $15 |
| Carl | $18 | $16 | $12 | $10 |
| Dave | $13 | $23 | $15 | |

**FCAT TESTED** SSS/GLEs MA.E.I.2.2.5.2 Uses range and measures of central tendency in real-world situations. *also* MA.E.I.2.3.5.I

**Chapter 5**

# Find the Median and Mode

## Quick Review

Give the number halfway between the numbers in each pair.

1. 6 and 8
2. 12 and 14
3. 14 and 18
4. 32 and 36
5. 68 and 72

VOCABULARY

median    mode

▶ **Learn**

**WHAT'S THE SCORE?**   The Eagles basketball team has played 9 games so far this season. The coach recorded their scores.

To analyze the data, the coach can find the median and mode of the scores.

The **median** is the middle number when the data are arranged in order.

The **mode** is the number or item that occurs most often in a set of data. There may be one mode, more than one mode, or no mode.

**HANDS ON**   **Activity**

**STEP 1**

Put the basketball points in order from least to greatest. Find the median.

**STEP 2**

Make a line plot of the points.

• Draw a horizontal line.
• Label vertical tick marks in units of 1 from 40–50.
• Plot the data. Then title the graph.

**STEP 3**

Use the line plot to find the mode.

• Where are the data clustered on the line plot?
• What if the Eagles score 45 points in their tenth game? Will that change the mode? Explain.

| GAME | POINTS | GAME | POINTS |
|------|--------|------|--------|
| 1 | 42 | 6 | 43 |
| 2 | 50 | 7 | 40 |
| 3 | 45 | 8 | 42 |
| 4 | 42 | 9 | 45 |
| 5 | 44 | 10 | |

• What fraction of the basketball points are greater than the median? What fraction are less than the median?

When there are two middle numbers, the median is the mean of the two numbers.

The median for 3, 5, 7, 9 is between 5 and 7.

$$(5 + 7) \div 2 = 12 \div 2 = 6$$   The median is 6.

**Technology Link**

More Practice:
Harcourt Mega Math
The Number Games,
*ArachnaGraph*, Level F

1. **Explain** how the median and the mode differ from the mean of a set of data.

**Find the median and the mode.**

2. 12, 14, 11, 11, 9, 16, 17, 19

3. 24, 32, 28, 45, 19, 24, 50, 32

▶ **Practice and Problem Solving** ( Extra Practice, page 110, Set C )

**Find the median and the mode.**

4.

| KATIE'S TEST SCORES | | | | | | | |
|---|---|---|---|---|---|---|---|
| **Test** | 1 | 2 | 3 | 4 | 5 | 6 | 7 |
| **Score** | 94 | 93 | 95 | 87 | 94 | 78 | 85 |

5.

| CARD COLLECTIONS | | | | | |
|---|---|---|---|---|---|
| **Name** | Tony | Kara | Ray | Sue | Jay |
| **Number** | 240 | 200 | 200 | 265 | 285 |

**Find the mean, median, mode, and range.**

6. 9, 6, 5, 9, 11

7. $4, $1, $8, $6, $3, $8

8. 124, 130, 100, 122, 124

9. 95, 84, 72, 73, 76

10. 202, 213, 315, 285, 285

11. 749, 751, 1,298, 202

**For 12–15, use the line plot.**

12. How many players were measured, and what is the range of their heights?

13. What is the most common height?

14. What is the median height for the basketball team?

15. Two players with heights of 56 in. and 63 in. join the team. How does this affect the median and the mode of the heights?

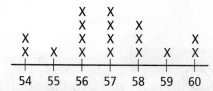

Heights of Fifth-Grade Basketball Players (in.)

16. **? What's the Error?** Julio said the median of the scores 90, 80, 82, 95, 78, 84, and 86 is 95. Explain Julio's error. What is the correct median of the scores?

**Getting Ready for FCAT**

17. Trevor made a list of the number of spelling words that he got correct each week. Which statement is true?

A. median > mode
B. median < mode
C. median = mode
D. range > median

| SPELLING WORDS CORRECT | | | |
|---|---|---|---|
| **Week** | **Words** | **Week** | **Words** |
| 1 | 17 | 4 | 20 |
| 2 | 19 | 5 | 15 |
| 3 | 17 | 6 | 17 |

# Problem Solving Strategy
## Make a Graph

**PROBLEM** A store recorded the ages of all the people who bought a pair of in-line skates last month. Which age group bought the most skates: people 10–19, people in their 20's, in their 30's, in their 40's, or in their 50's?

**Quick Review**

Find the following for this data set: 14, 15, 18, 14, 14, 16, 18, 19, 16.

1. Mean    2. Mode
3. Median    4. Range
5. Least number

**VOCABULARY**

**stem-and-leaf plot**

### UNDERSTAND

• What are you asked to find?

• What information will you use?

### PLAN

• What strategy can you use to solve the problem?

You can *make a graph* to organize the data.

### SOLVE

• How can you use the strategy to solve the problem?

You can make a **stem-and-leaf plot** to help you see how data are clustered, or grouped.

List the tens digits of the data in order from least to greatest. These are the stems.

Beside each tens digit, record the ones digits of the data, in order from least to greatest. These are the leaves.

So, the most skate buyers were in the 10–19 age group.

| Ages of People Who Bought In-Line Skates | | | |
|---|---|---|---|
| 26 | 18 | 41 | 51 |
| 12 | 34 | 23 | 19 |
| 31 | 44 | 45 | 14 |
| 34 | 16 | 37 | 23 |
| 13 | 27 | 12 | 22 |

The tens digit of each number is its stem.

The ones digit of each number is its leaf.

| Stem | Leaves |
|---|---|
| 1 | 2 2 3 4 6 8 9 |
| 2 | 2 3 3 6 7 |
| 3 | 1 4 4 7 |
| 4 | 1 4 5 |
| 5 | 1 |

4 | 5  represents 45.

**Ages of In-Line Skate Buyers**

### CHECK

• Look back. Does the answer make sense? Explain.

## Problem Solving Practice

### Make a graph to solve.

1. **What if** three more people, ages 25, 28, and 32, bought skates? Which age group would have bought the most skates then?

2. Angela's bowling scores are 71, 87, 96, 73, 76, 95, 84, 95, and 97. Does she bowl more often in the 70's, 80's, or 90's?

**Mr. Brown recorded the class test scores. Make a stem-and-leaf plot, using the table below. Check students' plots.**

| TEST SCORES | | | | | | | | | | |
|---|---|---|---|---|---|---|---|---|---|---|
| 84 | 81 | 85 | 75 | 81 | 87 | 70 | 90 | 82 | 92 | 86 |

3. Jim and Tamara got the same score on the test. What was their score?

   **A** 90            **C** 81
   **B** 85            **D** 75

4. Which is true about the test scores?

   **F** The mode for the test scores is 87.
   **G** The mean test score is 85.
   **H** The range for the test scores is 12.
   **J** The median test score is 84.

### Strategies

Draw a Diagram or Picture
Make a Model or Act It Out
Make an Organized List
Find a Pattern
▶ **Make a Table or Graph**
Predict and Test
Work Backward
Solve a Simpler Problem
Write an Equation
Use Logical Reasoning

## Mixed Strategy Practice

**For 5–6, use the table.**

5. Make a stem-and-leaf plot of the number of home runs. Which stem has the most leaves?

6. What are the range, median, and mode for the data set?

| NATIONAL LEAGUE HOME-RUN RECORDS 1992–2001 | | | |
|---|---|---|---|
| Year | Home Runs | Year | Home Runs |
| 1992 | 35 | 1997 | 49 |
| 1993 | 46 | 1998 | 70 |
| 1994 | 43 | 1999 | 65 |
| 1995 | 40 | 2000 | 50 |
| 1996 | 47 | 2001 | 73 |

7. ▰**FAST FACT** • **SPORTS** The New York Yankees won their first World Series championship in 1923. They won their twenty-sixth championship 77 years later. What year was that?

8. Brenda is older than June. Alice is younger than June. Cindy's age is between Alice's and June's. Write the names in order from oldest to youngest.

9. The Richardos family paid $14.00 for parking. Parking cost $5.00 for the first hour and $1.50 for each additional hour. How many hours were they parked?

10. Antonio has 6 coins that are dimes and quarters. He has a total of $1.05. What combination of coins does he have?

FCAT TESTED  SSS/GLEs MA.E.1.2.2.5.1 Uses a stem-and-leaf plot from a set of data to identify the range, median, mean, and mode. *also* MA.E.3.2.2.5.2, MA.E.1.2.1.5.1

Chapter 5  **105**

# Analyze Graphs

**GRAPHS GALORE!** A **pictograph** displays countable data with symbols or pictures. Pictographs have a *key* to show how many each picture represents.

Look at the Aerobics Class Size pictograph. How many people are in the 3:00 and 4:00 aerobics classes altogether?

| AEROBICS CLASS SIZE | |
|---|---|
| 3:00 | ⅄⅄⅄ |
| 4:00 | ⅄⅄⅄⅄⅄⅄ |
| 5:00 | ⅄⅄⅄⅄⅄⅄ |
| 6:00 | ⅄⅄⅄⅄⅄ |

Key: ⅄ = 2 people

There are 8 whole symbols and 1 half symbol in the 3:00 and 4:00 classes combined.

$$(8 \times 2) + 1 = 17$$

So, there are 17 people altogether.

A **bar graph** uses horizontal or vertical bars to display countable data. Bar graphs allow you to compare facts about groups of data.

Look at the exercise bar graph. Which type of exercise is more popular, jogging or weights?

The jogging bar is taller, so that exercise is more popular.

How many more students chose that exercise?

There were 14 students who chose it and 10 who chose weights.

$$14 - 10 = 4$$

So, 4 more students chose jogging.

FAVORITE TYPES OF EXERCISE

Number of Students / Type of Exercise: Aerobics, Treadmill, Jogging, Weights

## More Graphs

A **line graph** shows how data change over time. All or part of the graph may show a **trend**, or a pattern over time, such as increasing, decreasing, or staying the same.

Look at the line graph. The distance increases by 6 miles each hour. Predict how long it will take to travel 30 miles by bike if the trend continues.

You can extend the line to see that it will probably take 5 hours to travel 30 miles if the trend continues.

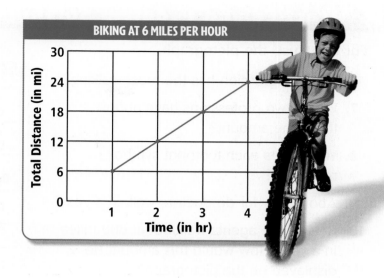

**BIKING AT 6 MILES PER HOUR**

**KAREN'S 60-MINUTE WORKOUT**

10 min Warm-up

10 min Stretch

30 min Jog

10 min Cool-Down

A **circle graph** shows how parts of the data are related to the whole and to each other.

Look at the circle graph of Karen's workout. On which activity does Karen spend the most time? How long does she spend on this activity?

Jogging fills half of the circle. So, Karen spends the most time jogging. Half of 60 minutes is 30 minutes. So, Karen jogs for 30 minutes.

 **MATH IDEA** When you know how to analyze graphs, you can draw conclusions, answer questions, and make predictions about the data.

## ▶ Check

1. **Explain** which type of graph would be the most appropriate to compare the high temperatures for a week.

**For 2–5, use the graphs above.**

2. How long does it take to travel 12 miles?

3. Estimate the distance that can be traveled in $1\frac{1}{2}$ hours.

4. How does the amount of time Karen jogs compare to the amount of time she stretches?

5. What fraction of her workout does Karen spend warming up?

**LESSON CONTINUES**

**For 6–10, use the pictograph.**

6. Which profession has the most walking?

7. Which two professions have about the same amount?

8. What does each footprint symbol represent?

9. About how far do doctors walk in a year?

10. Real estate agents walk about 600 miles in a year. How would this amount be displayed on the pictograph?

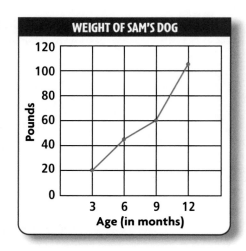

**PROFESSIONS WITH MUCH WALKING**

| Police Officer | 👣👣👣👣👣👣👣👣👣 |
| Mail Carrier | 👣👣👣👣👣( |
| TV Reporter | 👣👣👣👣 |
| Doctor | 👣👣👣 |

Key: 👣 = 200 mi/yr

**For 11–13, use the line graph.**

11. Between which ages did Sam's dog gain the most weight? About how much did the dog gain?

12. Estimate the dog's weight at 5 months and at 11 months.

13. **What if** Sam's dog stays at 105 pounds for the next 3 months? How would this trend be displayed on the line graph?

**WEIGHT OF SAM'S DOG**

(Line graph: Pounds (y-axis, 0 to 120) vs Age in months (x-axis: 3, 6, 9, 12))

14. Sam spent $30 on dog food, $20 on a collar, $15 on toys, and $35 for a dog bed. What type of graph would best display how Sam spent $100?

**For 15–16, use the circle graph.**

15. About what part of all the pets in the United States are either cats, birds, or fish?

16. Do dogs or fish account for about one quarter of all the pets in the United States?

**PETS IN THE U.S.**

(Circle graph with sections: Cats, Birds, Fish, Dogs, Other)

**17.** Rosa works at a dog kennel. She feeds each dog 0.2 pound of dry food each day. How much dry food does she use for 5 dogs in 2 weeks?

**18.** Of the 25 students in Mr. Reeve's class, 7 ride a bus to school, 8 ride in a carpool, and the rest walk to school. How many students walk to school?

## Getting Ready for FCAT — THINK SOLVE EXPLAIN

**19.** The line graph shows the sales at Shoe Mart for an 8-week period. Describe a trend for the data shown in the line graph. If the trend continues, what do you predict the amount of sales, in dollars, will be in Week 9?

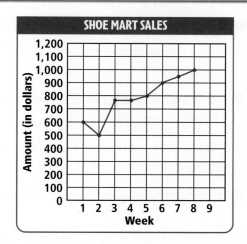

# Problem Solving LiNKUP... to Science

The cheetah is the fastest land animal, reaching speeds of 70 miles per hour. The slowest land animal is the snail, moving at top speeds of 0.03 miles per hour, or about 3 feet per minute.

**For 1–6, use the bar graph.**

**1.** Which animal runs faster, a rabbit or a zebra?

**2.** About how fast can an elephant run?

**3.** A slow-moving truck is traveling at 37 miles per hour. Which animals can run faster than the truck is moving?

**4.** A greyhound runs faster than a rabbit but slower than a zebra. How fast can a greyhound run?

**5.** ? **What's the Error?** Lisa read the graph and said that a pig can run about 20 miles per hour. How fast can a pig run? Explain Lisa's error.

**6.** ? **What's the Question?** The answer is 40 miles per hour.

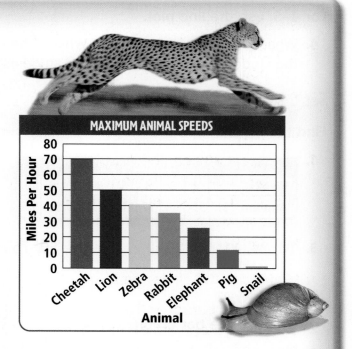

# Extra Practice

## Set A (pp. 96–99)

**For 1–4, use the frequency table.**

1. How many students eat 2 fruits each day? 5 fruits each day?

2. How many students eat fewer than 4 fruits each day?

3. What is the range of the fruits eaten each day?

4. How many students were surveyed?

| SCHOOL FRUIT SURVEY | | |
|---|---|---|
| **Fruits Eaten Each Day** | **Frequency** | **Cumulative Frequency** |
| 1 | 6 | 6 |
| 2 | 3 | 9 |
| 3 | 4 | 13 |
| 4 | 2 | 15 |
| 5 | 5 | 20 |

## Set B (pp. 96–99, 100–101)

**Find the mean for each set of data.**

1. 8, 21, 18, 17

2. 45, 31, 20, 27, 52

3. 15, 64, 33, 18, 22, 40

**For 4–5, use the line plot.**

4. What is the mean of the students' ages?

5. What is the range of the students' ages?

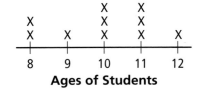

Ages of Students

## Set C (pp. 102–103)

**Find the median and the mode.**

1.

| SAVINGS | | | | | | | | | |
|---|---|---|---|---|---|---|---|---|---|
| Weeks | 1 | 2 | 3 | 4 | 5 | 6 | 7 | 8 | 9 |
| Amount | $10 | $14 | $8 | $7 | $10 | $12 | $10 | $12 | $12 |

2.

| POINTS SCORED | | | | | | | |
|---|---|---|---|---|---|---|---|
| Game | 1 | 2 | 3 | 4 | 5 | 6 | 7 |
| Points | 23 | 17 | 28 | 20 | 24 | 30 | 20 |

3. 16, 24, 11, 29, 20

4. 25, 50, 75, 25, 80

5. 26, 28, 28, 36, 40, 28

## Set D (pp. 106–109)

**For 1–3, use the bar graph.**

1. How many students voted for cake? ice cream?

2. Which two foods got the same number of total votes?

3. How many more students voted for cake than for popcorn?

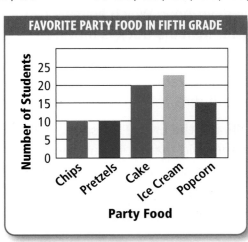

**110**

# Review/Test

## ✓ CHECK VOCABULARY AND CONCEPTS

**Choose the best term from the box.**

1. When you add all of the data and divide by the number of addends, you find the __?__ of the data. (p. 100)

2. To find the __?__ for a data set, subtract the least value from the greatest value. (p. 97)

3. In a survey, the whole group is known as the __?__. (p. 96)

| mean |
| mode |
| range |
| population |
| sample |

## ✓ CHECK SKILLS

**For 4–6, use the tally table.** (pp. 96–99)

4. Make a cumulative frequency table for the data.

5. During which hour were the most salads sold? the fewest?

6. How many more salads were sold during the first two hours than in the last two hours?

| SALADS SOLD ||
|---|---|
| **Hour** | **Salads** |
| 1 | ⊪ I |
| 2 | ⊪ ⊪ II |
| 3 | ⊪ IIII |
| 4 | ⊪ |

**Find the range, mean, median, and mode for each.** (pp. 96–103)

7. $8, $9, $11, $5, $8, $7

8. 15, 11, 20, 12, 12

9. 635, 499, 717, 601

**For 10–12, use the circle graph.** (pp. 106–109)

10. In which activity does Austin spend the most time?

11. Which two activities take up about the same part of Austin's day?

12. Does Austin spend more than or less than half the day sleeping?

HOW AUSTIN SPENDS A TYPICAL DAY

## ✓ CHECK PROBLEM SOLVING

**Solve. Use the test score data.** (pp. 104–105)

13. Make a stem-and-leaf plot for the data.

14. What are the range, median, mean, and mode for the test scores?

15. Two more students score 79 and 97 on the test. How does this affect the range, median, mean, and mode of the scores? Explain.

| 5th Grade Test Scores ||||
|---|---|---|---|
| 76 | 92 | 82 | 88 |
| 89 | 68 | 72 | |
| 70 | 94 | 89 | |

# Getting Ready for ⭐FCAT

## ⭐ DATA ANALYSIS AND PROBABILITY

1. Jan's table shows the high and low temperatures for the past five days. What was the median low temperature?

| DAILY TEMPERATURES (in °F) | | |
|---|---|---|
| **Day** | **High** | **Low** |
| Monday | 76° | 60° |
| Tuesday | 84° | 64° |
| Wednesday | 75° | 57° |
| Thursday | 77° | 60° |
| Friday | 83° | 64° |

**A.** 60°F      **C.** 62°F

**B.** 61°F      **D.** 64°F

2. Look at the table above. What was the mean high temperature?

**F.** 77°F

**G.** 78°F

**H.** 79°F

**I.** 84°F

3. **Explain It** Thomas is playing a game with these spinners. He spins both pointers.

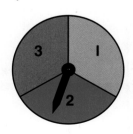 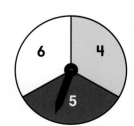

If his total is greater than 7, he wins a prize. List all the possible outcomes of the two spins. Explain the ways that Thomas can win.

## ⭐ MEASUREMENT

**TIP**   **Look for important words.** See item 4. *About* is an important word. You do not need to find the exact length in yards of the average blue whale. You can estimate the number of yards in 110 feet.

4. The table shows facts about blue whales. About how many yards long is the average blue whale?

| BLUE WHALE | |
|---|---|
| Average length | 110 feet |
| Average weight | 209 tons |

**A.** 10      **C.** 300

**B.** 40      **D.** 1,320

5. Look at the table above. How many pounds does an average blue whale weigh?

**F.** 418,000 pounds

**G.** 209,000 pounds

**H.** 41,800 pounds

**I.** 2,090 pounds

6. **Explain It** Heather went to the store to buy a gallon of milk.

$2.89

She gave the clerk $10 to pay for the milk and received $5.11 in change. ESTIMATE to explain how much change Heather should have received.

## NUMBER SENSE, CONCEPTS, AND OPERATIONS

**7.** The table shows the prices of four electronic items. Which costs less than $18.90?

| ELECTRONICS STORE PRICE LIST | |
|---|---|
| **Item** | **Price** |
| Headphones | $18.89 |
| Portable radio | $18.99 |
| Clock radio | $19.98 |
| CD player | $19.95 |

**A.** headphones

**B.** portable radio

**C.** clock radio

**D.** CD player

**8.** Look at the table above. Jared bought a CD player and a set of headphones. He gave the clerk two $20 bills. How much change did he get?

**F.** $0.16

**G.** $1.06

**H.** $1.16

**I.** $2.16

**9.** What is the **greatest** 4-digit number that can be made from the digits 7, 0, 1, and 6?

**A.** 6,017    **C.** 7,061

**B.** 6,701    **D.** 7,610

**10. Explain It** Marilee went on a 5-hour beach walk to collect shells. Her goal was to collect 500 shells to make a wreath. She collected 108 shells the first hour, 83 the second hour, 78 the third hour, 84 the fourth hour, and 103 the fifth hour. ESTIMATE to decide whether she reached her goal. Explain your solution.

 ## ALGEBRAIC THINKING

**11.** Cleo gained 3 pounds and then lost 7 pounds. If $p$ represents Cleo's beginning weight, which expression represents Cleo's weight now?

**F.** $(p + 3) + 7$

**G.** $(p + 3) - 7$

**H.** $(p - 3) + 7$

**I.** $(p - 3) - 7$

**12.** Shania spent $45 on a pair of new shoes. She had $13 left. Let $m$ represent the amount of money Shania started with. Which equation could be used to find the amount of money she started with?

**A.** $45 - m = 13$

**B.** $m + 13 = 45$

**C.** $13 - m = 45$

**D.** $m - 45 = 13$

**13.** Which is a rule for this pattern?

54, 62, 70, 78, 86

**F.** Add 18.

**G.** Add 16.

**H.** Add 8.

**I.** Subtract 8.

**14. Explain It** Look at the equations in the chart.

| | | |
|---|---|---|
| ○ + ○ = ☆ | | |
| ☆ + ○ = ▢ | | |
| ▢ + ☆ = 10 | | |

Find the number represented by each symbol. Explain your reasoning.

### CHAPTER 6

# Make Graphs

Polar bear at the
North Carolina
Zoological Park
in Asheboro,
North Carolina

**≡FAST FACT • SCIENCE** The world population of polar bears is estimated to be between 22,000 and 27,000. Polar bears spend much of their lives on the arctic ice.

**PROBLEM SOLVING** The graph shows how the amount of arctic ice in the Nordic Sea area of the Arctic Ocean has changed. Approximately how many fewer square kilometers of ice were in the Nordic Sea area in 2000 than in 1900?

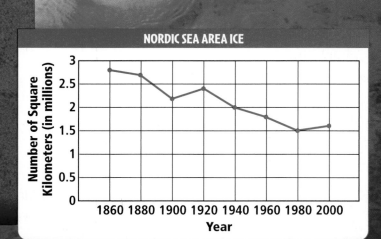

**NORDIC SEA AREA ICE**

Use this page to help you review and remember important skills needed for Chapter 6.

## NUMBER PATTERNS

Write a rule for each pattern. Then find the missing numbers.

**1.** 0, 6, 12, 18, ▪, ▪, ▪

**2.** 0, 10, 20, 30, ▪, ▪, ▪

**3.** 0, 3, 6, 9, ▪, ▪, ▪

**4.** 0, 4, 8, 12, ▪, ▪, ▪

**5.** 0, 50, 100, 150, ▪, ▪, ▪

**6.** 0, 25, 50, 75, ▪, ▪, ▪

**7.** 0, 12, 24, 36, ▪, ▪, ▪

**8.** 0, 100, 200, 300, ▪, ▪, ▪

**9.** 0, 15, 30, 45, ▪, ▪, ▪

**10.** 0, 500, 1,000, 1,500, ▪, ▪, ▪

**11.** 0, 200, 400, 600, ▪, ▪, ▪

**12.** 0, 150, 300, 450, ▪, ▪, ▪

## IDENTIFY POINTS ON A GRID

For 13–22, use the ordered pair to name the point on the grid.

**13.** (1,3)

**14.** (2,6)

**15.** (5,4)

**16.** (4,1)

**17.** (6,8)

**18.** (0,5)

**19.** (7,5)

**20.** (2,9)

**21.** (9,10)

**22.** (8,0)

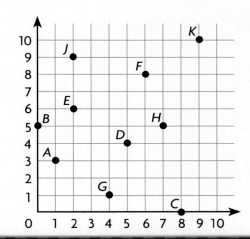

## VOCABULARY POWER

### REVIEW

**mean** [mēn] *noun*
**median** [mē′•dē•ən] *noun*

In math, the mean is sometimes confused with the median. This is not surprising because both words come from the same root word, *medhyo*, and both words originally meant the same thing, "middle." Explain the difference between the mean and the median.

### PREVIEW

scale
interval
ordered pair
histogram

www.harcourtschool.com/mathglossary

LESSON

# Choose a Reasonable Scale

## ▶ Learn

**SEAL SIZES** For her report, Helen made a graph of the lengths of 5 different types of seals. Her data are shown in the table.

First, Helen decided what scale and interval she would use. The **scale** is the set of numbers placed at fixed distances to help label the graph. The **interval** is the difference between one number and the next on the scale.

**LENGTHS OF SEALS**

| Seal | Average Length |
|---|---|
| Ribbon seal | 58 in. |
| Harbor seal | 65 in. |
| Ringed seal | 67 in. |
| Hooded seal | 95 in. |
| Bearded seal | 85 in. |

The data range from 58 to 95 inches. So, Helen used a scale of 0–100 because the greatest number in the data was 95. She used an interval of 10 because most of the data had different digits in the tens place.

▲ Harbor seal

## Examples

Choose a reasonable scale and interval for the data.

**A** 12, 15, 18, 30, 22, 16

The data range from 12 to 30.

Scale: 0–35

Interval: 5

**B** 50, 100, 200, 225, 120, 60

The data range from 50 to 225.

Scale: 0–250

Interval: 50

# Horizontal or Vertical

The scale on a bar graph can run horizontally or vertically.

The fifth graders at Westhill School voted for their favorite sea mammal. Will's and Anthony's bar graphs show the results in different ways.

**Anthony's Bar Graph**

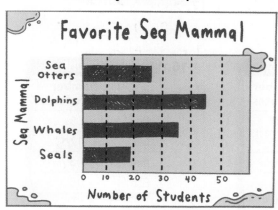

**Will's Bar Graph**

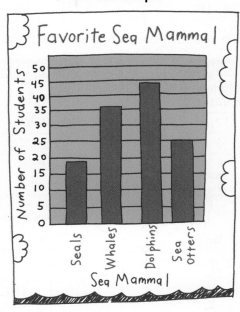

Both graphs have a scale of 0 to 50.

Each graph shows that dolphins are the most popular sea mammal.

• How are the graphs different?

## ▶ Check

1. **Tell** what scale and interval you would use for these data: 16, 20, 24, 28, 35, 42, 50.

**Choose 10, 25, 50, or 100 as the most reasonable interval for the data.**

2. 10, 62, 18, 21, 31

3. 105, 200, 990, 800, 620

4. 45, 100, 95, 50, 150

5. 20, 31, 40, 78, 85

**Choose the more reasonable scale for the data.**

6.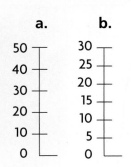

| GAME SCORES | |
|---|---|
| **Game** | **Score** |
| 1 | 32 |
| 2 | 15 |
| 3 | 28 |
| 4 | 45 |

a.
50
40
30
20
10
0

b.
30
25
20
15
10
5
0

7.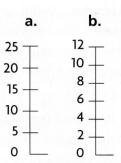

| FAVORITE PLACE | |
|---|---|
| **Place** | **Votes** |
| Zoo | 9 |
| Beach | 5 |
| Park | 12 |
| Museum | 7 |

a.
25
20
15
10
5
0

b.
12
10
8
6
4
2
0

**LESSON CONTINUES**

**FCAT TESTED** SSS/GLEs MA.E.1.2.1.5.3 *Chooses reasonable titles, labels, scales and intervals for organizing data on graphs.*

**Chapter 6 117**

**Choose 1, 5, 10, or 25 as the most reasonable interval for the data.**

**8.** 2, 5, 6, 3, 1, 4, 7

**9.** 6, 3, 3, 5, 4

**10.** 75, 25, 50, 100, 110

**11.** 10, 35, 40, 20, 30

**12.** 27, 24, 50, 74, 101

**13.** 10, 5, 20, 15, 17, 25

**Choose the more reasonable scale for the data.**

**14.**

| FAVORITE ZOO ANIMALS | |
|---|---|
| **Animal** | **Number of Votes** |
| Lion | 12 |
| Bear | 19 |
| Elephant | 8 |
| Zebra | 5 |

a.
```
25
20
15
10
5
0
```
b.
```
12
10
8
6
4
2
0
```

**15.**

| FAVORITE SPORTS | |
|---|---|
| **Sport** | **Number of Votes** |
| Baseball | 20 |
| Soccer | 28 |
| Basketball | 16 |
| Softball | 25 |
| Other | 5 |

a.
```
50
40
30
20
10
0
```
b.
```
25
20
15
10
5
0
```

**16.**

| PETS AT HOME | |
|---|---|
| **Pet** | **Number of Students** |
| Dog | 9 |
| Cat | 12 |
| Bird | 8 |
| Fish | 5 |

a.
```
25
20
15
10
5
0
```
b.
```
12
10
8
6
4
2
0
```

**USE DATA   For 17–19, use the table.**

**17.** What is a reasonable scale for the data?

**18.** What is a reasonable interval for the data?

**19.** Make a double-bar graph for the data. Then compare your graph to that of a classmate. Did you use the same scale and interval?

**20. REASONING**   What is the relationship between the heights of two vertical graphs of the same data if one uses an interval of 20 and the other uses an interval of 10?

**21.** ≣**FAST FACT** • **SCIENCE** The great gray owl is one of the world's largest owls. The female weighs about 49.5 ounces. A female elf owl weighs only about 1.5 ounces. What is the difference in their weights?

| AVERAGE LENGTHS OF OWLS | | |
|---|---|---|
| **Owl** | **Female** | **Male** |
| Elf | 16 cm | 18 cm |
| Great gray | 72 cm | 69 cm |
| Long-eared | 37 cm | 34 cm |
| Eastern screech | 23 cm | 21 cm |
| Spotted | 48 cm | 46 cm |

▲ Great gray owl

**22. Vocabulary Power** *Range* comes from the old French word *rangier,* meaning "place in a row, or arrange." Explain how this meaning can be used to describe a data range.

**23.** John is twice as old as Enrico. The sum of their ages is 21. How old is John?

**24.** Shareen made a table to show the results of her survey. She wants to display the data in a bar graph. Which is NOT a reasonable scale and interval for the data?

**A.** scale 0–30, interval of 10

**B.** scale 0–40, interval of 10

**C.** scale 0–36, interval of 2

**D.** scale 0–40, interval of 5

| FAVORITE ICE CREAM FLAVOR | |
|---|---|
| **Flavor** | **Number of Votes** |
| Chocolate | 34 |
| Vanilla | 15 |
| Strawberry | 12 |
| Rocky Road | 5 |
| Other | 24 |

# Problem Solving  THINKER'S CORNER

**REASONING** The graph represents the top speeds of three roller coasters in the United States.

**1.** Use the clues to determine the scale and interval for the graph.

- The scale starts at 0.

- There is a difference of 10 miles per hour between the top speeds of the Scorpion and the Montu.

**2.** What is the top speed of the Scorpion roller coaster?

**3.** What is the top speed of the Kraken roller coaster?

**4.** Would an interval of 1 make sense for this graph? Explain your answer.

ROLLER COASTER TOP SPEEDS

Roller Coaster

Kraken

Montu

Scorpion

Speed
(in miles per hour)

# Graph Ordered Pairs

## Quick Review

Find the median.

1. 8, 12, 8, 9, 7, 11

2. 37, 35, 40, 41, 38

3. 63, 60, 60, 71, 68

4. 53, 58, 53, 54, 58, 60

5. 24, 18, 26, 24, 29

**VOCABULARY**

**ordered pair**

## ▶ Learn

**SIGHTSEEING** Reading a map of a city is like finding a point on a coordinate grid. A grid is formed by horizontal lines and vertical lines.

Each point on the coordinate grid can be located by using an **ordered pair** of numbers.

- The first number tells how far to move horizontally.
- The second number tells how far to move vertically.

The horizontal and vertical axes intersect at the point (0,0). To get to point *A*, start at (0,0). Move 4 units to the right and 2 units up. The ordered pair (4,2) gives the location of point *A*.

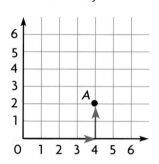

**Example** Graph the ordered pair (5,3).

**STEP 1**

Start at (0,0).

**STEP 2**

Move 5 units to the right.

**STEP 3**

Move 3 units up.

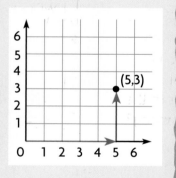

 **MATH IDEA** A point on a grid can be graphed or identified by using an ordered pair of numbers.

L'Enfant's design for Washington, D.C. is based on a grid pattern of streets. ▼

## ▶ Check

1. **Explain** why you think the numbers used to graph a point on a grid are called an ordered pair.

**Graph and label the following points on a coordinate grid.**

2. *A* (3,1)  3. *B* (1,3)  4. *C* (0,5)  5. *D* (2,7)

**Technology Link**

More Practice: Harcourt Mega Math The Number Games, *ArachnaGraph*, Level G

**Graph and label the following points on a coordinate grid.**

**6.** *L* (1,6)  **7.** *M* (2,1)  **8.** *N* (3,4)  **9.** *P* (3,8)

**10.** *Q* (8,6)  **11.** *R* (5,7)  **12.** *S* (0,3)  **13.** *T* (4,6)

**14.** *U* (6,3)  **15.** *V* (6,0)  **16.** *W* (8,2)  **17.** *Z* (7,5)

**Name the ordered pair for each point.**

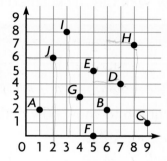

**18.** *A*  **19.** *B*

**20.** *C*  **21.** *D*

**22.** *E*  **23.** *F*

**24.** *G*  **25.** *H*

**26.** *I*  **27.** *J*

**Use the map grid for 28–32.**

**28.** What ordered pair gives the location of the Capitol?

**29.** The National Air and Space Museum is 6 blocks east and 1 block south of the Washington Monument. What ordered pair gives the location of the museum?

**30.** Write directions on how to walk from the White House to the FBI building.

**31.** **? What's the Error?** Myra walked 6 blocks east and 1 block north from the Washington Monument to get to the White House. What did Myra do wrong?

**32.** Doug bought popcorn for $1.65 and 3 pretzels. He spent $3.90. If each pretzel costs the same amount, how much did 1 pretzel cost?

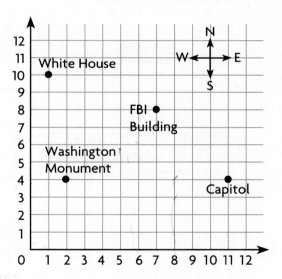

**Getting Ready for FCAT** **THINK SOLVE EXPLAIN**

**33.** What are the coordinates of the point that is 2 units to the right and 3 units down from point *A*? Explain how you know.

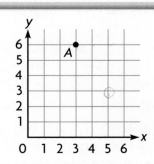

FCAT TESTED  SSS/GLEs MA.C.3.2.2.5.1 Knows how to identify, locate, and plot ordered pairs of whole numbers on a graph or on the first quadrant of a coordinate system.

**Chapter 6  121**

# Make Line Graphs

▶ **Learn**

**BAKED APPLE!** The table below shows normal monthly temperatures for New York City, nicknamed the Big Apple.

| NEW YORK CITY MONTHLY NORMAL TEMPERATURE (°F) | | | | | | |
|---|---|---|---|---|---|---|
| **Month** | Jun | Jul | Aug | Sep | Oct | Nov |
| **Temperature** | 72 | 77 | 76 | 68 | 58 | 48 |

You can make a line graph to show how data change over time.

◀ Statue of Liberty on July 4

**HANDS ON**  **Activity**  **MATERIALS:** line graph pattern

**STEP 1**

Choose an appropriate scale and interval for the data. Since there are no data between 0°F and 48°F, show a break in the scale using a zigzag line.

**STEP 2**

Write the months along the bottom of the graph. Label the vertical and horizontal axes. Write a title for the graph.

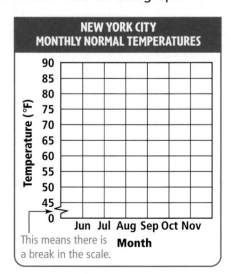

This means there is a break in the scale.

**STEP 3**

Plot a point to show each month's temperature. Connect the points with straight lines.

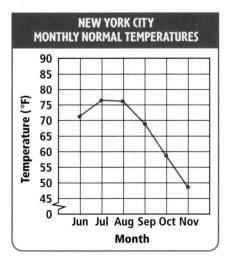

• What does the graph tell you about how the temperatures in New York City change over time?

# Double-Line Graph

A double-line graph shows two different sets of data on one graph. Include the data for the monthly normal temperatures in Miami Beach, Florida in your line graph from page 122.

| MIAMI BEACH MONTHLY NORMAL TEMPERATURE (°F) | | | | | | |
|---|---|---|---|---|---|---|
| **Month** | Jun | Jul | Aug | Sep | Oct | Nov |
| **Temperature** | 83 | 84 | 85 | 82 | 79 | 74 |

## STEP 4

Change the title to include the new data. Write a key to tell which line represents each city.

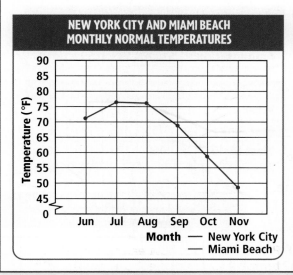

## STEP 5

Plot a point to show each temperature for Miami Beach. Connect the points with straight lines.

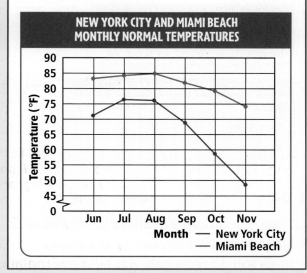

## Check

1. **Explain** the purpose of the title and the labels on a graph.

**USE DATA** Use the graph above for 2–4.

2. In New York City, which three months have about the same normal temperature?

3. During which month is the temperature difference between the two cities the least?

4. What trend do you notice in the temperatures for New York City and Miami Beach? If the trend continues, what will happen to the temperatures in these two cities in December?

▲ New York City's Central Park in October

LESSON CONTINUES

FCAT TESTED  SSS/GLEs MA.E.1.2.1.5.6 Analyzes and explains orally or in writing the implications of graphed data. *also* MA.E.3.2.2.5.1, MA.E.3.2.2.5.3

Chapter 6  **123**

**USE DATA** **For 5–7, use the data in the table.**

5. How would you label and title a graph of this data?

6. What would be an appropriate scale and interval for the wages?

7. What years would you show on the bottom of the graph?

| FEDERAL MINIMUM WAGE | | | | | |
|---|---|---|---|---|---|
| **Year** | 1960 | 1970 | 1980 | 1990 | 2000 |
| **Amount** | $1.15 | $2.30 | $3.25 | $3.80 | $5.15 |

**For 8–11, make a line graph or double-line graph for each set of data. Describe the data shown on your graph.**

8.

| INCHES OF RAINFALL | | | | |
|---|---|---|---|---|
| **Month** | Jun | Jul | Aug | Sep |
| **Inches** | 3 | 5 | 6 | 4 |

9.

| WEEKLY FOOD COST | | | | | |
|---|---|---|---|---|---|
| **Week** | 1 | 2 | 3 | 4 | 5 |
| **Amount** | $80 | $100 | $95 | $90 | $105 |

10.

| ABLE AUTO MONTHLY SALES | | | | |
|---|---|---|---|---|
| **Month** | Jan | Feb | Mar | Apr |
| **Cars Sold** | 25 | 18 | 23 | 32 |
| **Trucks Sold** | 12 | 20 | 25 | 18 |

11.

| NUMBER OF PEOPLE ATTENDING THE SKATING RINKS | | | | | |
|---|---|---|---|---|---|
| **Week** | 1 | 2 | 3 | 4 | 5 |
| **East Rink** | 150 | 155 | 165 | 180 | 185 |
| **West Rink** | 140 | 160 | 175 | 190 | 200 |

**USE DATA** **For 12–17, use the graph.**

12. Does the monthly average precipitation in New York City increase or decrease from July to October? How can you tell from the graph?

13. During which months was the monthly average precipitation for New York City and Asheville the same?

14. **What if** the data for Asheville included the month of December with a monthly average precipitation of 3.5 inches? How would the graph change?

15. Describe the precipitation trends in the data for New York City and for Asheville.

16. **Write About It** Tell what the zigzag line on the left of the graph represents.

17. **Write a problem** using the data in the graph.

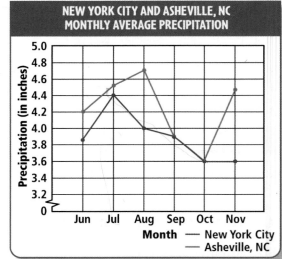

**124**

**18.** Shara and her dad paid a total of $175 for their train fare to New Orleans. Shara's fare was $39 less than her dad's. How much was her dad's fare?

**19.** The temperature on Friday at 12 noon was 23°F. A cold front moved through, and by midnight the temperature had dropped 19 degrees. What was the temperature at midnight?

## Getting Ready for FCAT

**20.** Jake's mother kept a record of how tall Jake was at each of his birthdays. She made a line graph to show his growth. Between which two ages did Jake grow the most?

**A.** birth to 1
**B.** 1 to 2
**C.** 7 to 8
**D.** 10 to 11

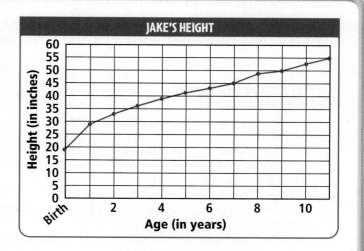

## Problem Solving LINKUP... to Reading

**STRATEGY • DRAW CONCLUSIONS** This line graph shows the number of active bald eagle nests recorded in Florida during an 8-year period.

Use the information shown on the graph to draw conclusions.

**1.** How did the number of active bald eagle nests change from 1993 to 2001?

**2.** Between what years did the number of active nests increase by 81 nests?

**3.** How many active bald eagle nests do you predict there will be in Florida in 2007? How did you make your prediction?

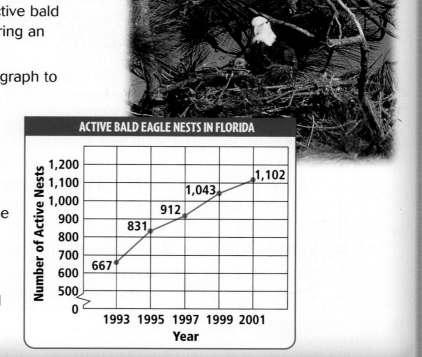

# Problem Solving Strategy
## Draw a Diagram

**PROBLEM** A café surveyed customers about all the cookie ingredients they like. The results showed 9 like fruit, 12 like nuts, 16 like chocolate, 3 like fruit and nuts, 5 like nuts and chocolate, 3 like fruit and chocolate, and 2 like all three. How many customers were surveyed?

### UNDERSTAND

- What are you asked to find?
- What information will you use?

### PLAN

- What strategy can you use to solve the problem?

  You can *draw a diagram* to display the results.

### SOLVE

- How can you use the strategy to solve the problem?

a. Draw a Venn diagram with three overlapping ovals. Two customers like all three ingredients, so write 2 in the part common to all three ovals.

Look at the two parts where the fruit and nuts ovals overlap. Three customers like fruit and nuts, so the sum of these parts must be 3. Since $3 - 2 = 1$, write 1 in the part where only the fruit and nuts ovals overlap. Use the same process to complete the other two middle parts.

b. Look at the four parts of the fruit oval. Since 9 customers like fruit, the sum of these parts must be 9. Since $9 - 4 = 5$, write 5 in the remaining part of the fruit oval. Use the same process to complete the diagram.

c. Add all the numbers in the diagram to find how many customers were surveyed: $5 + 1 + 6 + 1 + 2 + 3 + 10 = 28$. So, 28 customers were surveyed.

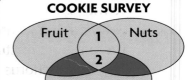
a.

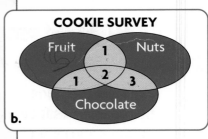
b.

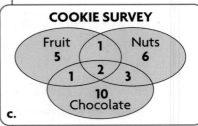
c.

### CHECK

- What other strategy could you use?

## Problem Solving Practice

**Strategies**

▶ Draw a Diagram or Picture
Make a Model or Act It Out
Make an Organized List
Find a Pattern
Make a Table or Graph
Predict and Test
Work Backward
Solve a Simpler Problem
Write an Equation
Use Logical Reasoning

**Draw a Venn diagram to solve.**

1. **What if** 15 customers at the café like fruit, 25 like nuts, 30 like chocolate, and all other results are the same? How many customers were surveyed?

2. How many numbers less than 20 are nonzero multiples of both 2 and 3?

**USE DATA** For 3–4, use the diagram.

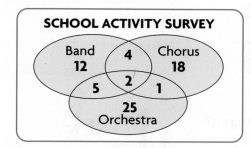

SCHOOL ACTIVITY SURVEY
Band 12 — 4 — Chorus 18
5 — 2 — 1
25 Orchestra

3. Which of the following is not true?

   **A** Two students are in all three activities.

   **B** Twelve students are only in the band.

   **C** There are more students in the band than in the chorus.

   **D** Twenty-three students are in the band.

4. Which equation could you use to find the number of students surveyed?

   **F** $12 + 18 + 25 = 45$

   **G** $4 + 2 + 5 + 1 = 12$

   **H** $12 + 4 + 18 + 5 + 2 + 1 + 25 = 67$

   **J** $12 + 4 + 18 + 5 + 1 + 25 = 65$

## Mixed Strategy Practice

**USE DATA** For 5–6, use the table.

5. Both students and parents voted for their choice of food. Make a double-bar graph showing their votes. What was the favorite choice of students? of parents?

6. How many people voted altogether?

7. The Tigers sold 1,018 tickets to the first game and 650 tickets to the second game. Their other games had sales of 835; 1,186; and 946 tickets. What are the mean and the range of the data?

| FALL FESTIVAL FOOD CHOICES | | |
|---|---|---|
| **Food** | **Parents** | **Students** |
| Burgers | 60 | 72 |
| Hot Dogs | 48 | 65 |
| Chicken | 78 | 75 |
| Ribs | 50 | 42 |

8. **REASONING** Jason forgot his locker number. The sum of its digits is 11 and the digits are all odd numbers. The locker numbers are from 1 to 120. What is Jason's locker number?

FCAT TESTED  MA.E.I.2.I The student solves problems by generating, collecting, organizing, displaying, and analyzing data using histograms, bar graphs, circle graphs, line graphs, pictographs, and charts.

Chapter 6  **127**

# Histograms

▶ **Explore**

A **histogram** is a bar graph that shows the number of times data occur within intervals.

The data show the number of minutes some students spent on homework each night.

| MINUTES SPENT ON HOMEWORK | | | | | | |
|---|---|---|---|---|---|---|
| 15 | 20 | 25 | 35 | 10 | 10 | 45 |
| 30 | 20 | 15 | 40 | 25 | 5 | 10 |
| 20 | 25 | 20 | 30 | 45 | 35 | |

### Quick Review

**What interval would you use to graph the data?**

1. 3, 8, 4, 2, 5

2. 25, 52, 75, 99

3. 10, 16, 35, 42, 26

4. 20, 15, 30, 50, 41

5. 4, 10, 7, 18, 21

### VOCABULARY

**histogram**

## Activity

Follow the steps to make a histogram of the data.

**STEP 1**

- Find the range of the data.

  Range: 45 − 5 = 40

- Decide on the scale.

  The scale could be 0 to 50 minutes.

- Select a reasonable interval.

  Use 5 intervals of 10 minutes.

The intervals are used to show the number of times data occur within them.

**STEP 2**

- Make a frequency table with the intervals you chose.
- Tally the data for each interval.
- Record the frequencies.

| Number of Minutes | Tally | Frequency |
|---|---|---|
| 0–10 minutes | IIII | 4 |
| 11–20 minutes | ЖГ I | 6 |
| 21–30 minutes | ЖГ | 5 |
| 31–40 minutes | III | 3 |
| 41–50 minutes | II | 2 |

**STEP 3**

- Use the frequency table to make the histogram.
- The intervals are along one axis. The scale for the frequencies is along the other axis.

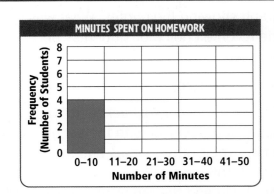

## Try It

**a.** Copy the histogram on page 128.

**b.** Graph the frequency for each interval to complete the histogram. The bars should be connected side-by-side.

## ▶ Connect

Look at the bar graph and histogram at the right.

- In which graph can you compare the number of people listening to each type of music?
- What is the same about both graphs? What is different?

## ▶ Practice and Problem Solving

**Decide which graph would better represent the data below, a bar graph or histogram. Then make each graph.**

**1.**

| Height | Number of Students |
|---|---|
| 48–51 inches | 2 |
| 52–55 inches | 5 |
| 56–59 inches | 12 |
| 60–63 inches | 7 |

**2.**

| Name of Trail | Time to Complete |
|---|---|
| Nature | 30 minutes |
| Challenge | 90 minutes |
| Stroller | 25 minutes |
| Scenic | 35 minutes |

**3.** Give five intervals that you could use to make a histogram for this data.

| MINUTES SPENT DOING CHORES | | | | | | | |
|---|---|---|---|---|---|---|---|
| 20 | 25 | 30 | 15 | 40 | 55 | 60 | 42 |
| 90 | 80 | 45 | 30 | 25 | 20 | 40 | 65 |

**4.** **REASONING** How do you think the number of students in each interval would change in Problem 1 if you made six height intervals?

**5.** Victor has to practice 50 hours before every swim meet. If Victor practices for 5 hours each day, how many days does he need to practice for 2 swim meets?

## ⌐Getting Ready for ★FCAT

**6.** Hank made a stem-and-leaf plot from the data in the table. How many stems will Hank's stem-and-leaf plot have?

**A.** 5      **B.** 6      **C.** 7      **D.** 21

| AGES OF PEOPLE IN THE LIBRARY | | | | | | |
|---|---|---|---|---|---|---|
| 13 | 30 | 24 | 15 | 19 | 11 | 15 |
| 67 | 32 | 48 | 51 | 12 | 34 | 19 |
| 17 | 38 | 36 | 40 | 55 | 13 | 31 |

FCAT TESTED ⬦ SSS/GLEs MA.E.I.2.I.5.3 Chooses reasonable titles, labels, scales and intervals for organizing data on graphs.

**Chapter 6** **129**

# Choose the Appropriate Graph

▶ **Learn**

**BEST CHOICE** To choose the best graph for a set of data, determine what type of data they are and how to analyze them. Using the correct graph makes it easier to interpret data and solve problems.

## Examples

**A**

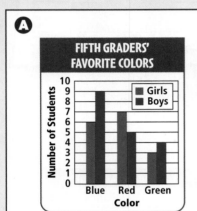

Use a bar graph or a double-bar graph to compare data by category.

**B**

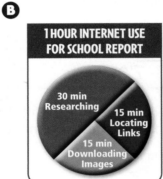

Use a circle graph to compare parts of a group to the whole group.

**C**

| Stem | Leaves |
|------|--------|
| 7 | 1 3 6 |
| 8 | 4 7 |
| 9 | 5 5 6 7 |

**Angela's Bowling Scores**

Use a stem-and-leaf plot to organize data by place value.

**D**

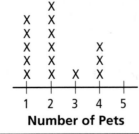

Use a line plot to keep count of data as they are collected or to show frequencies of repeated amounts.

**E**

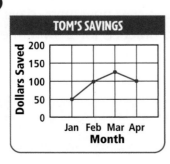

Use a line graph or a double-line graph to show how data change over time.

**F**

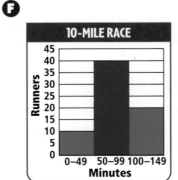

Use a histogram to show the number of times data occur within certain intervals.

# What Is the Best Graph for the Data?

Dexter, Kelly, and Mario are giving a report on weather. Each used a different way to display the data in the table. Who chose the best graph or plot?

| NORMAL JANUARY PRECIPITATION | |
|---|---|
| City | Precipitation |
| Boise, ID | 1.5 in. |
| Orlando, FL | 2.3 in. |
| Richmond, VA | 3.2 in. |
| Indianapolis, IN | 2.3 in. |

**Dexter's Line Plot**

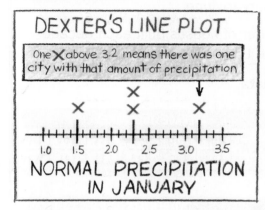

You do not need to count the precipitation frequencies. You need to list the cities. So, a line plot is *not* the best way to display the data.

**Mario's Line Graph**

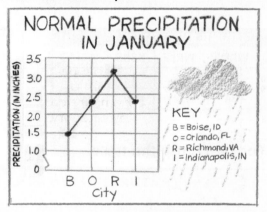

**Kelly's Bar Graph**

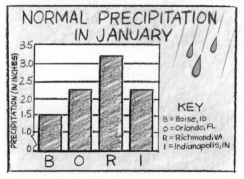

The table compares the precipitation in different cities in the same month. So, a bar graph is an appropriate way to display the data.

The precipitation amounts are for different cities, not over periods of time. So, a line graph is *not* the best way to display the data.

• Why is Kelly's graph the best way to display the data?

## Check

1. **Describe** the kind of temperature data that would be appropriate for a line graph.

**For 2–5, choose the best type of graph or plot for the data. Explain your choice.**

2. scores for a math test

3. number of students in four schools

4. yearbook sales over a four-week period

5. minutes spent on each activity in a one-hour class

LESSON CONTINUES

FCAT TESTED  SSS/GLEs MA.E.3.2.1.5.3 Creates an appropriate graph to display data, including titles, labels, scales, and intervals. *also* MA.E.1.2.1.5.1

Chapter 6  **131**

**For 6–9, choose the best type of graph or plot for the data. Explain your choice.**

6. favorite ice-cream flavors of fifth and sixth graders

7. money a business earned from January to June

8. survey of the number of CDs your friends own

9. number of houses built each decade in the United States

**Draw the graph or plot that best displays each set of data.**

10.

| NUMBER OF FAMILY MEMBERS | | | | | |
|---|---|---|---|---|---|
| Number of Members | 2 | 3 | 4 | 5 | 6 |
| Frequency | 9 | 7 | 4 | 2 | 1 |

11.

| AVERAGE STOCK PRICES | | | | | | |
|---|---|---|---|---|---|---|
| Stock A | Jul | Aug | Sep | Oct | Nov | Dec |
| | $34 | $36 | $37 | $32 | $31 | $31 |

12.

| FAVORITE RADIO STATIONS | | | | |
|---|---|---|---|---|
| Station | WRDK | WRLF | KSRS | WEMD |
| Boys | 24 | 16 | 12 | 28 |
| Girls | 36 | 22 | 20 | 4 |

13.

| DVD RENTALS | | | | |
|---|---|---|---|---|
| Week | 1 | 2 | 3 | 4 |
| Store A | 156 | 95 | 122 | 118 |
| Store B | 170 | 143 | 131 | 97 |

**USE DATA** For 14–17, use the table.

| TEMPERATURES IN WILMINGTON, NC, ON SEPTEMBER 22 | | | | | | |
|---|---|---|---|---|---|---|
| Time | 5:00 A.M. | 8:00 A.M. | 11:00 A.M. | 2:00 P.M. | 5:00 P.M. | 8:00 P.M. |
| Temperature | 70°F | 70°F | 81°F | 84°F | 83°F | 77°F |

14. What type of graph would you choose to display the data? Explain.

15. Would it be reasonable to use an interval of 1°? Explain.

16. When did the least change in temperature occur? How would the line between those hours look?

17. **What if** another row of data is added to the table to show the temperatures on September 23? Could you display the new data on the same graph? Explain.

18. Caryn received $5.51 in change. She bought 1 pocket folder for $0.99 and 3 pens for $3.50. How much did she start with?

19. You recorded the high and low temperatures for your city during one week. What type of graph will best show these data?

20. Reina surveyed students to find their favorite type of birthday party. There were 5 choices. What type of graph will show the choices of boys and girls?

21. ✎ **Write a problem** using the data about favorite radio stations.

**22.** Keith took a survey about the cost to join a health club for one year. The results are shown in the table.

| COST FOR ANNUAL HEALTH CLUB MEMBERSHIP | |
|---|---|
| **Health Club** | **Cost** |
| Fit for Life | $99 |
| Exercise Away | $175 |
| Platinum Fitness | $325 |
| Great Body | $250 |

Draw a graph to display the data. Explain your choice of graph.

**23.** Maya is collecting data about the favorite and least favorite subjects of middle-school students. Is "What is your favorite subject?" a good survey question for Maya to use to collect her data? Explain.

**24.** Which set of data would be best displayed in a line graph?

**A.**

| ANNUAL RAINFALL IN INCHES | | | | |
|---|---|---|---|---|
| **Year** | 2000 | 2001 | 2002 | 2003 |
| **Amount** | 56 | 52 | 59 | 50 |

**B.**

| KRISTEN'S BUDGET | | | | |
|---|---|---|---|---|
| **Food** | **Power** | **Rent** | **Savings** | **Other** |
| 25% | 20% | 40% | 10% | 5% |

**C.**

| ANNUAL HEATING COSTS | | | | |
|---|---|---|---|---|
| **Gas** | **Oil** | **Wood** | **Coal** | **Electricity** |
| $1,500 | $1,800 | $900 | $800 | $2,000 |

**D.**

| NUMBER OF PETS | | | | | | |
|---|---|---|---|---|---|---|
| **Number** | 0 | 1 | 2 | 3 | 4 | 5 |
| **Frequency** | 7 | 10 | 8 | 6 | 3 | 1 |

# Problem Solving LINKUP...to Social Studies

Four states with names that begin with the letter *N* were among the original 13 colonies of the United States.

Today, 8 states begin with the letter *N*. Design a survey to find out how many people can name all 8 states. Survey a random sample of 20 people. Part of a possible recording sheet is shown.

**1.** Make a frequency table showing the number of people who correctly named each possible number of states, from 0 through 8.

**2.** Make a line plot of the survey results. Find the range, mean, median, and mode. How is the mode displayed on the line plot?

**3.** If you repeat the survey with 20 boys and 20 girls, what type of graph should you choose to display the results?

| Person | States Named |
|---|---|
| 1 | |
| 2 | |
| 3 | |
| 4 | |

# Extra Practice

## Set A (pp. 116–119)

**Choose 5, 10, 15, or 20 as the most reasonable interval for the data.**

**1.** 30, 16, 60, 45, 75    **2.** 3, 6, 10, 14, 22    **3.** 10, 30, 40, 60, 20

**Choose the more reasonable scale for the data.**

**4.**

| FAVORITE ANIMAL | |
|---|---|
| **Animal** | **Number** |
| Cat | 20 |
| Dog | 40 |
| Horse | 30 |
| Bird | 10 |
| Rabbit | 9 |

a. 50, 40, 30, 20, 10, 0    b. 25, 20, 15, 10, 5, 0

**5.**

| FAVORITE COLOR | |
|---|---|
| **Color** | **Number** |
| Red | 6 |
| Blue | 8 |
| Green | 2 |
| Purple | 5 |
| Yellow | 4 |

a. 25, 20, 15, 10, 5, 0    b. 12, 10, 8, 6, 4, 2, 0

## Set B (pp. 120–121)

**Graph and label the following points on a coordinate grid.**

**1.** A (0,6)    **2.** B (1,3)    **3.** C (2,2)    **4.** D (3,4)

**5.** E (4,1)    **6.** F (5,3)    **7.** G (6,5)    **8.** H (7,2)

## Set C (pp. 122–125)

**USE DATA For 1–4, use the table.**

| TIME MARIA SPENT ON HOMEWORK | | | | | |
|---|---|---|---|---|---|
| **Day** | Mon | Tue | Wed | Thu | Fri |
| **Time** | 20 min | 45 min | 60 min | 75 min | 0 min |

**1.** Make a line graph for the data in the table.

**2.** Between which days did Maria increase her homework time the most?

**3.** On which day or days did Maria spend 1 hour or more on homework?

**4.** How many more minutes did Maria spend on homework on Thursday than on Monday?

## Set D (pp. 130–133)

**Choose the best type of graph or plot for the data. Explain your choice.**

**1.** how you spend your allowance

**2.** results of a survey to find the most popular running shoes

**3.** the number and types of sports cards

**4.** daily store earnings during a month

# Review/Test

 **CHECK VOCABULARY AND CONCEPTS**

**Choose the best term from the box.**

> histogram
> line graph
> scale

1. The set of numbers placed at fixed distances to help label the graph is the __?__. (p. 116)

2. A __?__ shows how data change over time. (p. 122)

 **CHECK SKILLS**

**Choose 1, 5, 20, or 50 as the most reasonable interval for the data.** (pp. 116–119)

3. 35, 15, 20, 45, 60, 55

4. 75, 48, 100, 125, 150, 200

5. 85, 100, 61, 20, 45, 80

6. 3, 13, 10, 7, 5, 12

**Name a reasonable scale for the data.** (pp. 116–119)

7. Josie found information on the price of in-line skates. The prices were $30, $45, $48, and $53.

8. The average miles per gallon for several new cars are 26, 17, 32, 12, and 28.

**Graph and label the following points on a coordinate grid.** (pp. 120–121)

9. A (1,2)  10. B (2,4)  11. C (3,6)  12. D (4,5)  13. E (0,3)

**Tell whether a bar graph or a histogram is more appropriate.** (pp. 128–129)

14. ages of 75 ice-skating competitors

15. frequency of five girls' names

16. scores of 50 students on a math test

**Choose the best type of graph or plot for the data. Explain your choice.** (pp. 130–133)

17. money earned working one summer

18. number of skyscrapers in four cities

 **CHECK PROBLEM SOLVING**

**For 19–20, draw a Venn diagram and solve.** (pp. 126–127)

19. A survey showed 12 students liked both broccoli and carrots, 14 liked both peas and carrots, 7 liked only peas, and 4 liked all three vegetables. How many students were surveyed?

20. Of the letters in the words *mathematics*, *multiplication*, and *percentages*, how many appear in all three words?

# Getting Ready for  FCAT

 **DATA ANALYSIS AND PROBABILITY**

**1.** Abraham Lincoln was elected President of the United States in 1860. The table shows the number of electoral votes that he and his opponents received.

| 1860 PRESIDENTIAL ELECTION ||
| Candidate | Electoral Votes |
| --- | --- |
| Lincoln | 180 |
| Douglas | 12 |
| Breckinridge | 72 |
| Bell | 38 |

Which type of graph would **best** display this data?

**A.** line plot

**B.** bar graph

**C.** line graph

**D.** histogram

**2.** Look at the table above. How many more votes did Lincoln receive than Breckinridge?

**F.** 92

**G.** 98

**H.** 108

**I.** 252

**3. Explain It** Eli surveyed 100 people about their eye color. There were 75 people with brown eyes, 20 with blue eyes and 5 with green eyes. Draw a graph to represent these data. Explain your choice of graph.

 **NUMBER SENSE, CONCEPTS, AND OPERATIONS**

**4.** The table shows the number of miles Derek jogged.

| DISTANCE DEREK JOGGED (in miles) ||||
| Day | Mon | Tue | Wed |
| --- | --- | --- | --- |
| Distance | 3.8 | 4.5 | 5.4 |

How much farther did Derek jog on Wednesday than on Monday?

**A.** 1.6 miles

**B.** 2.4 miles

**C.** 2.6 miles

**D.** 9.2 miles

**5.** Look at the table above. During the three days, how many miles did Derek jog in all?

**F.** 8.3 miles

**G.** 12.7 miles

**H.** 13.7 miles

**I.** 14.3 miles

**6. Explain It** The table below shows the frequent flyer points Marina received.

| FREQUENT FLYER POINTS ||
| Trip | Points |
| --- | --- |
| Washington, DC, to Atlanta, GA | 547 |
| Atlanta, GA, to Ft. Lauderdale, FL | 581 |
| Ft. Lauderdale, FL, to Cincinnati, OH | 932 |
| Cincinnati, OH, to Albany, NY | 623 |

ESTIMATE the total number of points she received for the four trips. Explain how you found your answer.

**GEOMETRY AND SPATIAL SENSE**

**7.** Marco used a coordinate grid to mark where he planted each kind of vegetable in his garden.

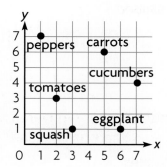

Which vegetable did he plant at (5,6)?

**A.** carrots

**B.** cucumbers

**C.** peppers

**D.** eggplant

**8.** Look at the coordinate grid above. Which ordered pair names the point where Marco planted tomatoes?

**F.** (3,2)

**G.** (2,2)

**H.** (2,3)

**I.** (3,3)

**9. Explain It** Ursula wants to draw a figure with four congruent sides and two pairs of parallel sides. Draw and name two figures that she can draw. Explain how the figures you drew are different.

 **ALGEBRAIC THINKING**

**10.** Nick has $8 more than Ashley. Let $x$ represent the amount of money Ashley has in dollars. Which expression shows how many dollars Nick will have left if he gives $5 to Ashley?

**A.** $x - 8 - 5$     **C.** $x + 8 - 5$

**B.** $x - 8 + 5$     **D.** $8 - 5 - x$

> **TIP**   **Check your work.** See item 10. Look at your answer choice. Substitute a value for $x$, the amount of money Ashley has, in the expression you chose. Evaluate the expression. Does your answer make sense?

**11.** Maya forgot to write the amount of her check for her phone bill in her check register. Her checking account balance was $98 before she wrote the check. The balance is now $59. Let $c$ represent the amount of the check for the phone bill. Which equation can Maya use to find the amount of the check?

| Number | Date | Description | Payment | Deposit | Balance |
|--------|------|-------------|---------|---------|---------|
| | 10/25 | Deposit | | $50.00 | $98.00 |
| 475 | 10/27 | Phone Company | ▓ | | $59.00 |

    **F.** $c - 98 = 59$

    **G.** $98 - c = 59$

    **H.** $c + 98 = 59$

    **I.** $59 - c = 98$

**12. Explain It** Explain why $x = 9$ is a solution of the inequality $x - 3 < 7$ but $x = 10$ is not a solution.

# IT'S IN THE BAG

## Data and Graphing in a Snap

**PROJECT** Make a booklet to review data and graphing skills.

### Materials

- 1 thin plastic CD case
- 2 half sheets of construction paper
- Markers
- Glue, tape
- Colored paper
- Magazines and newspapers

### Directions

1. Tape two half sheets of construction paper together to form a 22-inch strip.

2. Accordion-fold the strip of paper. Fold the left side forward about $3\frac{5}{8}$ inches, and then fold it back about $3\frac{5}{8}$ inches. Continue until there are six panels. *(Picture A)*

3. On the front of the first panel, explain how to choose an appropriate graph for a set of data. On the inside six panels, make a line plot, stem-and-leaf plot, double-bar graph, line graph, histogram, and circle graph. Describe the type of data for which each graph is appropriate. *(Picture B)*

4. Glue a piece of colored paper on the front of the CD case for a cover. Decorate the cover and write on it the title "Choose an Appropriate Graph." *(Picture C)*

5. Find data from magazines and newspapers that can be displayed as a graph and make an appropriate graph.

# Challenge

## Relationships in Graphs

**Graphs can show relationships between two different variables, such as distance and time.**

**A** Suppose you shoot an arrow toward a target.

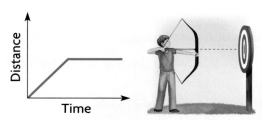

- The graph begins with a sloped line, which shows that the distance of the arrow from you is increasing at a constant rate after it is shot.
- The flat part of the graph begins when the arrow hits the target and stops. After this time, the distance does not change.

**B** Suppose you fire a model rocket into the air.

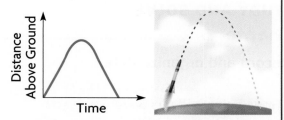

- The graph begins with a line that soon curves. The line curves because the rocket slows as it goes higher into the air.
- The graph curves downward as the rocket comes back to Earth. The distance is 0 when the rocket hits the ground.

- How would the appearance of Graph A change if the target were only half as far away?

## Try It

**For 1–4, tell which graph illustrates the situation that is described. Explain.**

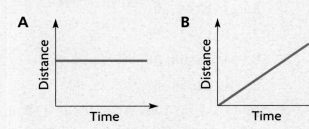

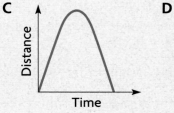

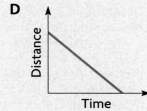

**1.** a rocket's distance from the launch pad during liftoff

**2.** a carousel rider's distance from the center of the carousel

**3.** a hot air balloon's distance from the ground when descending

**4.** the distance from the ground of a ball thrown upward

# Study Guide and Review

## VOCABULARY

**Choose the best term from the box.**

population
sample
interval
mean
median

1. A part of a group, or __?__, is chosen to represent the whole group, or __?__. (p. 96)

2. The difference between one number and the next on a scale is the __?__. (p. 97)

## STUDY AND SOLVE
### Chapter 5

**Record and organize data.**

How many students were surveyed?

| MOVIES SEEN LAST MONTH | | |
|---|---|---|
| Number of Movies | Number of Students | Cumulative Frequency |
| 0 | 7 | 7 |
| 1 | 12 | 19 |
| 2 | 22 | 41 |
| 3 | 18 | 59 |
| 4 | 4 | 63 |

Read the last entry in the cumulative frequency column. Sixty-three students were surveyed.

**Interpret data by finding the mean, median, mode, and range.**

Data: 4, 6, 7, 8, 8, 9
**mean:** Add data; then divide by number of addends.
4 + 6 + 7 + 8 + 8 + 9 = 42
42 ÷ 6 = 7
**median:** Arrange the data in order; then find the middle number. 7.5
**mode:** Find the number that occurs most often. 8
**range:** Subtract the least number from the greatest.
9 − 4 = 5

**For 3–5, use the table below.** (pp. 96–99)

| NUMBER OF BOOKS READ IN 1 MONTH | | | | |
|---|---|---|---|---|
| 6 | 9 | 10 | 7 | 3 |
| 5 | 4 | 8 | 7 | 6 |
| 4 | 3 | 3 | 2 | 1 |
| 2 | 5 | 4 | 5 | 6 |

3. Make a cumulative frequency table.

4. How many students were surveyed?

5. Make a line plot. Find the range.

**Find the mean, median, mode, and range for each set of data.** (pp. 100–103)

6. 24, 10, 4, 10
7. 11, 12, 31, 28
8. 44, 36, 38, 38, 39
9. 84, 82, 84, 89, 92, 95, 90
10. 113, 115, 126, 101, 99, 98, 118

# Chapter 6

## Choose appropriate scales and intervals.

Choose a reasonable scale and interval for this data set: 12, 15, 18, 30, 22, 16.
The data range from 12 to 30.
Scale: 0 to 30
Interval: 5

## Display data in tables and graphs.

| FIVE-DAY FORECAST (IN °F) | | | | | |
|---|---|---|---|---|---|
| October | 4 | 5 | 6 | 7 | 8 |
| Chicago, IL | 74 | 62 | 62 | 58 | 60 |
| Tampa, FL | 89 | 90 | 89 | 87 | 89 |

You can make a double-line graph to show how data change over time.

## Choose an appropriate graph.

Choose the best type of graph or plot to show a city's daily rainfall for one week.

A bar graph compares data by category. | A line graph shows how data change over time.

A line graph would be the best graph to display the data since the rainfall was recorded over a period of one week.

## Name a reasonable scale and interval for the data. (pp. 116–119)

**11.** 74, 100, 55, 125, 27

**12.** 20, 10, 5, 15, 30, 25

**13.** 50, 10, 40, 20, 30, 60

**14.** 120, 80, 60, 100, 40

## Use the data in the table. (pp. 122–125)

**15.** How would you label the graph?

**16.** What dates would you show along the bottom of the graph?

**17.** Make a double-line graph to determine when the greatest difference in temperature between Chicago and Tampa is expected to occur.

## Choose the best type of graph or plot for the data. (pp. 130–133)

**18.** the number of boys and girls in grades 3, 4, and 5

**19.** number of medals won by the United States in the last 5 Winter Olympic Games

**20.** number of brothers and sisters of students in your class

## PROBLEM SOLVING PRACTICE

**Solve.** (pp. 104–105, 126–127)

**21.** Connie's math test scores are 87, 82, 91, 88, 93, 81, 84, 78, 92, and 90. Are her scores most often in the 70's, 80's, or 90's? Make a stem-and-leaf plot.

**22.** The football team has 19 players, 14 who play defense and 11 who play offense. Six players play both offense and defense. How many players play offense but not defense? Make a Venn diagram.

# PERFORMANCE ASSESSMENT

## TASK A • TICKET SALES

Two local theaters sell advertising space on the back of their tickets.

| Month | Number of Tickets Sold | |
| --- | --- | --- |
| | Theater A | Theater B |
| March | 200 | 300 |
| April | 500 | 50 |
| May | 150 | 600 |
| June | 500 | 500 |
| July | 450 | 650 |

**a.** Use the data in the table to find the mean, median, mode, and range of ticket sales for each theater.

**b.** Compare the ticket sales at the two theaters. Based on this data, which theater should you choose if you want to advertise? Explain.

**c.** Decide what kind of graph would be best to organize and display the data in the table. Make the graph. Write a question that can be answered by using the data in your graph.

## TASK B • HISTOGRAM RUN

The table shows the number of runs each player on a Little League team scored in one season.

| RUNS SCORED | | | | |
| --- | --- | --- | --- | --- |
| 12 | 15 | 8 | 21 | 32 |
| 16 | 17 | 15 | 7 | 23 |
| 24 | 19 | 23 | 9 | 14 |

**a.** Put the data into equal-sized intervals. Explain how you chose the intervals.

**b.** Use your intervals to make a frequency table of the data.

**c.** Use your frequency table to make a histogram.

**d.** Write a question that can be answered using the data in your graph. Then solve.

# Technology Linkup

## Use a Spreadsheet to Make Graphs

The table at the right shows the number of sports cards four friends have in their collections. Enter the names and the number of cards into a spreadsheet. Then use the spreadsheet to make a bar graph of the data.

To make a graph using the spreadsheet, highlight all the names and numbers of cards you entered. Then click [icon]. This icon or a similar icon in the toolbar opens the graph-making program.

| SPORTS CARDS COLLECTIONS | |
|---|---|
| **Name** | **Number of Cards** |
| Denise | 45 |
| Samuel | 92 |
| Amber | 67 |
| Juan | 84 |

**Step 1** Choose *Column* to make a vertical bar graph. Then click *Next*.

**Step 2** This shows a preview of the graph. Click *Next*.

**Step 3** Fill in the labels for the graph.
- Chart title: SPORTS CARDS COLLECTIONS
- Category (X) axis: Name
- Category (Y) axis: Number of Cards
  Click *Next*.

**Step 4** Click *As object in:* to place the graph and data on the spreadsheet. You can also click *As new sheet* to place the graph on a new page. Click *Finish* to view the completed graph.

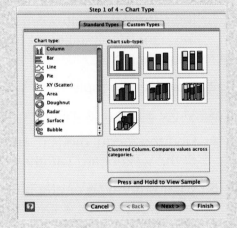

## Practice and Problem Solving

**Use a spreadsheet to make each graph.**

1. Use the sports cards data to make a horizontal bar graph.

2. In a survey about favorite vacation spots, 29 students chose the beach, 33 chose the mountains, and 18 chose an amusement park. Make a bar graph of the data.

3. **STRETCH YOUR THINKING** In Exercise 2, what other type of graph could you use to show the favorite vacation data?

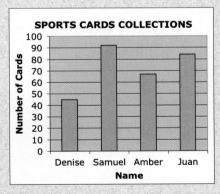

**GO ON-LINE** **Multimedia Math Glossary** www.harcourtschool.com/mathglossary
**Vocabulary Power** Look up *bar graph* and *histogram* in the Multimedia Math Glossary. Compare the definitions of the terms.

# PROBLEM SOLVING IN FLORIDA

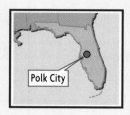

Polk City

## WAKEBOARDING

Florida is a popular spot for one of the country's fastest growing sports, wakeboarding. Wakeboarding is a combination of surfing, skateboarding, snowboarding, and trick waterskiing.

**USE DATA** For 1–6, use the frequency table.

| WAKEBOARD LENGTH SURVEY | |
|---|---|
| **Length (in cm)** | **Frequency** |
| 125 | 2 |
| 134 | 4 |
| 137 | 5 |
| 138 | 6 |
| 142 | 2 |
| 143 | 1 |

1. Make a cumulative frequency table of the survey data. How is a cumulative frequency table different from a frequency table?

2. How many people were surveyed?

3. Make a line plot using the survey data.

4. Find the range, median, and mode of the wakeboard lengths.

5. What other type of graph could you use to display the data in the survey?

6. **Write a problem** using the frequency table data. Then solve the problem.

# SKI FLYING

Ski flying is another popular water sport in Florida. Ski flying is somewhat like traditional ski jumping, but as the name suggests, the jumps are higher and farther.

**2002 SKI FLYING NATIONAL CHAMPIONSHIPS**

(Bar graph — Jump Distance (in ft) vs Division: B3, G3, M3, W1, OM, OW)

| QUALIFICATIONS | |
|---|---|
| **Division** | **Ages** |
| B3 | Boys 13–16 |
| G3 | Girls 13–16 |
| M3 | Men 35–44 |
| W1 | Women 17–24 |
| OM | Men any age |
| OW | Women any age |

**USE DATA** The graph shows the record jumps from the 2002 Ski Flying National Championships in Polk City, Florida. The table shows the qualifications for each division. For 1–4, use the graph and table.

1. Which three divisions had the longest jumps?

2. What is the age of the person who jumped a distance of 200 feet?

3. Would you make a line graph using this data? Explain.

4. How would the bar graph look if the scale were broken between 0 and 150?

5. The rules of ski flying say that the part of the take-off ramp that is above the water must be longer than 7.35 meters but shorter than 7.5 meters. Write two inequalities that show $g$, the length of the part of the ramp that is above the water.

# Multiply Whole Numbers

The twin Keck Telescopes stand eight stories tall on the 13,800-foot Mauna Kea summit.

**≡FAST FACT** • SCIENCE The largest reflecting telescopes are the twin Keck Telescopes, weighing 300 tons each. Reflecting telescopes use mirrors to help us see distant objects in our solar system and beyond. Each telescope has an opening that allows light to be gathered by a mirror. The larger the opening, the more powerful the telescope and the farther you can see.

PROBLEM SOLVING The mirror diameter of the twin Keck telescopes is about two times the Hale Telescope's mirror diameter, which is shown in the graph. How big are the mirrors of the Keck I and Keck II?

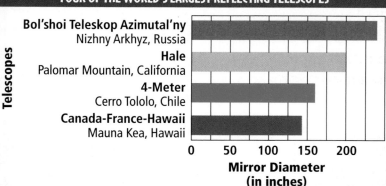

**FOUR OF THE WORLD'S LARGEST REFLECTING TELESCOPES**

Telescopes

**Bol'shoi Teleskop Azimutal'ny**
Nizhny Arkhyz, Russia

**Hale**
Palomar Mountain, California

**4-Meter**
Cerro Tololo, Chile

**Canada-France-Hawaii**
Mauna Kea, Hawaii

0    50    100    150    200

**Mirror Diameter**
**(in inches)**

Use this page to help you review and remember
important skills needed for Chapter 7.

### MULTIPLY BY TENS AND HUNDREDS

Find the product.

| | | | |
|---|---|---|---|
| **1.** $1 \times 100$ | **2.** $2 \times 10$ | **3.** $5 \times 40$ | **4.** $7 \times 60$ |
| **5.** $8 \times 90$ | **6.** $9 \times 600$ | **7.** $3 \times 700$ | **8.** $6 \times 300$ |
| **9.** $2 \times 600$ | **10.** $5 \times 300$ | **11.** $4 \times 800$ | **12.** $7 \times 900$ |

### MULTIPLY 2-DIGIT NUMBERS

Find the product.

| | | | |
|---|---|---|---|
| **13.** $\begin{array}{r} 12 \\ \times\ 6 \\ \hline \end{array}$ | **14.** $\begin{array}{r} 19 \\ \times\ 9 \\ \hline \end{array}$ | **15.** $\begin{array}{r} 14 \\ \times 12 \\ \hline \end{array}$ | **16.** $\begin{array}{r} 17 \\ \times\ 4 \\ \hline \end{array}$ |
| **17.** $\begin{array}{r} 50 \\ \times\ 9 \\ \hline \end{array}$ | **18.** $\begin{array}{r} 24 \\ \times 15 \\ \hline \end{array}$ | **19.** $\begin{array}{r} 28 \\ \times\ 3 \\ \hline \end{array}$ | **20.** $\begin{array}{r} 20 \\ \times\ 6 \\ \hline \end{array}$ |
| **21.** $\begin{array}{r} 32 \\ \times\ 7 \\ \hline \end{array}$ | **22.** $\begin{array}{r} 64 \\ \times\ 2 \\ \hline \end{array}$ | **23.** $\begin{array}{r} 54 \\ \times 23 \\ \hline \end{array}$ | **24.** $\begin{array}{r} 94 \\ \times\ 7 \\ \hline \end{array}$ |
| **25.** $\begin{array}{r} 29 \\ \times 24 \\ \hline \end{array}$ | **26.** $\begin{array}{r} 34 \\ \times 27 \\ \hline \end{array}$ | **27.** $\begin{array}{r} 72 \\ \times 31 \\ \hline \end{array}$ | **28.** $\begin{array}{r} 93 \\ \times 45 \\ \hline \end{array}$ |

## VOCABULARY POWER

### REVIEW

**factor** [fak´•tər] *noun*

The Latin root of *factor* means "to do."
Factories are used to put goods together
to make something. How are factors used
in multiplication?

### PREVIEW

multiples

 www.harcourtschool.com/mathglossary

# Estimation: Patterns in Multiples

**Quick Review**

Round to the nearest 10.

**1.** 93 **2.** 16

**3.** 139 **4.** 147

**5.** 998

**VOCABULARY**

multiples

## ▶ Learn

**ORBITING NUMBERS** The **multiples** of a whole number are all of the whole numbers that are products of the given number and another whole number. For example, multiples of 10 include 10, 20, 30, and 40 since $1 \times 10 = 10$, $2 \times 10 = 20$, $3 \times 10 = 30$, and $4 \times 10 = 40$.

Use multiples of 10 to help you estimate mentally.

Each hour, the Hubble Space Telescope transmits enough data to fill about 83 computer floppy disks. About how many computer floppy disks are filled with data in a day?

Estimate. $24 \times 83$

↓ ↓

$20 \times 80$ Round each factor.

$2 \times 8 = 16$ **Think:** Use the basic fact $2 \times 8$.
$2 \times 80 = 160$ Look for patterns in multiples of 10.
$20 \times 80 = 1,600$

So, about 1,600 computer floppy disks are filled.

• Look for a pattern in the factors and products. What do you notice?

▲ Each day, the Hubble Space Telescope collects enough data to fill an encyclopedia. Since 1990, over 2.5 terabytes of data (1 terabyte = 1 million megabytes) have been collected.

## Examples

**A** Estimate. $8 \times 522$

$8 \times 500$ Think: $8 \times 5 = 40$
$8 \times 500 = 4,000$
↑ ↑
2 zeros 2 zeros
So, $8 \times 522$ is about 4,000.

**B** Estimate. $73 \times 862$

$70 \times 900$ Think: $7 \times 9 = 63$
$70 \times 900 = 63,000$
↑ ↑ ↑
1 zero + 2 zeros 3 zeros
So, $73 \times 862$ is about 63,000.

 **MATH IDEA** You can use multiples of 10 to estimate products mentally. Count the number of zeros in the rounded factors. Place that number of zeros at the end of the product of the basic fact.

► **Check**

1. **Explain** why 400 × 5 has more zeros in the product than 300 × 5.

**Estimate each product.**

2. 4 × 1,453    3. 67 × 824    4. 32 × 1,839    5. 8 × 2,347

6. 6 × 3,609    7. 42 × 690    8. 99 × 2,092    9. 23 × 3,041

► **Practice and Problem Solving** ⟩ Extra Practice, page 158, Set A

**Estimate each product.**

10. 34 × 123    11. 5 × 960    12. 82 × 53    13. 69 × 681

14. 58 × 2,234    15. 2 × 490    16. 7 × 2,589    17. 42 × 524

18.  301    19.  291    20.  341    21.  915    22.  5,451
   × 12        ×  8        × 86        × 52        ×   83

23.  290    24.  723    25.  963    26.  389    27.  6,715
   × 82        ×  3        × 42        × 49        ×   39

28. The product 20 × 600 has 3 zeros. How many zeros does the product 20 × 600,000 have?

29. How can you tell without multiplying that 3,000,000 × 6,000 = 30,000 × 600,000?

30.  **What's the Question?** Juan bought 52 bicycles for his store. Each bicycle cost $117. The estimate is $5,000.

31. The product of two 2-digit numbers is 2,000. Their sum is 90. What are the numbers?

32. Gail received $10 as a gift. She bought a magazine that cost $2 and a marker set. She has $3.45 left. How much did she spend on the marker set?

33. ✎ **Write About It** Explain how you can tell if the estimated products in the Examples on page 148 are greater than or less than the actual product.

**Getting Ready for** ✦FCAT **THINK SOLVE EXPLAIN**

34. The table shows the air distance from New York City, NY to two different cities. Mr. Johnson flies round-trip from New York City to Chicago once a month on business. Estimate how many miles he flies round-trip to Chicago each year. Explain how you made your estimate.

| ONE-WAY AIR DISTANCES (in miles) | |
|---|---|
| New York City, New York to Chicago, Illinois | 714 miles |
| New York City, NY to Honolulu, Hawaii | 4,969 miles |

FCAT TESTED  SSS/GLEs MA.A.4.2.1.5.1 The student chooses, describes, and explains estimation strategies used to determine the reasonableness of solutions to real-world problems. *also* MA.A.2.2.1.5.1, MA.A.3.2.1.5.3, MA.A.5.2.1.5.5

Chapter 7  **149**

# Multiply by 1-Digit Numbers

▶ **Learn**

**HEAVYWEIGHTS**   An African elephant, the heaviest land mammal, weighs 14,632 pounds. A humpback whale weighs as much as 4 African elephants. How much might a humpback whale weigh?

## Example 1

Find $4 \times 14,632$.

$4 \times 15,000 = 60,000$    Estimate. Round 14,632 to the nearest thousand.

| STEP 1 | STEP 2 | STEP 3 | STEP 4 |
|---|---|---|---|
| Multiply the ones and tens. $4 \times 2 = 8$ ones $4 \times 3 = 12$ tens Regroup. | Multiply the hundreds. $4 \times 6 = 24$ hundreds Add the 1 regrouped hundred. Regroup. | Multiply the thousands. $4 \times 4 = 16$ thousands Add the 2 regrouped thousands. Regroup. | Multiply the ten thousands. $4 \times 1 = 4$ ten thousands Add the 1 regrouped ten thousand. |
| $\begin{array}{r} 1 \\ 14,632 \\ \times\quad 4 \\ \hline 28 \end{array}$ | $\begin{array}{r} 2\;1 \\ 14,632 \\ \times\quad 4 \\ \hline 528 \end{array}$ | $\begin{array}{r} 1\,2\,1 \\ 14,632 \\ \times\quad 4 \\ \hline 8,528 \end{array}$ | $\begin{array}{r} 1\,2\,1 \\ 14,632 \\ \times\quad 4 \\ \hline 58,528 \end{array}$ |

So, a humpback whale might weigh about 58,528 pounds. This is close to the estimate of 60,000, so the answer is reasonable.

 **MATH IDEA**   To multiply a greater number by a 1-digit number, use the same method you use for 2-digit numbers. Just repeat the same steps for all the digits.

▼ The heaviest known 90-foot female blue whale weighed 418,000 pounds. That's about 29 African elephants!

## Example 2

Use place value and expanded form.

$5 \times 3,014 = n$    Think: $3,014 = 3,000 + 10 + 4$

$(5 \times 3,000) + (5 \times 10) + (5 \times 4) = n$

$\quad 15,000 \quad + \quad 50 \quad + \quad 20 \quad = n$

$\qquad\qquad\qquad\qquad 15,070 = n$

So, $n = 15,070$.

## Check

1. **Explain** how you know that 115,275 is a reasonable product for 38,425 × 3.

**Find the product. Estimate to check.**

| 2. | 3. | 4. | 5. | 6. |
|---|---|---|---|---|
| 2,231 | 348 | 52,113 | 608,123 | 391,224 |
| × 3 | × 5 | × 2 | × 7 | × 4 |

7. 36,825 × 9    8. 5 × 309,224    9. 649,321 × 4

**Practice and Problem Solving** ( Extra Practice, page 158, Set B )

**Find the product. Estimate to check.**

| 10. | 11. | 12. | 13. | 14. |
|---|---|---|---|---|
| 4,567 | 8,112 | 24,531 | 417,263 | 882,917 |
| × 8 | × 7 | × 9 | × 4 | × 6 |

15. 8 × 52,379    16. 826,243 × 3    17. 7,952,344 × 5

 **Solve for *n*.**

18. $20,450 \times 6 = n$         19. $292,453 \times 9 = n$

**USE DATA**  For 20–21, use the table.

20. To ship animals to new locations, a zoo needs to estimate how much the animals weigh. About how much would 8 hippopotamuses weigh?

21. **MENTAL MATH**  Suppose the shipping weight limit is 50,000 pounds. Can a zoo ship 6 white rhinoceroses together? Explain.

22. **Write About It**  Explain the steps you follow to multiply by a 1-digit number.

| ANIMAL WEIGHTS | |
|---|---|
| **Animal** | **Average Weight (in pounds)** |
| Hippopotamus | 5,512 |
| White rhinoceros | 7,937 |
| Whale shark | 46,297 |
| Blue whale | 286,600 |

## Getting Ready for FCAT

23. Mr. Kay sold a 57-inch and a 53-inch television during the sale. Which of the following operations should you use to find his sales total?

   **A.** subtraction          **C.** addition

   **B.** multiplication        **D.** division

HURRY-IN ELECTRONICS

| 53-inch | $2,198 |
|---|---|
| 57-inch | $2,798 |
| 65-inch | $2,998 |

Big-Screen TV Sale

FCAT TESTED  SSS/GLEs MA.A.3.2.2.5.1  Use problem-solving strategies to determine the operation(s) needed to solve one- and two-step problems involving addition, subtraction, multiplication, and division of whole numbers, . . . *also* MA.A.3.2.3.5.1, MA.A.4.2.1.5.1

**Chapter 7  151**

# Multiply by 2-Digit Numbers

▶ **Learn**

**PEDAL POWER**  Eugene is starting a cycling training program. He plans to ride a total of 315 minutes each week for the next 26 weeks. How many minutes does he plan to ride altogether?

## Example

Find $26 \times 315$.

$30 \times 300 = 9{,}000$  Estimate. Round each factor.

| STEP **1** | STEP **2** | STEP **3** |
|---|---|---|
| Multiply by the ones. | Multiply by the tens. | Add the partial products. |
| $\begin{array}{r} 3 \\ 315 \\ \times\ 26 \\ \hline 1890 \end{array}$ ← 6 × 315 | $\begin{array}{r} 1 \\ 3 \\ 315 \\ \times\ 26 \\ \hline 1890 \\ 6300 \end{array}$ ← 20 × 315 | $\begin{array}{r} 1 \\ 3 \\ 315 \\ \times\ 26 \\ \hline 1890 \\ +6300 \\ \hline 8{,}190 \end{array}$ ← partial products |

So, Eugene will ride 8,190 minutes altogether. This is close to the estimate of 9,000, so the answer is reasonable.

## More Examples

**Ⓐ**
$\begin{array}{r} 7 \\ 29 \\ \times 18 \\ \hline 232 \\ +290 \\ \hline 522 \end{array}$
← 8 × 29
← 10 × 29

**Ⓑ**
$\begin{array}{r} 1 \\ 705 \\ \times\ 23 \\ \hline 2115 \\ +14100 \\ \hline 16{,}215 \end{array}$
← 3 × 705
← 20 × 705

**Ⓒ**
$\begin{array}{r} 1\ 1 \\ 2{,}342 \\ \times\ \ \ 14 \\ \hline 9368 \\ +23420 \\ \hline 32{,}788 \end{array}$
← 4 × 2,342
← 10 × 2,342

• In Example B, what happens to the regrouped digit, 1, when there is a zero in the factor?

**MATH IDEA**  To multiply by a 2-digit number, first multiply by the ones and then the tens. Add the partial products.

▲ In 2002 Lance Armstrong became the first American to win four Tour de France titles (for 1999–2002).

## ▶ Check

1. **Explain** why the second partial product is always greater than the first partial product when you multiply two 2-digit numbers.

**Technology Link**

**More Practice:**
Harcourt Mega Math
The Number Games,
*Tiny's Think Tank,*
Level F

**Find the product. Estimate to check.**

2.   91
   ×43

3.   348
   ×  15

4.   24
   ×16

5.   1,924
   ×   21

6. 710 × 13

7. 801 × 61

8. 4,506 × 94

## ▶ Practice and Problem Solving   ( Extra Practice, page 158, Set C )

**Find the product. Estimate to check.**

9.   78
   ×53

10.   159
   ×  16

11.   500
   ×  43

12.   2,391
   ×   62

13.   8,705
   ×   98

14. 16 × 52

15. 119 × 54

16. 2,610 × 63

17. 3,059 × 72

**ALGEBRA  Find the missing digit. Explain your solution.**

18. 508 × 3■ = 17,780

19. 653 × 4■ = 31,997

20. 45■ × 27 = 12,258

**USE DATA**  For 21–24, copy and complete the table.

| | **WINGBEATS** | |
| **Animal** | **Beats per min** | **Beats per hr** |
| --- | --- | --- |
| 21. Hummingbird | 5,400 | ■ |
| 22. Bat | 1,200 | ■ |
| 23. Butterfly | 640 | ■ |
| 24. Stork | 180 | ■ |

For 25–26, use the table.

25. **REASONING**  A swift beats its wings 2 times as fast as a stork. How many times does a swift beat its wings in 30 minutes?

26. ✎ **Write a problem** that can be solved using multiplication with the data about wingbeats.

27. **Vocabulary Power**  One meaning of the word *partial* is "being part of." How does this definition apply to the term *partial product*?

## ▶ Getting Ready for FCAT

28. If 162 passengers paid the advertised airfare from Miami to Washington, how much did they pay in all?

   **A.** less than $13,000
   **B.** between $13,000 and $14,000
   **C.** between $14,000 and $15,000
   **D.** more than $15,000

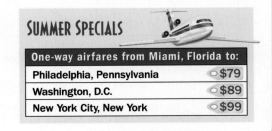

**SUMMER SPECIALS**

| One-way airfares from Miami, Florida to: | |
| --- | --- |
| Philadelphia, Pennsylvania | ○ $79 |
| Washington, D.C. | ○ $89 |
| New York City, New York | ○ $99 |

**FCAT TESTED**  SSS/GLEs MA.A.3.2.1 The student understands and explains the effects of addition, subtraction, and multiplication on whole numbers . . . . *also* MA.A.3.2.1.5.3, MA.A.4.2.1.5.1

**Chapter 7  153**

▶ **Learn**

**STARDUST**  Every hour 5 tons of cosmic dust—debris from outer space—enter Earth's atmosphere. If it could be shoveled onto one heap, it would be as big as a two-story house. How many tons of cosmic dust enter Earth's atmosphere every day?

◀ In 1986 the Vega probes were hit and damaged by 12,000 dust specks from Halley's Comet.

**Use Mental Math**

Find $24 \times 5$.

$5 \times 24 = 5 \times (20 + 4) = (5 \times 20) + (5 \times 4) = 100 + 20 = 120$

So, 120 tons of cosmic dust enter Earth's atmosphere every day.

**Use a Calculator**  How many tons of cosmic dust enter Earth's atmosphere per year?

Find $365 \times 120$.

     **3 6 5 × 1 2 0 =**  | 43,800 |

**Use Paper and Pencil**

| STEP 1 | STEP 2 | STEP 3 | STEP 4 |
|---|---|---|---|
| Multiply by the ones. | Multiply by the tens. | Multiply by the hundreds. | Add the partial products. |
| 365<br>×120<br>000 ← 0 × 365 | 1<br>365<br>×120<br>000<br>7300 ← 20 × 365 | 11<br>365<br>×120<br>000<br>7300<br>36500 ← 100 × 365 | 11<br>365<br>×120<br>000 ←  These<br>7300       zeros<br>+36500    can be<br>43,800    omitted. |

So, 43,800 tons of cosmic dust enter Earth's atmosphere every year.

 **MATH IDEA**  When an exact answer is needed, try mental math. If mental math is too difficult, choose a calculator or paper and pencil.

1. **Explain** how you multiply a 3-digit number by a 3-digit number. How do you multiply a 4-digit number by a 4-digit number?

**Find the product. Choose mental math, paper and pencil, or a calculator.**

2. $36 \times 5$

3. $80 \times 4{,}004$

4. $400 \times 789$

5. $105{,}874 \times 36$

6. $923 \times 202$

7. $5{,}500 \times 60$

8. $10{,}248 \times 32$

9. $200{,}800 \times 50$

▶ **Practice and Problem Solving** Extra Practice, page 158, Set D

**Find the product. Choose mental math, paper and pencil, or a calculator.**

10. $400 \times 142$

11. $28{,}000 \times 50$

12. $403 \times 830$

13. $3{,}000 \times 300$

14. $908{,}056 \times 60$

15. $973{,}204 \times 30$

16. $28 \times 69{,}434$

17. $21{,}002 \times 93$

18.
$$\begin{array}{r} 2{,}318 \\ \times \quad 47 \\ \hline \end{array}$$

19.
$$\begin{array}{r} 9{,}289 \\ \times \quad 106 \\ \hline \end{array}$$

20.
$$\begin{array}{r} 3{,}008 \\ \times \quad 23 \\ \hline \end{array}$$

21.
$$\begin{array}{r} 36{,}100 \\ \times \quad 800 \\ \hline \end{array}$$

22.
$$\begin{array}{r} 4{,}271 \\ \times 1{,}000 \\ \hline \end{array}$$

23.
$$\begin{array}{r} 482{,}763 \\ \times \quad 89 \\ \hline \end{array}$$

24.
$$\begin{array}{r} 72{,}315 \\ \times \quad 556 \\ \hline \end{array}$$

25.
$$\begin{array}{r} 56{,}403 \\ \times \quad 1{,}000 \\ \hline \end{array}$$

26. **NUMBER SENSE** Which estimate—14,000,000 or 24,000,000—is a closer estimate for the product of 79,321 and 260? Explain.

27. Mr. Calvin sells sheets of stamps at the post office. There are 100 stamps on each sheet. Each sheet costs $37. Last week he sold a total of 192 sheets. How much money did he collect for the sheets?

28. **≡FAST FACT • SCIENCE** The 140,000-acre Merritt Island National Wildlife Refuge has more than 1,500 plant and wildlife species. Kennedy Space Center uses 6,000 acres and the rest is wildlife habitat. Find the number of acres of wildlife habitat.

29. ✎ **Write About It** Why is it a good idea to estimate the product when finding the exact product?

30. Which circle is larger?

31. If Rio earned the same pay each week, how much did he earn for the year?

   **A.** $28,000   **C.** $32,500

   **B.** $29,120   **D.** $33,800

| YUBA FOOD COMPANY | | | |
|---|---|---|---|
| EMPLOYEE | WEEK ENDING | TOTAL PAY | YEAR TO DATE FOR 52 WEEKS |
| Rio Montoya | Dec. 31, 2003 | $560 | |

FCAT TESTED ⬦ SSS/GLEs MA.A.3.2.3.5.1 The student solves real-world problems involving . . . multiplication, and division of whole numbers, . . . using an appropriate method (for example, mental math, pencil and paper, calculator). *also* MA.A.3.2.2.5.1

Chapter 7 **155**

# Problem Solving Skill
## Evaluate Answers for Reasonableness

UNDERSTAND > PLAN > SOLVE > CHECK

**PAPER PRODUCTS** An important part of solving any problem is to check whether or not your answer is reasonable. You can use estimation to check the reasonableness of an answer.

One cord of hardwood weighs about 2 tons. Each cord can make an average of 2,700 copies of an average daily newspaper. Tyler says 32 cords will make 86,400 copies. Elena says 32 cords will make 13,500 copies. Whose answer is reasonable?

| Tyler |
| :---: |
| 2,700 |
| × 32 |
| 5400 |
| +81000 |
| 86,400 |

| Elena |
| :---: |
| 2,700 |
| × 32 |
| 5400 |
| + 8100 |
| 13,500 |

Estimate $2,700 \times 32$.

$3,000 \times 30 = 90,000$   Round each factor.

Compare Tyler's and Elena's answers to the estimate. Tyler's answer of 86,400 is close to the estimate of 90,000. Elena's answer of 13,500 is not close to the estimate of 90,000. So, Tyler's answer is reasonable.

▲ More than 5 new trees are planted each year for every man, woman, and child in the United States, and millions more regrow naturally from seeds and sprouts.

## Talk About It

• Why is it a good idea to determine if an answer is reasonable?

• What error do you think Elena made?

# ▶ Problem Solving Practice

1. An average of 1,096 commemorative-sized postage stamps can be made from one pound of hardwood. There are 2,000 pounds in one ton. Is it reasonable to say a ton of hardwood can make more than a million stamps? Explain.

2. **REASONING** What if you round both factors in a multiplication problem up to a greater number? How does your estimate compare to the exact answer? How do you know?

**Choose the most reasonable answer without doing an exact calculation.**

3. One cord of hardwood makes 942 hardcover books. Each book has 100 pages. How many pages does one cord make?

   **A** 942      **C** 94,200
   **B** 9,420     **D** 942,000

4. A newspaper company prints 28,231 newspapers daily. About how many newspapers does it print in July?

   **F** 9,000,000     **H** 93,000
   **G** 900,000      **J** 90,000

## Mixed Applications

**USE DATA** For 5–6, use the graph.

5. How many more letters are mailed in Vatican City than in the U.S. per person each year?

6. ? **What's the Error?** There are about 970 people in Vatican City. Lee says they mail about 925,865 letters each year. Describe and correct his error.

   | Lee |
   |---|
   | 9,545 |
   | × 970 |
   | 0000 |
   | 66815 |
   | + 859050 |
   | 925,865 |

7. The first place to issue postage stamps was Great Britain in 1840. How many years ago did Great Britain first issue postage stamps?

8. Luis worked for 18 hours. He earned $5.00 each hour. He bought a helmet for $15.95 and a skateboard for twice that amount. How much money did Luis have left?

9. 📓 **Write About It** How does estimation help you determine if your answer is reasonable?

**COUNTRIES SENDING THE MOST LETTERS PER PERSON**

Number of Letters (per person per year)

9,000 — 9,545
8,000
7,000
6,000
5,000
4,000
3,000
2,000
1,000 — 689 – 573 – 525 – 503
0

Vatican City, United States, Liechtenstein, Norway, Sweden

**Countries**

# Extra Practice

## Set A (pp. 148–149)

**Estimate the product.**

1. $73 \times 403$
2. $6 \times 7,834$
3. $32 \times 8,561$
4. $93 \times 468$
5. $702 \times 69$
6. $855 \times 28$
7. $276 \times 82$
8. $807 \times 51$
9. $1,231 \times 28$

## Set B (pp. 150–151)

**Find the product. Estimate to check.**

1. $\begin{array}{r} 2,335 \\ \times\ \ \ \ 6 \\ \hline \end{array}$
2. $\begin{array}{r} 3,584 \\ \times\ \ \ \ 4 \\ \hline \end{array}$
3. $\begin{array}{r} 5,824 \\ \times\ \ \ \ 5 \\ \hline \end{array}$
4. $\begin{array}{r} 4,854 \\ \times\ \ \ \ 3 \\ \hline \end{array}$

5. $\begin{array}{r} 530,944 \\ \times\ \ \ \ \ \ 4 \\ \hline \end{array}$
6. $\begin{array}{r} 90,256 \\ \times\ \ \ \ \ 3 \\ \hline \end{array}$
7. $\begin{array}{r} 6,993,028 \\ \times\ \ \ \ \ \ \ \ \ 7 \\ \hline \end{array}$
8. $\begin{array}{r} 3,511,824 \\ \times\ \ \ \ \ \ \ \ \ 8 \\ \hline \end{array}$

9. A theater complex has 9 theaters. Each theater seats 1,275 people. How many people can be seated at one time?

## Set C (pp. 152–153)

**Find the product. Estimate to check.**

1. $\begin{array}{r} 343 \\ \times\ 29 \\ \hline \end{array}$
2. $\begin{array}{r} 89 \\ \times 37 \\ \hline \end{array}$
3. $\begin{array}{r} 612 \\ \times\ 52 \\ \hline \end{array}$
4. $\begin{array}{r} 4,261 \\ \times\ \ \ 83 \\ \hline \end{array}$

5. $\begin{array}{r} 872 \\ \times\ 21 \\ \hline \end{array}$
6. $\begin{array}{r} 4,002 \\ \times\ \ \ 43 \\ \hline \end{array}$
7. $\begin{array}{r} 860 \\ \times\ 80 \\ \hline \end{array}$
8. $\begin{array}{r} 9,089 \\ \times\ \ \ 67 \\ \hline \end{array}$

9. $27 \times 63$
10. $312 \times 74$
11. $92 \times 859$
12. $532 \times 84$

## Set D (pp. 154–155)

**Find the product. Choose mental math, paper and pencil, or a calculator.**

1. $\begin{array}{r} 506 \\ \times 500 \\ \hline \end{array}$
2. $\begin{array}{r} 239,518 \\ \times\ \ \ \ \ 68 \\ \hline \end{array}$
3. $\begin{array}{r} 4,093 \\ \times\ \ 406 \\ \hline \end{array}$

4. $\begin{array}{r} 42,521 \\ \times\ \ \ \ 687 \\ \hline \end{array}$
5. $\begin{array}{r} 53,632 \\ \times\ \ 1,000 \\ \hline \end{array}$
6. $\begin{array}{r} 89,898 \\ \times\ \ \ 898 \\ \hline \end{array}$

7. $62,000 \times 40$
8. $399,017 \times 96$
9. $30,605 \times 20$

# Review/Test

## ✓ CHECK VOCABULARY AND CONCEPTS

**Choose the best term from the box.**

1. The __?__ of a whole number are all of the whole numbers that are products of the given number and another whole number. (p. 148)

2. You can use an __?__ to determine if an exact answer is reasonable. (p. 156)

> estimate
> factor
> multiples

## ✓ CHECK SKILLS

**Estimate the product.** (pp. 148–149)

3. $6 \times 1,239$

4. $84 \times 1,849$

5. $57 \times 6,236$

**Find the product. Estimate to check.** (pp. 150–155)

6. $5,631 \times 3$

7. $7,406 \times 6$

8. $12,648 \times 7$

9. $\begin{array}{r} 43 \\ \times 27 \\ \hline \end{array}$

10. $\begin{array}{r} 682 \\ \times 484 \\ \hline \end{array}$

11. $\begin{array}{r} 2,167 \\ \times\ \ \ 51 \\ \hline \end{array}$

12. $\begin{array}{r} 4,260 \\ \times\ \ \ 83 \\ \hline \end{array}$

13. $\begin{array}{r} 9,853 \\ \times\ \ \ 37 \\ \hline \end{array}$

14. $\begin{array}{r} 4,101 \\ \times\ \ 500 \\ \hline \end{array}$

15. $\begin{array}{r} 8,760 \\ \times\ \ \ 45 \\ \hline \end{array}$

16. $\begin{array}{r} 6,533 \\ \times\ \ 620 \\ \hline \end{array}$

17. $69,833 \times 9$

18. $1,265 \times 88$

19. $86,685 \times 7$

## ✓ CHECK PROBLEM SOLVING

20. Myra says the product of 26,547 and 269 is 7,141,143. Is this a reasonable answer? Explain. (pp. 156–157)

21. Bert says the product of 6,704 and 43 is 46,928. Is this a reasonable answer? Explain. (pp. 156–157)

22. A factory produces 342 vans every week. How many vans does the factory produce in a year? (pp. 152–153)

23. The product of 60 and 900 has 3 zeros. How many zeros does the product of 60 and 9,000,000 have? (pp. 148–149)

24. On average, a museum has 182,469 visitors per year. How many visitors does the museum have in 3 years? in 8 years? (pp. 150–151)

25. For the past 15 years, Tanya has jogged 10 miles per day. How many miles has she jogged altogether? Use 365 days for a year. (pp. 152–153)

# Getting Ready for FCAT

 **NUMBER SENSE, CONCEPTS, AND OPERATIONS**

1. The table shows the mean distance in miles of some planets from the sun.

| MEAN DISTANCE FROM THE SUN ||
| Planet | Mean Distance |
| --- | --- |
| Mercury | 36 million miles |
| Mars | 141 million miles |
| Jupiter | 480 million miles |
| Saturn | 900 million miles |

How many miles **farther** from the sun is Jupiter than Mercury?

A. 454,000,000 miles

B. 444,000,000 miles

C. 344,000,000 miles

D. 44,400,000 miles

2. Which of the following is **greater than** 948,026 and has a 5 in the ten thousands place?

F. 965,160

G. 958,347

H. 947,051

I. 943,529

3. **Explain It** There are 12 inches in 1 foot and 5,280 feet in 1 mile. Explain how you would ESTIMATE the number of inches in 1 mile. Then find the exact answer.

 **ALGEBRAIC THINKING**

4. Jacob bought 12 doughnuts. He ate 1 and gave some to his brother. Let $d$ represent the number of doughnuts Jacob gave to his brother. Which expression shows how many doughnuts Jacob has left?

A. $(d - 12) - 1$　　C. $(12 - 1) + d$

B. $(d - 12) + 1$　　D. $(12 - 1) - d$

5. The pictures on the wall of an art classroom are arranged in rows, with one picture in the first row, two in the second row, three in the third row, and so on. If there are 7 rows of pictures, how many pictures are on the wall?

F. 8　　　　　　　H. 28

G. 21　　　　　　I. 36

6. **Explain It** Carly is saving money to buy a new bike. In January she saved $3, in February she saved $9, in March she saved $27. This pattern continued for the next two months.

| CARLY'S SAVINGS |||||||
| Month | Jan | Feb | Mar | Apr | May |
| --- | --- | --- | --- | --- | --- |
| Amount Saved | $3 | $9 | $27 | ▨ | ▨ |

How much money did Carly save in May? Explain how you solved the problem.

## DATA ANALYSIS AND PROBABILITY

**7.** The graph shows the number of sneakers sold by Joe during 5 months. During which month were sales the **greatest**?

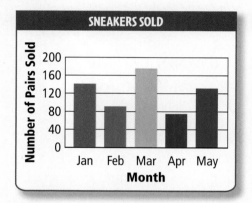

**SNEAKERS SOLD**

**A.** January   **C.** March

**B.** February   **D.** May

**8.** Mrs. Green bought sneakers for each of her children. The table shows the price she paid for each child's sneakers.

| Child | Price Paid |
|---|---|
| Matthew | $45 |
| Lisa | $56 |
| Daniel | $38 |
| Julie | $29 |

What was the average price Mrs. Green paid for a pair of sneakers?

**F.** $27   **H.** $42

**G.** $41.50   **I.** $56

**9. Explain It** Marliss is going on vacation. She can travel by bus, train, or car. She can leave on Monday, Tuesday, Wednesday, or Thursday. How many possible choices for type of transportation and day does she have? Explain your answer.

## GEOMETRY AND SPATIAL SENSE

**10.** Which of the following describes how the figure was moved?

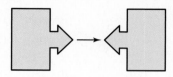

**A.** translation   **C.** rotation

**B.** reflection   **D.** tessellation

**TIP**   **Decide on a plan.**  See item 11. Use the strategy *draw a diagram* to help you find the dimensions of the picture frame.

**11.** Kira's dad is making a picture frame. The length is 8 inches. The width is 2 inches greater than the length. Which of the following shows the perimeter of the picture frame?

**F.** 80 inches   **H.** 28 inches

**G.** 36 inches   **I.** 18 inches

**12. Explain It** Josh has plotted two of three points that form a right triangle when connected.

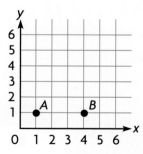

Name an ordered pair for a third point that can be used to form a right triangle. Then, name the ordered pairs for *A* and *B*. Explain what you notice about the *x*- and *y*-coordinates of the ordered pairs.

# Multiply Decimals

There are about 10 million different kinds of animals in the world. Some are very light. A bee hummingbird and a golf ball are about the same size, but the weight of a golf ball is about 28 times as great as that of a bee hummingbird.

The bee hummingbird measures 60 millimeters long.

**PROBLEM SOLVING**
The table lists some of the lightest and heaviest animals. About how much does a golf ball weigh?

| ANIMAL WEIGHTS | | |
|---|---|---|
| **Record** | **Animal** | **Weight (kilograms)** |
| Lightest bird | Bee hummingbird | 0.0016 |
| Lightest land mammal | Bumblebee bat | 0.002 |
| Heaviest insect | Goliath beetle | 0.099 |
| Heaviest bird | Ostrich | 148.5 |
| Heaviest bony fish | Ocean sunfish | 1,980 |
| Heaviest land mammal | African elephant | 7,000 |

Use this page to help you review and remember important skills needed for Chapter 8.

## MULTIPLY 2-DIGIT NUMBERS

Find the product.

| | | | |
|---|---|---|---|
| **1.** $\begin{array}{r} 13 \\ \times\ 8 \\ \hline \end{array}$ | **2.** $\begin{array}{r} 24 \\ \times\ 5 \\ \hline \end{array}$ | **3.** $\begin{array}{r} 52 \\ \times\ 7 \\ \hline \end{array}$ | **4.** $\begin{array}{r} 76 \\ \times 49 \\ \hline \end{array}$ |
| **5.** $\begin{array}{r} 39 \\ \times\ 3 \\ \hline \end{array}$ | **6.** $\begin{array}{r} 67 \\ \times\ 4 \\ \hline \end{array}$ | **7.** $\begin{array}{r} 53 \\ \times 83 \\ \hline \end{array}$ | **8.** $\begin{array}{r} 84 \\ \times\ 8 \\ \hline \end{array}$ |
| **9.** $\begin{array}{r} 48 \\ \times 27 \\ \hline \end{array}$ | **10.** $\begin{array}{r} 17 \\ \times 26 \\ \hline \end{array}$ | **11.** $\begin{array}{r} 92 \\ \times 56 \\ \hline \end{array}$ | **12.** $\begin{array}{r} 63 \\ \times 15 \\ \hline \end{array}$ |

## MULTIPLY MONEY

Multiply.

**13.** $\$0.10 \times 2$   **14.** $\$0.05 \times 20$   **15.** $\$0.25 \times 4$

**16.** $\$0.25 \times 3$   **17.** $\$0.10 \times 10$   **18.** $\$0.50 \times 5$

| | | |
|---|---|---|
| **19.** $\begin{array}{r} \$0.01 \\ \times\ \ \ \ 9 \\ \hline \end{array}$ | **20.** $\begin{array}{r} \$0.05 \\ \times\ \ \ \ 5 \\ \hline \end{array}$ | **21.** $\begin{array}{r} \$0.25 \\ \times\ \ \ \ 8 \\ \hline \end{array}$ |
| **22.** $\begin{array}{r} \$0.25 \\ \times\ \ \ \ 2 \\ \hline \end{array}$ | **23.** $\begin{array}{r} \$0.10 \\ \times\ \ \ \ 8 \\ \hline \end{array}$ | **24.** $\begin{array}{r} \$0.05 \\ \times\ \ \ \ 9 \\ \hline \end{array}$ |
| **25.** $\begin{array}{r} \$0.01 \\ \times\ \ \ 12 \\ \hline \end{array}$ | **26.** $\begin{array}{r} \$0.25 \\ \times\ \ \ \ 6 \\ \hline \end{array}$ | **27.** $\begin{array}{r} \$0.50 \\ \times\ \ \ \ 6 \\ \hline \end{array}$ |

# VOCABULARY POWER

## REVIEW

**decimal** [de′sə•məl] *noun*

*Decimal* is derived from the Latin *decimus*, meaning "tenth." Explain why this meaning helps you understand decimals.

 www.harcourtschool.com/mathglossary

# Multiply Decimals and Whole Numbers

**Quick Review**

1. 50¢ × 9
2. $60 × 8
3. $12 × 5
4. 75¢ × 4
5. $50 × 8

**MATERIALS**
decimal models
markers or colored pencils

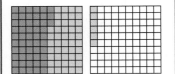

The red kangaroo, the world's largest marsupial, uses its tail for balance when jumping. Its tail is about 0.53 times as long as its body. Its body is about 2 meters long. How long is its tail to the nearest meter?

## Activity 1

Make a model to show how to multiply 2 by 0.53.

What is 2 × 0.53?

### STEP 1

Use hundredths models. Shade 0.53, or 53 hundredths, two times. Use a different color each time.

### STEP 2

Count the number of shaded hundredths. There are 106 shaded hundredths. This is 1 whole and 6 hundredths.

So, 2 × 0.53 = 1.06.

So, the red kangaroo's tail is about 1 meter long.

- How is multiplying 2 × 0.53 similar to multiplying 2 × 53?

- Is the product of 3 and 0.53 greater than or less than 3? Why?

## Try It

Make a model to find the product.

a. 4 × 0.12
b. 3 × 0.03
c. 5 × 0.5
d. 3 × 0.3

The orange squares show 1 × 0.12. How do you show 4 × 0.12?

You can write a multiplication sentence for your model.

## Activity 2

What is $3 \times 0.6$?

| **Model** | **Record** |
|---|---|
| Use tenths models. Shade 0.6, or 6 tenths, three times. Use a different color each time. Count the number of shaded tenths. There are 18 shaded tenths, or 1 whole and 8 tenths. 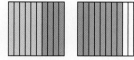 | Record. $$\begin{array}{r} 0.6 \\ \times\ \ \ 3 \\ \hline 1.8 \end{array}$$ Use the model to place the decimal point. $3 \times 0.6$ is $3 \times 6$ tenths, or 18 tenths, which is 1.8. So, $3 \times 0.6 = 1.8$. |

► **Practice and Problem Solving**

**Make a model to find each product.**

**1.** $3 \times 0.8$    **2.** $6 \times 0.4$    **3.** $5 \times 0.6$    **4.** $2 \times 0.82$

**5.** $7 \times 0.03$    **6.** $2 \times 0.12$    **7.** $4 \times 0.19$    **8.** $9 \times 0.18$

**Joy is shopping at the pet store. For 9–12, use the table to find the total cost.**

**9.** 3 neon tetras, 2 zebra danios

**10.** 2 albino danios, 3 leopard danios

**11.** 4 neon tetras, 2 zebra danios, 1 leopard danio

**12.** 5 albino danios, 3 zebra danios

**13.** ✎ **Write about it** Explain how to draw a picture to find $3 \times 0.9$.

| TROPICAL FISH | |
|---|---|
| **Item** | **Price** |
| Neon tetra | $0.74 |
| Zebra danio | $0.89 |
| Albino danio | $0.99 |
| Leopard danio | $0.95 |

## Getting Ready for ★FCAT

**14.** Mrs. Washburn does her laundry at the laundromat. How much does it cost her to wash 2 loads of laundry twice a week?

**A.** $1.50

**B.** $3.00

**C.** $4.00

**D.** $4.50

CLEAN AS A WHISTLE

Laundromat Wash

**$0.75**

per load

# Algebra: Patterns in Decimal Factors and Products

**Quick Review**

1. $10 \times 12$
2. $100 \times 12$
3. $1{,}000 \times 12$
4. $10{,}000 \times 12$
5. $100{,}000 \times 12$

▶ **Learn**

**MEASURE UP** The smallest frog in the Northern Hemisphere is found in Cuba and grows to about 0.98 centimeters in body length. The photos show the frog at its actual size and enlarged 5 times. What would be the length of the frog in a photo enlarged 1,000 times?

▲ Frog enlarged 5 times

▲ Actual size of frog

### Example

What is $0.98 \times 1{,}000$?

Look for a pattern.

$0.98 \times 1 = 0.98$

$0.98 \times 10 = 9.8$ ← The decimal point moves 1 place to the right.

$0.98 \times 100 = 98.$ ← The decimal point moves 2 places to the right.

$0.98 \times 1{,}000 = 980.$ ← The decimal point moves 3 places to the right.

So, in the photo enlarged 1,000 times, the frog would be 980 centimeters long.

• What if you enlarge the frog photo 100 times? What will be the length of the frog in the photo?

 **MATH IDEA** The decimal point moves one place to the right when you multiply by 10, two places to the right when you multiply by 100, and three places to the right when you multiply by 1,000.

### More Examples

**A**
$\$3.25 \times 1 = \$3.25$
$\$3.25 \times 10 = \$32.50$
$\$3.25 \times 100 = \$325.00$
$\$3.25 \times 1{,}000 = \$3{,}250.00$

**B**
$0.478 \times 1 = 0.478$
$0.478 \times 10 = 4.78$
$0.478 \times 100 = 47.8$
$0.478 \times 1{,}000 = 478$

**C**
$0.0009 \times 1 = 0.0009$
$0.0009 \times 10 = 0.009$
$0.0009 \times 100 = 0.09$
$0.0009 \times 1{,}000 = 0.9$

• **REASONING** How can you use the pattern to place the decimal point in $\$32.50 \times 100$?

## ▶ Check

1. **Explain** why the product 4.56 × 100 is the same as the product 4.56 × 10 × 10? What is 4.56 × 100?

**Use mental math to complete.**

2. 1 × 0.3 = 0.3
   10 × 0.3 = 3
   100 × 0.3 = ■
   1,000 × 0.3 = ■

3. 1 × 2.845 = 2.845
   10 × 2.845 = 28.45
   100 × 2.845 = ■
   1,000 × 2.845 = 2,845

4. 1 × 0.3459 = 0.3459
   10 × 0.3459 = ■
   100 × 0.3459 = 34.59
   1,000 × 0.3459 = 345.9

## ▶ Practice and Problem Solving ⟩ Extra Practice, page 178, Set A

**Use mental math to complete.**

5. 1 × 0.005 = 0.005
   10 × 0.005 = ■
   100 × 0.005 = 0.5
   1,000 × 0.005 = 5

6. 1 × 4.761 = 4.761
   10 × 4.761 = 47.61
   100 × 4.761 = ■
   1,000 × 4.761 = ■

7. 1 × 0.45 = 0.45
   10 × 0.45 = ■
   100 × 0.45 = ■
   1,000 × 0.45 = ■

**Multiply each number by 10, by 100, and by 1,000.**

8. 0.9
9. 0.51
10. 0.007
11. 0.015
12. 0.2178
13. $0.25
14. 45.69
15. 1.0608

**ALGEBRA** **Find the value of $n$.**

16. $10 \times 0.009 = n$
17. $n \times 0.08 = 0.8$
18. $100 \times n = 4.5$
19. $1.5 \times n = 15$
20. $n \times 100 = 1.9$
21. $n \times 1,000 = 3.1$

22. A half dollar is 0.50 of a dollar. What is the value of 100 half dollars? of 1,000 half dollars?

23. If a snail moves 8 inches a minute, how many minutes would it take it to move 12 feet?

24. ✎ **Write About It** Explain why multiplying a decimal by 10, by 100, and by 1,000 is easy to compute mentally.

25. **REASONING** How does the position of the decimal point change when you multiply 6.7 by 10,000?

## ⌐ Getting Ready for ◆FCAT

26. Justin just passed this road sign. How far is it to Melbourne?

   **A.** 0.62 mi
   **C.** 620 mi
   **B.** 62 mi
   **D.** 6,200 mi

| Orlando, FL | 10 kilometers or 6.2 miles |
| Melbourne, FL | 100 kilometers or ■ miles |

**FCAT TESTED** SSS/GLEs MA.A.3.2.1.5.2 Explains and demonstrates the multiplication of decimals to hundredths using concrete materials, drawings, story problems, symbols, and algorithms.

Chapter 8 **167**

# Model Decimal Multiplication

**Quick Review**

1. 0.4 + 0.4
2. 0.6 + 0.6
3. 0.7 + 0.7
4. 0.4 + 0.4 + 0.4
5. 0.1 + 0.1 + 0.1

▶ **Learn**

**FAST FOOD**   The bee hummingbird weighs about 0.2 dekagram. It needs to eat half its body weight in food every day to stay alive. About how much food does a bee hummingbird need to eat every day?

**Example**

Find $0.2 \times 0.5$.   ← **Think:** One half can be written as 0.5.

| STEP 1 | STEP 2 | STEP 3 |
|---|---|---|
| Divide a square into 10 equal columns. Shade 5 of the columns to show 0.5. | Divide the square into 10 equal rows to make 100 equal parts. Shade 2 of the rows to show 0.2. | The area in which the shading overlaps shows the product, or $0.2 \times 0.5$. |
|  |  |  |
| | | So, $0.2 \times 0.5 = 0.10$. |

So, a bee hummingbird eats about 0.10, or 0.1 dekagram, of food every day.

Since hummingbirds can rotate their wings in a figure-eight pattern, they can fly backward, and even hover like a helicopter! ▼

- **REASONING**   What relationship do you see between the product and the size of the two decimal factors less than 1?

▶ **Check**

1. **Tell** whether the product $0.2 \times 0.4$ is greater than or less than 1. Explain your reasoning.

**Complete the multiplication sentence for each model.**

2.

$0.5 \times 0.7 = n$

3.

$y \times 0.8 = 0.24$

4.

$0.3 \times 0.5 = p$

5.

$0.9 \times n = 0.27$

**Make a model to find the product.**

**6.** $0.1 \times 0.5$
**7.** $0.4 \times 0.7$
**8.** $0.3 \times 0.3$
**9.** $0.8 \times 0.4$

## Practice and Problem Solving    Extra Practice, page 178, Set B

**Complete the multiplication sentence for each model.**

**10.**

$0.4 \times 0.6 = n$

**11.**

$0.5 \times y = 0.25$

**12.**

$p \times 0.9 = 0.18$

**13.**

$0.1 \times 0.4 = n$

**Make a model to find the product.**

**14.** $0.8 \times 0.8$
**15.** $0.1 \times 0.9$
**16.** $0.6 \times 0.2$
**17.** $0.8 \times 0.3$

**Find the product.**

**18.** $0.7 \times 0.8$
**19.** $0.2 \times 0.8$
**20.** $0.9 \times 0.6$
**21.** $0.6 \times 0.7$

**22.** $0.5 \times 0.6$
**23.** $0.8 \times 0.9$
**24.** $0.5 \times 0.4$
**25.** $0.3 \times 0.6$

 **ALGEBRA**    **For 26–29, find the value of $n$.**

**26.** $n \times 0.2 = 0.14$
**27.** $0.6 \times n = 0.48$
**28.** $0.9 \times n = 0.63$
**29.** $n \times 0.7 = 0.35$

**30. Vocabulary Power** *Deca-* and *deka-* are variations of the same prefix. A *decagon* is a polygon with 10 sides. Use the meaning of *decagon* to explain the meaning of *dekagram*.

**31.** At the pet store, Jason bought 2 birdcages at $12.98 each and 5 boxes of birdseed at $3.49 each. If he gave the clerk five $10-bills, what would be his change?

**32.** **? What's the Error?** Marco said $0.1 \times 0.6 = 0.6$. Describe his error. Draw a model.

**33.** **FAST FACT • SCIENCE** A grasshopper can leap about 0.7 meter. A flea can jump 0.5 times as far. About how far can a flea jump?

## Getting Ready for FCAT

**34.** Ray modeled a decimal multiplication problem on the chalkboard. Which problem did he model?

**A.** $0.2 \times 0.9 = 0.18$
**B.** $0.6 \times 0.3 = 0.18$
**C.** $0.5 \times 0.4 = 0.20$
**D.** $0.1 \times 0.2 = 0.02$

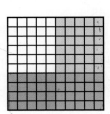

FCAT TESTED    SSS/GLEs MA.A.3.2.1.5.2 Explains and demonstrates the multiplication of decimals to hundredths using concrete materials, drawings, story problems, symbols, and algorithms.
*also* MA.A.1.2.3.5.1, MA.A.3.2.1.5.3

Chapter 8    **169**

# Place the Decimal Point

 **Learn**

**TIP TO TIP**   From the tip of its nose to the end of its tail, a pygmy shrew measures 6.1 centimeters long. A house mouse is 2.7 times as long. How long is the house mouse?

You can use estimation to help you place the decimal point in a decimal product and to determine if your answer is reasonable.

**Example 1**   Find $2.7 \times 6.1$.

**STEP 1**

Estimate the product. Round each factor.

$2.7 \times 6.1$
 ↓      ↓
$3 \times 6 = 18$

**STEP 2**

Multiply as with whole numbers.

```
   6.1
 ×2.7
   427
+1220
 1647
```

**STEP 3**

Use the estimate to place the decimal point in the product.

```
   6.1
 ×2.7
   427
+1220
 16.47
    ↑
```
Since the estimate is 18, place the decimal point so there is a two-digit whole number in the product.

So, the house mouse is 16.47 centimeters long.

The pygmy shrew, one of the world's smallest mammals, could sleep in a spoon! And it weighs about as much as a table-tennis ball! ▼

## More Examples

**A** Find $12 \times 0.48$.

$10 \times 0.5 = 5 \leftarrow$ Estimate.

```
   0.48
 ×   12
     96
 +480
   5.76
    ↑
```
Since the estimate is 5, place the decimal point so there is a one-digit whole number in the product.

**B** Find $0.75 \times \$1.25$.

$0.8 \times \$1 = \$0.8$, or $\$0.80 \leftarrow$ Estimate.

```
  $1.25
 × 0.75
    625
 +8750
 $0.9375
    ↑
```
Since the estimate is $0.80, place the decimal point so there is less than 1 dollar in the product.

## Count Decimal Places

You can also place the decimal point by finding the total number of decimal places in the factors. Then count that many places from the right in the product.

**Technology Link**

More Practice: Harcourt Mega Math The Number Games, *Buggy Bargains*, Levels K, L

**Example 2** Find 0.7 × 0.2.

| STEP 1 | STEP 2 |
|---|---|
| Multiply as with whole numbers. | Find the total number of decimal places in the factors. Place the decimal point that number of places from the right in the product. |
| 0.7<br>×0.2<br>14 | 0.7 ← 1 decimal place in the factor<br>×0.2 ← 1 decimal place in the factor<br>0.14 ← 1 + 1, or 2 decimal places in the product |

So, 0.7 × 0.2 is 0.14.

## More Examples

**C**

```
    23 ← 0 decimal places in the factor
×0.04 ← 2 decimal places in the factor
 0.92 ← 0 + 2, or 2 decimal places in
          the product
```

**D**

```
  7.52 ← 2 decimal places in the factor
 ×0.23 ← 2 decimal places in the factor
  2256
+15040
1.7296 ← 2 + 2, or 4 decimal places in
           the product
```

 **MATH IDEA** You can use estimation or the total number of decimal places in the factors to determine where to place the decimal point in the product.

▼ House mouse

## Check

1. **Explain** how you can check that the answer to Example D is reasonable.

**Choose the better estimate. Write *a* or *b*.**

**2.** 34 × 0.8    **a.** 24    **b.** 2.4    **3.** 4.2 × 3.9    **a.** 16    **b.** 1.6

**Copy each exercise. Place the decimal point in the product.**

| **4.** | **5.** | **6.** | **7.** |
|---|---|---|---|
| 29<br>×0.7<br>203 | 2.98<br>× 0.7<br>2086 | 1.8<br>×0.2<br>36 | 0.37<br>×0.64<br>2368 |

**Find the product. Estimate to check.**

**8.** 9 × 1.7     **9.** 0.2 × 12     **10.** 95 × 0.64     **11.** 1.25 × 0.5

**12.** 0.9 × 0.4     **13.** 0.37 × 0.6     **14.** 0.211 × 18

LESSON CONTINUES

FCAT TESTED  SSS/GLEs MA.A.3.2.1.5.2 Explains and demonstrates the multiplication of decimals to hundredths using concrete materials, drawings, story problems, symbols, and algorithms. *also* MA.A.1.2.3.5.1, MA.A.4.2.1.5.1

Chapter 8  **171**

**Choose the better estimate. Write *a* or *b*.**

**15.** 22 × 0.6    **a.** 12   **b.** 1.2      **16.** 2.3 × 4.8    **a.** 10   **b.** 1.0

**17.** 0.82 × 6    **a.** 0.48   **b.** 4.8      **18.** 42 × 0.5    **a.** 20   **b.** 2.0

**Copy each exercise. Place the decimal point in the product.**

**19.**
$$\begin{array}{r} 3.4 \\ \times\ 5 \\ \hline 170 \end{array}$$

**20.**
$$\begin{array}{r} 0.58 \\ \times\ 2 \\ \hline 116 \end{array}$$

**21.**
$$\begin{array}{r} 5.48 \\ \times 0.726 \\ \hline 397848 \end{array}$$

**22.**
$$\begin{array}{r} 2.32 \\ \times 4.68 \\ \hline 108576 \end{array}$$

**Find the product. Estimate to check.**

**23.** 0.3 × 14      **24.** 0.5 × 1,206      **25.** 6.8 × 4.5      **26.** 7.25 × 3.8

**27.** 5.1 × 2.7      **28.** 12.92 × 7.2      **29.** 19 × 0.21      **30.** 38.8 × 4.62

**31.** 0.7 × 0.8      **32.** 6.9 × 3.1      **33.** 0.12 × 0.9      **34.** 0.325 × 82

**35.** 0.68 × 0.4      **36.** 2.36 × 0.9      **37.** 0.3 × 0.918      **38.** 9.2 × 0.07

**39.** 0.25 × 0.75      **40.** 0.8 × 0.201      **41.** 2.7 × 5.6      **42.** 43.3 × 6.2

**43.** 24.37 × 0.8      **44.** 0.848 × 3.2      **45.** 9.748 × 0.42      **46.** 436.3 × 0.181

**47.** Which product will have 6 decimal places?

     **a.** 0.12 × 0.0456      **b.** 1.2 × 0.0456      **c.** 12 × 0.0456

**48.** Which product will have 5 decimal places?

     **a.** 0.283 × 1.078      **b.** 2.83 × 1.078      **c.** 28.3 × 1.078

**49.** **Write About It** How can you use an estimate to help you place the decimal point? Give an example.

**USE DATA** For 50–52, use the graph.

**50.** Which aquarium has a capacity that is 0.20 times as great as that of the shark aquarium?

**51.** Is the total capacity of the five aquariums greater than or less than 500,000 gallons? Explain.

**52.** Which aquariums have capacities that are greater than twice that of the river otter aquarium?

**53.** The largest male killer whale weighed 55 times the weight of a dolphin. If an average dolphin weighs 400 lb, how much did the largest killer whale weigh?

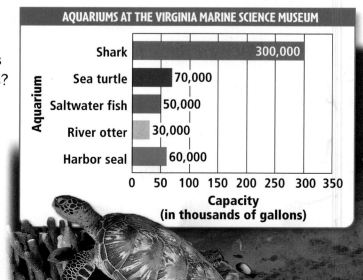

AQUARIUMS AT THE VIRGINIA MARINE SCIENCE MUSEUM

**54.** Four students shared 6 boxes of markers equally. Each of the boxes had the same number of markers. Each student received 6 markers. How many markers were in each box?

**55.** The largest frog is the Goliath frog. With its legs stretched out, it is about 0.8 meter long. When its legs are not stretched out, its body is about 0.5 times that length. How long is its body?

## Getting Ready for FCAT

**56.** Four students each multiplied 6.4 × 8.3. Who had the correct answer?

- **A.** Ann
- **B.** Beth
- **C.** Carl
- **D.** David

| | |
|---|---|
| Ann | 6.4 x 8.3 = 53.12 |
| Beth | 6.4 x 8.3 = 531.2 |
| Carl | 26.4 x 8.3 = 5,312 |
| David | 6.4 x 8.3 = 0.5312 |

# Problem Solving  LiNKUP...to Reading

**STRATEGY • SUMMARIZE** To *summarize,* you restate information in a shortened form. You include only the most important information.

Gwen runs her computer 8 hours each day, 5 days each week. How much does the electricity cost for 4 weeks?

| Summary | Solve |
|---|---|
| **A.** Electricity costs $0.01 per hour. | |
| **B.** The computer runs 8 hours a day. | 8 × $0.01 = $0.08 |
| **C.** The computer runs 5 days a week. | 5 × $0.08 = $0.40 |
| **D.** How much does it cost for 4 weeks? | 4 × $0.40 = $1.60 |

| ELECTRICITY COST (based on a 2001 average electric rate) | |
|---|---|
| **Appliances** | **Cost per hour** |
| Computer | $0.01 |
| Lamp, 100 watt | $0.01 |
| Refrigerator/freezer | $0.02 |
| Hair dryer | $0.12 |
| Television | $0.02 |
| Water heater | $0.40 |

So, it costs Gwen $1.60.

**USE DATA** For 1–2, use the table.

**1.** Mr. Ramos' water heater is on a timer. It runs a total of 3 hours each day. How much does it cost to run his water heater each week?

**2.** A fluorescent lamp costs $0.003 per hour to run. How much more does it cost to run the 100-watt lamp for 10 hours than the fluorescent lamp for 10 hours?

# Zeros in the Product

**Quick Review**

1. $1 \times 0.4$
2. $2 \times 0.4$
3. $10 \times 0.4$
4. $20 \times 0.4$
5. $125 \times 0.5$

 **Learn**

Sometimes when you multiply with decimals, there are zeros in the product.

**SUPER ANT** A *Formica japonica* worker ant weighs 0.004 gram. It can walk while holding in its mouth an object weighing 5 times as much as its own body. How many grams can a worker ant carry?

Find $5 \times 0.004$.

$$\begin{array}{r} 0.004 \\ \times \quad 5 \\ \hline 0.020 \end{array}$$

← Since there are 3 decimal places in the factors, you will need 3 decimal places in the product.
Write a zero at the left in the product to place the decimal point.

So, a worker ant can carry 0.020, or 0.02, gram.

## Examples

**A** Find $0.003 \times \$18$.

$$\begin{array}{r} \$18 \\ \times 0.003 \\ \hline \$0.054 \end{array}$$
↑

Since 3 decimal places are needed in the product, write a zero in this place.

**B** Find $0.09 \times 0.07$.

$$\begin{array}{r} 0.07 \\ \times 0.09 \\ \hline 0.0063 \end{array}$$
↑↑

Since 4 decimal places are needed in the product, write zeros in these places.

**C** Find $0.002 \times 9.27$.

$$\begin{array}{r} 9.27 \\ \times 0.002 \\ \hline 0.01854 \end{array}$$
↑

Since 5 decimal places are needed in the product, write a zero in this place.

**D** You can use a calculator to multiply decimals.

Find $0.06 \times 0.34$.

 ×  Enter

```
.06 x .34 =
        0.0204
```

• In Example A, what is the product to the nearest cent?

 **MATH IDEA** You may need to insert zeros at the left in the product to keep the same number of decimal places in the product as in the factors.

1. **Explain** how you know when to insert a zero in a product to place a decimal point.

**Find the product.**

2. $8 \times 0.003$     3. $0.04 \times 0.4$     4. $0.018 \times 9$     5. $6 \times 0.0006$

► **Practice and Problem Solving**    ( Extra Practice, page 178, Set D )

**Find the product.**

6. $9 \times 0.007$     7. $0.02 \times 2$     8. $0.016 \times 0.5$     9. $0.8 \times 0.03$

10.
$$\begin{array}{r} 0.006 \\ \times\quad 9 \\ \hline \end{array}$$

11.
$$\begin{array}{r} 0.08 \\ \times 0.02 \\ \hline \end{array}$$

12.
$$\begin{array}{r} 0.004 \\ \times\quad 24 \\ \hline \end{array}$$

13.
$$\begin{array}{r} 0.12 \\ \times 0.09 \\ \hline \end{array}$$

14.
$$\begin{array}{r} 54.07 \\ \times\ 0.04 \\ \hline \end{array}$$

15.
$$\begin{array}{r} 0.007 \\ \times\quad 8 \\ \hline \end{array}$$

16.
$$\begin{array}{r} 0.032 \\ \times\quad 17 \\ \hline \end{array}$$

17.
$$\begin{array}{r} 0.014 \\ \times\ 0.06 \\ \hline \end{array}$$

**Find the product. Round to the nearest cent.**

18. $\$0.89 \times 0.08$     19. $\$0.95 \times 0.05$     20. $\$3.09 \times 0.05$     21. $\$5.05 \times 0.06$

**Write <, >, or = for each** ●.

22. $0.008 \times 9$ ● $0.009 \times 8$     23. $3 \times 0.025$ ● $3.01 \times 0.02$

24.  **What's the Question?** Eileen bought 2 gallons of milk at $3.02 per gallon and one loaf of bread at $0.99. The answer is $7.03.

25. **Write a problem** including this information: a dozen eggs costs $0.78, a loaf of bread costs $1.03, a pound of bananas costs $0.63.

26. You can draw a line 35 miles long with a standard pencil. That's 0.9 of the distance from Baltimore to Washington, D.C. How long a line can you draw with 3 pencils?

27. The price of an ant farm is $28.00. The computer multiplies the price by 1.07 to find your total cost including tax. What change would you get from two $20-bills?

28. **Write About It** To find $0.05 \times 0.06$, would you use a calculator, paper and pencil, or mental math? Explain.

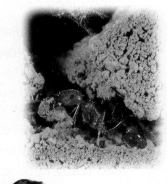

**Getting Ready for FCAT**

29. A hair on your head grows about 0.013 inch per day. How much does your hair grow in seven days?

    **A.** 91 inches       **C.** 0.91 inch
    **B.** 9.1 inches       **D.** 0.091 inch

# Problem Solving Skill
## Make Decisions

UNDERSTAND › PLAN › SOLVE › CHECK

**ARTIST'S CHOICE**  Suppose you are planning to take art lessons. You can sign up for either painting or sculpture. To help you make a decision on which to take, there are several things that you need to think about before you decide.

| THINGS TO CONSIDER | PAINTING | SCULPTURE |
|---|---|---|
| Time | Wednesday, 4:00 P.M. to 6:00 P.M. | Saturday, 10 A.M. to 11:30 A.M. |
| Number of lessons | 6 | 9 |
| Cost per lesson | $12.75 | $9.50 |
| Cost of general supplies | $10 | $25 |
| Cost per project | $2.35 per canvas panel | $1.45 per 5-lb bag of clay |

**Use the information in the table to help you answer the following questions.**

**A.** For each choice, how much will it cost for lessons and general supplies? Which costs less?

**B.** What is the difference in cost for general supplies for each choice?

**C.** How many total hours will each choice last? What is the difference in the amount of time?

**D.** You will complete a total of 4 painting projects or 6 sculpture projects. How much will you spend on project supplies for painting? for sculpture? In which project would supplies cost less?

## Talk About It

• If you had to take the one that costs less, would you take painting or sculpture? Explain the reasons for your decision.

• Make a list of other things you may consider before deciding which to take.

 **MATH IDEA**  To help you make a decision, compare facts and data.

**USE DATA** For 1–3, use the information in the table.

1. You have a coupon from Store A for $2.00 off if you purchase $10.00 worth of art supplies. You plan to buy 12 sheets of charcoal paper and 10 pastels. Would you spend more at Store A or Store B? How much more?

**You are buying art supplies for a drawing class. You need 4 sticks of charcoal, 3 kneaded erasers, and 2 pastels. You do not have any store coupons.**

| WHICH STORE HAS THE BEST BUY? | | | |
|---|---|---|---|
| **Items** | **Store A** | **Store B** | **Store C** |
| **Charcoal** | 2 for $0.75 | $0.33 each | 4 for $1.40 |
| **Kneaded eraser** | $0.47 each | 3 for $1.50 | $0.51 each |
| **Charcoal paper** | 3 for $1.89 | $0.57 each | 2 for $1.36 |
| **Pastels** | $0.98 each | 2 for $1.80 | $0.92 each |

2. You need to buy all the supplies from the same store. At which store would you spend the least?

   **A** Store A
   **B** Store B
   **C** Store C
   **D** The cost is the same at each store.

3. **What if** you could go to more than one store? What is the least amount you could spend?

   **F** $4.53   **H** $4.77
   **G** $4.62   **J** $4.87

 **Mixed Applications**

4. On an average day, 450 cars pass through the toll plaza. Val says about 164,250 cars pass through the toll plaza in a year. Chuck says about 42,750 pass through the toll plaza in a year. Whose answer is reasonable? Explain.

5. ✎ **Write a problem** in which you need to make a decision that can be answered with information in the table above.

6. Use the diagram above. Al's balloon is not next to Maggie's. Clem's balloon is larger than Maggie's. Who has the striped balloon?

# Extra Practice

## Set A (pp. 166–167)

**Multiply each number by 10, by 100, and by 1,000.**

**1.** 0.7        **2.** 0.32        **3.** 0.003        **4.** 0.152

**ALGEBRA** Find the value of $n$.

**5.** $100 \times 0.1 = n$      **6.** $10 \times 5.643 = n$      **7.** $1,000 \times 0.9023 = n$

**8.** $10 \times n = 0.06$      **9.** $n \times 10 = 0.27$      **10.** $100 \times n = 0.45$

**11.** In 1910, it cost about $0.80 per week to educate a public school student in the United States. By 1920, the weekly cost had doubled. How much did it cost to educate a student for 1 week in 1920?

## Set B (pp. 168–169)

**Make a model to find the product.**

**1.** $0.6 \times 0.6$      **2.** $0.1 \times 0.8$      **3.** $0.5 \times 0.3$      **4.** $0.7 \times 0.3$

**Find the product.**

**5.** $0.6 \times 0.8$      **6.** $0.3 \times 0.8$      **7.** $0.9 \times 0.5$      **8.** $0.4 \times 0.9$

**9.** $0.2 \times 0.9$      **10.** $0.5 \times 0.4$      **11.** $0.2 \times 0.3$      **12.** $0.2 \times 0.2$

## Set C (pp. 170–173)

**Find the product. Estimate to check.**

**1.** $0.3 \times 14$      **2.** $0.5 \times 1,206$      **3.** $6.8 \times 4.5$      **4.** $7.25 \times 3.8$

**5.** $\begin{array}{r} 0.67 \\ \times\ \ \ 8 \\ \hline \end{array}$      **6.** $\begin{array}{r} 3.94 \\ \times 0.04 \\ \hline \end{array}$      **7.** $\begin{array}{r} 0.53 \\ \times\ \ 58 \\ \hline \end{array}$      **8.** $\begin{array}{r} 5.06 \\ \times\ \ 28 \\ \hline \end{array}$

**9.** Gustavo has a pumpkin with a mass of 4.8 kilograms. If 0.9 of its mass is water, how much of its mass is water? How much is not water?

**10.** Bernadette bought 2 loaves of bread at $0.97 each and a carton of milk for $1.18. How much did she spend?

## Set D (pp. 174–175)

**Find the product.**

**1.** $8 \times 0.006$      **2.** $0.03 \times 2$      **3.** $0.02 \times 4$      **4.** $7 \times 0.004$

**5.** $0.7 \times 0.07$      **6.** $0.025 \times 0.6$      **7.** $0.075 \times 0.9$      **8.** $0.5 \times 0.024$

# Review/Test

## ✓ CHECK VOCABULARY AND CONCEPTS

**Choose the best term from the box.**

greater than
less than
one tenth
one hundredth
one thousandth

1. 0.1 represents __?__ . (p. 164)

2. The product of 9 and 0.65 is __?__ 9. (p. 164)

3. 0.01 represents __?__ . (p. 164)

**Make a model to find the product.** (pp. 168–169)

4. $0.6 \times 5$      5. $0.51 \times 3$      6. $2 \times 0.25$      7. $0.82 \times 4$

## ✓ CHECK SKILLS

**Multiply each number by 10, by 100, and by 1,000.** (pp. 166–167)

8. 0.3      9. 0.64      10. 0.002      11. 0.0225

**Copy each exercise. Place the decimal point in each product.** (pp. 170–173)

12. $0.5 \times 0.5 = 25$      13. $1.6 \times 3.34 = 5344$      14. $0.152 \times 0.78 = 11856$

15. $0.28 \times 0.7 = 196$      16. $0.9 \times 2.186 = 19674$      17. $25.4 \times 0.92 = 23368$

**Find the product.** (pp. 174–175)

18. $6.50 \times 0.8$      19. $2.85 \times 22$      20. $4.15 \times 0.6$      21. $4.34 \times 0.3$

22. $0.62 \times 0.07$      23. $0.7 \times 0.1$      24. $0.4 \times 0.5$      25. $0.76 \times 65$

26. $\begin{array}{r} 0.96 \\ \times\ \ \ 5 \\ \hline \end{array}$   27. $\begin{array}{r} 7.62 \\ \times 0.08 \\ \hline \end{array}$   28. $\begin{array}{r} 0.9 \\ \times 0.09 \\ \hline \end{array}$   29. $\begin{array}{r} 3.96 \\ \times\ \ 28 \\ \hline \end{array}$

## ✓ CHECK PROBLEM SOLVING

**For 30–31, use the table.** (pp. 176–177)

30. Janet needs to mail a 1-oz letter. Today is Monday. What is the least amount she could spend and guarantee it will arrive by Wednesday?

31. Which service is the fastest? How much does it cost?

| SERVICE | DELIVERY SCHEDULE | RATE (in 2002) |
|---|---|---|
| First-Class Mail | varies | $0.37 for the first ounce, $0.23 for each additional ounce |
| Priority Mail | 2 days | $3.85 |
| Express Mail | next day | $13.65 |

32. Jorge earns $24.65 a week. How much does he earn in 12 weeks? (pp. 170–173)

33. What is the value of 100 quarters? of 1,000 quarters? (pp. 166–167)

# Getting Ready for FCAT

 **NUMBER SENSE, CONCEPTS, AND OPERATIONS**

1. Becky buys 10 one-way bus tickets each week to get to work and back home. How much does she spend each week on bus fare?

| BUS TICKETS | |
|---|---|
| One-Way Ticket | $ 0.95 |
| 20-Trip Commuter Booklet | $16.00 |

   A. $95.00        C. $9.50
   B. $10.95        D. $0.95

   **TIP** **Decide on a plan.** See item 2. This problem involves more than one step, since you need to find the cost of 40 one-way tickets and the cost of two 20-trip commuter booklets.

2. Look at the sign in Problem 1. In one month Becky buys 40 one-way tickets. How much will Becky save each month by buying two 20-trip commuter booklets?

   F. $3
   G. $6
   H. $32
   I. $38

3. **Explain It** Marisa read that a blue whale weighs 4.9 times as much as a humpback whale. A humpback whale weighs 26.5 tons. About how much does a blue whale weigh? Explain how you would use estimation to solve the problem.

4. A dipstick is used to check the oil level in a car. The distance between the two marks shown on the dipstick at the right represents 1 quart. How many cups of oil would be needed to increase the oil level from the ADD mark to the FULL mark?

   A. 2 cups        C. 6 cups
   B. 4 cups        D. 8 cups

5. Peter wants to frame the painting he just finished. What length of wood will he need for the frame?

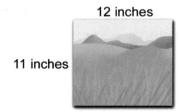

   12 inches
   11 inches

   F. 23 inches       H. 46 inches
   G. 36 inches       I. 132 inches

6. **Explain It** Shane's goal was to pick 25 pounds of tomatoes from his garden last week. The table shows the number of pounds of tomatoes he picked.

| TOMATOES PICKED | | | | | |
|---|---|---|---|---|---|
| Day | Mon | Tue | Wed | Thu | Fri |
| Weight (pounds) | 5.2 | 2.5 | 3.1 | 3.8 | 5.3 |

   Explain how to use estimation strategies to decide whether Shane reached his goal.

**ALGEBRAIC THINKING**

**7.** After writing this check, Mark had a balance of $85 in his account.

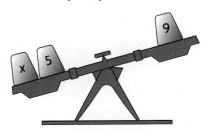

If *b* equals Mark's balance before he wrote the check, which equation could be used to find Mark's balance before he wrote the check?

**A.** $15b = 85$

**B.** $b - 15 = 85$

**C.** $15 - b = 85$

**D.** $85 - b = 15$

**8.** Leigh put weights on the balance to solve the inequality $x + 5 > 9$.

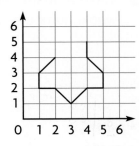

Which weights could she have used for *x*?

**F.** 1, 2, 3

**G.** 1, 2, 3, 4

**H.** 1, 2, 3, 4, 5, 6, 7, 8

**I.** 5, 6, 7, 8

**9. Explain It** Cara baked some brownies. She gave away 10 brownies, and then ate 3 of the remaining brownies. Let *n* represent the number of brownies Cara baked. Write an expression using *n* to show this. Explain your answer.

 **GEOMETRY AND SPATIAL SENSE**

**10.** Alana is making a symmetrical design on a grid. Which ordered pair names the point she should plot so she can complete the design?

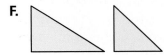

**A.** (5,2)     **C.** (2,4)

**B.** (2,5)     **D.** (4,5)

**11.** Which of the following pairs of figures appears to be congruent?

**F.**
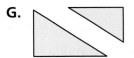

**G.**

**H.**
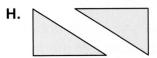

**I.**
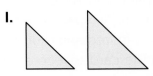

**12. Explain It** Fred drew a figure inside a circle. Name each radius he drew. Explain how you know.

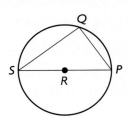

Chapter 8 **181**

# IT'S IN THE BAG

## Multiplication Trail

**PROJECT** Make a board game to practice multiplication of whole numbers and decimals.

### Materials

- 1 file folder
- Construction paper
- Markers or crayons
- Scissors, glue
- Card stock
- Spinner or number cube
- Game pieces

### Directions

1. Choose a theme for your multiplication game. Decorate the front of a file folder to match the theme. *(Picture A)*

2. Cut strips for the game path out of construction paper, and glue onto the inside of the folder. Draw the playing spaces on the path, and write *Start* and *Finish* on the appropriate spaces. All spaces should be the same size. Draw a $1\frac{1}{2}$-in. × 2-in. rectangle on the board to show where to place the cards. Decorate the folder around the path. *(Picture B)*

3. Cut $1\frac{1}{2}$-in. × 2-in. pieces of cardstock. On each card, write a multiplication problem using whole numbers or decimals. Place these cards face down on the rectangle you drew on the gameboard. *(Picture C)*

4. Write the directions for playing your game and glue them on the back of the file folder. Players can use paper and pencil to solve the problems and keep score.

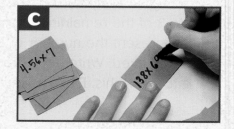

# Challenge

## Lattice Multiplication

Lattice multiplication is another way to find products.

Multiply. 295 × 731

### STEP 1

Draw a 3 × 3 lattice like the one shown. Write 295 across the top. Write 731 down the right side. Write an × above 731 as shown. Draw a diagonal line through each of the boxes.

### STEP 2

For each box, multiply the number at the top of that column by the number at the right of that row. Write the digits of the product above and below the diagonal. If the product has only one digit, write a zero above the diagonal.

### STEP 3

Add along the diagonals. Start with the lower right corner. If needed, regroup to the next diagonal. Write the sums along the bottom and left side of the lattice.

### STEP 4

Read the product by moving down the left side and across the bottom.

So, 295 × 731 = 215,645.

## Try It

**Use lattice multiplication to find the product.**

1. 124 × 562   2. 552 × 601   3. 759 × 106   4. 324 × 651   5. 944 × 293

6.  783      7.  342      8.  427      9.  135      10.  246
  × 504        × 175        × 899        × 975          × 806

# Study Guide and Review

## VOCABULARY

Choose the best term from the box.

> estimate
> factors
> multiples
> decimal
> product

1. All of the whole numbers that are products of the given whole number and another whole number are __?__. (p. 148)

2. To determine if an exact answer is reasonable, you can use a(n) __?__. (p. 156)

## STUDY AND SOLVE
### Chapter 7

**Estimate products.**

$43 \times 184$
$\downarrow \quad \downarrow$
$40 \times 200$

$4 \times 2 = 8 \leftarrow$ basic fact
$4 \times 20 = 80$
$40 \times 20 = 800$
$40 \times 200 = 8,000$   So, $43 \times 184$ is about 8,000.

**Estimate the product.** (pp. 148–149)

3. $32 \times 145$

4. $7 \times 861$

5. $56 \times 724$

6. $5,387 \times 31$

7. $\begin{array}{r} 864 \\ \times\ 43 \end{array}$    8. $\begin{array}{r} 7,613 \\ \times\ 68 \end{array}$

**Multiply by 1-digit and 2-digit numbers.**

$\begin{array}{r} 642 \\ \times 23 \\ \hline 1\,926 \\ +12\,840 \\ \hline 14,766 \end{array}$  Multiply by the ones.
Multiply by the tens.
Add the partial products.

So, $642 \times 23$ is 14,766.

**Find the product.** (pp. 150–151, 152–153)

9. $\begin{array}{r} 12,354 \\ \times\ 4 \end{array}$  10. $\begin{array}{r} 248,021 \\ \times\ 5 \end{array}$  11. $\begin{array}{r} 617,324 \\ \times\ 6 \end{array}$

12. $\begin{array}{r} 626 \\ \times 38 \end{array}$  13. $\begin{array}{r} 597 \\ \times 54 \end{array}$  14. $\begin{array}{r} 2,847 \\ \times\ 18 \end{array}$

15. $59,702 \times 8$   16. $10,287 \times 9$

17. $24,984 \times 32$   18. $58,701 \times 12$

**Multiply greater numbers.**

$\begin{array}{r} 375 \\ \times 149 \\ \hline 3\,375 \\ 15\,000 \\ +37\,500 \\ \hline 55,875 \end{array}$  Multiply by the ones.
Multiply by the tens.
Multiply by the hundreds.
Add the partial products.

So, $375 \times 149$ is 55,875.

**Find the product.** (pp. 154–155)

19. $\begin{array}{r} 539 \\ \times 843 \end{array}$  20. $\begin{array}{r} 792 \\ \times 154 \end{array}$  21. $\begin{array}{r} 4,703 \\ \times\ 238 \end{array}$

22. $6,178 \times 297$   23. $5,087 \times 964$

24. $4,532 \times 102$   25. $5,908 \times 309$

## Chapter 8

**Use mental math and patterns to multiply decimals.**

> Multiply 0.32 by 10, 100, and 1,000.
>
> 0.32 × 10 = 3.2
> 0.32 × 100 = 32
> 0.32 × 1,000 = 320

**Multiply decimals.**

> 35.48 × 0.72    Multiply as with whole numbers. Find the total number of decimal places in the factors. Place the decimal point that number of places from the right in the product.
>
> 35.48 ←2 decimal places in the factor
> × 0.72 ←2 decimal places in the factor
> 7096
> + 24 8360
> 25.5456 ←2 + 2, or 4 decimal places in the product

**Multiply each number by 10, 100, and 1,000.** (pp. 166–167)

26. 0.6            27. 0.82

28. 0.003          29. 0.213

30. 3.145          31. 0.014

**Find the product.** (pp. 168–175)

32. 0.6 × 0.8      33. 0.4 × 0.7

34. 0.08 × 8       35. 7 × 0.09

36. $0.76 × 4      37. $0.94 × 0.5

38.   0.05         39.   1.50
    ×    4             × 2.5

40.   0.007        41.   1.006
    ×     2             ×     8

42.   2.506        43.   84.11
    × 0.37             × 0.12

44.   $25.68       45.   $3.99
    ×    0.5            ×    6

46.      47        47.   6.03
    × 0.05             × 0.34

48.   20.09        49.   9.8
    ×     17            ×0.4

## PROBLEM SOLVING PRACTICE

**Solve.** (pp. 156–157; 176–177)

50. Ted works for a magazine that prints 712,245 copies each week. He calculates that 37,036,740 copies are printed each year. Is this reasonable? Explain.

51. Jiffy Market sells 12 cans of juice for $4.10. C&G Store sells each can of juice for $0.35. Which store has the better price for 12 cans of juice?

# PERFORMANCE ASSESSMENT

## TASK A • AT THE STADIUM

The diagram shows the football stadium at City College.

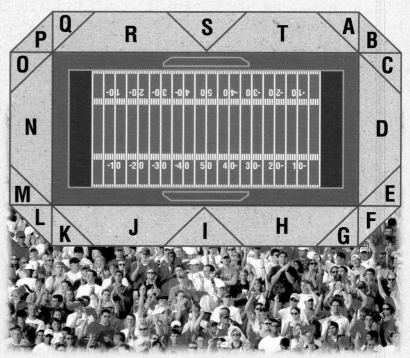

a. There are 615 seats in section A. What would be a good estimate for the number of seats in section D?

b. At the next football game, 30,000 fans are expected. How can you determine if there are enough seats?

c. The tickets cost $5 and $10. The stadium operators want to take in at least $200,000 on the sale of tickets for a full stadium. How many seats should sell for $10, and how many should sell for $5?

## TASK B • JEWELRY STORE

Suni uses glass beads to make jewelry. The beads come in six colors. Each color is a different size.

| Glass Beads | |
| --- | --- |
| Color | Size (in cm) |
| red | 1.2 |
| blue | 0.5 |
| green | 0.7 |
| yellow | 0.4 |
| orange | 1.3 |
| purple | 0.6 |

a. Design a bracelet using no fewer than 10 and no more than 20 beads. Include beads of at least two colors. Find the length of the bracelet.

b. Suni sells her bracelets and necklaces for $0.95 per centimeter. How much would the bracelet you designed cost?

c. Suni designs a necklace of 40 beads with red, orange, and yellow colors. What could be the length of the necklace?

# Technology Linkup

## Calculator • Multiplication Patterns

You can use a calculator to extend number patterns involving operations with whole numbers and decimals.

**Example** The numbers in the multiplication pattern below are increasing. What are the next three numbers in the pattern?

76; 304; 1,216; 4,864; ▓; ▓; ▓

You can divide the first two numbers in the pattern to find a multiplication rule.

**3 0 4 ÷ 7 6 =** | = 4.

So, a rule for the pattern is multiply by 4.

You can use the constant function on a calculator to extend a pattern.

- Press 4 ✕ ✕ .
  This sets 4 as the constant value for multiplying each number in the pattern. The *K* on the display shows that the value and operation have been set.

- Enter 4,864 and press = three times to find the next three numbers in the pattern.

So, the next three numbers in the pattern are 19,456; 77,824; and 311,296.

| Press | Display |
|---|---|
| 4 ✕ ✕ | = 4.X |
| 4864 = | K 19'456.X |
| = | K 77'824.X |
| = | K 311'296.X |

## Practice and Problem Solving

For 1–4, tell whether the pattern is increasing or decreasing. Find a rule. Use the rule and a calculator to find the next three numbers in the pattern.

**1.** 42; 252; 1,512; 9,072; ▓; ▓; ▓

**2.** 12; 15.6; 20.28; 26.364; ▓; ▓; ▓

**3.** 54; 32.4; 19.44; 11.664; ▓; ▓; ▓

**4.** 16.8; 134.4; 1,075.2; 8,601.6; ▓; ▓; ▓

**GO ON-LINE**

**Multimedia Math Glossary** www.harcourtschool.com/mathglossary

**Vocabulary Power** Using the Multimedia Math Glossary, tell how factors and products are related. Give an example to support your answer.

# PROBLEM SOLVING IN FLORIDA

Zebra longwing

## BUTTERFLY WORLD

Butterfly World, located near Fort Lauderdale, is the largest single butterfly habitat in the world. There you can walk through screened aviaries and enjoy the flight of thousands of live butterflies.

Fort Lauderdale

1. About 80 butterfly species from around the world are found at Butterfly World. In one aviary there are about 90 times as many butterflies as the number of species. About how many butterflies are in the aviary?

2. If Butterfly World is open from 9 A.M. to 5 P.M. six days a week and from 1 P.M. to 5 P.M. on Sundays, how many hours is Butterfly World open each week?

3. One of the smallest butterflies is the pygmy blue. It has a wingspan of about 0.375 inch. The largest butterfly has a wingspan more than 30 times as great. About how wide is the wingspan of the largest butterfly?

▼ Malachite

### For 4–6, use the table.

4. The Blackwells live in Tampa. If they leave home at 9 A.M. and drive an average of 55 miles per hour, will they arrive at Butterfly World by 1:30 P.M.? Explain how you know.

5. Josh drove round-trip from Naples to Butterfly World. Jackie drove from Orlando to Butterfly World and then to Miami. Who drove farther? How much farther?

6. ✎ **Write a problem** that can be solved using multiplication with the data in the table. Solve the problem.

| DISTANCE FROM FLORIDA CITIES TO BUTTERFLY WORLD | |
|---|---|
| **City** | **Distance (in miles)** |
| Jacksonville | 309.0 |
| Miami | 38.2 |
| Naples | 117.1 |
| Orlando | 198.2 |
| Tampa | 234.4 |

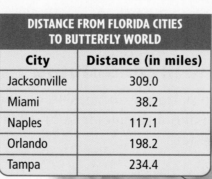

Birdwing

Paradise tanager

# HUMMINGBIRDS

In another aviary at Butterfly World you will find the largest live collection of hummingbirds in the world as well as tanagers. Hummingbirds can fly right, left, up, down, backward, and upside down.

Streamertail hummingbird

1. Hummingbird wings beat about 60 times a second. How many times do they beat in a minute? in an hour?

2. The average speed of a hummingbird during flight is 35 miles per hour. At this speed, how far can a hummingbird travel in 3.5 hours?

3. On average, male hummingbirds live 2.5 years. Female hummingbirds live 1.4 times as long. On average, how long do females live?

4. The United States has 24 recognized species of hummingbirds. There are more than 14 times this number of species in the world. How many species are there in the world?

5. Hummingbirds sip the nectar from tubular flowers with their long tongues, which move into and out of a flower about 13 times per second. How many times do their tongues move into and out of a flower in 0.5 minute?

6. A hummingbird's heart beats about 50 beats per minute during the night and about 25 times as many times per minute during the day. About how many times per minute does a hummingbird's heart beat during the day?

# Divide by 1-Digit Divisors

**≡FAST FACT •**

## SOCIAL STUDIES

Since history was first recorded, beads have been used for trade, adornment, and decoration. Beads were also used in ceremonies and to confirm treaties.

## PROBLEM SOLVING

The table shows the number of beads of various sizes that are needed to string a bracelet approximately 7 inches long. For each bead size, about how many beads are needed for 1 inch?

| BEADS PER 7-INCH BRACELET | |
|---|---|
| **Bead Size** | **Number of Beads** |
| 2 mm | 91 |
| 3 mm | 56 |
| 4 mm | 42 |
| 6 mm | 28 |
| 8 mm | 21 |

# CHECK WHAT YOU KNOW

Use this page to help you review and remember
important skills needed for Chapter 9.

## ESTIMATE QUOTIENTS
Estimate the quotients.

1. $3\overline{)260}$
2. $9\overline{)830}$
3. $8\overline{)580}$
4. $6\overline{)400}$

5. $6\overline{)290}$
6. $7\overline{)450}$
7. $4\overline{)340}$
8. $8\overline{)650}$

9. $640 \div 7$
10. $380 \div 9$
11. $470 \div 3$
12. $87 \div 9$

13. $270 \div 4$
14. $58 \div 4$
15. $190 \div 3$
16. $510 \div 8$

## DIVIDE 2-DIGIT NUMBERS
Divide.

17. $3\overline{)85}$
18. $7\overline{)93}$
19. $2\overline{)61}$
20. $6\overline{)92}$
21. $6\overline{)29}$

22. $4\overline{)83}$
23. $8\overline{)54}$
24. $3\overline{)81}$
25. $9\overline{)95}$
26. $8\overline{)36}$

27. $7\overline{)84}$
28. $2\overline{)58}$
29. $6\overline{)44}$
30. $8\overline{)97}$
31. $5\overline{)52}$

# VOCABULARY POWER

### REVIEW

**quotient** [kwō′shənt] *noun*

A *quotient* is the answer in a division
problem. *Quotient* comes from the Latin
root word *quot*, which means "how many."
Find how many equal groups of 9 can
be made from 450.

### PREVIEW

**compatible numbers**

www.harcourtschool.com/mathglossary

# Estimate Quotients

**Quick Review**

**1.** 28 ÷ 7    **2.** 48 ÷ 8
**3.** 20 ÷ 4    **4.** 36 ÷ 6
**5.** 24 ÷ 3

**VOCABULARY**

compatible numbers

## ▶ Learn

**CLOSE ENCOUNTERS** Musa Manarov is a famous Soviet cosmonaut who spent a total of 541 days in space during two space flights. About how many weeks did Manarov spend in space?

Estimate.   541 ÷ 7    7)541

**Compatible numbers** are numbers that are easy to compute mentally. Compatible numbers for 7 are multiples of 7, such as 14, 21, 28, 35, 42, 49, and 56.

Use 2 sets of compatible numbers to estimate 541 ÷ 7.

541 ÷ 7    or  541 ÷ 7    **Think:** 541 is between
490 ÷ 7 = 70    560 ÷ 7 = 80    490 and 560. So, use 490 and 560 as dividends.

So, Manarov spent between 70 and 80 weeks in space.

**MATH IDEA** To estimate quotients, use compatible numbers.

▲ **Soyuz TM-4:** Cosmonauts Levchenko, Manarov, and Titov

### Examples

**A** Estimate 4,126 ÷ 8.

**Think:** 40 is close to 41 and is a multiple of 8.

4,126 ÷ 8
4,000 ÷ 8 = 500

So, 4,126 ÷ 8 is about 500.

**B** Estimate 23,078 ÷ 4.

**Think:** 24 is close to 23 and is a multiple of 4.

23,078 ÷ 4
24,000 ÷ 4 = 6,000

So, 23,078 ÷ 4 is about 6,000.

**C** Estimate 462,028 ÷ 7.

**Think:** 49 is close to 46 and is a multiple of 7.

462,028 ÷ 7
490,000 ÷ 7 = 70,000

So, 462,028 ÷ 7 is about 70,000.

• **What if** you use two sets of compatible numbers, 180 ÷ 6 and 240 ÷ 6, to estimate 239 ÷ 6? Which estimate will be closer to the exact answer? Explain.

## Check

1. **Explain** how compatible numbers help you estimate quotients. Give an example.

**Estimate the quotient. Tell what compatible numbers you used.**

2. $5\overline{)263}$

3. $7\overline{)1,502}$

4. $8\overline{)1,389}$

5. $9\overline{)61,409}$

6. $11,583 \div 2$

7. $451,133 \div 9$

8. $337,028 \div 4$

9. $58,074 \div 8$

## Practice and Problem Solving  (Extra Practice, page 202, Set A)

**Estimate the quotient. Tell what compatible numbers you used.**

10. $8\overline{)316}$

11. $9\overline{)5,536}$

12. $4\overline{)3,306}$

13. $7\overline{)34,072}$

14. $372 \div 6$

15. $125,703 \div 6$

16. $78,305 \div 7$

17. $2,500,823 \div 4$

**Estimate the quotient, using two sets of compatible numbers.**

18. $8,219 \div 9$

19. $25,316 \div 7$

20. $50,068 \div 4$

21. $172,388 \div 5$

22. $6,358 \div 8$

23. $71,269 \div 9$

24. $1,369,168 \div 5$

25. $800,625 \div 9$

**USE DATA  For 26–28, use the table.**

26. About how many Earth weeks does it take Mars to complete one revolution around the sun?

27. Estimate how many Earth weeks it takes Pluto to complete one revolution around the sun.

28. About how many times does Mercury revolve around the sun during one Earth revolution?

| PLANET REVOLUTIONS AROUND THE SUN (based on Earth days) | |
|---|---|
| **Planet** | **Number of Days** |
| Mars | 687 |
| Mercury | 88 |
| Pluto | 90,465 |

29. **REASONING**   When I am divided by 4, the quotient has two digits and the remainder is 0. When I am divided by 6, the quotient has one digit and the remainder is 0. My ones digit is 8. What number am I?

▲ Mars

## Getting Ready for FCAT

30. Mr. Leone is driving from Tallahassee to Ft. Pierce. Which is the best estimate of the speed he should drive in order to reach Ft. Pierce in 7 hours?

  A. 30 miles per hour       C. 50 miles per hour

  B. 40 miles per hour       D. 60 miles per hour

| Welcome to Tallahassee | |
|---|---|
| St. Augustine | 205 miles |
| Sarasota | 289 miles |
| Ft. Pierce | 354 miles |
| West Palm Beach | 412 miles |

FCAT TESTED   SSS/GLEs MA.A.4.2.1.5.1. Chooses, describes, and explains estimation strategies used to determine the reasonableness of solutions to real-world problems. *also* MA.A.3.2.1.5.3

Chapter 9   **193**

# Divide 3-Digit Dividends

▶ **Learn**

**WEIGHT LOSS**   The moon's weaker gravity causes things to weigh one-sixth as much on the moon as they weigh on Earth. Suppose some of the rocks brought back from the moon weigh 102 pounds on Earth. How much did they weigh on the moon?

◀ Between 1969 and 1972, Apollo missions brought back 382 kg (843 lb) of lunar rocks and soil from the moon's surface.

**One Way** Use estimation to place the first digit in the quotient.

Find $102 \div 6$.

**STEP 1**

Estimate.

Think: $6\overline{)60}$ $\overset{10}{}$  or  $6\overline{)120}$ $\overset{20}{}$

$6\overline{)102}$ $\overset{\blacksquare}{}$  So, place the first digit in the tens place.

**STEP 2**

Divide the 10 tens.

$\begin{array}{r} 1 \\ 6\overline{)102} \\ -\ 6 \\ \hline 4 \end{array}$

Divide. $6\overline{)10}$
Multiply. $6 \times 1$
Subtract. $10 - 6$
Compare. $4 < 6$

**STEP 3**

Bring down the 2 ones. Divide the 42 ones.

$\begin{array}{r} 17 \\ 6\overline{)102} \\ -\ 6\downarrow \\ \hline 42 \\ -42 \\ \hline 0 \end{array}$

Divide. $6\overline{)42}$
Multiply. $6 \times 7$
Subtract. $42 - 42$
Compare. $0 < 6$

So, the rocks weighed 17 pounds on the moon.

**Another Way** Use place value to place the first digit.

Find $893 \div 9$.

**STEP 1**

Look at the hundreds.

$9\overline{)893}$  $8 < 9$, so look at the tens.

$9\overline{)893}$ $\overset{\blacksquare}{}$  $89 > 9$, so use 89 tens. Place the first digit in the tens place.

**STEP 2**

Divide the 89 tens.

$\begin{array}{r} 9 \\ 9\overline{)893} \\ -81 \\ \hline 8 \end{array}$

Divide.
Multiply.
Subtract.
Compare.

**STEP 3**

Bring down the 3 ones. Divide the 83 ones.

$\begin{array}{r} 99\ \text{r2} \\ 9\overline{)893} \\ -81\downarrow \\ \hline 83 \\ -81 \\ \hline 2 \end{array}$

Divide.
Multiply.
Subtract.
Compare.

**CHECK ✓**

Multiply the quotient by the divisor. Then add the remainder.

$\begin{array}{r} 99 \\ \times\ 9 \\ \hline 891 \\ +\ 2 \\ \hline 893 \end{array}$ ← dividend

## ▶ Check

**1. Explain** how you can tell without dividing whether the quotient of 539 ÷ 6 will have 2 digits or 3.

**Name the position of the first digit of the quotient.**

**2.** 9)117  **3.** 5)213  **4.** 2)472  **5.** 6)917  **6.** 9)526

## ▶ Practice and Problem Solving    Extra Practice, page 202, Set B

**Name the position of the first digit of the quotient.**

**7.** 8)504  **8.** 2)724  **9.** 4)183  **10.** 7)857  **11.** 6)176

**Divide.**

**12.** 2)408  **13.** 7)489  **14.** 5)516  **15.** 4)844  **16.** 8)246

**17.** 8)113  **18.** 9)912  **19.** 3)607  **20.** 2)526  **21.** 4)223

**22.** 348 ÷ 8  **23.** 905 ÷ 5  **24.** 124 ÷ 6  **25.** 414 ÷ 5  **26.** 807 ÷ 4

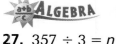 **Find the value of $n$.**

**27.** 357 ÷ 3 = $n$  **28.** $n$ ÷ 5 = 35 r4  **29.** $n$ ÷ 7 = 47 r3  **30.** 269 ÷ $n$ = 134 r1

**USE DATA**  For 31–32, use the table.

**31.** If there are 7 crew members, how many servings of each food type does each crew member receive? Copy and complete the table.

**32.** Which food type has the most servings per crew member?

| SPACE FLIGHT FOOD (based on a standard 7-day shuttle menu) | | |
|---|---|---|
| Food Type | Number of Servings | Servings Per Crew Member |
| Rehydratable Beverage | 203 | ■ |
| Fresh Food | 175 | ■ |
| Rehydratable Food | 238 | ■ |

**33.** The weight allowed for food is 3.8 pounds per crew member per day. How does the weight of the food supply for 7 crew members for 6 days compare to the weight for 6 crew members for 7 days?

**34. ≡FAST FACT • SCIENCE** The diameter of the moon, 2,160 miles, is 2 times as great as the radius. Find the radius of the moon.

## Getting Ready for ★FCAT

**35.** An arch on a parade float is made with 258 balloons. There are an equal number of balloons in 6 different colors. How many balloons of each color are there?

**A.** 33   **C.** 52
**B.** 43   **D.** 63

FCAT TESTED   SSS/GLEs MA.A.3.2.3.5.1 Solves real-world problems involving addition, subtraction, multiplication, and division of whole numbers . . . using an appropriate method. *also* MA.A.3.2.1.5.4

Chapter 9  **195**

# Zeros in Division

## Learn

**LOONY TUNES**  Mr. Knowles owns 4 music stores. He ordered 432 kazoos. He wants each store to have the same number of kazoos. How many will each store receive?

### Example

Divide.    $432 \div 4$    4)432

Estimate.    $440 \div 4 = 110$ ← Use compatible numbers.

**STEP 1**

Divide the 4 hundreds.

**Think:** 4 hundreds can be divided by 4. So, place the first digit in the hundreds place in the quotient.

```
   1
4)432   Divide.
 -4     Multiply.
  0     Subtract.
        Compare. 0 < 4
```

**STEP 2**

Bring down the tens. Divide the 3 tens.

**Think:** Since 4 > 3, write 0 in the quotient.

```
  10
4)432   Divide.
 -4↓    Multiply.
   3    Subtract.
  -0    Compare. 3 < 4
   3
```

**STEP 3**

Bring down the ones. Divide the 32 ones.

**Think:** $32 \div 4 = 8$

```
  108
4)432   Divide.
 -4  |  Multiply.
   3    Subtract.
  -0↓   Compare. 0 < 4
   32
  -32
    0
```

Since 108 is close to the estimate of 110, the answer is reasonable. So, each store will receive 108 kazoos.

• What happens to your answer if you forget to write the zero in the quotient?

**MATH IDEA**  In division, if the divisor is greater than the number to be divided, place a zero in the quotient.

## Check

1. **Explain** how you decide when to write a zero in the quotient. Give an example.

**Divide. Estimate to check.**

**2.** $5\overline{)250}$          **3.** $7\overline{)73}$          **4.** $4\overline{)801}$

## Practice and Problem Solving     Extra Practice, page 202, Set C

**Divide. Estimate to check.**

**5.** $9\overline{)87}$          **6.** $7\overline{)440}$          **7.** $4\overline{)82}$          **8.** $5\overline{)726}$          **9.** $6\overline{)91}$

**10.** $3\overline{)309}$          **11.** $5\overline{)54}$          **12.** $6\overline{)635}$          **13.** $4\overline{)816}$          **14.** $3\overline{)908}$

**15.** $6\overline{)612}$          **16.** $8\overline{)255}$          **17.** $5\overline{)525}$          **18.** $6\overline{)624}$          **19.** $7\overline{)745}$

**20.** $61 \div 2$          **21.** $528 \div 9$          **22.** $744 \div 8$          **23.** $606 \div 3$          **24.** $401 \div 5$

**25.** $122 \div 4$          **26.** $504 \div 5$          **27.** $824 \div 8$          **28.** $631 \div 6$          **29.** $801 \div 2$

**ALGEBRA** **Find the value of *n*.**

**30.** $305 \div 5 = n$          **31.** $n \div 8 = 110 \text{ r}7$          **32.** $n \div 7 = 101 \text{ r}3$          **33.** $209 \div n = 104 \text{ r}1$

**ALGEBRA** **Complete each table and write a division rule.**

**34.**

| Input, *n* | 49 | 107 | 239 | 564 |
|---|---|---|---|---|
| Output | 7 | 15 r2 | ■ | ■ |

**35.**

| Input, *n* | 83 | ■ | 404 | 412 |
|---|---|---|---|---|
| Output | 20 r3 | 24 r3 | 101 | ■ |

**36.** Felipe's family is planning to see a "Kazoo Band" show at a festival 306 miles away. It takes them 6 hours to drive there. On average, how many miles do they drive each hour?

**37.** At the "Kazoo Band" shows, everyone in the audience is given a kazoo for the grand finale. There were 357 adults and 529 children at the first show and 644 adults and 496 children at the second show. Did more adults or more children attend the shows? How many more?

**38.** **REASONING** Are there any zeros in the quotient $884 \div 4$? How can you tell without dividing?

**39.** **? What's the Error?** Jackie says $6 \div 6$ equals 1, so $606 \div 6$ equals 11. Find her error and write the correct division sentence.

## Getting Ready for FCAT

**40.** Janie ordered 432 T-shirts for the Walk for Your Heart Walk-a-thon. The T-shirts arrived in 4 boxes, each containing the same number of shirts. How many T-shirts were in each box?

   **A.** 18          **C.** 118
   **B.** 108          **D.** 180

# LESSON 4

# Choose a Method

## ▶ Learn

**DRAMATIC PARTS**  The Sunrise Drama Club has 1,240 beads to make necklaces for the costumes for the school play. If there are 4 beads to an inch, how long would a single strand of all the beads be?

**Use Mental Math**  Divide. 1,240 ÷ 4

Think:  1,240 = 1,200 + 40

$1,200 ÷ 4 = 300$    $40 ÷ 4 = 10$    $300 + 10 = 310$

So, a single strand would be 310 inches long.

Suppose the beads are used to make 6 necklaces that are equal in length. How many beads will be in each necklace?

**Use a Calculator**  Divide. 1,240 ÷ 6

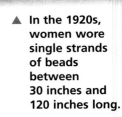

| 1 | 2 | 4 | 0 | ÷R | 6 | = |   *206 R4*   |

So, each necklace will have 206 beads; there will be 4 beads left over.

▲ In the 1920s, women wore single strands of beads between 30 inches and 120 inches long.

**Use Paper and Pencil**  For 4-digit numbers, use the same steps that you used for dividing 3-digit numbers. Just repeat the steps for all the digits.

## Example

**STEP 1**

The first digit will be in the hundreds place.

$$\begin{array}{r} 2 \\ 6\overline{)1{,}240} \\ -1\,2 \\ \hline 0 \end{array}$$

Divide.
Multiply.
Subtract.
Compare.
0 < 6

**STEP 2**

Bring down the 4 tens. Divide the 4 tens.

$$\begin{array}{r} 20 \\ 6\overline{)1{,}240} \\ -1\,2\downarrow \\ \hline 04 \\ -0 \\ \hline 4 \end{array}$$

Divide.
Multiply.
Subtract.
Compare.
4 < 6

**STEP 3**

Bring down the 0 ones. Divide the 40 ones.

$$\begin{array}{r} 206 \text{ r4} \\ 6\overline{)1{,}240} \\ -1\,2\phantom{\downarrow} \\ \hline 04\phantom{|} \\ -0\downarrow \\ \hline 40 \\ -36 \\ \hline 4 \end{array}$$

Divide.
Multiply.
Subtract.
Compare.
4 < 6

**MATH IDEA**  You can find a quotient by using mental math, paper and pencil, or a calculator. Choose the method that works best with the numbers in the problem.

**198**

**Technology Link**

More Practice: Harcourt Mega Math The Number Games, *Up, Up, & Array*, Level O

1. **Explain** when you might choose mental math instead of paper and pencil.

**Divide. Choose mental math, paper and pencil, or a calculator.**

2. $3\overline{)2,424}$    3. $8,100 \div 4$    4. $2\overline{)8,345}$    5. $19,145 \div 5$

▶ **Practice and Problem Solving**   Extra Practice, page 202, Set D

**Divide. Choose mental math, paper and pencil, or a calculator.**

6. $6\overline{)4,200}$    7. $3\overline{)3,012}$    8. $6\overline{)6,459}$    9. $8\overline{)3,348}$

10. $8\overline{)4,762}$    11. $2\overline{)3,760}$    12. $4\overline{)11,286}$    13. $7\overline{)700,000}$

14. $4,294 \div 3$    15. $5,407 \div 7$    16. $32,700 \div 4$    17. $4,000,000 \div 5$

18. $9,088 \div 3$    19. $12,422 \div 6$    20. $45,090 \div 9$    21. $74,608 \div 6$

**USE DATA**   For 22–23, use the circle graph.

22. The Booster Club donates money for costumes and props each year. If the Booster Club matches each dollar in the budget for costumes and props, how much money will the Sunrise Drama Club have for costumes and props?

23. The club members plan to print 28,620 programs. If they print an equal number for each of 4 plays, how many will they print for 1 play? How much money is budgeted per play for printing programs?

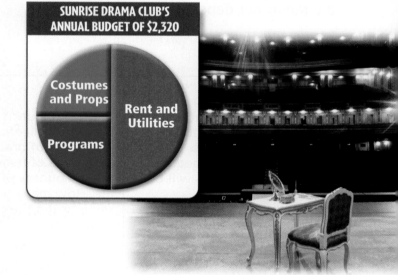

**SUNRISE DRAMA CLUB'S ANNUAL BUDGET OF $2,320**

Costumes and Props

Rent and Utilities

Programs

24. **? What's the Question?**   An embossing machine stamps 20 sheets of paper in one minute. The answer is 300 sheets.

25. **Vocabulary Power**   The word *calculator* has the suffix *-or*. When this suffix is attached to a word, it means that a person (or thing) does something. What other words contain the suffix *-or*?

▬ **Getting Ready for FCAT** ▬

26. The O'Brien family took a vacation in Orlando for 8 nights. The total cost of the hotel was $1,272. What was the cost of the hotel for each night?

    **A.** $159      **B.** $169      **C.** $179      **D.** $189

| ORLANDO BEST HOTEL |
|---|
| Mr. and Mrs. O'Brien |
| 8 Nights |
| Total: $1,272 |

FCAT TESTED   SSS/GLEs MA.A.3.2.3.5.1 Solves real-world problems involving addition, subtraction, multiplication, and division of whole numbers . . . using an appropriate method (for example, mental math, pencil and paper, calculator). *also* MA.A.1.2.3.5.1

**Chapter 9   199**

# Problem Solving Skill
## Interpret the Remainder

UNDERSTAND 〉 PLAN 〉 SOLVE 〉 CHECK

**FIGURE IT OUT** Determine how the remainder was used to solve each of the problems below. The situation determines when to drop the remainder, round the quotient to the next greater number, or use the remainder as a part of the answer.

**MATH IDEA** When you solve a division problem with a remainder, the way you interpret the remainder depends on the situation.

## Examples

**A**

There are 1,853 athletes and parents signed up for a sports picnic. Each table will seat 6 people. How many tables will be needed?

```
     308 r5
6)1,853
  −18
    05
   − 0
    53
   −48
     5
```

Since 308 tables will not be enough to seat everyone, 309 tables will be needed.

**B**

Erik made punch with 3 ounces of lemon juice, 32 ounces of orange juice, 32 ounces of lemonade, and 64 ounces of ginger ale. How many 6-ounce servings did the punch recipe make?

```
              21 r5
   3  → 6)131
  32     −12
  32      11
 +64     − 6
 131←     5
```

It made 21 six-ounce servings. The 5 ounces left over are not enough for another 6-ounce serving.

**C**

Mrs. Clarke brought a 145-inch rope to demonstrate tying knots. She divided the rope into 4 pieces of equal length. How long was each piece of rope?

Write the remainder as a fraction.

```
    36¼  ← Use the
4)145      remainder as
 −12       the numerator
  25       and the
 −24       divisor as the
   1       denominator.
```

So, each piece of rope was $36\frac{1}{4}$ inches long.

## Talk About It

• Explain how the remainder was used to answer Examples A–C.

• Explain why a fractional remainder was appropriate for Example C, but not for Examples A or B.

**200**

**Solve and then explain how you interpreted the remainder.**

1. Jake has 172 books to display on 5 shelves in the bookstore. If Jake places an equal number of books on each shelf, what is the maximum number of books on each? How many books will be left over?

2. The nursery assistant has 124 roses to arrange in vases. There are 18 vases on the shelves. Will there be enough roses for each vase to have 7 roses in it?

**USE DATA** Use the table. At the concession stand, the popcorn machine pops 80 cups of popcorn at a time.

| BAGS OF POPCORN | |
|---|---|
| **Size** | **Amount per serving** |
| Large | 4 cups |
| Jumbo | 6 cups |

3. Marci calculated that she could fill 13 jumbo popcorn bags from one batch. Explain how she interpreted the remainder.
   A There is no remainder.
   B She dropped the remainder.
   C She rounded the quotient.
   D She used the remainder.

4. Marci sold 8 jumbo bags. Does she have enough popcorn left to fill 9 large popcorn bags? How many large bags can she fill?
   F no; 8 bags
   G no; 3 bags
   H yes; 10 bags
   J yes; 9 bags

## Mixed Applications

5. Elena has a $20 bill. She buys 5 cookies for $2.00 each, a cup of tea for $1.50, and a sandwich for $2.35. How much change should she get?

6. Chiano bought a 50-page photo album. Each page holds 6 photos. She took 288 photos on her trip. Will the album hold all of her photos? Explain.

7. Mr. Jones is planning for buses for the school trip. A total of 105 students signed up. If each bus holds 42 students, will 2 buses be enough for the trip? Explain.

8. **PATTERNS** Carla is designing a necklace. She plans to repeat the pattern 1 red bead, 1 blue bead, and 1 green bead until she strings a total of 60 beads. What color will the 31st bead be?

9. Brian's model train track is 4 times as long as Mario's track. Brian's track is 1,247 inches long. How long is Mario's track?

10. ✎ **Write three problems** in which the remainder is used in three different ways.

# Extra Practice

## Set A (pp. 192–193)

**Estimate the quotient. Tell what compatible numbers you used.**

1. $8\overline{)902}$
2. $7\overline{)2,936}$
3. $9\overline{)1,989}$
4. $7\overline{)51,409}$
5. $7\overline{)313,084}$

**Estimate the quotient, using two sets of compatible numbers.**

6. $2,958 \div 3$
7. $46,133 \div 5$
8. $172,506 \div 8$
9. $217,028 \div 2$

10. Maria wants to put 468 stickers into a book. If each page gets 8 stickers, about how many pages will she need?

## Set B (pp. 194–195)

**Name the position of the first digit of the quotient.**

1. $2\overline{)417}$
2. $5\overline{)213}$
3. $3\overline{)697}$
4. $6\overline{)489}$
5. $2\overline{)526}$

**Divide.**

6. $4\overline{)448}$
7. $5\overline{)615}$
8. $6\overline{)212}$
9. $7\overline{)488}$
10. $8\overline{)568}$

11. Bailey and his family went on a 108-mile hiking trip in the mountains. They hiked 9 miles each day. How many days did they hike?

## Set C (pp. 196–197)

**Divide. Estimate to check.**

1. $7\overline{)714}$
2. $5\overline{)54}$
3. $9\overline{)936}$
4. $9\overline{)725}$
5. $8\overline{)167}$
6. $3\overline{)92}$
7. $2\overline{)815}$
8. $6\overline{)628}$
9. $8\overline{)105}$
10. $7\overline{)425}$

11. Tickets to the school basketball game cost $5. If the sale of tickets brought in $2,040, how many tickets were sold?

## Set D (pp. 198–199)

**Divide. Choose mental math, paper and pencil, or a calculator.**

1. $7\overline{)4,900}$
2. $3\overline{)4,005}$
3. $8\overline{)32,880}$
4. $5\overline{)26,253}$
5. $6\overline{)36,305}$
6. $3\overline{)75,249}$
7. $2\overline{)3,269}$
8. $4\overline{)8,400,000}$

9. The Tropical Tour Company has 2,375 programs to distribute equally among its 7 resort hotels. How many programs will each resort receive?

# Review/Test

 **CHECK VOCABULARY AND CONCEPTS**

Choose the best term from the box.

> compatible numbers
> place value
> remainder
> zero

1. To decide where to place the first digit in the quotient, you can estimate or use __?__. (p. 194)

2. Numbers that are close to the actual numbers and are easy to compute mentally are __?__. (p. 192)

3. The amount left over when you find a quotient is called the __?__. (p. 200)

 **CHECK SKILLS**

Estimate the quotient. Tell what compatible numbers you used. (pp. 192–193)

4. 3)3,296
5. 5)13,158
6. 2)23,498
7. 4)29,746

8. 7)4,387
9. 3)24,472
10. 8)56,703
11. 9)89,436

Divide. (pp. 194–199)

12. 9)504
13. 7)4,308
14. 8)998
15. 6)1,241

16. 5)421
17. 5)120,250
18. 4)2,872
19. 9)18,081

20. 6)704
21. 4)38,632
22. 8)105,687
23. 4)82,053

 **CHECK PROBLEM SOLVING**

Solve. Explain how you interpreted the remainder. (pp. 200–201)

24. A group of 123 students will take a swimming course. Each class can have 11 students. What is the least number of classes needed?

25. Mark has 300 miniature cars that he would like to display equally in 7 cases. Will 7 cases hold all of his collection? Explain.

# Getting Ready for ⭐FCAT

## ⭐ NUMBER SENSE, CONCEPTS, AND OPERATIONS

1. Greg is putting his vacation photos into an album. He has 284 photos. If two sides of a sheet of paper in the album can hold 8 photos in all, how many sheets will he need?

   A. 32

   B. 35

   C. 36

   D. 71

2. The table shows the number of cans of food that students at Sandpiper Elementary School collected for a food drive.

   | FOOD DRIVE COLLECTION | | | |
   |---|---|---|---|
   | Grade | 3 | 4 | 5 |
   | Number of Cans Collected | 390 | 400 | 425 |

   What was the average number of cans collected per grade?

   F. 405

   G. 406

   H. 450

   I. 460

   > **TIP** **Eliminate choices.**
   > See item 2. You can eliminate choices H and I since the average number of cans collected per grade cannot be greater than 425.

3. **Explain It** Bottles of grape juice are on sale at 2 for $2.89. Tyler has $15.00. Can he buy 10 bottles of juice? ESTIMATE to solve. Explain your answer.

## ⭐ ALGEBRAIC THINKING

4. There are 18 apples in a bowl. Five of the apples are green, and the rest are red.

   Suppose *r* represents the number of red apples. Which equation can be used to find the number of red apples in the bowl?

   A. $r + 5 = 18$

   B. $r - 5 = 18$

   C. $r - 18 = 5$

   D. $r + 18 = 5$

5. Cara is building bridges with connecting cubes. If the pattern continues, how many cubes will be in Bridge 5?

   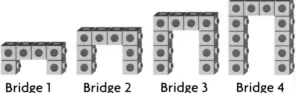

   Bridge 1    Bridge 2    Bridge 3    Bridge 4

   F. 13          H. 15

   G. 14          I. 16

6. **Explain It** Find a rule for the table below. Explain how you found the rule. Then use the rule to find the output when the input is 40.

   | INPUT | x | 4 | 7 | 15 | 29 |
   |---|---|---|---|---|---|
   | OUTPUT | y | 21 | 24 | 32 | 46 |

**DATA ANALYSIS AND PROBABILITY**

**7.** The graph shows Miguel's practice times. On which day did Miguel practice 35 minutes more than he practiced on Friday?

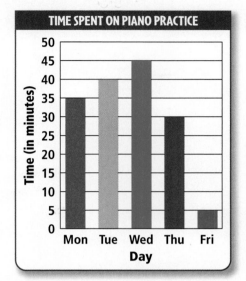

**A.** Monday

**B.** Tuesday

**C.** Wednesday

**D.** Thursday

**8.** Use the graph in Problem 7. For the week, what is the mean amount of time that Miguel practiced per day?

**F.** 40 minutes

**G.** 37.5 minutes

**H.** 35 minutes

**I.** 31 minutes

**9. Explain It** The Lake Bear basketball scores are shown below. Find the median of the five scores. Explain how to find the median, and tell what the median shows.

| BASKETBALL SCORES | | | | | |
|---|---|---|---|---|---|
| Game | 1 | 2 | 3 | 4 | 5 |
| Points Scored | 35 | 42 | 52 | 36 | 47 |

 **GEOMETRY AND SPATIAL SENSE**

**10.** The Blakes are planting sod around their house and driveway. How many square feet of sod do they need?

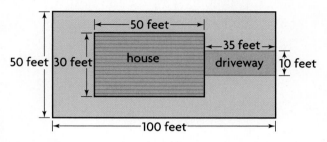

**A.** 5,000 square feet

**B.** 3,500 square feet

**C.** 3,150 square feet

**D.** 350 square feet

**11.** What term **best** describes how the figure was moved?

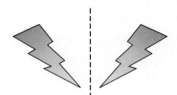

**F.** translation    **H.** rotation

**G.** reflection    **I.** tessellation

**12. Explain It** Find the area and perimeter of the rectangle below. Then draw another figure that has the same area but a different perimeter. Explain how you found your answer.

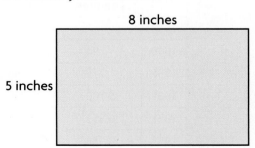

8 inches

5 inches

# Divide by 2-Digit Divisors

**≡FAST FACT • SOCIAL STUDIES** Little League Baseball was founded in 1939 with 45 participants. A $35 donation purchased the uniforms for the first three teams. Today almost 3,000,000 children participate in Little League around the world. The table shows the number of Little League participants since its founding.

**PROBLEM SOLVING** Find the average number of players who participated in each league in 1948.

In 2001, the U.S. Champion team from Apopka, Florida, played the team from Japan in the 55th Little League World Series.

| LITTLE LEAGUE PARTICIPANTS | | |
|---|---|---|
| Year | Number of Leagues | Number of Participants |
| 1939 | 1 | 45 |
| 1948 | 94 | 5,600 |
| 1951 | 775 | 46,600 |
| 1961 | 5,700 | 896,000 |
| 1971 | 6,552 | 1,447,200 |
| 1981 | 6,984 | 1,908,608 |
| 1991 | 7,056 | 2,534,355 |
| 2001 | 7,330 | 2,748,765 |

# CHECK WHAT YOU KNOW

Use this page to help you review and remember
important skills needed for Chapter 10.

## MULTIPLY WHOLE NUMBERS

Find the product. Estimate to check.

| 1. | 84 | 2. | 949 | 3. | 24 | 4. | 845 |
|---|---|---|---|---|---|---|---|
| | ×22 | | × 16 | | ×19 | | × 67 |

| 5. | 150 | 6. | 8,864 | 7. | 2,611 | 8. | 5,200 |
|---|---|---|---|---|---|---|---|
| | × 74 | | × 14 | | × 69 | | × 45 |

## COMPATIBLE NUMBERS

Estimate by using compatible numbers.

**9.** 9)660   **10.** 8)702   **11.** 4)122   **12.** 6)5,568

**13.** 359 ÷ 5   **14.** 2,662 ÷ 3   **15.** 820 ÷ 4   **16.** 9,074 ÷ 3

## DIVIDE BY 1-DIGIT NUMBERS

Divide.

**17.** 3)85   **18.** 4)907   **19.** 8)47   **20.** 4)556

**21.** 806 ÷ 5   **22.** 75 ÷ 4   **23.** 882 ÷ 7   **24.** 3)624

# VOCABULARY POWER

## REVIEW

**divide** [di•vīd′] *verb*

In the word *divide*, the prefix, *di-*, means "through" or "apart." The
root word *-videre* means "to separate." When you combine these
you get "separated apart." Name other math words in which the
prefix *di-* appears.

www.harcourtschool.com/mathglossary

# Algebra: Patterns in Division

## Learn

**ON THE ROAD AGAIN**   Last summer, Emilie's family drove 6,000 miles round trip from Portland, OR, to Richmond, VA. On the trip, the car averaged 30 miles per gallon (mpg). How many gallons of gasoline did the car use?

Divide.   $6{,}000 \div 30$     $30\overline{)6{,}000}$

**Look for a pattern.**

$6 \div 3 = 2$   ← Think: Use the basic fact.
$60 \div 30 = 2$
$600 \div 30 = 20$
$6{,}000 \div 30 = 200$

So, the car used 200 gallons of gasoline.

- What pattern do you see in $60 \div 30 = 2$, $600 \div 30 = 20$, and $6{,}000 \div 30 = 200$?

▲ The average American car got about 15 mpg in 1980 and about 24 mpg in 2003.

## Examples

**A**
$8 \div 2 = 4$ ← basic
$80 \div 20 = 4$     fact
$800 \div 20 = 40$
$8{,}000 \div 20 = 400$
$80{,}000 \div 20 = 4{,}000$

**B**
$12 \div 6 = 2$ ← basic
$120 \div 60 = 2$     fact
$1{,}200 \div 60 = 20$
$12{,}000 \div 60 = 200$
$120{,}000 \div 60 = 2{,}000$

**C**
$30 \div 6 = 5$ ← basic
$300 \div 60 = 5$     fact
$3{,}000 \div 60 = 50$
$30{,}000 \div 60 = 500$
$300{,}000 \div 60 = 5{,}000$
$3{,}000{,}000 \div 60 = 50{,}000$

 **MATH IDEA**   Basic facts and patterns can help you divide mentally.

## Check

1. **Compare** the basic facts and patterns in Examples B and C. How are they different?

**Use mental math to complete. Write the basic fact you use.**

2. $320 \div 40 = 8$
   $3{,}200 \div 40 = 80$
   $32{,}000 \div 40 = \blacksquare$

3. $420 \div 60 = 7$
   $4{,}200 \div 60 = 70$
   $42{,}000 \div 60 = \blacksquare$

4. $400 \div 50 = \blacksquare$
   $4{,}000 \div 50 = 80$
   $40{,}000 \div 50 = 800$

**Use mental math to complete. Write the basic fact you use.**

**5.** $90 \div 30 = $ ▓
$900 \div 30 = 30$
$9,000 \div 30 = 300$

**6.** $100 \div 50 = 2$
$1,000 \div 50 = 20$
$10,000 \div 50 = $ ▓

**7.** $450 \div 90 = 5$
$4,500 \div 90 = $ ▓
$45,000 \div 90 = $ ▓

**✦ALGEBRA** **Use basic facts and patterns to solve for *n*.**

**8.** $90 \div 3 = n$

**9.** $160 \div 40 = n$

**10.** $280 \div 40 = n$

**11.** $360 \div 40 = n$

**12.** $540 \div 90 = n$

**13.** $3,000 \div 60 = n$

**14.** $7,200 \div 90 = n$

**15.** $36,000 \div 90 = n$

**16.** $n \div 80 = 30$

**17.** $1,000 \div n = 50$

**18.** $3,500 \div n = 70$

**19.** $18,000 \div n = 600$

**20.** $330,000 \div 10 = n$

**21.** $4,800,000 \div 80 = n$

**22.** $4,000,000 \div n = 50$

**Compare. Use <, >, or = for the ●.**

**23.** $400 \div 20$ ● $400 \div 200$

**24.** $5,600 \div 70$ ● $560 \div 7$

**25.** $80,000 \div 40$ ● $800 \div 4$

**USE DATA** **For 26–27, use the map.**

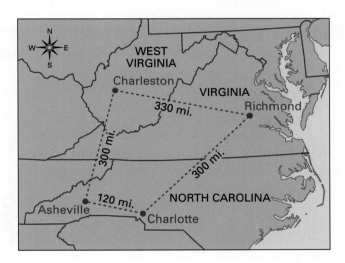

**26.** Mr. Fiori's truck route is round trip from Charlotte to Asheville, 4 days a week. On his route, he drives an average of 60 miles per hour. How many hours does he drive each week on his route?

**27.** Ricky's delivery van averages 30 miles per gallon. How many gallons of gas does the van use on the route from Asheville to Charleston to Richmond to Charlotte and back to Asheville?

**28.** A typical person will walk about 70,000 miles between childhood and senior years. If a person lives 70 years, how many miles will he or she walk, on average, a year?

**29.** ✷ **? What's the Error?** Tina says the quotient of $200,000 \div 40$ has four zeros. Describe Tina's error and find the correct quotient.

⌐ **Getting Ready for FCAT** ¬

**30.** A fifth-grade class has 18 students. Each day after school, one student gets to be a safety guard. When each student has had a turn, the list begins again.

How many times can each student be a safety guard if the school year consists of 180 days?

**A.** 8 **B.** 10 **C.** 12 **D.** 18

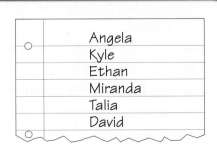

FCAT TESTED ◥ SSS/GLEs MA.A.3.2.3.5.1 Solves real-world problems involving addition, subtraction, multiplication, and division of whole numbers . . . using an appropriate method (for example, mental math, pencil and paper, calculator). *also* MA.D.1.2.1.5.1

**Chapter 10 209**

# 2 Estimate Quotients

 **Learn**

**WILD BLUE YONDER**   In 1927 Charles Lindbergh was the first person to fly solo across the Atlantic Ocean. He flew the 3,610 miles from New York to Paris in about 34 hours. About how many miles did Lindbergh fly per hour?

**MATH IDEA**   You can use compatible numbers to estimate quotients.

Estimate.    3,610 ÷ 34
$\qquad\qquad\downarrow\qquad\downarrow$
$\qquad$ 3,400 ÷ 34 = 100 ←   3,400 and 34 are compatible numbers, since 34 ÷ 34 = 1.

So, Lindbergh flew about 100 miles per hour.

You can also estimate a quotient by using two sets of compatible numbers to find two different reasonable estimates.

**Example**

Estimate.    3,281 ÷ 52

> **Think:** 3,281 is between 3,000 and 3,500.
> Use 3,000.
>
> 3,281 ÷ 52
> $\quad\downarrow\qquad\downarrow$
> 3,000 ÷ 50 = 60 ←   3,000 and 50 are compatible numbers, since 30 ÷ 5 = 6.

> **Think:** 3,281 is between 3,000 and 3,500.
> Use 3,500.
>
> 3,281 ÷ 52
> $\quad\downarrow\qquad\downarrow$
> 3,500 ÷ 50 = 70 ←   3,500 and 50 are compatible numbers, since 35 ÷ 5 = 7.

So, two reasonable estimates for 3,281 ÷ 52 are 60 and 70.

**Lindbergh's flight helped make air travel popular. Between 1926 and 1930, the number of people traveling by plane each year grew from about 6,000 to about 400,000.** ▼

• Will the quotient of 4,340 ÷ 62 be greater than or less than 100? Explain how you know.

▶ **Check**

**1. Show** two reasonable estimates for 2,652 ÷ 43.

Write two pairs of compatible numbers for each.
Give two possible estimates.

**2.** 524 ÷ 68       **3.** 329 ÷ 26       **4.** 171 ÷ 34       **5.** 2,548 ÷ 65

## Practice and Problem Solving    Extra Practice, page 222, Set B

Write two pairs of compatible numbers for each.
Give two possible estimates.

**6.** 186 ÷ 62       **7.** 1,275 ÷ 47       **8.** 20,725 ÷ 49

**Estimate the quotient.**

**9.** $42\overline{)508}$    **10.** $27\overline{)849}$    **11.** $64\overline{)532}$    **12.** $73\overline{)620}$    **13.** $86\overline{)743}$

**14.** $23\overline{)1,260}$    **15.** $47\overline{)3,524}$    **16.** $59\overline{)4,636}$    **17.** $77\overline{)8,199}$    **18.** $31\overline{)6,468}$

**19.** $81\overline{)2,417}$    **20.** $92\overline{)5,583}$    **21.** $34\overline{)27,925}$    **22.** $36\overline{)33,842}$    **23.** $53\overline{)48,574}$

**Name the compatible numbers used to find the estimate.**

**24.** 652 ÷ 18
estimate: 30

**25.** 423 ÷ 21
estimate: 20

**26.** 2,993 ÷ 75
estimate: 40

**27.** 37,642 ÷ 38
estimate: 900

**USE DATA** For 28–30, copy and complete the table.
Estimate each flight speed.

| | Year | Flight | Miles | Time (hours) | Speed (mph) |
|---|---|---|---|---|---|
| **28.** | 1931 | First Nonstop Trans-Pacific Flight | 4,458 | 42 | ■ |
| **29.** | 1932 | First Woman's Trans-Atlantic Solo | 2,026 | 15 | ■ |
| **30.** | 1949 | First Nonstop Round-the-World Flight | 23,452 | 94 | ■ |

**HISTORIC FLIGHTS**

**31. REASONING** A single-engine airplane can safely carry 5 people whose total weight is 857 pounds or less. Can the plane safely travel with 5 passengers if the average of their weights is 180 pounds? Explain.

▲ Amelia Earhart Putnam flew solo from Hawaii to California in a Wasp-powered Vega plane.

**32.** ✎ **Write About It** How do compatible numbers help you estimate quotients? Give an example.

## Getting Ready for FCAT [THINK SOLVE EXPLAIN]

**33.** Lynn is driving about 1,200 miles from Miami, FL, to Chicago, IL. She estimates that if she drives at an average speed of 55 miles per hour, she will have to drive for 20 hours. Which compatible numbers did she use? Explain.

Chicago

Miami

# Divide by 2-Digit Divisors

▶ **Learn**

**TAKE ME OUT TO THE BALL GAME**   Henry Louis "Hank" Aaron is American baseball's all-time champion home-run hitter. In his 23-year Major League career, Aaron hit 755 home runs. How many home runs did he average per year?

## Example

Divide.    755 ÷ 23       23)755

**STEP 1**

Estimate to place the first digit in the quotient.
**Think:**

$$\begin{array}{r} 30 \\ 25)\overline{750} \end{array} \quad \text{or} \quad \begin{array}{r} 40 \\ 20)\overline{800} \end{array}$$

$$\begin{array}{r} \blacksquare \\ 23)\overline{755} \end{array}$$  So, place the first digit in the tens place.

**STEP 2**

Divide the 75 tens.

$$\begin{array}{r} 3 \\ 23)\overline{755} \\ -69 \\ \hline 6 \end{array}$$

Divide. 23)75
Multiply. 23 × 3
Subtract. 75 − 69
Compare. 6 < 23

**STEP 3**

Bring down the 5 ones.
Divide the 65 ones.

$$\begin{array}{r} 32 \text{ r}19 \\ 23)\overline{755} \\ -69\downarrow \\ \hline 65 \\ -46 \\ \hline 19 \end{array}$$

Divide. 23)65
Multiply. 23 × 2
Subtract. 65 − 46
Compare. 19 < 23

So, Hank Aaron averaged between 32 and 33 home runs per year.

- Explain how to use multiplication to check 755 ÷ 23 = 32 r19.

💥 **MATH IDEA**   To divide by a 2-digit divisor, first estimate in order to place the first digit. Then follow the steps for division: divide, multiply, subtract, and compare. Repeat the steps until the remainder is zero or less than the divisor.

**Hank Aaron entered the record books on April 8, 1974, by breaking Babe Ruth's record of 714 home runs. Aaron' lifetime batting average was .305.** ▶

## More Examples

**A** Divide.

$$16\overline{)1,535}$$ 95 r15
$$-1\,44$$
$$\phantom{-}95$$
$$-80$$
$$\phantom{-}15$$

Check ✓

$$95$$
$$\times 16$$
$$\overline{570}$$
$$+950$$
$$\overline{1,520}$$
$$+\phantom{0}15$$
$$\overline{1,535}\,✓$$

**B** Divide.

$$24\overline{)31,294}$$ 1,303 r22
$$-24$$
$$\phantom{-}72$$
$$-72$$
$$\phantom{-}09$$
$$-\phantom{0}0$$
$$\phantom{-}94$$
$$-72$$
$$\phantom{-}22$$

Check ✓

$$1,303$$
$$\times\phantom{0}24$$
$$\overline{5\,212}$$
$$+26\,060$$
$$\overline{31,272}$$
$$+\phantom{00}22$$
$$\overline{31,294}\,✓$$

- In Example B, what does the zero in the quotient indicate?

**Technology Link**

**More Practice: Harcourt Mega Math The Number Games,** *Up, Up, and Array,* **Levels R, S**

## ▶ Check

1. **Explain** how you can use an estimate to help you divide.

**Name the position of the first digit of the quotient.**

2. $36\overline{)209}$      3. $14\overline{)1,624}$      4. $53\overline{)2,369}$      5. $47\overline{)7,395}$

6. $89\overline{)8,969}$      7. $43\overline{)205}$      8. $38\overline{)7,268}$      9. $13\overline{)24,613}$

**Divide. Check by multiplying.**

10. $831 \div 38$      11. $2,816 \div 56$      12. $3,974 \div 23$      13. $694 \div 81$

14. $42\overline{)365}$      15. $38\overline{)4,031}$      16. $74\overline{)3,568}$      17. $54\overline{)34,078}$

## ▶ Practice and Problem Solving    Extra Practice, page 222, Set C

**Name the position of the first digit of the quotient.**

18. $47\overline{)310}$      19. $25\overline{)3,205}$      20. $63\overline{)1,824}$      21. $71\overline{)9,546}$

22. $42\overline{)42,785}$      23. $68\overline{)54,330}$      24. $21\overline{)458}$      25. $34\overline{)3,894}$

**Divide. Check by multiplying.**

26. $942 \div 49$      27. $5,690 \div 78$      28. $458 \div 45$      29. $10,675 \div 11$

30. $4,369 \div 74$      31. $12,362 \div 35$      32. $8,149 \div 41$      33. $30,362 \div 62$

**LESSON CONTINUES** ▶

FCAT TESTED   SSS/GLEs MA.A.3.2.3.5.I Solves real-world problems involving addition, subtraction, multiplication, and division of whole numbers . . . using an appropriate method (for example, mental math, pencil and paper, calculator).

**Chapter 10 213**

**Divide.**

**34.** $24\overline{)824}$    **35.** $50\overline{)545}$    **36.** $73\overline{)7,809}$    **37.** $29\overline{)6,932}$

**38.** $33\overline{)669}$    **39.** $43\overline{)759}$    **40.** $37\overline{)4,801}$    **41.** $58\overline{)9,286}$

**42.** $73\overline{)5,841}$    **43.** $29\overline{)31,803}$    **44.** $26\overline{)5,330}$    **45.** $37\overline{)3,363}$

**46.** $399 \div 26$    **47.** $2,904 \div 45$    **48.** $4,598 \div 61$    **49.** $35,718 \div 13$

**Match each check with a division problem.**

**50.** Check: $(66 \times 14) + 60 = 984$

**51.** Check: $(82 \times 108) + 71 = 8,927$

**52.** Check: $(98 \times 1,010) + 9 = 98,989$

**53.** Check: $(69 \times 115) + 47 = 7,982$

**a.** $7,982 \div 69 = 115 \text{ r}47$

**b.** $984 \div 66 = 14 \text{ r}60$

**c.** $8,927 \div 82 = 108 \text{ r}71$

**d.** $98,989 \div 98 = 1,010 \text{ r}9$

**ALGEBRA** **For 54–57, find the missing digit that makes each equation true.**

**54.** $1,288 \div 23 = 5\blacksquare$

**55.** $3,580 \div (\blacksquare \times 10) = 89 \text{ r}20$

**56.** $(456 - 18) \div 42 = 1\blacksquare \text{ r}18$

**57.** $452 \div 22 = 20 \text{ r}\blacksquare$

**58.** **? What's the Error?** In the student paper on the right, which is incorrect, the problem or the check? Describe and correct the error.

**59.** **REASONING** What is the greatest remainder you can have if you divide by 48? Explain.

**60.** **NUMBER SENSE** Two numbers have a sum of 64. The quotient is 7. What are the two numbers?

**61.** An adult ticket to the baseball game costs $9. A student ticket is $6. Anna paid a total of $153 for tickets to a game. She bought 11 adult tickets. How many student tickets did she buy?

```
       15 r12    Check ✓
18)282              15
   18              ×12
   102              30
  - 90            +150
   12              180
                  + 18
                   198
```

**USE DATA** **For 62–64, use the table.**

**62.** Estimate how many games Cy Young won in an average season.

**63.** **? What's the Question?** The answer is Warren Spahn won 10 fewer games.

**64.** **REASONING** Who averaged more wins per season, Alexander or Spahn?

| PITCHER WINS | | |
|---|---|---|
| Pitcher | Seasons Pitched | Games Won |
| Cy Young | 22 | 511 |
| Walter Johnson | 21 | 416 |
| Christy Mathewson | 17 | 373 |
| Grover Alexander | 20 | 373 |
| Warren Spahn | 21 | 363 |

**Walter Johnson** ▶

**65.** The Crestview School had an "Eat Apples" fund-raising activity and sold 2,485 apples. The apples were sold by 87 students. If an equal number of apples were sold by each student, about how many apples did each student sell?

**66. Vocabulary Power** Compatible numbers work easily together. The prefix *com-* in *compatible* means "with" or "together." Name other words you know that have the prefix *com-*.

## Getting Ready for FCAT

**67.** The Tovars are buying a used car that costs $9,792. They will pay for it by making 24 equal monthly payments. How much will each monthly payment be?

    **A.** $48

    **B.** $408

    **C.** $480

    **D.** $488

**68.** The Reed Company ordered 16,072 calendars for their offices. How many calendars can the Reed Company send to each of its 28 offices?

    **F.** 274

    **G.** 574

    **H.** 682

    **I.** 834

## Problem Solving   Thinker's Corner

### REMAINDER SCOREBOARD

**Materials:** 5 blank number cubes

**Getting Ready:** Label 2 number cubes 0–5. Label 3 number cubes 4–9.

**Let's Play!**

- One player tosses all the cubes, using the results as digits to write a 3-digit by 2-digit division problem that has a high remainder. Then the player divides.

- The other players check the quotient and remainder. If both are correct, the player records the remainder as the score for that round. If both are incorrect, the remainder is not recorded.

- Players continue alternating turns, writing division problems, and adding the remainders (if correct) to their scores. The player with the highest score after ten rounds wins.

$$3\ r76$$
$$90\overline{)346}$$

$$(90 \times 3) + 76 = 346$$

# Correcting Quotients

▶ **Learn**

**DRAMATIC DIVISION**   The Civic Youth Theater has a total of 238 seats on the main floor and in the balcony. Each row on the main floor has 32 seats. The rest of the seats are in the balcony. What is the maximum number of rows on the main floor? How many balcony seats are there?

## Example 1

Divide.          $238 \div 32$                    $32\overline{)238}$
                      ↓      ↓
Estimate.      $240 \div 30 = 8$ or $210 \div 30 = 7$

**STEP 1**

Divide, using your first estimate.

$$\begin{array}{r} 8 \\ 32\overline{)238} \\ -256 \end{array}$$  Divide. $238 \div 32$
Multiply. $32 \times 8$

**Think:** Since $256 > 238$, this estimate is too high.

**STEP 2**

Adjust. Divide, using your second estimate.

$$\begin{array}{r} 7\ r14 \\ 32\overline{)238} \\ -224 \\ \hline 14 \end{array}$$  Divide. $238 \div 32$
Multiply. $32 \times 7$
Subtract. $238 - 224$
Compare. $14 < 32$

So, the main floor has 7 rows, and there are 14 seats in the balcony.

## Example 2

Divide.     $5,867 \div 65$     $65\overline{)5,867}$

Estimate.
Use compatible numbers.

$5,867 \div 65$
   ↓        ↓
$5,600 \div 70 = 80$
or
$6,300 \div 70 = 90$

Divide.

$$\begin{array}{r} 8 \\ 65\overline{)5,867} \\ -5\ 20 \\ \hline 66 \end{array}$$

**Think:** Since $66 > 65$, the estimate is too low.

Adjust.

$$\begin{array}{r} 90\ r17 \\ 65\overline{)5,867} \\ -5\ 85 \\ \hline 17 \\ -\ 0 \\ \hline 17 \end{array}$$

Shakespeare's plays were first performed in London, England's Globe Theatre in 1599. It seated about 1,500 people, with a ground area and three tiers of seats. ▼

- How do you adjust an estimated quotient that is too high? too low?

 **MATH IDEA**   Sometimes when you divide, your estimate is too high or too low. Then you need to adjust the first digit of your quotient to complete the division.

1. **Explain** how you can tell if each digit in the quotient is large enough.

**Write** *too high*, *too low*, or *just right* **for each estimate.**

2. $\overset{4}{25\overline{)83}}$   3. $\overset{1}{32\overline{)61}}$   4. $\overset{90}{78\overline{)6,778}}$   5. $\overset{3}{57\overline{)239}}$   6. $\overset{500}{95\overline{)54,362}}$

► **Practice and Problem Solving**   ( Extra Practice, page 222, Set D )

**Write** *too high*, *too low*, or *just right* **for each estimate.**

7. $\overset{7}{42\overline{)321}}$   8. $\overset{7}{64\overline{)519}}$   9. $\overset{20}{88\overline{)3,265}}$   10. $\overset{800}{39\overline{)34,527}}$   11. $\overset{700}{54\overline{)34,563}}$

**Choose the better estimate to use for the quotient. Write *a* or *b*.**

12. $19\overline{)84}$   **a.** 3 **b.** 4   13. $34\overline{)276}$   **a.** 8 **b.** 9   14. $24\overline{)158}$   **a.** 6 **b.** 7

15. $46\overline{)463}$   **a.** 9 **b.** 10   16. $59\overline{)283}$   **a.** 3 **b.** 4   17. $62\overline{)506}$   **a.** 8 **b.** 9

18. $78\overline{)314,674}$   **a.** 3,000 **b.** 4,000   19. $38\overline{)2,736,214}$   **a.** 60,000 **b.** 70,000

**Divide.**

20. $32\overline{)154}$   21. $25\overline{)278}$   22. $29\overline{)3,275}$   23. $28\overline{)3,582}$

24. $53\overline{)45,320}$   25. $47\overline{)842}$   26. $15\overline{)485}$   27. $26\overline{)5,206}$

28. $31,827 \div 56$   29. $89,345 \div 89$   30. $38,568 \div 47$   31. $749 \div 62$

32. A total of 131 students are planning to go to Asolo Theatre in Florida to see *The Rivals*. For every 14 students, one adult chaperone is required. How many chaperones are required?

33. Barnie has $25. He buys a shirt for $12.75 and a hat for $8.39. How much change should he get back?

34. **Write About It** Explain how finding two estimates for a division problem helps you find a quotient.

► **Getting Ready for** ⭐**FCAT**

35. Four students in Mrs. Lincoln's class were dividing 5,583 by 63. Each had a different estimate. Which is the **most** reasonable estimate for $5,583 \div 63$?

   **A.** 9   **C.** 200
   **B.** 90   **D.** 800

36. Chung Press attaches about 12,800 locks to diaries weekly. Each of 62 workers averages the same number of locks. About how many diaries can each worker complete per week?

   **F.** about 100   **H.** about 300
   **G.** about 200   **I.** about 400

# 5 Practice Division

## Quick Review

1. 345 ÷ 4
2. 781 ÷ 11
3. 628 ÷ 9
4. 6,760 ÷ 38
5. 1,232 ÷ 12

▶ **Learn**

**ALL YOU CAN EAT** An adult giant panda in the wild eats about 10,220 pounds of bamboo shoots and leaves a year. On average, how many pounds of bamboo does a giant panda eat each month?

◀ **Bamboo makes up 99 percent of a giant panda's diet. A panda sometimes consumes as much as 80 pounds of fresh bamboo shoots per day.**

## Example

Divide. 10,220 ÷ 12    12)10,220

**STEP 1**

Estimate.

**Think:**

$$\frac{800}{12)9,600} \text{ or } \frac{900}{12)10,800}$$

$$\frac{\blacksquare}{12)10,220}$$

So, place the first digit in the hundreds place.

**STEP 2**

Divide the 102 hundreds. Use your first estimate.

$$\begin{array}{r} 8 \\ 12)\overline{10,220} \\ -\,9\,6 \\ \hline 6 \end{array}$$

**STEP 3**

Bring down the 2 tens. Divide the 62 tens.

$$\begin{array}{r} 85 \\ 12)\overline{10,220} \\ -\,9\,6\downarrow \\ \hline 62 \\ -60 \\ \hline 2 \end{array}$$

**STEP 4**

Bring down the 0 ones. Divide the 20 ones.

$$\begin{array}{r} 851 \text{ r8} \\ 12)\overline{10,220} \\ -\,9\,6 \\ \hline 62 \\ -60\downarrow \\ \hline 20 \\ -12 \\ \hline 8 \end{array}$$

Express the remainder as a fraction. So, a giant panda eats an average of $851\frac{8}{12}$, or $851\frac{2}{3}$, pounds of bamboo each month.

## More Examples

**A**

$$\begin{array}{r} 24 \text{ r3 or } 24\frac{3}{35} \\ 35)\overline{843} \\ -70 \\ \hline 143 \\ -140 \\ \hline 3 \end{array}$$

**Check ✓**

$$\begin{array}{r} 24 \\ \times 35 \\ \hline 120 \\ +720 \\ \hline 840 \\ +\quad 3 \\ \hline 843\checkmark \end{array}$$

**B**

$$\begin{array}{r} 61 \text{ r17 or } 61\frac{17}{42} \\ 42)\overline{2,579} \\ -2\,52 \\ \hline 59 \\ -42 \\ \hline 17 \end{array}$$

**Check ✓**

$$\begin{array}{r} 61 \\ \times 42 \\ \hline 122 \\ +2\,440 \\ \hline 2,562 \\ +\quad 17 \\ \hline 2,579\checkmark \end{array}$$

You can use a calculator to divide.

2  5  7  9  Int÷  4  2  Enter

2579÷42=
61r17

## ▶ Check

**1. Explain** how to express the remainder as a fraction in a division problem.

**Divide. Check by multiplying.**

**2.** 851 ÷ 15

**3.** 93 ÷ 14

**4.** 1,242 ÷ 48

**5.** 84 ÷ 17

**6.** 42)‾23,898

**7.** 61)‾36,182

**8.** 29)‾1,073

**9.** 28)‾5,016

## ▶ Practice and Problem Solving ⟨ Extra Practice, page 222, Set E ⟩

**Divide.**

**10.** 402 ÷ 65

**11.** 4,161 ÷ 19

**12.** 4,591 ÷ 37

**13.** 89 ÷ 23

**14.** 71)‾7,171

**15.** 33)‾1,877

**16.** 51)‾4,095

**17.** 92)‾46,235

**18.** 91)‾5,396

**19.** 69)‾2,109

**20.** 48)‾24,916

**21.** 42)‾23,911

**22.** 25)‾424,867

**23.** 32)‾306,452

**24.** 24)‾6,809

**25.** 76)‾3,965

**ALGEBRA** **For 26–31, find the missing digit that makes each equation true.**

**26.** 4■4 ÷ 23 = 18

**27.** 1,065 ÷ ■1 = 15

**28.** 7,■22 ÷ 99 = 78

**29.** 12,084 ÷ 76 = 15■

**30.** (1,188 − 18) ÷ 90 = 1■

**31.** 1,860 ÷ (■ × 15) = 62

**32.** About 31,000 people visited the San Diego Zoo's website the day the live "Panda Cam" was launched. On average, how many people visited the website each hour?

**33. NUMBER SENSE** What is the least 4-digit number that can be divided by 20 and have a remainder of 5?

**34.** ☰**FAST FACT • SCIENCE** A newborn panda is about the size of a stick of butter. An adult panda weighs about 200 lb, about 800 times as great as the weight of a newborn. Find the weight of a newborn. (16 oz = 1 lb)

## Getting Ready for ⫸FCAT

**35.** The first 30 days that the International Spy Museum in Washington, D.C. was open, there were over 100,000 visitors. Which operation should be used for ● to find the average attendance per day?

100,000 ● 30

**A.** addition

**C.** multiplication

**B.** subtraction

**D.** division

FCAT TESTED ▼ SSS/GLEs MA.A.3.2.3.5.1 Solves real-world problems involving addition, subtraction, multiplication, and division of whole numbers, . . . using an appropriate method (for example, mental math, pencil and paper, calculator) *also* MA.A.1.2.3.5.1

**Chapter 10 219**

# Problem Solving Strategy
## Predict and Test

**PROBLEM** A collector has 158 world's fair souvenirs. He wants to sell them in equal groups with no more than 25 in each group. After he divides them into equal groups, there are 20 souvenirs left over that he will sell individually. How many groups was he able to make? How many souvenirs are in each group?

**UNDERSTAND**

• What are you asked to find?

• What information will you use?

**PLAN**

• What strategy can you use to solve the problem?

Since you know the dividend is 158, you can use *predict and test* to find equal groups with no more than 25 souvenirs in each.

**SOLVE**

• How can you use the strategy to solve the problem?

Since there are 20 souvenirs left over, there must be more than 20 souvenirs in each group. So, start by predicting different divisors greater than 20. Then test each prediction to see if the remainder is 20.

| Predict the number of souvenirs in each group. | Divide to find the number of groups. | Compare the remainder to 20. | Does the remainder equal 20? |
|---|---|---|---|
| 21 | 158 ÷ 21 = 7 r11 | 11 < 20 | No |
| 22 | 158 ÷ 22 = 7 r4 | 4 < 20 | No |
| 23 | 158 ÷ 23 = 6 r20 | 20 = 20 √ | Yes |

So, the collector made 6 groups, each with 23 souvenirs.

**CHECK**

• How can you decide if your answer is correct?

**Strategies**

Draw a Diagram or Picture
Make a Model or Act It Out
Make an Organized List
Find a Pattern
Make a Table or Graph
► **Predict and Test**
Work Backward
Solve a Simpler Problem
Write an Equation
Use Logical Reasoning

**Predict and test to solve.**

1. **What if** there were 18 souvenirs left over? How many groups would he be able to make? How many souvenirs would be in each group?

2. Tim spent $22.50 on souvenirs at the fair. He bought 2 souvenirs. One of them cost $4.50 more than the other. How much was each souvenir?

The fifth-grade students had 181 paintings to be displayed in equal groups on walls throughout the school. No more than 30 paintings would fit on each wall. After the paintings were placed, 20 were left over and were placed on the office wall.

3. How many groups were formed? How many paintings were in each group?

  **A** 6 groups of 30 paintings
  **B** 7 groups of 23 paintings
  **C** 8 groups of 21 paintings
  **D** 9 groups of 20 paintings

4. Which equation models this situation?

  **F** 181 ÷ 30 = 6 r1
  **G** 181 ÷ 20 = 9 r1
  **H** 181 ÷ 23 = 7 r20
  **J** 181 ÷ 7 = 25 r6

## Mixed Strategy Practice

**USE DATA** For 5–6, use the table.

5. If a tour boat travels 19 miles per hour down the Colorado River and another tour boat travels 25 miles per hour down the Rio Grande, which tour boat will travel the length of its river first?

6. Suppose there are rescue stations every 35 miles along the Yenisey River. If the first station is located at the beginning of the river, how many stations are there in all?

7. Karen left her house and drove 35 miles north and then 15 miles west to the mall. When she left the mall, she drove 5 miles east and then 20 miles south to the library. How far north and west was Karen from her house?

8. **NUMBER SENSE** The sum of two numbers is 36. Their product is 320. What are the two numbers?

9. ✎ **Write a problem** using the table above. Explain the strategy you would use to solve the problem.

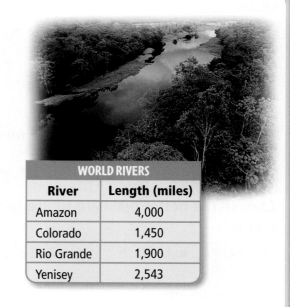

| WORLD RIVERS | |
|---|---|
| **River** | **Length (miles)** |
| Amazon | 4,000 |
| Colorado | 1,450 |
| Rio Grande | 1,900 |
| Yenisey | 2,543 |

FCAT
TESTED  SSS/GLEs MA.A.3.2.2.5.1 Uses problem-solving strategies to determine the operation(s) needed to solve one- and two-step problems involving addition, subtraction, multiplication, and division of whole numbers, and addition, subtraction, and multiplication of decimals and fractions.

**Chapter 10  221**

# Extra Practice

## Set A (pp. 208–209)

**Use mental math to complete. Write the basic fact you use.**

1. $200 \div 40 = 5$
   $2,000 \div 40 = 50$
   $20,000 \div 40 = \blacksquare$

2. $160 \div 40 = 4$
   $1,600 \div 40 = \blacksquare$
   $16,000 \div 40 = 400$

3. $180 \div 30 = \blacksquare$
   $1,800 \div 30 = 60$
   $18,000 \div 30 = \blacksquare$

4. A tour group traveled 6,000 miles in 30 days. How many miles a day did it average?

5. If you average 50 miles per hour for 550 miles, how many hours will you travel?

## Set B (pp. 210–211)

**Write two pairs of compatible numbers for each. Give two possible estimates.**

1. $198 \div 28$
2. $336 \div 46$
3. $1,344 \div 87$

**Estimate the quotient.**

4. $22\overline{)215}$
5. $33\overline{)605}$
6. $42\overline{)1,378}$
7. $51\overline{)9,750}$
8. $41\overline{)8,261}$

## Set C (pp. 212–215)

**Divide.**

1. $842 \div 27$
2. $2,946 \div 76$
3. $8,888 \div 62$
4. $15,432 \div 18$
5. $23\overline{)532}$
6. $31\overline{)8,461}$
7. $18\overline{)2,468}$
8. $27\overline{)16,798}$
9. $23\overline{)86,698}$

## Set D (pp. 216–217)

**Write *too high, too low,* or *just right* for each estimate.**

1. $34\overline{)26,163}$ → 800
2. $41\overline{)325}$ → 6
3. $29\overline{)23,007}$ → 800
4. $69\overline{)698}$ → 10
5. $76\overline{)1,826}$ → 20

**Choose the better estimate to use for the quotient. Write *a* or *b.***

6. $14\overline{)92}$   **a.** 6   **b.** 5
7. $18\overline{)138}$   **a.** 6   **b.** 7
8. $61\overline{)192}$   **a.** 3   **b.** 4

## Set E (pp. 218–219)

**Divide.**

1. $12\overline{)58}$
2. $18\overline{)79}$
3. $24\overline{)9,168}$
4. $33\overline{)234}$
5. $84\overline{)31,164}$
6. $36\overline{)24,469}$
7. $21\overline{)6,954}$
8. $26\overline{)635,204}$

# Review/Test

 ## CHECK VOCABULARY AND CONCEPTS

Choose the best term from the box.

| estimate |
| multiples |
| multiplication |
| patterns |

1. You can use basic facts and ___?___ to divide mentally. (p. 208)

2. You can use compatible numbers to ___?___ quotients. (p. 210)

3. You can use ___?___ to check division. (p. 212)

## CHECK SKILLS

Use mental math to complete. Write the basic fact you use. (pp. 208–209)

4.  $490 \div 70 = 7$
    $4,900 \div 70 = 70$
    $49,000 \div 70 = \blacksquare$

5.  $640 \div 80 = 8$
    $6,400 \div 80 = \blacksquare$
    $64,000 \div 80 = 800$

6.  $810 \div 90 = \blacksquare$
    $8,100 \div 90 = \blacksquare$
    $81,000 \div 90 = 900$

Write two pairs of compatible numbers for each. Give two possible estimates. (pp. 210–211)

7. $263 \div 43$

8. $1,456 \div 37$

9. $5,063 \div 81$

Write *too high, too low,* or *just right* for each estimate. (pp. 216–217)

10. $13\overline{)667}$ → 40

11. $26\overline{)3,521}$ → 90

12. $41\overline{)37,651}$ → 900

13. $75\overline{)49,036}$ → 700

Divide. (pp. 212–215 and pp. 218–219)

14. $17\overline{)64}$
15. $22\overline{)90}$
16. $36\overline{)184}$
17. $47\overline{)2,943}$
18. $34\overline{)3,294}$

19. $27\overline{)344}$
20. $36\overline{)645}$
21. $45\overline{)4,292}$
22. $42\overline{)8,325}$
23. $71\overline{)685,210}$

## CHECK PROBLEM SOLVING

Predict and test to solve. (pp. 220–221)

24. The Trader Card Store has 161 baseball cards. The store wants to sell the cards in equal groups, with no more than 30 cards in each group. There will be 17 cards left over that they will sell individually. How many equal groups can be made? How many cards will be in each group?

25. **NUMBER SENSE** The sum of two numbers is 35 and their difference is 7. What are the two numbers?

# Getting Ready for FCAT

## ⭐ NUMBER SENSE, CONCEPTS, AND OPERATIONS

1. Last month Steve earned $378 mowing lawns. He has 7 customers, and he mowed each lawn 3 times during the month. How much money does Steve charge to mow one lawn?

   A. $18

   B. $21

   C. $54

   D. $126

2. Joan is buying the dining room set shown below.

   $2,025

   She will make a down payment of $225 and monthly payments of $75. How many monthly payments does Joan have to make to pay for the dining room set?

   F. 7

   G. 9

   H. 24

   I. 27

3. **Explain It** Sara's class sold pencils for 20¢ each as a fund-raising project. They collected $28.40. Is the total number of pencils they sold closer to 100, 150, 200, or 250? ESTIMATE to solve. Explain your estimate.

## ⭐ ALGEBRAIC THINKING

4. Jamie earned $d$ dollars baby-sitting on Friday and $15 baby-sitting on Saturday. Which expression represents how much Jamie earned baby-sitting?

   A. $d - 15$       C. $d + 15$

   B. $15 - d$       D. $15d$

   > **TIP** **Understand the problem.** See item 5. The number of used books and total number of books are given. You do not know the number of new books.

5. Trevor sold 127 used books and some new books at a book sale. He sold 221 books in all.

   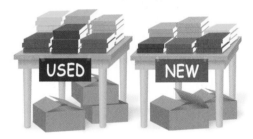

   USED       NEW

   Suppose $n$ represents the number of new books sold. Which equation could be used to find the number of new books sold?

   F. $127 + n = 221$

   G. $n + 221 = 127$

   H. $221 + 127 = n$

   I. $n - 221 = 127$

6. **Explain It** Janelle is 2 years younger than Hannah and 6 years older than Sal. Write two expressions with different variables to represent Janelle's age.

**MEASUREMENT**

**7.** Noah planted a bush that was 30 centimeters tall. Six months later, the bush was 1 meter tall. How much had the bush grown?

   **A.** 70 millimeters

   **B.** 7 centimeters

   **C.** 70 centimeters

   **D.** 700 centimeters

**8.** Briana went to the post office to mail the package shown below.

How many ounces did the package weigh?

   **F.** 18 ounces

   **G.** 22 ounces

   **H.** 26 ounces

   **I.** 34 ounces

**9. Explain It** To make a trail mix, Jeff bought 3 pounds of raisins at $2.15 per pound. He also bought 2 pounds of walnuts at $3.90 per pound. Did Jeff spend more on raisins or more on walnuts? ESTIMATE to find the answer. Explain your answer.

 **DATA ANALYSIS AND PROBABILITY**

**10.** The graph shows the number of ice skating lessons offered at Jo's Ice Rink.

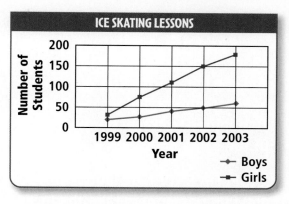

What conclusion can you make about the data?

   **A.** The number of lessons for boys decreased from 1999 to 2000.

   **B.** The number of lessons for girls decreased from 2001 to 2003.

   **C.** The number of students taking lessons stayed the same every year.

   **D.** More girls than boys took lessons each year from 1999 to 2003.

**11.** Parker's math quiz scores are 7, 10, 8, 10, 9, 10, and 9. Which of the following is true about his scores?

   **F.** The median equals the mode.

   **G.** The range equals the median.

   **H.** The mode equals the range.

   **I.** The mode, median, and range are all equal.

**12. Explain It** Evan is deciding what clothes to wear. He has a red shirt, a blue shirt, and a white shirt. He has black, brown, and blue pants. Draw a diagram to show how many choices he has. Explain the diagram.

# Divide Decimals by Whole Numbers

**≡FAST FACT** • SOCIAL STUDIES  In the 1800s, it took four hours to travel by horse and carriage to the top of Lookout Mountain in Chattanooga, Tennessee. Today it takes 10 minutes to travel by the Incline Railway to the same point.

PROBLEM SOLVING   Between 350,000 and 450,000 passengers take the Incline Railway during an average year. The graph shows the fraction of passengers who ride from April to October. Write this fraction as a decimal.

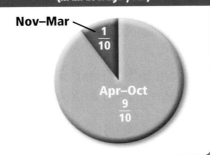

THE INCLINE RAILWAY PASSENGER TRIPS
(in an average year)

Nov–Mar
$\frac{1}{10}$

Apr–Oct
$\frac{9}{10}$

The Incline Railway is the steepest and safest passenger incline in the world.

# CHECK WHAT YOU KNOW

Use this page to help you review and remember
important skills needed for Chapter 11.

## ✓ DIVISION PATTERNS

Complete the pattern.

1.  $350 \div 50 = 7$
    $3,500 \div 50 = 70$
    $35,000 \div 50 = n$

2.  $180 \div 30 = 6$
    $1,800 \div 30 = n$
    $18,000 \div 30 = 600$

3.  $360 \div 40 = n$
    $3,600 \div 40 = 90$
    $36,000 \div 40 = 900$

4.  $300 \div 60 = 5$
    $3,000 \div 60 = 50$
    $n \div 60 = 500$

5.  $320 \div 80 = 4$
    $n \div 80 = 40$
    $32,000 \div 80 = 400$

6.  $400 \div 50 = 8$
    $4,000 \div n = 80$
    $40,000 \div 50 = 800$

## ✓ DIVIDE WHOLE NUMBERS

Divide.

7. $7\overline{)84}$

8. $4\overline{)92}$

9. $5\overline{)485}$

10. $9\overline{)207}$

11. $6\overline{)288}$

12. $4\overline{)824}$

13. $3\overline{)1,620}$

14. $8\overline{)3,248}$

15. $144 \div 16$

16. $832 \div 32$

17. $3,825 \div 45$

18. $1,365 \div 91$

## ✓ EQUIVALENT DECIMALS

Write two equivalent decimals for each.

19. 8

20. 0.25

21. 1.3

22. 2.60

# VOCABULARY POWER

## REVIEW

**hundredth** [hun′drədth] *adjective* or *noun*

One whole can be divided into 100 equal parts, or 100 hundredths.
One dollar can be divided into hundredths. What is another name for
one hundredth of one dollar?

 www.harcourtschool.com/mathglossary

# Algebra: Patterns in Decimal Division

 **Learn**

**POP! POP! POP!**   Roderic read that the average person in the United States eats about 16 gallons of popcorn each year. Roderic bought 4 cans of popcorn for $2. What is the cost for one can?

Find 2 ÷ 4.

**Look for a pattern in these quotients.**

200 ÷ 4 = 50  ← Pattern in the zeros
 20 ÷ 4 = 5   ← Basic fact
  2 ÷ 4 = 0.5 ← Decimal quotient

So, one can of popcorn costs $0.50.

**Examples**   Use a pattern to solve.

| **A** Find 2 ÷ 5. | **B** Find 1.8 ÷ 6. | **C** Find 3.2 ÷ 4. |
|---|---|---|
| 200 ÷ 5 = 40 | 180 ÷ 6 = 30 | 320 ÷ 4 = 80 |
| 20 ÷ 5 = 4 | 18 ÷ 6 = 3 | 32 ÷ 4 = 8 |
| 2 ÷ 5 = 0.4 | 1.8 ÷ 6 = 0.3 | 3.2 ÷ 4 = 0.8 |

**MATH IDEA**   When the divisor is greater than the dividend, the quotient is a decimal less than 1.

**Remember**

In any whole number, a decimal point is to the right of the ones place.

50 = 50.
        ↑

 **Check**

1. **Explain** what happens to the quotient in Examples A–C as the dividend gets smaller.

**Copy and complete each pattern.**

2. 100 ÷ 5 = ■
   10 ÷ 5 = ■
   1 ÷ 5 = ■

3. 400 ÷ 8 = ■
   40 ÷ 8 = ■
   4 ÷ 8 = ■

4. 600 ÷ 8 = ■
   60 ÷ 8 = ■
   6 ÷ 8 = ■

**Copy and complete each pattern.**

**5.** $300 \div 5 = \blacksquare$
$30 \div 5 = \blacksquare$
$3 \div 5 = \blacksquare$

**6.** $160 \div 4 = \blacksquare$
$16 \div 4 = \blacksquare$
$1.6 \div 4 = \blacksquare$

**7.** $720 \div 8 = \blacksquare$
$72 \div 8 = \blacksquare$
$7.2 \div 8 = \blacksquare$

**8.** $400 \div 5 = \blacksquare$
$40 \div 5 = \blacksquare$
$4 \div 5 = \blacksquare$

**9.** $250 \div 5 = \blacksquare$
$25 \div 5 = \blacksquare$
$2.5 \div 5 = \blacksquare$

**10.** $630 \div 9 = \blacksquare$
$63 \div 9 = \blacksquare$
$6.3 \div 9 = \blacksquare$

✹**ALGEBRA**   **Copy and complete each table. Use patterns and mental math.**

**11.** Divide by 25.

| Input | Output |
|-------|--------|
| 10,000 | $\blacksquare$ |
| 1,000 | $\blacksquare$ |
| 100 | $\blacksquare$ |
| 10 | $\blacksquare$ |

**12.** Divide by 40.

| Input | Output |
|-------|--------|
| 28,000 | $\blacksquare$ |
| $\blacksquare$ | 70 |
| $\blacksquare$ | 7 |
| 28 | $\blacksquare$ |

**13.** Divide by 8.

| Input | Output |
|-------|--------|
| 2,000 | $\blacksquare$ |
| 200 | $\blacksquare$ |
| $\blacksquare$ | 2.5 |
| 2 | $\blacksquare$ |

**Write the check for each division problem.**

**14.** $10 \div 2 = 5$
$1 \div 2 = 0.5$

**15.** $5,000 \div 10 = 500$
$5 \div 10 = 0.5$

**16.** $360 \div 6 = 60$
$3.6 \div 6 = 0.6$

**17. REASONING**   Continue the pattern until the quotient extends to the hundredths place:

$560 \div 7 = 80$
$56 \div 7 = 8$

**18.** Amy bought 5 bags of peanuts for $3.00. Did she pay more or less than $0.50 for each bag? Explain.

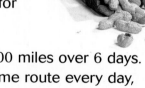

**19.** 📖 **Write About It**   Show how a pattern beginning with $640 \div 8 = 80$ leads to a decimal quotient of 0.8.

**20.** A bus traveled 3,000 miles over 6 days. If it covered the same route every day, how long was the route?

**21.** Find values for ♦ and ▼ that make the equation true. ♦ $\div$ ▼ $= 0.5$

**22.** John boarded his dog at the kennel and paid $72. It costs $20 for the first day and $13 for each additional day. How many days did he board his dog?

**◖ Getting Ready for ✦FCAT**

**23.** At Rudy's Dress Factory, a machine separates 25,000,000 buttons into groups of 1,000. Use the pattern shown to find how many buttons are in each group.

| | |
|---|---|
| $25,000,000 \div 1,000,000 = 25$ |
| $25,000,000 \div 100,000 = 250$ |
| $25,000,000 \div 10,000 = 2,500$ |
| $25,000,000 \div 1,000 = \blacksquare$ |

  **A.** 205     **C.** 250,000
  **B.** 25,000   **D.** 25,000,000

**FCAT TESTED** ✎ SSS/GLEs MA.D.1.2.1.5.1 Describes, extends, creates, predicts, and generalizes numerical and geometric patterns . . . . *also* MA.A.1.2.3.5.1, MA.A.3.2.1.5.3

**Chapter 11   229**

 **Decimal Division**

**MATERIALS**
decimal models
markers
scissors

▶ **Explore**

You can make a model to find the quotient of a decimal divided by a whole number.

## Activity 1

Find $1.5 \div 3$.     $3\overline{)1.5}$

### STEP 1
Show 1.5 by shading tenths models.

### STEP 2
Cut each model to show the tenths.

### STEP 3
Divide the tenths into 3 groups of the same size. Each group has 5 tenths.

### STEP 4
Record a division equation for your model.

$1.5 \div 3 = 0.5$

So, $1.5 \div 3$ is 0.5.

 **MATH IDEA**    A model can help you visualize division of decimals.

- Explain how you can use this pattern to show that your quotient is correct.

$150 \div 3 = 50$
$15 \div 3 = 5$
$1.5 \div 3 = \blacksquare$

How can you show equal groups for $1.4 \div 2$?

## Try It

Make a model to show the division. Record an equation for the model.

**a.** $1.4 \div 2$        **b.** $0.9 \div 3$
**c.** $2.5 \div 5$        **d.** $1.6 \div 4$

## ▶ Connect

### Activity 2    You can use a hundredths model to show 0.24 ÷ 6.

| STEP 1 | STEP 2 | STEP 3 | STEP 4 |
|---|---|---|---|
| Show 0.24 by shading a hundredths model.  | Cut the model to show the hundredths. 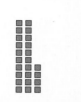 | Divide the hundredths into 6 groups of the same size. Each group has 4 hundredths.  | Record a division equation for your model. $0.24 \div 6 = 0.04$ |

## ▶ Practice and Problem Solving

**Make a model and find the quotient.**

**1.** $0.08 \div 2$

**2.** $\$0.24 \div 2$

**3.** $0.15 \div 3$

**4.** $1.2 \div 4$

**5.** $\$0.12 \div 4$

**6.** $3.5 \div 5$

**7.** $2.4 \div 3$

**8.** $0.08 \div 8$

**9.** $\$0.39 \div 3$

**10.** $\$0.44 \div 2$

**11.** $0.18 \div 9$

**12.** $0.18 \div 6$

**Technology Link**

More Practice:
Harcourt Mega Math
*The Number Games,*
*Tiny's Think Tank,*
Level S
*Buggy Bargains,*
Levels N, O, and P

**Use the model to find the value of n.**

**13.**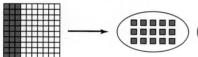

$0.30 \div 2 = n$

**14.**

$0.12 \div 3 = n$

**15.** Mario bought 4 pieces of wood for a total of $7.20. If two of the pieces together cost $4.20, and each of the other two pieces had the same cost, how much was each remaining piece?

**16.**  ? **What's the Error?**  Look at the model below for $0.16 \div 4$. Describe and correct the error.

## Getting Ready for FCAT

**17.** Bruce paid $4.80 for 3 boxes of nails. Each box was the same price. Which expression can he use to find the cost of each box?

**A.** $\$4.80 \div 3$

**C.** $\$4.80 - 3$

**B.** $3 \times \$4.80$

**D.** $\$4.80 + 3$

# 3 Divide Decimals by Whole Numbers

▶ **Learn**

**UP, UP, AND AWAY**  Paulo and his friends are making 3 kites. To make the tails for the kites, they will cut a narrow piece of cloth that is 4.2 meters long into 3 equal lengths. How long will each piece of cloth be?

◀ One of the largest kites ever flown had an area of 5,952 square feet.

## Example

Find 4.2 ÷ 3.
Estimate. 3 ÷ 3 = 1

**One Way**  You can divide by using a model.

**STEP 1**

Shade decimal models to show 4.2.

**STEP 2**

Divide the models into 3 groups of the same size.

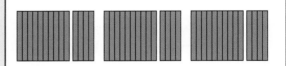

• Explain how you know how many wholes and how many tenths to put in each of the 3 equal groups.

**Another Way**  You can divide by using paper and pencil.

**STEP 1**

Write the decimal point of the quotient above the decimal point of the dividend.

3)4.2

**STEP 2**

Divide as you would divide whole numbers.

```
   1.4
3)4.2
 -3
  12
 -12
   0
```

So, each piece of cloth will be 1.4 meters long. Since the answer is close to the estimate, the answer is reasonable.

## More Examples

**A**

Find 2.49 ÷ 3.

```
  0.83
3)2.49
 -0
  24
 -24
  09
  -9
   0
```
← The divisor is greater than the dividend, so place a zero in the ones place.

You can multiply to check your answer.

**Check ✓**
```
 0.83
×   3
 2.49
```

**B**

Find $18.45 ÷ 15.

```
    $1.23
15)$18.45
  -15
   34
  -30
   45
  -45
    0
```
← When you divide money, remember to include a dollar sign in the quotient.

**Check ✓**
```
  $1.23
×    15
   615
 +123
 $18.45
```

**C**

Find 5.628 ÷ 4.

```
  1.407
4)5.628
 -4
  16
 -16
  02
  -0
  28
 -28
   0
```
← Since 4 > 2, place a zero in the hundredths place.

**Check ✓**
```
 1.407
×    4
 5.628
```

 **MATH IDEA** When the dividend is a decimal and the divisor is a whole number, divide as with whole numbers. Line up the decimal point in the quotient with the decimal point in the dividend.

## Check

1. **Explain** where you place the decimal point in the quotient when you divide a decimal by a whole number.

**Draw a picture to show the quotient.**

2. 1.26 ÷ 3

3. 2.38 ÷ 7

**Copy the quotient and correctly place the decimal point.**

4.
```
  0 5 3
2)1.06
```

5.
```
  0 0 0 9
5)0.045
```

6.
```
   70
7)49.0
```

7.
```
   815
4)32.60
```

**Find the quotient. Check by multiplying.**

8. 6)4.8

9. 9)$9.09

10. 4)12.04

11. 2)$1.04

12. 35.7 ÷ 7

13. $0.80 ÷ 5

14. 4.355 ÷ 5

15. 115.2 ÷ 24

**LESSON CONTINUES**

**FCAT TESTED** SSS/GLEs MA.A.1.2.3.5.1 Translates problem situations into diagrams, models, and numerals using whole numbers, fractions, mixed numbers, decimals, and percents. *also* MA.A.3.2.3.5.1

**Chapter 11 233**

**Copy the quotient and correctly place the decimal point.**

16. $\overset{09}{7\overline{)6.3}}$

17. $\overset{202}{4\overline{)8.08}}$

18. $\overset{075}{8\overline{)6.00}}$

19. $\overset{027}{15\overline{)4.05}}$

20. $\overset{0712}{6\overline{)4.272}}$

21. $\overset{0122}{3\overline{)0.366}}$

22. $\overset{341}{8\overline{)27.28}}$

23. $\overset{1236}{5\overline{)61.80}}$

**Find the quotient. Check by multiplying.**

24. $8\overline{)74.4}$

25. $3\overline{)27.9}$

26. $5\overline{)\$55.55}$

27. $2\overline{)19.64}$

28. $7\overline{)85.4}$

29. $70\overline{)854.0}$

30. $3\overline{)\$93.66}$

31. $4\overline{)9.064}$

32. $8\overline{)\$33.04}$

33. $4\overline{)21.56}$

34. $14\overline{)59.22}$

35. $19\overline{)\$234.84}$

36. $12\overline{)39.0}$

37. $10\overline{)212.5}$

38. $9\overline{)343.89}$

39. $11\overline{)570.9}$

40. $24.6 \div 6$

41. $\$2.46 \div 6$

42. $0.93 \div 3$

43. $8.05 \div 7$

44. $0.54 \div 6$

45. $5.04 \div 8$

46. $72.64 \div 8$

47. $48.6 \div 9$

48. $48.3 \div 7$

49. $18.5 \div 5$

50. $21.6 \div 4$

51. $\$4.24 \div 8$

**USE DATA   For 52–55, use the data in the list.**

52. How much did Blair pay for 1 paintbrush?

53. How much did Bryan pay for 2 yards of ribbon?

54. Ian bought 6 silk flowers and 2 glue sticks. How much did he spend?

55. ✎ **Write a problem** that uses data in the list and is solved by dividing a decimal. Solve your problem.

56. **≡FAST FACT** • HISTORY The world record for the longest "kite fly" is 180 hours. How many days is 180 hours? Write the answer as a decimal. (HINT: 180 = 180.0)

57. **Vocabulary Power** The word *equation* comes from the Latin root word *aequus,* which means "level" or "equal." Write the equation that shows 8 wholes and 4 tenths divided into 2 equal groups.

**Price List**

Paintbrushes   3 for $7.47

Silk flowers   $15.48 per dozen

Glue sticks   5 for $9.45

Ribbon   $1.19 per yard

**58.** Tennis balls are 3 for $2.79 or $5.00 for a half dozen. Which is the better buy?

**59.** ? **What's the Question?** The difference between the prices of two bikes is $16. The sum of their prices is $232. The answer is $124.

---

## Getting Ready for FCAT

**60.** Jackie paid $14.22 for 9 gallons of gas at Station A. She paid $17.93 for 11 gallons of gas at Station B. Which of the following statements is true?

   **A.** Gas costs $0.15 less per gallon at Station A than at Station B.

   **B.** Gas costs $0.05 more per gallon at Station A than at Station B.

   **C.** Jackie spent a total of $31.15 for gas at Station A and Station B.

   **D.** Gas costs $0.05 more per gallon at Station B than at Station A.

**61.** The Shipley family is buying patio furniture for $498.50. They plan to pay for it in 12 equal monthly payments. Which expression represents the monthly payment?

   **F.** $498.50 ÷ 12

   **G.** 12 × $498.50

   **H.** 42 ÷ 12

   **I.** $42 × 12

---

# Problem Solving THINKER'S CORNER

**REASONING** Mr. Renard had $120 to buy supplies for his kite-making classes. After he finished shopping, he had $7.82 left. Mr. Renard lost his receipt and recorded what he remembered in the table below.

**For 1–2, choose the best answer. Then copy and complete the table.**

**1.** How can you find the total amount spent on all the supplies?

   **A** Find $17.88 + $25.50 + $14.80. Then subtract the sum from $120.00.

   **B** Subtract $7.82 from $120.00.

   **C** Add $120.00 and $7.82.

   **D** Add all the numbers in the table.

**2.** **ALGEBRA** If $b$ equals the cost per package for paintbrushes, which equation can you use to solve for $b$?

   **F** $b = \$14.80 \times 8$    **H** $b \div \$14.80 = 8$

   **G** $\$14.80 - b = 8$    **J** $\$14.80 \div 8 = b$

| KITE-MAKING SUPPLIES | | | |
|---|---|---|---|
| **Item Bought** | **Cost per Package** | **Number of Packages** | **Total Amount Spent** |
| Kite fabric | $1.49 | 12 | $17.88 |
| Paints | $2.55 | ■ | $25.50 |
| Balsa wood | $3.00 | ■ | ■ |
| Paintbrushes | ■ | 8 | $14.80 |
| **Total Spent →** | | | ■ |

# Problem Solving Skill
## Choose the Operation

UNDERSTAND ▷ PLAN ▷ SOLVE ▷ CHECK

**"WEIGH OUT" IN SPACE**  Beth used data she found on a class trip to the Space Museum to make this table. The table shows how much a 1-pound weight on Earth would weigh on other planets.

| ONE EARTH POUND IN SPACE | |
|---|---|
| Planet | Weight (in pounds) |
| Mercury | 0.38 |
| Venus | 0.91 |
| Earth | 1 |
| Mars | 0.38 |
| Jupiter | 2.53 |
| Saturn | 1.07 |
| Uranus | 0.90 |
| Neptune | 1.10 |
| Pluto | 0.07 |

**MATH IDEA**  The way numbers in a problem are related can help you choose the operation needed to solve the problem.

| Add | To join groups. |
|---|---|
| Subtract | To take away or compare groups. |
| Multiply | To join equal-sized groups. |
| Divide | To separate into equal-sized groups. To find out how many in each group. |

**Decide how the numbers in the problem are related. Name the operation needed to solve the problem. Then solve.**

**A.** A cocker spaniel weighs 35 pounds on Earth. To the nearest pound, how much would it weigh on Jupiter?

**B.** The 9 moon rocks on display at the museum weigh a total of 3.69 pounds. What is the average weight of one moon rock?

**C.** How much more would a kitten that weighs 1 pound on Earth weigh on Jupiter?

**D.** How much would 2 hamsters weigh on Mercury if they weigh 1 pound each on Earth?

## Talk About It

• Explain how you decided which operation to use to solve each problem.

• **What if** the cocker spaniel in Problem A weighed 27.5 pounds on Earth? To the nearest pound, how much would it weigh on Jupiter?

## Problem Solving Practice

**Solve. Name the operation or operations you used.**
**For 1–2, use the table on page 236.**

**1.** On Earth, an astronaut's suit weighed 65.2 pounds, and the life-support systems weighed 41.6 pounds. About how much weight would this be on Saturn?

**2.** If a blue whale weighs 286,600 pounds on Earth, how much would it weigh on Mars?

**3.** Suppose a polar bear weighs 1,323 pounds and a walrus weighs 1,503 pounds. How much more does the walrus weigh than the polar bear?

**4.** Suppose 3 giant pandas weigh a total of 1,056 pounds. What is the average weight of the pandas?

**In 1999, the record was set for the most animals on a space mission. On board the shuttle *Columbia* were 1,500 crickets, 18 mice, 152 rats, 135 snails, 4 oyster toadfish, and 229 swordtail fish.**

◄ Laika, the first living creature in space, was launched aboard *Sputnik 2* in 1957.

**5.** What operation would you use to find the total number of creatures on the mission?
  **A** multiplication  **C** subtraction
  **B** division  **D** addition

**6.** How many more crickets were there than all other animals combined?
  **F** 538  **H** 962
  **G** 872  **J** 1,500

## Mixed Applications

**USE DATA** For 7–8, use the bar graph.

**7.** What is the difference in speed between the fastest and slowest fish on the graph?

**8.** How long would it take a marlin to travel 1,000 miles?

**9.** The sixth-fastest fish is the wahoo. It swims 66 kilometers per hour. How many miles per hour does it swim? (1 kilometer equals 0.62 mile)

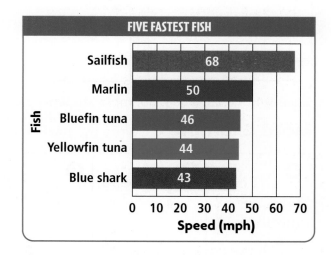

**FIVE FASTEST FISH**

Fish / Speed (mph):
Sailfish 68
Marlin 50
Bluefin tuna 46
Yellowfin tuna 44
Blue shark 43

0 10 20 30 40 50 60 70
**Speed (mph)**

**10.** Anthony has a total of 74 inches of string to wrap 6 boxes. He uses 12 inches of string for each of the boxes. Find how many inches of string Anthony will have left after wrapping 6 boxes.

**11.** ✎ **Write a problem** using the information in the graph above. Exchange problems with a classmate and solve.

**FCAT TESTED** SSS/GLEs MA.A.3.2.2.5.1 Uses problem-solving strategies to determine the operation(s) needed to solve one- and two-step problems involving addition, subtraction, multiplication, and division of whole numbers, and addition, subtraction, and multiplication of decimals and fractions.

**Chapter 11 237**

# Divide to Change a Fraction to a Decimal

 **Learn**

**HAVING FUN!** The students at Lakeville School are planning their school carnival. After school, $\frac{2}{5}$ of the students planned the game booths and $\frac{1}{4}$ of the students planned the food booths. Did more students plan the food or the game booths?

One way to compare fractions that have different denominators is to change the fractions to decimals.

**MATH IDEA** Change a fraction to an equivalent decimal by dividing the numerator by the denominator.

**Example** Compare $\frac{2}{5}$ and $\frac{1}{4}$.

**STEP 1**

Write each fraction as a division problem.

$$\frac{2}{5} \rightarrow 5\overline{)2}$$

$$\frac{1}{4} \rightarrow 4\overline{)1}$$

**STEP 2**

Divide as with whole numbers. Place a decimal point and zeros as needed in the dividend. Place a decimal point and a zero in the quotient.

$$\begin{array}{r} 0.4 \\ 5\overline{)2.0} \\ -2\,0 \\ \hline 0 \end{array}$$

$$\begin{array}{r} 0.25 \\ 4\overline{)1.00} \\ -8 \\ \hline 20 \\ -20 \\ \hline 0 \end{array}$$

 **Remember**

$\frac{1}{4}$ can be read as one fourth, one quarter, one out of four, or one divided by four.

Since $0.4 > 0.25$, $\frac{2}{5} > \frac{1}{4}$. So, more students planned the games.

**More Examples** Write the fraction as a decimal.

**A**
$$\frac{1}{5} \rightarrow \begin{array}{r} 0.2 \\ 5\overline{)1.0} \\ -1\,0 \\ \hline 0 \end{array}$$

**B**
$$\frac{3}{4} \rightarrow \begin{array}{r} 0.75 \\ 4\overline{)3.00} \\ -2\,8 \\ \hline 20 \\ -20 \\ \hline 0 \end{array}$$

**C**
$$\frac{7}{8} \rightarrow \begin{array}{r} 0.875 \\ 8\overline{)7.000} \\ -6\,4 \\ \hline 60 \\ -56 \\ \hline 40 \\ -40 \\ \hline 0 \end{array}$$

 You can also use a calculator to change a fraction to a decimal.

$\frac{2}{5} =$         0.4

1. **Explain** how you know that $\frac{1}{4}$ and 0.25 are equivalent.

**Write as a decimal.**

2. $\frac{2}{10}$     3. $\frac{3}{5}$     4. $\frac{3}{8}$     5. $\frac{4}{8}$     6. $\frac{6}{10}$     7. $\frac{3}{20}$

▶ **Practice and Problem Solving**    Extra Practice, page 240, Set C

**Write as a decimal.**

8. $\frac{7}{10}$     9. $\frac{23}{25}$     10. $\frac{9}{12}$     11. $\frac{2}{5}$     12. $\frac{2}{4}$     13. $\frac{2}{8}$

14. $\frac{3}{10}$     15. $\frac{17}{20}$     16. $\frac{5}{8}$     17. $\frac{1}{8}$     18. $\frac{4}{5}$     19. $\frac{6}{8}$

**USE DATA**   For 20–22, use the circle graph.

20. Use a decimal to name the part of the money Jake's family spent on souvenirs.

21. Use a decimal to name the part of the money Jake's family spent on rides and games.

22. **What if** Jake's family had bought food for $15 and saved the extra money? Use a decimal to name the part of their money they would have saved.

23. Jenny ran $\frac{6}{25}$ mile. Greg ran 0.21 mile. Who ran farther? Explain how you know.

24. Write a fraction that has a decimal equivalent that is greater than 0.5 and less than 0.75.

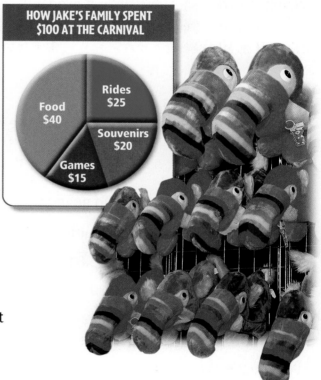

**HOW JAKE'S FAMILY SPENT $100 AT THE CARNIVAL**

Food $40   Rides $25   Souvenirs $20   Games $15

▬ **Getting Ready for FCAT** ▬

25. The table shows the distance in miles that each student lives from the science center. Who lives second farthest from the science center?

   A. Christa
   B. Nola
   C. Steve
   D. Lexi

| DISTANCE FROM THE SCIENCE CENTER | |
|---|---|
| **Student** | **Miles** |
| Christa | $\frac{2}{5}$ |
| Nola | 0.25 |
| Steve | $\frac{3}{8}$ |
| Lexi | 0.3 |

# Extra Practice

## Set A (pp. 228–229)

**Copy and complete each pattern.**

**1.** 300 ÷ 6 = ■
30 ÷ 6 = ■
3 ÷ 6 = ■

**2.** 200 ÷ 5 = ■
20 ÷ 5 = ■
2 ÷ 5 = ■

**3.** 180 ÷ 3 = ■
18 ÷ 3 = ■
1.8 ÷ 3 = ■

**4.** 100 ÷ 4 = ■
10 ÷ 4 = ■
1 ÷ 4 = ■

**5.** 400 ÷ 8 = ■
40 ÷ 8 = ■
4 ÷ 8 = ■

**6.** 240 ÷ 8 = ■
24 ÷ 8 = ■
2.4 ÷ 8 = ■

**7.** 900 ÷ 10 = ■
90 ÷ 10 = ■
9 ÷ 10 = ■

**8.** 100 ÷ 5 = ■
10 ÷ 5 = ■
1 ÷ 5 = ■

**9.** 200 ÷ 4 = ■
20 ÷ 4 = ■
2 ÷ 4 = ■

## Set B (pp. 232–235)

**Copy the quotient and correctly place the decimal point.**

**1.** 685; 2)13.70

**2.** 1143; 3)34.29

**3.** 0587; 4)2.348

**4.** 0015; 5)0.075

**5.** 9564; 6)57.384

**6.** 01234; 7)0.8638

**7.** 8888; 8)71.104

**8.** 2112; 9)190.08

**Find the quotient. Check by multiplying.**

**9.** 5)$4.45

**10.** 4)$5.84

**11.** 3)1.92

**12.** 7)10.5

**13.** 7.92 ÷ 6

**14.** 3.29 ÷ 7

**15.** $0.32 ÷ 8

**16.** 75.36 ÷ 3

**17.** $0.64 ÷ 4

**18.** 10.92 ÷ 7

**19.** 0.265 ÷ 5

**20.** 51.56 ÷ 4

## Set C (pp. 238–239)

**Write as a decimal.**

**1.** $\frac{7}{8}$
**2.** $\frac{2}{5}$
**3.** $\frac{7}{28}$
**4.** $\frac{7}{20}$
**5.** $\frac{9}{10}$
**6.** $\frac{17}{20}$

**7.** $\frac{19}{20}$
**8.** $\frac{6}{10}$
**9.** $\frac{9}{12}$
**10.** $\frac{6}{16}$
**11.** $\frac{13}{20}$
**12.** $\frac{5}{10}$

**13.** $\frac{3}{10}$
**14.** $\frac{18}{24}$
**15.** $\frac{3}{8}$
**16.** $\frac{16}{40}$
**17.** $\frac{5}{8}$
**18.** $\frac{3}{12}$

**19.** Carol ate $\frac{2}{5}$ of the cake, and Evelyn ate $\frac{1}{5}$ of the cake. Write as a decimal the part of the cake they ate.

**20.** Brett ate $\frac{3}{4}$ of a pizza. Write as a decimal the part of the pizza that is left.

# Review/Test

## ✓ CHECK CONCEPTS

Copy and complete each pattern. (pp. 228–229)

1. $210 \div 7 =$ ▨
   $21 \div 7 =$ ▨
   $2.1 \div 7 =$ ▨

2. $400 \div 5 =$ ▨
   $40 \div 5 =$ ▨
   $4 \div 5 =$ ▨

3. $240 \div 6 =$ ▨
   $24 \div 6 =$ ▨
   $2.4 \div 6 =$ ▨

## ✓ CHECK SKILLS

Find the quotient. Check by multiplying. (pp. 232–235)

4. $8\overline{)7.2}$

5. $7\overline{)5.6}$

6. $9\overline{)0.81}$

7. $2\overline{)3.66}$

8. $3.95 \div 5$

9. $109.2 \div 6$

10. $218.4 \div 8$

11. $5,716.8 \div 9$

12. $33.68 \div 8$

13. $28.44 \div 9$

14. $81.84 \div 6$

15. $58.75 \div 5$

Write as a decimal. (pp. 238–239)

16. $\dfrac{4}{16}$

17. $\dfrac{6}{12}$

18. $\dfrac{5}{25}$

19. $\dfrac{3}{40}$

20. $\dfrac{6}{24}$

21. $\dfrac{7}{35}$

## ✓ CHECK PROBLEM SOLVING

Solve. Name the operation or operations you used. (pp. 236–237)

22. Ben earned $40.00 by doing lawn work. He used his earnings and bought two CDs for $12.98 each. The tax was $2.10. How much did Ben have left?

23. Blanche has $16.87 and Carl has $19.54. How much more money does Carl have than Blanche?

24. Arturo worked 5 hours at $5.75 per hour. Christine worked 3 hours at $6.50 per hour. Who made more money? How much more?

25. Mr. Huang bought 32.4 pounds of chicken during the month of June. What was the average number of pounds of chicken Mr. Huang bought per week?

# Getting Ready for FCAT

## ★ NUMBER SENSE, CONCEPTS, AND OPERATIONS

**1.** A stack of 9 identical math textbooks is 30.6 centimeters tall. How thick is each book?

  **A.** 0.34 centimeter

  **B.** 3.4 centimeters

  **C.** 34 centimeters

  **D.** 275.4 centimeters

**2.** At the deli, Mrs. Dawson asked for $\frac{1}{4}$ pound of roast beef. The clerk weighed that amount and printed a label showing the weight as a decimal. Which of the following was shown on the label?

  **F.** 0.75

  **G.** 0.60

  **H.** 0.50

  **I.** 0.25

**3. Explain It** A small wedge of cheese costs $3.75. About how much does the whole wheel of cheese cost? Explain how you found your answer.

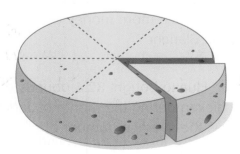

## ★ ALGEBRAIC THINKING

**4.** Brooke and Jamie each have a collection of troll dolls. Brooke has 8 more dolls than Jamie. If $d$ represents the number of dolls that Jamie has, which expression describes the number of dolls that Brooke has?

  **A.** $d - 8$

  **B.** $8d$

  **C.** $8 - d$

  **D.** $d + 8$

**5.** Yuko is shorter than Sue. Sue is no more than 3 inches taller than Yuko. Sue is 51 inches tall. Which are the possible heights, in inches, for Yuko?

  **F.** 48, 49, 50, 51

  **G.** 49, 50, 51

  **H.** 48, 49, 50

  **I.** 47, 48, 49, 50

**6. Explain It** Name a rule for the table. Write the rule as an equation. Then copy and complete the table. Explain how you know your rule is correct.

| n | p |
|----|----|
| 21 | 6 |
| 33 | 18 |
| 15 | ■ |
| 47 | ■ |
| 59 | 44 |

## ⭐ MEASUREMENT

**7.** What is the volume of this toy box?

3 feet
TOYS
2 feet
6 feet

Volume of rectangular prism $= l \times w \times h$

  **A.** 11 feet

  **B.** 36 cubic feet

  **C.** 36 square feet

  **D.** 150 feet

**8.** The area of a rectangular rug is 84 square feet. The width of the rug is 7 feet. What is the length of the rug?

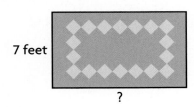

7 feet

?

Area of rectangle $= l \times w$

  **F.** 12 feet

  **G.** 28 feet

  **H.** 77 feet

  **I.** 91 feet

**9. Explain It** ESTIMATE the area of the figure. Each square on the grid represents 1 square foot. Explain how you found your estimate.

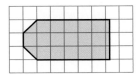

## ⭐ DATA ANALYSIS AND PROBABILITY

> **TIP** **Get the information you need.** See item 10. Look at the graph. Read the scale to determine the lengths of the bars. A bar halfway between 8 miles and 10 miles represents 9 miles.

**10.** The bar graph shows the results of the Annual Walk-a-Thon.

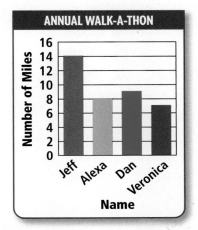

**ANNUAL WALK-A-THON**

Number of Miles

Jeff  Alexa  Dan  Veronica

**Name**

How many more miles did Jeff walk than Alexa?

  **A.** 6 miles      **C.** 7.5 miles

  **B.** 7 miles      **D.** 8.5 miles

**11.** Look at the graph in Problem 10. Suppose $2.00 is pledged for every mile walked. In all, how much money will the four friends raise?

  **F.** $7.50      **H.** $76.00

  **G.** $37.50      **I.** $750.00

**12. Explain It** Three fifth-grade students are running for class president. Ron wants to take a survey to predict the most likely winner of the election. Describe one way Ron can select a fair sample for his survey. Explain your choice.

# Algebra: Use Multiplication and Division

**≡FAST FACT** • SOCIAL STUDIES

The largest flying flag in the United States is in Gastonia, NC. It covers 7,410 square feet, weighs 180 pounds, and takes at least 6 people to raise and lower it.

PROBLEM SOLVING   The flag is 65 feet wide. Write and solve an equation to find the length of the flag, using $A = l \times w$. See the table. Write and solve equations to find the missing dimensions for some United States flags.

| DIMENSIONS OF SOME UNITED STATES FLAGS | | | |
|---|---|---|---|
| Flag | Length (*l*) | Width (*w*) | Area (*A*) |
| Gastonia, NC | ▪ | 65 ft | 7,410 ft² |
| U.S. Capitol Building | 8 ft | ▪ | 40 ft² |
| Betsy Ross Flag | 3 ft | 5 ft | ▪ |
| Ft. McHenry Flag | 42 ft | ▪ | 1,260 ft² |

# CHECK WHAT YOU KNOW

Use this page to help you review and remember
important skills needed for Chapter 12.

## RELATE MULTIPLICATION AND DIVISION

Find the value of the variable. Write a related division equation.

**1.** $2 \times 6 = n$     **2.** $8 \times 4 = n$     **3.** $7 \times 9 = n$     **4.** $6 \times 8 = n$

**5.** $5 \times 6 = n$     **6.** $7 \times 8 = n$     **7.** $9 \times 6 = n$     **8.** $9 \times 9 = n$

## USE PARENTHESES

Choose the expression that shows the given value.

**9.** 32
   **a.** $2 + (10 \times 3)$
   **b.** $(2 + 10) \times 3$

**10.** 0
   **a.** $15 - (3 \times 5)$
   **b.** $(15 - 3) \times 5$

**11.** 24
   **a.** $4 + (8 \times 2)$
   **b.** $(4 + 8) \times 2$

**12.** 12
   **a.** $12 + (0 \times 4)$
   **b.** $(12 + 0) \times 4$

## MULTIPLICATION PROPERTIES

Write the letter of the multiplication property used
in each equation.

**a.** Order Property        **c.** Identity Property
**b.** Grouping Property      **d.** Zero Property

**13.** $8 \times 5 = 5 \times 8$

**14.** $(4 \times 2) \times 5 = 4 \times (2 \times 5)$

**15.** $(8 \times 2) \times 5 = 8 \times (2 \times 5)$

**16.** $25 \times 1 = 25$

**17.** $78 \times 0 = 0$

**18.** $4 \times 11 = 11 \times 4$

# VOCABULARY POWER

## REVIEW

**algebra** [al′ jə brə] *noun*

Algebra is a branch of mathematics
that deals with the relationships among
numbers. The word *algebra* comes from
an Arabic word meaning "the reunion of
broken parts, such as broken bones".
Explain how this definition relates to an
equation such as $4 + n + 8 = 15$.

## PREVIEW

evaluate      Commutative Property
order of operations      Associative Property
function      Distributive Property
               Identity Property

 www.harcourtschool.com/mathglossary
ON-LINE

# Expressions and Equations

▶ **Learn**

**SIGN IN** Tina collects autographs. After a recent trip, she had 2 times as many autographs in her collection as she had before her trip. You can use an expression to represent how many autographs Tina has.

**VOCABULARY**

**evaluate**

---

**One Way**   Use models.

Model the expression.

Let  represent the number of autographs she had before the trip.

 → number of autographs she has now

_____

Suppose Tina had 5 autographs before the trip. How many does she have now?

Replace each ⬡ with 5 ⬛'s.

So, she has 10 autographs now.

**Another Way**   Use paper and pencil.

Write an expression. Let *n* represent the number of autographs she had before the trip.

2 × *n* → number of autographs she has now

You can also write 2 × *n* as 2 • *n*, 2(*n*), or 2*n*.

_____

Suppose Tina had 5 autographs before the trip. How many does she have now? Find the value when *n* = 5.

$2n$

2 × 5     Replace *n* with 5.

10

So, she has 10 autographs now.

---

 **MATH IDEA** To **evaluate** an expression with a variable, replace the variable with any number. Then perform the operations to find the value of the expression for that number.

• Explain how to evaluate the expression 2*n* + 1 if *n* = 3.

## Examples

**A** Evaluate 6*y* if
*y* = 5.

6 × 5 ← Replace *y*
           with 5.

30

The value of the expression is 30.

**B** Evaluate *n* ÷ 3 − 7 if
*n* = 27.

27 ÷ 3 − 7 ← Replace *n*
                 with 27.

9 − 7 = 2

The value of the expression is 2.

**C** Evaluate 3*a* + 1 if
*a* = 9.

3 × 9 ← Replace *a*
           with 9.

27 + 1 = 28

The value of the expression is 28.

# Write and Solve Equations

Antoni has collected 84 autographs. He filled 14 pages in his new autograph album. Each page holds an equal number of autographs. How many autographs fit on a page?

Write an equation with a variable to model this problem.

Let $a$ = the number of autographs per page.

| number of pages | multiplied by | number of autographs per page | equals | number of autographs |
|:---:|:---:|:---:|:---:|:---:|
| ↓ | ↓ | ↓ | ↓ | ↓ |
| 14 | × | $a$ | = | 84 |

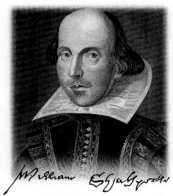

▲ Experts believe that William Shakespeare's autograph would sell for $5,000,000.

When you solve an equation, you find the value of the variable that makes the equation true.

**One Way** Which of the values 3, 4, or 6 is the solution of $84 \div a = 14$? Substitute each of the values for $a$.

| | | |
|---|---|---|
| $14 \times a = 84$   Try 3. | $14 \times a = 84$   Try 4. | $14 \times a = 84$   Try 6. |
| $14 \times 3 \overset{?}{=} 84$   Replace<br>$42 \neq 84$   $a$ with 3. | $14 \times 4 \overset{?}{=} 84$   Replace<br>$56 \neq 84$   $a$ with 4. | $14 \times 6 \overset{?}{=} 84$   Replace<br>$84 = 84$   $a$ with 6. |
| The two sides are not the same, so $a = 3$ is not a solution. | The two sides are not the same, so $a = 4$ is not a solution. | The two sides are the same, so $a = 6$ is the solution. |

So, each page of Antoni's autograph album holds 6 autographs.

**Another Way** You can also solve an equation by using mental math.

**D** Solve $72 \div c = 12$.

$72 \div c = 12$    **Think:** 72 divided by
$c = 6$        what number equals 12?

**Check:** $72 \div 6 = 12$   Replace $c$
$12 = 12 \checkmark$   with 6.

So, $c = 6$.

**E** Solve $5 \times n = 35$.

$5 \times n = 35$    **Think:** 5 times
$n = 7$        what number equals 35?

**Check:** $5 \times 7 = 35$   Replace $n$
$35 = 35 \checkmark$   with 7.

So, $n = 7$.

• **REASONING** How could you use inverse operations to solve Examples D and E?

• Write a problem that can be represented by the equation $n \times 3 = 24$.

**LESSON CONTINUES** ⊙

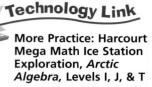
**Technology Link**

More Practice: Harcourt
Mega Math Ice Station
Exploration, *Arctic
Algebra*, Levels I, J, & T

1. **Model** the expression *5n*. Then evaluate the expression if *n* = 4.

**Evaluate the expression *n* ÷ 8 for each value of *n*.**

**2.** *n* = 96　　　**3.** *n* = 856　　　**4.** *n* = 112　　　**5.** *n* = 488

**Determine which value is a solution for the given equation.**

**6.** 9 × *n* = 72
　*n* = 7, 8, or 9

**7.** 147 ÷ *y* = 21
　*y* = 6, 7, or 8

**8.** *n* × 4 = 92
　*n* = 23 or 24

**9.** *m* ÷ 7 = 16
　*m* = 112 or 119

▶ **Practice and Problem Solving**　　Extra Practice, page 262, Set A

**Evaluate the expression 1,080 ÷ *n* for each value of *n*.**

**10.** *n* = 2　　　**11.** *n* = 3　　　**12.** *n* = 216　　　**13.** *n* = 9

**Evaluate the expression for each value of *n*.**

**14.** 2,700 ÷ *n*
　*n* = 3, 4, 5

**15.** *n* × 13
　*n* = 14, 15, 16

**16.** 168 ÷ *n*
　*n* = 6, 7, 8

**17.** *n* × 3
　*n* = 79, 81

**Determine which value is the solution for the given equation.**

**18.** 3 × *n* = 27
　*n* = 7, 8, or 9

**19.** 248 ÷ *n* = 62
　*n* = 4, 5, or 6

**20.** *p* ÷ 6 = 31
　*p* = 184 or 186

**21.** *w* ÷ 9 = 23
　*w* = 207 or 208

**22.** 60 ÷ *n* = 12
　*n* = 3, 4, or 5

**23.** *y* ÷ 5 = 28
　*y* = 135 or 140

**24.** *n* ÷ 8 = 31
　*n* = 248 or 256

**25.** 63 × *n* = 189
　*n* = 2, 3, or 4

**Solve the equation. Then check the solution.**

**26.** 24 ÷ *n* = 12　　**27.** 5 × *m* = 45　　**28.** *n* ÷ 9 = 12　　**29.** *s* ÷ 6 = 3

**30.** 9 × *n* = 81　　**31.** *p* ÷ 8 = 4　　**32.** *n* ÷ 3 = 12　　**33.** 5 × *n* = 55

**34. REASONING** Find the value of each symbol by using the given equations. A symbol always has the same value.

♥ ÷ 4 = 10　　　5 × ♦ = ♥　　　(♥ + 8) ÷ 3 = ♣　　　♠ ÷ 2 = ♣

**USE DATA** For 35–37, use the table.

**35.** How many kids were surveyed?

**36.** Collecting cards is how many more times as popular as collecting stamps?

**37.** What type of graph would you use to show these data? Explain.

**38.** 📕 **Write About It** Describe how you evaluate *p* ÷ 11 if *p* = 132.

| KIDS' FAVORITE COLLECTIBLES | |
|---|---|
| **Collectible** | **Number of Kids** |
| Cards | 36 |
| Coins | 20 |
| Dolls | 24 |
| Model cars | 14 |
| Stamps | 6 |

**Stamps from the Space
Achievement and Exploration series.**

**39.** Sean stopped at the mall for lunch. He had a $10 bill. He bought the Lunch Special for $3.59, a drink for $1.50, and 3 cookies for $0.65 each. How much change should he get?

**40.** ≡**FAST FACT** • SCIENCE An autographed photo of the *Apollo 11* astronauts was sold at auction for $1,783. An autographed photo of Buzz Aldrin as he stepped onto the moon sold for $1,066. Write an equation to show the difference in the prices.

## Getting Ready for FCAT

**41.** Nolan was asked to write four equations that have a solution of 6. Which one of his equations was NOT correct?

**A.** $13 \times n = 72$   **C.** $16 \times n = 96$

**B.** $9 \times n = 54$   **D.** $18 \times n = 108$

**42.** Julia had a piece of ribbon that was 90 inches long. She cut the ribbon into 6 equal pieces. Which equation can be used to find the length of each piece?

**F.** $p \div 6 = 90$   **H.** $p \div 90 = 6$

**G.** $90 \div p = 6$   **I.** $6 + p = 90$

# Problem Solving LiNKUP . . . to Reading

**STRATEGY • ANALYZE INFORMATION** When you *analyze information*, look for the important details. Then think about how to use the details to solve the problem.

People all over the world collect pencil sharpeners. One of the largest collections of pencil sharpeners belongs to Gemma Dickmann of Holland. By 1999, she owned a total of 4,275 bronze, plastic, wood, stone, and rubber pencil sharpeners. She had 2,200 plastic sharpeners. She had twice as many plastic sharpeners as stone ones. About how many stone sharpeners did Gemma have?

- List the important details. about 2,200 plastic sharpeners; twice as many plastic sharpeners as stone sharpeners

- Tell what you need to find. the number of stone sharpeners she had

- Look for clues. *Twice as many* tells you to multiply or divide. Since you know the number of plastic sharpeners, divide.

- Solve. $2,200 \div 2 = 1,100$; So, Gemma had about 1,100 stone sharpeners.

**Write the details you need to solve each problem. Then solve.**

**1.** Rob has 177 baseball cards. Rob has 3 times as many cards as Jen. How many cards does Jen have?

**2.** In the past year, Jack has doubled the size of his stamp collection to 568 stamps. How many stamps did he have last year?

# Order of Operations

**VOCABULARY**
order of operations

## Learn

**FIRST THINGS FIRST**   Lamar is saving the money he earns to buy a new bicycle. One week he earned $7 for cleaning the garage. For the next 8 weeks he earned $3 a week for mowing the lawn. How much did Lamar save?

$$7 + (8 \times 3)$$

When you evaluate an expression with more than one operation, you need to know which operation to do first.

A special set of rules, called the **order of operations**, is used to solve an expression with more than one operation.

1. First, operate inside parentheses.
2. Next, multiply and divide from left to right.
3. Then, add and subtract from left to right.

### Example
Use the order of operations to evaluate $7 + (8 \times 3)$.

| | |
|---|---|
| $7 + (8 \times 3)$ | Operate inside the parentheses. $8 \times 3$ |
| $7 + 24$ | Add. $7 + 24$ |
| 31 | |

So, Lamar saved $31.

**MATH IDEA**   When you find the value of an expression with more than one operation, you use the rules called the order of operations.

### More Examples

**A** $(16 + 4) \times 3 + 9$   Operate inside parentheses. $16 + 4$
  $20 \times 3 + 9$   Multiply. $20 \times 3$
  $60 + 9$   Add. $60 + 9$
  $69$

**B** $32 \div 4 - 2 \times 3$   Divide. $32 \div 4$
  $8 - 2 \times 3$   Multiply. $2 \times 3$
  $8 - 6$   Subtract. $8 - 6$
  $2$

## Check

1. **Explain** which operation to do first, second, and third in evaluating this expression. $100 - 6 \times (4 + 7)$

**Evaluate the expression.**

2. $12 + 9 \times 6 + 4$      3. $12 \times (9 + 6) + 4$      4. $12 \div 6 \times (9 - 4)$

**Evaluate the expression.**

**5.** $10 + 8 \times 5 + 20$

**6.** $20 \times (10 + 1) + 4$

**7.** $20 \times 10 + 1 + 4$

**8.** $12 \times 3 \div 6 + 4$

**9.** $15 \times (5 + 5) \div 15$

**10.** $40 \div 5 \times (11 - 7)$

**11.** $3 - (3 - 3) \times 3$

**12.** $16 - (9 \div 3) \times 4$

**13.** $90 \div 15 - (8 - 2)$

**Write *correct* if the order of operations is correct. Otherwise, give the correct sequence of operations.**

**Technology Link**

More Practice: Harcourt Mega Math Ice Station Exploration, *Arctic Algebra*, Level R

**14.** $18 + 16 - 2 \times 5$   Multiply, add, and then subtract.

**15.** $3 \times (7 + 4) \div 5$   Multiply, divide, and then add.

**16.** $5 + 14 \div 2 \times 5$   Divide, add, and then multiply.

**For 17–19, insert parentheses in the expression to get the given value for *a*, *b*, and *c*.**

**17.** $24 + 8 \times 4 + 3$   **a.** 59   **b.** 80   **c.** 131

**18.** $24 - 8 - 4 - 3$   **a.** 9   **b.** 15   **c.** 17

**19.** $24 + 8 \div 4 - 3$   **a.** 32   **b.** 23   **c.** 5

**Evaluate each expression if *n* = 10 and 11.**

**20.** $2 + n \times 6 + 4$

**21.** $(2 + n) \times 6 + 4$

**22.** $2 + n \times (6 + 4)$

**23.** At a neighborhood yard sale, Derek spent $8 for a bike helmet and $3 each for two sets of kneepads. How much did he spend in all?

**24.** Find the value of *n* that makes the expression $2 \times (n - 4)$ equal to 10.

**25.** **? What's the Error?** Jacques wrote $8 + 12 \div 2 - 4 = 6$. Identify and correct his error.

**26.** **Write About It** Explain the order of operations in your own words. Then give an example of how you might use these rules.

**27.** **Vocabulary Power** *Parentheses* are sometimes called "fences." Why do you think "fence" is a good name for *parentheses* in a math problem?

**Getting Ready for FCAT**

**28.** Lance wrote down his practice schedule for his recital on Saturday. Which expression shows the total number of hours he will practice?

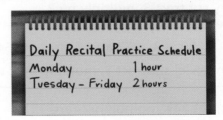

Daily Recital Practice Schedule
Monday            1 hour
Tuesday – Friday  2 hours

   **A.** $(1 + 2) \times 4$   **C.** $1 \times (2 + 4)$
   **B.** $(1 \times 2) + 4$   **D.** $1 + (2 \times 4)$

FCAT TESTED   SSS/GLEs MA.A.3.2.2 Selects the appropriate operation to solve specific problems involving addition, subtraction, and multiplication of whole numbers, decimals, and fractions, and division of whole numbers.

**Chapter 12 251**

# Number Patterns

**Quick Review**

1. $8 \times 6$    2. $36 \div 3$
3. $9 \times 4$    4. $28 - 9$
5. $16 + 14$

▶ **Learn**

**TELEPHONE TREE** The students at West Side School use a telephone tree to pass important news. The tree starts with one student. On the second round, 3 calls are made, on the third round, 9 calls, and on the fourth round 27 calls are made. How many calls are made on the fifth and sixth rounds?

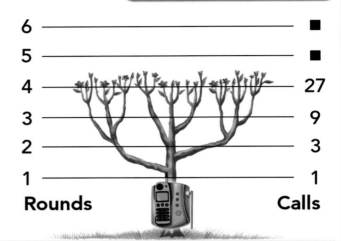

**Example 1** Find a rule. Then find the next two numbers in the pattern. 1, 3, 9, 27, ▪, ▪

**STEP 1**

Find a rule for the pattern.

**Think:** What rule changes 1 to 3?

Try **add 2** because $1 + 2 = 3$.
         $3 + 2 = 5$, but $5 \neq 9$.

The rule, **add 2** doesn't work.

Try **multiply by 3** since $1 \times 3 = 3$.
The rule, **multiply by 3**, works.

**STEP 2**

Now, use the rule to solve the problem.

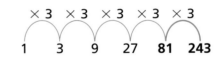

$$1 \quad 3 \quad 9 \quad 27 \quad \mathbf{81} \quad \mathbf{243}$$

$27 \times 3 = 81$      $81 \times 3 = 243$

So, 81 calls were made on the fifth round, and 243 calls were made on the sixth round.

**Example 2** Find a rule. Then find the missing numbers in the pattern.
43, 40, 80, 77, 154, ▪, ▪, 299, 598

**STEP 1**

Look at the first two numbers. Since they decrease and increase, try two operations.

Try **subtract 3, multiply by 2,** because $43 - 3 = 40$ and $40 \times 2 = 80$.

$80 - 3 = 77$ and $77 \times 2 = 154$

The rule, **subtract 3, multiply by 2** works.

**STEP 2**

Now, use the rule to solve the problem.

$154 - \mathbf{3} = 151$ and $151 \times \mathbf{2} = 302$

Check the last numbers in the pattern:

$302 - 3 = 299$ and $299 \times 2 = 598$

So, the missing numbers are 151 and 302.

1. **Explain** how you can find the missing number in the pattern
   2, 5, 8, 11, ■, 17.

**Write a rule for each pattern. Then find the missing number(s).**

2. 1, 2, 4, 8, 16, ■, ■
3. 90, 89, 87, ■, 80, 75
4. 105, 90, 75, 60, ■, 30

---

▶ **Practice and Problem Solving** ( Extra Practice, page 262, Set C )

**Write a rule for each pattern. Then find the missing number(s).**

5. 20, 17, 14, 11, ■
6. 5, 10, 15, 20, ■, ■
7. 93, 99, 33, 39, ■, 19
8. 1, 4, 16, 64, ■, ■
9. 11, 21, 41, ■, 111, 161
10. 486, 162, 54, 18, ■, ■
11. 5.8, 5.7, ■, 5.5, 5.4
12. 98, 80, 62, ■, 26, 8
13. 75, 25, 150, ■, 300, 100
14. 6, 18, ■, 162, 486
15. 37, 54, 71, 88, ■, ■
16. 4.2, 16.8, 8.4, 33.6, ■, ■
17. 2, 3, 5, 8, ■, ■,
18. 50, 25, 30, 15, 20, ■, ■
19. 35, 70, 60, 120, ■, ■

20. Make a pattern using the rule *add 10, subtract 5.* Start with 5 and write the first six numbers in the pattern.

21. ✎ **Write a Problem** about a pattern that has 20 as its second number. Tell the rule you used.

22. Find a pattern in the tile designs. If the pattern continues, how many tiles will there be in the eighth tile design? Draw a picture of the eighth tile design.

23. Kira made a long-distance telephone call to her grandmother. The first 10 minutes cost $1.50, and each minute after that cost $0.29 per minute. They talked for 16 minutes. How much did the call cost?

24. **REASONING** The pattern 1, 1, 2, 3, 5, 8, 13, . . . is called the Fibonacci sequence. Write a rule for the pattern and find the next two numbers.

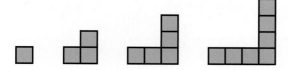

---

**Getting Ready for FCAT** | THINK SOLVE EXPLAIN |

25. Mr. Hall wrote a pattern on the chalkboard. He asked the class to think about how the numbers in the pattern are related.

   Write a rule for the pattern, and tell how to find the next number in the pattern.

FCAT TESTED  SSS/GLEs MA.D.1.2.2.5.2 Analyzes and generalizes number patterns and states the rule for relationships . . . . *also* MA.D.2.2.1.5.2

Chapter 12  **253**

# Functions

 **Learn**

**DOG WALKER**   After school, Selena walks some of her neighbors' dogs. She earns $2 for each day she walks a dog. Last week, she walked Bandit on 4 days. How much money did Selena earn walking Bandit last week?

You can use a function table to show the number of dollars Selena earns for walking dogs for different numbers of days. The table matches each input value, *t* (days), with an output value, *d* (dollars). It shows a function.

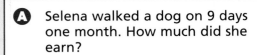

| days, *t* | 1 | 2 | 3 | 4 | 5 | 8 |
|---|---|---|---|---|---|---|
| dollars, *d* | 2 | 4 | 6 | 8 | 10 | 16 |

← Rule: multiply the number of days by 2.

So, Selena earned $8.

**MATH IDEA**   A **function** is a relationship between two quantities in which one quantity depends on the other.

In this problem, the number of dollars earned, *d*, depends on the number of days walked, *t*. You can use an equation to represent this function.

$d = 2 \times t$, or $d = 2t$

## Examples

**A**   Selena walked a dog on 9 days one month. How much did she earn?

$d = 2 \times t$   Write the equation.

$d = 2 \times 9$   Replace *t* with 9. Multiply.

$d = 18$

She earned $18.

**B**   One week, Selena charged $5 for washing a dog and $2 for each of the 3 days she walked the dog. How much did she earn?

$d = 5 + 2 \times t$   Write an equation for this function.

$d = 5 + 2 \times 3$   Replace *t* with 3. Multiply.

$d = 5 + 6$   Add.

$d = 11$

She earned $11.

## Check

**1. Explain** what it means to say that this equation is a function. $f = 3e - 2$

**Copy and complete the function table.**

**2.** $d = 6c$

| c | 0 | 5 | 10 | 15 | 20 |
|---|---|---|----|----|----|
| d |   |   |    |    |    |

**3.** $g = 11h - 12$

| h | 9 | 8 | 7 | 6 | 5 |
|---|---|---|---|---|---|
| g |   |   |   |   |   |

**4.** $y = 5x + 4$

| x | 0 | 5 | 10 | 15 | 20 |
|---|---|---|----|----|----|
| y |   |   |    |    |    |

## Practice and Problem Solving   Extra Practice, page 262, Set D

**Copy and complete the function table.**

**5.** $p = 8q$

| q | 7 | 8 | 9 | 10 | 11 |
|---|---|---|---|----|----|
| p |   |   |   |    |    |

**6.** $t = 9s - 13$

| s | 3 | 6 | 9 | 12 | 15 |
|---|---|---|---|----|----|
| t |   |   |   |    |    |

**7.** $y = 5 + 4x$

| x | 0 | 5 | 10 | 15 | 20 |
|---|---|---|----|----|----|
| y |   |   |    |    |    |

**Use the function. Find the output, $y$, for each input, $x$.**

**8.** $y = 2 + 3x - 4$ for $x = 5, 6, 7$

**9.** $y = 12 + 13x - 14$ for $x = 1, 2, 3$

**10.** $y = 9x - 40$ for $x = 7, 8, 9$

**11.** $y = 150 + 12x$ for $x = 1, 20, 300$

**For 12–13, write a function to solve.**

**12.** Last week, Selena charged $6 for washing a dog and then $2 each day for walking the dog on 4 days. How much did she earn?

**13.** Ross charged $6 to wash a dog and then $3 each day to walk the dog. He earned $21. How many days did he walk the dog?

**14.** Suppose one week you wash a dog once and walk the dog on 4 days. Would you earn more money if you charged $3 to wash the dog and $2 for each day walked, or $2 to wash the dog and $3 for each day walked?

**15.** Write an equation that shows how the number of days worked relates to the amount of money earned. Complete the table.

| Days, x | 1 | 2 | 3 | 4 | 5 | 6 |
|---------|---|---|---|---|---|---|
| Money earned, y | $7 | $13 | $19 |   |   |   |

## Getting Ready for FCAT

**THINK SOLVE EXPLAIN**

**16.** Erica made a table to show how much she earns babysitting. Complete the pattern in the table to show how much she earns in 5 hours and 6 hours.

| Number of Hours | 2 | 3 | 4 | 5 | 6 |
|-----------------|---|---|---|---|---|
| Money earned | $5.60 | $8.40 | $11.20 |   |   |

Explain your thinking.

FCAT TESTED   SSS/GLEs MA.D.1.2.2.5.3 Applies the appropriate rule to complete a table or chart.

**Chapter 12  255**

# Problem Solving Strategy
## Compare Strategies

**PROBLEM** Erica and her father paid $7.50 for tickets to the Hot-Air Balloon Festival. An adult's ticket costs $3.00 more than a child's ticket. What was the cost of each ticket?

## Quick Review

1. $(3 + 4) \times 2$
2. $10 + (25 \div 5)$
3. $(42 \div 6) + 4$
4. $84 \div (7 + 5)$
5. $4 \times (3 + 6)$

### UNDERSTAND

• What are you asked to find?

• What information will you use?

### PLAN

• What strategy can you use?

Often you can use more than one strategy to solve a problem. Use *work backward* or *draw a diagram*.

### SOLVE

• How will you solve the problem?

*Work Backward* Show how to find the total, and use *work backward* and inverse operations to find the cost of the child's ticket.

| ( ■ | × | 2) | + | $3.00 | = | $7.50 |
|---|---|---|---|---|---|---|
| ↑ | | ↑ | | ↑ | | ↑ |
| price of child's ticket | | total number of tickets | | additional cost for adult ticket | | total cost |

■ × 2 = $7.50 − $3.00
■ × 2 = $4.50
　　■ = $4.50 ÷ 2
　　■ = $2.25 ← the cost of a child's ticket

$2.25
+ 3.00
$5.25 ← the cost of an adult's ticket

*Draw a Diagram* Show the relationship of 2 tickets for $7.50. Let $t$ = the cost of the child's ticket.

| adult | $t$ | $3.00 |
|---|---|---|
| child | $t$ | |

← $2t + \$3.00 = \$7.50$  Subtract $3.00 from the total cost to find the cost of 2 tickets. Divide $4.50 by 2 to find the cost of 1 child's ticket.

So, the adult's ticket cost $5.25 and the child's ticket cost $2.25.

### CHECK

• Look back at the problem. How can you decide if your answer makes sense for the problem? Explain.

## Problem Solving Practice

### Strategies

▶ **Draw a Diagram or Picture**
Make a Model or Act It Out
Make an Organized List
Find a Pattern
Make a Table or Graph
Predict and Test
▶ **Work Backward**
Solve a Simpler Problem
Write an Equation
Use Logical Reasoning

**Work backward or draw a diagram to solve.**

1. **What if** Erica and her father had paid $7.00 for tickets and the adult's ticket was $1.50 more than the child's ticket? How much would each ticket have cost?

2. After buying 3 postcards for $0.25 each and a book about hot-air balloons for $3.65, Erica had $5.60 left. How much did Erica have before she made her purchases?

**Brian came home from a baseball game with $7.26. At the game, he spent $7.50 for a ticket, $2.25 for lunch, and $3.99 for a souvenir. During the game, his brother gave him $1.00.**

3. How much money did Brian have when he left for the game?

   **A** $19.00    **C** $21.00
   **B** $20.00    **D** $22.00

4. How much money would Brian have come home with if he had also spent $1.73 for a poster but not had lunch?

   **F** $11.24    **H** $7.78
   **G** $9.51    **J** $6.74

## Mixed Strategy Practice

5. The pretzels booth at the fair is on the left end of the row. The popcorn booth is between pretzels and ice cream. The cotton candy booth is between ice cream and popcorn. The lemonade booth is between cotton candy and popcorn. List the booths in order from left to right.

6. Ali has been keeping track of her plant's growth since she bought it 2 weeks ago. It grew 2.5 centimeters the first week and twice as much the second week. If it is 12.0 centimeters tall now, how tall was it when Ali bought it?

7. Marian made a phone call that cost $0.99 for the first 10 minutes and $0.25 for each additional minute. She was on the phone for 20 minutes. What was the cost of the phone call?

8. Ana needs $130 to buy a coat. She has $45. If she saves $5 each week, how many weeks will it take her to save enough money to buy the coat?

9. Two buses will transport 1,225 people to the stadium. If each bus holds 52 people, how many trips will each bus make?

FCAT TESTED ▶ SSS/GLEs MA.A.3.2.2.5.1 Uses problem-solving strategies to determine the operation(s) needed to solve one- and two-step problems involving addition, subtraction, multiplication, and division of whole numbers, and addition, subtraction, and multiplication of decimals and fractions.

**Chapter 12  257**

**Quick Review**
1. $7 \times 6$    2. $70 \times 6$
3. $700 \times 6$    4. $7{,}000 \times 6$
5. $70{,}000 \times 6$

## ▶ Learn

**DIGITAL DILEMMA**   Keri has 8 shelves with the same number of DVDs on each shelf. Malik has 5 shelves with 8 DVDs on each shelf. They have the same number of DVDs. How many DVDs does Keri have on each shelf?

You can write an equation to model this problem.

Let $d$ = the number of DVDs Keri has on each shelf.

**VOCABULARY**
**Commutative Property**
**Associative Property**

| Keri's DVDs | | | | Malik's DVDs | | |
|---|---|---|---|---|---|---|
| number of shelves | × | DVDs on each shelf | = | number of shelves | × | DVDs on each shelf |
| ↓ | ↓ | ↓ | | ↓ | ↓ | ↓ |
| 8 | × | $d$ | = | 5 | × | 8 |

$8 \times d = 5 \times 8$    Think about the Order Property.
$8 \times 5 = 5 \times 8$    $d$ must equal 5.
$d = 5$

So, Keri has 5 DVDs on each shelf.

The Order Property is also called the **Commutative Property**.
The Grouping Property is also called the **Associative Property**.

**Remember**

You can use mental math and the properties of multiplication to solve problems.

**Order Property**
$4 \times 3 = 3 \times 4$

**Grouping Property**
$(8 \times 2) \times 6 = 8 \times (2 \times 6)$

**Identity Property**
$7 \times 1 = 7$

**Zero Property**
$9 \times 0 = 0$

**Examples** Solve the equation.

**A**

$(8 \times 6) \times 5 = 8 \times (6 \times p)$   Associative Property
$(8 \times 6) \times 5 = 8 \times (6 \times 5)$

So, $p = 5$.

**B**

$16 \times c = 16$   Identity Property
$16 \times 1 = 16$

So, $c = 1$.

• How is the Commutative Property different from the Associative Property?

⚠ **MATH IDEA**   The properties of multiplication can help you solve problems.

1. **Explain** how one of the properties can help make it easier to find the value of $n$. $(16 \times 72) \times n = 0$

**Solve the equation. Identify the property used.**

2. $(7 \times y) \times 8 = 7 \times (3 \times 8)$     3. $n \times 3 = 3 \times 9$     4. $h \times 7 = 0$

▶ **Practice and Problem Solving**     Extra Practice, page 262, Set E

**Solve the equation. Identify the property used.**

5. $4 \times (8 \times d) = (4 \times 8) \times 7$     6. $9 \times y = 0$     7. $n \times 43 = 43 \times 3$

8. $(6 \times 7) \times 2 = 6 \times (n \times 2)$     9. $5 \times n = 5$     10. $1 \times k = 165$

11. $5 \times (n \times 13) = (5 \times 4) \times 13$     12. $112 \times 9 = n \times 112$     13. $n \times 1 = n$

**ALGEBRA    Identify the property or properties shown.**

14. $a \times b = b \times a$     15. $a \times 0 = 0$     16. $a \times 1 = a$

17. $a \times (b \times c) = (a \times b) \times c$     18. $(a \times b) \times c = b \times (a \times c)$

**USE DATA    For 19–20, use the graph.**

19. Estimate the number of DVD players sold from 1997 through 1999.

20. In what year were the most DVD players sold?

21. Tell where to place parentheses to make the equation $8 \times 5 + 6 \div 2 = 44$ true.

22. Tamar took her pulse for 20 seconds. She counted 29 heartbeats. How many beats per minute is that?

23. A group of goats and ducks have a total of 99 heads and legs among them. There are twice as many ducks as there are goats. How many are there of each?

24. ✎ **Write About It**   Give an example to show how the Associative Property of Multiplication can help you solve problems mentally.

**Getting Ready for FCAT**

25. Which is an example of the Commutative Property of Multiplication?

   A. $8 \times 14 \times 21 = 8 \times 21 \times 14$
   B. $2 \times (5 \times 8) = (2 \times 5) \times 8$
   C. $9 \times 0 = 0$
   D. $4 \times 1 = 4$

26. Which is an example of the Identity Property of Multiplication?

   F. $7 \times 2 \times 13 = 2 \times 7 \times 13$
   G. $(3 \times 6) \times 5 = 3 \times (6 \times 5)$
   H. $8 \times 0 = 0$
   I. $5 \times 1 = 5$

# The Distributive Property

**VOCABULARY**

Distributive Property

 ▶ **Learn**

**PIECE BY PIECE** You can break apart one factor in a multiplication problem to make a problem simpler.

**HANDS ON**

**Activity** Find 5 × 16.

**MATERIALS:** grid paper

**STEP 1**

On grid paper, outline a rectangle that is 5 units high and 16 units wide. Think of the area as the product.

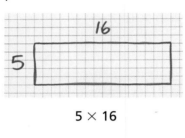

5 × 16

**STEP 2**

Count over 10 units from the left and draw a line to break apart the rectangle.

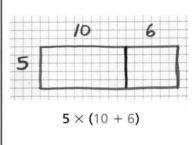

5 × (10 + 6)

**STEP 3**

Use the Distributive Property to show a sum of two products. Multiply what is in parentheses first. Add the products.

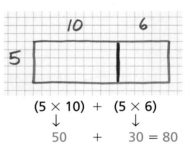

(5 × 10) + (5 × 6)
↓            ↓
50    +    30 = 80

So, 5 × 16 = 80.

• Use grid paper to show 12 × 17 = n.

The Activity shows the Distributive Property. The **Distributive Property** states that multiplying a sum by a number is the same as multiplying each addend in the sum by the number and then adding the products. You can use the Distributive Property to find the value of expressions with variables.

**Example** Find the value of 6 × (n + 5) if n = 10.

| | |
|---|---|
| 6 × (n + 5) = (6 × n) + (6 × 5) | Use the Distributive Property. |
| = (6 × 10) + (6 × 5) | Replace n with 10. |
| = 60 + 30 | |
| = 90 | |

So, 6 × (n + 5) = 90 if n = 10.

1. **Explain** how you can use the Distributive Property to find the value of $7 \times 82$. Show your steps.

**Use grid paper to show the product.**

2. $10 \times 18$      3. $20 \times 15$      4. $23 \times 6$      5. $30 \times 14$

**Use the Distributive Property to restate each expression. Find the product.**

6. $7 \times 26$      7. $9 \times 24$      8. $26 \times 3$      9. $7 \times 15$

▶ **Practice and Problem Solving**  Extra Practice, page 262, Set F

**Use grid paper to show the product.**

10. $5 \times 17$      11. $9 \times 16$      12. $20 \times 14$      13. $33 \times 6$

**Use the Distributive Property to restate each expression. Find the product.**

14. $14 \times 8$      15. $8 \times 34$      16. $9 \times 37$      17. $6 \times 35$

18. $9 \times 28$      19. $10 \times 32$      20. $12 \times 26$      21. $50 \times 12$

**ALGEBRA**  Restate the expression, using the Distributive Property. Then find the value of the expression.

22. $9 \times (y + 8)$ if $y$ is 10      23. $8 \times (4 + n)$ if $n$ is 20

24. $3 \times (6 + n)$ if $n$ is 40      25. $5 \times (d + 20 + 7)$ if $d$ is 300

26. Ida has 4 tomato plants. For 3 weeks in a row, each plant produced 4 tomatoes. Then Ida shared her tomatoes equally with 3 friends. How many tomatoes did each person get?

27. **? What's the Error?** Jill wrote $7 \times (30 + 7) = 210 + 7 = 217$. Identify and correct her error.

28. Use the Distributive Property to check if the equation $5 \times (n + 6) = 130$ is true if $n = 20$.

29. ✎ **Write About It** Explain the Distributive Property in your own words. Give an example.

## Getting Ready for FCAT

30. Kim found the solution for the equation shown on the chalkboard by using the Distributive Property. What is the solution?

   **A.** $n = 2$      **C.** $n = 12$
   **B.** $n = 5$      **D.** $n = 30$

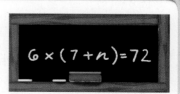

$6 \times (7 + n) = 72$

FCAT TESTED  SSS/GLEs MA.A.3.2.1.5.5 Explains and demonstrates the commutative, associative, and distributive properties of multiplication. *also* MA.D.2.2.1.5.2

Chapter 12  **261**

# Extra Practice

## Set A (pp. 246–249)

**Write an expression. If you use a variable, tell what it represents.**

**1.** Stan had 8 board games. He got 3 more for his birthday.

**2.** George did the same number of sit-ups each day for 5 days.

**Evaluate the expression.**

**3.** $30 + n$ if $n = 18$

**4.** $(8 \times n) - 15$ if $n = 4$

**5.** $3 \times (n + 12)$ if $n = 22$

## Set B (pp. 250–251)

**Evaluate the expression.**

**1.** $5 + 4 \times 4 - 6$

**2.** $3 \times 2 + 9 \div 3$

**3.** $5 \times 4 \div 10 + 8$

**4.** $25 - (5 \div 5) \times 2$

**5.** $48 \div 6 \times (8 - 3)$

**6.** $15 - (9 - 3) - 2$

**Insert parentheses in the expression to get the given value for $a$, $b$, and $c$.**

**7.** $36 + 8 \div 2 + 2$    **a.** 38          **b.** 24          **c.** 42

## Set C (pp. 252–253)

**Write a rule for each pattern. Then find the missing number(s).**

**1.** 5, 15, ■, 135, 405

**2.** 49, 63, 126, 140, ■, ■

**3.** 729, 243, 81, ■, 9, 3

## Set D (pp. 254–255)

**Complete the function table.**

**1.** $b = 6a$

| a | 2 | 4 | 6 | 8 | 10 |
|---|---|---|---|---|----|
| b | ■ | ■ | ■ | ■ | ■ |

**2.** $t = 2s - 4$

| s | 3 | 5 | 9 | 10 | 12 |
|---|---|---|---|----|----|
| t | ■ | ■ | ■ | ■ | ■ |

**Use the function. Find the output, $y$, for each input, $x$.**

**3.** $y = 5x + 10$ for $x = 9, 10, 11$

**4.** $y = 6 + 3x - 1$ for $x = 1, 3, 5$

## Set E (pp. 258–259)

**Solve the equation. Identify the property used.**

**1.** $y \times 35 = 0$

**2.** $n \times 10 = 10$

**3.** $4 \times 2 = z \times 4$

## Set F (pp. 260–261)

**Use the Distributive Property to restate each expression. Find the product.**

**1.** $33 \times 4$

**2.** $8 \times 17$

**3.** $22 \times 6$

**4.** $5 \times 24$

# Review/Test

## ✓ CHECK VOCABULARY AND CONCEPTS

Choose the best term from the box.

> Associative Property
> Distributive Property
> equation
> evaluate
> expression
> function

1. The __?__ states that multiplying a sum by a number is the same as multiplying each addend in the sum by the number and then adding the products. (p. 260)

2. When you replace the variable with a number and perform the operations, you __?__ an expression. (p. 246)

## ✓ CHECK SKILLS

Evaluate the expression. (pp. 246–249, 250–251)

3. $n + 56$ if $n = 11$

4. $12 \times y$ if $y = 8$

5. $72 \div n$ if $n = 9$

6. $12 \times (4 + 6) + 8$

7. $36 \div (9 + 3) - 3$

8. $5 \times 8 \div (8 - 6)$

Copy and complete the function table. (pp. 254–255)

9. $y = 15 + 5x$

| x | 0 | 2 | 4 | 6 | 8 |
|---|---|---|---|---|---|
| y | ■ | ■ | ■ | ■ | ■ |

10. $b = 6a - 4$

| a | 1 | 3 | 5 | 7 | 9 |
|---|---|---|---|---|---|
| b | ■ | ■ | ■ | ■ | ■ |

Write a rule for each pattern. Then find the missing number(s). (pp. 252–253)

11. 23, 38, 53, 68, ■, ■

12. 13, 52, ■, 832, 3,328

13. 448, 224, 112, 56, 28, 14, ■

14. 234, 205, 176, ■, 118, 89

Solve the equation. Identify the property used. (pp. 258–259)

15. $0 = 19 \times n$

16. $(5 \times 4) \times 9 = 5 \times (n \times 9)$

17. $16 = m \times 16$

18. $6 \times f = 13 \times 6$

Use the Distributive Property to restate each expression. Find the product. (pp. 260–261)

19. $24 \times 7$

20. $9 \times 44$

21. $11 \times 23$

22. $6 \times 32$

23. $54 \times 5$

## ✓ CHECK PROBLEM SOLVING

Solve. Name the operation or operations you used. (pp. 256–257)

24. The total rainfall for the week was 2.14 inches. For 4 days it did not rain at all. On 2 days it rained 0.5 inch each day. How much rain fell on the last day?

25. Sally came home from the fair with $3.86. She spent $5.50 for a ticket, $4.35 for food, and $7.29 for rides. How much money did Sally have before she went to the fair?

# Getting Ready for FCAT

## ★ ALGEBRAIC THINKING

**1.** At the sporting goods store, Dan bought 3 cans of tennis balls and 1 box of golf balls.

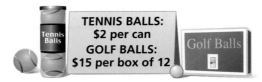

Which expression can be used to find out how much he spent in all?

**A.** $3 \times 2 + 15$

**B.** $3 \times (3 + 15)$

**C.** $2 \times (3 + 15)$

**D.** $3 \times 2 + 12 \times 15$

**2.** Robbie made this pattern of dots.

How many dots will there be in the sixth figure of his pattern?

**F.** 6 **G.** 9 **H.** 12 **I.** 13

**3. Explain It** Tina bought some T-shirts and 3 pairs of shorts at the End-of-Season Sale. Write an expression to show the number of dollars Tina spent for the clothing she bought. Let *n* represent the number of T-shirts she bought. Explain how to evaluate the expression if $n = 4$.

## ★ DATA ANALYSIS AND PROBABILITY

**4.** Ariel used the line graph below to record the temperature at noon every day for a week for a science project. What was the temperature on Tuesday?

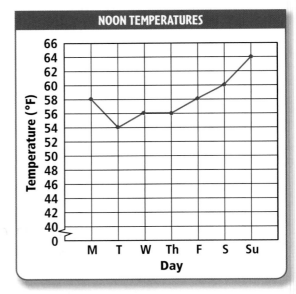

**A.** 60°F **C.** 56°F

**B.** 58°F **D.** 54°F

**5.** Look at the graph above. Between which two days did the temperature increase the most?

**F.** Wednesday and Thursday

**G.** Thursday and Friday

**H.** Friday and Saturday

**I.** Saturday and Sunday

**6. Explain It** Look at the graph in Problem 4. Ariel said that the mean, median, and mode of the temperatures for the seven days were the same number. Do you agree? Explain your answer.

**MEASUREMENT**

**7.** What is the length of the key to the nearest centimeter?

**A.** 5 centimeters

**B.** $5\frac{3}{4}$ centimeters

**C.** 6 centimeters

**D.** $6\frac{1}{2}$ centimeters

**8.** Pat ran a 5-mile race. The race began at 8:30 A.M. At what time did he cross the finish line?

| PAT'S RACE | |
|---|---|
| **Mile** | **Time (each mile)** |
| 1 and 2 | 8 minutes |
| 3 | 9 minutes |
| 4 and 5 | 10 minutes |

**F.** 8:57 A.M.

**G.** 9:10 A.M.

**H.** 9:15 A.M.

**I.** 9:20 A.M.

**9. Explain It** Janine estimated that each soup bowl would hold about 12 ounces of soup. If each soup can contains 8 ounces, about how many cans of soup does she need to serve 9 people? Explain your thinking.

 **GEOMETRY AND SPATIAL SENSE**

**10.** Which of these figures appears to have a right angle?

**A.**

**C.**

**B.**

**D.**

> **TIP** **Check your work.** See item 10. A right angle has a measure of 90° and forms a square corner. Use a corner of an index card or a piece of paper to check that the angles in the figure you chose are right angles.

**11.** Roxy drew this figure. Which solid figure did she draw?

**F.** cube

**G.** triangular prism

**H.** square pyramid

**I.** triangular pyramid

**12. Explain It** The perimeter of a rectangle is 36 inches. The length is 12 inches. What is the width of the rectangle? Explain how you found the answer.

# IT'S IN THE BAG

## Shoot for the Moon

**PROJECT** Make a rocket and play a game to practice evaluating expressions.

### Materials

- 1 9-in. tall snack can with lid
- Construction paper
- Tape, glue, ruler
- Compass
- Markers, crayons, and color pencils
- Brass fastener
- Small paper clip
- Directions, game board
- Game pieces

### Directions

1. Cover the snack can with construction paper. Cut out 2 paper wings for the bottom of the rocket, and tape them to the sides of the can. Color the rocket, and label it Shoot for the Moon. *(Picture A)*

2. Make a spinner with 4 equal sections. On white construction paper, trace the lid of the can and cut out the circle. Write 2, 3, 4, and 6, in the four sections. Insert the brass fastener through the center of the paper and the lid. Attach the paper clip to the fastener to use as the pointer. Color the spinner. *(Picture B)*

3. To complete the rocket, make a 6-inch-diameter circle by using white construction paper and a compass. Decorate the edge of the circle, and then form a cone by taping the sides of the paper together. *(Picture C)*

4. Use the directions and game board to play the game with a partner. You can also use crayons and color pencils to decorate the game board.

# Challenge

## Divide a Decimal by a Decimal

Look at the multiplication equations and their related division equations below.

| **Multiplication Equations** | | **Related Division Equations** |
|---|---|---|
| $12 \times 4 = 48$ | $\rightarrow$ | $48 \div 12 = 4$ |
| $1.2 \times 4 = 4.8$ | $\rightarrow$ | $4.8 \div 1.2 = 4$ |
| $0.12 \times 4 = 0.48$ | $\rightarrow$ | $0.48 \div 0.12 = 4$ |

Notice that all the division equations have the same quotient. You could write $48 \div 12 = 4.8 \div 1.2 = 0.48 \div 0.12$.

To divide by a decimal, you can write an equivalent problem that has a whole-number divisor. Multiply both the divisor and the dividend by 10, 100, or more.

> **Remember**
>
> When you multiply by 10 or 100, the number of places the decimal point moves to the right is the same as the number of zeros.
>
> $0.32 \times 10 = 3.2$
> $0.32 \times 100 = 32$

$$0.2\overline{)2.6} \quad \rightarrow \quad 2.\overline{)26.}$$ **Think:** $0.2 \times 10 = 2$
$2.6 \times 10 = 26$

---

### Example  Find $2.15 \div 0.5$.

**STEP 1**

0.5 has one decimal place. So, to change it to a whole number, multiply it by 10.

$0.5 \times 10 = 5$

Multiply the dividend **and** the divisor by 10.

$0.5\overline{)2.15}$

**STEP 2**

In the quotient, place the decimal point directly above the decimal point in the dividend.

$$5.\overline{)21.5}$$

Divide as with whole numbers.

$$\begin{array}{r} 4.3 \\ 5.\overline{)21.5} \\ -20 \phantom{.} \\ \hline 1\,5 \\ -1\,5 \\ \hline 0 \end{array}$$

---

- By what number would you multiply both the dividend and the divisor to divide 6.02 by 0.02?

## Try It

**Divide.**

**1.** $2.1 \div 0.7$ **2.** $0.24 \div 1.2$ **3.** $3.6 \div 0.06$ **4.** $0.09 \div 0.3$

**5.** $0.7\overline{)5.32}$ **6.** $0.02\overline{)2.16}$ **7.** $2.5\overline{)0.75}$ **8.** $1.1\overline{)1.32}$

# Study Guide and Review

## VOCABULARY

Choose the best term from the box.

| compatible numbers |
| evaluate |
| remainder |
| quotients |
| function |

1. Pairs of numbers that are easy to compute mentally are __?__. (p. 192)

2. You can use compatible numbers to estimate __?__. (p. 192)

3. A relationship between two quantities in which one depends on the other is called a __?__. (p. 254)

4. To __?__ an expression, replace the variable with a number and perform the operations. (p. 246)

## STUDY AND SOLVE

### Chapter 9

**Divide by 1-digit divisors.**

652 ÷ 8
↓     ↓
640 ÷ 8 = 80 Estimate.

```
   81 r4
8)652    Divide the 65 tens.
 −64
  12    Divide the 12 ones.
 − 8
   4
```

**Divide.** (pp. 194–199)

5. 4)628          6. 3)250

7. 6)687          8. 7)219

9. 6)3,648        10. 8)845

11. 4)807         12. 9)5,042

13. 7)496         14. 5)68,515

15. 8)16,048      16. 9)180,981

### Chapter 10

**Divide by 2-digit divisors.**

625 ÷ 22
↓      ↓
600 ÷ 20 = 30 Estimate.

```
    28 r9
22)625    Divide the 62 tens.
 −44
  185    Divide the 185 ones.
 −176
    9
```

**Divide.** (pp. 210–219)

17. 15)249        18. 26)13,761

19. 37)5,082      20. 41)2,506

21. 52)3,124      22. 88)91,669

23. 30)48,843     24. 63)83,405

## Chapter 11

**Divide decimals by whole numbers.**

Place the decimal point for the quotient above the decimal point in the dividend.

$$\begin{array}{r} 64.1 \\ 5\overline{)320.5} \\ -30 \\ \hline 20 \\ -20 \\ \hline 05 \\ -\ 5 \\ \hline 0 \end{array}$$

Divide the 32 tens.

Divide the 20 ones.

Divide the 5 tenths.

**Divide.** (pp. 230–235)

**25.** $73.6 \div 8$ **26.** $42.6 \div 5$

**27.** $18.6 \div 4$ **28.** $53.2 \div 7$

**29.** $6\overline{)36.072}$ **30.** $16\overline{)134.4}$

**31.** $9\overline{)1,148.4}$ **32.** $17\overline{)209.1}$

## Chapter 12

**Evaluate algebraic expressions.**

$8 \times d$ Evaluate the expression if $d = 4$.
$\downarrow$
$8 \times 4$ Replace $d$ with 4.
$\downarrow$
$32$

**Evaluate each expression.** (pp. 246–247)

**33.** $15 \times n$ if $n = 3$

**34.** $37 - n$ if $n = 15$

**35.** $(7 - n) \times 2$ if $n = 1$

**36.** $(4 \times n) - 3$ if $n = 3$

**Evaluate expressions using the order of operations.**

$6 + (7 \times 3)$ Operate inside parentheses.

$6 + 21$ Add.

$27$

**Evaluate each expression.** (pp. 250–251)

**37.** $4 \times (5 + 2) \div 2$

**38.** $45 \div 9 + (16 \div 2)$

**39.** $6 - (18 \div 9) \times 4$

**40.** $20 \div 5 + (4 - 2)$

## PROBLEM SOLVING PRACTICE

**Solve.** (pp. 200–201, 256–257)

**41.** Henry spent $6.50 on a movie ticket, $2.50 on popcorn, and $1.25 for a drink. He had $3.85 left. How much money did he have at the start?

**42.** Ana has 24.5 feet of rope that she would like to divide into 7 equal pieces. How long will each piece be?

# PERFORMANCE ASSESSMENT

## TASK A • AT THE FAIR

You are in charge of renting tables and buying hot dogs and hamburgers for the Fall Fair. You want to have enough food, but not much left over. Use the notes from last year's fair committee to help you plan.

a. Estimate how many people will eat at the fair. You need to seat about half of the people at one time. How many tables should you rent?

b. How many packages of hot dogs and hamburgers should you buy? Explain why you think these are good estimates.

c. This year you decide to order packages of cheese slices so that half of the hamburger orders can have a slice of cheese. Cheese slices come in packages of 24. How many packages of cheese will you need?

**Notes from the Fair**
- 475 people ate at the fair.
- More people bought hamburgers than hot dogs. Some people bought both.
- Hot dogs: 8 per package.
- Hamburgers: 12 per package.
- Tables seat 10 people.

## TASK B • ROLLING PRICES

Uma, Thad, and Jeremy are shopping for gifts at the Sports Palace.

| ITEM | PRICE |
|------|-------|
| Scooter | $39.90 |
| Skateboard | $54.00 |
| In-line skates | $78.75 |

a. Uma earns $10.00 per week. She plans to save the same amount of money each week to buy the scooter for her younger sister. Decide how much Uma should save each week. For how many weeks must she save that amount in order to buy the scooter?

b. If Jeremy saves $6.00 each week for *n* weeks, for how many weeks will he save to purchase the skateboard? Write and solve an equation using a variable.

c. Thad plans to save the same amount of money each week for 15 weeks to buy the scooter or the in-line skates. How much more must he save each week to buy the in-line skates than to buy the scooter? Explain.

# Technology Linkup

## Calculator • Order of Operations

Evaluate $5 + (92 + 79) \times 3 - 12 \div 4$ using the order of operations.

| ORDER OF OPERATIONS | |
|---|---|
| 1. | Perform operations in parentheses. |
| 2. | Multiply and divide from left to right. |
| 3. | Add and subtract from left to right. |

$5 + (92 + 79) \times 3 - 12 \div 4$     *Perform addition in parentheses.*

$5 + 171 \times 3 - 12 \div 4$     *Multiply and divide.*

$5 + 513 - 3$     *Add and subtract.*

$515$

Some calculators automatically follow the order of operations.
Test your calculator to see if it follows the order of operations.

[ 5 ] [ + ] [ ( ] [ 9 ] [ 2 ] [ + ] [ 7 ] [ 9 ] [ ) ]

[ × ] [ 3 ] [ − ] [ 1 ] [ 2 ] [ ÷ ] [ 4 ] [ Enter ]

```
'5 + (92 + 79) × 3
 - 12 ÷ 4 =   515
```

The solution is correct, so the calculator follows the order of operations.

## Practice and Problem Solving

**Use a calculator that follows the order of operations to evaluate
each expression.**

**1.** $18 + 9 \times (4 + 32) - 42 \div 6$

**2.** $23 \times 8 + (100 - 72) \div 4 + 9$

**3.** $15 \div 3 + (14 \times 3) - 16$

**4.** $36 \times (29 + 3) \div 12 + 4$

**5.** **? What's the Error?** Selena and Betsy
evaluated $7 + 3 \times 4 + 3 + 19$. Selena said the
answer is 41. Betsy said the answer is 62. Who
made the error, and what is it?

**GO ON-LINE**

**Multimedia Math Glossary** www.harcourtschool.com/mathglossary

**Vocabulary Power** Look up *order of operations* in the Multimedia Math
Glossary. Write a problem that uses all four operations and solve it.

# PROBLEM SOLVING IN FLORIDA

Tampa Bay

## WEEDON ISLAND PRESERVE

Weedon Island, on Tampa Bay, was once the home of early Native Americans. Today it is a nature preserve. Canoeing through its mangrove forests is like going through a maze of tunnels. Visitors see many birds, fish, and black crabs.

1. There is a 9,000-foot trail system on Weedon Island. If you divided the system into 6 equal sections, how long would each section be?

2. Visitors can walk along a boardwalk through a mangrove forest to an observation tower. The 50-foot tower has 4 stories. If each story is the same height, about how tall is each story in the tower?

▲ The 50-foot observation tower

3. **REASONING** Access to Weedon Island is limited to 300 people at a time. Suppose 5,300 people visit Weedon Island during a two-week period. About how many people would have visited the island each day? Explain how this is possible.

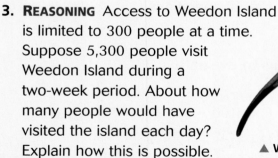

▲ White Ibises

# SUNSHINE SKYWAY BRIDGE

The Sunshine Skyway Bridge goes across Tampa Bay and connects St. Petersburg and Bradenton. The bridge is 29,040 feet long, making it the world's longest concrete bridge held up by cables.

An important part of the bridge's design was a way to protect it from being damaged by ships. There are 36 concrete islands called dolphins installed around the bridge to form a "bumper system" of protection.

◀ The bridge's cables are colored bright yellow because of Florida's nickname, the Sunshine State.

1. Construction on the bridge began in 1980. It was completed in 1987. The cost of the bridge was $244 million. Estimate the average yearly cost for the bridge's construction.

2. The longest span of the bridge is 1,200 feet. If 2,430 feet of the bridge is evenly divided into 18 spans, what is the length of each span?

**USE DATA** The table shows the average daily number of vehicles using the Sunshine Skyway Bridge for a given month. For 4–6, use the table.

3. During a one-week period in the month of February, 338,800 vehicles crossed the bridge. How many vehicles crossed the bridge per day?

4. About how many vehicles crossed the bridge during the entire month of April?

| AVERAGE NUMBER OF VEHICLES PER DAY IN 2001 | |
| --- | --- |
| **Month** | **Number of Vehicles Per Day** |
| February | |
| March | 50,200 |
| April | 47,100 |
| May | 43,100 |
| June | 42,100 |

# Factors and Multiples

**≡FAST FACT • SCIENCE** Seed Savers Exchange in Decorah, Iowa, maintains 135 varieties of eggplant seeds. The exchange is an organization that gathers, grows, and distributes heirloom seeds. Heirloom seeds are rare vegetable, fruit, and flower seeds that have been passed down from generation to generation.

**PROBLEM SOLVING** How many packages of 50 seeds can be made from 1,500 heirloom eggplant seeds?

| PACKAGES OF EGGPLANT SEEDS FROM 1,500 SEEDS | |
|---|---|
| **Seeds per Package** | **Complete Package? (Yes or No)** |
| 20 | ▣ |
| 30 | Yes |
| 40 | No |
| 50 | ▣ |
| 60 | ▣ |
| 70 | No |
| 80 | ▣ |

1. **Explain** why a number that is divisible by 10 is also divisible by 2 and by 5.

**Tell if each number is divisible by 2, 3, 4, 5, 6, 9, or 10.**

**2.** 10      **3.** 18      **4.** 30      **5.** 56      **6.** 72

▶ **Practice and Problem Solving**    Extra Practice, page 286, Set A

**Tell if each number is divisible by 2, 3, 4, 5, 6, 9, or 10.**

**7.** 24      **8.** 45      **9.** 108      **10.** 308      **11.** 519

**12.** 3,750      **13.** 2,604      **14.** 605      **15.** 1,896      **16.** 12,035

**Leap years have 366 days. Every year whose number is divisible by 4 is a leap year, except years that end in two zeros. These years are leap years only when they are divisible by 400. Write *yes* or *no* to tell whether the year was a leap year.**

**Technology Link**

More Practice: Harcourt Mega Math Ice Station Exploration, *Arctic Algebra*, Levels M, N

**17.** 1985      **18.** 2000      **19.** 1776      **20.** 1492

**21. REASONING** For what values of ■ is 2,3■1 divisible by 9? by 3?

**22.** Is the statement, "All numbers that are divisible by 3 are also divisible by 9" *true* or *false*? Explain.

**USE DATA** For 23–24, use the table.

**23.** The printer wants to package the "How to Care for a Tree" brochures into stacks with none left over. Can he put them in stacks of 6? stacks of 10?

| ARBOR DAY CELEBRATION MATERIALS | |
|---|---|
| **Item** | **Number** |
| Tree Seedlings | 1,764 |
| Brochures | 504 |
| Shovels | 9 |

**24.** The tree seedlings for the celebration come in trays of 28. If each tray costs $7, how much will be spent on seedlings?

**25. Vocabulary Power** The word *remainder* means "part left over." Explain how a remainder is used to determine divisibility.

**26.** ✎ **Write About It** What is the least number that is divisible by 2, 3, 5, and 10? Explain.

**Getting Ready for FCAT**

**27.** Jake picked 56 apples. How many friends can he give an equal number of apples to so that no apples are left over?

**A.** 3    **B.** 4    **C.** 6    **D.** 9

# Greatest Common Factor

▶ **Learn**

**GREEN THUMB**   Kevin and Celia are selling boxes of red petunia and pansy plants. Each box will have one type of plant, and all boxes will have the same number of plants. There are 12 red petunia plants and 18 pansy plants. What is the greatest number of plants Kevin and Celia can put in each box?

To find how many plants they can put in each box, Kevin and Celia found all the common factors of 12 and 18. Common factors for a set of numbers are factors of each number in the set.

**Kevin listed the factors.**          **Celia made a Venn diagram.**

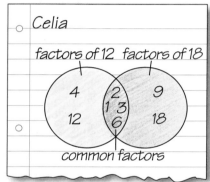

Kevin

Factors of 12: 1, 2, 3, 4, 6, 12

Factors of 18: 1, 2, 3, 6, 9, 18

Common factors: 1, 2, 3, 6

Celia

factors of 12    factors of 18

4    2    9
12   1 3   18
     6
common factors

The greatest number of plants can be found by using the greatest common factor. The **greatest common factor**, or **GCF**, is the greatest factor that two or more numbers share. The greatest common factor of 12 and 18 is 6.

So, the greatest number of plants they can put in each box is 6 plants.

## GCF of Three Numbers

**What if** there are 15 purple petunia plants to put into boxes? Now what is the greatest number of plants Kevin and Celia can put in each box?

**Factors of 12:** 1, 2, 3, 4, 6, 12
**Factors of 18:** 1, 2, 3, 6, 9, 18
**Factors of 15:** 1, 3, 5, 15

The GCF of 12, 18, and 15 is 3. So, they can put 3 plants in each box.

- **REASONING** Explain how you can tell if a number is a factor of another number.

**MATH IDEA** You can find the greatest common factor of two or more numbers by listing the factors and finding the greatest factor shared by all of the numbers.

### Examples

**A** Find the GCF of 10 and 25.

10:  1, 2, 5, 10
25:  1, 5, 25

GCF: 5

**B** Find the GCF of 36 and 81.

36:  1, 2, 3, 4, 6, 9, 12, 18, 36
81:  1, 3, 9, 27, 81

GCF: 9

**C** Find the GCF of 8, 24, and 30.

 8:  1, 2, 4, 8
24:  1, 2, 3, 4, 6, 8, 12, 24
30:  1, 2, 3, 5, 6, 10, 15, 30

GCF: 2

### Check

1. **Explain** how divisibility rules can help you find common factors.

**List the factors for each number.**

| | | | | |
|---|---|---|---|---|
| **2.** 32 | **3.** 55 | **4.** 21 | **5.** 17 | **6.** 100 |
| **7.** 37 | **8.** 42 | **9.** 56 | **10.** 63 | **11.** 77 |

**Write the common factors for each set of numbers.**

| | | | | |
|---|---|---|---|---|
| **12.** 6, 14 | **13.** 8, 16 | **14.** 30, 45 | **15.** 18, 22 | **16.** 5, 9, 18 |
| **17.** 5, 25 | **18.** 4, 24 | **19.** 36, 54 | **20.** 13, 19 | **21.** 8, 12, 18 |

**Write the greatest common factor for each set of numbers.**

**22.** 4, 12    **23.** 5, 25    **24.** 3, 12, 18

LESSON CONTINUES

FCAT TESTED SSS/GLEs MA.A.5.2.1.5.3 Determines the greatest common factor of two numbers. also MA.A.5.2.1.5.6.

Chapter 13 **279**

**List the factors for each number.**

**25.** 16     **26.** 20     **27.** 23     **28.** 28     **29.** 80

**30.** 15     **31.** 51     **32.** 31     **33.** 49     **34.** 50

**Write the common factors for each set of numbers.**

**35.** 2, 14     **36.** 11, 15     **37.** 30, 50     **38.** 13, 26     **39.** 5, 20, 45

**40.** 16, 20     **41.** 12, 14     **42.** 36, 45     **43.** 34, 51     **44.** 8, 16, 20

**Write the greatest common factor for each set of numbers.**

**45.** 6, 15     **46.** 12, 21     **47.** 7, 35     **48.** 18, 45     **49.** 6, 8, 12

**50.** 9, 15     **51.** 12, 36     **52.** 16, 24     **53.** 42, 49     **54.** 6, 50, 60

**55.** 14, 21     **56.** 12, 28     **57.** 8, 32     **58.** 21, 56     **59.** 4, 8, 16

**USE DATA** For 60–61, use the table. Mr. Torres collected marbles. He is placing all the marbles in bags. Each bag will have only one kind of marble. All bags of the same color will have the same number of marbles.

| MR. TORRES'S MARBLE COLLECTION | | | | | |
|---|---|---|---|---|---|
| **Type** | Swirl | Helmet Patch | Patch | Slag | Sunburst |
| **Number** | 18 | 20 | 12 | 32 | 30 |

**60.** Mr. Torres is placing swirl and sunburst marbles in green bags. What is the greatest number of marbles he can put in a bag?

**62.** ? **What's the Question?** Eva is making gift baskets. She has 18 ribbons, 36 barrettes, and 12 bracelets. All baskets must have the same number of each item with no items left over. Eva can make 6 baskets.

**64.** A total of 90 students were divided into 15 groups. In each group, there were 3 boys. How many girls were there in all?

**66.** Write About It Explain how to find the greatest common factor of three numbers.

**61.** Mr. Torres is placing helmet patch, patch, and slag marbles in red bags. What is the greatest number of marbles he can put in a bag?

**63.** **REASONING** I am thinking of two numbers. Each number is between 20 and 30. The greatest common factor of the numbers is 4. What are the numbers?

**65.** **REASONING** What is the greatest factor any number can have? What is the least factor any number can have?

**67.** ≡**FAST FACT** • **SCIENCE** Bamboo grows an average of 30 cm a day. Castor bean plants grow an average of 0.2125 cm an hour. Which grows more in an hour? Explain.

**68.** Four friends plan to hike a 102-mile section of the Appalachian Trail in 9 days. If they walk 10 miles each day, will they walk the length of the entire 102-mile section? If not, how many more miles will they have to walk?

## Getting Ready for FCAT

**69.** Lily made a row of square tiles that was 72 inches long. Tom's row was 56 inches long. If they used tiles of the same size, what is the largest size they could have used?

    **A.** 24-inch square

    **B.** 16-inch square

    **C.** 8-inch square

    **D.** 2-inch square

**70.** A florist has 12 carnations, 36 roses, and 42 daisies. What is the greatest number of bouquets that can be made with the same number of each flower?

    **F.** 12        **H.** 4

    **G.** 6         **I.** 2

# Problem Solving LiNKUP . . . to History

Euclid, a Greek mathematician who lived more than 2,000 years ago, described another method for finding the greatest common factor, in his book *Elements*. The method is now known as the **Euclidean algorithm.** He used division to find the GCF. Follow the steps to find the GCF of 220 and 60.

## Example

| **STEP 1** | **STEP 2** | **STEP 3** | **STEP 4** |
|---|---|---|---|
| Divide the greater number by the lesser number. | Divide the divisor, 60, by the remainder, 40. | Continue dividing the divisors by the remainders until the remainder is 0. | The divisor in the last division problem is the GCF. |
| $$\begin{array}{r} 3 \\ 60)\overline{220} \\ -180 \\ \hline 40 \end{array}$$ | $$\begin{array}{r} 1 \\ 40)\overline{60} \\ -40 \\ \hline 20 \end{array}$$ | $$\begin{array}{r} 2 \\ 20)\overline{40} \\ -40 \\ \hline 0 \end{array}$$ | Since $40 \div 20$ has a remainder of 0, the GCF of 220 and 60 is 20. |

**Use the Euclidean algorithm to find the GCF for each pair of numbers.**

   **1.** 16, 60      **2.** 190, 36     **3.** 27, 40     **4.** 45, 330     **5.** 90, 105

# Multiples and the Least Common Multiple

HANDS ON

## Quick Review

Count by

1. fives from 5 to 30.
2. threes from 3 to 18.
3. fours from 4 to 24.
4. sixes from 6 to 36.
5. eights from 8 to 40.

▶ **Explore**

A multiple is the product of two or more nonzero whole numbers.

When a number is a multiple of two or more numbers in a set, it is a **common multiple**.

The least number that is a common multiple of two or more numbers is the **least common multiple**, or **LCM**.

## Activity

You can make a model to find the least common multiple of 3 and 5.

**STEP 1**

Place 3 red counters in a row. Place 5 yellow counters in a row directly below.

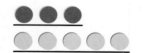

**STEP 2**

Continue placing groups of 3 red counters and groups of 5 yellow counters until both rows have the same number of counters. At that point, the number of counters in each row is the least common multiple, or LCM, of 3 and 5.

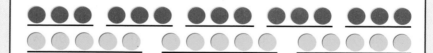

There are 15 counters in each row. So, the least common multiple of 3 and 5 is 15.

## Try It

Use counters to find the least common multiple for each set of numbers.

What should you do next to find the LCM of 2 and 7?

a. 2, 7    b. 4, 5    c. 4, 8

d. 3, 4    e. 2, 3, 6    f. 2, 3, 9

## Connect

You can also find the LCM of two or more numbers by
making a list or by using a number line.

| Make a List | Use a Number Line |
|---|---|
| Multiples of 4: 4, 8, 12, 16, 20, 24<br>Multiples of 6: 6, 12, 18, 24, 30, 36<br>LCM of 4 and 6: 12 | 0 2 4 6 8 10 **12** 14 16 18 20 22 24 |
| Multiples of 3: 3, 6, 9, 12, 15, 18, 21, 24<br>Multiples of 6: 6, 12, 18, 24, 30, 36, 42<br>Multiples of 9: 9, 18, 27, 36, 45, 54, 63<br>LCM of 3, 6, and 9: 18 | 0 2 4 6 8 10 12 14 16 **18** |

## Practice and Problem Solving

**List the first six multiples of each number.**

**1.** 4        **2.** 5        **3.** 6        **4.** 8        **5.** 9

**Write the least common multiple for each set of numbers.**

**6.** 2, 3        **7.** 3, 7        **8.** 16, 48        **9.** 4, 16, 96    **10.** 24, 27, 108

USE DATA    For 11–12, use the graph.

**11.** What are the least numbers of packs of glass
and ceramic beads you have to buy to have
the same number of each type of bead?

**12.** What are the least numbers of packs of glass,
wooden, and silver beads you have to buy to
have the same number of each type of bead?

**13.** The LCM of two numbers is 24. Their GCF is 4.
The numbers differ by 4. What are the numbers?

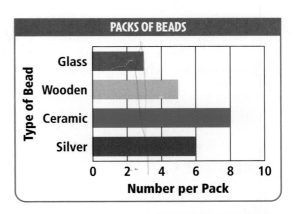

## Getting Ready for FCAT

**14.** Nick jogs every third day. Mia jogs every fifth
day. If they jog together today, in how many
days will they jog together again?

   **A.** 2                **C.** 15

   **B.** 8                **D.** 30

FCAT
TESTED    SSS/GLEs MA.A.5.2.1.5.4 Determines the least common multiple of two numbers up to
100 or more.

Chapter 13    **283**

# Problem Solving Skill
## Identify Relationships

**UNDERSTAND** > **PLAN** > **SOLVE** > **CHECK**

**THEY'RE RELATED!**   When you test numbers for divisibility or find the least common multiple (LCM) or greatest common factor (GCF), you are *identifying relationships* between numbers.

Lynn and Lynda used this table to help them find relationships between two numbers and their LCM and GCF.

| First Number, *a* | Second Number, *b* | *a* × *b* | GCF | LCM | GCF × LCM |
|---|---|---|---|---|---|
| 2 | 3 | 6 | 1 | 6 | 6 |
| 4 | 6 | 24 | 2 | 12 | 24 |
| 5 | 10 | 50 | 5 | 10 | 50 |
| 7 | 3 | 21 | 1 | 21 | 21 |
| 9 | 3 | 27 | 3 | 9 | 27 |
| 60 | 3 | 180 | 3 | 60 | 180 |

## Talk About It

- Look at 2 and 3 in the first row of the table. When 1 is the GCF of two numbers, what is the LCM?

- Look at 5 and 10. If the GCF of two numbers is one of the numbers, what is the LCM?

- Look at 9 and 3. If one number is divisible by the other number, what are the GCF and LCM?

- What is the relationship between the product of two numbers and the product of their GCF and LCM?

## Examples

**A** The GCF of 3 and another number is 1. The LCM is 15. What is the other number?

**Think:** When 1 is the GCF of two numbers, the LCM is the product of the numbers, *a* × *b*.

$3 \times b = 15$ ← 3 times what number equals 15?

$b = 5$

So, the other number is 5.

**B** The GCF of 4 and 20 is 4. What is the LCM of 4 and 20?

**Think:** When the GCF of two numbers is one of the numbers, the LCM is the other number.

So, the LCM is 20.

## ▶ Problem Solving Practice

**Use the relationships between the given numbers to find the missing number.**

1. The GCF of 7 and another number is 1. The LCM is 28. What is the other number?

2. The GCF of 3 and 21 is 3. What is the LCM of 3 and 21?

3. The LCM of 25 and 75 is 75. What is the GCF of 25 and 75?

4. The LCM of 12 and 36 is 36. What is the GCF of 12 and 36?

5. Which statement describes a relationship between 14 and 17?

    A The GCF is 2.
    B The LCM is 238.
    C Both numbers are multiples of 2.
    D Both numbers are even.

6. Which statement does *not* describe a relationship between 8 and 14?

    F The GCF is 2.
    G The LCM is 112.
    H GCF × LCM = 112
    J Both numbers are even.

## Mixed Applications

7. Carlos divided 60 by a number and got 2.5 for an answer. Is the number greater than or less than 70? Explain.

8. What is the number of pieces of string you can get by using 16 cuts to cut apart a straight piece of string?

9. How many angles are in 3 triangles, 4 squares, and 1 pentagon?

10. What is the average of all the numbers from 1 to 50 that are divisible by 4?

**USE DATA   For 11–12, use the table.**

11. Find the range, mean, median, and mode for the data.

12. **What if** the membership of each club doubles? What are the range, mean, median, and mode for the new set of data?

13. Dave packed oranges into boxes, 36 oranges per box. He then packed the boxes into crates, 16 boxes per crate. When he finished, he had 4 crates, 11 boxes, and 23 loose oranges. How many oranges did he have when he started?

14. ✎ **Write a problem** about a relationship between a pair of numbers. Use the GCF or LCM.

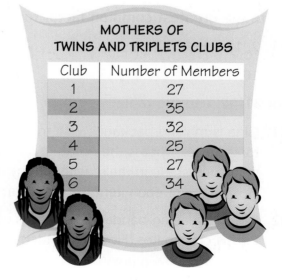

MOTHERS OF
TWINS AND TRIPLETS CLUBS

| Club | Number of Members |
|------|-------------------|
| 1 | 27 |
| 2 | 35 |
| 3 | 32 |
| 4 | 25 |
| 5 | 27 |
| 6 | 34 |

# Extra Practice

## Set A (pp. 276–277)

**Tell if each number is divisible by 2, 3, 4, 5, 6, 9, or 10.**

| | | | | |
|---|---|---|---|---|
| **1.** 15 | **2.** 26 | **3.** 60 | **4.** 132 | **5.** 725 |
| **6.** 1,410 | **7.** 135 | **8.** 109 | **9.** 15,324 | **10.** 378 |
| **11.** 1,618 | **12.** 16,836 | **13.** 855 | **14.** 740 | **15.** 234 |
| **16.** 489 | **17.** 1,971 | **18.** 2,538 | **19.** 620 | **20.** 396 |

**Is the statement true or false? Explain.**

**21.** All even numbers are divisible by 4.　　**22.** All odd numbers are divisible by 3.

**23.** All numbers divisible by 6 are divisible by 3.　　**24.** Some even numbers are divisible by 5.

## Set B (pp. 278–281)

**List the factors for each number.**

| | | | | |
|---|---|---|---|---|
| **1.** 3 | **2.** 17 | **3.** 32 | **4.** 75 | **5.** 100 |
| **6.** 36 | **7.** 56 | **8.** 120 | **9.** 60 | **10.** 132 |

**Write the common factors for each set of numbers.**

| | | | | |
|---|---|---|---|---|
| **11.** 17, 18 | **12.** 12, 32 | **13.** 10, 50 | **14.** 35, 75 | **15.** 60, 100 |
| **16.** 18, 20 | **17.** 15, 63 | **18.** 25, 80 | **19.** 6, 24 | **20.** 27, 54 |

**Write the greatest common factor for each set of numbers.**

| | | | | |
|---|---|---|---|---|
| **21.** 2, 12 | **22.** 6, 21 | **23.** 14, 28 | **24.** 30, 36 | **25.** 9, 27 |
| **26.** 16, 18 | **27.** 27, 33 | **28.** 48, 72 | **29.** 24, 54 | **30.** 20, 35 |

**For 31–32, use the table.**

**31.** Gina is making packages with toothbrushes and toothpaste. What is the greatest number of identical packages she can make without any items left over? How many of each item will be in each package?

**32.** Kevin is placing bandages and bars of soap in bags for his classmates. How many identical bags can he make, and how many of each item will be in each bag if none are left over?

| HEALTH FAIR SAMPLES | |
|---|---|
| **Item** | **Number** |
| Toothbrushes | 72 |
| Toothpaste | 48 |
| Bars of soap | 75 |
| Adhesive bandages | 100 |

# Review/Test

 **CHECK VOCABULARY AND CONCEPTS**

Choose the best term from the box.

| common multiples |
| divisible |
| greatest common factor (GCF) |
| least common multiple (LCM) |

1. The least number that is a common multiple of two or more numbers is called the __?__. (p. 282)

2. Multiples of one number that are also multiples of another number are called __?__. (p. 282)

3. The number 45 is __?__ by 9 because the remainder is 0 when 45 is divided by 9. (p. 276)

4. The __?__ of 20 and 30 is 10. (p. 278)

**CHECK SKILLS**

Tell if each number is divisible by 2, 3, 4, 5, 6, 9, or 10. (pp. 276–277)

5. 42  6. 48  7. 56  8. 63  9. 66

10. 90  11. 264  12. 681  13. 1,245  14. 6,460

Write the common factors for each set of numbers. (pp. 278–281)

15. 8, 14  16. 24, 28  17. 4, 12, 20  18. 8, 16, 32

Write the greatest common factor for each set of numbers. (pp. 278–281)

19. 6, 12  20. 18, 32  21. 3, 15, 30  22. 6, 12, 36

List the first six multiples of each number. (pp. 282–283)

23. 3  24. 7  25. 9  26. 12

Write the least common multiple for each set of numbers. (pp. 282–283)

27. 5, 30  28. 8, 36  29. 10, 24, 120  30. 8, 32, 160

**CHECK PROBLEM SOLVING**

31. Baseball cards come in packs of 20; race car cards, packs of 40; and football cards, packs of 50. What is the least number of packs of each that will give you the same number of each kind of card? (pp. 278–281)

32. The GCF of 11 and another number is 1. The LCM is 99. What is the other number? (pp. 284–285)

33. The LCM of 7 and 14 is 14. What is the GCF of 7 and 14? (pp. 284–285)

# Getting Ready for FCAT

## ⭐ NUMBER SENSE, CONCEPTS, AND OPERATIONS

**1.** Which of the following shows 0.125 written in expanded form?

  **A.** 100 + 20 + 5

  **B.** 1 + 2 + 5

  **C.** 0.1 + 0.2 + 0.5

  **D.** 0.1 + 0.02 + 0.005

> **TIP** **Get the information you need.**
> See item 2. To find the first day they will volunteer on the same day, find the least common multiple of 4 and 6.

**2.** Mel and Jo volunteer at the hospital in March. Mel volunteers every fourth day beginning on March 4. Jo volunteers every sixth day beginning on March 6. Which is the first day they will volunteer on the same day?

  **F.** March 6          **H.** March 10

  **G.** March 8          **I.** March 12

**3.** A group of 90 students went on a field trip. The students were put into groups, with an equal number of boys and an equal number of girls in each group. If 48 boys went on the field trip, how many groups were there?

  **A.** 6          **C.** 7

  **B.** 9          **D.** 9

**4. Explain It** Feather eats 4 pounds of dog food each week. The food is sold in 20-pound bags. ESTIMATE to determine whether it will take more than 9 bags to feed Feather for one year. Explain your answer.

## ⭐ MEASUREMENT

**5.** The Dolphins show lasts 45 minutes. At what time does it end?

| ANIMAL REVIEW | SHOW | TIME |
|---|---|---|
| | Flying Friends | 10:30 A.M. |
| | Dolphins | 10:45 A.M. |
| | Amazing Animals | 11:00 A.M. |
| | Monkeys | 11:15 A.M. |

  **F.** 11:00 A.M.

  **G.** 11:30 A.M.

  **H.** 11:45 A.M.

  **I.** 12:00 P.M.

**6.** Look at the schedule above. The Amazing Animals show starts in 20 minutes. What time is it now?

  **A.**           **C.**

  **B.**           **D.**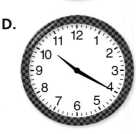

**7. Explain It** Randy estimates that the height of the classroom door is about 800 centimeters. Is this estimate reasonable? Explain how you know.

## ⭐ ALGEBRAIC THINKING

**8.** There were 9 people at a party. After some other people arrived, there were 15 people at the party. If *n* represents the number of people who arrived later, which equation can be used to find *n*?

**F.** $9 + n = 15$

**G.** $n - 9 = 15$

**H.** $15 + n = 9$

**I.** $9 - n = 15$

**9.** The number line below shows the value of *x*.

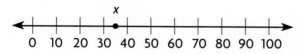

Which of the following number lines shows the value of $x + 25$?

**A.**

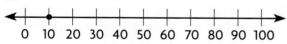

**B.**

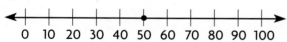

**C.**

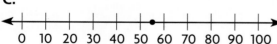

**D.**

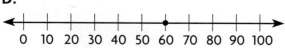

**10. Explain It** What are the next two numbers in the pattern?

50, 43, 36, 29, ▪, ▪

Explain how you decided.

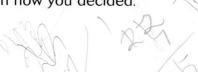

## ⭐ DATA ANALYSIS AND PROBABILITY

**11.** The graph below shows sources of energy used in the United States. Hydroelectric and nuclear energy are used half as much as which other energy source?

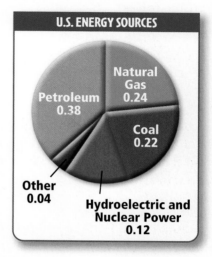

**U.S. ENERGY SOURCES**

Natural Gas 0.24

Petroleum 0.38

Coal 0.22

Other 0.04

Hydroelectric and Nuclear Power 0.12

**F.** coal

**G.** natural gas

**H.** petroleum

**I.** other sources

**12.** Look at the graph above. Which shows the part of energy sources from petroleum and coal together?

**A.** 0.22

**B.** 0.38

**C.** 0.50

**D.** 0.60

**13. Explain It** The ages of seven people at a picnic are 10, 6, 13, 20, 9, 25, and 15. If the 10-year-old leaves the picnic and a 17-year-old arrives, how will the mean age of the people at the picnic change? Explain your answer.

# Exponents and Prime Numbers

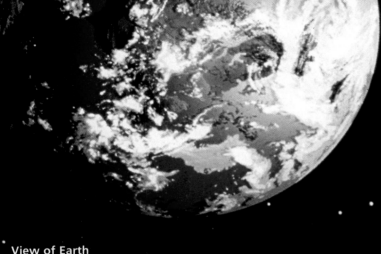

View of Earth
from near the moon

**≡FAST FACT • SCIENCE** Our solar system consists of
the sun and nine planets. Earth is 150 million kilometers,
or about 93 million miles, from the sun.

PROBLEM SOLVING  Numbers can be written in
word form, standard form, and expanded form with
or without exponents. The table shows the average
distances, from the sun, of the other eight planets in our
solar system. Write the average distances for Mercury
and Mars using expanded form with exponents.

| AVERAGE DISTANCE TO SUN | |
|---|---|
| **Planet** | **Average Distance to Sun (km)** |
| Mercury | 58,000,000 |
| Venus | 108,000,000 |
| Mars | 228,000,000 |
| Jupiter | 778,000,000 |
| Saturn | 1,429,000,000 |
| Uranus | 2,871,000,000 |
| Neptune | 4,500,000,000 |
| Pluto | 5,900,000,000 |

Use this page to help you review and remember
important skills needed for Chapter 14.

## MULTIPLICATION AND DIVISION FACTS

**Find the product.**

**1.** $3 \times 5$     **2.** $5 \times 12$     **3.** $7 \times 2$     **4.** $9 \times 1$

**5.** $2 \times 0$     **6.** $4 \times 8$     **7.** $6 \times 7$     **8.** $8 \times 9$

**Find the quotient.**

**9.** $16 \div 2$     **10.** $21 \div 7$     **11.** $36 \div 6$     **12.** $44 \div 11$

**13.** $108 \div 9$     **14.** $144 \div 12$     **15.** $80 \div 10$     **16.** $64 \div 8$

## FACTORS

**Write all the factors for each number.**

**17.** 9     **18.** 12     **19.** 18     **20.** 21

**21.** 36     **22.** 32     **23.** 20     **24.** 24

# VOCABULARY POWER

## REVIEW

**array** [ə•rā′] *noun*

An array is an arrangement of objects in
rows and columns. Describe a real-life
example of an array.

## PREVIEW

exponent     prime number

base     prime factorization

square number     factor tree

composite number     square root

**GO ON-LINE**     www.harcourtschool.com/mathglossary

# Introduction to Exponents

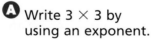

**VOCABULARY**

exponent
base
square number

**ONE, TWO, FOUR, EIGHT . . .** An amoeba is a one-celled organism that reproduces by splitting. After 1 amoeba split 5 times, there were $2 \times 2 \times 2 \times 2 \times 2$, or 32 amoebas.

You can use words, pictures, and numerical expressions to represent a number. The following all represent the number 5.

five    5    V    $4 + 1$    $(12 - 10) + 3$

You can also represent a number by using an exponent and a base. An **exponent** shows how many times a number, called the **base**, is used as a factor.

exponent
↓

$$32 = \underbrace{2 \times 2 \times 2 \times 2 \times 2}_{5 \text{ factors}} = 2^{\overset{5}{\underset{\uparrow}{}}}_{\text{base}}$$

Read the expression $2^5$ as "the fifth power of two."

So, 32 can be written as $2 \times 2 \times 2 \times 2 \times 2$, or $2^5$.

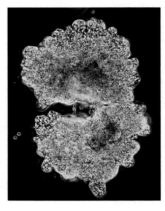

▲ Some freshwater amoebas travel between 0.5 and 3 microns per second. A micron is 0.001 millimeter. So, the fastest time for an amoeba 1-millimeter dash is about 5 minutes.

## Examples

**A** Write $3 \times 3$ by using an exponent.
**Think:** 3 is used as a factor 2 times. The base is 3 and the exponent is 2.

So, $3 \times 3 = 3^2$.
**Read:** "the second power of 3," or "three squared."

**B** Find the value of $7^3$.
$7^3 = 7 \times 7 \times 7$
   $= (7 \times 7) \times 7$
   $= 49 \times 7$
   $= 343$

So, $7^3 = 343$.
**Read:** "the third power of 7," or "seven cubed."

**C** Find the value of $1^7$.
$1^7 = 1 \times 1 \times 1 \times 1 \times 1 \times 1 \times 1$
   $= 1$

So, $1^7 = 1$.
**Read:** "the seventh power of 1."

• Explain how you can use $4^3 = 64$ to find $4^4$.

• What is the value of $1^3$? of $1^5$? of $1^9$? Explain a rule for finding the value of any power of 1.

## Square Numbers

A square number is the product of a number and itself. A
**square number** can be expressed with the exponent 2.

### Activity

**MATERIALS:** square tiles or grid paper

- Make a square array with 3 square tiles on each side.
  How many tiles did you use?

- Make a square array with 4 square tiles on each side.
  Continue to make square arrays, using tiles or grid paper,
  until you have a square array with 12 tiles on each side. Copy,
  complete, and continue the table to show arrays with 1 to
  12 tiles on each side.

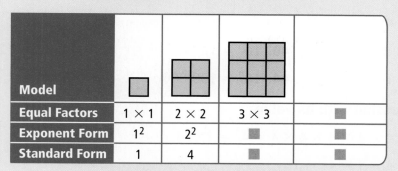

| Model |  |  |  | |
|---|---|---|---|---|
| Equal Factors | $1 \times 1$ | $2 \times 2$ | $3 \times 3$ | ■ |
| Exponent Form | $1^2$ | $2^2$ | ■ | ■ |
| Standard Form | 1 | 4 | ■ | ■ |

- Write a rule for the number of tiles in each array.

- Suppose you have a square array with *n* square tiles on
  each side. How many tiles would be in the square array?

You can use a calculator to find the value of a number with an
exponent.

 $13^2 \rightarrow$ ( 1 ) ( 3 ) ( ^ ) ( 2 ) (Enter =)  $13^2 = 169$

### ▶ Check

1. **Explain** how you would rewrite $3^4$ as a multiplication problem.
   What is the value of $3^4$?

2. **Explain** how $2^6$ and $6^2$ are different.

**Write in exponent form. Then find the value.**

3. 9 cubed          4. $6 \times 6 \times 6 \times 6$          5. $4 \times 4 \times 4 \times 4 \times 4 \times 4$

**Find the value.**

6. $9^2$          7. $4^3$          8. $10^2$          9. $4^4$          10. $7^2$

11. $2^4$          12. $2^7$          13. $1^5$          14. $3^3$          15. $5^3$

**LESSON CONTINUES**

**FCAT
TESTED** SSS/GLEs MA.A.1.2.4 The student understands that numbers can be represented in a variety
of equivalent forms using whole numbers, decimals, fractions, and percents.          **Chapter 14  293**

**Write in exponent form. Then find the value.**

**16.** seven squared    **17.** the sixth power of 2    **18.** 11 cubed

**19.** $7 \times 7 \times 7 \times 7$    **20.** $3 \times 3 \times 3 \times 3 \times 3 \times 3 \times 3$    **21.** $15 \times 15$

**Find the value.**

**22.** $3^2$    **23.** $8^3$    **24.** $1^4$    **25.** $4^5$    **26.** $9^4$

**27.** $11^2$    **28.** $10^6$    **29.** $3^4$    **30.** $6^3$    **31.** $10^3$

**32.** $2^3$    **33.** $0^5$    **34.** $7^5$    **35.** $14^2$    **36.** $5^4$

**37.** Use the expressions in the box. Write three pairs of expressions that have the same value.

| $4^2$ | $1^7$ | $2^6$ | $4^3$ | $1^5$ | $2^4$ |

**ALGEBRA** Find the value of $n$.

**38.** $3^n = 81$    **39.** $n^5 = 32$    **40.** $10^n = 1{,}000$    **41.** $n^3 = 125$

**42.** $n^2 = 121$    **43.** $8^n = 64$    **44.** $10^n = 100{,}000$    **45.** $n^4 = 1$

**For 46–49, match the word expression with its value.**

**46.** four cubed    **a.** $4 \times 4 \times 4 \times 4 \times 4 = 4^5 = 1{,}024$

**47.** four squared    **b.** $4 \times 4 = 4^2 = 16$

**48.** the fifth power of four    **c.** $4 \times 4 \times 4 = 4^3 = 64$

**49.** the sixth power of four    **d.** $4 \times 4 \times 4 \times 4 \times 4 \times 4 = 4^6 = 4{,}096$

**USE DATA** For 50–51, use the schedule.

**50.** Class B is in the science lab for 45 minutes. What time does Class B leave the lab?

**51.** Class D spends 50 minutes in the lab. How much time is there between the time Class C leaves the lab and Class D enters the lab?

| SCIENCE LAB SCHEDULE | | |
|---|---|---|
| **Class** | **Start Time** | **End Time** |
| Class A | 9:30 A.M. | 10:15 A.M. |
| Class B | 10:35 A.M. | ■ |
| Class C | 12:15 P.M. | 1:05 P.M. |
| Class D | ■ | 2:15 P.M. |

**52. REASONING** Maria thinks that $5^4 = 625$. How can she use division to check her work?

**53.** ✍ **Write a problem** involving a number pattern. Explain how to find the sixth number in the pattern.

**54. Vocabulary Power** Many words used in mathematics also have meanings outside mathematics. Write a mathematical definition and a nonmathematical definition for *power*.

**55.** A bacterium cell splits into 2 every hour. How many cells will there be in 4 hours? in 7 hours?

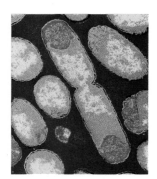

**56.** Jacob has 18.75 meters of fencing that he needs to cut into 3 equal sections. After he has cut off one section, how long is the remaining fencing?

**57. REASONING** How can you use what you know about exponents to find the values of $(1.2)^3$ and $(0.4)^2$?

**58.** A company puts $10^3$ pencils in each carton. Which number is equal to the number of pencils in each carton?

   **A.** 10
   **B.** 100
   **C.** 1,000
   **D.** 10,000

**59.** A bacterium reproduces by splitting in two every hour. How many bacteria will there be after 6 hours?

   **F.** 6      **H.** 36
   **G.** 12      **I.** 64

**60.** Marco is combining cubes. Each large cube contains $3^3$ small cubes. How many small cubes are in each large cube?

   **A.** 9      **C.** 18
   **B.** 12      **D.** 27

# Problem Solving ✦ THINKER's CORNER 💡

**PATTERNS WITH EXPONENTS** You can make models of cubes to help visualize numbers with an exponent of 3. Look at the cube at the right. You can write the volume of the cube as $4^3$.

Copy and complete the table.

**1.**

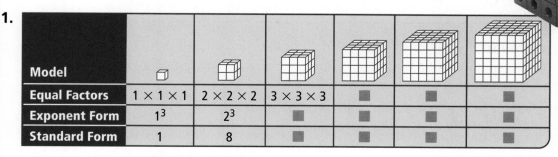

| Model | □ | ⧈ | ⬚ | ⬚ | ⬚ | ⬚ |
|---|---|---|---|---|---|---|
| Equal Factors | $1 \times 1 \times 1$ | $2 \times 2 \times 2$ | $3 \times 3 \times 3$ | ■ | ■ | ■ |
| Exponent Form | $1^3$ | $2^3$ | ■ | ■ | ■ | ■ |
| Standard Form | 1 | 8 | ■ | ■ | ■ | ■ |

**2.** How many small cubes do you need to make a large cube that is 25 small cubes along each edge?

**3.** Describe a pattern in the models shown in the table.

**4.** What is the exponent form for the volume of a cube with 50 tiles on a side?

**5.** Suppose you have a large cube with $n$ small cubes along each edge. How many small cubes would be in the large cube?

# Exponents and Expanded Form

▶ **Learn**

You have learned how to find the value of expressions such as $2^2$, $2^4$, $10^3$, and $10^5$ that have 2 or a greater number as an exponent. How can you find the value of expressions that have 1 or 0 as an exponent?

**HANDS ON**

## Activity

Look at the patterns below. What are the values of $2^1$, $2^0$, $10^1$, and $10^0$?

$2^5 = 2 \times 2 \times 2 \times 2 \times 2 = 32$
$2^4 = 2 \times 2 \times 2 \times 2 \quad = 16 = 32 \div 2$ **Think:** Divide by 2
$2^3 = 2 \times 2 \times 2 \quad\quad\quad = 8 = 16 \div 2$ each time.
$2^2 = 2 \times 2 \quad\quad\quad\quad\quad = 4 = 8 \div 2$
$2^1 = 2 \quad\quad\quad\quad\quad\quad\quad = 2 = 4 \div 2$
$2^0 = 1 \quad\quad\quad\quad\quad\quad\quad = 1 = 2 \div 2$

$10^5 = 10 \times 10 \times 10 \times 10 \times 10 = 100,000$ **Think:** Divide by 10 each time.
$10^4 = 10 \times 10 \times 10 \times 10 \quad\quad = 10,000 = 100,000 \div 10$
$10^3 = 10 \times 10 \times 10 \quad\quad\quad\quad = 1,000 = 10,000 \div 10$
$10^2 = 10 \times 10 \quad\quad\quad\quad\quad\quad = 100 = 1,000 \div 10$
$10^1 = 10 \quad\quad\quad\quad\quad\quad\quad\quad = 10 = 100 \div 10$
$10^0 = 1 \quad\quad\quad\quad\quad\quad\quad\quad = 1 = 10 \div 10$

- Explain how to use the values of $2^2$ and $10^2$ to find $2^1$ and $2^0$ and $10^1$ and $10^0$.

- Start with $3^5$ and make a similar pattern to find $3^1$ and $3^0$.

- Predict the values of the first power and zero power of any number greater than zero.

You can use these rules to find the value of numbers with 0 or 1 as an exponent.

| The zero power of any number, except 0, is 1. | The first power of any number equals that number. |
|---|---|
| $2^0 = 1$    $9^0 = 1$    $10^0 = 1$ | $2^1 = 2$    $9^1 = 9$    $10^1 = 10$ |

# Expanded Form

The continent of Antarctica has a land area of about 5,404,000 square miles and is bordered by the South Atlantic, Indian, and South Pacific Oceans.

You can use powers of ten to show numbers in expanded form. The value of each digit in 5,404,000 can be expressed with or without an exponent. For example, the value of 5 can be written as 5,000,000, as $5 \times 1,000,000$, or as $5 \times 10^6$.

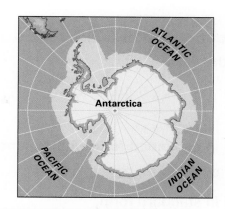

| MILLIONS | THOUSANDS | | | ONES | | |
|---|---|---|---|---|---|---|
| Ones | Hundreds | Tens | Ones | Hundreds | Tens | Ones |
| 5, | 4 | 0 | 4, | 0 | 0 | 0 |
| $5 \times 1,000,000$, or 5,000,000 | $4 \times 100,000$ or 100,000 | $0 \times 10,000$, or 0 | $4 \times 1,000$, or 0 | $0 \times 100$, or 0 | $0 \times 10$, or 0 | $0 \times 1$, or 0 |
| $5 \times 10^6$ | $4 \times 10^5$ | $0 \times 10^4$ | $4 \times 10^3$ | $0 \times 10^2$ | $0 \times 10^1$ | $0 \times 10^0$ |

You do not need to write the value of a place with a zero digit. The land area of Antarctica can be written in expanded form with exponents as $(5 \times 10^6) + (4 \times 10^5) + (4 \times 10^3)$.

## Examples

**A** Write 40,503 in expanded form with exponents.

$$40,000 = 4 \times 10^4$$
$$500 = 5 \times 10^2$$
$$40,503 \leftarrow 3 = 3 \times 10^0$$

$$40,503 = (4 \times 10^4) + (5 \times 10^2) + (3 \times 10^0)$$

**B** Write $(5 \times 10^5) + (6 \times 10^3) + (7 \times 10^2) + (8 \times 10^1) + (9 \times 10^0)$ in standard form.

Think:
$$(5 \times 10^5) = 5 \times 100,000 = 500,000$$
$$(6 \times 10^3) = 6 \times 1,000 = 6,000$$
$$(7 \times 10^2) = 7 \times 100 = 700$$
$$(8 \times 10^1) = 8 \times 10 = 80$$
$$(9 \times 10^0) = 9 \times 1 = 9$$

$$500,000 + 6,000 + 700 + 80 + 9 = 506,789$$

## Check

1. **Explain** how you know the value of $5^1$ and $5^0$.

**Find the value.**

2. $3^0$  3. $12^1$  4. $10^1$  5. $16^1$  6. $7^0$

7. Write 4,062,035 in expanded form with exponents.

8. Write $(2 \times 10^6) + (4 \times 10^5) + (7 \times 10^3) + (9 \times 10^1) + (5 \times 10^0)$ in standard form.

**LESSON CONTINUES**

FCAT TESTED  SSS/GLEs MA.A.2.2.1.5.2 Expresses numbers to millions or more in expanded form using powers of ten, with or without exponential notation.

Chapter 14  **297**

**Find the value.**

**9.** $8^1$     **10.** $10^7$     **11.** $2^0$     **12.** $10^9$     **13.** $12^0$

**14.** $13^1$     **15.** $5^6$     **16.** $9^0$     **17.** $10^1$     **18.** $11^1$

**Write in expanded form with exponents.**

**19.** 734,261     **20.** 15,934     **21.** 127,803     **22.** 25,000,005     **23.** 396,047

**Write in standard form.**

**24.** $(4 \times 10^6) + (5 \times 10^5) + (1 \times 10^3) + (2 \times 10^1) + (9 \times 10^0)$

**25.** $(1 \times 10^6) + (7 \times 10^4) + (4 \times 10^3) + (2 \times 10^0)$

**26.** $(2 \times 10^5) + (4 \times 10^4) + (9 \times 10^2)$

**Copy and complete each table.**

**27.**

| Exponent Form | Standard Form |
|---|---|
| $3^4$ | 81 |
| $3^3$ | ■ |
| $3^2$ | ■ |
| $3^1$ | ■ |
| $3^0$ | ■ |

**28.**

| Exponent Form | Standard Form |
|---|---|
| $5^4$ | 625 |
| $5^3$ | ■ |
| $5^2$ | ■ |
| $5^1$ | ■ |
| $5^0$ | ■ |

**29.**

| Exponent Form | Standard Form |
|---|---|
| $10^4$ | ■ |
| $10^3$ | ■ |
| $10^2$ | ■ |
| $10^1$ | ■ |
| $10^0$ | ■ |

 **ALGEBRA** Compare. Write $<$, $>$, or $=$ for each ●.

**30.** $6^0$ ● $2^0$     **31.** $10^3$ ● $2^{10}$     **32.** $1^7$ ● $7^1$

**33.** $10^2$ ● $100^1$     **34.** $1^0$ ● $1^1$     **35.** $8^0$ ● $0^8$

**USE DATA For 36–37, use the graph.**

**36.** Between which years did the population of Florida become greater than $10^7$?

**37.** If the pattern continues, what is a reasonable estimate for the population of Florida in 2010?

**38.** Elianne earned $10 each week for 10 weeks of baby-sitting. Ricardo earned $17 each week for 6 weeks of mowing lawns. How much money did they earn altogether?

**39.** Cal puts 56 marbles into 7 bags so that each bag contains the same number of marbles. How many marbles are in 4 bags?

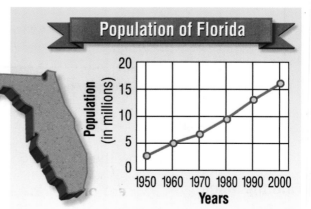

**40.** ≡**FAST FACT** • SOCIAL STUDIES

Tallgrass prairie in North America once covered 142 million acres. Write the number of acres in standard form and in expanded form using exponents.

**41.** After Kelly paid $26.50 for books, $3.55 for paper, and $4.36 for pens, she had $5.98 left. How much money did she have to start?

## Getting Ready for FCAT

**42.** Four students wrote the expanded form of a number on the chalkboard. Who wrote the expanded form of 300,401?

| Lynn | $(3 \times 10^5) + (4 \times 10^3) + (1 \times 10^0)$ |
| Evan | $(3 \times 10^3) + (4 \times 10^4) + (1 \times 10^1)$ |
| Matt | $(3 \times 10^5) + (4 \times 10^2) + (1 \times 10^0)$ |
| Gina | $(3 \times 10^6) + (4 \times 10^3) + (1 \times 10^1)$ |

**A.** Lynn      **C.** Matt

**B.** Evan      **D.** Gina

**43.** Veronica computed that there are $(8 \times 10^3) + (7 \times 10^2) + (6 \times 10^1)$ hours in a year. What is the standard form of the number of hours in a year?

**F.** 876

**G.** 8,706

**H.** 8,760

**I.** 87,600

## Problem Solving   Thinker's Corner

**ALGEBRA** The binary, or base-two, number system uses only the digits 0 and 1.

| decimal | 0 | 1 | 2 | 3 | 4 | 5 | 6 | 7 | 8 | 9 | 10 |
|---------|---|---|---|---|---|---|---|---|---|---|----|
| binary | 0 | 1 | 10 | 11 | 100 | 101 | 110 | 111 | 1000 | 1001 | 1010 |

In the decimal system, each place value is ten times the place value to the right. In the binary system, each place value is two times the place value to the right. You can use powers of 2 to find the decimal equivalent of a binary number.

$$10100_{two} = (1 \times 2^4) + (0 \times 2^3) + (1 \times 2^2) + (0 \times 2^1) + (0 \times 2^0)$$
$$= (1 \times 16) + (0 \times 8) + (1 \times 4) + (0 \times 2) + (0 \times 1)$$
$$= 16 + 0 + 4 + 0 + 0$$
$$= 20$$

**Find the decimal equivalent of each binary number.**

**1.** $1111_{two}$   **2.** $10001_{two}$   **3.** $11000_{two}$   **4.** $11111_{two}$   **5.** $101010_{two}$

**6.** Explain the similarities and differences between the decimal number system and the binary number system.

# Prime and Composite Numbers

**Quick Review**

List the factors for each number.

**1.** 4    **2.** 8    **3.** 12
**4.** 36    **5.** 15

**VOCABULARY**

composite number
prime number

**MATERIALS**
square tiles

▶ **Explore**

You can make rectangular arrays to find factors.

## Activity 1

Show all the ways 6 tiles can be arranged in an array.

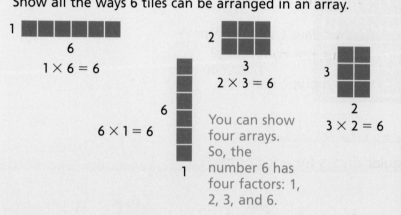

1
6
$1 \times 6 = 6$

$6 \times 1 = 6$

2
3
$2 \times 3 = 6$

3
2
$3 \times 2 = 6$

You can show four arrays. So, the number 6 has four factors: 1, 2, 3, and 6.

If a whole number has more than two factors, it is a **composite number**. So, 6 is a composite number.

## Activity 2

Show all the ways 5 tiles can be arranged in an array.

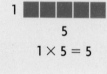

1
5
$1 \times 5 = 5$

$5 \times 1 = 5$

You can show two arrays. So, the number 5 has two factors: 1 and 5.

If a whole number has exactly two factors, 1 and the number itself, it is a **prime number**. So, 5 is a prime number.

How many arrays can you show for the number 15?

### Try It

Use tiles to show all the arrays for each number. Write *prime* or *composite*.

**a.** 15    **b.** 9    **c.** 13    **d.** 7

Use tiles to show all the rectangular arrays you can make for the numbers 2–12. Copy and complete the table below.

| Number | Rows × Columns for Arrays | Factors | Prime or Composite? |
|--------|---------------------------|---------|---------------------|
| 2 | 1 × 2<br>2 × 1 | 1, 2 | prime |
| 3 | 1 × 3<br>3 × 1 | 1, 3 | prime |
| 4 | 1 × 4<br>■ × ■<br>■ × ■ | ■, ■, ■ | ___?___ |

 **MATH IDEA** Every whole number greater than 1 is either prime or composite. The number 1 is neither prime nor composite.

• **REASONING** Explain why 2 is the only even prime number.

▶ **Practice and Problem Solving**

Use tiles to show all the rectangular arrays for each number. Write *prime* or *composite*.

**1.** 3          **2.** 10          **3.** 11          **4.** 12          **5.** 17

Write *prime* or *composite* for each number.

**6.** 7          **7.** 14          **8.** 21          **9.** 25          **10.** 23

**11.** 41          **12.** 32          **13.** 37          **14.** 49          **15.** 19

**16.** List all the prime numbers from 1 to 100.

**17.** List all the composite factors of 72.

**18.** Chris spent $24.00 at the pet store. He bought a toy for $4.50 and 2 bags of dog food. If the bags of food cost the same, how much did he spend on each bag?

**19.** 📖 **Write About It** Explain the difference between a prime number and a composite number. Use examples in your explanation.

**Getting Ready for FCAT**

**20.** Alma has 33 stamps, Brendan has 31, Courtney has 39, and David has 35. Which person will NOT be able to line up his or her stamps in two or more equal rows?

  **A.** Alma
  **B.** Brendan
  **C.** Courtney
  **D.** David

# Prime Factors and Exponents

**Quick Review**

Write *prime* or *composite* for each.

1. 6                  2. 5
3. 8                  4. 12
5. 13

## Learn

**PRIME TIME**   All composite numbers can be written as the product of prime factors. This is called the **prime factorization** of the number. To find the prime factorization of a number, you can use a diagram called a **factor tree**.

To use a factor tree to find the prime factorization of 36, first choose any two factors of 36. Continue factoring until only prime factors are left.

**VOCABULARY**

**prime factorization**
**factor tree**
**square root**

David and Luisa each made a factor tree.

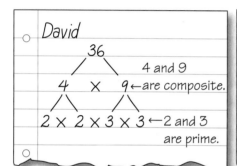

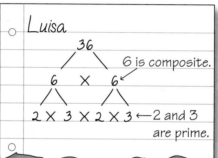

Because of the Commutative Property of Multiplication, $2 \times 2 \times 3 \times 3 = 2 \times 3 \times 2 \times 3$. Order the prime factors from least to greatest. So, the prime factorization of 36 is $2 \times 2 \times 3 \times 3$.

## Examples

**A** What is the prime factorization of 40?

```
        40
       /  \
      8 × 5
     / \
    4 × 2
   / \
  2 × 2
```

So, $40 = 2 \times 2 \times 2 \times 5$.

**B** What is the prime factorization of 27?

```
      27
     /  \
    9 × 3
   / \
  3 × 3
```

So, $27 = 3 \times 3 \times 3$.

**C** What is the prime factorization of 630?

```
          630
         /   \
       63  ×  10
      / \    / \
     9 × 7 × 2 × 5
    / \
   3 × 3
```

So, $630 = 2 \times 3 \times 3 \times 5 \times 7$.

# Exponents in Prime Factorizations

Sometimes you can use exponents to write the prime factorization of a number.

When a prime factor is repeated in a factorization, use the prime as the base and use the number of times it is repeated as the exponent.

$$36 = \underline{2 \times 2} \times \underline{3 \times 3} \quad \leftarrow \text{2 is a factor two times.}$$
$$\phantom{36 = 2 \times 2 \times 3 \times 3 \quad \leftarrow} \text{3 is a factor two times.}$$

$$36 = 2^2 \times 3^2 \quad \leftarrow \text{So, use 2 for the exponents.}$$

Examples D, E, and F show how you can write the prime factorization by using exponents for the numbers in Examples A, B, and C on page 302.

## Examples

**D** $40 = \underline{2 \times 2 \times 2} \times 5$

$40 = 2^3 \times 5$

**E** $27 = \underline{3 \times 3 \times 3}$

$27 = 3^3$

**F** $630 = 2 \times \underline{3 \times 3} \times 5 \times 7$

$630 = 2 \times 3^2 \times 5 \times 7$

Notice in Examples D and F that exponents of 1 are not written.

## Check

**Technology Link**

More Practice: Harcourt Mega Math Ice Station Exploration, *Arctic Algebra*, Levels O, W

1. **Explain** why you would not use the number 1 as a factor in a factor tree.

**Copy and complete to find the prime factorization.**

2. $5 \times 4 = 5 \times \blacksquare \times \blacksquare$

3. $6 \times 9 = \blacksquare \times 3 \times 3 \times 3$

4. $4 \times 4 = \blacksquare \times \blacksquare \times \blacksquare \times 2$

5. $2 \times 6 = 2 \times \blacksquare \times \blacksquare$

6. $35 \times 2 = \blacksquare \times \blacksquare \times 2$

7. $98 = \blacksquare \times \blacksquare \times \blacksquare$

**Rewrite the prime factorization by using exponents.**

8. $125 = 5 \times 5 \times 5$

9. $24 = 2 \times 2 \times 2 \times 3$

10. $100 = 2 \times 2 \times 5 \times 5$

11. $147 = 3 \times 7 \times 7$

12. $150 = 2 \times 3 \times 5 \times 5$

13. $5{,}929 = 7 \times 7 \times 11 \times 11$

**Find the prime factorization of the number. Use exponents when possible.**

14. 4

15. 21

16. 24

17. 19

18. 65

19. 10

20. 16

21. 28

22. 100

23. 155

**LESSON CONTINUES** ▶

FCAT TESTED  SSS/GLEs MA.A.5.2.1.5.2 Expresses a whole number as a product of its prime factors.

Chapter 14  **303**

**Copy and complete to find the prime factorization.**

**24.** $3 \times 9 = 3 \times \blacksquare \times \blacksquare$

**25.** $5 \times 6 = 5 \times \blacksquare \times \blacksquare$

**26.** $8 \times 7 = \blacksquare \times \blacksquare \times \blacksquare \times 7$

**27.** $50 = 2 \times \blacksquare \times \blacksquare$

**28.** $6 \times 7 = \blacksquare \times \blacksquare \times 7$

**29.** $39 = \blacksquare \times \blacksquare$

**Rewrite the prime factorization by using exponents.**

**30.** $242 = 2 \times 11 \times 11$

**31.** $100 = 5 \times 2 \times 2 \times 5$

**32.** $338 = 2 \times 13 \times 13$

**33.** $275 = 11 \times 5 \times 5$

**34.** $220 = 2 \times 5 \times 2 \times 11$

**35.** $342 = 2 \times 3 \times 3 \times 19$

**Find the prime factorization of the number. Use exponents when possible.**

**36.** 18

**37.** 46

**38.** 22

**39.** 35

**40.** 243

**41.** 38

**42.** 44

**43.** 26

**44.** 196

**45.** 225

**46.** 125

**47.** 294

**48.** 135

**49.** 224

**50.** 686

**ALGEBRA** **Complete the prime factorization. Find the value of the variable.**

**51.** $2 \times 2 \times 2 = 2^n$

**52.** $2^2 \times m = 28$

**53.** $3^s \times 5 = 45$

**54.** $3 \times 3 \times r = 3^3$

**55.** $5^n \times 11 = 275$

**56.** $5^2 \times s = 1{,}225$

**57. NUMBER SENSE** What is the greatest square number that is a factor of 72 and a whole number?

**58.** Find the prime factorizations of all the composite numbers from 4 to 20. Use exponents when possible.

**59. NUMBER SENSE** The prime factors of a number are the first three prime numbers. No factor is repeated. What is the number?

**60. REASONING** Jen says the prime factorization of 24 is $2 \times 2 \times 2 \times 3$. Ralph says it is $2 \times 3 \times 2 \times 2$. Who is right? Explain.

**61.** Tamika spent \$4.35, \$14.15, and \$19.45 at the mall. Did she spend more than \$37? Explain.

**62.** Bill has to wait 98 days for his vacation. How many weeks does Bill have to wait?

**For 63–64, use the factor tree.**

**63.** ? **What's the Error?** Tyler made this factor tree for 72. Describe and correct his error.

**64.** Make two other factor trees for 72.

**65.** Ohio has a population of about 11 million. Is the population greater than or less than $10^7$?

**66.** Is $10^4$ greater than, less than, or equal to $2^4 \times 5^4$? Explain.

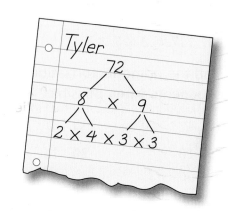

**67.** Josh is shipping 4 cases of water. Each case holds 24 bottles. The 4 cases hold 1,536 ounces in all. How many ounces does each bottle hold?

**68.** Of 314 runners entered in a race, 29 were unable to finish. If those who finished ran a combined total of 2,280 km, how long was the race?

## Getting Ready for FCAT

**69.** During math class, four students each wrote the prime factorization of 150 on the chalkboard.

| Tami | $150 = 2 \times 3^2 \times 5$ |
| Hugh | $150 = 6 \times 5^2$ |
| Briana | $150 = 10 \times 3 \times 5$ |
| Drew | $150 = 2 \times 3 \times 5^2$ |

Which student was correct?

**A.** Tami

**B.** Hugh

**C.** Briana

**D.** Drew

**70.** Joe's homework got wet, and some of the numbers got smudged. What is the missing factor for the prime factorization of 108?

$108 = 2^2 \times$

**F.** $9^2$

**G.** $3^3$

**H.** $3^2$

**I.** 3

## Problem Solving LiNKUP . . . to History

Ancient Egyptian mathematicians understood the idea of the square root. They used square roots to help solve geometric puzzles. Other cultures, including the Greeks, Chinese, and Babylonians, also studied square roots.

The **square root** of a number is a number that, when multiplied by itself, equals the original number.

### Example

Find the square root of 9.
Think of the factors of 9: 9 × 1 and 3 × 3
You see that 3, when multiplied by itself, equals 9.
So, the square root of 9 is 3.

**Find the square root of each number.**

**1.** 16          **2.** 1          **3.** 100          **4.** 36          **5.** 144

# Problem Solving Strategy
## Make a Table

**PROBLEM** Liz is studying number patterns at school. For her project, she saves two pennies on Day 1, four pennies on Day 2, and eight pennies on Day 3. If she continues to double the number of pennies she saves each day for 10 days, how many pennies will she save on the tenth day? How much will she save in all?

### UNDERSTAND

- What are you asked to find?
- What information will you use?

### PLAN

- What strategy can you use to solve the problem?

  You can make a table to organize the data. Then you can use the table to answer the questions.

### SOLVE

- How can you organize the table?

  Decide on a title and row labels. Find the daily amount represented by each number of pennies. Add the daily amounts to find the total amount Liz will save in 10 days.

| AMOUNT OF MONEY SAVED | | | | | | | | | | |
|---|---|---|---|---|---|---|---|---|---|---|
| Day | 1 | 2 | 3 | 4 | 5 | 6 | 7 | 8 | 9 | 10 |
| Number of Pennies | 2 | 4 | 8 | 16 | 32 | 64 | 128 | 256 | 512 | 1024 |
| Daily Amount | $0.02 | $0.04 | $0.08 | $0.16 | $0.32 | $0.64 | $1.28 | $2.56 | $5.12 | $10.24 |
| Total Amount | $0.02 | $0.06 | $0.14 | $0.30 | $0.62 | $1.26 | $2.54 | $5.10 | $10.22 | $20.46 |

  Next, use the table to answer the questions. Liz will save 1,024 pennies, or $10.24, on the tenth day. She will save $20.46 in all.

### CHECK

- Look back at the problem. Do the answers make sense?

## Problem Solving Practice

1. **What if** Liz continued saving pennies in the same way for 14 days? How much would she save in all?

2. Don saves $1 on Day 1 and continues to save one dollar more each day than the previous day for 14 days. How much will he save in all?

**USE DATA** Jane's mother buys her 4 sheets of stickers for every 5 days that Jane completes her chores. Copy and complete the table. Then use the table for questions 3–4.

| STICKER SHEETS | | | | | | | | | | |
|---|---|---|---|---|---|---|---|---|---|---|
| **Days of Doing Chores** | 5 | 10 | 15 | ■ | ■ | ■ | ■ | ■ | ■ | ■ |
| **Total Number of Sheets** | 4 | 8 | 12 | ■ | ■ | ■ | ■ | ■ | ■ | ■ |

3. How many days will it take Jane to have 40 sheets of stickers?

   **A** 15     **B** 20     **C** 40     **D** 50

4. If there are 10 stickers on each sheet, in how many days could Jane earn 200 stickers?

   **F** 16     **G** 20     **H** 25     **J** 200

## Mixed Strategy Practice

5. Sal walked 1.25 miles on Saturday, 1.75 miles on Sunday, and 1.75 miles on Monday. His goal was to walk a total of 5 miles. Did he reach his goal? How far did he walk in all?

6. **What's the Question?** Cheri wants to buy equal numbers of lemons and limes. Lemons are sold in packages of 4. Limes are sold in bags of 10. The answer is 20 lemons.

7. Ben's dad builds 3-legged stools and 4-legged tables. He used 60 legs to build 6 more stools than tables. How many stools and tables did he build?

8. Jack's family plans to cook 2 turkey burgers for every 3 people at a picnic. How many turkey burgers should they cook for 15 people?

9. Marshall is counting the number of people at the assembly. So far, he has counted 8 rows, with 8 people in each row, in each of 8 sections. How many people has he counted so far?

10. Les and his two brothers collect stamps. Les has twice as many stamps as his older brother, who has 42 stamps. Les has three times as many stamps as his younger brother. How many stamps do they have in all?

FCAT TESTED   SSS/GLEs MA.A.3.2.2.5.1 Uses problem-solving strategies to determine the operation(s) needed to solve one- and two-step problems involving addition, subtraction, multiplication, and division of whole numbers, and addition, subtraction, and multiplication of decimals and fractions.

**Chapter 14**   **307**

# Extra Practice

## Set A (pp. 292–295)

**Write in exponent form. Then find the value.**

1. $5 \times 5 \times 5 \times 5 \times 5$
2. 8 cubed
3. $10 \times 10 \times 10 \times 10$
4. $3 \times 3 \times 3 \times 3$
5. 4 squared
6. $4 \times 4 \times 4 \times 4$

**Find the value.**

7. $2^8$
8. $4^6$
9. $10^7$
10. $7^4$
11. $12^3$
12. $1^7$
13. $11^3$
14. $9^4$
15. $10^5$
16. $3^5$
17. $6^4$
18. $10^8$
19. $8^4$
20. $3^6$
21. $2^5$

## Set B (pp. 296–299)

**Find the value.**

1. $5^0$
2. $4^1$
3. $14^0$
4. $8^0$
5. $7^1$

**Write in standard form.**

6. $(3 \times 10^6) + (2 \times 10^5) + (8 \times 10^2) + (1 \times 10^1) + (6 \times 10^0)$
7. $(9 \times 10^6) + (7 \times 10^5) + (4 \times 10^3) + (5 \times 10^0)$
8. $(1 \times 10^5) + (8 \times 10^3) + (2 \times 10^2)$

**Write in expanded form with exponents.**

9. 3,005
10. 5,120
11. 6,409
12. 7,158
13. 9,224
14. 12,504
15. 22,009
16. 18,030
17. 34,559
18. 80,003

## Set C (pp. 302–305)

**Rewrite the prime factorization by using exponents.**

1. $45 = 3 \times 3 \times 5$
2. $150 = 2 \times 3 \times 5 \times 5$
3. $686 = 2 \times 7 \times 7 \times 7$
4. $882 = 2 \times 3 \times 3 \times 7 \times 7$
5. $120 = 2 \times 2 \times 2 \times 3 \times 5$
6. $825 = 3 \times 5 \times 5 \times 11$

**Find the prime factorization of the number. Use exponents when possible.**

7. 49
8. 54
9. 23
10. 36
11. 84
12. 25
13. 52
14. 60

# Review/Test

## CHECK VOCABULARY AND CONCEPTS

Choose the best term from the box.

base
composite number
exponent
prime factorization
prime number

1. The __?__ of a number is the number written as the product of prime numbers. (p. 302)

2. For $10^2$, 10 is the __?__. (p. 292)

3. A number that has more than two factors is a __?__. (p. 300)

## CHECK SKILLS

Find the value. (pp. 292–295, 296–299)

4. $7^3$
5. $15^0$
6. $6^4$
7. $10^2$
8. $10^1$

9. $12^2$
10. $1^0$
11. $9^3$
12. $2^0$
13. $5^4$

14. $0^6$
15. $13^1$
16. $8^5$
17. $4^6$
18. $15^3$

Write in expanded form with exponents. (pp. 296–299)

19. 16,741
20. 24,053
21. 340,204
22. 605,489
23. 701,039

Write prime or composite for each number. (pp. 300–301)

24. 13
25. 21
26. 101
27. 2
28. 57

29. 61
30. 85
31. 87
32. 47
33. 94

Find the prime factorization of the number. Use exponents when possible. (pp. 302–305)

34. 33
35. 30
36. 63
37. 42
38. 48

39. 72
40. 225
41. 150
42. 85
43. 96

44. 112
45. 166
46. 144
47. 210
48. 240

## CHECK PROBLEM SOLVING

49. Pam earns $6.50 an hour at a grocery store. Every six months, she will earn an increase of $0.50 an hour. What will her hourly pay be after 2 years? (pp. 306–307)

50. Kia has $15.00. If she saves $2.50 each week, how much money will she have after 8 weeks? (pp. 306–307)

# Getting Ready for FCAT

 **NUMBER SENSE, CONCEPTS, AND OPERATIONS**

1. The table shows packaging and price information about hot dogs and buns.

| Item | Number per Package | Price per Package |
|---|---|---|
| Hot dogs | 10 | $2.75 |
| Buns | 8 | $1.50 |

What is the **least** number of packages of hot dogs and buns Ted needs to buy to have as many hot dogs as buns?

A. 4 packs of hot dogs and 5 packs of buns

B. 5 packs of hot dogs and 6 packs of buns

C. 7 packs of hot dogs and 9 packs of buns

D. 8 packs of hot dogs and 10 packs of buns

**TIP** **Decide on a plan.** Look at item 2. Using the strategy *work backward,* find the cost of the buns, and subtract it from the total cost. Then find how many packages of hot dogs were bought.

2. Look at the table above. Shana spent $14.25 on hot dogs and buns. If she bought 4 packages of buns, how many packages of hot dogs did she buy?

F. 6       H. 4

G. 5       I. 3

3. **Explain It** Explain how to ESTIMATE the number of students who will buy lunch at school in one week if 488 students bought lunch today.

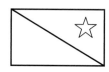 **GEOMETRY AND SPATIAL SENSE**

4. Noah drew the figure shown below.

Which is Noah's figure after he flipped it vertically?

A.

B.

C.

D.

5. A band is marching due north. During the routine the band members make a 180° turn. In which direction are they marching now?

F. north

G. south

H. east

I. west

6. **Explain It** Evan has a rectangular patio with a perimeter of 20 feet. He knows that the width of the patio is 3 feet. Explain how he can find the length of the patio.

**DATA ANALYSIS AND PROBABILITY**

**7.** The graph shows the types of sports equipment sold during May.

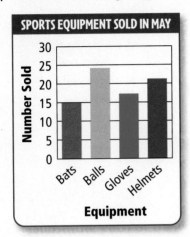

SPORTS EQUIPMENT SOLD IN MAY

About how many pieces of equipment were sold in May?

**A.** 24

**B.** 60

**C.** 80

**D.** 90

**8.** Look at the graph above. Which type of sports equipment had the **most** sales in May?

**F.** bats

**G.** balls

**H.** gloves

**I.** helmets

**9. Explain It** Ariel has a spinner with 8 equal sections. Four of the sections are blue, 2 are yellow, and 2 are green. About how many times will Ariel have to spin the pointer of the spinner for it to stop on the blue section 5 times? Explain your answer.

 **ALGEBRAIC THINKING**

**10.** Jean has $130 in her checking account. After making a deposit, she has $200 in the account. If $d$ equals the amount of her deposit, which equation could be used to find the amount of the deposit?

**A.** $130d = $200

**B.** $\frac{$200}{d} = $130$

**C.** $130 - d = $200

**D.** $130 + d = $200

**11.** Mr. White challenged his class to find the missing number in this table.

| Input | 1 | 2 | 3 | 7 |
|-------|---|---|---|---|
| Output | 1 | 4 | 9 | ■ |

If the pattern continues, which is the missing number?

**F.** 49

**G.** 16

**H.** 14

**I.** 13

**12. Explain It** Ivan and Irene were playing a number game that used a rule. Ivan called out a number, and Irene called out another number. The results are shown in the table.

| Ivan | 4 | 7 | 19 | 13 |
|------|---|---|----|----|
| Irene | 9 | 12 | 24 | 18 |

What is a rule for the game? Explain how you found it.

# Fraction Concepts

**FAST FACT** • SOCIAL STUDIES
In 1607, 104 passengers from 3 ships came ashore at Jamestown, Virginia. This was 13 years before the colony at Plymouth, Massachusetts, was established.

PROBLEM SOLVING   Spoon bread was a favorite of some early Americans. Rewrite the list of ingredients so that the amounts are in order from least to greatest.

**Spoon Bread**

$1\frac{1}{2}$ cups water

2 cups milk

$1\frac{1}{2}$ cups cornmeal

$1\frac{1}{4}$ teaspoons salt

$1\frac{1}{2}$ teaspoons sugar

2 tablespoons butter

5 eggs (about $\frac{2}{3}$ cup)

1 tablespoon baking powder

# CHECK WHAT YOU KNOW

Use this page to help you review and remember
important skills needed for Chapter 15.

## ✓ UNDERSTAND FRACTIONS

Write the fraction for the shaded part.

1.

2.

3.

4.

Write in words.

5. $\frac{2}{3}$

6. $\frac{4}{5}$

7. $\frac{1}{6}$

8. $\frac{3}{8}$

## ✓ COMPARE FRACTIONS

Compare the fractions. Write <, >, or = for each ●.

9.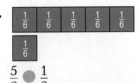

$\frac{5}{6}$ ● $\frac{1}{6}$

10.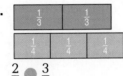

$\frac{2}{3}$ ● $\frac{3}{4}$

11.

$\frac{5}{8}$ ● $\frac{3}{4}$

12.

$\frac{5}{6}$ ● $\frac{5}{8}$

13.

$\frac{1}{4}$ ● $\frac{1}{3}$

14.

$\frac{2}{5}$ ● $\frac{3}{10}$

15.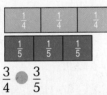

$\frac{3}{4}$ ● $\frac{3}{5}$

16.

$\frac{3}{8}$ ● $\frac{2}{3}$

17.

$\frac{5}{6}$ ● $\frac{7}{10}$

# VOCABULARY POWER

## REVIEW

**denominator** [di•nä′mə•nā•tər] *noun*

*Denominator* comes from the root *nomen,*
for *name.* The bottom number of a fraction
"names" the type of fraction being counted.
What part of speech names a person,
place, thing, or idea that can be described?

## PREVIEW

**equivalent fractions**

**simplest form**

**mixed number**

www.harcourtschool.com/mathglossary

# Equivalent Fractions

▶ **Learn**

**SUB DIVISION!**   Sharonda bought two sub sandwiches. She cut one into halves and the other into fourths. She noticed that one half of a sub and two fourths of a sub are the same amount.

You can use a number line to represent a fraction. On the number lines, the fractions $\frac{1}{2}$ and $\frac{2}{4}$ name the same amount because they are the same distance from 0.

Fractions that name the same amount are called **equivalent fractions**. So, $\frac{1}{2} = \frac{2}{4}$.

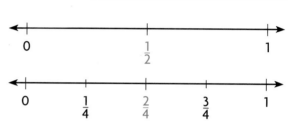

**MATH IDEA**   You can find equivalent fractions by multiplying or dividing both the numerator and denominator of a fraction by the same number.

## Examples

**A** *Multiply* the numerator and the denominator by the same number.

$$\frac{4}{6} = \frac{4 \times 2}{6 \times 2} = \frac{8}{12}$$

**B** *Divide* the numerator and the denominator by the same common factor.

$$\frac{6}{18} = \frac{6 \div 3}{18 \div 3} = \frac{2}{6}$$

**C** Find a fraction equivalent to $\frac{5}{8}$.

$$\frac{5}{8} = \frac{5 \times 3}{8 \times 3} = \frac{15}{24}$$

**D** Find a fraction equivalent to $\frac{8}{12}$.

$$\frac{8}{12} = \frac{8 \div 4}{12 \div 4} = \frac{2}{3}$$

▶ **Check**

1. **Explain** how you could use number lines to show that $\frac{8}{12}$ and $\frac{2}{3}$ are equivalent.

**Use the number lines to name an equivalent fraction for each.**

2. $\frac{3}{4}$    3. $\frac{2}{8}$    4. $\frac{2}{4}$    5. $\frac{6}{8}$

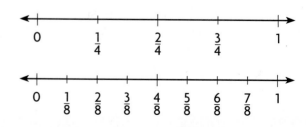

Use the number lines to name an equivalent fraction for each.

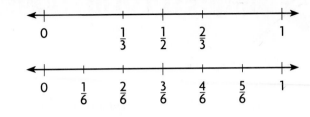

6. $\frac{1}{3}$    7. $\frac{2}{3}$    8. $\frac{3}{6}$    9. $\frac{2}{6}$

Write an equivalent fraction. Use multiplication or division.

10. $\frac{2}{6}$    11. $\frac{2}{12}$    12. $\frac{1}{3}$    13. $\frac{4}{8}$    14. $\frac{5}{25}$    15. $\frac{9}{12}$

16. $\frac{2}{9}$    17. $\frac{5}{6}$    18. $\frac{3}{15}$    19. $\frac{7}{21}$    20. $\frac{2}{7}$    21. $\frac{4}{11}$

Which fraction is *not* equivalent to the given fraction?
Write *a*, *b*, or *c*.

22. $\frac{3}{4}$    a. $\frac{6}{8}$    b. $\frac{12}{16}$    c. $\frac{6}{12}$    23. $\frac{1}{2}$    a. $\frac{4}{8}$    b. $\frac{4}{7}$    c. $\frac{7}{14}$

24. $\frac{8}{12}$    a. $\frac{2}{3}$    b. $\frac{10}{18}$    c. $\frac{4}{6}$    25. $\frac{5}{15}$    a. $\frac{2}{3}$    b. $\frac{1}{3}$    c. $\frac{4}{12}$

Copy and complete to make a true statement.

26. $\frac{2}{7} = \frac{\blacksquare}{14}$    27. $\frac{7}{8} = \frac{\blacksquare}{24}$    28. $\frac{9}{12} = \frac{3}{\blacksquare}$    29. $\frac{3}{4} = \frac{6}{\blacksquare}$

30. $\frac{2}{\blacksquare} = \frac{6}{9}$    31. $\frac{10}{25} = \frac{\blacksquare}{5}$    32. $\frac{\blacksquare}{12} = \frac{1}{3}$    33. $\frac{1}{6} = \frac{3}{\blacksquare}$

USE DATA   For 34, use the table at the right.

34. Sayre has $7.50 to spend at the bakery. She wants to buy 2 loaves of wheat bread. Does she have enough money to also buy one each of the other weekly specials? Explain.

35. Mr. Florez had 10 cans of juice. He gave 3 cans to Greg and 5 cans to Meg. Write two equivalent fractions to describe the fraction of the cans that are left.

36. Describe the pattern. Then write the next two numbers in the pattern.

$\frac{2}{5}, \frac{4}{10}, \frac{6}{15}, \frac{8}{20}, \blacksquare, \blacksquare, \dots$

37.   **? What's the Error?** Rita used $\frac{2}{5}$ of her pet-food supply last week. She said that was the same as $\frac{4}{25}$. Describe and correct her error.

## Getting Ready for FCAT

38. Mary used a ruler to measure the width of her thumb. The width is $\frac{8}{16}$ inch. Which fraction is NOT equal to $\frac{8}{16}$?

A. $\frac{2}{4}$    B. $\frac{3}{9}$    C. $\frac{1}{2}$    D. $\frac{4}{8}$

FCAT TESTED   SSS/GLEs MA.A.1.2.4.5.1 Knows that numbers in different forms are equivalent or nonequivalent, using whole numbers, decimals, fractions, mixed numbers, and percents. *also* MA.A.1.2.1.5.1

Chapter 15   **315**

# Simplest Form

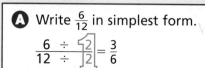

## Quick Review

Find the greatest common factor, or GCF, for each set of numbers.

**1.** 6, 9     **2.** 12, 24

**3.** 3, 9, 15   **4.** 12, 16, 20

**5.** 6, 12, 18, 24

**MUFFIN MAN!** Andy increased a recipe for muffins and decided he needs $\frac{4}{8}$ cup of butter. He doesn't have a $\frac{1}{8}$-cup measure. What fraction can he use instead of $\frac{4}{8}$?

A fraction is in **simplest form** when the numerator and denominator have 1 as their only common factor.

**VOCABULARY**
simplest form

## Example 1

**One Way** You can divide by common factors to write $\frac{4}{8}$ in simplest form.

Divide both the numerator and the denominator by a common factor of 4 and 8.

**Try 2.** $\frac{4 \div 2}{8 \div 2} = \frac{2}{4}$ ← not in simplest form

**Try 2 again.** $\frac{2 \div 2}{4 \div 2} = \frac{1}{2}$   The numerator and denominator have 1 as their only common factor.

So, $\frac{4}{8}$ in simplest form is $\frac{1}{2}$. Andy needs $\frac{1}{2}$ cup of butter.

▲ Measuring cups used for cooking are often in sets of 1, $\frac{3}{4}$, $\frac{2}{3}$, $\frac{1}{2}$, $\frac{1}{3}$, and $\frac{1}{4}$ cup.

## More Examples

**A** Write $\frac{6}{12}$ in simplest form.

$\frac{6 \div 2}{12 \div 2} = \frac{3}{6}$

$\frac{3 \div 3}{6 \div 3} = \frac{1}{2}$

So, $\frac{6}{12}$ in simplest form is $\frac{1}{2}$.

**B** Write $\frac{15}{18}$ in simplest form.

$\frac{15 \div 3}{18 \div 3} = \frac{5}{6}$

So, $\frac{15}{18}$ in simplest form is $\frac{5}{6}$.

**C** Write $\frac{30}{45}$ in simplest form.

$\frac{30 \div 5}{45 \div 5} = \frac{6}{9}$

$\frac{6 \div 3}{9 \div 3} = \frac{2}{3}$

So, $\frac{30}{45}$ in simplest form is $\frac{2}{3}$.

You can also use a calculator to find simplest form.

## Example 2

**Another Way** You can use the greatest common factor, or GCF, to help you write a fraction in simplest form.

Write $\frac{12}{16}$ in simplest form.

**STEP 1**

List the factors of 12 and 16. Find the GCF.

Factors of 12: 1, 2, 3, 4, 6, 12
Factors of 16: 1, 2, 4, 8, 16
The GCF is 4.

**STEP 2**

Divide the numerator and the denominator of $\frac{12}{16}$ by the GCF.

$$\frac{12 \div 4}{16 \div 4} = \frac{3}{4}$$

So, $\frac{12}{16}$ in simplest form is $\frac{3}{4}$.

## More Examples

**A** Write $\frac{9}{16}$ in simplest form.

$\frac{9}{16}$  1 is the only common factor for 9 and 16.

So, $\frac{9}{16}$ is in simplest form.

**B** Write $\frac{21}{42}$ in simplest form.

$$\frac{21 \div 21}{42 \div 21} = \frac{1}{2}$$

So, $\frac{21}{42}$ in simplest form is $\frac{1}{2}$.

**C** Write $\frac{18}{45}$ in simplest form.

$$\frac{18 \div 9}{45 \div 9} = \frac{2}{5}$$

So, $\frac{18}{45}$ in simplest form is $\frac{2}{5}$.

 **MATH IDEA** You can divide by using common factors until 1 is the only common factor, or you can divide by the GCF one time to write a fraction in simplest form.

## Check

1. **Explain** how you would find the simplest form of $\frac{16}{24}$ by using both the common factor method and the GCF method.

**Tell whether the fraction is in simplest form.**
**Write *yes* or *no*.**

2. $\frac{2}{6}$  3. $\frac{1}{10}$  4. $\frac{5}{12}$  5. $\frac{6}{18}$  6. $\frac{8}{20}$  7. $\frac{25}{32}$

**Name the GCF of the numerator and the denominator.**

8. $\frac{2}{6}$  9. $\frac{8}{24}$  10. $\frac{12}{15}$  11. $\frac{15}{45}$  12. $\frac{18}{30}$  13. $\frac{50}{100}$

**Write each fraction in simplest form.**

14. $\frac{4}{10}$  15. $\frac{8}{14}$  16. $\frac{8}{20}$  17. $\frac{12}{36}$  18. $\frac{8}{8}$  19. $\frac{24}{32}$

**LESSON CONTINUES**

**FCAT TESTED** SSS/GLEs MA.A.1.2.4.5.1 Knows that numbers in different forms are equivalent or nonequivalent, using whole numbers, decimals, fractions, mixed numbers, and percents. *also* MA.A.1.2.1.5.1

Chapter 15  **317**

**Tell whether the fraction is in simplest form. Write *yes* or *no*.**

20. $\frac{3}{8}$    21. $\frac{4}{10}$    22. $\frac{10}{32}$    23. $\frac{7}{15}$    24. $\frac{20}{45}$    25. $\frac{48}{50}$

**Name the GCF of the numerator and the denominator.**

26. $\frac{8}{22}$    27. $\frac{9}{30}$    28. $\frac{8}{12}$    29. $\frac{21}{33}$    30. $\frac{9}{54}$    31. $\frac{36}{60}$

**Write each fraction in simplest form.**

32. $\frac{6}{16}$    33. $\frac{14}{49}$    34. $\frac{40}{75}$    35. $\frac{24}{26}$    36. $\frac{15}{45}$    37. $\frac{8}{12}$

38. $\frac{27}{36}$    39. $\frac{4}{4}$    40. $\frac{8}{72}$    41. $\frac{48}{54}$    42. $\frac{30}{25}$    43. $\frac{60}{32}$

**Complete.**

44. $\frac{4}{16} = \frac{1}{\blacksquare}$

45. $\frac{21}{24} = \frac{\blacksquare}{8}$

46. $\frac{\blacksquare}{36} = \frac{1}{2}$

47. $\frac{15}{18} = \frac{\blacksquare}{6}$

48. $\frac{\blacksquare}{20} = \frac{3}{5}$

49. $\frac{7}{\blacksquare} = \frac{1}{8}$

**USE DATA** Use the graph for 50–53. The graph shows the number of boxes of cookies four students have sold. Each student set a goal of selling 20 boxes of each kind of cookie.

50. What fraction of Carol's goal for the sale of chocolate chip cookies has she met? Write the fraction in simplest form.

51. What fraction of Luis's goal for the sale of peanut butter cookies has he *not* met? Write the fraction in simplest form.

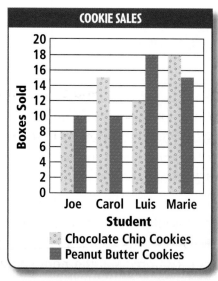

52. How many more boxes of cookies does Marie need to sell to meet her goal for both kinds of cookies?

53. The cookies sell for $2.50 a box. How much money have the students collected so far?

54. **REASONING** Colette looked at fractions in simplest form and said that any fraction that had both an odd and an even number was in simplest form. Do you agree with Colette? Explain.

55. Kyle earns $12.00 per week for baby-sitting. He saves $8.00 per week. Write the fraction, in simplest form, for the part he saves.

56. Hannah used $\frac{3}{4}$ cup of sugar, $\frac{2}{3}$ cup of cornmeal, and $\frac{1}{2}$ cup of flour for muffins. Of which ingredient did she use the greatest amount?

57. ✎ **Write About It** Describe the way you would find the simplest form of $\frac{32}{40}$.

**58.** Cyril works at a health food store. On Mondays he makes 24 cups of a snack mix. He uses the ingredients listed in the chart.

| SNACK MIX | |
|---|---|
| **Ingredients** | **Cups** |
| Raisins | 3 |
| Sunflower Seeds | 4 |
| Cashew Nuts | 8 |
| Peanuts | 9 |

What fractional part of the mix are peanuts?

**A.** $\frac{1}{3}$     **B.** $\frac{1}{4}$     **C.** $\frac{3}{8}$     **D.** $\frac{3}{5}$

**59.** Rita works in a hospital. She needs to order rubber tubing. The chart shows the different diameters available.

| RUBBER TUBING | | | | |
|---|---|---|---|---|
| **Model** | 102 | 104 | 108 | 203 |
| **Diameter (in inches)** | $\frac{1}{2}$ | $\frac{1}{4}$ | $\frac{1}{8}$ | $\frac{2}{3}$ |

Which model should Rita order if she needs tubing with a diameter of $\frac{4}{16}$ inch?

**F.** 102          **H.** 108

**G.** 104          **I.** 203

## Problem Solving  THINKER'S CORNER

**DATA AND GRAPHING** You can show factors graphically and then use the graph to find the greatest common factor of two numbers.

**MATERIALS:** grid paper, ruler

Make a line graph. Show the numbers 1–20 on the horizontal axis and the factors 1–20 on the vertical axis. Use points to show all the factors of each number. The graph at the right shows the factors for 1–10. The factors for 4 are 1, 2, and 4.

1. Study your graph. Look up the vertical lines for 6 and 9. What factors have points in both lines? What is the greatest common factor?

2. Use your graph to find the greatest common factor for 8 and 20.

3. Explain how to use your graph to help you write $\frac{12}{18}$ in simplest form.

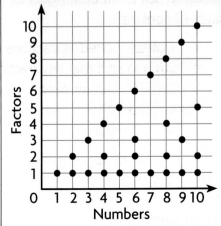

# Understand Mixed Numbers

### Quick Review

1. $(3 \times 9) + 2$
2. $(2 \times 8) + 1$
3. $14 \div 3$
4. $15 \div 2$
5. $24 \div 5$

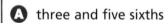

**Learn**

**BAGEL MANIA**   A baker packages bagels in boxes that each hold one dozen. Stephanie bought one full box of bagels and 5 more bagels, or $1\frac{5}{12}$ dozen bagels.

A **mixed number** is made up of a whole number and a fraction.

**Read:** one and five twelfths   **Write:** $1\frac{5}{12}$

Use models and number lines to show mixed numbers.

## Examples

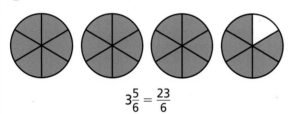

**A** three and five sixths

$$3\frac{5}{6} = \frac{23}{6}$$

**B** two and one fourth

$2\frac{1}{4}$

0   1   2   3

$$2\frac{1}{4} = \frac{9}{4}$$

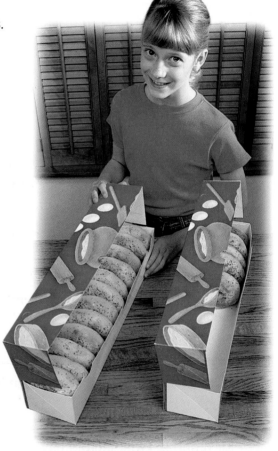

**MATH IDEA**   A fraction that is greater than 1 can be renamed as a mixed number. A mixed number can be renamed as a fraction.

## More Examples

**C** Rename $2\frac{3}{4}$ as a fraction.

$2\frac{3}{4} = \frac{2 \times 4}{1 \times 4} + \frac{3}{4}$   Write a fraction for the whole number by using the denominator, 4. Find the sum of the fractions.

$= \frac{8}{4} + \frac{3}{4}$

$= \frac{11}{4}$

**D** Rename $\frac{11}{4}$ as a mixed number.

$4\overline{)11} \;\rightarrow\; 2\frac{3}{4}$   Divide the numerator by the denominator. Use the remainder and the divisor to write a fraction.

$\phantom{4)}\underline{-8}$

$\phantom{4)11}3$

A fraction greater than 1 is sometimes called an *improper fraction*.

**Technology Link**

More Practice:
Harcourt Mega Math
Fraction Action,
*Number Line Mine,*
Level H

▶ **Check**

1. **Explain** how you can tell whether a fraction is greater than or less than 1.

**Write a mixed number and a fraction for each.**

2. four and three fourths

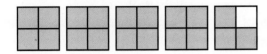

3. one and five eighths

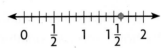

**Write each mixed number as a fraction. Write each fraction as a mixed number.**

4. $4\frac{1}{4}$    5. $3\frac{2}{5}$    6. $2\frac{3}{7}$    7. $\frac{9}{8}$    8. $\frac{31}{6}$    9. $\frac{7}{3}$

▶ **Practice and Problem Solving**    Extra Practice, page 332, Set C

**Write a mixed number and a fraction for each.**

10. three and two thirds

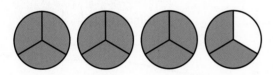

11. two and one fifth

**Write each mixed number as a fraction.**

12. $4\frac{1}{3}$    13. $6\frac{3}{5}$    14. $2\frac{7}{11}$    15. $9\frac{2}{9}$    16. $1\frac{11}{12}$    17. $5\frac{3}{4}$

**Write each fraction as a mixed number.**

18. $\frac{5}{2}$    19. $\frac{10}{3}$    20. $\frac{11}{6}$    21. $\frac{15}{4}$    22. $\frac{11}{8}$    23. $\frac{11}{5}$

24. Dan used $2\frac{1}{2}$ cups of flour to make bread. Write as a fraction the number of cups he used.

25. **REASONING** Ashley thinks $2\frac{1}{4} = \frac{7}{4}$. Is she correct? Explain by using a model and a number line.

26. Which of the fractions $\frac{13}{8}$, $\frac{16}{8}$, $\frac{8}{8}$, and $\frac{7}{8}$ is less than 1? Explain.

**Getting Ready for FCAT**

27. Mr. Barbero's pizzeria sells pizza by the slice. Each large pizza is cut into eighths. After lunch, Mr. Barbero has 11 slices left. How many pizzas does this represent?

A. $1\frac{1}{8}$    C. $1\frac{1}{2}$

B. $1\frac{3}{8}$    D. $1\frac{5}{8}$

FCAT TESTED    SSS/GLEs MA.A.1.2.4.5.1 Knows that numbers in different forms are equivalent or nonequivalent, using whole numbers, decimals, fractions, mixed numbers, and percents. *also* MA.A.1.2.1.5.1

Chapter 15    **321**

# Compare and Order Fractions and Mixed Numbers

▶ **Learn**

**WET PAINT!** Joe and Ricardo are painting the walls of their clubhouse. By noon Joe had painted $\frac{5}{6}$ of his wall and Ricardo had painted $\frac{3}{4}$ of his wall. Who had painted more of his wall?

## Example 1

**One Way** You can use fraction bars to compare.

| $\frac{1}{6}$ | $\frac{1}{6}$ | $\frac{1}{6}$ | $\frac{1}{6}$ | $\frac{1}{6}$ |

| $\frac{1}{4}$ | $\frac{1}{4}$ | $\frac{1}{4}$ |

$\frac{5}{6} > \frac{3}{4}$

**Remember**

To compare fractions with like denominators, compare the numerators.

Since $3 > 1$, $\frac{3}{4} > \frac{1}{4}$.

So, Joe had painted more of his wall.

## Example 2

**Another Way** You can rename fractions with unlike denominators, such as $\frac{5}{6}$ and $\frac{3}{4}$, so they have like denominators for easy comparison.

**STEP 1**

Find the least common multiple, or LCM, of the denominators.

**6:** 6, 12, 18, 24
**4:** 4, 8, 12, 16

So, the LCM is 12.

**STEP 2**

Rename as equivalent fractions with denominators of 12.

$\frac{5 \times 2}{6 \times 2} = \frac{10}{12}$

$\frac{3 \times 3}{4 \times 3} = \frac{9}{12}$

**STEP 3**

Compare the numerators of the new fractions.

Since $10 > 9$, $\frac{10}{12} > \frac{9}{12}$.

So, $\frac{5}{6} > \frac{3}{4}$.

• Explain how to compare $1\frac{4}{5}$ and $1\frac{2}{3}$.

## Order Fractions

By noon Mr. Banak had painted $\frac{5}{8}$ of his wall. Order the fractions $\frac{5}{6}, \frac{3}{4}$, and $\frac{5}{8}$ from least to greatest to find who painted the least amount.

When you have three or more fractions to order, rename the fractions so they have like denominators. Then put them in order.

### Example 1

**STEP 1**

Find the LCM of 6, 4, and 8.

**6:** 6, 12, 18, 24, 30, 36
**4:** 4, 8, 12, 16, 20, 24, 28
**8:** 8, 16, 24, 32, 40, 48

The LCM is 24.

**STEP 2**

Rename as equivalent fractions with denominators of 24.

$$\frac{5 \times 4}{6 \times 4} = \frac{20}{24}$$

$$\frac{3 \times 6}{4 \times 6} = \frac{18}{24}$$

$$\frac{5 \times 3}{8 \times 3} = \frac{15}{24}$$

**STEP 3**

Compare the numerators. Put them in order from least to greatest.

Since 15 < 18 < 20,

$$\frac{15}{24} < \frac{18}{24} < \frac{20}{24}.$$

So, the order is $\frac{5}{8}, \frac{3}{4}$, and $\frac{5}{6}$.

So, Mr. Banak painted the least amount.

- Order the fractions above from greatest to least.

To order mixed numbers, compare the whole numbers. Then, compare the fractions.

### Example 2

Order $3\frac{2}{3}, 2\frac{7}{9}$, and $3\frac{5}{6}$ from least to greatest.

**STEP 1**

Compare the whole numbers.

$3\frac{2}{3}$ $\qquad$ $2\frac{7}{9}$ $\qquad$ $3\frac{5}{6}$

Since 2 < 3, $2\frac{7}{9}$ is the least.

**STEP 2**

Compare the other two fractions. Use equivalent fractions.

$3\frac{2}{3} = 3\frac{8}{12}$ $\qquad$ $3\frac{5}{6} = 3\frac{10}{12}$

Since 8 < 10, $3\frac{8}{12} < 3\frac{10}{12}$.

The order is $2\frac{7}{9}, 3\frac{2}{3}$, and $3\frac{5}{6}$.

### Check

1. **Describe** a situation in which the LCM of two numbers is one of the numbers.

LESSON CONTINUES

FCAT TESTED  SSS/GLEs MA.A.1.2.2.5.3 Compares and orders commonly used fractions, percents, and decimals to thousandths using concrete materials, number lines, drawings, and numerals.
also MA.A.1.2.1.5.1, MA.A.1.2.2.5.1

**Compare the fractions. Write <, >, or = for each ⬤.**

**2.**

| $\frac{1}{6}$ | $\frac{1}{6}$ | $\frac{1}{6}$ | $\frac{1}{6}$ | $\frac{1}{6}$ |

| $\frac{1}{8}$ | $\frac{1}{8}$ | $\frac{1}{8}$ | $\frac{1}{8}$ | $\frac{1}{8}$ | $\frac{1}{8}$ | $\frac{1}{8}$ |

$\frac{5}{6}$ ⬤ $\frac{7}{8}$

**3.**

| $\frac{1}{4}$ | $\frac{1}{4}$ | $\frac{1}{4}$ |

| $\frac{1}{3}$ | $\frac{1}{3}$ |

$\frac{3}{4}$ ⬤ $\frac{2}{3}$

**Write in order from least to greatest.**

**4.** $\frac{3}{4}, \frac{3}{6}, \frac{3}{5}$

**5.** $\frac{1}{4}, \frac{5}{6}, \frac{5}{12}$

**6.** $4\frac{3}{4}, 4\frac{1}{6}, 3\frac{2}{3}$

**7.** $2\frac{1}{5}, 2\frac{1}{2}, 2\frac{3}{10}$

**Practice and Problem Solving**    Extra Practice, page 332, Set D

**Compare. Write <, >, or = for each ⬤.**

**8.** $\frac{3}{10}$ ⬤ $\frac{1}{4}$

**9.** $\frac{2}{3}$ ⬤ $\frac{3}{4}$

**10.** $\frac{4}{9}$ ⬤ $\frac{2}{6}$

**11.** $\frac{1}{3}$ ⬤ $\frac{3}{8}$

**12.** $\frac{4}{6}$ ⬤ $\frac{8}{12}$

**13.** $\frac{7}{8}$ ⬤ $\frac{3}{4}$

**14.** $3\frac{2}{7}$ ⬤ $3\frac{5}{14}$

**15.** $6\frac{1}{4}$ ⬤ $6\frac{2}{8}$

**Write in order from least to greatest.**

**16.** $\frac{1}{10}, \frac{3}{5}, \frac{1}{2}$

**17.** $\frac{2}{3}, \frac{3}{4}, \frac{7}{12}$

**18.** $2\frac{9}{14}, 3\frac{2}{4}, 2\frac{5}{7}$

**19.** $4\frac{4}{5}, 4\frac{7}{10}, 4\frac{1}{2}$

**20.** $\frac{2}{3}, \frac{5}{9}, \frac{1}{2}$

**21.** $\frac{1}{6}, 2\frac{1}{12}, 1\frac{1}{12}$

**22.** $5\frac{6}{10}, 5\frac{2}{5}, 5\frac{2}{7}$

**23.** $1\frac{2}{5}, \frac{3}{5}, 1\frac{1}{2}$

**USE DATA**   For 24–25, use the table.

**24.** Order the fractions from greatest to least. On which day were the most rooms painted? On which day were the fewest rooms painted?

**25.** There are 20 classrooms in all, and 9 still need to be painted. What fraction of the total have been painted?

**26.** How can you compare fractions with *like* numerators and *unlike* denominators, such as $\frac{2}{3}$ and $\frac{2}{5}$, without renaming or using fraction strips?

**27.** Liza needs music for her gymnastics routine. The selection needs to be less than $3\frac{1}{2}$ min. *Changes* is $3\frac{2}{3}$ min, and *Dreaming* is $3\frac{2}{5}$ min. Which should she choose? Explain.

**28.** **VOCABULARY POWER** The word *order* comes from the Latin word *ordinem,* meaning "arrangement." List things other than numbers that you can order.

| CLASSROOMS PAINTED | |
|---|---|
| **Day** | **Fraction of Total** |
| Monday | $\frac{1}{5}$ |
| Tuesday | $\frac{1}{4}$ |
| Wednesday | $\frac{1}{10}$ |

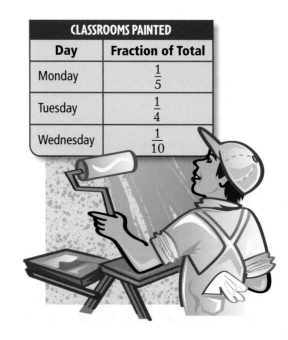

**29.** Judy has four notebooks.

| NOTEBOOK THICKNESS | |
|---|---|
| **Notebook** | **Thickness** |
| Red | $\frac{1}{2}$ inch |
| Black | $\frac{1}{4}$ inch |
| Green | $\frac{1}{3}$ inch |
| Blue | $\frac{1}{5}$ inch |

Which notebook is the thickest?

**A.** red      **C.** green

**B.** black      **D.** blue

**30.** Four friends compared how long they studied for a math quiz.

| MATH STUDY TIME | |
|---|---|
| **Name** | **Study Time** |
| Caleb | $\frac{2}{3}$ hour |
| Margarita | $\frac{2}{5}$ hour |
| Natasha | $\frac{2}{6}$ hour |
| Darrin | $\frac{2}{4}$ hour |

Who studied the **least** amount of time?

**F.** Caleb      **H.** Natasha

**G.** Margarita      **I.** Darrin

# Problem Solving LiNKUP . . . to Reading

**STRATEGY • COMPARE AND CONTRAST** You can compare to see how things are alike. You can also contrast to see how they are different. Read the following problem.

A recipe for hot chocolate calls for $\frac{1}{2}$ cup of cocoa, $\frac{1}{8}$ cup of sugar, and $\frac{3}{4}$ cup of milk. List the ingredients in order from greatest amount to least amount.

| Compare | Contrast |
|---|---|
| All the ingredients are measured in cups. | The amounts are not equal. |
| All the amounts are fractions less than 1. | The fractions have different denominators. |

Order the fractions. Think: $\frac{3}{4} > \frac{1}{2} > \frac{1}{8}$

So, the ingredients in order are milk, cocoa, and sugar.

**Compare and contrast the data to solve.**

**1.** Latoya used $\frac{1}{2}$ cup of milk for icing, $\frac{7}{8}$ cup for a cake, and $\frac{3}{4}$ cup for hot chocolate. For which item did she use the most milk?

**2.** A recipe for apple pie calls for $\frac{5}{8}$ tsp of nutmeg. Kara has $\frac{1}{2}$ tsp of nutmeg. Does she have enough for the recipe? Explain.

LESSON 5

# Problem Solving Strategy
## Make a Model

**Quick Review**

**Compare. Write <, >, or = for each ●.**

1. $\frac{4}{4}$ ● $\frac{3}{4}$
2. $\frac{2}{4}$ ● $\frac{1}{2}$
3. $\frac{1}{2}$ ● $\frac{1}{3}$
4. $\frac{2}{3}$ ● $\frac{3}{4}$
5. $\frac{1}{4}$ ● $\frac{2}{9}$

**PROBLEM** Minh made a table to record the number of miles he walked each day. On which day did Minh walk the greatest distance? On which day did he walk the least distance?

| Day | Mon | Tue | Wed | Thu |
|---|---|---|---|---|
| Miles Walked | $2\frac{1}{2}$ | $3\frac{1}{4}$ | $2\frac{3}{4}$ | $2\frac{3}{8}$ |

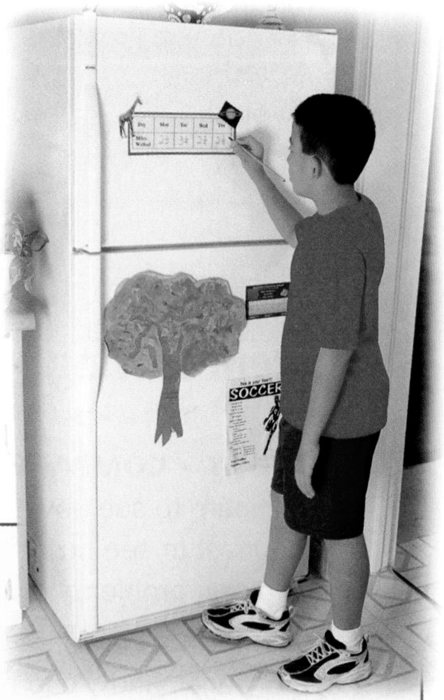

**UNDERSTAND**

- What are you asked to find?
- What information will you use?
- Is there any information you will not use?

**PLAN**

- What strategy can you use to solve the problem?

You can *make a model* with fraction bars.

**SOLVE**

- How can you use the strategy to solve the problem?

You can use fraction bars to help you compare the numbers.

First, look at the whole numbers: $2\frac{1}{2}$, $3\frac{1}{4}$, $2\frac{3}{4}$, $2\frac{3}{8}$. Since 3 is the greatest whole number, $3\frac{1}{4}$ miles is the greatest distance.

Now use fraction bars to compare the fractional parts of $2\frac{1}{2}$, $2\frac{3}{4}$, and $2\frac{3}{8}$. Since $\frac{3}{8}$ is the shortest, $2\frac{3}{8}$ miles is the least distance.

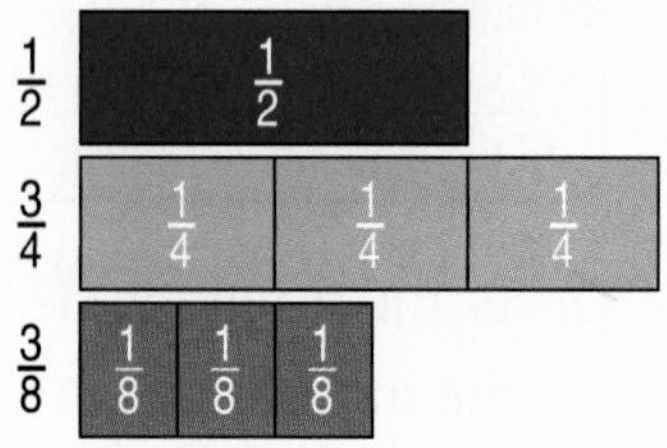


So, Minh walked the greatest distance on Tuesday and the least distance on Thursday.

**CHECK**

- What other strategy can you use?

## Strategies

Draw a Diagram or Picture
**Make a Model or Act It Out**
Make an Organized List
Find a Pattern
Make a Table or Graph
Predict and Test
Work Backward
Solve a Simpler Problem
Write an Equation
Use Logical Reasoning

**Problem Solving**

**Make a model to solve.**

1. **What if** Minh had walked only $2\frac{1}{4}$ miles on Tuesday? How would this change the answers?

2. The five planets closest to the sun are Earth, Venus, Mars, Mercury, and Jupiter. Earth is the only planet between Venus and Mars. Mercury is the only planet between Venus and the sun. Which of these planets is next to Jupiter?

**USE DATA** Use the table for 3 and 4.

3. How do you know that April had the most rainfall?

   **A** The greatest rainfall is always in April.

   **B** April has the greatest whole-number part.

   **C** April has the greatest fractional part.

   **D** April is the last month listed.

| MONTHLY RAINFALL | | | | |
|---|---|---|---|---|
| **Month** | **Jan** | **Feb** | **Mar** | **Apr** |
| **Rainfall (in inches)** | $3\frac{3}{8}$ | $2\frac{2}{4}$ | $3\frac{1}{2}$ | $5\frac{7}{8}$ |

4. What is the order of the months from greatest rainfall to least rainfall?

   **F** Apr, Mar, Feb, Jan

   **G** Jan, Mar, Feb, Apr

   **H** Apr, Mar, Jan, Feb

   **J** Apr, Jan, Mar, Feb

## Mixed Strategy Practice

5. **GEOMETRY** Alex is enclosing his pentagon-shaped garden with fencing. If each side is 8 meters long, how much fencing does he need?

6. If 2 people can be seated on each side of a square table, how many people can be seated at 12 square tables that are pushed together end to end to form a rectangle?

7. Aiko had $20.00 to buy candles. She returned 2 candles for which she had paid $4.75 each. Then she bought 3 candles for $3.50 each and 1 candle for $5.00. How much money did Aiko have then?

8. In Ted's class, students were asked to name their favorite sport. Football was the response of $\frac{1}{8}$ of them. If 3 students said football, how many students are in Ted's class?

FCAT TESTED SSS/GLEs MA.A.1.2.2.5.3 Compares and orders commonly used fractions, percents, and decimals to thousandths using concrete materials, number lines, drawings, and numerals. *also* MA.A.1.2.1.5.1

**Chapter 15 327**

# Relate Fractions and Decimals

 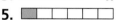
## ▶ Learn

**KICK OFF!** At the World Cup soccer tournament, each match has two 45-minute halves. The times can be expressed as fractions, mixed numbers, or decimals.

|  | FRACTION | MIXED NUMBER | DECIMAL |
|---|---|---|---|
| **First Half** | $\frac{3}{4}$ hr |  | 0.75 hr |
| **Match** | $\frac{3}{2}$ hr | $1\frac{1}{2}$ hr | 1.50 hr |

**MATH IDEA** The same number can be represented as a fraction or as a decimal. If the number is greater than 1, it can be represented as a mixed number, a fraction, or a decimal.

One way to show a number both ways is to use a number line.

Fraction or mixed number:

$\frac{3}{4}$   $\frac{3}{2}$, or $1\frac{1}{2}$

```
0   0.10 0.20 0.30 0.40 0.50 0.60 0.70 0.80 0.90  1  1.10 1.20 1.30 1.40 1.50 1.60 1.70 1.80 1.90  2
```

Decimal:          0.75                    1.50

Another way to show numbers as fractions, mixed numbers, or decimals is to use grids.

**Remember**

There are three ways to think of a fraction. $\frac{3}{4}$ is three fourths, three out of four, or three divided by four.

## Examples

---

**A** Write a fraction and a decimal for the model.

**fraction**
Three out of ten equal parts are shaded.

$\frac{3}{10}$, or three tenths, is shaded.

**decimal**
Three out of ten equal parts are shaded.

0.3, or three tenths, is shaded.

---

**B** Write a mixed number and a decimal for the model.

**mixed number**
One whole plus three out of four equal parts are shaded.

$1\frac{3}{4}$, or one and three-fourths, is shaded.

**decimal**
One whole plus seventy-five out of one hundred equal parts are shaded.

1.75, or one and seventy-five hundredths, is shaded.

---

## Place Value and Division

Here are other ways you can change a decimal to a fraction or a fraction to a decimal.

### Examples

**Decimal to Fraction** You can use place value to change a decimal to a fraction.

| 0.24 | Identify the place value of the last digit. The 4 is in the hundredths place. |
| $\frac{24}{100}$ | Use that place value for the denominator. |

So, $0.24 = \frac{24}{100}$.

**Fraction to Decimal** You can use division to change a fraction to a decimal.

$\frac{2}{5}$ Divide the numerator by the denominator.

$$\begin{array}{r} 0.4 \\ 5\overline{)2.0} \\ -2\,0 \\ \hline 0 \end{array}$$

Place the decimal point. Since 5 does not divide into 2, place a zero. Then divide as with whole numbers.

So, $\frac{2}{5} = 0.4$.

### More Examples

**A** Write 0.375 as a fraction.

0.375 The 5 is in the thousandths place.

So, $0.375 = \frac{375}{1,000}$.

**B** Write $\frac{3}{4}$ as a decimal.

$$\begin{array}{r} 0.75 \\ 4\overline{)3.00} \\ -2\,8 \\ \hline 20 \\ -20 \\ \hline 0 \end{array}$$

So, $\frac{3}{4} = 0.75$.

**C** Write $3\frac{5}{8}$ as a decimal.

$$\begin{array}{r} 0.625 \\ 8\overline{)5.000} \\ -4\,8 \\ \hline 20 \\ -16 \\ \hline 40 \\ -40 \\ \hline 0 \end{array}$$

Rename the fraction as a decimal. Then add the whole number to the decimal.

So, $3\frac{5}{8} = 3.625$.

### Check

1. **Describe** two ways you can change a decimal to a fraction and two ways you can change a fraction to a decimal.

**Identify a decimal and a fraction or mixed number for the point.**

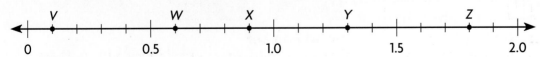

2. Point *X*      3. Point *W*      4. Point *Z*      5. Point *V*      6. Point *Y*

**Write a fraction or mixed number in simplest form.**

7. 0.8      8. 0.63      9. 1.2      10. 1.55      11. 2.305

FCAT TESTED  SSS/GLEs MA.A.1.2.4.5.1 Knows that numbers in different forms are equivalent or nonequivalent, using whole numbers, decimals, fractions, mixed numbers, and percents. *also* MA.A.1.2.1.5.1, MA.A.1.2.2.5.4

**Write a decimal for each fraction or mixed number.**

**12.** $\frac{1}{100}$    **13.** $\frac{3}{10}$    **14.** $\frac{1}{5}$    **15.** $1\frac{2}{4}$    **16.** $4\frac{3}{8}$

## Practice and Problem Solving    Extra Practice, page 332, Set E

**Identify a decimal and a fraction or mixed number for the point.**

K        H    F            G              E
0   0.10 0.20 0.30 0.40 0.50 0.60 0.70 0.80 0.90   1   1.10 1.20 1.30 1.40 1.50 1.60 1.70 1.80 1.90   2

**17.** Point *E*    **18.** Point *F*    **19.** Point *G*    **20.** Point *H*    **21.** Point *K*

**Write a fraction or mixed number in simplest form.**

**22.** 0.8    **23.** 0.37    **24.** 0.90    **25.** 2.125    **26.** 1.33

**Write a decimal for each fraction or mixed number.**

**27.** $\frac{8}{100}$    **28.** $\frac{7}{10}$    **29.** $\frac{1}{4}$    **30.** $2\frac{4}{5}$    **31.** $3\frac{7}{8}$

**Compare. Write <, >, or = for each ●.**

**32.** $\frac{1}{2}$ ● 0.75    **33.** 0.25 ● $\frac{2}{8}$    **34.** $\frac{3}{5}$ ● 0.52    **35.** 0.65 ● $\frac{3}{4}$

**36.** $1\frac{1}{5}$ ● 1.23    **37.** $2\frac{7}{10}$ ● 1.75    **38.** $\frac{1}{4}$ ● 0.50    **39.** 2.30 ● $2\frac{3}{10}$

**For 40–41, draw a number line and label points for the numbers described.**

**40.** the number that is halfway between 0.2 and the number that is twice 0.2

**41.** the number $1\frac{7}{10}$ and the number that is 0.3 less than it

**42.** Order $\frac{5}{12}$, 1.60, 0.50, $1\frac{3}{4}$, $\frac{3}{8}$ from greatest to least.

**43.** **? What's the Error?** Harvey says $\frac{1}{4}$ is equivalent to 0.4 because they both have a 4. Explain and correct the error.

**44.** Kelly walks her dog 0.8 of a mile every day. Write as a fraction the number of miles Kelly walks her dog.

**45.** **FAST FACT • SCIENCE** The world's smallest vegetable is a snow pea, measuring about 0.25 inch in diameter. Write the diameter as a fraction.

**46.** Mariko hoped to sell a used book for $0.80 but accepted $\frac{3}{4}$ of a dollar for it. What is the difference in the two amounts?

**47.**  **Write a problem** about someone who walks more than 1 mile. Express as both a mixed number and a decimal.

**48.** Which decimal represents the part of the states admitted into the Union from 1751 to 1800?

   **A.** 0.08
   **B.** 0.32
   **C.** 0.8
   **D.** 0.825

**49.** During which time period were 0.28 of the states admitted to the Union?

   **F.** 1751–1800
   **G.** 1801–1850
   **H.** 1851–1900
   **I.** 1901–1950

| ADMISSION OF STATES TO THE UNION | |
| --- | --- |
| **Time Period** | **Fraction of 50 States** |
| 1751–1800 | $\frac{8}{25}$ |
| 1801–1850 | $\frac{3}{10}$ |
| 1851–1900 | $\frac{7}{25}$ |
| 1901–1950 | $\frac{3}{50}$ |
| 1951–2000 | $\frac{1}{25}$ |

# Problem Solving | Thinker's Corner

**REASONING** Think about the number of numbers that you can represent on a number line.

**1.** Are there numbers between 0 and 0.1? If so, name some of them.

**2.** Are there numbers between 0 and 0.01? If so, name some of them.

**3.** What are some numbers between 0.08 and 0.09? between 0.09 and 0.10?

**4.** How many numbers can be represented on a number line? Explain.

# Extra Practice

## Set A (pp. 314–315)

Write three equivalent fractions for each.

1. $\frac{2}{4}$   2. $\frac{3}{8}$   3. $\frac{4}{5}$   4. $\frac{6}{9}$   5. $\frac{12}{15}$   6. $\frac{22}{33}$

7. $\frac{8}{24}$   8. $\frac{2}{8}$   9. $\frac{1}{2}$   10. $\frac{6}{7}$   11. $\frac{2}{12}$   12. $\frac{2}{3}$

## Set B (pp. 316–319)

Write each fraction in simplest form.

1. $\frac{4}{16}$   2. $\frac{6}{18}$   3. $\frac{12}{18}$   4. $\frac{6}{10}$   5. $\frac{6}{36}$   6. $\frac{15}{20}$

7. $\frac{19}{38}$   8. $\frac{8}{24}$   9. $\frac{18}{72}$   10. $\frac{18}{24}$   11. $\frac{30}{45}$   12. $\frac{25}{125}$

## Set C (pp. 320–321)

Write each fraction as a mixed number. Write each mixed number as a fraction.

1. $\frac{9}{7}$   2. $5\frac{2}{3}$   3. $\frac{13}{4}$   4. $6\frac{4}{5}$   5. $\frac{16}{6}$   6. $6\frac{3}{4}$

7. $4\frac{1}{2}$   8. $\frac{8}{3}$   9. $\frac{25}{8}$   10. $5\frac{1}{4}$   11. $\frac{8}{5}$   12. $4\frac{2}{7}$

## Set D (pp. 322–325)

Compare. Write <, >, or = for each ●.

1. $\frac{1}{2}$ ● $\frac{2}{6}$   2. $\frac{2}{3}$ ● $\frac{4}{6}$   3. $5\frac{5}{7}$ ● $6\frac{3}{5}$   4. $2\frac{5}{6}$ ● $3\frac{2}{4}$   5. $7\frac{4}{8}$ ● $7\frac{2}{4}$

Write in order from least to greatest.

6. $\frac{1}{6}, \frac{2}{5}, \frac{1}{3}$   7. $\frac{4}{8}, \frac{2}{3}, \frac{1}{6}$   8. $2\frac{1}{4}, 3\frac{2}{12}, 2\frac{4}{6}$   9. $6\frac{4}{6}, 5\frac{9}{11}, 6\frac{7}{12}$   10. $1\frac{8}{9}, \frac{2}{5}, 1\frac{12}{18}$

## Set E (pp. 328–331)

Write a fraction or mixed number in simplest form.

1. 0.55   2. 0.7   3. 0.26   4. 11.751   5. 6.2   6. 8.305

Write a decimal for each fraction or mixed number.

7. $\frac{1}{4}$   8. $\frac{17}{20}$   9. $\frac{3}{8}$   10. $4\frac{6}{10}$   11. $2\frac{35}{100}$   12. $7\frac{1}{8}$

# Review/Test

##  CHECK VOCABULARY AND CONCEPTS

Choose the best term from the box.

> equivalent fractions
> fraction
> mixed number
> simplest form

1. Fractions that name the same amount are called __?__. (p. 314)

2. A fraction is in __?__ when the greatest common factor of the numerator and denominator is 1. (p. 316)

3. A number, like $2\frac{1}{2}$, that has a whole-number part and a fraction part is a(n) __?__. (p. 320)

##  CHECK SKILLS

Write an equivalent fraction. (pp. 314–315)

4. $\frac{1}{7}$    5. $\frac{3}{9}$    6. $\frac{6}{42}$    7. $\frac{2}{9}$    8. $\frac{21}{49}$

Write each fraction in simplest form. (pp. 316–319)

9. $\frac{4}{16}$    10. $\frac{8}{12}$    11. $\frac{20}{45}$    12. $\frac{16}{56}$    13. $\frac{63}{81}$

Write each fraction as a mixed number. Write each mixed number as a fraction. (pp. 320–321)

14. $\frac{9}{4}$    15. $\frac{17}{8}$    16. $\frac{13}{4}$    17. $2\frac{1}{5}$    18. $3\frac{3}{8}$

Compare. Write <, >, or = for each ●. (pp. 322–325)

19. $\frac{2}{4}$ ● $\frac{5}{8}$    20. $\frac{3}{4}$ ● $\frac{6}{12}$    21. $1\frac{7}{28}$ ● $1\frac{4}{7}$    22. $2\frac{7}{8}$ ● $2\frac{14}{16}$

Write in order from least to greatest. (pp. 322–325)

23. $\frac{1}{6}, \frac{15}{18}, \frac{2}{3}$    24. $\frac{3}{6}, \frac{1}{3}, \frac{8}{12}$    25. $\frac{1}{4}, 1\frac{1}{3}, \frac{1}{2}$    26. $3\frac{2}{5}, 3\frac{1}{2}, 3\frac{3}{4}$

Write a fraction or mixed number in simplest form for each decimal. Write a decimal for each fraction or mixed number. (pp. 328–331)

27. 0.4    28. $\frac{3}{5}$    29. 0.042    30. $4\frac{3}{4}$    31. 13.65

##  CHECK PROBLEM SOLVING

Make a model to solve. (pp. 326–327)

32. Dave's practice swims were $1\frac{3}{8}$ miles, $1\frac{2}{6}$ miles, and $1\frac{3}{4}$ miles. Which was the greatest distance?

33. Rosa bought $1\frac{2}{5}$ lb of chocolate, $2\frac{1}{2}$ lb of fudge, and $1\frac{5}{8}$ lb of caramels. Of which candy did she buy the least amount?

# Getting Ready for FCAT

##  NUMBER SENSE, CONCEPTS, AND OPERATIONS

> **TIP** **Understand the problem.** See item 1. Each fraction represents a part of a pound of cheese. Compare and order the fractions to find the second greatest amount.

1. Mrs. Gold wants to buy $\frac{1}{3}$ pound of Muenster cheese, $\frac{1}{4}$ pound of American cheese, $\frac{1}{2}$ pound of Swiss cheese, and $\frac{1}{5}$ pound of Cheddar cheese.

   Of which cheese does she plan to buy the **second** greatest amount?

   **A.** Swiss      **C.** American

   **B.** Muenster      **D.** Cheddar

2. Look at the cheese list in Problem 1. Which statement is true about the cheeses in the list?

   **F.** The amount of Cheddar cheese is greater than the amount of American cheese.

   **G.** The amount of American cheese is greater than the amount of Muenster cheese.

   **H.** The amount of Swiss cheese is greater than the amount of Cheddar cheese.

   **I.** The amount of Cheddar cheese is greater than the amount of Muenster cheese.

3. **Explain It** Tim is making a circle graph to show how he spent his day yesterday. He worked for 8 hours. In the circle graph, should the fractional part for work be greater than or less than one half the circle? Explain how you know.

## MEASUREMENT

4. According to the airline schedule, how long is the flight from Albany to Baltimore?

   > Albany, NY, to Baltimore, MD
   > Leaves 10:05 A.M. Arrives 11:30 A.M.
   >
   > Baltimore, MD, to Miami, FL
   > Leaves 1:00 P.M. Arrives 3:35 P.M.

   **A.** 1 hour 25 minutes

   **B.** 1 hour 35 minutes

   **C.** 2 hours 35 minutes

   **D.** 5 hours 30 minutes

5. Use the table in Problem 4. How long is the layover in Baltimore before the plane takes off for Miami?

   **F.** 10 hours 30 minutes

   **G.** 2 hours 35 minutes

   **H.** 2 hours 30 minutes

   **I.** 1 hour 30 minutes

6. **Explain It** A professional soccer team left town on August 16 for a trip. The team returned on September 1. Was the team gone for more than or less than two weeks? Explain how you know.

   | August | | | | | | |
   |---|---|---|---|---|---|---|
   | Sun | Mon | Tue | Wed | Thu | Fri | Sat |
   | 1 | 2 | 3 | 4 | 5 | 6 | 7 |
   | 8 | 9 | 10 | 11 | 12 | 13 | 14 |
   | 15 | 16 | 17 | 18 | 19 | 20 | 21 |
   | 22 | 23 | 24 | 25 | 26 | 27 | 28 |
   | 29 | 30 | 31 | | | | |

**GEOMETRY AND SPATIAL SENSE**

**7.** The diagram shows Mitch's four vegetable gardens.

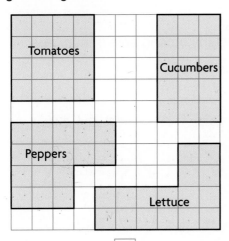

Tomatoes

Cucumbers

Peppers

Lettuce

☐ = 1 square foot

Which garden does NOT have the same area as the others?

**A.** tomato

**B.** pepper

**C.** cucumber

**D.** lettuce

**8.** Look at the diagram above. Which garden has the greatest perimeter?

**F.** tomato

**G.** pepper

**H.** cucumber

**I.** lettuce

**9. Explain It** Tyler drew this diagram of his new tent.

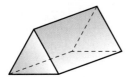

Tyler said the tent is shaped like a triangular pyramid. Mackenzie said the tent is shaped like a triangular prism. Who is correct? Explain how you know.

 **DATA ANALYSIS AND PROBABILITY**

**10.** Lou made a circle graph to show the deductions taken out of his paycheck for each dollar he earns.

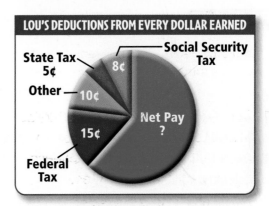

**LOU'S DEDUCTIONS FROM EVERY DOLLAR EARNED**

State Tax 5¢

Social Security Tax 8¢

Other 10¢

Net Pay ?

Federal Tax 15¢

Out of every dollar Lou earns, how much is left after all the deductions?

**A.** 38¢

**C.** 62¢

**B.** 48¢

**D.** 72¢

**11.** Look at the circle graph above. Which two deductions make up $\frac{1}{4}$ of the whole circle?

**F.** Social Security Tax and Other

**G.** Social Security Tax and State Tax

**H.** State Tax and Other

**I.** Federal Tax and Other

**12. Explain It** A movie rental store wants to display the data below in a graph. What type of graph is best for displaying the data? Explain your choice.

| DAILY RENTALS | | |
|---|---|---|
| **Day** | **DVDs Rented** | **Videos Rented** |
| Monday | 623 | 430 |
| Tuesday | 582 | 550 |
| Wednesday | 791 | 702 |
| Thursday | 807 | 598 |
| Friday | 1,045 | 825 |

# IT'S IN THE BAG

## Venn Diagrams

**PROJECT** Make a Venn diagram to show relationships among sets of numbers.

### Materials

- 1 page protector cut in half
- $8\frac{1}{2}$-in. x $5\frac{1}{2}$-in. sheet of construction paper
- Permanent markers
- Stapler
- Venn diagram worksheet

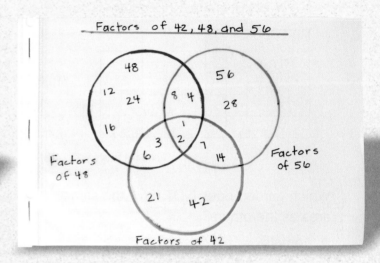

### Directions

1. For each half of the page protector, cut off the closed top or bottom edge, if present. Cut between the sheets, along the fold at the right edge of each half, separated to form a total of 4 sheets. *(Picture A)*

2. Place the sheet of construction paper on the table. Place both halves of the protector over the construction paper, with the hole-punched sides on the left. Staple along the left side. *(Picture B)*

3. Insert the Venn diagram worksheet underneath all 4 protector sheets. Trace a different circle onto each of the three bottom sheets. On the top sheet, trace the line for the title. *(Picture C)*

4. Using each description once, label the circles *Factors of 42*, *Factors of 48*, *Factors of 56*. Title the Venn diagram *Factors of 42, 48, and 56*. Write the factors of each number in the appropriate parts of the diagram.

# Challenge

## Scientific Notation

Today's biggest and fastest computers can perform more than 850,000,000,000 operations in 1 second. The number 850,000,000,000 is written in standard form. You can use **scientific notation** to write a large number like 850,000,000,000 more easily.

A number written in scientific notation is expressed as a product of two factors.

The first factor is a number that is at least 1 but less than 10.    The second factor is a power of 10.

$$8.5 \times 10^{11}$$

Follow these steps to write a number in scientific notation.

### Example

**STEP 1**

Count the number of places the decimal point must be moved to the left to form a number that is at least 1 but less than 10.

$$850{,}000{,}000{,}000 \rightarrow 8.5$$

11 places

**STEP 2**

Since the decimal point moved 11 places, the exponent of 10 is 11. Write the number as the product of the two factors.

$$8.5 \times 10^{11}$$

So, $850{,}000{,}000{,}000 = 8.5 \times 10^{11}$.

### More Examples

**A** $5{,}470{,}000 = 5.47 \times 10^6$

6 places

**B** $38{,}211{,}000{,}000 = 3.8211 \times 10^{10}$

10 places

## Talk About It

- Tell why each of these numbers is not written in scientific notation: $12 \times 10^4$, $2.7 \times 5^4$, and $9.4 + 10^4$.

- **STRETCH YOUR THINKING** By 2002, more than $5.8 \times 10^8$ people around the world were using the Internet. Explain how you can write $5.8 \times 10^8$ in standard form.

## Try It

**Write the number in scientific notation.**

1. 4,000,000

2. 73,000

3. 682,100,000

4. 100,000

5. 3,140,000

6. 9,502,000,000

# Study Guide and Review

## VOCABULARY

Choose the best term from the box.

1. A number that tells how many times the base is used as a factor is called a(n) __?__. (p. 292)

2. All composite numbers can be written as the product of __?__. (p. 302)

3. When a fraction's numerator and denominator have 1 as their only common factor, the fraction is in __?__. (p. 316)

## STUDY AND SOLVE

## Chapter 13

**Find the greatest common factor of two numbers.**

Find the GCF of 16 and 24.
Factors of 16: 1, 2, 4, 8, 16
Factors of 24: 1, 2, 3, 4, 6, 8, 12, 24
So, the GCF is 8.

**Write the GCF for each set of numbers.** (pp. 278–281)

4. 14 and 28      5. 15 and 35

6. 18 and 42      7. 6, 12, and 45

8. 9 and 12       9. 7, 14, and 35

**Find the least common multiple of two numbers.**

Find the LCM of 6 and 9.
Multiples of 6: 6, 12, 18, 24, 30, 36, . . .
Multiples of 9: 9, 18, 27, 36, 45, 54, . . .
So, the LCM is 18.

**Write the LCM for each set of numbers.** (pp. 282–283)

10. 2 and 14      11. 6 and 32

12. 3 and 18      13. 3, 5, and 20

14. 5 and 6       15. 2, 7, and 14

## Chapter 14

**Write and evaluate exponents.**

exponent
Base → $3^5 = 3 \times 3 \times 3 \times 3 \times 3 = 243$

**Find the value.** (pp. 292–299)

16. $10^3$  17. $8^3$  18. $2^2$  19. $1^0$

20. $4^3$  21. $3^1$  22. $5^2$  23. $2^6$

**Find the prime factorization of a number.**

What is the prime factorization of 54?
$54 = 2 \times 3 \times 3 \times 3$
$54 = 2 \times 3^3$ ← Use 3 for the exponent.

**Find the prime factorization of the number. Use exponents when possible.** (pp. 302–305)

24. 30        25. 80

26. 33        27. 126

## Chapter 15

**Write equivalent fractions.**

| Multiply the numerator and the denominator by the same number. | Divide the numerator and the denominator by a common factor. |
|---|---|
| $\frac{4}{6} = \frac{4 \times 2}{6 \times 2} = \frac{8}{12}$ | $\frac{8}{12} = \frac{8 \div 4}{12 \div 4} = \frac{2}{3}$ |

**Write an equivalent fraction.**

(pp. 314–315)

**28.** $\frac{9}{21}$ **29.** $\frac{10}{12}$

**30.** $\frac{2}{5}$ **31.** $\frac{4}{7}$

**32.** $\frac{11}{12}$ **33.** $\frac{16}{20}$

**Write the fraction in simplest form.**

Write $\frac{12}{16}$ in simplest form.

$\frac{12}{16} = \frac{12 \div 4}{16 \div 4} = \frac{3}{4}$ ← Divide the numerator and the denominator by the GCF.

So, $\frac{12}{16}$ in simplest form is $\frac{3}{4}$.

**Write each fraction in simplest form.** (pp. 316–319)

**34.** $\frac{9}{24}$ **35.** $\frac{7}{49}$

**36.** $\frac{6}{24}$ **37.** $\frac{15}{48}$

**38.** $\frac{10}{42}$ **39.** $\frac{6}{28}$

**Write fractions as decimals and decimals as fractions.**

To write $\frac{2}{5}$ as a decimal, divide 2 by 5.

$2 \div 5 = 0.4$

To write 0.125 as a fraction, use place value.

$0.125 = \frac{125}{1,000}$ ← 125 thousandths

**Write a fraction for each decimal.**

(pp. 328–331)

**40.** 0.16 **41.** 0.5 **42.** 0.012

**Write a decimal for each fraction.**

(pp. 328–331)

**43.** $\frac{3}{4}$ **44.** $\frac{1}{5}$ **45.** $\frac{5}{8}$

**46.** $\frac{2}{5}$ **47.** $\frac{3}{8}$ **48.** $\frac{1}{4}$

## PROBLEM SOLVING PRACTICE

**Solve.** (pp. 284–285, 326–327)

**49.** The GCF of 8 and another number is 1. The LCM is 24. What is the other number?

**50.** Shawn rode his bike $\frac{5}{8}$ mi on Monday, $1\frac{2}{3}$ mi on Tuesday, $\frac{3}{2}$ mi on Wednesday, $2\frac{1}{9}$ mi on Thursday, and $\frac{7}{16}$ mi on Friday. On which day did he ride the least distance? the greatest distance?

# PERFORMANCE ASSESSMENT

## TASK A • BAKE SALE

Ariel, Brad, and Curt baked cookies for the school bake sale. The students want to put the cookies in bags. Each bag will contain all three kinds of cookies. All of the bags will have the same number of each kind of cookie.

| Baker | Number of Cookies | Kind of Cookie |
|-------|-------------------|----------------|
| Ariel | 24 | Peanut |
| Brad | 18 | Raisin |
| Curt | 12 | Oatmeal |

**a.** Find all the ways each kind of cookie can be divided so there is the same number in each bag.

**b.** What is the greatest number they can put in each bag? How many bags of cookies does this make?

**c.** Other students want to bring in cookies. Name two other numbers of cookies that can be divided in the same way.

## TASK B • CLOWNING AROUND

Jolynn and her mother are making a clown costume for the class play. They found some pieces of fabric at a yard sale. Help them choose fabric pieces for the costume.

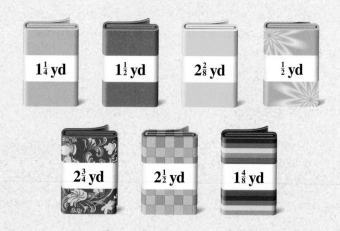

$1\frac{1}{4}$ yd  $1\frac{1}{2}$ yd  $2\frac{2}{8}$ yd  $\frac{1}{2}$ yd

$2\frac{3}{4}$ yd  $2\frac{1}{2}$ yd  $1\frac{4}{8}$ yd

**a.** They can use the shortest piece of fabric for the hat. Which piece should they choose for the hat?

**b.** They need $2\frac{5}{8}$ yards for the top of the costume. Is there a piece large enough for the top? If so, which is it?

**c.** Decide what other pieces of fabric they might buy for the sleeves and the pants of the costume. The pants will take more fabric than the top or the sleeves.

GARAGE SALE

# Technology Linkup

## Bases and Exponents

You can use a calculator to find the missing base or missing exponent in an equation.

On the Casio *fx-55* calculator, use $x^y$ to evaluate equations with exponents.

Find the missing numbers. Use the strategy *predict and test*.

**MISSING BASE**

$$x^4 = 625$$

• Try $x = 6$.

1,296 > 625
Try a lesser number for the base.

• Try $x = 5$.

625 = 625

So, $x = 5$. $5^4 = 625$.

**MISSING EXPONENT**

$$5^y = 15,625$$

• Try $y = 5$.

3,125 < 15,625
Try a greater number for the exponent.

• Try $y = 6$.

15,625 = 15,625

So, $y = 6$. $5^6 = 15,625$.

## Practice and Problem Solving

Use the $x^y$ key to find the missing exponent or base.

**1.** $b^5 = 1,024$     **2.** $y^4 = 2,401$     **3.** $n^6 = 46,656$     **4.** $a^8 = 65,536$

**5.** $w^7 = 128$     **6.** $x^9 = 19,683$     **7.** $3^q = 6,561$     **8.** $7^s = 16,807$

**9.** $8^r = 512$     **10.** $12^y = 20,736$     **11.** $15^x = 3,375$     **12.** $9^m = 59,049$

**13. REASONING** Find $10^x$ on your calculator. What do you think this key is used to evaluate? Use the key to check your thinking.

**GO ON-LINE**

**Multimedia Math Glossary** www.harcourtschool.com/mathglossary
**Vocabulary Power** Look up *base* and *exponent* in the Multimedia Math Glossary. Write a sentence that uses *exponent* to explain *base*.

St. Augustine
Plant City

## STRAWBERRY FESTIVAL

The Florida Strawberry Festival®, one of Florida's most famous festivals, dates back to 1930. This festival takes place every year in Plant City, Florida. Originally started to celebrate the harvest of strawberries, this festival has grown to include a variety of events and activities.

**USE DATA** For 1–3, use the table.

1. Arrange the events from least to greatest amount of time Alberto spent at each. Explain.

2. What type of graph would you use to show the data in the table? Make the graph, and explain why you chose it.

3. ✎ **Write a problem** that can be solved using the data in the table. Then solve the problem.

4. During the Strawberry Shortcake Eating Contest, entrants can use a spoon for the first 8 minutes but must eat with their hands for the last 2 minutes. For what fraction of the total contest time do entrants have to eat with their hands? Write the answer in simplest form.

| TIME ALBERTO SPENT AT THE FESTIVAL | |
|---|---|
| **Event** | **Time Spent** |
| Dog Show | $1\frac{1}{4}$ hr |
| Baby Parade | $\frac{1}{4}$ hr |
| Grand Parade | $\frac{1}{2}$ hr |
| Poultry Show | $\frac{3}{4}$ hr |

▲ Strawberries are not the only items sold at the annual Florida Strawberry Festival®. You can also enjoy foods made with strawberries, such as shortcake, milkshakes, and ice cream.

# ANASTASIA STATE PARK

In addition to the festivals held throughout the year, thousands of visitors enjoy boating, hiking, fishing, and other outdoor activities in Florida's state parks and recreation areas.

▲ Gulf fritillary

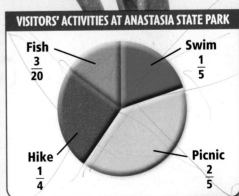

▲ Gray hairstreak

1. Anastasia State Park, in St. Augustine, has 104 campsites with electricity. Write the prime factorization of 104 using exponents.

2. The nightly camping rate is $16.00. There is also a nightly charge of $2.00 for each pet. In November the Smith family went camping with their dog. They paid $126 for a campsite. For how long did the Smiths camp at the park? Explain.

3. There are 7 species of butterflies commonly found in Anastasia State Park. If you saw 3 different species on a recent visit, did you see more than or less than half of the species of butterflies in the park? Explain.

**USE DATA** Bob surveyed 60 visitors to the state park. His results are shown in the circle graph. Use the circle graph for 4–5.

4. How could you draw a circle graph using decimals instead of fractions to show the same information?

5. Which activity has the greatest number of visitors? Explain how you know.

**VISITORS' ACTIVITIES AT ANASTASIA STATE PARK**

Fish $\frac{3}{20}$

Swim $\frac{1}{5}$

Hike $\frac{1}{4}$

Picnic $\frac{2}{5}$

# Add and Subtract Fractions

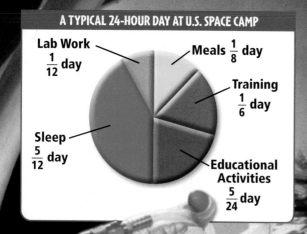

**A TYPICAL 24-HOUR DAY AT U.S. SPACE CAMP**

Lab Work $\frac{1}{12}$ day

Meals $\frac{1}{8}$ day

Training $\frac{1}{6}$ day

Sleep $\frac{5}{12}$ day

Educational Activities $\frac{5}{24}$ day

**≡FAST FACT • SOCIAL STUDIES** The White House began the Young Astronaut Program in 1984. Since then, more than 2,000,000 students worldwide have participated in programs developed by the Young Astronaut Council.

**PROBLEM SOLVING** What part of a typical day at U.S. Space Camp is spent doing lab work and sleeping? Write the answer in simplest form.

Use this page to help you review and remember important skills needed for Chapter 16.

## ✔ EQUIVALENT FRACTIONS

Write an equivalent fraction.

1. $\frac{15}{20}$    2. $\frac{1}{3}$    3. $\frac{5}{10}$    4. $\frac{2}{6}$    5. $\frac{9}{21}$

6. $\frac{2}{5}$    7. $\frac{3}{12}$    8. $\frac{3}{8}$    9. $\frac{2}{3}$    10. $\frac{5}{6}$

11. $\frac{7}{8}$    12. $\frac{2}{9}$    13. $\frac{3}{10}$    14. $\frac{4}{12}$    15. $\frac{1}{7}$

## ✔ SIMPLEST FORM

Write each fraction in simplest form.

16. $\frac{6}{42}$    17. $\frac{7}{56}$    18. $\frac{10}{32}$    19. $\frac{8}{12}$    20. $\frac{4}{30}$

21. $\frac{5}{40}$    22. $\frac{4}{28}$    23. $\frac{16}{18}$    24. $\frac{7}{35}$    25. $\frac{9}{72}$

Tell whether the fraction is in simplest form. Write *yes* or *no*.

26. $\frac{5}{12}$    27. $\frac{6}{18}$    28. $\frac{8}{20}$    29. $\frac{12}{15}$    30. $\frac{12}{56}$

31. $\frac{2}{8}$    32. $\frac{6}{7}$    33. $\frac{9}{12}$    34. $\frac{8}{11}$    35. $\frac{9}{31}$

# VOCABULARY POWER

### REVIEW

**numerator** [nōō′mə•rā•tər] *noun*

*Numerator* is from the Latin word *enumerate*, "to count out." The top number of a fraction shows how many parts of the whole are being "counted." What other words come from the Latin *enumerate*?

### PREVIEW

least common denominator (LCD)

www.harcourtschool.com/mathglossary

# Add and Subtract Like Fractions

▶ **Learn**

**WHOOSH!** Damon's basketball team practices each afternoon. The team works on free throws for $\frac{3}{8}$ hour and runs plays for $\frac{5}{8}$ hour. How long does the team practice last?

## Example 1  Add. $\frac{3}{8} + \frac{5}{8}$

**One Way** Use a model.

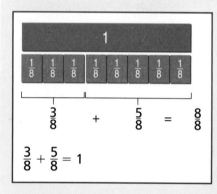

$\frac{3}{8} + \frac{5}{8} = 1$

**Another Way** Use paper and pencil.

$$\begin{array}{r} \frac{3}{8} \\ + \frac{5}{8} \\ \hline \frac{8}{8} = 1 \end{array}$$

- Add the numerators.
- Write the sum over the denominator.
- Write the sum in simplest form.

$\frac{3}{8} + \frac{5}{8} = 1$

So, the team practice lasts 1 hour.

## Example 2  How much more time does the team spend on plays than on free throws?

Subtract. $\frac{5}{8} - \frac{3}{8}$

**One Way** Use a model.

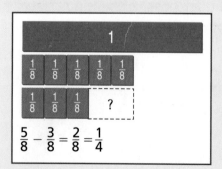

$\frac{5}{8} - \frac{3}{8} = \frac{2}{8} = \frac{1}{4}$

**Another Way** Use mental math.

Think: $5 - 3 = 2$

So, $\frac{5}{8} - \frac{3}{8} = \frac{2}{8}$.

$\frac{2}{8} = \frac{1}{4} \rightarrow$ simplest form

$\frac{5}{8} - \frac{3}{8} = \frac{2}{8}$, or $\frac{1}{4}$

So, the team spends $\frac{1}{4}$ hour longer on plays than on free throws.

**Technology Link**

More Practice: Harcourt Mega Math Fraction Action, *Fraction Flare-Up*, Levels G, H

On May 10, 1997, Karl Malone set a record for the most free throws made in a play-off game. He made 18 free throws without missing one! ▼

1. **Explain** what is true about the numerators of two like fractions with a sum of 1.

**Find the sum or difference. Write it in simplest form.**

2. $\frac{2}{3} + \frac{1}{3}$　　　3. $\frac{1}{4} + \frac{2}{4}$　　　4. $\frac{5}{10} + \frac{2}{10}$

5. $\frac{2}{3} - \frac{1}{3}$　　　6. $\frac{7}{8} - \frac{1}{8}$　　　7. $\frac{5}{6} - \frac{2}{6}$

▶ **Practice and Problem Solving**

**Find the sum or difference. Write it in simplest form.**

8. $\frac{1}{6} + \frac{3}{6}$　　　9. $\frac{3}{10} - \frac{1}{10}$　　　10. $\frac{5}{7} + \frac{2}{7}$

11. $\frac{4}{5} - \frac{1}{5}$　　　12. $\frac{7}{12} + \frac{1}{12}$　　　13. $\frac{4}{9} - \frac{1}{9}$

14. $\frac{2}{8} + \frac{3}{8}$　　　15. $\frac{5}{12} - \frac{2}{12}$　　　16. $\frac{1}{10} + \frac{4}{10}$

 **ALGEBRA**　Find the value of $n$.

17. $n + \frac{4}{9} = \frac{7}{9}$　　　18. $\frac{9}{10} - n = \frac{7}{10}$　　　19. $1 - n = \frac{8}{11}$

20. **MEASUREMENT**　Karla is using $\frac{3}{8}$ yard of ribbon for one craft project and $\frac{5}{8}$ yard for another. How much ribbon is she using in all?

21. Sara and Matt each ordered a medium pizza. Sara ate $\frac{3}{8}$ of her pizza for lunch and $\frac{2}{8}$ for a snack. Matt ate $\frac{2}{4}$ of his pizza for lunch and $\frac{1}{4}$ for a snack. Who ate more pizza? Explain.

22. **REASONING**　Pat made $\frac{3}{5}$ of her free throws in the basketball game. What part of her free throws did she not make?

23. ✏ **Write About It** When you add or subtract two like fractions, when does the final answer have a different denominator?

**Getting Ready for FCAT**

24. Jeff is training for a swim meet. How much farther did he swim on Monday than on Tuesday?

A. $\frac{1}{5}$ mile　　C. $\frac{3}{5}$ mile

B. $\frac{2}{5}$ mile　　D. $\frac{4}{5}$ mile

| JEFF'S SWIMMING LOG | |
|---|---|
| **Day** | **Miles** |
| Monday | $\frac{9}{10}$ |
| Tuesday | $\frac{3}{10}$ |

FCAT TESTED 🏴 SSS/GLEs MA.A.3.2.3.5.1 Solves real-world problems involving . . . addition, subtraction . . . of decimals, fractions, and mixed numbers using an appropriate method (for example, mental math, pencil and paper, calculator). *also* MA.A.1.2.3.5.1

Chapter 16　**347**

# Add and Subtract Unlike Fractions

**Quick Review**

Write an equivalent fraction.

1. $\frac{1}{2}$     2. $\frac{3}{9}$

3. $\frac{5}{20}$    4. $\frac{2}{5}$    5. $\frac{6}{24}$

**MATERIALS**
fraction bars

**BEST FRIENDS FOREVER!** At a crafts class, Liz and Whitney are making bracelets using beads and colored string. Liz is using $\frac{1}{2}$ cup of large red beads and $\frac{1}{4}$ cup of yellow beads. How many cups of beads is she using in all?

## Activity 1

Use fraction bars to add fractions with unlike denominators.

Add. $\frac{1}{2} + \frac{1}{4}$

**STEP 1**

Place a $\frac{1}{2}$ bar and a $\frac{1}{4}$ bar under a 1 whole bar.

| 1 |
| $\frac{1}{2}$ | $\frac{1}{4}$ |

**STEP 2**

Find like fraction bars that fit exactly under the sum $\frac{1}{2} + \frac{1}{4}$.

| 1 |
| $\frac{1}{2}$ | $\frac{1}{4}$ |
| $\frac{1}{4}$ | $\frac{1}{4}$ | $\frac{1}{4}$ |

$$\frac{1}{2} + \frac{1}{4} = \frac{2}{4} + \frac{1}{4}$$
$$= \frac{3}{4}$$

So, Liz is using $\frac{3}{4}$ cup of beads.

In the second step of your model, the $\frac{1}{2}$ bar was replaced with two $\frac{1}{4}$ bars. The fractions $\frac{2}{4}$ and $\frac{1}{4}$ have like denominators. To add fractions with unlike denominators, you need to find equivalent fractions with like denominators.

• What fraction bars can you use to show equivalent fractions for $\frac{1}{3}$ and $\frac{1}{2}$?

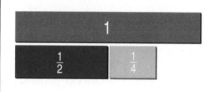

| 1 |
| $\frac{1}{3}$ | $\frac{1}{2}$ |

## Subtract Unlike Fractions

Whitney cut colored string to make a bracelet.
A piece of blue string is $\frac{2}{3}$ yard long.
Whitney cut $\frac{1}{2}$ yard from it. How much string was left?

**HANDS ON**

### Activity 2

Use fraction bars to subtract fractions with unlike denominators.

Subtract. $\frac{2}{3} - \frac{1}{2}$

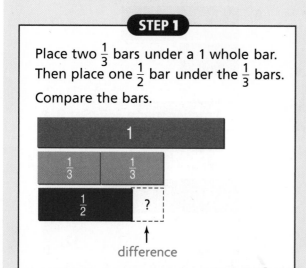

**STEP 1**

Place two $\frac{1}{3}$ bars under a 1 whole bar.
Then place one $\frac{1}{2}$ bar under the $\frac{1}{3}$ bars.
Compare the bars.

difference

**STEP 2**

Find like fraction bars that fit exactly under the difference $\frac{2}{3} - \frac{1}{2}$.

$$\frac{2}{3} - \frac{1}{2} = \frac{1}{6}$$

So, Whitney had $\frac{1}{6}$ yard of string left.

When you use fraction bars to subtract fractions with unlike denominators, you can think of equivalent fractions with like denominators.

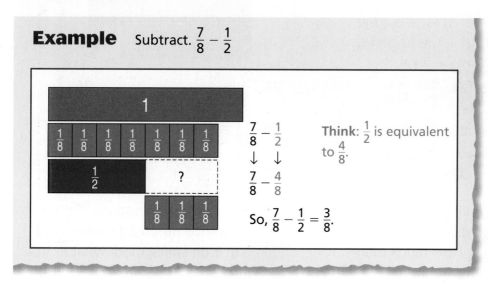

**Example** Subtract. $\frac{7}{8} - \frac{1}{2}$

$$\frac{7}{8} - \frac{1}{2}$$
$$\downarrow \quad \downarrow$$
$$\frac{7}{8} - \frac{4}{8}$$

**Think:** $\frac{1}{2}$ is equivalent to $\frac{4}{8}$.

So, $\frac{7}{8} - \frac{1}{2} = \frac{3}{8}$.

**FCAT TESTED** SSS/GLEs MA.A.1.2.3.5.1 Translates problem situations into diagrams, models, and numerals using whole numbers, fractions, mixed numbers, decimals, and percents. *also* MA.A.1.2.4.5.1, MA.A.3.2.2.5.1

1. **Explain** how to find $\frac{1}{3} + \frac{3}{6}$ using fraction bars.

2. **Explain** how to find $\frac{5}{6} - \frac{1}{2}$ using fraction bars.

**Use fraction bars to find the sum.**

3.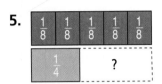

4. | $\frac{1}{5}$ | $\frac{1}{10}$ | $\frac{1}{10}$ | $\frac{1}{10}$ |

**Use fraction bars to find the difference.**

5. | $\frac{1}{8}$ | $\frac{1}{8}$ | $\frac{1}{8}$ | $\frac{1}{8}$ | $\frac{1}{8}$ |

   | $\frac{1}{4}$ | ? |

6. | $\frac{1}{5}$ | $\frac{1}{5}$ | $\frac{1}{5}$ |

   | $\frac{1}{10}$ | $\frac{1}{10}$ | $\frac{1}{10}$ | ? |

▷ **Practice and Problem Solving**   Extra Practice, page 362, Set B

**Use fraction bars to find the sum.**

7.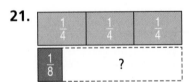

8. | $\frac{1}{10}$ | $\frac{1}{10}$ | $\frac{1}{2}$ |

9. $\frac{1}{4} + \frac{1}{6}$

10. $\frac{2}{5} + \frac{3}{10}$

11. $\frac{5}{6} + \frac{1}{12}$

12. $\frac{3}{10} + \frac{1}{2}$

13. $\frac{1}{6} + \frac{2}{3}$

14. $\frac{4}{10} + \frac{1}{2}$

15. $\frac{2}{3} + \frac{1}{4}$

16. $\frac{1}{8} + \frac{3}{4}$

17. $\frac{1}{4} + \frac{1}{3}$

18. $\frac{1}{6} + \frac{1}{2}$

19. $\frac{3}{5} + \frac{1}{10}$

20. $\frac{1}{4} + \frac{3}{8}$

**Use fraction bars to find the difference.**

21. | $\frac{1}{4}$ | $\frac{1}{4}$ | $\frac{1}{4}$ |

    | $\frac{1}{8}$ | ? |

22. | $\frac{1}{6}$ | $\frac{1}{6}$ | $\frac{1}{6}$ | $\frac{1}{6}$ | $\frac{1}{6}$ |

    | $\frac{1}{3}$ | $\frac{1}{3}$ | ? |

23. $\frac{4}{6} - \frac{1}{4}$

24. $\frac{5}{6} - \frac{1}{12}$

25. $\frac{7}{10} - \frac{1}{2}$

26. $\frac{6}{8} - \frac{1}{4}$

27. $\frac{2}{3} - \frac{1}{12}$

28. $\frac{1}{2} - \frac{1}{5}$

29. $\frac{11}{12} - \frac{3}{4}$

30. $\frac{4}{5} - \frac{1}{10}$

31. $\frac{5}{8} - \frac{1}{2}$

32. $\frac{2}{3} - \frac{1}{6}$

33. $\frac{9}{10} - \frac{1}{2}$

34. $\frac{5}{6} - \frac{2}{3}$

35. Amy is making a burrito dish that calls for $\frac{3}{4}$ cup of grated cheddar cheese. She has grated $\frac{1}{2}$ cup. How much more cheese does Amy have to grate?

36. Every week Tim spends $\frac{1}{2}$ of his allowance on entertainment and $\frac{1}{3}$ of it on snack food. What fraction of Tim's weekly allowance is this in all?

**37. REASONING** John has to mix $\frac{1}{2}$ cup of flour and $\frac{1}{4}$ cup of sugar. He has a container that holds $\frac{7}{8}$ cup. Can John mix the flour and sugar in the container? Explain.

**38.** **? What's the Question?** Carl worked for $\frac{5}{6}$ hour. He tilled his garden for $\frac{1}{2}$ hour, planted seeds for $\frac{1}{6}$ hour, and watered for the rest of the time. The answer is $\frac{1}{6}$ hour.

## Getting Ready for FCAT

**39.** Matt walked $\frac{2}{5}$ mile to Brad's house and then $\frac{3}{10}$ mile to school. Which shows how to find how far he walked in all?

Matt's House        Brad's House        School

**A.** $\frac{2}{5} - \frac{3}{10} = \frac{1}{10}$

**B.** $\frac{2}{5} + \frac{3}{10} = \frac{7}{10}$

**C.** $\frac{1}{5} - \frac{1}{10} = \frac{1}{10}$

**D.** $\frac{2}{10} + \frac{3}{10} = \frac{5}{10}$

**40.** Lewis needs 2 pieces of wood, each $\frac{1}{2}$ foot long, for his birdhouse. He has these pieces of wood.

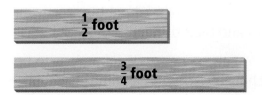

How much does he need to cut off the second piece to get the length he needs?

**F.** $\frac{3}{4}$ foot

**G.** $\frac{1}{2}$ foot

**H.** $\frac{1}{4}$ foot

**I.** $\frac{1}{8}$ foot

## Problem Solving    LiNKUP... to History

The earliest known writing about fractions is called the Rhind Papyrus. It is a roll of papyrus paper 18 feet long and 1 foot high. The Rhind Papyrus was written 3,600 years ago by Egyptian mathematicians. In 1858 it was discovered by a Scottish man, Alexander Henry Rhind.

Egyptian fractions were expressed as sums of "unit" fractions. A unit fraction is a fraction that has a 1 in the numerator. To write $\frac{3}{4}$, for example, the Egyptians would write $\frac{1}{2} + \frac{1}{4}$.

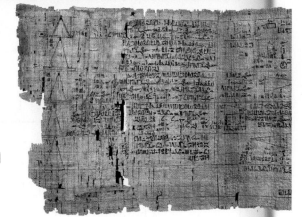

**Find the fraction represented by the unit fractions.**

**1.** $\frac{1}{2} + \frac{1}{5}$     **2.** $\frac{1}{3} + \frac{1}{4}$     **3.** $\frac{1}{5} + \frac{1}{10}$     **4.** $\frac{1}{8} + \frac{1}{4}$

**5.** Find Egyptian fractions for $\frac{2}{7}$ and $\frac{5}{6}$.

# Estimate Sums and Differences

▶ **Learn**

**HAPPY TRAILS**   On a weekend camping trip, Ken, Eric, and their dad went for a 2-hour walk on the Woodland Trail to look for the trail markings. The first hour, they walked $\frac{3}{8}$ mile. The second hour, they walked $\frac{4}{5}$ mile. About how many miles did the boys and their dad walk?

**MATH IDEA**   Rounding fractions to benchmarks such as $0$, $\frac{1}{2}$, or $1$ on a number line can help you estimate sums and differences.

**Example** Estimate. $\frac{3}{8} + \frac{4}{5}$

**STEP 1**

The fraction $\frac{3}{8}$ is close to $\frac{1}{2}$. Round to $\frac{1}{2}$.

$\frac{1}{8}$ $\frac{2}{8}$ $\frac{3}{8}$ $\frac{4}{8}$ $\frac{5}{8}$ $\frac{6}{8}$ $\frac{7}{8}$

0 $\frac{1}{2}$ 1

**STEP 2**

The fraction $\frac{4}{5}$ is close to $1$. Round to $1$.

$\frac{1}{5}$ $\frac{2}{5}$ $\frac{3}{5}$ $\frac{4}{5}$

0 $\frac{1}{2}$ 1

**STEP 3**

Add the rounded fractions.

$$\frac{3}{8} \rightarrow \frac{1}{2}$$
$$+\frac{4}{5} \rightarrow +1$$
$$\overline{\qquad 1\frac{1}{2}}$$

So, Ken, Eric, and their dad walked about $1\frac{1}{2}$ miles.

## More Examples

**A** Estimate. $\frac{2}{3} + \frac{4}{5}$

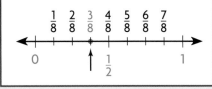

$\frac{1}{5}$ $\frac{2}{5}$ $\frac{3}{5}$ $\frac{4}{5}$

0 $\frac{1}{3}$ $\frac{1}{2}$ $\frac{2}{3}$ 1

$\frac{2}{3} \rightarrow \frac{1}{2}$  $\frac{2}{3}$ is between $\frac{1}{2}$ and 1, but closer to $\frac{1}{2}$.

$+\frac{4}{5} \rightarrow +1$  $\frac{4}{5}$ is between $\frac{1}{2}$ and 1, but closer to 1.

$\overline{\quad 1\frac{1}{2}}$  The sum is greater than 1, but less than 2.

**B** Estimate. $\frac{3}{8} - \frac{1}{6}$

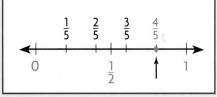

$\frac{1}{6}$ $\frac{2}{6}$ $\frac{3}{6}$ $\frac{4}{6}$ $\frac{5}{6}$

0 $\frac{1}{8}$ $\frac{2}{8}$ $\frac{3}{8}$ $\frac{1}{2}$ $\frac{5}{8}$ $\frac{6}{8}$ $\frac{7}{8}$ 1

$\frac{3}{8} \rightarrow \frac{1}{2}$  $\frac{3}{8}$ is between 0 and $\frac{1}{2}$, but closer to $\frac{1}{2}$.

$-\frac{1}{6} \rightarrow -0$  $\frac{1}{6}$ is between 0 and $\frac{1}{2}$, but closer to 0.

$\overline{\quad \frac{1}{2}}$  The difference is greater than 0, but less than $\frac{1}{2}$.

## ▶ Check

1. **Compare** the numerators and denominators of fractions that round to 1, such as $\frac{11}{12}, \frac{8}{9}, \frac{7}{8},$ and $\frac{8}{10}$. What do you notice?

**Write whether the fraction is closest to 0, $\frac{1}{2}$, or 1. Use the number lines.**

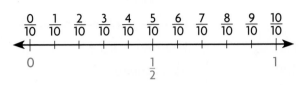
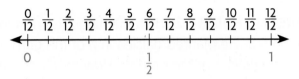

2. $\frac{7}{10}$     3. $\frac{1}{12}$     4. $\frac{3}{10}$     5. $\frac{5}{12}$     6. $\frac{9}{10}$     7. $\frac{2}{10}$

## ▶ Practice and Problem Solving   Extra Practice, page 362, Set C

**Write whether the fraction is closest to 0, $\frac{1}{2}$, or 1.**

8. $\frac{4}{7}$     9. $\frac{2}{9}$     10. $\frac{6}{7}$     11. $\frac{8}{9}$     12. $\frac{3}{7}$     13. $\frac{5}{6}$

**Estimate each sum or difference.**

14. $\frac{1}{9} + \frac{5}{6}$     15. $\frac{2}{3} + \frac{5}{7}$     16. $\frac{3}{8} - \frac{1}{5}$     17. $\frac{9}{10} - \frac{3}{8}$     18. $\frac{7}{12} + \frac{1}{7}$

19. $\frac{8}{10} - \frac{2}{3}$     20. $\frac{6}{7} + \frac{3}{5}$     21. $\frac{7}{9} - \frac{2}{6}$     22. $\frac{7}{8} + \frac{2}{3}$     23. $\frac{10}{12} - \frac{1}{10}$

**Estimate to compare. Write < or > for each ●.**

24. $\frac{6}{8} + \frac{2}{3}$ ● 1       25. $\frac{1}{2}$ ● $\frac{3}{5} - \frac{1}{3}$       26. $\frac{2}{5} + \frac{1}{7}$ ● 1

27. **REASONING** The number ♣ is three times the number ♥. What is the fraction $\frac{♥}{♣}$ in simplest form?

28. ✎ **Write About It** Explain how you can estimate the sum of $\frac{4}{5}$ and $\frac{1}{10}$.

29. Yoko added $\frac{3}{4}$ cup cashews, $\frac{1}{2}$ cup pecans, $\frac{5}{6}$ cup banana chips, and $\frac{1}{3}$ cup peanuts to the trail mix. Did she add more nuts or more fruit?

## Getting Ready for FCAT [THINK SOLVE EXPLAIN]

30. Trudi and Melissa are making hats for the class play. They are cutting pieces of ribbon to tie on the hats. Each hat will need $\frac{5}{6}$ yard of yellow ribbon and $\frac{2}{3}$ yard of blue ribbon. Use the number line to ESTIMATE the number of yards needed for each hat. Explain how you made your estimate.

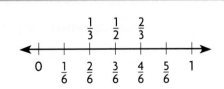

# Use Common Denominators

▷ **Learn**

**GREEN THUMB** Zach is planting a garden in his backyard. He planted daisies in $\frac{3}{8}$ of the garden and marigolds in $\frac{1}{2}$ of the garden. How much of the garden did Zach use?

To add or subtract unlike fractions, you need to rename them as like fractions with a common denominator.

### VOCABULARY

**least common denominator (LCD)**

**Example** Add. $\frac{3}{8} + \frac{1}{2}$

Estimate. $\frac{3}{8}$ is close to $\frac{1}{2}$, so the sum is close to 1.

**One Way** Use a common denominator.

Multiply the denominators to find a common denominator.

$8 \times 2 = 16 \leftarrow$ common denominator

Use the common denominator to write equivalent fractions. Then add.

$$\frac{3}{8} = \frac{6}{16}$$
$$+ \frac{1}{2} = + \frac{8}{16}$$
$$\overline{\phantom{+\frac{1}{2}=+}\frac{14}{16}} = \frac{7}{8} \leftarrow \text{simplest form}$$

**Another Way** Use the least common denominator.

The **least common denominator**, or **LCD**, is the least common multiple of two or more denominators. List multiples of each denominator. Then find the least common multiple of the denominators.

Multiples of 8: 8, 16, 32, 40, 48, 56
Multiples of 2: 2, 4, 6, 8, 10, 12

The LCM is 8. So, the LCD of $\frac{3}{8}$ and $\frac{1}{2}$ is 8. Write equivalent fractions. Then add.

$$\frac{3}{8} = \frac{3}{8}$$
$$+ \frac{1}{2} = + \frac{1 \times 4}{2 \times 4} = + \frac{4}{8}$$
$$\overline{\phantom{+\frac{1}{2}=+}\frac{7}{8}} \leftarrow \text{simplest form}$$

So, Zach used $\frac{7}{8}$ of the garden. The answer is close to the estimate, so the answer is reasonable.

- What would the least common denominator be for $\frac{3}{4} - \frac{2}{5}$? Explain.

 **MATH IDEA** To add or subtract unlike fractions, write equivalent fractions with a common denominator.

1. **Explain** how you can use multiples to find the LCD for $\frac{2}{3} + \frac{3}{5}$.

**Find the sum. Write it in simplest form.**

2. $\frac{1}{5} + \frac{1}{10}$     3. $\frac{1}{4} + \frac{1}{3}$     4. $\frac{1}{3} + \frac{2}{9}$     5. $\frac{1}{6} + \frac{2}{4}$     6. $\frac{1}{5} + \frac{5}{10}$

**Find the difference. Write it in simplest form.**

7. $\frac{2}{3} - \frac{1}{2}$     8. $\frac{3}{4} - \frac{3}{8}$     9. $1 - \frac{1}{4}$     10. $\frac{11}{12} - \frac{1}{6}$     11. $\frac{7}{10} - \frac{1}{5}$

▶ **Practice and Problem Solving**    Extra Practice, page 362, Set D

**Find the sum or difference. Write it in simplest form.**

12. $\frac{1}{8} + \frac{3}{4}$     13. $\frac{1}{2} + \frac{2}{5}$     14. $\frac{5}{6} - \frac{3}{4}$     15. $1 - \frac{3}{5}$     16. $\frac{7}{8} + \frac{1}{4}$

17. $\frac{2}{3} + \frac{1}{6}$     18. $\frac{2}{3} - \frac{1}{9}$     19. $\frac{7}{8} - \frac{1}{2}$     20. $\frac{1}{4} + \frac{2}{3}$     21. $\frac{1}{4} + \frac{2}{8}$

22. $\frac{4}{5} + \frac{2}{10}$     23. $\frac{3}{12} - \frac{1}{6}$     24. $\frac{9}{10} - \frac{1}{2}$     25. $\frac{1}{4} + \frac{1}{12}$     26. $\frac{1}{4} - \frac{3}{16}$

**ALGEBRA    Find the value of $n$.**

27. $\frac{2}{10} + n = 1$     28. $n + \frac{1}{12} = \frac{7}{12}$     29. $\frac{5}{8} - n = \frac{3}{8}$     30. $\frac{9}{10} - n = \frac{1}{5}$

**USE DATA    For 31–32, use the table.**

31. Which type of plant grew more during the first week?

32. ✏ **Write a problem** that uses subtraction, using the data from the second week.

| GARDEN PLANT GROWTH (in inches) | | |
|---|---|---|
|  | **First Week** | **Second Week** |
| Tulips | $\frac{7}{8}$ | $\frac{3}{4}$ |
| Daffodils | $\frac{1}{4}$ | $\frac{1}{2}$ |

33. Dan wrote a report. He found $\frac{1}{8}$ of the information for the report on the Internet and $\frac{1}{2}$ at the library. How much of his information did he get from sources other than the Internet and the library?

**Getting Ready for FCAT**

34. The circle graph shows the expenses for the fifth-grade party. What part of the expenses are for decorations?

   A. $\frac{1}{5}$     B. $\frac{3}{10}$     C. $\frac{1}{2}$     D. $\frac{3}{5}$

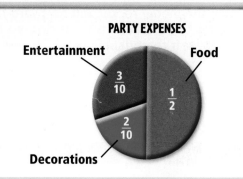

PARTY EXPENSES

Entertainment $\frac{3}{10}$

Food $\frac{1}{2}$

Decorations $\frac{2}{10}$

# Use the Least Common Denominator

▶ **Learn**

**LIFT OFF!** Kevin and Stuart are building a model rocket at U.S. Space Camp. The body tube is $\frac{1}{2}$ yard long and the nose cone is $\frac{1}{6}$ yard long. How tall will the rocket be when the parts are joined?

**Quick Review**

Write a common denominator.

**1.** $\frac{1}{3}$ and $\frac{1}{10}$    **2.** $\frac{2}{3}$ and $\frac{1}{9}$

**3.** $\frac{2}{5}$ and $\frac{1}{7}$    **4.** $\frac{2}{8}$ and $\frac{7}{6}$

**5.** $\frac{2}{3}$ and $\frac{1}{6}$

## Example 1

Add. $\frac{1}{6} + \frac{1}{2}$

Estimate. $\frac{1}{6}$ is a little more than 0, so the sum is close to $\frac{1}{2}$.

**STEP 1**

The LCM of 2 and 6 is 6. So, the LCD of $\frac{1}{2}$ and $\frac{1}{6}$ is 6. Use the LCD to write like fractions.

$$\frac{1}{6} = \frac{1}{6}$$
$$+\ \frac{1 \times \boxed{3}}{2 \times \boxed{3}} = +\ \frac{3}{6}$$

**STEP 2**

Add the fractions. Write the answer in simplest form.

$$\frac{1}{6} = \frac{1}{6}$$
$$+\ \frac{1 \times \boxed{3}}{2 \times \boxed{3}} = +\ \frac{3}{6}$$
$$\frac{4}{6} = \frac{2}{3}$$

So, the model rocket will be $\frac{2}{3}$ yard tall when the parts are joined. The exact answer is close to the estimate, so the answer is reasonable.

You can also use a calculator that operates with fractions.

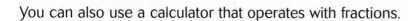

## Example 2

Subtract. $\frac{3}{4} - \frac{1}{6}$

Estimate. $\frac{3}{4}$ is halfway between $\frac{1}{2}$ and 1, and $\frac{1}{6}$ is a little more than 0, so the difference is close to $\frac{1}{2}$.

**STEP 1**

The LCM of 4 and 6 is 12. So, the LCD of $\frac{3}{4}$ and $\frac{1}{6}$ is 12. Use the LCD to change the fractions to like fractions.

$$\frac{3}{4} = \frac{3 \times 3}{4 \times 3} = \frac{9}{12}$$
$$-\frac{1}{6} = -\frac{1 \times 2}{6 \times 2} = -\frac{2}{12}$$

**STEP 2**

Subtract the fractions.
Write the answer in simplest form.

$$\frac{3}{4} = \frac{3 \times 3}{4 \times 3} = \frac{9}{12}$$
$$-\frac{1}{6} = -\frac{1 \times 2}{6 \times 2} = -\frac{2}{12}$$
$$\frac{7}{12} \leftarrow \text{simplest form}$$

## More Examples

**A** Find $\frac{3}{4} + \frac{5}{8}$.

$$\frac{3 \times 2}{4 \times 2} = \frac{6}{8}$$
$$+\frac{5}{8} \quad = +\frac{5}{8}$$
$$\frac{11}{8}, \text{ or } 1\frac{3}{8}$$

**B** Find $1 - \frac{2}{5}$.

$$\frac{1 \times 5}{1 \times 5} = \frac{5}{5}$$
$$-\frac{2}{5} \quad = -\frac{2}{5}$$
$$\frac{3}{5}$$

 **MATH IDEA** To add or subtract unlike fractions, you need to find the least common denominator (LCD) to write equivalent fractions. Then add or subtract the numerators.

## Check

**1. Explain** what the least common denominator is.

**Find the LCD. Then add or subtract.**

2. $\quad \frac{6}{12}$
$\quad -\frac{1}{3}$

3. $\quad \frac{1}{5}$
$\quad +\frac{1}{2}$

4. $\quad \frac{5}{7}$
$\quad -\frac{1}{2}$

5. $\quad \frac{8}{9}$
$\quad -\frac{2}{3}$

6. $\quad \frac{1}{2}$
$\quad +\frac{1}{3}$

**Find the sum or difference. Write the answer in simplest form.**

7. $\frac{2}{3} + \frac{1}{6}$

8. $\frac{2}{3} - \frac{1}{9}$

9. $\frac{7}{8} - \frac{1}{2}$

10. $\frac{1}{4} + \frac{2}{3}$

11. $\frac{1}{4} + \frac{2}{8}$

12. $\frac{7}{12} - \frac{1}{3}$

13. $\frac{3}{8} + \frac{3}{4}$

14. $1 - \frac{5}{6}$

15. $\frac{3}{9} + \frac{1}{3}$

16. $1 - \frac{7}{10}$

**LESSON CONTINUES**

FCAT TESTED SSS/GLEs MA.A.3.2.3.5.I Solves real-world problems involving . . . addition, subtraction, and multiplication of decimals, fractions, and mixed numbers using an appropriate method (for example, mental math, pencil and paper, calculator). *also* MA.A.I.2.3.5.I

Chapter 16 **357**

**Find the LCD. Then add or subtract.**

17. $\frac{1}{6}$
$+\frac{1}{3}$

18. $\frac{7}{10}$
$+\frac{1}{2}$

19. $\frac{5}{9}$
$-\frac{1}{6}$

20. $\frac{2}{8}$
$+\frac{3}{4}$

21. $\frac{2}{3}$
$-\frac{1}{4}$

**Find the sum or difference. Write it in simplest form.**

22. $\frac{1}{8} + \frac{3}{4}$

23. $\frac{1}{2} + \frac{2}{5}$

24. $\frac{5}{6} - \frac{3}{4}$

25. $1 - \frac{3}{5}$

26. $\frac{2}{3} + \frac{1}{4}$

27. $1 - \frac{5}{7}$

28. $\frac{4}{5} + \frac{3}{10}$

29. $\frac{7}{8} - \frac{1}{2}$

30. $\frac{3}{4} + \frac{1}{12}$

31. $\frac{4}{5} + \frac{1}{10}$

32. $\frac{7}{14} - \frac{1}{7}$

33. $\frac{2}{5} + \frac{6}{10}$

34. $1 - \frac{8}{9}$

35. $\frac{4}{18} + \frac{2}{6}$

36. $\frac{6}{8} - \frac{1}{4}$

37. $\frac{1}{3} + \frac{5}{12}$

38. $\frac{2}{3} - \frac{5}{9}$

39. $\frac{1}{3} + \frac{2}{5}$

40. $\frac{5}{6} - \frac{1}{8}$

41. $\frac{4}{9} + \frac{1}{3}$

 **ALGEBRA**   **Compare. Write < or > for each ●.**

42. $\frac{1}{2} + \frac{2}{3}$ ● $\frac{1}{6} + \frac{1}{3}$

43. $\frac{2}{4} - \frac{2}{8}$ ● $\frac{1}{2} - \frac{1}{8}$

44. $\frac{7}{12} - \frac{1}{2}$ ● $\frac{4}{6} + \frac{1}{12}$

45. **REASONING** Jake and Libby both made streamers for the nose cones of their model rockets from the same piece of ribbon. Jake said he used $\frac{3}{8}$ of the ribbon, and Libby said she used $\frac{3}{4}$ of the ribbon. Was this possible? Explain.

46. **?** **What's the Error?** Ramon says $\frac{2}{3} - \frac{1}{2} = \frac{1}{1} = 1$. Describe his error. Write the correct answer.

**For 47–50, use the drawing.**

47. What fraction of the square is red?

48. What fraction of the square is green or orange?

49. What subtraction equation can you write to find the fraction of the square that is yellow? Solve the equation.

50. What fraction of the square is white, blue, or yellow?

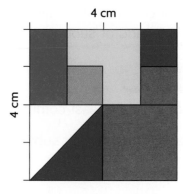

4 cm

4 cm

51. **FAST FACT • SCIENCE** On the surface of the moon, gravity is only about $\frac{1}{6}$ of what it is on Earth because the moon is smaller than Earth. How much would a person weigh on the moon if he weighs 90 pounds on Earth?

52. **Vocabulary Power** Some words show a comparison when *-er* or *-est* is added to them. An example of this comparison is *simple*, *simpler*, and *simplest*. Write the comparison for the word *great*. Then use one form of *great* in a sentence that describes how numbers compare.

**53.** Edward says that if you add $\frac{2}{3}$ and $\frac{3}{4}$, the sum will be greater than 1. Is he correct? Explain.

**54.** Mitchell paid $94 for ten tickets to the concert. Adult tickets cost $15 each. Student tickets cost $8 each. How many of each kind of ticket did he buy?

## Getting Ready for FCAT

**55.** Four students each found a different sum for $\frac{1}{12} + \frac{3}{4}$. Who had the correct answer?

| | |
|---|---|
| Monica | $\frac{4}{16}$ |
| Corey | $\frac{2}{3}$ |
| Joshua | $\frac{5}{6}$ |
| Britney | $\frac{11}{12}$ |

**A.** Monica      **C.** Joshua

**B.** Corey      **D.** Britney

**56.** The table shows how far from school four students live. Who lives farthest from the school?

| DISTANCE TO SCHOOL | |
|---|---|
| **Student** | **Miles** |
| Dana | $\frac{1}{4}$ |
| Jason | $\frac{1}{8}$ |
| Felicia | $\frac{1}{3}$ |
| Mario | $\frac{1}{2}$ |

**F.** Dana      **H.** Felicia

**G.** Jason      **I.** Mario

# Problem Solving   Thinker's Corner

**PATTERNS** You can use models to help you look at patterns in fractions.

### Examples      MATERIALS: fraction strips

**A** How do the values of these fractions change as the denominators increase?

$$\frac{1}{2}, \frac{1}{3}, \frac{1}{4}, \frac{1}{5}, \frac{1}{6}$$

**Use fraction strips to model the fractions.**

As the denominators increase, the values of the fractions decrease.

**B** How do the values of these fractions change as the numerators increase?

$$\frac{3}{10}, \frac{4}{10}, \frac{5}{10}, \frac{6}{10}, \frac{7}{10}$$

**Use fraction strips to model the fractions.**

As the numerators increase, the values of the fractions increase.

**Use fraction strips to model the fractions. Then describe how the values of the fractions change.**

**1.** $\frac{8}{8}, \frac{7}{8}, \frac{6}{8}, \frac{5}{8}, \frac{4}{8}$

**2.** $\frac{1}{12}, \frac{1}{10}, \frac{1}{8}, \frac{1}{6}, \frac{1}{4}$

**3.** $\frac{3}{3}, \frac{3}{4}, \frac{3}{5}, \frac{3}{6}, \frac{3}{7}$

**4.** $\frac{1}{2}, \frac{2}{2}, \frac{3}{2}, \frac{4}{2}, \frac{5}{2}$

# Problem Solving Strategy
## Work Backward

**PROBLEM** Jessica built a tower out of building blocks for a craft fair. She worked on her tower for three weeks. After three weeks, the tower was $\frac{9}{10}$ meter tall. This was $\frac{1}{5}$ meter taller than it was after two weeks. The height at two weeks was $\frac{1}{2}$ meter taller than it was after the first week. How tall was Jessica's tower after the first week?

**UNDERSTAND**

- What are you asked to find?

- What information will you use?

**PLAN**

- What strategy can you use to solve this problem?

  You can *work backward* to find out how tall Jessica's tower was after the first week.

**SOLVE**

- How can you work backward to solve?

  The growth can be shown by this equation: $n + \frac{1}{2} + \frac{1}{5} = \frac{9}{10}$.

  To work backward, start with $\frac{9}{10}$ and subtract.

  $$\frac{9}{10} - \frac{1}{5} - \frac{1}{2} = n$$

  $$\frac{9}{10} - \frac{2}{10} - \frac{5}{10} = n \quad \text{Find a common denominator.}$$

  $$\frac{7}{10} - \frac{5}{10} = n \quad \text{Subtract.}$$

  $$\frac{2}{10} = n, \text{ or } \frac{1}{5} = n$$

  So, Jessica's tower was $\frac{1}{5}$ meter tall after one week.

▲ Miniature model of Manhattan skyline

**CHECK**

- How can you determine if your answer is reasonable?

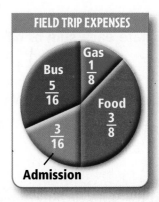

**Strategies**

Draw a Diagram or Picture
Make a Model or Act It Out
Make an Organized List
Find a Pattern
Make a Table or Graph
Predict and Test
▶ **Work Backward**
Solve a Simpler Problem
Write an Equation
Use Logical Reasoning

**Problem Solving**

**Work backward to solve.**

1. What if Jessica's tower was $\frac{11}{12}$ yard tall after 3 weeks? This was $\frac{1}{6}$ yard taller than it was after 2 weeks. The height at 2 weeks was $\frac{1}{4}$ yard taller than it was after the first week. How tall was the tower after the first week?

2. On Friday, Michael's plant was $\frac{5}{6}$ foot tall. It had grown $\frac{1}{3}$ foot from Wednesday to Friday. It had grown $\frac{3}{8}$ foot from Monday to Wednesday. How tall was Michael's plant on Monday?

3. Lisa came home from the toy store with $2.26. At the store she spent $7.38 on blocks, $4.17 on a book, and $8.55 on a science kit. She used a gift certificate worth $3.00 to help pay the bill. How much money did Lisa have before she went to the toy store?

**USE DATA** Mrs. Balog's class raised money for a field trip. The circle graph shows the field trip expenses.

4. Which expression shows what fraction of the money was used for the bus and gas?

   **A** $\frac{3}{16} - \frac{1}{8}$     **B** $\frac{5}{16} + \frac{1}{8}$     **C** $\frac{3}{16} + \frac{3}{8}$     **D** $\frac{5}{16} - \frac{1}{8}$

5. What fraction of the money was not for the bus and gas?

   **F** $\frac{5}{16}$     **G** $\frac{3}{8}$     **H** $\frac{7}{16}$     **J** $\frac{9}{16}$

**FIELD TRIP EXPENSES**

Bus $\frac{5}{16}$
Gas $\frac{1}{8}$
Food $\frac{3}{8}$
$\frac{3}{16}$
Admission

## Mixed Strategy Practice

6. Charity gave 12 baseball cards to Rhonda and 18 to James. Then she traded 5 of her cards for 3 of Andy's cards. Charity now has 48 cards. How many cards did she have to start with?

7. A rectangular fence has a perimeter of 20 feet. If the width is 2 feet, what is the length?

8. Carlotta bought 9 packages of lemonade for $1.10 each and 2 packages of cups for $1.09 each. She sold 23 cups of lemonade every hour for 4 hours at $0.40 per cup. How much more money did Carlotta earn than she spent on supplies?

9. Sherwood earned $35 last week. He earned twice as much for baby-sitting as he did for mowing lawns. He earned twice as much for mowing lawns as he did for washing cars. How much did Sherwood earn for each job?

# Extra Practice

## Set A (pp. 346–347)

**Find the sum or difference. Write it in simplest form.**

1. $\frac{3}{6} + \frac{1}{6}$
2. $\frac{4}{10} + \frac{1}{10}$
3. $\frac{1}{3} + \frac{2}{3}$
4. $\frac{3}{8} + \frac{4}{8}$

5. $\frac{1}{4} + \frac{2}{4}$
6. $\frac{4}{5} - \frac{1}{5}$
7. $\frac{5}{8} - \frac{3}{8}$
8. $\frac{5}{12} + \frac{2}{12}$

## Set B (pp. 348–351)

**Use fraction bars to find the sum or difference.**

1. $\frac{2}{5} + \frac{5}{10}$
2. $\frac{2}{4} + \frac{1}{6}$
3. $\frac{2}{8} + \frac{1}{4}$
4. $\frac{1}{6} + \frac{3}{9}$

5. $\frac{9}{10} - \frac{1}{2}$
6. $\frac{7}{8} - \frac{3}{4}$
7. $\frac{10}{12} - \frac{5}{6}$
8. $\frac{4}{5} - \frac{3}{10}$

## Set C (pp. 352–353)

**Estimate each sum or difference.**

1. $\frac{5}{6} - \frac{1}{8}$
2. $\frac{3}{7} + \frac{7}{9}$
3. $\frac{10}{11} - \frac{2}{4}$
4. $\frac{2}{3} + \frac{7}{8}$
5. $\frac{6}{10} - \frac{1}{5}$

**Estimate to compare. Write < or > for each ●.**

6. $\frac{2}{3} + \frac{3}{4}$ ● $\frac{4}{5} + \frac{1}{10}$
7. $\frac{5}{8} - \frac{1}{9}$ ● $\frac{4}{10} + \frac{5}{12}$
8. $\frac{5}{6} - \frac{3}{7}$ ● $0$

## Set D (pp. 354–355)

**Find the sum or difference. Write it in simplest form.**

1. $\frac{1}{3} + \frac{1}{6}$
2. $\frac{1}{5} + \frac{4}{10}$
3. $\frac{7}{8} - \frac{1}{4}$
4. $\frac{2}{3} + \frac{1}{4}$

5. $\frac{1}{3} + \frac{1}{4}$
6. $\frac{5}{8} - \frac{1}{2}$
7. $\frac{8}{9} - \frac{1}{3}$
8. $\frac{4}{5} - \frac{3}{4}$

## Set E (pp. 356–359)

**Find the sum or difference. Write it in simplest form.**

1. $\frac{2}{3} + \frac{2}{9}$
2. $\frac{1}{4} + \frac{3}{8}$
3. $\frac{1}{3} + \frac{2}{4}$
4. $\frac{4}{5} - \frac{1}{2}$
5. $\frac{8}{9} - \frac{2}{3}$

6. Eva used $\frac{3}{4}$ yard, $\frac{7}{8}$ yard, and $\frac{1}{2}$ yard of ribbon to make a hair bow. How much ribbon did she use?

7. The sauce has $\frac{3}{4}$ teaspoon basil, $\frac{1}{2}$ teaspoon oregano, and $\frac{3}{4}$ teaspoon parsley. How many teaspoons of herbs does the sauce have in all?

# Review/Test

## ✓ CHECK VOCABULARY AND CONCEPTS

Choose the best term from the box.

| denominators |
|---|
| numerators |
| least common denominator (LCD) |

1. The least common multiple of two or more denominators is the __?__. (p. 354)

2. When you add or subtract fractions with unlike denominators, first write equivalent fractions with like __?__. (p. 348)

## ✓ CHECK SKILLS

Estimate each sum or difference. (pp. 352–353)

3. $\frac{5}{6} - \frac{3}{8}$

4. $\frac{3}{9} + \frac{5}{8}$

5. $\frac{7}{8} - \frac{2}{3}$

6. $\frac{1}{3} + \frac{1}{5}$

Find the sum or difference. Write it in simplest form. (pp. 346–347, 348–351, 354–355, 356–359)

7. $\frac{2}{8} + \frac{4}{8}$

8. $\frac{7}{9} - \frac{4}{9}$

9. $\frac{4}{12} + \frac{2}{12}$

10. $\frac{5}{8} - \frac{1}{8}$

11. $\begin{array}{r} \frac{3}{4} \\ + \frac{2}{3} \\ \hline \end{array}$

12. $\begin{array}{r} \frac{3}{4} \\ - \frac{4}{6} \\ \hline \end{array}$

13. $\begin{array}{r} \frac{1}{2} \\ + \frac{4}{5} \\ \hline \end{array}$

14. $\begin{array}{r} \frac{2}{5} \\ - \frac{1}{3} \\ \hline \end{array}$

15. $\frac{1}{7} + \frac{1}{2}$

16. $\frac{4}{6} - \frac{1}{4}$

17. $1 - \frac{3}{8}$

18. $\frac{4}{5} - \frac{1}{4}$

19. $\frac{1}{4} + \frac{2}{3}$

20. $\frac{5}{8} - \frac{1}{3}$

21. $\frac{4}{5} + \frac{1}{3}$

22. $\frac{6}{7} - \frac{1}{3}$

## ✓ CHECK PROBLEM SOLVING (pp. 360–361)

23. On Friday, Kayla's bean plant was $\frac{7}{8}$ in. tall. It had grown $\frac{3}{8}$ in. from Wednesday to Friday. It had grown $\frac{1}{4}$ in. from Monday to Wednesday. How tall was the plant on Monday?

24. From 9 A.M. to 4 P.M., $\frac{1}{3}$ foot of snow fell on the mountain. At 8 P.M., the snow was $\frac{5}{6}$ foot deep, which was $\frac{1}{4}$ foot deeper than it was at 4 P.M. How much snow was on the ground at 9 A.M.?

25. Blaine has $2.05 left after going on a field trip. He spent $4.95 on lunch, $5.35 on a souvenir, and $12.65 on a T-shirt. How much money did Blaine have before he left for the field trip?

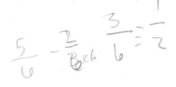

# Getting Ready for FCAT

 **NUMBER SENSE, CONCEPTS, AND OPERATIONS**

1. Carl went to the fair with $20.00. Admission to the fair was $4.50. While he was there, his friend Anna gave him $6.00. He spent $8.25 on food and rides. How much money did Carl have when he left the fair?

    A. $1.25

    B. $7.25

    C. $13.25

    D. $29.75

2. How long would it take the elevator of the Metropolitan Life Tower Building to go from the first floor to the top of the building if it moves 25 feet per second?

| FAMOUS NEW YORK CITY BUILDINGS | | |
|---|---|---|
| **Building** | **Number of Stories** | **Height (in feet)** |
| Park Row | 30 | 386 |
| Empire State | 103 | 1,250 |
| Metropolitan Life Tower | 50 | 700 |
| Chrysler | 77 | 1,047 |

    F. 2 seconds

    G. 28 seconds

    H. 50 seconds

    I. 200 seconds

3. **Explain It** Use the table in Problem 2. About how tall is each story in the Park Row Building? Explain how you found your answer.

 **ALGEBRAIC THINKING**

4. Haley created this pattern with triangles. If the pattern continues, how many triangles will be in the next figure?

    A. 12

    B. 13

    C. 14

    D. 15

> **TIP** **Check your work.**
> See item 4. Draw the next figure in the pattern. Count the triangles in the figure to see if it matches your answer choice.

5. Suppose *m* represents the number of miles from Jay's house to the mall. Which expression represents the number of miles in a round trip from Jay's house to the mall?

    F. $m - 2$

    G. $2 \times m$

    H. $2 + m$

    I. $m \div 2$

6. **Explain It** Rosa paid $108 for 9 cans of paint. If each can costs the same amount, how much did she pay for each can of paint? Write an equation with a variable to solve. Explain what the variable represents and how you solved the equation.

## ⭐ DATA ANALYSIS AND PROBABILITY

**7.** The circle graph shows the results of a survey about the type of transportation families use when they travel on vacation.

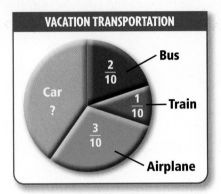

VACATION TRANSPORTATION

Which fraction of those surveyed travel by car?

**A.** $\frac{3}{10}$

**B.** $\frac{4}{10}$

**C.** $\frac{6}{10}$

**D.** $\frac{10}{10}$

**8.** There are 6 red marbles, 5 blue marbles, and 9 green marbles in a bag. What is the probability of drawing a marble that is NOT green?

**F.** $\frac{9}{11}$

**G.** $\frac{11}{20}$

**H.** $\frac{9}{20}$

**I.** $\frac{11}{9}$

**9. Explain It** Pete, Rose, and Sara are competing in the 50-yard dash. In how many different ways can they finish first, second, and third in the race? Explain your answer.

## ⭐ MEASUREMENT

**10.** The clock shows the time Wesley finished his homework. It took him 15 minutes to do his homework. At what time did Wesley begin his homework?

**A.** 3:45      **C.** 3:55

**B.** 3:50      **D.** 4:25

**11.** Jeff is not feeling well. Which tool would be **best** to measure his body temperature?

**F.**       **H.**

**G.**       **I.**

**12. Explain It** Yoriko drew this 2-inch line segment.

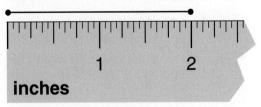

inches

ESTIMATE to determine whether the line segment is greater than or less than 8 centimeters. Explain how you know.

| 1 inch ≈ 2.5 centimeters |
| --- |

# Add and Subtract Mixed Numbers

**≣FAST FACT** • HEALTH Every year between 2,000 and 3,000 hikers set off with the intention of completing the Appalachian Trail. However, only 200 to 300 hikers are successful because it takes the average person more than six months to complete it.

PROBLEM SOLVING Look at the graph. How many more miles of the Appalachian Trail are in North Carolina than in Georgia?

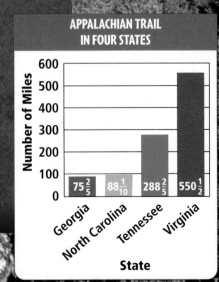

APPALACHIAN TRAIL IN FOUR STATES

| State | Number of Miles |
|-------|-----------------|
| Georgia | $75\frac{2}{5}$ |
| North Carolina | $88\frac{1}{10}$ |
| Tennessee | $288\frac{2}{5}$ |
| Virginia | $550\frac{1}{2}$ |

# CHECK WHAT YOU KNOW ✓

Use this page to help you review and remember
important skills needed for Chapter 17.

## ✓ UNDERSTAND MIXED NUMBERS

Write a mixed number for each picture.

1. 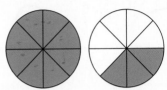   2. 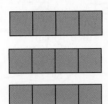   3.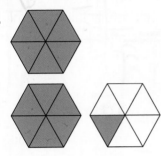

Rename each fraction as a mixed number. You may wish
to draw a picture.

4. $\frac{4}{3}$        5. $\frac{5}{2}$        6. $\frac{11}{5}$        7. $\frac{13}{4}$        8. $\frac{22}{5}$

## ✓ ADD AND SUBTRACT FRACTIONS

Find the sum or difference. Write it in simplest form.

9. $\begin{array}{r} \frac{3}{4} \\ +\frac{1}{4} \\ \hline \end{array}$
10. $\begin{array}{r} \frac{3}{5} \\ +\frac{4}{5} \\ \hline \end{array}$
11. $\begin{array}{r} \frac{5}{7} \\ -\frac{1}{2} \\ \hline \end{array}$
12. $\begin{array}{r} \frac{8}{9} \\ -\frac{2}{3} \\ \hline \end{array}$
13. $\begin{array}{r} \frac{1}{2} \\ +\frac{1}{3} \\ \hline \end{array}$

14. $\frac{2}{3} + \frac{5}{6}$
15. $\frac{2}{3} - \frac{1}{9}$
16. $\frac{7}{8} - \frac{1}{2}$
17. $\frac{1}{4} + \frac{2}{8}$
18. $\frac{3}{4} + \frac{2}{3}$

# VOCABULARY POWER ✓

## REVIEW

**mixed number** [mikst num′bər] *noun*

A mixed number is the combination of two types of numbers: a whole
number and a fraction. Give an example of a situation in which mixed
numbers are used.

 www.harcourtschool.com/mathglossary

# Add Mixed Numbers

## Quick Review

Find the least common denominator (LCD) for each pair of fractions.

1. $\frac{1}{2}$ and $\frac{1}{4}$    2. $\frac{1}{6}$ and $\frac{2}{3}$

3. $\frac{3}{4}$ and $\frac{3}{5}$    4. $\frac{7}{9}$ and $\frac{5}{6}$

5. $\frac{8}{11}$ and $\frac{4}{7}$

## ▶ Learn

**A MIGHTY PATH** From Georgia to Maine, the footpath called the Appalachian Trail winds for 2,168 miles across the ridges and valleys of the Appalachian Mountains. Madison and her family hiked $2\frac{3}{8}$ miles on the trail before lunch and $1\frac{1}{4}$ miles after lunch. How many miles did they hike in all?

### HANDS ON Activity

You can use fraction bars to find $2\frac{3}{8} + 1\frac{1}{4}$.

**MATERIALS:** fraction bars

**STEP 1**

Model the problem.

**STEP 2**

Find like fraction bars for $\frac{3}{8}$ and $\frac{1}{4}$. Add the fractions and add the whole numbers.

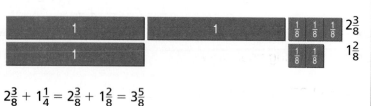

$$2\frac{3}{8} + 1\frac{1}{4} = 2\frac{3}{8} + 1\frac{2}{8} = 3\frac{5}{8}$$

So, Madison and her family hiked $3\frac{5}{8}$ miles.

• Use fraction bars to find the sum.

   **a.** $3\frac{1}{8} + 1\frac{3}{4}$          **b.** $1\frac{2}{5} + 1\frac{7}{10}$

   **c.** $2\frac{1}{3} + 2\frac{1}{4}$          **d.** $1\frac{2}{3} + 1\frac{1}{6}$

# Least Common Denominator

You can find and use the least common denominator (LCD) to add mixed numbers.

## Example

Find $2\frac{1}{3} + 1\frac{5}{12}$.

Estimate. $2\frac{1}{2} + 1\frac{1}{2} = 4$

**STEP 1**

Find the LCD. Write equivalent fractions.

$$2\frac{1}{3} = 2\frac{4}{12}$$
$$+1\frac{5}{12} = +1\frac{5}{12}$$

**STEP 2**

Add the fractions.

$$2\frac{1}{3} = 2\frac{4}{12}$$
$$+1\frac{5}{12} = +1\frac{5}{12}$$
$$\frac{9}{12}$$

**STEP 3**

Add the whole numbers. Write the answer in simplest form if needed.

$$2\frac{1}{3} = 2\frac{4}{12}$$
$$+1\frac{5}{12} = +1\frac{5}{12}$$
$$3\frac{9}{12} = 3\frac{3}{4}$$

So, $2\frac{1}{3} + 1\frac{5}{12} = 3\frac{3}{4}$. Since $3\frac{3}{4}$ is close to the estimate, 4, the answer is reasonable.

## More Examples

**A**

$$2\frac{2}{3} = 2\frac{10}{15}$$
$$+1\frac{4}{5} = +1\frac{12}{15}$$
$$3\frac{22}{15} = 3 + 1\frac{7}{15} = 4\frac{7}{15}$$

**B**

$$5\frac{7}{9} = 5\frac{7}{9}$$
$$+4\frac{1}{3} = +4\frac{3}{9}$$
$$9\frac{10}{9} = 10\frac{1}{9}$$

**C**

$$14\frac{3}{4} = 14\frac{9}{12}$$
$$+12\frac{1}{6} = +12\frac{2}{12}$$
$$26\frac{11}{12}$$

• Why is estimating a good method for checking your answer?

 **MATH IDEA** Make a model or use the LCD to add mixed numbers.

## Check

1. **Explain** why in Example B, $9\frac{10}{9}$ was renamed as $10\frac{1}{9}$.

**Find the sum in simplest form. Estimate to check.**

2. $1\frac{1}{4}$
   $+2\frac{1}{2}$

3. $2\frac{5}{8}$
   $+1\frac{1}{2}$

4. $5\frac{1}{3}$
   $+2\frac{1}{6}$

5. $4\frac{5}{9}$
   $+2\frac{2}{3}$

6. $8\frac{5}{6}$
   $+3\frac{1}{3}$

7. $4\frac{5}{12} + 1\frac{1}{6}$

8. $1\frac{1}{5} + 3\frac{2}{5}$

9. $9\frac{3}{4} + 8\frac{1}{2}$

10. $9\frac{4}{5} + 2\frac{3}{10}$

**LESSON CONTINUES** ▶

FCAT TESTED  SSS/GLEs MA.A.1.2.3.5.1 Translates problem situations into diagrams, models, and numerals using whole numbers, fractions, mixed numbers, decimals, and percents. *also* MA.A.3.2.1.5.3, MA.E.1.2.1.5.2

Chapter 17  **369**

Find the sum in simplest form. Estimate to check.

11. $4\frac{2}{3}$
$+2\frac{1}{3}$

12. $3\frac{1}{2}$
$+1\frac{1}{4}$

13. $5\frac{7}{9}$
$+3\frac{1}{3}$

14. $5\frac{2}{5}$
$+1\frac{3}{10}$

15. $4\frac{7}{12}$
$+1\frac{2}{3}$

16. $2\frac{3}{5}$
$+2\frac{3}{10}$

17. $3\frac{2}{3}$
$+4\frac{1}{12}$

18. $5\frac{1}{6}$
$+1\frac{11}{12}$

19. $2\frac{1}{8}$
$+3\frac{1}{2}$

20. $1\frac{1}{5}$
$+1\frac{3}{4}$

21. $7\frac{3}{4} + 4\frac{7}{12}$

22. $4\frac{5}{8} + 2\frac{1}{4}$

23. $5\frac{5}{8} + 2\frac{1}{4}$

24. $4\frac{3}{4} + 3\frac{5}{12}$

25. $6\frac{1}{3} + 3\frac{1}{4}$

26. $5\frac{11}{12} + 2\frac{1}{4}$

27. $4\frac{3}{4} + 2\frac{3}{8}$

28. $7\frac{1}{2} + 1\frac{1}{16}$

⭐**ALGEBRA**  Find the value of *n*. Identify the addition property used.

29. $0 + n = 3\frac{1}{2}$

30. $5\frac{1}{3} + 8 = n + 5\frac{1}{3}$

31. $\frac{2}{7} + (n + \frac{4}{7}) = (\frac{2}{7} + 6\frac{2}{7}) + \frac{4}{7}$

⭐**ALGEBRA**  Find the value of *n*.

32. $4\frac{4}{5} + n = 4\frac{4}{5}$

33. $n + n = 3\frac{1}{2}$

34. $n + 2\frac{3}{5} = 4$

35. $3\frac{1}{6} + n = 11\frac{5}{6}$

**USE DATA**  For 36–38, use the line graph.

The Appalachian Trail goes through Damascus in southwest Virginia. Damascus is known as the "friendliest town on the Appalachian Trail."

36. Does the precipitation in Damascus increase or decrease from January to March? Explain how you know.

37. Find the total precipitation for 3 consecutive months of the year, beginning in January.

38. 📓 Write a problem, using the information in the graph, that you can solve by adding mixed numbers.

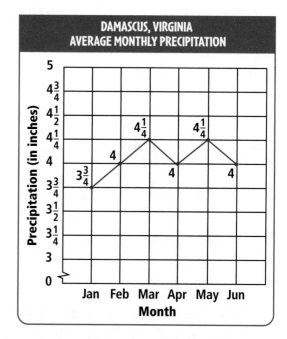

39. This week, Amanda worked $2\frac{1}{2}$ hours on Monday, $1\frac{2}{3}$ hours on Tuesday, and $2\frac{1}{3}$ hours on Wednesday. How many hours did she work this week?

40. **Vocabulary Power** Sometimes companies advertise that they will give a free estimate. Explain what a free estimate is.

**41.** A turnover recipe calls for $\frac{3}{4}$ cup of biscuit mix and $\frac{1}{2}$ cup of whole wheat flour. If Kevin doubles the recipe, what is the total number of cups of biscuit mix and flour he will need?

**42.** Felicia paid $4.80 for a roll of film and $11.52 for developing and prints. If she received 24 prints, how much did each print cost?

## Getting Ready for FCAT

**43.** Nicole and Tracey are sewing suits. The table at the right shows the number of yards of fabric needed for each size. If Nicole wears a size 6 jacket and a size 8 skirt, how many yards of fabric does she need to buy?

**A.** $3\frac{3}{8}$ yards

**B.** $3\frac{3}{4}$ yards

**C.** $3\frac{7}{8}$ yards

**D.** $4\frac{1}{4}$ yards

**44.** How many yards of fabric does Tracey need to buy if she wears a size 8 jacket and a size 8 skirt?

**F.** $3\frac{1}{2}$ yards

**G.** $3\frac{7}{8}$ yards

**H.** $4\frac{1}{8}$ yards

**I.** $4\frac{1}{4}$ yards

| YARDS OF FABRIC | | | |
|---|---|---|---|
| Size | 6 | 8 | 10 |
| Jacket | $2\frac{5}{8}$ | $2\frac{3}{4}$ | $2\frac{7}{8}$ |
| Skirt | $\frac{7}{8}$ | $1\frac{1}{8}$ | $1\frac{3}{8}$ |

# Problem Solving  LiNKUP ... to Reading

**STRATEGY • SEQUENCE**  Placing events in order, or in sequence, can help you solve a problem. Words like *first*, *next,* and *then* can help show the order. Compare the problem below with the sequence shown in the table.

Soccer practice starts at 3:00 P.M. Rosa played a practice game for $\frac{2}{3}$ hour at the end of practice. She spent the first part of the practice stretching. Then she spent $\frac{1}{3}$ hour passing the ball. Practice lasted $1\frac{1}{4}$ hours. What time did Rosa finish stretching?

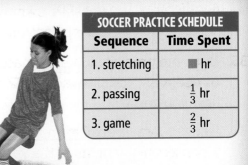

| SOCCER PRACTICE SCHEDULE | |
|---|---|
| Sequence | Time Spent |
| 1. stretching | ▮ hr |
| 2. passing | $\frac{1}{3}$ hr |
| 3. game | $\frac{2}{3}$ hr |

**1.** What must you find before you can find the time Rosa finished stretching? Solve the problem.

**2.** Steve went to the mall at 11:30 A.M. and arrived back home at 4:00 P.M. After shopping at the mall, he walked 30 min to get to the baseball field. He stayed at the field for 1 hr. Next, he walked 20 min to get home. What time did Steve leave the mall?

# Subtract Mixed Numbers

▶ **Learn**

**ALL ABOARD!**   Jacob collects model trains. He is setting up the track for one of his models. He bought $3\frac{1}{2}$ feet of new track, but $1\frac{1}{4}$ feet of it were damaged. How many feet of new track were not damaged?

**Example**  Subtract. $3\frac{1}{2} - 1\frac{1}{4}$

First, make an estimate. $3\frac{1}{2} - 1 = 2\frac{1}{2}$

**One Way**  Use a model.

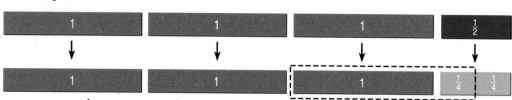

To subtract $1\frac{1}{4}$, replace the $\frac{1}{2}$ bar with $\frac{1}{4}$ bars.

Subtract $1\frac{1}{4}$.     $3\frac{1}{2} - 1\frac{1}{4} = 3\frac{2}{4} - 1\frac{1}{4} = 2\frac{1}{4}$

**Another Way**  Use the LCD.

$$3\frac{1}{2} = \phantom{-}3\frac{2}{4}$$
$$\underline{-1\frac{1}{4} = -1\frac{1}{4}}$$
$$\phantom{-}2\frac{1}{4}$$

Find the LCD. Write equivalent fractions.

Subtract the fractions and the whole numbers.

Write the difference in simplest form.

So, $2\frac{1}{4}$ feet of new track were not damaged. Since $2\frac{1}{4}$ is close to the estimate of $2\frac{1}{2}$, $2\frac{1}{4}$ is reasonable.

You can also use a calculator that operates with fractions to subtract mixed numbers.

▲ **The Toy Train Museum in Kenner, Louisiana**

            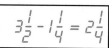

$3\frac{1}{2} - 1\frac{1}{4} = 2\frac{1}{4}$

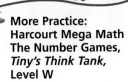

**Technology Link**

More Practice:
Harcourt Mega Math
The Number Games,
*Tiny's Think Tank,*
Level W

1. **Explain** how you can tell your answer is reasonable when subtracting mixed numbers.

**Find the difference in simplest form. Estimate to check.**

2. $5\frac{3}{4}$
   $-2\frac{1}{8}$

3. $9\frac{1}{2}$
   $-2\frac{2}{5}$

4. $5\frac{7}{9}$
   $-3\frac{1}{9}$

5. $3\frac{2}{3}$
   $-1\frac{5}{12}$

▷ **Practice and Problem Solving**  Extra Practice, page 380, Set B

**Find the difference in simplest form. Estimate to check.**

6. $7\frac{11}{12}$
   $-4\frac{5}{6}$

7. $5\frac{5}{8}$
   $-2\frac{1}{4}$

8. $6\frac{1}{3}$
   $-3\frac{1}{4}$

9. $4\frac{7}{10}$
   $-2\frac{3}{10}$

10. $8\frac{3}{5}$
    $-3\frac{3}{10}$

11. $5\frac{7}{12} - 4\frac{1}{3}$

12. $6\frac{3}{4} - 2\frac{5}{16}$

13. $3\frac{8}{9} - 1\frac{5}{9}$

14. $7\frac{3}{5} - 2\frac{1}{4}$

**ALGEBRA**  Find the value of *n*.

15. $n - 1\frac{1}{2} = 3$

16. $3\frac{5}{n} - 1\frac{3}{8} = 2\frac{1}{4}$

17. $4\frac{3}{5} - n = 1\frac{2}{15}$

18. $8\frac{n}{6} - 3\frac{1}{6} = 5\frac{2}{3}$

**USE DATA**  For 19–20, use the table.

19. How much longer is the S scale caboose than the HO scale caboose?

20. In which scale is the caboose $2\frac{7}{10}$ inches longer than a caboose in N scale?

| MODEL TRAIN CABOOSE SIZES | | | | | |
|---|---|---|---|---|---|
| Scale | O | S | HO | N | Z |
| Size (in.) | 6 | $4\frac{1}{2}$ | $3\frac{1}{3}$ | $1\frac{4}{5}$ | $\frac{3}{4}$ |

21. **? What's the Error?**  Marty compared the length of four Z scale cabooses with the length of one HO scale caboose. He said they are the same. Describe his error and write the correct answer.

**Getting Ready for FCAT**

22. Each week students volunteer at a local hospital. They record their hours in a table. Find the difference between the greatest number of volunteer hours and the least number of hours.

   **A.** $2\frac{1}{6}$ hours
   **C.** 3 hours
   **B.** $2\frac{1}{3}$ hours
   **D.** $3\frac{1}{6}$ hours

| MOUNT HOPE HOSPITAL | |
|---|---|
| **Student** | **Volunteer Hours** |
| George | $5\frac{2}{3}$ |
| Jake | $3\frac{1}{2}$ |
| Erica | $5\frac{1}{4}$ |
| Tina | $2\frac{5}{6}$ |
| Zach | $2\frac{1}{2}$ |

FCAT TESTED  SSS/GLEs MA.A.1.2.3.5.1 Translates problem situations into diagrams, models, and numerals using whole numbers, fractions, mixed numbers, decimals, and percents. *also* MA.A.3.2.1.5.3, MA.A.3.2.3.5.1

Chapter 17  **373**

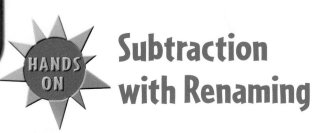

# Subtraction with Renaming

## Quick Review

Write each mixed number as a fraction.

**1.** $1\frac{1}{2}$    **2.** $1\frac{5}{6}$    **3.** $3\frac{3}{4}$

**4.** $2\frac{7}{9}$    **5.** $3\frac{6}{7}$

**MATERIALS**
fraction bars

▶ **Explore**

Sometimes you need to rename the whole number to subtract with mixed numbers.

**Activity 1** Find $2 - 1\frac{3}{8}$.

Model 2 by using two whole bars.

| 1 | 1 | 2 |

To subtract $1\frac{3}{8}$, model 2 another way by renaming one of the whole bars with eight $\frac{1}{8}$ bars.

| 1 | $\frac{1}{8}$ $\frac{1}{8}$ $\frac{1}{8}$ $\frac{1}{8}$ $\frac{1}{8}$ $\frac{1}{8}$ $\frac{1}{8}$ $\frac{1}{8}$ | $1\frac{8}{8}$ |

**STEP 3**

Subtract $1\frac{3}{8}$. Write the answer in simplest form.

| 1 | $\frac{1}{8}$ $\frac{1}{8}$ $\frac{1}{8}$ $\frac{1}{8}$ $\frac{1}{8}$ $\frac{1}{8}$ $\frac{1}{8}$ $\frac{1}{8}$ | $1\frac{8}{8} - 1\frac{3}{8}$ |

So, $2 - 1\frac{3}{8} = 1\frac{8}{8} - 1\frac{3}{8} = \frac{5}{8}$.

- In Step 2, why did 2 have to be renamed as $1\frac{8}{8}$?

## Try It

Use fraction bars to find the difference. Write it in simplest form.

**a.** $2\frac{1}{6} - 1\frac{4}{6}$     **b.** $6\frac{1}{4} - 2\frac{3}{4}$

**c.** $4\frac{3}{8} - 3\frac{7}{8}$     **d.** $7\frac{1}{3} - 2\frac{2}{3}$

How can you rename one whole bar to subtract $1\frac{4}{6}$?

▶ **Connect**

Sometimes you need to rename when the denominators are *unlike*.

**Activity 2** Find $2\frac{1}{3} - 1\frac{5}{6}$.

**STEP 1**

Model $2\frac{1}{3}$, using two whole bars and one $\frac{1}{3}$ bar.

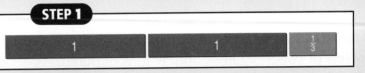

**STEP 2**

To subtract, think of the LCD for $\frac{5}{6}$ and $\frac{1}{3}$. Rename $\frac{1}{3}$ as $\frac{2}{6}$.

**STEP 3**

Rename one whole bar as $\frac{6}{6}$.
$2\frac{1}{3} = 1\frac{8}{6}$

**STEP 4**

Subtract $1\frac{5}{6}$. Write the answer in simplest form.
So, $2\frac{1}{3} - 1\frac{5}{6} = 1\frac{8}{6} - 1\frac{5}{6} = \frac{3}{6}$, or $\frac{1}{2}$.

 **MATH IDEA** When subtracting mixed numbers, you can rename part of the whole number as a fraction.

▶ **Practice and Problem Solving**

**Use fraction bars to find the difference. Write it in simplest form.**

1. $5\frac{2}{9} - 4\frac{1}{3}$  
2. $6\frac{5}{12} - 5\frac{3}{4}$  
3. $3\frac{1}{4} - 1\frac{3}{4}$  
4. $4\frac{2}{5} - 2\frac{1}{2}$

5. $3\frac{1}{8} - 2\frac{7}{8}$  
6. $4\frac{2}{3} - 2\frac{5}{6}$  
7. $8\frac{4}{10} - 2\frac{3}{5}$  
8. $3\frac{1}{2} - 2\frac{2}{3}$

9. ❓ **What's the Error?** Larry had $4\frac{1}{2}$ quarts of apple cider. He used $3\frac{4}{5}$ quarts for punch. Larry says that he has $1\frac{3}{10}$ quarts left. Describe his error and write the correct amount.

10. Kim's father drives $17\frac{1}{3}$ miles to work each day. Her mother drives 32 miles on a round-trip between home and work. How much farther is Kim's father's round-trip than her mother's?

11. ✏️ **Write About It** Explain how to find $2\frac{1}{3} - 1\frac{2}{3}$.

**Getting Ready for FCAT**

12. Heather bought $3\frac{1}{2}$ pounds of grapes and $2\frac{3}{4}$ pounds of cherries. How much more did the grapes weigh?

   **A.** $\frac{1}{4}$ pound  **B.** $\frac{1}{2}$ pound  **C.** $\frac{3}{4}$ pound  **D.** $1\frac{1}{2}$ pounds

# Practice with Mixed Numbers

**Quick Review**

Write each as a mixed number in simplest form.

**1.** $\dfrac{7}{6}$  **2.** $\dfrac{12}{8}$  **3.** $\dfrac{10}{3}$

**4.** $\dfrac{17}{5}$  **5.** $\dfrac{26}{6}$

▶ **Learn**

**PUMPKINS APLENTY**  A farmer produces crops of $4\frac{3}{4}$ tons of sweet potatoes and $5\frac{1}{3}$ tons of pumpkins. How many tons does the farmer produce in all?

## Example 1

Add. $4\frac{3}{4} + 5\frac{1}{3}$        Estimate. $5 + 5\frac{1}{2} = 10\frac{1}{2}$

| **STEP 1** | **STEP 2** | **STEP 3** |
|---|---|---|
| Find the LCD. Write equivalent fractions. $$\begin{aligned} 4\tfrac{3}{4} &= \ \ 4\tfrac{9}{12} \\ +5\tfrac{1}{3} &= +5\tfrac{4}{12} \end{aligned}$$ | Add the fractions. $$\begin{aligned} 4\tfrac{3}{4} &= \ \ 4\tfrac{9}{12} \\ +5\tfrac{1}{3} &= +5\tfrac{4}{12} \\ \hline &\quad\ \ \tfrac{13}{12} \end{aligned}$$ | Add the whole numbers. Write the answer in simplest form. $$\begin{aligned} 4\tfrac{3}{4} &= \ \ 4\tfrac{9}{12} \\ +5\tfrac{1}{3} &= +5\tfrac{4}{12} \\ \hline 9\tfrac{13}{12} &= 10\tfrac{1}{12} \end{aligned}$$ |

So, $10\frac{1}{12}$ tons of sweet potatoes and pumpkins were produced.

Since $10\frac{1}{12}$ is close to the estimate of $10\frac{1}{2}$, the answer is reasonable.

## Example 2

Subtract. $5\frac{1}{2} - 1\frac{2}{3}$        Estimate. $5\frac{1}{2} - 2 = 3\frac{1}{2}$

| **STEP 1** | **STEP 2** | **STEP 3** |
|---|---|---|
| Find the LCD. Write equivalent fractions. $$\begin{aligned} 5\tfrac{1}{2} &= \ \ 5\tfrac{3}{6} \\ -1\tfrac{2}{3} &= -1\tfrac{4}{6} \end{aligned}$$ | Rename the mixed numbers. Subtract the fractions. $$\begin{aligned} 5\tfrac{1}{2} &= \ \ 5\tfrac{3}{6} = \ \ 4\tfrac{9}{6} \\ -1\tfrac{2}{3} &= -1\tfrac{4}{6} = -1\tfrac{4}{6} \\ \hline && \tfrac{5}{6} \end{aligned}$$ | Subtract the whole numbers. Write the answer in simplest form. $$\begin{aligned} 5\tfrac{1}{2} &= \ \ 5\tfrac{3}{6} = \ \ 4\tfrac{9}{6} \\ -1\tfrac{2}{3} &= -1\tfrac{4}{6} = -1\tfrac{4}{6} \\ \hline && 3\tfrac{5}{6} \end{aligned}$$ |

So, $5\frac{1}{2} - 1\frac{2}{3} = 3\frac{5}{6}$. Since $3\frac{5}{6}$ is close to the estimate of $3\frac{1}{2}$, the answer is reasonable.

Pumpkins are warm-season crops that grow best during hot weather. ▶

1. **Explain** how you can check your answer when adding or subtracting fractions.

**Add or subtract. Write the answer in simplest form. Estimate to check.**

2. $2\frac{1}{4}$
$+4\frac{7}{16}$

3. $7\frac{1}{8}$
$-2\frac{1}{2}$

4. $1\frac{2}{3}$
$+1\frac{7}{9}$

5. $5\frac{9}{10}$
$-4\frac{4}{5}$

**Practice and Problem Solving** (Extra Practice, page 380, Set C)

**Add or subtract. Write the answer in simplest form. Estimate to check.**

6. $6\frac{1}{2}$
$+7\frac{3}{5}$

7. $4\frac{5}{8}$
$+2\frac{14}{16}$

8. $6\frac{1}{4}$
$-3\frac{10}{12}$

9. $5\frac{2}{3}$
$-1\frac{3}{4}$

10. $4\frac{3}{8} - 3\frac{7}{8}$

11. $4\frac{1}{3} + 2\frac{3}{4}$

12. $9\frac{3}{8} - 3\frac{12}{16}$

13. $2\frac{2}{7} + 1\frac{1}{2} + 1\frac{3}{7}$

14. $6\frac{4}{15} - 2\frac{1}{5}$

15. $3\frac{3}{20} + 5\frac{3}{10}$

16. $8\frac{1}{18} - 2\frac{4}{9}$

17. $1\frac{2}{5} + 4\frac{2}{3} + 1\frac{1}{3}$

 **Find the value of $n$.**

18. $4\frac{3}{8} + n = 6$

19. $n + 2\frac{1}{4} = 5$

20. $3\frac{1}{6} - 1\frac{2}{n} = 1\frac{1}{2}$

21. $n\frac{1}{3} + 1\frac{3}{4} = 4\frac{1}{12}$

22. Mrs. Kelly is making matching outfits. She needs $4\frac{1}{2}$ yards for her dress and 3 yards for her daughter's dress. If she buys 8 yards of fabric, will she have enough to make a matching doll dress that requires $\frac{1}{2}$ yard of fabric? Explain.

23. A 9-inch cake pan holds $5\frac{3}{4}$ cups of batter. Latasha's cake recipe makes 10 cups of batter. Will she need to use 2 pans or 3 pans? Explain.

24. **≡FAST FACT • SOCIAL STUDIES** The world's largest pumpkin in 2001 weighed 1,262 pounds. Was the weight of the pumpkin greater than or less than $10^3$ pounds?

**Getting Ready for FCAT** THINK SOLVE EXPLAIN

25. Dustin needs to buy two pieces of lumber to use in his greenhouse. One piece should be $5\frac{3}{4}$ feet and the other piece should be $4\frac{7}{8}$ feet. If the store sells lumber in the lengths shown, what length should he buy? Explain your answer.

LUMBER LENGTHS:
8 feet
10 feet
12 feet

FCAT TESTED SSS/GLEs MA.A.1.2.3.5.1 Translates problem situations into diagrams, models, and numerals using whole numbers, fractions, mixed numbers, decimals, and percents. *also* MA.A.3.2.1.5.3

Chapter 17 **377**

# Problem Solving Skill
## Multistep Probems

UNDERSTAND ▸ PLAN ▸ SOLVE ▸ CHECK

**Quick Review**

1. $1\frac{2}{3} + 1\frac{1}{3}$  2. $2\frac{1}{2} - 1\frac{1}{4}$

3. $3\frac{2}{5} + 2\frac{7}{10}$  4. $2\frac{3}{4} + 4\frac{5}{6}$

5. $5\frac{5}{8} - 3\frac{1}{4}$

**STEPPIN' OUT**  Kaitlin is making costumes for the dance recital. She made a table to keep track of the amount of fabric she buys and uses. Kaitlin forgot to record some of the information in the table. How many yards of fabric does she have left?

**FABRIC FOR COSTUMES**

| Fabric | Purchased | Used | Remaining |
|---|---|---|---|
| blue | $12\frac{7}{12}$ yd | $3\frac{5}{6}$ yd | ▪ |
| gold | $11\frac{3}{4}$ yd | ▪ | $9\frac{5}{12}$ yd |
| striped | ▪ | $5\frac{11}{12}$ yd | ▪ |
| TOTAL | 40 yd | ▪ | ▪ |

## Example

**STEP 1**

Find the amount of gold fabric used.

$11\frac{3}{4}$  gold fabric purchased

$-9\frac{5}{12}$  gold fabric remaining

$2\frac{1}{3}$ yd  gold fabric used

**STEP 2**

Add to find the total amount of fabric used.

$3\frac{5}{6}$  blue fabric used

$2\frac{1}{3}$  gold fabric used

$+5\frac{11}{12}$  striped fabric used

$12\frac{1}{12}$ yd  total fabric used

**STEP 3**

Subtract the total amount used from the total purchased.

$40$
$-12\frac{1}{12}$

$27\frac{11}{12}$ yd

So, she has $27\frac{11}{12}$ yd left.

A *multistep problem* requires more than one step to solve.

## Talk About It

• Is there another way this problem could have been solved? Explain.

• How could you find the amount of striped fabric Kaitlin has left?

1. **Explain** how you know when a problem requires more than one step to solve.

2. **What if** Kaitlin had used $4\frac{1}{6}$ yards of gold fabric and $4\frac{3}{4}$ yards of blue fabric? How many total yards of fabric would she have left?

**USE DATA** For 3–4, use the table. At Snyder's Dance Supply Store, Vince records how many dozens of each item are sold every day. Some entries are missing from Vince's record book for today's sales. Choose the best answer. Then copy and complete the table.

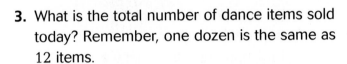

| SALES RECORDS | | | |
|---|---|---|---|
| Item | Start | Sold | Remaining |
| Tights | ■ | $10\frac{2}{3}$ | ■ |
| Sweat Pants | $8\frac{2}{3}$ | ■ | $2\frac{5}{6}$ |
| Leotards | $5\frac{5}{6}$ | $2\frac{1}{2}$ | ■ |
| TOTAL | 28 | ■ | ■ |

3. What is the total number of dance items sold today? Remember, one dozen is the same as 12 items.

   **A** 2,228   **B** 228   **C** 128   **D** 28

4. What is the total number of dance items that Snyder's Dance Supply Store has left?

   **F** 1,118   **G** 208   **H** 180   **J** 108

## Mixed Applications

**USE DATA** For 5–6, use the graph.

5. On average, how many more hours a week do girls spend doing homework than boys?

6. Find the average number of hours all students in this age group spend doing homework each week.

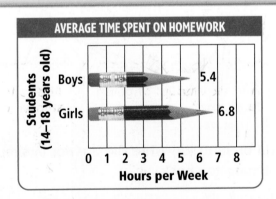

**AVERAGE TIME SPENT ON HOMEWORK**

Students (14–18 years old)

Boys 5.4
Girls 6.8

Hours per Week

7. Trina made a four-by-four grid. She colored the corner squares blue and any square that shared a side with a blue square green. The remaining squares she colored yellow. How many squares were colored green? yellow?

8. At the concession stand, customers can choose between a hot dog and a hamburger. The concession stand offers soda, lemonade, and water. How many different combinations of food and drink are there?

9. **What's the Question?** Ellen has a goal of running 12 miles this week. She ran $2\frac{1}{3}$ miles Monday, $3\frac{1}{2}$ miles Tuesday, and $4\frac{1}{4}$ miles Thursday. The answer is $1\frac{11}{12}$ miles.

FCAT TESTED ▸ SSS/GLEs MA.A.3.2.2.5.1 Uses problem-solving strategies to determine the operation(s) needed to solve one- and two-step problems involving addition, subtraction, multiplication, and division of whole numbers, and addition, subtraction, and multiplication of decimals and fractions.

Chapter 17 **379**

# Extra Practice

## Set A (pp. 368–371)

**Find the sum in simplest form.**
**Estimate to check.**

1. $2\frac{1}{2} + \frac{1}{6}$
2. $3\frac{2}{5} + 1\frac{1}{10}$
3. $4\frac{1}{3} + 2\frac{5}{9}$
4. $1\frac{5}{8} + 2\frac{1}{2}$

5. $6\frac{2}{3}$
   $+4\frac{1}{6}$
6. $5\frac{1}{4}$
   $+2\frac{1}{2}$
7. $7\frac{1}{4}$
   $+1\frac{4}{5}$
8. $9\frac{1}{3}$
   $+1\frac{1}{4}$
9. $10\frac{2}{5}$
   $+ 6\frac{1}{2}$

10. The contractor built $1\frac{1}{2}$ miles of road in June and $1\frac{1}{4}$ miles in July. How many miles of road did the contractor build in June and July?

11. Vic and his teammates had $1\frac{1}{10}$ hours to practice drills and run laps. If they ran for $\frac{2}{5}$ hour, how long did they practice drills?

## Set B (pp. 372–373)

**Find the difference in simplest form.**
**Estimate to check.**

1. $3\frac{5}{7} - 2\frac{3}{14}$
2. $10\frac{4}{5} - 6\frac{3}{10}$
3. $8\frac{1}{3} - 3\frac{5}{6}$
4. $5\frac{1}{2} - 2\frac{7}{12}$

5. $5\frac{1}{2}$
   $-2\frac{1}{3}$
6. $7\frac{5}{6}$
   $-6\frac{2}{3}$
7. $3\frac{3}{4}$
   $-1\frac{1}{2}$
8. $10\frac{7}{8}$
   $- 6\frac{1}{2}$
9. $12\frac{2}{3}$
   $- 4\frac{5}{6}$

## Set C (pp. 376–377)

**Add or subtract. Write the answer in simplest form.**
**Estimate to check.**

1. $4\frac{2}{3} + 5\frac{5}{6}$
2. $12\frac{1}{3} - 6\frac{5}{9}$
3. $7\frac{1}{5} + 8\frac{3}{4}$
4. $15\frac{1}{6} - 10\frac{3}{4}$

5. $2\frac{1}{8}$
   $+1\frac{3}{4}$
6. $7\frac{7}{9}$
   $-6\frac{2}{3}$
7. $14\frac{2}{3}$
   $- 5\frac{1}{2}$
8. $8\frac{7}{8}$
   $-5\frac{3}{4}$
9. $7\frac{1}{6}$
   $+4\frac{5}{9}$

10. There are $7\frac{7}{8}$ cups of flour in the canister. If $2\frac{1}{4}$ cups are used to make muffins, how much will be left?

11. Marilyn bought $4\frac{1}{2}$ pounds of hazelnut coffee and $2\frac{1}{4}$ pounds of chocolate-flavored coffee. How much coffee did she buy in all?

# Review/Test

##  CHECK VOCABULARY AND CONCEPTS

**Choose the best term from the box.**

| |
|---|
| least common denominator (LCD) |
| mixed numbers |
| renaming |
| simplest form |

1. When you add or subtract mixed numbers, make sure your answer is in __?__. (p. 368)

2. To add or subtract mixed numbers, first find the __?__ to make equivalent fractions. (p. 368)

3. When you change $9\frac{1}{4}$ to $8\frac{5}{4}$, you are __?__ the mixed number. (p. 374)

## CHECK SKILLS

**Find the sum in simplest form.** (pp. 368–371)

4. $3\frac{1}{4}$
$+6\frac{1}{8}$

5. $3\frac{5}{12}$
$+1\frac{1}{6}$

6. $5\frac{7}{8}$
$+3\frac{1}{4}$

7. $2\frac{1}{3}$
$+5\frac{8}{9}$

8. $6\frac{1}{8}$
$+1\frac{1}{4}$

**Find the difference in simplest form.** (pp. 372–373)

9. $4\frac{3}{4}$
$-1\frac{1}{7}$

10. $5\frac{17}{18}$
$-4\frac{8}{9}$

11. $10\frac{11}{12}$
$-5\frac{8}{9}$

12. $6\frac{1}{2}$
$-3\frac{2}{3}$

13. $9\frac{1}{6}$
$-3\frac{1}{2}$

**Find the sum or difference in simplest form.** (pp. 368–377)

14. $4\frac{1}{4} + 1\frac{1}{2}$

15. $5\frac{2}{5} + 3\frac{1}{2}$

16. $4\frac{3}{4} - 1\frac{1}{3}$

17. $8\frac{1}{8} - 4\frac{1}{4}$

## CHECK PROBLEM SOLVING (pp. 378–379)

18. Mary volunteered $3\frac{2}{3}$ hours on Monday, 5 hours on Tuesday, and $2\frac{1}{12}$ hours on Wednesday. How many more hours must she work to meet her weekly goal of 15 hours?

19. On April 3, Jan's plant was $3\frac{1}{4}$ in. tall and Bob's was $3\frac{3}{8}$ in. tall. On May 3, Jan's had grown to $8\frac{7}{8}$ in. and Bob's measured $8\frac{5}{8}$ in. Whose plant grew more during the month? How much more?

20. Sam's grandmother baked 2 apple pies and 1 peach pie. The family ate one apple pie and $\frac{1}{3}$ of the second apple pie. They ate $\frac{3}{8}$ of the peach pie. What part of the 3 pies is left?

# Getting Ready for FCAT

##  NUMBER SENSE, CONCEPTS, AND OPERATIONS

1. The table shows the amount of flour and sugar needed to make two kinds of bread.

| SOME BREAD INGREDIENTS | | |
|---|---|---|
| Type of Bread | Flour | Sugar |
| Banana | $1\frac{1}{2}$ cups | $\frac{3}{4}$ cup |
| Wheat | $2\frac{1}{4}$ cups | $\frac{1}{2}$ cup |

How many cups of flour are needed to make 1 loaf of banana bread and 1 loaf of wheat bread?

A. $3\frac{1}{4}$ cups     C. $3\frac{3}{4}$ cups

B. $3\frac{1}{2}$ cups     D. $4\frac{1}{4}$ cups

2. Use the table in Problem 1. How much more sugar is needed to make 2 loaves of banana bread than 2 loaves of wheat bread?

F. $\frac{1}{4}$ cup     H. $1\frac{1}{4}$ cups

G. $\frac{1}{2}$ cup     I. $2\frac{1}{2}$ cups

3. Ben wrote $\frac{1}{2}$ of his book report on Monday and $\frac{1}{3}$ on Tuesday. He finished the report on Wednesday. What part of the book report did he write on Wednesday?

A. $\frac{1}{6}$     B. $\frac{2}{5}$     C. $\frac{3}{5}$     D. $\frac{5}{6}$

4. **Explain It** Joe has 36 inches of wood trim. He wants to make a frame for a rectangular picture that is $7\frac{3}{4}$ inches by $10\frac{7}{8}$ inches. ESTIMATE to decide if he has enough trim to make a frame. Explain your answer.

##  MEASUREMENT

5. The clocks show the time Janet's airplane leaves Charlotte, North Carolina and the time it arrives in Miami, Florida.

How long is the flight?

F. 1 hour 5 minutes

G. 1 hour 55 minutes

H. 2 hours 5 minutes

I. 2 hours 55 minutes

6. Hannah placed a 10-ounce weight on one side of a balance. She placed 5 marbles on the other side of the balance. Each marble is the same weight.

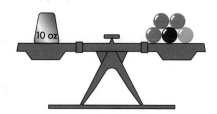

How much does each marble weigh?

A. 0.5 ounce

B. 2 ounces

C. 5 ounces

D. 50 ounces

7. **Explain It** Walter eats 3 meals a day, 7 days a week. ESTIMATE how many meals Walter eats in one year. Explain how you found your estimate.

**DATA ANALYSIS AND PROBABILITY**

**8.** The list shows the weights, in pounds, of some large dogs.

88, 94, 91, 79, 84, 99, 92, 90, 88

What is the median weight?

**F.** 88 pounds          **H.** 90 pounds

**G.** 89 pounds          **I.** 99 pounds

**9.** Look at the graph.

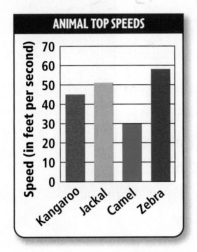

Which of the following statements is true about animal top speeds?

**A.** A kangaroo runs 45 feet in one minute.

**B.** A jackal runs almost as fast as a kangaroo.

**C.** A camel runs almost two times as fast as a zebra.

**D.** A zebra runs almost two times as fast as a camel.

**10. Explain It** Use the graph in Problem 9. Suppose a jackal runs for 30 seconds. How many seconds will a camel have to run to go the same distance? Explain your answer.

 **GEOMETRY AND SPATIAL SENSE**

**11.** Which two parts of this figure appear to be congruent?

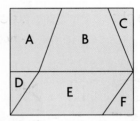

**F.** A and B          **H.** C and D

**G.** B and E          **I.** D and F

**12.** Becky plotted points A and B on the grid below.

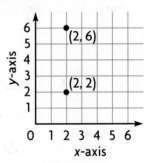

Which of these pairs of coordinates should Becky plot to make a rectangle?

**A.** (3,2) and (3,4)

**B.** (0,1) and (2,4)

**C.** (4,2) and (4,6)

**D.** (2,4) and (6,4)

**TIP** **Check your work.** See item 12. On a grid, plot the two ordered pairs in the diagram and the two ordered pairs in the answer you chose. If you can join the four points to form a rectangle, your answer is correct.

**13. Explain It** Which of the following letters do NOT have a line of symmetry? Explain how you know.

# F H L M T Z

# CHAPTER 18 Multiply Fractions

**≡FAST FACT • SOCIAL STUDIES**

In Ohio, more than 500 volunteer leaders helped begin and maintain 212 community gardens. Community and school gardens are becoming more and more popular. Gardeners are encouraged to share their harvest with a neighborhood family.

PROBLEM SOLVING   Look at the garden diagram. If $\frac{1}{4}$ of the garden is planted with tomatoes, how many square feet are planted with tomatoes?

| Tomatoes | Corn | Squash |
| Green beans | Green peppers | Lettuce |
| Peas | Flowers | |

20 feet

20 feet

Use this page to help you review and remember
important skills needed for Chapter 18.

## ✓ PARTS OF A WHOLE

Write a fraction to represent the shaded part.

**1.**

**2.**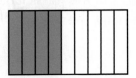

**3.**

**4.**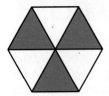

**5.**

**6.**

## ✓ RENAME FRACTIONS AND MIXED NUMBERS

Write the mixed number as a fraction. Write each fraction as
a mixed number.

**7.** $1\frac{4}{5}$

**8.** $2\frac{1}{3}$

**9.** $\frac{17}{5}$

**10.** $5\frac{1}{2}$

**11.** $\frac{14}{3}$

**12.** $\frac{25}{4}$

**13.** $1\frac{9}{10}$

**14.** $8\frac{5}{6}$

**15.** $\frac{31}{8}$

**16.** $2\frac{5}{9}$

**17.** $7\frac{3}{4}$

**18.** $\frac{22}{3}$

**19.** $9\frac{6}{7}$

**20.** $13\frac{1}{2}$

**21.** $\frac{31}{9}$

### REVIEW

**fraction** [frak′ shən] *noun*

*Fraction* comes from the Latin word *frangere,* which means "to break."
A fraction represents a broken part of a whole. Explain how this
meaning applies to the fraction $\frac{1}{4}$.

 www.harcourtschool.com/mathglossary

# Multiply a Fraction by a Fraction

**HIGH-STRUNG**   In an orchestra, $\frac{2}{3}$ of the musicians play stringed instruments. In the string section, $\frac{1}{4}$ of the musicians play the viola. What part of the orchestra plays the viola?

**Quick Review**

Write in simplest form.

1. $\frac{12}{21}$    2. $\frac{9}{24}$

3. $\frac{5}{15}$    4. $\frac{12}{16}$

5. $\frac{18}{30}$

**Example**   Multiply. $\frac{1}{4} \times \frac{2}{3}$

**One Way**   You can make a model to find the product.

**STEP 1**

Fold a piece of paper vertically into 3 equal parts. Color 2 columns to represent $\frac{2}{3}$ of the whole.

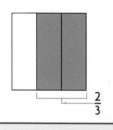

$\frac{2}{3}$

**STEP 2**

Fold the paper horizontally into fourths so that each of the thirds is divided into 4 equal parts.

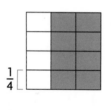

$\frac{1}{4}$

**STEP 3**

Use the other color to shade 1 of the fourths rows to represent $\frac{1}{4}$. The overlapped shading shows the product.

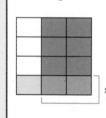

$\frac{2}{12}$

Since 2 of the 12 parts are shaded both colors, $\frac{1}{4}$ of $\frac{2}{3} = \frac{2}{12}$, or $\frac{1}{6}$.

• Look at the numerators and denominators of the factors and the product. What relationship do you see?

**Another Way**   You can compute the product $\frac{1}{4} \times \frac{2}{3}$.

**STEP 1**

Multiply the numerators. Then multiply the denominators.

$\frac{1}{4} \times \frac{2}{3} = \frac{1 \times 2}{4 \times 3} = \frac{2}{12}$

**STEP 2**

Write the product in simplest form.

$\frac{2 \div 2}{12 \div 2} = \frac{1}{6}$

So, $\frac{1}{6}$ of the musicians in the orchestra play the viola.

Some problems can be solved with mental math.

$\frac{2}{3} \times \frac{1}{5}$   Think: $2 \times 1 = 2$ and $3 \times 5 = 15$. So, $\frac{2}{3} \times \frac{1}{5} = \frac{2}{15}$.

⚡ **MATH IDEA**   To multiply a fraction by a fraction, multiply the numerators and then multiply the denominators. Write the product in simplest form.

1. **Explain** why the product of two fractions less than one is less than each of its factors.

**Find the product. Write it in simplest form.**

2. $\frac{1}{4} \times \frac{1}{3}$      3. $\frac{2}{3} \times \frac{1}{3}$      4. $\frac{1}{3} \times \frac{3}{4}$      5. $\frac{1}{5} \times \frac{2}{5}$      6. $\frac{1}{4} \times \frac{2}{5}$

▷ **Practice and Problem Solving**   ( Extra Practice, page 396, Set B )

**Find the product. Write it in simplest form.**

7. $\frac{2}{3} \times \frac{1}{5}$      8. $\frac{1}{5} \times \frac{1}{4}$      9. $\frac{1}{3} \times \frac{3}{5}$      10. $\frac{5}{6} \times \frac{3}{4}$      11. $\frac{1}{4} \times \frac{3}{4}$

12. $\frac{3}{7} \times \frac{2}{3}$      13. $\frac{8}{9} \times \frac{5}{6}$      14. $\frac{4}{5} \times \frac{8}{11}$      15. $\frac{7}{10} \times \frac{3}{8}$      16. $\frac{6}{7} \times \frac{11}{18}$

17. $\frac{2}{3} \times \frac{3}{4}$      18. $\frac{1}{5} \times \frac{3}{4}$      19. $\frac{2}{7} \times \frac{1}{2}$      20. $\frac{7}{8} \times \frac{4}{5}$      21. $\frac{5}{6} \times \frac{1}{3}$

**Write the number sentence each model represents.**

22.       23.       24.       25.

26. ✏️ **Write About It**  Explain how to multiply $\frac{3}{8} \times \frac{1}{3} \times \frac{2}{3}$. Then find the product.

28. Mel ate $\frac{1}{3}$ of $\frac{1}{2}$ of the pizza. Sue ate $\frac{1}{2}$ of $\frac{1}{4}$ of the pizza. Who ate more pizza? Explain.

29. **Vocabulary Power** Some words have several meanings. Write a mathematical and a nonmathematical definition for *product*.

27. Of the 50 students in the school band, $\frac{2}{5}$ play woodwind instruments. In the woodwind section, $\frac{1}{2}$ of the students play the clarinet. How many students play the clarinet?

**Getting Ready for FCAT**

30. Tom had $\frac{3}{4}$ pound of ground beef. He used $\frac{2}{3}$ of it to make burgers. How much ground beef did Tom use?

    A. $\frac{1}{12}$ pound      C. $\frac{5}{8}$ pound

    B. $\frac{1}{2}$ pound       D. $\frac{11}{12}$ pound

31. Maggie grated $\frac{2}{3}$ cup of cheese for a casserole. The recipe said to set aside $\frac{1}{2}$ of the cheese for the topping. How much of the cheese did she set aside?

    F. $\frac{1}{3}$ cup       H. $\frac{1}{6}$ cup

    G. $\frac{1}{2}$ cup       I. $\frac{1}{4}$ cup

FCAT TESTED  SSS/GLEs MA.A.3.2.3 The student adds, subtracts, and multiplies whole numbers, decimals and fractions, including mixed numbers . . . . *also* MA.A.1.2.3

Chapter 18  **387**

# Multiply Fractions and Whole Numbers

**Learn**

**BAKER'S DOZEN** A chef is making 3 batches of doughnuts. The recipe calls for $\frac{3}{4}$ cup of sugar for each batch. How many cups of sugar does the chef need?

## Example

Find $3 \times \frac{3}{4}$, or 3 groups of $\frac{3}{4}$.

**One Way** You can draw a picture.

| STEP 1 | STEP 2 | STEP 3 |
|---|---|---|
| Use circles to show 3 groups of $\frac{3}{4}$. 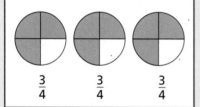 $\frac{3}{4}$   $\frac{3}{4}$   $\frac{3}{4}$ | Count the shaded fourths. 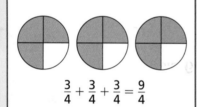 $\frac{3}{4} + \frac{3}{4} + \frac{3}{4} = \frac{9}{4}$ | Write the answer as a mixed number. 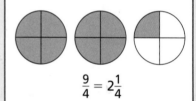 $\frac{9}{4} = 2\frac{1}{4}$ |

**Another Way** You can multiply.

| STEP 1 | STEP 2 | STEP 3 |
|---|---|---|
| Write the whole number as a fraction. Think: $3 = \frac{3}{1}$   $\frac{3}{1} \times \frac{3}{4}$ | Multiply the numerators. Then multiply the denominators. $\frac{3 \times 3}{1 \times 4} = \frac{9}{4}$ | Write the answer as a mixed number. $\frac{9}{4} = 2\frac{1}{4}$ |

So, the chef needs $2\frac{1}{4}$ cups of sugar.

## More Examples

**A**

$$12 \times \frac{2}{3} = \frac{12}{1} \times \frac{2}{3}$$
$$= \frac{12 \times 2}{1 \times 3}$$
$$= \frac{24 \div 3}{3 \div 3} = \frac{8}{1} = 8$$

**B**

$$\frac{2}{5} \times 3 = \frac{2}{5} \times \frac{3}{1}$$
$$= \frac{2 \times 3}{5 \times 1}$$
$$= \frac{6}{5}, \text{ or } 1\frac{1}{5}$$

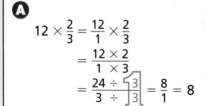

**Technology Link**

More Practice: Harcourt Mega Math Fraction Action, *Number Line Mine,* Level L

1. **Explain** how to draw a model to show the product $4 \times \frac{2}{3}$.

**Write the multiplication number sentence each model represents.**

2.

3.

4.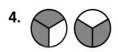

**Find the product.**

5. $\frac{1}{4} \times 8$

6. $6 \times \frac{2}{3}$

7. $\frac{3}{5} \times 5$

8. $\frac{1}{4} \times 15$

9. $15 \times \frac{2}{5}$

► **Practice and Problem Solving**    Extra Practice, page 396, Set A

**Write the multiplication number sentence each model represents.**

10.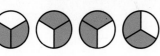

11.

12.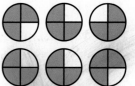

**Find the product.**

13. $\frac{3}{5} \times 25$

14. $\frac{2}{3} \times 15$

15. $\frac{2}{9} \times 8$

16. $16 \times \frac{7}{8}$

17. $20 \times \frac{2}{5}$

18. $30 \times \frac{5}{6}$

19. $\frac{3}{7} \times 10$

20. $14 \times \frac{5}{7}$

21. $9 \times \frac{3}{8}$

22. $\frac{2}{7} \times 35$

**ALGEBRA** Find the missing digit.

23. $\frac{\blacksquare}{2} \times 8 = 4$

24. $\frac{1}{2} \times \blacksquare = 30$

25. $\frac{1}{\blacksquare} \times 18 = 3$

26. $\frac{2}{9} \times 27 = \blacksquare$

**Evaluate each expression. Then write $<$, $>$, or $=$ for each ●.**

27. $\frac{1}{2} \times 14$ ● $\frac{1}{3}$ of 27

28. $\frac{2}{3} \times 21$ ● $\frac{1}{4} \times 24$

29. $\frac{3}{4} \times 16$ ● $\frac{1}{5}$ of 60

30. **? What's the Question?** Cyd saved $20 in quarters. The answer is 80 quarters.

31. Don is making 4 batches of fig bars and 3 batches of date bars. He needs $\frac{2}{3}$ c sugar for each batch. How much sugar does he need?

32. **REASONING** Will the product of a fraction less than one and a whole number be less than or greater than the whole number? Explain.

**Getting Ready for FCAT**

33. Of the 60 students in the Robinsville School orchestra, how many students play a brass instrument?

    **A.** 10

    **C.** 15

    **B.** 12

    **D.** 30

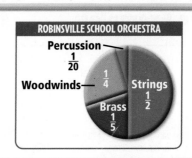

ROBINSVILLE SCHOOL ORCHESTRA
Percussion $\frac{1}{20}$
Woodwinds $\frac{1}{4}$
Strings $\frac{1}{2}$
Brass $\frac{1}{5}$

# Multiply Fractions and Mixed Numbers

▶ **Learn**

**CHEF'S GARDEN** Maria's parents run a bed-and-breakfast inn. They grow fresh produce in their garden, on $1\frac{1}{3}$ acres. They planted $\frac{1}{4}$ of the garden with herbs. How many acres of herbs did they plant?

**Remember**

You can write a mixed number as a fraction.

$$2\frac{1}{3} = 2 + \frac{1}{3} = \frac{6}{3} + \frac{1}{3} = \frac{7}{3}$$

## Example

Multiply.   $\frac{1}{4} \times 1\frac{1}{3}$

**One Way** Use models to multiply fractions and mixed numbers.

| **STEP 1** | **STEP 2** | **STEP 3** |
|---|---|---|
| Show 2 whole squares. Divide each square into thirds. Shade 1 whole square and $\frac{1}{3}$ of the other square yellow to show $1\frac{1}{3}$, or $\frac{4}{3}$. | Divide the squares into fourths the other way. Each of the squares is now divided into twelfths. | Shade $\frac{1}{4}$ of each whole square blue. The overlapped shading shows the product. $\frac{3}{12} + \frac{1}{12} = \frac{4}{12}$, or $\frac{1}{3}$ |

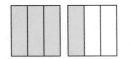

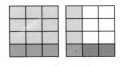

**Another Way** Compute the product $\frac{1}{4} \times 1\frac{1}{3}$.

| **STEP 1** | **STEP 2** | **STEP 3** |
|---|---|---|
| Rename the mixed number as a fraction. Think: $1\frac{1}{3} = \frac{4}{3}$ $\frac{1}{4} \times 1\frac{1}{3} = \frac{1}{4} \times \frac{4}{3}$ | Multiply. $\frac{1}{4} \times \frac{4}{3} = \frac{1 \times 4}{4 \times 3} = \frac{4}{12}$ | Write the product in simplest form. $\frac{4 \div 4}{12 \div 4} = \frac{1}{3}$ |

So, they planted $\frac{1}{3}$ acre of herbs.

## More Examples

**A**   $1\frac{1}{2} \times \frac{3}{4} = \frac{3}{2} \times \frac{3}{4} = \frac{9}{8}$, or $1\frac{1}{8}$

**B**   $\frac{2}{3} \times 3\frac{2}{5} = \frac{2}{3} \times \frac{17}{5} = \frac{34}{15}$, or $2\frac{4}{15}$

1. **Explain** how multiplying a fraction and a mixed number is different from multiplying a fraction by a fraction.

**Find the product. Draw fraction squares as needed.**

2. $\frac{1}{3} \times 1\frac{1}{5}$   3. $\frac{1}{2} \times 1\frac{2}{3}$   4. $\frac{1}{2} \times 2\frac{2}{5}$   5. $\frac{3}{5} \times 1\frac{1}{2}$   6. $2\frac{1}{4} \times \frac{1}{6}$

▶ **Practice and Problem Solving**   Extra Practice, page 396, Set C

**Find the product. Draw fraction squares as needed.**

7. $\frac{3}{4} \times 1\frac{1}{6}$   8. $\frac{2}{5} \times 3\frac{2}{3}$   9. $3\frac{1}{5} \times \frac{1}{4}$   10. $4\frac{1}{2} \times \frac{1}{9}$   11. $\frac{1}{4} \times 2\frac{1}{5}$

12. $\frac{1}{3} \times 3\frac{5}{8}$   13. $\frac{5}{12} \times 2\frac{2}{5}$   14. $6\frac{1}{4} \times \frac{3}{8}$   15. $5\frac{6}{7} \times \frac{1}{10}$   16. $\frac{1}{9} \times 3\frac{1}{2}$

17. $\frac{1}{2} \times 5\frac{3}{5}$   18. $1\frac{1}{8} \times \frac{2}{3}$   19. $\frac{1}{4} \times 6\frac{2}{7}$   20. $2\frac{5}{6} \times \frac{1}{9}$   21. $\frac{2}{5} \times 5\frac{1}{3}$

22. $3\frac{3}{4} \times \frac{1}{5}$   23. $4\frac{1}{6} \times \frac{1}{12}$   24. $\frac{3}{8} \times 2\frac{5}{6}$   25. $\frac{1}{3} \times 6\frac{3}{5}$   26. $4\frac{1}{4} \times \frac{2}{3}$

27. $\frac{2}{5} \times 4\frac{3}{4}$   28. $\frac{3}{7} \times 2\frac{1}{3}$   29. $1\frac{3}{4} \times \frac{2}{9}$   30. $3\frac{1}{5} \times \frac{1}{7}$   31. $\frac{5}{6} \times 2\frac{1}{3}$

32. ▤**FAST FACT** • **SCIENCE** Strawberries are the only fruit with seeds on the outside. One strawberry has about 200 seeds! At the market, strawberries cost $3.00 a pound. If you paid for $1\frac{1}{4}$ pounds with a $5 bill, how much change would you receive?

33. Chef Leo bought $1\frac{1}{2}$ pints of strawberries. He used $\frac{3}{4}$ of the strawberries to make tarts. How many pints of strawberries does he have left?

34. ✎ **Write a problem** about finding a fractional part of $3\frac{1}{2}$ dozen apples. Solve the problem.

▶ **Getting Ready for** ⭐**FCAT**

35. Brandon had a piece of lumber $11\frac{1}{4}$ feet long. He used $\frac{1}{3}$ of the lumber for a shelf. How long was the shelf?

   **A.** $3\frac{1}{4}$ feet   **C.** $3\frac{3}{4}$ feet

   **B.** $3\frac{1}{2}$ feet   **D.** $7\frac{1}{2}$ feet

**FCAT TESTED** SSS/GLEs MA.A.3.2.3 The student adds, subtracts, and multiplies whole numbers, decimals and fractions, including mixed numbers . . . . *also* MA.A.1.2.3, MA.E.1.2.1.5.5

**Chapter 18   391**

# Multiply with Mixed Numbers

**Quick Review**

1. $\dfrac{6 \div \blacksquare}{8 \div \blacksquare} = \dfrac{3}{4}$

2. $\dfrac{9 \div \blacksquare}{12 \div \blacksquare} = \dfrac{3}{4}$

3. $\dfrac{6 \div 6}{12 \div 6} = \dfrac{\blacksquare}{\blacksquare}$

4. $\dfrac{21 \div 7}{7 \div 7} = \dfrac{\blacksquare}{\blacksquare}$

5. $\dfrac{18 \div 6}{6 \div 6} = \dfrac{\blacksquare}{\blacksquare}$

## ▶ Learn

**PLAN AHEAD** To multiply two mixed numbers, follow the same steps you use to multiply a fraction and a mixed number.

**Example 1**  Multiply.  $2\frac{1}{4} \times 1\frac{2}{3}$

**STEP 1**

Rename both mixed numbers as fractions greater than 1.

$2\frac{1}{4} \times 1\frac{2}{3} = \frac{9}{4} \times \frac{5}{3}$

**STEP 2**

Multiply.

$\frac{9}{4} \times \frac{5}{3} = \frac{9 \times 5}{4 \times 3} = \frac{45}{12}$

**STEP 3**

Write the product as a mixed number in simplest form.

$\frac{45}{12} = 3\frac{9}{12} = 3\frac{3}{4}$

Sometimes you can simplify the factors by dividing by a common factor of a numerator and a denominator.

**Example 2**  Multiply.  $2\frac{1}{7} \times 1\frac{1}{6}$

$2\frac{1}{7} \times 1\frac{1}{6} = \dfrac{\overset{5}{\cancel{15}} \times \overset{1}{\cancel{7}}}{\underset{1}{\cancel{7}} \times \underset{2}{\cancel{6}}}$

$= \frac{5}{2}$, or $2\frac{1}{2}$

Look for a numerator and denominator with common factors.

Divide 15 and 6 by their GCF, 3.

Divide 7 and 7 by their GCF, 7.

**Remember**

The greatest common factor, or GCF, is the greatest number that is a factor of two or more numbers.

18: 1, 2, 3, 6, 9, 18
12: 1, 2, 3, 4, 6,12

GCF = 6

You can also use a calculator to multiply mixed numbers.
Find $7\frac{1}{4} \times 5\frac{3}{4}$.

  7 $a$ 1 b/c 4 × 5 $a$ 3 b/c 4 = | = $41\frac{11}{16}$

## ▶ Check

1. **Explain** how you can use division with a common factor before you compute $4 \times 5\frac{1}{4}$.

**Copy and complete each problem. Show how to simplify before you multiply.**

2. $4\frac{2}{3} \times 1\frac{3}{7} = \frac{14}{3} \times \frac{10}{7} = \frac{14 \times 10}{3 \times 7} = \blacksquare$

3. $2\frac{1}{2} \times 5\frac{1}{3} = \frac{5}{2} \times \frac{16}{3} = \frac{5 \times 16}{2 \times 3} = \blacksquare$

**Multiply. Write the answer in simplest form.**

**4.** $4\frac{1}{3} \times 2\frac{1}{2}$      **5.** $3\frac{3}{4} \times 1\frac{1}{10}$      **6.** $4\frac{1}{2} \times 1\frac{2}{3}$      **7.** $6 \times 3\frac{2}{3}$      **8.** $5\frac{1}{3} \times 3\frac{3}{4}$

## Practice and Problem Solving   Extra Practice, page 396, Set D

**Copy and complete each problem. Show how to simplify before you multiply.**

**9.** $2\frac{1}{4} \times 3\frac{2}{3} = \frac{9}{4} \times \frac{11}{3} = \frac{9 \times 11}{4 \times 3} = \blacksquare$      **10.** $3\frac{1}{3} \times 2\frac{2}{5} = \frac{10}{3} \times \frac{12}{5} = \frac{10 \times 12}{3 \times 5} = \blacksquare$

**Multiply. Write the answer in simplest form.**

**11.** $4\frac{2}{3} \times 1\frac{1}{2}$      **12.** $3\frac{1}{3} \times 2\frac{2}{5}$      **13.** $2\frac{3}{8} \times 1\frac{2}{5}$      **14.** $\frac{1}{2} \times 2\frac{2}{3}$      **15.** $\frac{4}{5} \times \frac{5}{6}$

**16.** $\frac{3}{8} \times 24$      **17.** $1\frac{2}{3} \times \frac{1}{4}$      **18.** $1\frac{1}{4} \times \frac{5}{6}$      **19.** $1\frac{1}{6} \times 4\frac{2}{3}$      **20.** $14 \times \frac{3}{7}$

**21.** $4 \times 2\frac{1}{3} \times \frac{1}{2}$      **22.** $3\frac{1}{5} \times \frac{2}{3} \times \frac{1}{4}$      **23.** $\frac{1}{6} \times 2\frac{2}{3} \times 1\frac{1}{3}$      **24.** $7\frac{1}{4} \times \frac{1}{2} \times 2\frac{1}{2}$

**Solve the equation. Identify the multiplication property used.**

**25.** $1\frac{1}{2} \times 3\frac{3}{4} = 3\frac{3}{4} \times n$      **26.** $(6\frac{3}{8} \times 8\frac{1}{3}) \times 4 = 6\frac{3}{8} \times (n \times 4)$      **27.** $5\frac{1}{4} \times n = 0$

**USE DATA For 28–30, use the circle graph.**

**28.** If Bob spent $\frac{1}{5}$ of his time at school in art class, how long was his art class?

**29.** Bob spent a quarter of his free time surfing the Internet. How much free time did he have left for other things?

**30.** How much more sleep time did he have than free time?

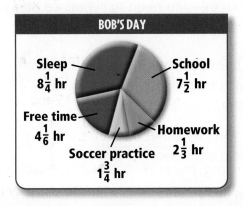

BOB'S DAY

Sleep $8\frac{1}{4}$ hr

School $7\frac{1}{2}$ hr

Free time $4\frac{1}{6}$ hr

Homework $2\frac{1}{3}$ hr

Soccer practice $1\frac{3}{4}$ hr

**31.**  **ALGEBRA**   Find $n$ if $\clubsuit = 2$, $\diamond = 2 \times \clubsuit$, $\heartsuit = \diamond \times 2$, and $\frac{\clubsuit}{\diamond} = \frac{n}{\heartsuit}$.

**32.** Write About It How is multiplying fractions different from adding fractions?

## Getting Ready for FCAT

**33.** Crystal is making flags for her class election campaign. Each flag is $7\frac{1}{2}$ inches wide and $4\frac{2}{3}$ inches high. How much fabric does she need for each flag?

   **A.** $24\frac{1}{3}$ square inches

   **B.** $28\frac{1}{3}$ square inches

   **C.** 32 square inches

   **D.** 35 square inches

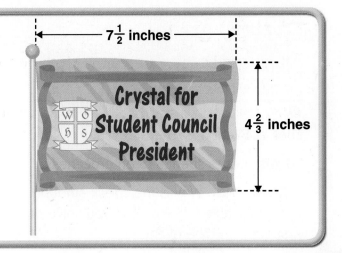

$7\frac{1}{2}$ inches

Crystal for Student Council President

$4\frac{2}{3}$ inches

FCAT TESTED   SSS/GLEs MA.A.3.2.3 The student adds, subtracts, and multiplies whole numbers, decimals and fractions, including mixed numbers . . . . *also* MA.A.1.2.3

Chapter 18   **393**

# Problem Solving Skill
## Sequence and Prioritize Information

**Quick Review**
1. $5 ÷ 2
2. $10 ÷ 10
3. $4.20 ÷ 4
4. $3.75 ÷ 3
5. $20 × \frac{3}{4}$

**UNDERSTAND** ❯ **PLAN** ❯ **SOLVE** ❯ **CHECK**

**BUDGET YOUR BUCKS!** Ms. James saved $\frac{1}{4}$ of her paycheck in the bank. Then she paid bills with half of what was left. She used a third of her remaining cash for tickets to a concert. After she went grocery shopping, she had $30 left. Her paycheck was $300. How much did she spend on groceries?

**MATH IDEA** Sometimes to solve a problem, you need to put events in order of time and importance—you need to *sequence and prioritize information*.

First, prioritize your information: The answer depends on the fact that Ms. James's check was for $300.

Then you can make a list or a table to sequence the amounts she spent.

| EXPENSE TABLE | | |
|---|---|---|
| Event | Amount Used | Balance |
| 1. She started with $300. | 0 | $300 |
| 2. She saved $\frac{1}{4}$ in bank. | $300 × $\frac{1}{4}$ = $75 | $300 – $75 = $225 |
| 3. She paid bills with $\frac{1}{2}$ of what was left. | $225 × $\frac{1}{2}$ = $112.50 | $225 – $112.50 = $112.50 |
| 4. She spent $\frac{1}{3}$ on concert tickets. | $112.50 × $\frac{1}{3}$ = $37.50 | $112.50 – $37.50 = $75 |
| 5. She bought groceries. | ■ | $75 – ■ = $30 |
| 6. She had $30 left. | 0 | $30 |

Look at Event 5. $75 − $45 = $30

So, Ms. James spent $45 on groceries.

• **REASONING** Why is the check amount an important fact in the problem? Why can't you solve the problem without sequencing the events?

## Problem Solving Practice

**Sequence and prioritize information to solve.**

1. **What if** Ms. James's paycheck had been for $350? How much would she have spent on groceries?

2. The United States produced 569 movies in one year. In the same year, England made $\frac{1}{2}$ the number of movies that France made and 499 fewer than the United States made. How many movies did France make that year?

**The compact disc (CD) was invented 273 years after the piano. The tape recorder was invented in 1898. Thomas Edison invented the phonograph 21 years before the tape recorder and 95 years before the compact disc.**

3. Which invention's date will you use to find the dates of all the others?

   **A** tape recorder
   **B** compact disc
   **C** piano
   **D** phonograph

4. Which list is in sequence from earliest invention to latest invention?

   **F** recorder, piano, phonograph, CD
   **G** piano, phonograph, CD, recorder
   **H** phonograph, piano, recorder, CD
   **J** piano, phonograph, recorder, CD

## Mixed Applications

**For 5–7, use the map.**

5. Morgan left home and drove 127 miles to Jacksonville. Then she continued 339 miles to Charlotte. In what city on the map does Morgan live?

6. Charlie drove from Nashville to Miami to attend college. About how many miles did he drive?

7. Lucy visits her grandparents in Asheville twice a year. If she lives in Savannah, about how many miles does she travel each year for these visits?

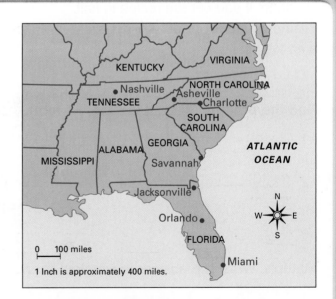

8. The Cineplex has 16 theaters. Each theater shows a different movie. Each movie is played 7 times a day on Saturdays and Sundays. How many shows are there in one weekend?

9. **NUMBER SENSE** Jim chose a number. Then he multiplied it by 3, added 5, and divided the sum by 2. After he subtracted 4 from the quotient, he got 6. What number did Jim choose?

**FCAT TESTED** SSS/GLEs MA.A.3.2.3.5.1 Solves real-world problems involving addition, subtraction, multiplication, and division of whole numbers, and addition, subtraction, multiplication of decimals, fractions, and mixed numbers . . . . *also* MA.A.I.2.3

**Chapter 18 395**

# Extra Practice

## Set A (pp. 386–387)

**Find the product.**

1. $\frac{2}{5} \times 10$
2. $\frac{1}{4} \times 12$
3. $15 \times \frac{3}{5}$
4. $\frac{4}{7} \times 28$
5. $32 \times \frac{5}{8}$

6. $30 \times \frac{5}{6}$
7. $\frac{7}{8} \times 16$
8. $\frac{3}{4} \times 20$
9. $\frac{1}{2} \times 22$
10. $24 \times \frac{1}{3}$

11. There are 15 cars in a parking lot. Of the 15 cars, $\frac{1}{3}$ are red. How many of the cars in the parking lot are red?

12. Mike has 22 baseball cards. Of the 22 cards, $\frac{1}{2}$ show rookie players. How many of the cards show rookie players?

## Set B (pp. 388–389)

**Find the product. Write it in simplest form.**

1. $\frac{3}{4} \times \frac{5}{6}$
2. $\frac{2}{3} \times \frac{4}{5}$
3. $\frac{3}{4} \times \frac{1}{3}$
4. $\frac{1}{3} \times \frac{3}{5}$
5. $\frac{3}{8} \times \frac{2}{3}$

6. $\frac{3}{10} \times \frac{1}{6}$
7. $\frac{1}{5} \times \frac{5}{12}$
8. $\frac{2}{3} \times \frac{5}{6}$
9. $\frac{5}{8} \times \frac{2}{5}$
10. $\frac{2}{3} \times \frac{3}{5}$

11. A muffin recipe calls for $\frac{3}{4}$ cup of flour. If you cut the recipe in half, how much flour do you need?

12. Julie bought $\frac{3}{4}$ yard of fabric. She used $\frac{1}{3}$ of it to make a doll dress. How much fabric does she have left?

## Set C (pp. 390–391)

**Find the product. Write it in simplest form.**

1. $\frac{1}{2} \times 1\frac{1}{2}$
2. $2\frac{1}{3} \times \frac{1}{4}$
3. $\frac{4}{5} \times 2\frac{1}{6}$
4. $2\frac{1}{2} \times \frac{2}{3}$
5. $\frac{3}{4} \times 3\frac{1}{2}$

6. $\frac{3}{4} \times 1\frac{2}{3}$
7. $2\frac{1}{3} \times \frac{1}{5}$
8. $\frac{5}{6} \times 3\frac{1}{5}$
9. $1\frac{3}{4} \times \frac{4}{7}$
10. $2\frac{1}{2} \times \frac{5}{8}$

## Set D (pp. 392–393)

**Multiply. Write the answer in simplest form.**

1. $2\frac{1}{4} \times 1\frac{2}{3}$
2. $3\frac{2}{3} \times 4\frac{1}{2}$
3. $1\frac{7}{8} \times 2\frac{2}{5}$
4. $2\frac{2}{3} \times 4\frac{1}{2}$
5. $4 \times 1\frac{7}{8}$

6. $3\frac{1}{2} \times 2\frac{3}{5}$
7. $1\frac{5}{7} \times 3\frac{1}{3}$
8. $4\frac{1}{3} \times 6\frac{3}{4}$
9. $5\frac{1}{4} \times 3\frac{2}{5}$
10. $2\frac{5}{8} \times 4\frac{2}{3}$

11. LaKeshia is training for a track meet. She walks $5\frac{3}{4}$ mi every day. How many miles does she walk in one week?

# Review/Test

## ✓ CHECK CONCEPTS

Write the multiplication number sentence each model represents.
(pp. 386–389)

1.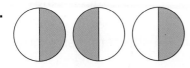

2.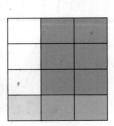

3.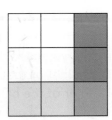

## ✓ CHECK SKILLS

Find the product. Write it in simplest form. (pp. 386–393)

4. $\frac{2}{5} \times 50$

5. $6 \times \frac{4}{9}$

6. $\frac{3}{4} \times 16$

7. $2 \times \frac{3}{10}$

8. $\frac{1}{3} \times \frac{1}{4}$

9. $\frac{3}{4} \times \frac{1}{2}$

10. $\frac{1}{6} \times \frac{3}{5}$

11. $\frac{1}{7} \times \frac{2}{3}$

12. $\frac{1}{6} \times \frac{2}{7}$

13. $\frac{1}{2} \times \frac{3}{10}$

14. $\frac{3}{8} \times \frac{1}{4}$

15. $\frac{2}{9} \times \frac{1}{4}$

16. $\frac{1}{2} \times 2\frac{1}{5}$

17. $3\frac{3}{4} \times \frac{1}{3}$

18. $\frac{5}{6} \times 5\frac{1}{2}$

19. $4\frac{1}{2} \times \frac{3}{7}$

20. $1\frac{2}{3} \times 3\frac{1}{5}$

21. $4 \times 2\frac{5}{8}$

22. $3\frac{1}{4} \times 1\frac{3}{5}$

23. $2\frac{2}{5} \times 3\frac{3}{4}$

## ✓ CHECK PROBLEM SOLVING

Sequence and prioritize information to solve. (pp. 394–395)

24. Colin has 2 hours before dinner is ready. He does homework for $\frac{3}{4}$ hour, plays basketball for $\frac{3}{4}$ hour, and then plays a computer game until dinner. How long does he play the computer game?

25. Karen had 100 beads. She used $\frac{3}{5}$ of the beads to make necklaces. Then she used $\frac{1}{2}$ of the leftover beads to make earrings. She used the rest to make a bracelet. How many beads are on the bracelet?

# Getting Ready for FCAT

 ## NUMBER SENSE, CONCEPTS, AND OPERATIONS

> **TIP**  **Get the information you need.**
> See item 1. To find the height of the can of tennis balls, you need the height of each ball. The height of the ball is the same as the diameter of the ball.

**1.** A tennis ball has a diameter of $2\frac{5}{8}$ inches. There are 3 tennis balls in a can. What is the least possible height for a can of tennis balls?

**A.** $5\frac{5}{8}$ inches     **C.** $7\frac{5}{8}$ inches

**B.** $6\frac{7}{8}$ inches     **D.** $7\frac{7}{8}$ inches

**2.** Use the data in the table. How much more does a tennis ball weigh than a golf ball?

| WEIGHTS OF BALLS | |
|---|---|
| **Ball** | **Weight (in ounces)** |
| Baseball | $4\frac{4}{5}$ |
| Tennis ball | 2 |
| Golf ball | $1\frac{3}{5}$ |

**F.** $1\frac{2}{5}$ ounces     **H.** $\frac{2}{5}$ ounce

**G.** $1\frac{3}{5}$ ounces     **I.** $\frac{3}{5}$ ounce

**3. Explain It** A bottle of cranberry juice that holds $40\frac{3}{4}$ ounces is $\frac{2}{3}$ full. Is there enough juice in the bottle to fill two 12-ounce glasses? Explain how you know.

## ALGEBRAIC THINKING

**4.** The table shows how much Cindy will earn if she mows up to 5 lawns. How much will she earn if she mows 8 lawns?

| AMOUNT EARNED MOWING LAWNS | |
|---|---|
| **Number of Lawns** | **Amount Earned** |
| 1 | $9 |
| 2 | $18 |
| 3 | $27 |
| 4 | $36 |
| 5 | $45 |

**A.** $54

**B.** $63

**C.** $72

**D.** $81

**5.** Suppose the number of students in a class is represented by $x$. Which expression shows the number of students present on Tuesday?

| STUDENTS ABSENT | | | | | |
|---|---|---|---|---|---|
| **Day** | M | T | W | Th | F |
| **Number Absent** | 1 | 4 | 3 | 2 | 5 |

**F.** $x + 4$

**G.** $x - 4$

**H.** $4 - x$

**I.** $4x$

**6. Explain It** Alex had 40¢. He bought a pencil and gave the cashier three of the same coin to pay for it. Then he had a quarter left. What coins did Alex give the cashier? Explain how you know.

## GEOMETRY AND SPATIAL SENSE

**7.** Which line is perpendicular to $\overleftrightarrow{BE}$?

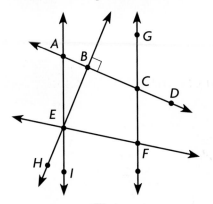

**A.** $\overleftrightarrow{AE}$

**B.** $\overleftrightarrow{DE}$

**C.** $\overleftrightarrow{AD}$

**D.** $\overleftrightarrow{AI}$

**8.** Use the drawing in Exercise 7. Which of these is an obtuse angle?

**F.** angle ADE

**G.** angle HEF

**H.** angle CBE

**I.** angle DAB

**9.** What part of the figure below does the letter C name?

**A.** a side

**B.** a vertex

**C.** a plane

**D.** a base

**10. Explain It** Rita said that Figure 2 shows a reflection of Figure 1. Did she name the transformation correctly? Explain your answer.

Figure 1

Figure 2

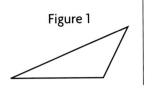
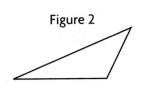

 ## MEASUREMENT

**11.** The Johnsons marked Frank's height on the doorway every year on his birthday.

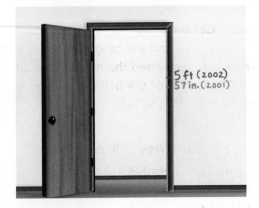

How much did Frank grow from 2001 to 2002?

**F.** 1 inch

**G.** 3 inches

**H.** 7 inches

**I.** 11 inches

**12.** How long is line segment AB?

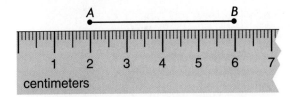

**A.** 5 centimeters

**B.** 4 centimeters

**C.** 5 millimeters

**D.** 4 millimeters

**13. Explain It** Elena has solved the first three of the 20 math problems in her homework. To solve the problems, it took her $1\frac{1}{2}$ minutes, $1\frac{1}{4}$ minutes, and $1\frac{1}{2}$ minutes. If each of the remaining problems take about the same amount of time, about how long will it take her to solve all 20 problems? Explain your answer.

# Divide Fractions

**FAST FACT • SOCIAL STUDIES**

The explorers, Meriwether Lewis and William Clark, crossed into Idaho in August 1805. They traveled over mountains and took canoes down rock-strewn rapids on the Snake River.

PROBLEM SOLVING Today people ride the same rapids as Lewis and Clark rode. With stops for resting and lunch, a team of rafters averages $\frac{3}{4}$ mile per hour down Milner Gorge. About how long will the trip take?

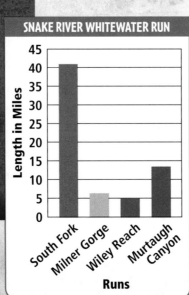

**SNAKE RIVER WHITEWATER RUN**

Length in Miles

45
40
35
30
25
20
15
10
5
0

South Fork   Milner Gorge   Wiley Reach   Murtaugh Canyon

Runs

Use this page to help you review and remember
important skills needed for Chapter 19.

## RENAME FRACTIONS AND MIXED NUMBERS

Write each fraction as a mixed number. Write each
mixed number or whole number as a fraction.

1. $\frac{13}{3}$     2. $\frac{7}{4}$     3. $\frac{46}{5}$     4. $\frac{28}{8}$     5. $\frac{17}{6}$

6. $3$     7. $1\frac{1}{6}$     8. $4$     9. $7\frac{1}{2}$     10. $7$

11. $\frac{16}{5}$     12. $4\frac{2}{3}$     13. $6$     14. $\frac{31}{8}$     15. $2\frac{3}{5}$

## MULTIPLY FRACTIONS

Find the product. Write it in simplest form.

16. $\frac{1}{3} \times \frac{3}{4}$     17. $\frac{2}{3} \times \frac{1}{6}$     18. $\frac{2}{5} \times \frac{3}{8}$     19. $\frac{1}{2} \times \frac{2}{6}$     20. $\frac{7}{8} \times \frac{3}{5}$

21. $\frac{1}{8} \times \frac{3}{4}$     22. $\frac{3}{5} \times \frac{1}{2}$     23. $\frac{5}{6} \times \frac{1}{3}$     24. $\frac{1}{9} \times \frac{3}{4}$     25. $\frac{3}{8} \times \frac{2}{3}$

26. $\frac{5}{8} \times \frac{1}{5}$     27. $\frac{1}{9} \times \frac{2}{5}$     28. $\frac{1}{4} \times \frac{5}{6}$     29. $\frac{6}{10} \times \frac{1}{5}$     30. $\frac{3}{4} \times \frac{1}{12}$

## VOCABULARY POWER

**REVIEW**

**inverse** [in´vərs] *adjective*

In math, *inverse* means "opposite." For
example, two inverse operations that are
opposites are addition and subtraction,
since $5 + 8 = 13$ and $13 - 5 = 8$. Give
an example to show that multiplication and
division are inverse operations.

**PREVIEW**

reciprocal

ON-LINE

www.harcourtschool.com/mathglossary

**HANDS ON**

# Explore Division of Fractions

## ▶ Explore

Kari has 2 yards of ribbon to use for a craft project.
She needs to cut the ribbon into pieces that are $\frac{1}{3}$ yard long.
How many pieces of ribbon will Kari have?

### Activity 1

Divide 2 by $\frac{1}{3}$.　　$2 \div \frac{1}{3}$

Use fraction bars to show how many thirds are in 2.

---

**STEP 1**

Model the bars for 2.
Model the bar for $\frac{1}{3}$.

| 1 | 1 |

| $\frac{1}{3}$ |

---

**STEP 2**

See how many $\frac{1}{3}$ bars are equal to 2 whole bars.
So, six $\frac{1}{3}$ bars are equal to 2 whole bars.

| 1 | 1 |

| $\frac{1}{3}$ | $\frac{1}{3}$ | $\frac{1}{3}$ | $\frac{1}{3}$ | $\frac{1}{3}$ | $\frac{1}{3}$ |

---

**STEP 3**

Record a number sentence for the model.

$2 \div \frac{1}{3} = 6$

---

So, Kari will have 6 pieces of ribbon.

## Try It

**Write a number sentence for each model.**

**a.**

| 1 |
| $\frac{1}{5}$ |

**b.**

| 1 |
| $\frac{1}{8}$ | $\frac{1}{8}$ |

How many $\frac{1}{4}$ bars are equal to 1 whole bar?

**Use fraction bars to find the quotient.**

**c.** $1 \div \frac{1}{4}$　　**d.** $3 \div \frac{1}{6}$　　**e.** $5 \div \frac{1}{2}$

You can also use fraction bars to help you divide a fraction by a fraction.

**Technology Link**
More Practice: Harcourt Mega Math
Fraction Action, *Fraction Flare Up*,
Level O

**Activity 2**  Divide $\frac{1}{2}$ by $\frac{1}{8}$.  $\frac{1}{2} \div \frac{1}{8}$

**STEP 1**

Model $\frac{1}{2}$ and $\frac{1}{8}$ with fraction bars.

**STEP 2**

See how many $\frac{1}{8}$ bars are equal to a $\frac{1}{2}$ bar.

So, four $\frac{1}{8}$ bars are equal to a $\frac{1}{2}$ bar.

**STEP 3**

Record a number sentence for the model.

$\frac{1}{2} \div \frac{1}{8} = 4$

▶ **Practice and Problem Solving**

**Write a division number sentence for each model.**

**1.**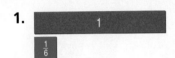

**2.**

**3.**

**Use fraction bars to find the quotient.**

**4.** $\frac{9}{10} \div \frac{1}{10}$

**5.** $1 \div \frac{1}{3}$

**6.** $\frac{3}{4} \div \frac{3}{12}$

**7.** $5 \div \frac{2}{4}$

**8.** $\frac{3}{4} \div \frac{1}{4}$

**9.** $3 \div \frac{2}{8}$

**10.** $\frac{1}{3} \div \frac{1}{6}$

**11.** $\frac{10}{2} \div \frac{1}{2}$

**12.** Cindy used $\frac{3}{4}$ yard of wire to make earrings. Each pair of earrings took $\frac{1}{12}$ yard of wire and sold for \$2.98. If she sold all the earrings, how much money would Cindy earn?

**13.** **REASONING**  If you divide $\frac{1}{10}$ of a dollar into parts that are each $\frac{1}{100}$ of a dollar, how many parts are there? What are they called?

**14.** Compare the answers for **a** and **b**. What did you find?  **a.** $12 \times \frac{4}{3}$  **b.** $12 \div \frac{3}{4}$

**Getting Ready for FCAT**

**15.** What division number sentence does the model show?

**A.** $2 \div 5 = n$

**C.** $2 \div \frac{2}{5} = n$

**B.** $2 \div \frac{1}{5} = n$

**D.** $2\frac{2}{5} \div 5 = n$

**FCAT TESTED**  SSS/GLEs MA.A.1.2.3 Understands concrete and symbolic representations of whole numbers, fractions, decimals, and percents in real-world situations.

**Chapter 19  403**

# Reciprocals

▷ **Learn**

**WORKING FOR PEANUTS!** Hanh and three friends visited the elephant exhibit at the zoo. Hanh divided a 4-pound bag of peanuts into four smaller bags. He put $\frac{1}{4}$ of the peanuts into each bag. How many pounds of peanuts did Hanh put into each bag?

Think: $\frac{1}{4}$ of $4 \rightarrow \frac{1}{4} \times 4 = \frac{1}{4} \times \frac{4}{1}$

$$= \frac{4}{4} = 1$$

So, Hanh put 1 pound of peanuts into each bag.

The product of a number and its **reciprocal** is 1. $\frac{1}{4}$ and 4 are reciprocals because $\frac{1}{4} \times 4 = 1$.

 **MATH IDEA** To write the reciprocal of a fraction, write a new fraction by exchanging the numerator and denominator.

### Quick Review

Write each whole number or mixed number as a fraction.

1. 6     2. $2\frac{2}{3}$

3. $1\frac{7}{10}$     4. $4\frac{3}{8}$     5. 2

### VOCABULARY

reciprocal

---

## Examples

**Ⓐ** The reciprocal of $2\frac{2}{3}$, or $\frac{8}{3}$, is $\frac{3}{8}$.

$$\frac{8}{3} \times \frac{3}{8} = \frac{24}{24} = 1$$

**Ⓑ** The reciprocal of 6, or $\frac{6}{1}$, is $\frac{1}{6}$.

$$\frac{6}{1} \times \frac{1}{6} = \frac{6}{6} = 1$$

**Ⓒ** The reciprocal of $\frac{14}{7}$ is $\frac{7}{14}$.

$$\frac{\overset{1}{\cancel{14}}}{\underset{1}{\cancel{7}}} \times \frac{\overset{1}{\cancel{7}}}{\underset{1}{\cancel{14}}} = \frac{1}{1} = 1$$

---

▷ **Check**

1. **Explain** how to find the reciprocal of 3 and the reciprocal of $3\frac{5}{8}$.

**Are the two numbers reciprocals? Write _yes_ or _no._**

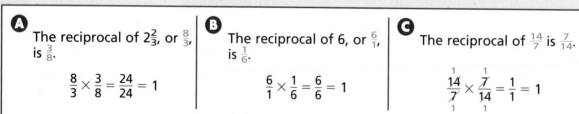

2. $\frac{5}{4}$ and $\frac{4}{5}$     3. $\frac{1}{7}$ and $\frac{7}{3}$     4. $\frac{1}{8}$ and 8     5. $\frac{5}{7}$ and $1\frac{2}{5}$     6. $2\frac{3}{4}$ and $12\frac{4}{3}$

**Are the two numbers reciprocals? Write *yes* or *no*.**

**7.** $\frac{5}{9}$ and $\frac{9}{5}$     **8.** $\frac{3}{10}$ and $\frac{10}{3}$     **9.** 4 and $\frac{1}{4}$     **10.** $\frac{3}{4}$ and $3\frac{1}{3}$     **11.** $2\frac{1}{4}$ and $\frac{4}{9}$

**Write the reciprocal of each number.**

**12.** $\frac{3}{5}$     **13.** $1\frac{3}{4}$     **14.** $\frac{1}{9}$     **15.** $\frac{12}{7}$     **16.** 7

**17.** 12     **18.** $3\frac{1}{5}$     **19.** $\frac{23}{6}$     **20.** $\frac{1}{13}$     **21.** $\frac{2}{9}$

**ALGEBRA**    **Find the value of *n*.**

**22.** $\frac{1}{8} \times \frac{n}{1} = 1$    **23.** $\frac{1}{n} \times \frac{6}{1} = 1$    **24.** $\frac{8}{9} \times \frac{n}{8} = 1$    **25.** $\frac{7}{n} \times \frac{4}{7} = 1$    **26.** $8 \times \frac{1}{n} = 1$

**27.** $5 \times \frac{1}{n} = 1$    **28.** $\frac{9}{28} \times 3\frac{1}{n} = 1$    **29.** $\frac{1}{n} \times \frac{n}{1} = 1$    **30.** $5\frac{2}{3} \times \frac{n}{17} = 1$    **31.** $\frac{2}{n} \times 3\frac{1}{2} = 1$

**Multiply. Use the Associative and Commutative Properties to help you.**

**32.** $\frac{1}{5} \times \frac{5}{1} \times \frac{2}{7}$      **33.** $\frac{7}{8} \times \frac{6}{1} \times \frac{8}{7}$      **34.** $\frac{2}{5} \times \frac{5}{6} \times \frac{5}{2}$

**35.** $\frac{1}{5} \times \frac{11}{4} \times \frac{4}{11} \times 5$      **36.** $\frac{3}{4} \times \frac{10}{3} \times \frac{3}{10} \times 8$      **37.** $\frac{3}{2} \times \frac{2}{3} \times \frac{2}{3} \times 9$

**Which is greater, the number or its reciprocal?**

**38.** $\frac{1}{5}$      **39.** 8      **40.** $\frac{4}{7}$      **41.** $1\frac{1}{2}$      **42.** $\frac{97}{98}$

**43.** **? What's the Error?** Blair said that the reciprocal of $3\frac{1}{3}$ is $\frac{3}{7}$. Describe and correct her error.

**44.** **? What's the Question?** Christy has $\frac{3}{4}$ pound of peanuts. Alex has $\frac{4}{3}$ pounds of peanuts. The answer is $\frac{7}{12}$. What is the question?

**45.** **REASONING** If a number is greater than 1, what can you say about its reciprocal?

**46.** Mr. Ross bought 1.5 pounds of tomatoes for spaghetti sauce and 8 ounces for salad. Tomatoes cost $2.49 a pound. How much did Mr. Ross pay for the tomatoes?

**Getting Ready for FCAT**

**47.** On the first day of the trip, Jason hiked $\frac{3}{4}$ of the way from Base Camp to Warm Springs. Sara hiked from Base Camp to High Rocks. How much farther did Sara hike?

   **A.** 1 mile      **C.** $\frac{1}{2}$ mile

   **B.** $1\frac{1}{4}$ mile      **D.** $\frac{1}{4}$ mile

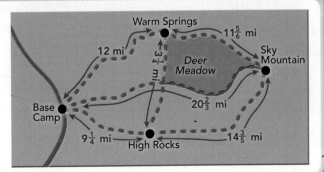

# Divide Whole Numbers By Fractions

**Quick Review**

Write each fraction as a whole number or a mixed number.

1. $\frac{6}{1}$   2. $\frac{14}{3}$

3. $\frac{8}{2}$   4. $\frac{9}{4}$   5. $\frac{13}{10}$

▶ **Learn**

**SLOW MOTION**   If a giant tortoise walks $\frac{1}{5}$ mile per hour, how many hours will it take the tortoise to walk 2 miles?

**Example 1**

Find $2 \div \frac{1}{5}$.   ←**Think:** How many $\frac{1}{5}$ miles are in 2 miles?

**One Way**   Use a model.

| 1 | 1 |
|---|---|

| $\frac{1}{5}$ | $\frac{1}{5}$ | $\frac{1}{5}$ | $\frac{1}{5}$ | $\frac{1}{5}$ | $\frac{1}{5}$ | $\frac{1}{5}$ | $\frac{1}{5}$ | $\frac{1}{5}$ | $\frac{1}{5}$ |

**Another Way**   Use patterns.

$2 \times \frac{1}{1} = 2$     $2 \div 1 = 2$

$2 \times \frac{2}{1} = 4$     $2 \div \frac{1}{2} = 4$

$2 \times \frac{3}{1} = 6$     $2 \div \frac{1}{3} = 6$

$2 \times \frac{4}{1} = 8$     $2 \div \frac{1}{4} = 8$

$2 \times \frac{5}{1} = 10$     $2 \div \frac{1}{5} = 10$

So, it will take a giant tortoise 10 hours.

You can also use a reciprocal to divide by a fraction. Look at the patterns at the right. The patterns show that dividing by a number is the same as multiplying by its reciprocal.

$6 \div 2 = 3$     $6 \times \frac{1}{2} = 3$

$6 \div 1 = 6$     $6 \times \frac{1}{1} = 6$

$6 \div \frac{1}{2} = 12$     $6 \times 2 = 12$

**Example 2**   Find $5 \div \frac{2}{3}$.

**STEP 1**

Write the whole number as a fraction.

$5 \div \frac{2}{3} = \frac{5}{1} \div \frac{2}{3}$

**STEP 2**

Use the reciprocal of the divisor to write a multiplication problem.

$\frac{5}{1} \div \frac{2}{3} = \frac{5}{1} \times \frac{3}{2}$

↑         ↑

reciprocals

**STEP 3**

Multiply.

$\frac{5}{1} \times \frac{3}{2} = \frac{15}{2}$, or $7\frac{1}{2}$

So, $5 \div \frac{2}{3} = \frac{15}{2}$, or $7\frac{1}{2}$.

 **MATH IDEA**   To divide a whole number by a fraction, write the whole number as a fraction and then multiply it by the reciprocal of the divisor.

**1. Explain** two ways you can find $3 \div \frac{1}{6}$.

**Use fraction bars, patterns, or reciprocals to divide.**

**2.** $2 \div \frac{1}{4}$     **3.** $3 \div \frac{1}{6}$     **4.** $5 \div \frac{1}{3}$     **5.** $1 \div \frac{1}{6}$     **6.** $4 \div \frac{1}{3}$

**Divide.**

**7.** $8 \div \frac{1}{2}$     **8.** $9 \div \frac{2}{5}$     **9.** $7 \div \frac{3}{4}$     **10.** $3 \div \frac{1}{5}$     **11.** $5 \div \frac{3}{10}$

▶ **Practice and Problem Solving**   Extra Practice, page 414, Set B

**Use fraction bars, patterns, or reciprocals to divide.**

**12.** $5 \div \frac{1}{2}$     **13.** $3 \div \frac{1}{3}$     **14.** $8 \div \frac{2}{3}$     **15.** $1 \div \frac{1}{8}$     **16.** $7 \div \frac{1}{4}$

**Divide.**

**17.** $9 \div \frac{3}{8}$     **18.** $8 \div \frac{6}{7}$     **19.** $4 \div \frac{4}{5}$     **20.** $6 \div \frac{3}{4}$     **21.** $1 \div \frac{2}{5}$

**Find the missing number.**

**22.** $4 \div \frac{2}{9} = \blacksquare$     **23.** $\blacksquare \div \frac{1}{2} = 16$     **24.** $5 \div \frac{1}{\blacksquare} = 30$     **25.** $3 \div \frac{\blacksquare}{4} = 12$

**26.** How many halves are in 4?     **27.** How many thirds are in 5?

**28.** How many three-fourths are in 6?     **29.** How many twos are in 9?

**30.** What if a tortoise travels $\frac{2}{12}$ miles per hour? How many hours will it take the tortoise to walk 6 miles?

**31.** ✎ **Write a problem** that has a whole number divided by a fraction, with a quotient of 4.

**32.** ✎ **Write About It** Show how you can use multiplication to solve $4 \div \frac{1}{2}$.

**33. Vocabulary Power** The word *quotient* comes from the Latin word *quotiens* meaning "how many times." Explain why that meaning makes sense for $18 \div 3 = 6$.

▲ **Giant tortoises have one of the longest life spans of any animal, sometimes more than 200 years.**

▶ **Getting Ready for ★FCAT**

**34.** Mrs. Bates rides her bicycle $2\frac{2}{3}$ miles every day. Her husband rides 2 times as far as she does. How many miles does Mr. Bates ride his bicycle?

  **A.** $5\frac{1}{3}$ miles     **B.** $4\frac{1}{3}$ miles     **C.** $4\frac{1}{4}$ miles     **D.** $3\frac{5}{8}$ miles

# Divide Fractions

▶ **Learn**

**BUZZZY WORK!**   If one honeybee makes $\frac{1}{12}$ teaspoon of honey during its lifetime, how many honeybees are needed to make $\frac{1}{2}$ teaspoon of honey?

## Example 1

Find $\frac{1}{2} \div \frac{1}{12}$. ←**Think:** How many $\frac{1}{12}$ teaspoons are in $\frac{1}{2}$ teaspoon?

**One Way**  You can use fraction bars to help you divide fractions by fractions.

See how many $\frac{1}{12}$ bars are equal to a $\frac{1}{2}$ bar.

**Another Way**  You can find the quotient of two fractions by using what you know about reciprocals.

**STEP 1**

Use the reciprocal of the divisor to write a multiplication problem.

$$\frac{1}{2} \div \frac{1}{12} = \frac{1}{2} \times \frac{12}{1}$$
$$\uparrow \qquad \uparrow$$
reciprocals

**STEP 2**

Multiply. Write the answer in simplest form.

$$\frac{1}{2} \times \frac{12}{1} = \frac{12}{2}, \text{ or } 6$$

So, $\frac{1}{2} \div \frac{1}{12} = 6$.

So, 6 honeybees are needed to make $\frac{1}{2}$ teaspoon of honey.

▲ A honeybee would have to visit over 2,000,000 flowers in order to collect enough nectar to produce 1 pound of honey.

• What multiplication problem could you write for $\frac{3}{5} \div \frac{1}{5}$? What is the quotient?

  **MATH IDEA**   To find the quotient of two fractions, multiply the dividend by the reciprocal of the divisor.

# Use Reciprocals to Divide

You can use reciprocals to divide mixed numbers by fractions and fractions by whole numbers.

## Example 2

Find $2\frac{1}{4} \div \frac{1}{3}$.

**STEP 1**

Write the mixed number as a fraction.

$$2\frac{1}{4} \div \frac{1}{3} = \frac{9}{4} \div \frac{1}{3}$$

**STEP 2**

Use the reciprocal of the divisor to write a multiplication problem.

$$\frac{9}{4} \div \frac{1}{3} = \frac{9}{4} \times \frac{3}{1}$$
$$\uparrow \qquad \uparrow$$
reciprocals

**STEP 3**

Multiply. Write the answer in simplest form if needed.

$$\frac{9}{4} \times \frac{3}{1} = \frac{27}{4}, \text{ or } 6\frac{3}{4}$$

So, $2\frac{1}{4} \div \frac{1}{3} = \frac{27}{4}$, or $6\frac{3}{4}$.

### More Examples

**A**

Find $1\frac{2}{3} \div \frac{2}{5}$.

$$1\frac{2}{3} \div \frac{2}{5} = \frac{5}{3} \div \frac{2}{5} = \frac{5}{3} \times \frac{5}{2}$$

$$\frac{5}{3} \times \frac{5}{2} = \frac{25}{6}, \text{ or } 4\frac{1}{6}$$

**B**

Find $1\frac{1}{4} \div 2\frac{1}{3}$.

$$1\frac{1}{4} \div 2\frac{1}{3} = \frac{5}{4} \div \frac{7}{3} = \frac{5}{4} \times \frac{3}{7}$$

$$\frac{5}{4} \times \frac{3}{7} = \frac{15}{28}$$

**C**

Find $\frac{5}{6} \div 3$.

$$\frac{5}{6} \div 3 = \frac{5}{6} \times \frac{1}{3}$$

$$\frac{5}{6} \times \frac{1}{3} = \frac{5}{18}$$

## Check

1. **Explain** whether the dividend is greater than or less than the divisor in Examples A, B, and C. When is the quotient greater than 1?

**Write a division sentence for each model.**

2.

3.

4.

**Use a reciprocal to write a multiplication problem for the division problem.**

5. $\frac{3}{4} \div \frac{1}{3}$

6. $\frac{1}{3} \div \frac{1}{2}$

7. $2 \div \frac{2}{5}$

8. $3\frac{2}{3} \div \frac{3}{8}$

9. $2\frac{1}{5} \div 1\frac{1}{4}$

**Divide. Write the answer in simplest form.**

10. $\frac{1}{4} \div \frac{1}{2}$

11. $\frac{2}{5} \div \frac{1}{10}$

12. $\frac{1}{2} \div 2$

13. $1\frac{3}{4} \div \frac{1}{2}$

14. $1\frac{1}{3} \div 1\frac{1}{2}$

LESSON CONTINUES ▶

FCAT TESTED  SSS/ GLEs MA.A.3.2.3 The student adds, subtracts, and multiplies whole numbers, decimals and fractions, including mixed numbers . . . . MA.A.I.2.3, MA.E.I.2.I.5.5

Chapter 19  **409**

Write a division sentence for each model.

**15.**

**16.**

**17.**

Use a reciprocal to write a multiplication problem for the division problem.

**18.** $\frac{3}{8} \div \frac{1}{2}$

**19.** $\frac{7}{8} \div \frac{1}{3}$

**20.** $4 \div \frac{3}{8}$

**21.** $1\frac{2}{5} \div \frac{1}{4}$

**22.** $2\frac{2}{7} \div 1\frac{1}{5}$

Divide. Write the answer in simplest form.

**23.** $6 \div \frac{3}{8}$

**24.** $7 \div \frac{6}{7}$

**25.** $\frac{3}{5} \div \frac{1}{5}$

**26.** $\frac{4}{7} \div \frac{2}{3}$

**27.** $1\frac{1}{4} \div \frac{3}{4}$

**28.** $8 \div \frac{4}{5}$

**29.** $\frac{5}{6} \div \frac{1}{3}$

**30.** $\frac{7}{12} \div \frac{2}{3}$

**31.** $\frac{3}{4} \div \frac{1}{8}$

**32.** $\frac{3}{4} \div 2\frac{1}{4}$

**33.** $3\frac{7}{10} \div 2\frac{4}{5}$

**34.** $2\frac{3}{4} \div \frac{1}{8}$

**35.** $\frac{4}{5} \div 8$

**36.** $\frac{1}{3} \div 12$

**37.** $2\frac{4}{5} \div 1\frac{2}{3}$

★**ALGEBRA** For 38–40, copy and complete each rule table.

**38.**

| $n$ | $n \div \frac{1}{3}$ |
|---|---|
| $\frac{5}{6}$ | ▪ |
| $\frac{1}{2}$ | ▪ |
| $\frac{1}{9}$ | ▪ |

**39.**

| $y$ | $y \div \frac{1}{4}$ |
|---|---|
| $\frac{7}{8}$ | ▪ |
| ▪ | $2$ |
| ▪ | $\frac{16}{5}$, or $3\frac{1}{5}$ |

**40.**

| $n$ | $n \div \frac{1}{2}$ |
|---|---|
| ▪ | $\frac{6}{8}$, or $\frac{3}{4}$ |
| $3$ | ▪ |
| ▪ | $5$ |

**41.** If a bee travels $\frac{1}{8}$ mile on each trip it makes to gather nectar, how many trips will the bee make to travel $\frac{1}{2}$ mile?

**42.** **REASONING** If $\frac{3}{4} \div \frac{n}{8} = \frac{3}{4} \times \frac{n}{8}$, what is the value of $n$? Explain.

**43.** How many more $1\frac{1}{2}$-ounce servings are in the large jar of honey on the right than in the small jar?

**44.** ★**ALGEBRA** Find $n$ if $a = 4$, $b = 6$, and $c = 4$.     $\frac{a}{b} \div \frac{c}{n} = \frac{1}{2}$

**45.** Mrs. Banak bought a $12\frac{1}{2}$-ounce box of honeycomb cereal for \$3. How much does the cereal cost per ounce?

**46.** ≡**FAST FACT** • **SOCIAL STUDIES**
On average, each person in the United States eats $1\frac{1}{10}$ pounds of honey every year. At this rate, how much honey do 5 people eat in a year?

**47.** Scott uses $2\frac{1}{4}$ ounces of honey to make a loaf of bread. How many loaves can he make from a 12-ounce jar of honey? How much honey will be left?

**48.** Luke made a chart to compare the speeds that some animals move. How many more miles can a chicken travel in an hour than a spider?

   **A.** 10.17 miles

   **B.** 8.83 miles

   **C.** 8.17 miles

   **D.** 7.83 miles

**49.** Which of the following represents the distance a spider can travel in 2 hours?

   **F.** $1\frac{17}{100}$ miles    **H.** $2\frac{34}{100}$ miles

   **G.** $2\frac{17}{100}$ miles    **I.** $2\frac{7}{20}$ miles

| ANIMAL SPEEDS | |
|---|---|
| **Animal** | **Speed (in miles per hour)** |
| Chicken | 9 |
| Spider | 1.17 |
| Three-toed sloth | 0.15 |
| Giant tortoise | $\frac{17}{100}$ |
| Garden snail | $\frac{3}{100}$ |

# Problem Solving   LiNKUP . . . to Reading

**STRATEGY • IDENTIFY INFORMATION**  A careful reader must identify the details needed to solve a word problem. Read the following problem.

The average bee collects nectar for honey within 1 mile of its hive, makes up to 25 trips each day, and can carry a load of about 0.002 ounce—about half its weight. After the first half of their lives, bees eat only honey. In fact, for every pound of honey sold in stores, 8 pounds are used by the hive. About how much does a honeybee weigh?

**1.** What detail do you need to solve this problem?

**2.** Solve the problem.

**For 3–4, use the paragraph above. Write the detail you need to solve each problem. Then solve.**

**3.** If a bee visits 75 flowers during each nectar-collecting trip, about how many flowers does it visit each day?

**4.** For every $\frac{1}{4}$ pound of honey sold in stores, how many pounds are used by the hive?

# Problem Solving Strategy
## Solve a Simpler Problem

**PROBLEM** The greatest weight ever recorded for a great white shark was about 7,000 pounds. This is $\frac{4}{25}$ the weight of the world's largest shark, the whale shark. How much does a whale shark weigh?

▲ Great whites are the largest meat-eating sharks. They have 3,000 teeth that are triangular, razor-sharp, and up to 3 inches long.

**UNDERSTAND**

- What are you asked to find?
- What information will you use?

**PLAN**

- What strategy can you use to solve the problem?

  You can *solve a simpler problem* by using simpler numbers.

**SOLVE**

- How can you use the strategy to solve the problem?

  **Think:** ■ $\times \frac{4}{25} = 7{,}000$, so $7{,}000 \div \frac{4}{25} = $ ■.

  Use a simpler number instead of 7,000. Since $7 \times 1{,}000 = 7{,}000$, use the simpler number 7 to represent the weight of the great white shark.

  $$7 \div \frac{4}{25} = \frac{7}{1} \times \frac{25}{4} = \frac{175}{4}$$

  To find the actual weight of a whale shark, multiply by 1,000.

  $$\frac{175}{4} \times 1{,}000 = \frac{175{,}000}{4} = 43{,}750$$

  So, a whale shark weighs about 43,750 pounds.

**CHECK**

- Look back at the problem. How can you decide if your answer is correct?

**Use a simpler problem to solve.**

1. **What if** a whale shark is 1,500 centimeters long and a great white shark is $\frac{2}{5}$ as long? How long is the great white shark?

2. A Pacific gray whale can weigh 70,000 pounds. This is about $\frac{7}{30}$ the weight of a blue whale. How much does a blue whale weigh?

**A whale shark is 600 inches long. The world's smallest shark, the smalleye pygmy shark, is $\frac{1}{75}$ the length of a whale shark.**

3. Which equation can be used to find the length of a pygmy shark?

   **A** $600 \times \frac{1}{75} = n$

   **B** $600 \times n = \frac{1}{75}$

   **C** $600 \div \frac{1}{75} = n$

   **D** $600 - \frac{1}{75} = n$

4. How long is a smalleye pygmy shark in feet?

   **F** 80 feet   **G** 8 feet   **H** $1\frac{1}{2}$ feet   **J** $\frac{2}{3}$ foot

▲ **Whale shark**

### Strategies

Draw a Diagram or Picture
Make a Model or Act It Out
Make an Organized List
Find a Pattern
Make a Table or Graph
Predict and Test
Work Backward
**Solve a Simpler Problem**
Write an Equation
Use Logical Reasoning

---

## Mixed Strategy Practice

5. Cole's dresser is $5\frac{1}{4}$ feet wide. His bookcase is $\frac{2}{3}$ as wide as his dresser. How wide is his bookcase?

6. Rachel has $4.75 in coins. She has 6 dimes and twice as many quarters. The rest are nickels. How many of each coin does she have?

7. The city bought 48,000 tulip bulbs. Workers planted $\frac{1}{8}$ in parks and $\frac{2}{3}$ along roads. How many bulbs do they have left?

8. Chloe made a square design. She colored $\frac{1}{4}$ of the square blue, $\frac{1}{8}$ yellow, and $\frac{1}{8}$ green. She left $\frac{1}{2}$ of the square white. What might her design look like?

9. **NUMBER SENSE** Oren chose a number and multiplied it by 3. Then he added 6, divided by 9, and subtracted 5. The answer was 4. What number did Oren choose?

10. **? What's the Error?** Of the 398 species of sharks in the world, 199 are less than 39 inches long. Joe says the other $\frac{1}{3}$ are 39 inches or longer. Describe and correct his error.

FCAT TESTED **SSS/ GLEs MA.A.3.2.2.5.1** The student uses problem-solving strategies to determine the operation(s) needed to solve one- and two-step problems involving . . . , and addition, subtraction, and multiplication of decimals and fractions.

**Chapter 19 413**

# Extra Practice

## Set A (pp. 404–405)

**Are the two numbers reciprocals? Write *yes* or *no*.**

1. $\frac{2}{3}$ and 3
2. $\frac{3}{4}$ and $1\frac{1}{3}$
3. $\frac{4}{7}$ and $1\frac{4}{7}$
4. $1\frac{2}{3}$ and $\frac{3}{5}$
5. $\frac{3}{4}$ and $1\frac{1}{4}$

**Write the reciprocal of each number.**

6. $\frac{1}{3}$
7. 10
8. $\frac{7}{2}$
9. $1\frac{3}{4}$
10. $2\frac{1}{3}$

11. $\frac{6}{9}$
12. $1\frac{1}{4}$
13. $\frac{7}{8}$
14. 6
15. $5\frac{2}{5}$

16. Jane writes the reciprocal of $\frac{7}{10}$. What number does she write?

17. Is the reciprocal of $1\frac{2}{5}$ greater than or less than 1?

## Set B (pp. 406–407)

**Divide. Write the answer in simplest form.**

1. $9 \div \frac{3}{4}$
2. $4 \div \frac{1}{3}$
3. $2 \div \frac{4}{5}$
4. $7 \div \frac{2}{3}$
5. $10 \div \frac{1}{4}$

6. $3 \div \frac{3}{4}$
7. $8 \div \frac{1}{6}$
8. $6 \div \frac{3}{8}$
9. $1 \div \frac{5}{6}$
10. $15 \div \frac{2}{3}$

11. How many halves are in 7?

12. How many thirds are in 6?

13. There are 8 pounds of clay for projects. Each project uses $\frac{1}{2}$ pound of clay. How many projects can be made from the clay?

14. A pastry chef has 9 pounds of butter and uses $\frac{3}{4}$ pound for each batch of cookies. How many batches of cookies can he make?

## Set C (pp. 408–411)

**Use a reciprocal to write a multiplication problem for the division problem.**

1. $\frac{3}{4} \div \frac{1}{5}$
2. $\frac{3}{5} \div \frac{6}{7}$
3. $\frac{1}{3} \div \frac{5}{9}$
4. $\frac{6}{7} \div \frac{1}{8}$
5. $\frac{5}{8} \div \frac{2}{3}$

**Divide. Write the answer in simplest form.**

6. $\frac{4}{7} \div \frac{3}{4}$
7. $\frac{7}{8} \div \frac{5}{6}$
8. $\frac{5}{7} \div \frac{5}{9}$
9. $\frac{1}{6} \div \frac{3}{7}$
10. $\frac{2}{7} \div \frac{1}{4}$

11. $\frac{2}{3} \div \frac{4}{7}$
12. $\frac{3}{10} \div 4$
13. $\frac{5}{8} \div 2\frac{1}{2}$
14. $3\frac{1}{3} \div \frac{2}{3}$
15. $2\frac{2}{3} \div 1\frac{1}{6}$

16. Chris wants to build a fence $8\frac{1}{3}$ yards long. How many $1\frac{2}{3}$-yard pieces of fence will he need?

17. Mr. Cook wants to fence his rectangular garden which covers 100 ft². The width of the garden is $7\frac{1}{2}$ ft. What is the length of the garden? How much fencing will Mr. Cook need?

# Review/Test

 **CHECK VOCABULARY AND CONCEPTS**

Choose the best term from the box.

> denominator
> divisor
> fraction
> numerator
> reciprocal

1. To find the quotient of two fractions, multiply the dividend by the reciprocal of the __?__. (p. 408)

2. To find the reciprocal of a mixed number, first rename the mixed number as a __?__. (p. 404)

3. To divide a whole number by a fraction, first write the whole number as a fraction with a __?__ of 1. (p. 406)

4. The product of a number and its __?__ is 1. (p. 404)

 **CHECK SKILLS**

Write the reciprocal of each number. (pp. 404–405)

5. $\frac{3}{10}$

6. $8\frac{2}{3}$

7. $14$

8. $4\frac{2}{11}$

9. $\frac{2}{5}$

Divide. Write the answer in simplest form. (pp. 406–411)

10. $12 \div \frac{2}{3}$

11. $9 \div \frac{4}{5}$

12. $\frac{4}{5} \div 4$

13. $7 \div \frac{5}{9}$

14. $8 \div \frac{3}{7}$

15. $\frac{8}{9} \div 11$

16. $\frac{2}{7} \div \frac{2}{3}$

17. $\frac{5}{6} \div 1\frac{1}{9}$

18. $\frac{3}{5} \div \frac{3}{10}$

19. $1\frac{1}{2} \div \frac{1}{4}$

20. $2\frac{5}{8} \div \frac{1}{4}$

21. $2\frac{3}{4} \div 2\frac{1}{6}$

 **CHECK PROBLEM SOLVING**

Solve. (pp. 412–413)

22. The mustard factory has 20,000 ounces of mustard to put into small packets. If each packet holds $\frac{1}{4}$ ounce, how many packets can be filled?

23. Lydia needs $\frac{3}{4}$ cup of flour to make bread. She has only a $\frac{1}{8}$-cup measuring cup. How many times will she fill the $\frac{1}{8}$ cup to get the $\frac{3}{4}$ cup she needs?

24. The Sports Card Store has 200,000 cards. If $\frac{1}{10}$ of them are baseball cards, how many cards are *not* baseball cards?

25. Gretchen has 27 feet of ribbon. She needs to cut the ribbon into $\frac{3}{4}$-foot pieces. How many pieces of ribbon can she cut?

# Getting Ready for FCAT

## NUMBER SENSE, CONCEPTS, AND OPERATIONS

**1.** Theresa is thinking of a number. She wrote these clues for her number.

- The number has 5 digits.
- The sum of the digits is 19.
- The digit 0 is not used.
- All the digits are different.

What is the **greatest** number you can write using Theresa's clues?

**A.** 98,765

**C.** 95,320

**B.** 98,761

**D.** 94,321

**2.** The table shows the number of horses in four countries.

| HORSE POPULATIONS | |
| --- | --- |
| **Country** | **Number of Horses** |
| Brazil | 6,394,140 |
| China | 8,854,800 |
| Mexico | 6,250,000 |
| United States | 6,150,000 |

How many more horses are there in China than in the United States?

**F.** 1,704,800

**H.** 2,704,800

**G.** 2,604,800

**I.** 15,004,800

**3. Explain It** Use the table in Problem 2. ESTIMATE, to the nearest hundred thousand, the total horse population of the four countries. Explain how you found your answer.

## DATA ANALYSIS AND PROBABILITY

**4.** Joseph's average for four bowling games was 135. If his bowling scores for the first three games were 127, 149, and 130, what was his score for the last game?

**A.** 134

**C.** 406

**B.** 146

**D.** 540

**5.** The graph shows flower sales at Gala Flowers.

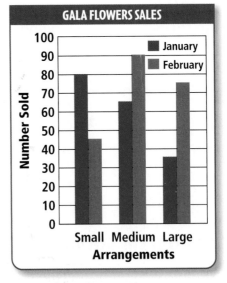

What was the total number of arrangements sold in February?

**F.** 125

**G.** 155

**H.** 180

**I.** 210

**6. Explain It** Look at the graph above. Medium arrangements sell for $15. How much more did Gala Flowers make on sales of medium floral arrangements in February than in January? Explain how you solved the problem.

**ALGEBRAIC THINKING**

**7.** Four students each wrote an expression using the numbers 3, 4, 6, and 8. Who wrote the expression with the **greatest** value?

| STUDENT EXPRESSIONS | |
|---|---|
| **Debra** | $(6 \div 3) \times (8 \div 4)$ |
| **Andrew** | $(6 + 8) \div (3 + 4)$ |
| **Tomoko** | $8 \times 3 \div 6 - 4$ |
| **Lacey** | $(4 + 8) - 6 \div 3$ |

**A.** Debra

**B.** Andrew

**C.** Tomoko

**D.** Lacey

**8.** A camp group went to the aquarium. The table shows the relationship between the number of campers and the cost of admission.

| AQUARIUM ADMISSION COSTS | | | | | |
|---|---|---|---|---|---|
| **Number of Campers** | 1 | 2 | 3 | 4 | 5 |
| **Cost (in dollars)** | 6 | 12 | 18 | 24 | 30 |

What is the cost of admission for a camp group with 8 campers?

**F.** $36

**G.** $42

**H.** $48

**I.** $54

**9. Explain It** Write a rule for this pattern.

16, 8, 24, 12, 36, 18, 54, ▌, ▌

Then write the next two numbers in the pattern. Explain your answer.

 **GEOMETRY AND SPATIAL SENSE**

**10.** Which figure does NOT have line symmetry?

 **TIP** **Look for important words.**
See item 10. The term *line symmetry* is important. If a figure has line symmetry, it can be folded along a line so that the two parts match exactly.

**A.**  **C.**

**B.** 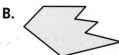 **D.**

**11.** The perimeter of a square rug is 32 feet. What is the area of the rug?

**F.** 16 square feet

**G.** 24 square feet

**H.** 48 square feet

**I.** 64 square feet

**12. Explain It** Name a diameter of the circle.

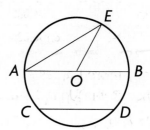

Explain how you know that the segment you named is a diameter.

# IT'S IN THE BAG

## Create-a-Meal Cookbook

**PROJECT** Make a cookbook to practice comparing fractions.

### Materials

- 3 to 9 recipes
- 3 sheets of white paper
- 1 piece of fabric (11 in. × 9 in.)
- Glue stick
- Colored paper for title
- Markers
- Cookbook comparisons worksheet

### Directions

1. Make the cookbook pages. Fold a white sheet of paper in half and cut a window down the folded side that is about $6\frac{1}{2}$ in. long and $\frac{1}{2}$ in. wide. *(Picture A)*

2. Fold the other two white papers in half and cut slits of 1 in. on each end of the fold. Fold these papers lengthwise and put them through the "window". Open them so the slits are at the top and bottom to form the pages of the book. *(Picture B)*

3. Open the book and lay it on the reverse side of the fabric. Glue the first and last pages of the book to the fabric, forming the cover. Make a label with colored paper, write the title on it, and glue it to the front of the book cover. Glue the cookbook comparisons worksheet inside the front cover of the book. Choose 3 to 9 recipes for your favorite meals and copy them into the book. *(Picture C)*

4. Suppose you are having a party. How much of each ingredient would you need to serve 12 people? 16 people? 24 people? Explain.

# Challenge

## Explore Patterns with Fractions

A **pattern** of fractions follows a rule. When you know the rule for the pattern, you can figure out the next fraction in the sequence.

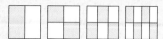

**Example**  Find the next fraction in this pattern. $\frac{1}{2}, \frac{2}{4}, \frac{3}{6}, \frac{4}{8}, \ldots$

**STEP 1**

Look for a pattern to find a rule.

**Think:** What do I do to $\frac{1}{2}$ to get $\frac{2}{4}$?

$\frac{1+1}{2+2} \begin{matrix} \leftarrow\text{add 1} \\ \leftarrow\text{add 2} \end{matrix} = \frac{2}{4}$

**STEP 2**

Test the rule for all the terms.

**Rule:** Add 1 to the numerator. Add 2 to the denominator.

$\frac{2+1}{4+2} = \frac{3}{6}, \frac{3+1}{6+2} = \frac{4}{8}$

**STEP 3**

Use the rule to find the next term.

$\frac{4}{8} \rightarrow \frac{4+1}{8+2} = \frac{5}{10}$

So, the next fraction in the pattern is $\frac{5}{10}$.

## More Examples

**Ⓐ** $\frac{1}{3}, \frac{2}{6}, \frac{3}{9}, \frac{4}{12}, \ldots$

**Rule:** Add 1 to the numerator. Add 3 to the denominator.

So, the next fraction in the pattern is $\frac{4+1}{12+3} = \frac{5}{15}$.

**Ⓑ** $\frac{3}{6}, \frac{6}{12}, \frac{12}{24}, \frac{24}{48}, \ldots$

**Rule:** Multiply the numerator and the denominator by 2.

So, the next fraction in the pattern is $\frac{24 \times 2}{48 \times 2} = \frac{48}{96}$.

## Talk About It

- What would you do if your rule in Step 1 did not work with the other fractions?

## Try It

Write a rule. Find the next fraction in the pattern.

**1.** $\frac{3}{4}, \frac{9}{12}, \frac{27}{36}, \frac{81}{108}, \ldots$

**2.** $\frac{6}{7}, \frac{7}{8}, \frac{8}{9}, \frac{9}{10}, \ldots$

**3.** $\frac{1}{2}, \frac{3}{5}, \frac{5}{8}, \frac{7}{11}, \ldots$

Create a pattern for the rule. Start with any fraction.

**4. Rule:** Multiply the numerator by 2. Add 1 to the denominator.

**5. Rule:** Add 2 to the numerator. Add 1 to the denominator.

**6. Rule:** Add 2 to the numerator and the denominator.

# Study Guide and Review

## VOCABULARY

Choose the best term from the box.

> equivalent fractions
> greatest common factor
> reciprocals
> rename
> least common denominator

1. The least common multiple of the denominators is the __?__ for the fractions. (p. 356)

2. Two numbers with a product of 1 are called __?__. (p. 404)

3. To simplify factors before you multiply them, you can divide by the __?__ of a numerator and a denominator. (p. 392)

## STUDY AND SOLVE

### Chapter 16

**Add and subtract fractions.**

Find $\frac{2}{3} + \frac{1}{4}$.

Use the LCD to write like fractions.

$$\frac{2}{3} = \frac{2 \times 4}{3 \times 4} = \frac{8}{12}$$   Add the numerators.

$$+\frac{1}{4} = +\frac{1 \times 3}{4 \times 3} = +\frac{3}{12}$$   Write the sum over the

$$\frac{11}{12}$$   denominator.

**Find the sum or difference. Write the answer in simplest form.** (pp. 346–359)

4. $\frac{3}{5} + \frac{2}{5}$

5. $\frac{5}{7} - \frac{3}{14}$

6. $\frac{7}{16} + \frac{3}{8}$

7. $\frac{2}{3} - \frac{5}{9}$

8. $\frac{1}{4} - \frac{1}{12}$

9. $\frac{1}{9} + \frac{5}{6}$

### Chapter 17

**Add and subtract mixed numbers.**

$$2\frac{3}{8} = 2\frac{3}{8}$$   Use the LCD to rename.
Subtract the fractions.

$$-1\frac{1}{4} = -1\frac{2}{8}$$   Then subtract the whole

$$1\frac{1}{8}$$   numbers. Simplify if possible.

**Find the sum or difference. Write the answer in simplest form.** (pp. 368–377)

10. $4\frac{7}{12} + 3\frac{1}{8}$

11. $3\frac{4}{6} - 2\frac{1}{6}$

12. $6\frac{2}{5} - 5\frac{3}{5}$

13. $6\frac{5}{8} + 7\frac{7}{8}$

### Chapter 18

**Multiply a fraction by a fraction.**

Multiply. $\frac{3}{4} \times \frac{2}{5}$

$$\frac{3}{4} \times \frac{2}{5} = \frac{3 \times 2}{4 \times 5}$$   Multiply the numerators.
Multiply the

$$= \frac{6}{20} = \frac{3}{10}$$   denominators.

**Find the product. Write the answer in simplest form.** (pp. 386–389)

14. $\frac{1}{2} \times \frac{2}{7}$

15. $\frac{1}{3} \times \frac{5}{9}$

16. $\frac{4}{9} \times \frac{6}{11}$

17. $\frac{3}{8} \times \frac{1}{6}$

## Multiply mixed numbers.

Multiply. $2\frac{2}{3} \times \frac{2}{3}$

$\frac{8}{3} \times \frac{2}{3} = \frac{16}{9}$, or $1\frac{7}{9}$   Rename the mixed number as a fraction. Multiply the fractions.

## Find the product. Write the answer in simplest form. (pp. 390–393)

18. $\frac{5}{6} \times 3\frac{1}{2}$   19. $2\frac{1}{4} \times \frac{3}{8}$

20. $4\frac{3}{4} \times 1\frac{1}{2}$   21. $2\frac{2}{3} \times 3\frac{1}{4}$

22. $5\frac{1}{2} \times \frac{1}{4}$   23. $1\frac{5}{8} \times \frac{2}{3}$

# Chapter 19

## Write the reciprocal of a number.

Write the reciprocals of $\frac{2}{3}$ and $2\frac{3}{4}$.
Exchange the numerators and denominators.
$\frac{2}{3} \to \frac{3}{2}$, or $1\frac{1}{2}$ ← reciprocal
$2\frac{3}{4} = \frac{11}{4} \to \frac{4}{11}$ ← reciprocal

## Write the reciprocal of each number.
(pp. 404–405)

24. 19   25. $2\frac{3}{7}$   26. $\frac{7}{12}$

27. $3\frac{2}{9}$   28. $\frac{14}{31}$   29. $4\frac{1}{3}$

## Divide with fractions.

Divide. $4 \div \frac{2}{3}$

$\frac{4}{1} \div \frac{2}{3} = \frac{4}{1} \times \frac{3}{2}$   Write the whole number as a fraction. Multiply using the reciprocal of the divisor.

$= \frac{12}{2} = 6$   Write the answer in simplest form.

## Find the quotient. Write the answer in simplest form. (pp. 408–411)

30. $5 \div \frac{2}{3}$   31. $\frac{9}{10} \div \frac{2}{5}$

32. $12 \div \frac{5}{6}$   33. $1\frac{3}{4} \div \frac{5}{8}$

## PROBLEM SOLVING PRACTICE

Solve. (pp. 378–379, 412–413)

34. Mrs. Catalanello made 3 loaves of bread. The first loaf was $10\frac{7}{8}$ inches long, the second loaf was $3\frac{1}{2}$ inches shorter than the first, and the third was $1\frac{3}{4}$ inches longer than the second. How long was the third loaf?

35. In 1998, the populations of Los Angeles, San Francisco, and San Diego totalled about 5,500,000. The population of Los Angeles was $\frac{2}{3}$ of this total. What was the population of Los Angeles in 1998?

# PERFORMANCE ASSESSMENT

## TASK A • PIZZA TIME

Dan bought a pizza to share with Kenny. Each boy ate a different number of pieces. Dan ate the most. When the boys were finished, there was one piece left for Dan to give to his grandmother.

a. Draw a diagram of the pizza. Write fractions on the diagram to show the amounts Dan and Kenny ate.

b. If the boys ate the amounts you suggested, what fraction of the pizza was left for Dan's grandmother?

c. Dan baked four strawberry tarts to share with his grandmother and Kenny. Use mixed numbers to suggest a way they could have shared the tarts if Dan ate the most and his grandmother ate the least.

## TASK B • ON THE JOB

A local grocery store has these part-time jobs available. Jon and Kate each want to apply for one of these jobs.

**HELP WANTED**

**JOB A**

Stock shelves after school for $2\frac{1}{2}$ hours per day, 4 days a week. Pays $6 per hour.

**HELP WANTED**

**JOB B**

Help at check-out counters for $3\frac{1}{2}$ hours every Friday and $5\frac{1}{2}$ hours every Saturday. Pays $6 per hour.

**HELP WANTED**

**JOB C**

Unload 3 delivery trucks every Saturday. Each truck requires about $2\frac{1}{2}$ hours to unload. Pays $20 per truck.

a. Jon wants to work 10 hours per week. Which job should he apply for?

b. Kate wants to work only on Saturdays to earn $100 as quickly as possible. Which job should she apply for?

c. Change the job descriptions so that Jon and Kate can choose between two part-time jobs.

# Technology Linkup

## Calculator • Operations with Fractions

You can use a calculator to extend number patterns involving operations with fractions.

**Example**   The rule is add $\frac{2}{3}$. The first number in the pattern is $\frac{2}{3}$. Each fraction is expressed in simplest form. What are the next three numbers in the pattern?

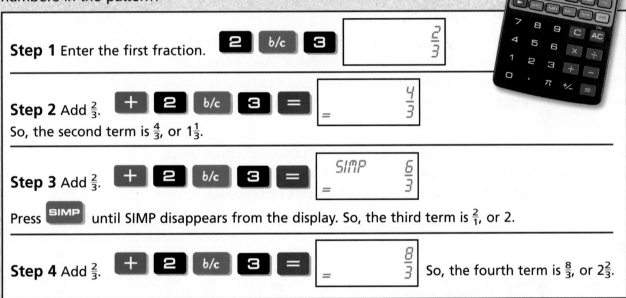

**Step 1** Enter the first fraction.   [2] [b/c] [3]   $\frac{2}{3}$

**Step 2** Add $\frac{2}{3}$.   [+] [2] [b/c] [3] [=]   $= \frac{4}{3}$
So, the second term is $\frac{4}{3}$, or $1\frac{1}{3}$.

**Step 3** Add $\frac{2}{3}$.   [+] [2] [b/c] [3] [=]   SIMP $= \frac{6}{3}$

Press [SIMP] until SIMP disappears from the display. So, the third term is $\frac{2}{1}$, or 2.

**Step 4** Add $\frac{2}{3}$.   [+] [2] [b/c] [3] [=]   $= \frac{8}{3}$   So, the fourth term is $\frac{8}{3}$, or $2\frac{2}{3}$.

So, the next three numbers in the pattern are $\frac{4}{3}$, 2, and $\frac{8}{3}$.

## Practice and Problem Solving

Use a calculator to find the next three numbers in the pattern. Express all fractions in simplest form.

**1. rule:** subtract $\frac{1}{6}$
**first number:** $\frac{19}{20}$

**2. rule:** mutiply by $\frac{3}{5}$
**first number:** $\frac{7}{10}$

**3. rule:** divide by $\frac{1}{8}$
**first number:** $\frac{1}{3}$

**4. REASONING**   The first four terms in the pattern are 3, $4\frac{1}{2}$, $6\frac{3}{4}$, and $10\frac{1}{8}$. What is a rule for the pattern?

**GO ON-LINE**

**Multimedia Math Glossary** www.harcourtschool.com/mathglossary

**Vocabulary Power**   Find *least common denominator* in the Multimedia Math Glossary. Its definition contains words that are also math vocabulary words. Make a list of the words and definitions. Then draw a diagram to show how these words are related.

Orange grove near
Winter Haven

# PROBLEM SOLVING IN FLORIDA

Winter Haven
Lake Okeechobee

## FLORIDA CITRUS

Florida is famous for its oranges, but it is also a major producer of other citrus fruits, including tangerines and tangelos. Also known as mandarins, tangerines are the sweetest citrus fruit. A tangelo is actually a cross between a tangerine and a grapefruit. Citrus fruits are a good source of vitamin C.

**A recent survey found that there are about 106,000,000 citrus trees in Florida. Of these, $\frac{4}{5}$ are orange trees, $\frac{3}{25}$ are grapefruit trees, and the rest are other citrus trees, such as tangerines or tangelos.**

**USE DATA** For 1–4, use the paragraph above and the graph.

1. What fraction of the Florida citrus trees are other types of trees, such as tangerines and tangelos?

2. About how many of the citrus trees in Florida are orange trees? About how many are grapefruit trees?

3. Most Florida oranges are used to make juice. What fraction of the Florida orange crop is used for frozen concentrate or chilled juice?

4. Write a fraction to show how much more of the orange crop is used for chilled juice than is used as fresh oranges.

5. Write a problem that can be solved using operations with fractions and the data in the graph. Solve the problem.

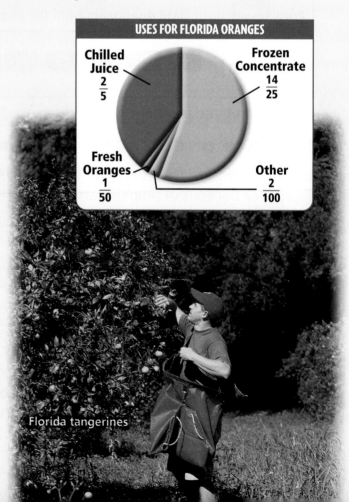

**USES FOR FLORIDA ORANGES**

Chilled Juice $\frac{2}{5}$

Frozen Concentrate $\frac{14}{25}$

Fresh Oranges $\frac{1}{50}$

Other $\frac{2}{100}$

Florida tangerines

# SUGARCANE

Sugarcane, another important agricultural crop in Florida, is grown near the southern and eastern shores of Lake Okeechobee. Almost $\frac{3}{4}$ of Florida's sugarcane acreage is in Palm Beach County, the leading county in the United States in sugar production.

1. An average sugarcane stalk weighs about 3 pounds and contains about $\frac{3}{10}$ lb of sugar. About how many pounds of sugar are contained in a ton of sugarcane stalks?

2. About $\frac{11}{20}$ of the sugarcane produced in the United States comes from Florida. About what fraction of the sugarcane comes from other states?

**USE DATA** For 3–5, use the recipe.

3. How much more flour than sugar is needed to make Florida Orange muffins?

4. If $\frac{2}{3}$ cup of raisins is put in a 1-cup measuring cup, how much of the cup is not filled?

5. If all the ingredients measured in cups were combined, would you have more than or less than 4 cups of ingredients? Explain.

> **Florida Orange Muffins**
>
> 1 whole orange
>
> $\frac{1}{2}$ cup orange juice
>
> 1 egg
>
> $\frac{1}{2}$ cup vegetable oil
>
> $\frac{3}{4}$ cup sugar
>
> $1\frac{1}{2}$ cups flour
>
> 1 teaspoon baking soda
>
> 1 teaspoon baking powder
>
> $\frac{1}{2}$ teaspoon salt
>
> $\frac{2}{3}$ cup raisins

# Geometric Figures

| SHAPE | MESSAGE |
|-------|---------|
| STOP | Stop |
| YIELD | Yield |
| R R | Railroad Warning |
| NO PASSING ZONE | No Passing Zone |
| PIER ENDS | Warning Signs |
| HANDICAPPED PARKING | Guide Signs |
| King Creek Falls | Recreational Area Signs |

**FAST FACT • SOCIAL STUDIES** Traffic signs regulate the flow of traffic for motor vehicles, bicycles, and pedestrians. The signs give information through their shape, color, message, and placement. There are road signs to meet the special needs of handicapped people. For example, there are road signs in Braille for the blind and signs that designate handicapped parking.

**PROBLEM SOLVING** Look at the table. Name the shape of each type of sign.

# CHECK WHAT YOU KNOW

Use this page to help you review and remember
important skills needed for Chapter 20.

## NAME POLYGONS

Name each polygon. Tell the number of sides and angles.

1.

2.

3.

4.

5.

6.

7.

8.

## PATTERNS

Draw the next 2 figures in each pattern.

9. ▯ o △ ▯ o △ ▯ o △

10. ◸ ◹ ◸ ◹ ◸ ◹ ◸ ◹

11. ◑• ◑• ◑• ◑• ◑•

12. ▭ ▪ ▭ ▪ ▭ ▪ ▪

13. △ ▯ o ◇ △ ▯ o ◇ △ ▯ o ◇ △

14. ◺• ■ ⬡ ◺• ■ ⬡ ◺• ■ ⬡

# VOCABULARY POWER

### REVIEW

**geometry** [jē am′ə trē] *noun*

The word *geometry* comes from *geo,* which means "Earth," and *metry,* which means "measure." So, *geometry* means "Earth measure." Think of another word that has *geo* or *metry* in it and explain what it means.

### PREVIEW

parallel lines
intersecting lines
perpendicular lines
central angle
line symmetry
rotational symmetry
corresponding angles
corresponding sides

degree
circle
radius
diameter
chord
similar
congruent
regular polygon

 www.harcourtschool.com/mathglossary

LESSON
1

# Lines and Angles

**WHAT'S THE ANGLE?** You can see basic geometric figures all around you. Some geometric figures have special names and symbols.

A **point** marks an exact location in space. Use a letter to name a point.

• *A*

point *A*

A **line** is an endless straight path. It has no endpoints. Use two points on the line to name the line.

*A* ← → *B*
line *AB* or $\overleftrightarrow{AB}$ or line *BA* or $\overleftrightarrow{BA}$

A **ray** is part of a line that has one endpoint and continues without end in one direction. Use an endpoint and one other point on the ray to name a ray.

*K* — *L* →
ray *KL* or $\overrightarrow{KL}$

A **line segment** is part of a line that includes two endpoints and all of the points between them. Use the two endpoints to name the line segment.

*C* — *D*
line segment *CD* or $\overline{CD}$ or line segment *DC* or $\overline{DC}$

A **plane** is an endless flat surface. Use three points that are not on a line to name the plane.

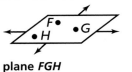
plane *FGH*

**Quick Review**

1. $7 \times 8$  2. $72 \div 9$
3. $10 \times 90$  4. $240 \div 80$
5. $130 \times n = 2{,}600$

**VOCABULARY**

| point | line segment |
| line | parallel lines |
| ray | intersecting lines |
| plane | perpendicular lines |
| angle | degree |

▲ Vehicle Assembly Building, Kennedy Space Center

An **angle** is formed by two rays with the same endpoint. An angle can be named by three letters—a point from each side and the vertex as the middle letter. It can also be named by a single letter, its vertex.

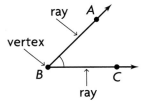
∠*ABC*, ∠*CBA*, or ∠*B*

Angles can be different sizes. The unit of measure for an angle is called a **degree** (°).

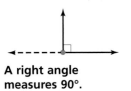
A right angle measures 90°.

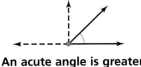
An acute angle is greater than 0° and less than 90°.

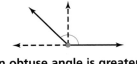
An obtuse angle is greater than 90° and less than 180°.

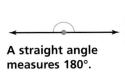
A straight angle measures 180°.

# Line Relationships

Within a plane, lines can have different relationships.

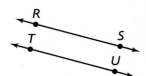

Lines in a plane that never intersect and are the same distance apart at every point are **parallel lines**. $\overleftrightarrow{RS} \parallel \overleftrightarrow{TU}$

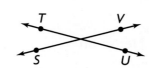

Lines that cross at one point are **intersecting lines**.

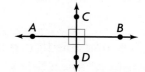

Lines that intersect to form four right angles are **perpendicular lines**. $\overleftrightarrow{AB} \perp \overleftrightarrow{CD}$

**HINT:** Remember that ‖ means "is parallel to" and ⊥ means "is perpendicular to."

- Are all intersecting lines perpendicular?

## Activity

**On the worksheet, draw and label parallel, perpendicular, and intersecting lines on each figure.**

**MATERIALS:** ruler, polygons worksheet, TR 56

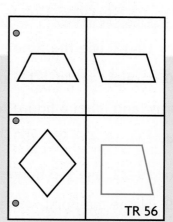

TR 56

### STEP 1

Label the vertices of your figure *A*, *B*, *C*, and *D*. Draw a line through points *A* and *D*. Draw arrowheads to show that the line is endless. Repeat through points *B* and *C* and points *D* and *C*. You have drawn $\overleftrightarrow{AD}$, $\overleftrightarrow{DC}$, and $\overleftrightarrow{BC}$. Now, draw a line from point *A* to point *B*.

### STEP 2

Classify the lines. Examples:

**Parallel:** $\overleftrightarrow{AB}$ is parallel to $\overleftrightarrow{DC}$, or $\overleftrightarrow{AB} \parallel \overleftrightarrow{DC}$.
**Perpendicular:** $\overleftrightarrow{AD}$ is perpendicular to $\overleftrightarrow{DC}$ or $\overleftrightarrow{AD} \perp \overleftrightarrow{DC}$.
**Intersecting:** $\overleftrightarrow{DC}$ intersects $\overleftrightarrow{BC}$.

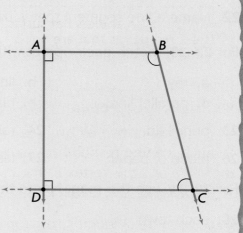

### STEP 3

Classify the angles. Examples:

**Right:** ∠A and ∠D     **Obtuse:** ∠B     **Acute:** ∠C

- If $\overleftrightarrow{AD}$ and $\overleftrightarrow{BC}$ were extended, would they be parallel, perpendicular, or intersecting? Explain.

- Repeat Steps 1–3 for each figure on the worksheet.

LESSON CONTINUES

**FCAT TESTED** SSS/GLEs MA.C.1.2.1.5.3 Knows the characteristics of and relationships among points, lines, line segments, rays, and planes. also MA.B.1.2.1.5.4

**Chapter 20   429**

1. **Explain** the difference between a line and a line segment.

**For 2–9, use the figure at the right. Name an example of each term.**

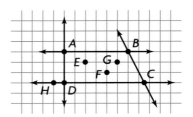

2. acute angle
3. parallel line segments

4. line segment
5. plane

6. ray
7. line
8. right angle
9. perpendicular lines

▶ **Practice and Problem Solving** ( Extra Practice, page 450, Set A )

**For 10–13, use the figure above. Name an example of each.**

10. straight angle
11. obtuse angle
12. point
13. intersecting lines

**Draw and label a figure for each.**

14. $\overline{LM}$
15. $\overrightarrow{CD}$
16. $\overleftrightarrow{AB}$
17. ∠BDE
18. point P

**For 19–22, use the figure at the right.**

19. Name the point where $\overline{AB}$ and $\overline{BC}$ intersect.

20. Name a line segment on plane ABC that is perpendicular to $\overline{AD}$.

21. Name a line segment on the plane that intersects but is not perpendicular to $\overline{DC}$.

22. Name a line segment that is parallel to $\overline{BC}$.

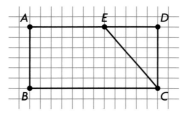

**For 23–28, match each object with a term.**

   **a.** ray
   **b.** line segment
   **c.** intersecting line segments
   **d.** parallel lines
   **e.** plane
   **f.** point

23. pencil tip
24. railroad tracks
25. the letter X

26. piece of paper
27. laser beam
28. flagpole

**For 29–31, use the map. Name the geometric figure suggested by**

29. each town.

30. Interstate 18 and Interstate 287.

31. Maple Avenue and Interstate 287.

32. ✎ **Write About It** Explain why parallel lines never meet.

**33.** Draw two rays that meet at a vertex. Label the rays, the vertex, the interior, and the exterior of the angle.

**34.** Mark one point on your paper. Label it *P*. How many lines can you draw through point *P*?

**35.** Sophia bought 5 packages of 8 hot dogs each and 3 packages of 12 buns each. Does she have enough buns for all the hot dogs? Explain.

**36.** Copy the points on your paper. Connect the points to make a closed figure. Find the perimeter and area of the figure.

## Getting Ready for FCAT  THINK SOLVE EXPLAIN

**37.** Mario drew a map of Elm Village on grid paper. Name two lines that appear to be parallel in Mario's map.

How many obtuse angles appear to be in Mario's map? Name them.

Which line segment is perpendicular to $\overleftrightarrow{AG}$?

**MAP OF ELM VILLAGE**

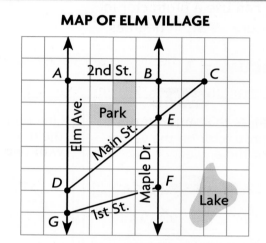

# Problem Solving  LINKÜP... to Science

Astronomers use star charts such as this one of the northern constellations to plot locations of stars.

1. What geometric figure represents each star?

2. What geometric figure represents the distance between two stars in a constellation?

3. Name an acute angle and an obtuse angle in Cepheus.

4. In the diagram of Cepheus, is $\overline{CD}$ parallel to $\overline{ED}$ or does it intersect $\overline{ED}$ at point *D*?

5. ✎ **Write a problem** using the star chart.

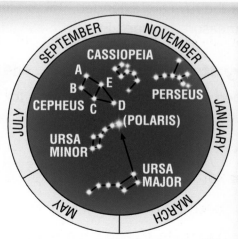

▲ To use the chart, face north soon after sunset and hold the chart in front of you with the current month at the top.

# Measure and Draw Angles

## Quick Review

1. $(110 + 70) - 90$
2. $120 + 240$    3. $270 - 180$
4. $4 \times 90$        5. $360 - 90$

### VOCABULARY

**protractor**

### MATERIALS
protractor

## ▶ Explore

A **protractor** is a tool used for measuring or drawing angles. You can use a protractor to measure ∠ABC in degrees.

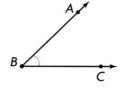

## Activity 1

| STEP 1 | STEP 2 | STEP 3 |
|---|---|---|
| Place the center of the protractor on the vertex of the angle. | Line up the center point and the 0° mark on the protractor with one ray of the angle. | Read the measure of the angle where the other ray passes through the scale. |

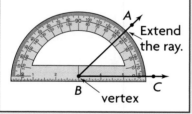 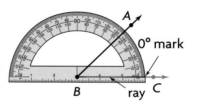 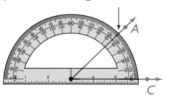

So, the measure of ∠ABC is 45°.

- If the rays are extended, will the angle measure change? Explain.

## Try It

Trace each angle. Use a protractor to measure each angle.

a.

b.

c.
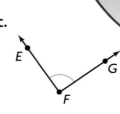

Which scale on the protractor do you read to find the measure of an angle?

You can use a protractor to draw a right angle. A right angle is 90°.

## Activity 2

**STEP 1**

Draw and label a ray. Place the center point of the protractor on the endpoint of the ray. Then line up the ray with the 0° mark on the protractor.

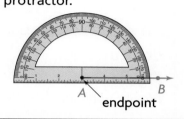

**STEP 2**

Find 90° on the protractor scale. Mark a point on your paper at 90°.

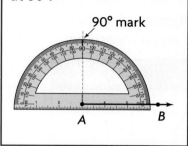

**STEP 3**

Draw the ray connecting the endpoint and your 90° mark. Label one point on this ray.

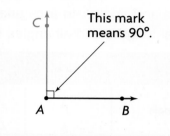

This mark means 90°.

• A right angle measures 90°. What can you conclude about the measures of acute and obtuse angles?

## ► Practice and Problem Solving

**For 1–8, use the figure at the right. Copy each angle. Then use a protractor to measure and classify each angle.**

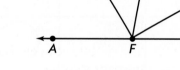

1. ∠AFB
2. ∠BFE
3. ∠AFE
4. ∠AFD
5. ∠AFC
6. ∠CFD
7. ∠DFE
8. ∠BFD

**Use a protractor to draw each angle. Then write _acute, right,_ or _obtuse_ for each angle.**

9. 40°
10. 90°
11. 120°
12. 15°
13. 95°

14. ❓ **What's the Error?**  Ben measured a 50° angle as 130°. Explain how Ben made this error.

15. ☰**FAST FACT** • SCIENCE The fastest sailing vessel in the world can sail at 46 knots. One knot equals 1.15 miles per hour. How much faster or slower is 46 knots than 50 miles per hour?

16. Draw a triangle with a 95° angle. Explain how you can find the measures of the other angles.

## Getting Ready for ◀FCAT

17. Which angle can be classified as obtuse?

   **A.** ∠ABD
   **C.** ∠DBC
   **B.** ∠DBE
   **D.** ∠ABC

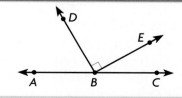

FCAT TESTED ⬟ SSS/GLEs MA.B.1.2.1.5.4 Classifies angle measures as acute, obtuse, right, or straight. _also_ MA.C.1.2.1.5.1

**Chapter 20  433**

# Angles and Polygons

 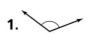
▶ **Learn**

**SIGNS OF THE TIMES**   When you recognize a stop sign
by its shape, you are classifying a polygon. A **polygon** is
a closed plane figure formed by three or more line
segments. Polygons are named by the number of their
sides and angles. In a **regular polygon**, all sides have
equal lengths and all angles have equal measures.

**VOCABULARY**

**polygon**

**regular polygon**

| | Sides and angles | Regular polygon | Polygon that is not regular |
|---|---|---|---|
| **Triangle** | 3 | | |
| **Quadrilateral** | 4 | | |
| **Pentagon** | 5 | | |
| **Hexagon** | 6 | | |
| **Octagon** | 8 | | |
| **Decagon** | 10 | | |

 **Activity 1**

**MATERIALS:** square and triangle dot paper, ruler

| **STEP 1** | **STEP 2** |
|---|---|
| Draw a regular polygon. 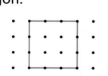 | Draw a polygon that is not regular. 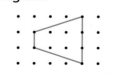 |

• Now, use the triangular dot paper to draw two 6-sided
polygons, one regular and one that is not regular. Name
the figures and explain how they are alike and how they
are different.

## Angles of Polygons

A straight angle measures 180°. You can use this fact to find the sums of the angles of polygons.

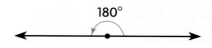

180°

## Activity 2

**Find the sum of the angles in a triangle.**

| STEP 1 | STEP 2 | STEP 3 |
|---|---|---|
| Draw a triangle. Label each angle. Cut out the triangle. 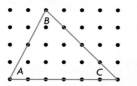 | Cut off the angles as shown. 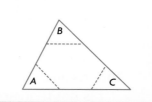 | The angles placed together at a point form a straight angle as shown. 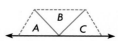 The sum of the angles appears to be 180°. |

- Repeat the steps with two different-shaped triangles. Write a rule about the sum of the angles in a triangle.

**Find the sum of the angles in a quadrilateral.**

| STEP 1 | STEP 2 | STEP 3 |
|---|---|---|
| Draw a quadrilateral on dot paper. Label each angle. Cut out the quadrilateral. 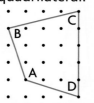 | Draw a line segment from C to A to make two triangles. 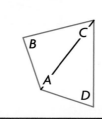 | Since the sum of the angles in each triangle is 180°, multiply. 108 × 2 = 360.  So, the sum of the angles in the quadrilateral is 360°. |

- Repeat the steps with two different-shaped quadrilaterals. Write a rule about the sum of the angles in a quadrilateral.

 **MATH IDEA** The sum of the angles in a triangle is 180°, and the sum of the angles in a quadrilateral is 360°.

## Check

1. **Explain** another way to show that the sum of the angles in a quadrilateral is 360°.

**Name each polygon and tell if it is regular or not regular.**

2.     3.     4.     5.

**LESSON CONTINUES**

FCAT TESTED    SSS/GLEs MA.C.1.2.1.5.1 Uses appropriate geometric vocabulary to describe properties and attributes of two- and three-dimensional figures.

Chapter 20    **435**

**Name each polygon and tell if it is *regular* or *not regular*.**

6.

7.

8.

9.

10.

11.

12.

13.

**Use dot paper to draw an example of each.**

14. regular triangle

15. regular octagon

16. hexagon that is not regular

17. quadrilateral that is not regular

**Find the unknown angle measure.**

18.

19.

20.

21.

22.

23.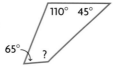

24.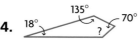

25.

**Find a pattern. Then write a rule. Use your rule to draw the next figure in the pattern.**

26.

27.

28. **Vocabulary Power** Polygon names include prefixes that tell how many sides the polygon has. For example, *penta-* means 5, and a pentagon has 5 sides. The prefix for 7 is *hepta-*, and for 10 it's *deca-*. What are the names of polygons with 7 and 10 sides?

29. How many triangles are in this figure?

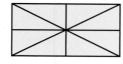

30. **? What's the Error?** Rhonda says all the angles in a regular hexagon are greater than 90°, so they are acute. Describe and correct her error.

**436**

**31.** A nonagon has 9 sides. Use the pattern in the table of polygons on page 434 to find how many angles a nonagon has.

**32.** Two angles in a triangle measure 40° and 47°. Tell whether the third angle is *acute, obtuse,* or *right.*

**Getting Ready for**

**33.** Look at the figures that have been sorted into two groups.

Use geometric terms to describe one characteristic that the figures in Group 1 have in common and one characteristic that the figures in Group 2 have in common.

Which figures could be in both Group 1 and Group 2? Explain.

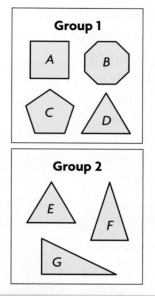

# Problem Solving    Thinker's Corner

**SUM IT UP!**   You can find the sum of the angles of any polygon.

Look at the pentagon.

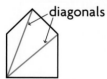

Diagonals have been drawn from one vertex to another to divide it into 3 parts.

**Remember**

The sum of the angles in a triangle is 180°.

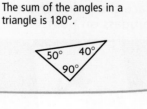

- What are the shapes of the 3 parts?

- What is the sum of the angle measures of each part?

- What do you think the sum of the angle measures of a pentagon is?

**Trace each figure. Find the sum of the angles in each figure.**

**1.**

**2.**

**3.**

# 4 Circles

**Quick Review**

1. 90° + 90°
2. 180° + 180°
3. 120° + 120° + 120°
4. 60° + 240° + 60°
5. 90° + 90° + 90° + 90°

## ▶ Learn

**ROUND AND ROUND** The largest Ferris wheel in the world, the London Eye, is shaped like a giant circle.

A **circle** is a closed plane figure with all points the same distance from the center. It has no beginning point and no ending point.

A line segment with one endpoint at the center of a circle and the other endpoint on the circle is called a **radius** (plural: *radii*). $\overline{BA}$ is a radius of Circle *A*.

**VOCABULARY**

| circle | chord |
|---|---|
| radius | compass |
| diameter | central angle |

A line segment that passes through the center of the circle and has its endpoints on the circle is called a **diameter**. $\overline{CD}$ is a diameter of Circle *A*.

A line segment with its endpoints on the circle is called a **chord**. $\overline{EF}$ is a chord of Circle *A*.

## Activity 1

**MATERIALS:** compass, centimeter ruler

A **compass** is a tool for constructing circles. You can use a compass to construct a circle with a radius of 7 centimeters to model the London Eye Ferris Wheel.

**STEP 1**

Draw and label a point, *P*. Place the point of the compass on point *P*.

**STEP 2**

Open the compass 7 cm, which is the length of the radius.

**STEP 3**

Use the compass to make the circle.

- Draw and label a chord, a diameter, and a radius of Circle *P*. Write the length of each.

- Draw three more circles of different sizes. Measure the lengths of each circle's radius and diameter. Record the measurements in a table.

- What relationship do you notice between the radius and diameter of a circle?

## Activity 2

When two radii of a circle meet at its center, they form a **central angle**. The measure of a central angle is less than or equal to 180°.

The sum of the angles in any circle is 360°.

How can you find the unknown measure of an angle in a circle?

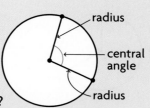

radius

central angle

radius

---

**STEP 1**

Find the sum of the angles that are given in the circle.

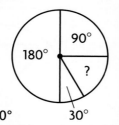

90°
180°
?
30°

$180° + 90° + 30° = 300°$

---

**STEP 2**

Then subtract that sum from 360°.

$360° - 300° = 60°$

---

So, the angle measure is 60°.

• Trace Figures A and B. Use a protractor to measure each central angle. Then find the sum of the angles in each circle.

A          B

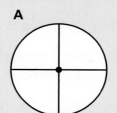  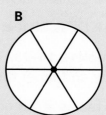

---

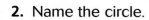

## Check

1. **Explain** how you can find the length of the diameter of the London Eye Ferris Wheel. HINT: The London Eye Ferris Wheel is about 1,000 times as large as your model.

**Use the circle for 2–5.**

2. Name the circle.

3. Name a radius of the circle.

4. Name a diameter of the circle.

5. Name a chord of the circle.

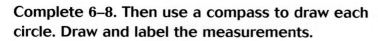

B
E
A
C
D
F

**Complete 6–8. Then use a compass to draw each circle. Draw and label the measurements.**

6. radius = 4 cm          diameter = ▨

7. radius = ▨          diameter = 6 cm

8. radius = 5 cm          diameter = ▨

**LESSON CONTINUES**

FCAT TESTED   SSS/GLEs MA.C.I.2.I.5.I Uses appropriate geometric vocabulary to describe properties and attributes of two- and three-dimensional figures.

**Chapter 20   439**

**Use a protractor to measure each central angle.**

9.

10.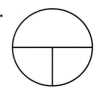

**Find the unknown angle measure.**

11.

12.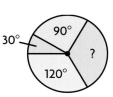

**Practice and Problem Solving**    Extra Practice, page 450, Set C

**For 13–17, use circle C.**

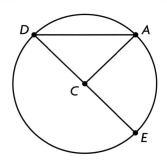

**13.** Name the three radii.

**14.** Name the two chords.

**15.** Name the diameter.

**16.** If $\overline{CD}$ is 5 inches long, how long is $\overline{DE}$?

**17.** If $\overline{DE}$ is 20 feet long, how long is $\overline{AC}$?

**Complete 18–23. Then use a compass to draw each circle. Draw and label the measurements.**

**18.** radius = 2.5 cm
diameter = ■

**19.** radius = ■
diameter = 9 cm

**20.** radius = 1.5 cm
diameter = ■

**21.** radius = ■
diameter = 7 cm

**22.** radius = 3 cm
diameter = ■

**23.** radius = ■
diameter = 11 cm

**Use a protractor to measure each central angle.**

24.

25.

26.

27.

**Find the unknown angle measure.**

28.

29.

30.

31.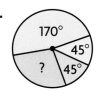

**32.** ⭐ **What's the Error?**  The radius of Ken's circle is 12 cm. The diameter of Tom's circle is 24 cm. Tom says his circle is bigger. Describe his error.

**33.** What line segments in a circle determine the size of the circle?

**34.** How many degrees are there in $\frac{1}{2}$ of a circle? $\frac{1}{4}$ of a circle? $\frac{1}{8}$ of a circle?

**35.** **REASONING** How many degrees are between the 2 and the 3 on a clock?

**36.** The second largest Ferris wheel in the world is in Japan. Its radius is about 42 meters. What is its diameter?

**37.** The largest Ferris wheel in the United States is the Texas Star in Dallas. Its radius is about 10 meters less than the radius of the Ferris wheel in Problem 36. What is the Texas Star's diameter?

---

**Getting Ready for FCAT**  THINK SOLVE EXPLAIN

**38.** Name the radii and the chords in the circle at the right. If $\overline{AB}$ is 7 inches long, how long is $\overline{AD}$? Explain how you know.

**39.** Jake drew another circle with a radius of 9 centimeters. On Jake's circle, chord $GH$ is 12 centimeters long. Explain why $GH$ cannot be a diameter.

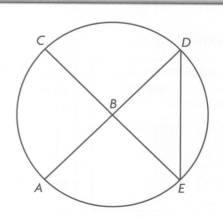

---

# Problem Solving  Thinker's Corner 💡

### YOU BE THE JUDGE!

**1.** Which is longer, $\overline{AB}$ or $\overline{BC}$?

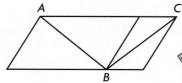

**2.** Which of the lines is the most curved?

**3.** What happened to the ruler? Are the sides parallel?

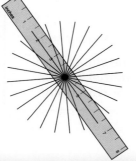

**4.** Look at the heavy lines in the figures. Which is longer?

# Congruent and Similar Figures

## ▶ Learn

**DOUBLE TAKE!** On the plaza of Philadelphia's City Hall, there are several giant sculptures of game pieces. All of these sculptures are similar to actual-sized game pieces.

### Examples

| | |
|---|---|
| **Congruent** figures have the same size and shape. 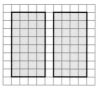 | **Similar** figures have the same shape but do not have to be the same size.  |

The green rectangles are also similar because they have the same shape.

- Does a real domino and the sculpture of a domino in Philadelphia appear to be *congruent, similar, both,* or *neither*? Explain.

### More Examples  Tell whether the figures appear to be *similar, congruent, both,* or *neither*.

| Ⓐ 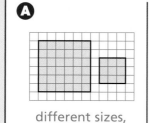 | Ⓑ 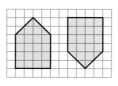 | Ⓒ 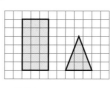 |
|---|---|---|
| different sizes, same shape | same size, same shape | different sizes, different shapes |
| The figures are **similar** but not congruent. | The figures are **both** similar and congruent. | The figures are **neither** similar nor congruent. |

- Are all similar figures congruent? Explain.

- Are all congruent figures similar? Explain.

# Investigating Similar Figures

Use a protractor and a ruler to investigate similar figures.

**Technology Link**

More Practice:
Harcourt Mega Math,
Ice Station Exploration,
*Polar Planes*, Level I

**HANDS ON**

## Activity

**MATERIALS:** centimeter grid paper, protractor, centimeter ruler

Triangle *ABC* and triangle *FGH* are similar. Similar polygons have corresponding angles and corresponding sides.

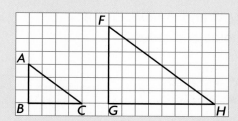

**Corresponding Angles**

∠*A* corresponds to ∠*F*.
∠*B* corresponds to ∠*G*.
∠*C* corresponds to ∠*H*.

**Corresponding Sides**

$\overline{AB}$ corresponds to $\overline{FG}$.
$\overline{BC}$ corresponds to $\overline{GH}$.
$\overline{CA}$ corresponds to $\overline{HF}$.

---

**STEP 1**

Copy △*ABC* and △*FGH* on grid paper. (The symbol for triangle is △.)

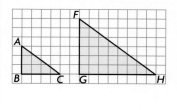

**STEP 2**

Use a protractor to measure the angles in each triangle.

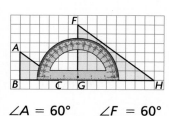

| | |
|---|---|
| ∠*A* = 60° | ∠*F* = 60° |
| ∠*B* = 90° | ∠*G* = 90° |
| ∠*C* = 30° | ∠*H* = 30° |

**STEP 3**

Use a centimeter ruler to measure the sides of each triangle.

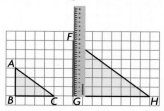

| | |
|---|---|
| $\overline{AB}$ = 3 cm | $\overline{FG}$ = 6 cm |
| $\overline{BC}$ = 4 cm | $\overline{GH}$ = 8 cm |
| $\overline{CA}$ = 5 cm | $\overline{HF}$ = 10 cm |

---

So, the angles in △*ABC* are congruent to the corresponding angles in △*FGH*, and the lengths of the sides in △*FGH* are 2 times the lengths of the corresponding sides in △*ABC*.

Now, copy △*JKL* and △*MNP* on grid paper.

Measure the angles and the sides.

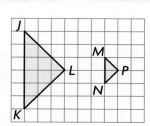

• Explain how the corresponding angles and the corresponding sides in △*JKL* and △*MNP* are related.

• Do △*JKL* and △*MNP* appear to be similar? Explain.

1. **Explain** why two congruent figures are also similar.

2. **Explain** why all squares are similar.

**Write whether the figures appear to be** *similar, congruent,* **both,** *or neither.*

**3.**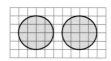

**4.**

**5.**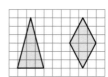

6. On grid paper, draw similar triangles △*KLM* and △*NOP*. Use a protractor and a ruler to measure the angles and sides.

▶ **Practice and Problem Solving** ( Extra Practice, page 450, Set D )

**Write whether the figures appear to be** *similar, congruent,* **both,** *or neither.*

**7.**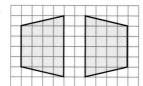

**8.**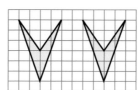

**9.**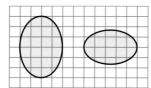

**10.**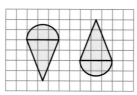

**11.**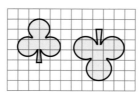

**12.**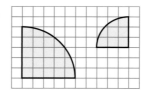

**For 13–16, use the figures below.**

 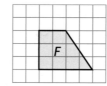 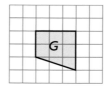 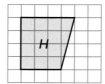 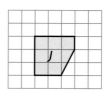

13. Write the letter of the figure that appears to be congruent to quadrilateral *ABCD*.

14. Write the letter of the figure that appears to be similar but not congruent to quadrilateral *ABCD*.

15. Write the letters of the two figures that appear to be neither congruent nor similar to quadrilateral *ABCD*.

16. What appears to be the same and what appears to be different about figures *G* and *H*?

**17. REASONING** Square *ABCD* has sides that are twice as long as the sides of square *EFGH*. The perimeter of square *ABCD* is 28 inches. What is the length of $\overline{EF}$?

**For 19–20, use the rectangles.**

**19.** Copy the rectangles on centimeter grid paper. Use a protractor and a centimeter ruler to measure the angles and the sides of each rectangle.

**20.** Do the rectangles appear to be similar? Explain.

**18.** Two sculptures are similar. The height of one is four times the height of the other. The smaller sculpture is 2.5 feet tall. How tall is the larger sculpture?

## Getting Ready for FCAT

**21.** Look at the pairs of quadrilaterals below. Which pair appears to be similar?

A.

B.

C.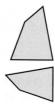

D.

## Problem Solving  LiNKUP...to Art

You can use different size grid paper to help you draw similar figures.
**MATERIALS:** 1-cm and 0.5-cm grid paper

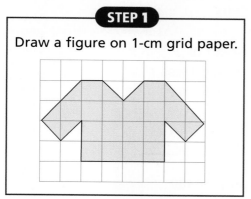

**STEP 1**

Draw a figure on 1-cm grid paper.

**STEP 2**

Draw the same figure on 0.5-cm grid paper.

**1.** Draw a polygon on 1-cm grid paper. Then draw a similar polygon on 0.5-cm grid paper. Explain how you know the polygons are similar.

**2.** Draw a figure on grid paper. Draw a smaller similar figure and a larger similar figure. Explain how you decided which grid paper to use for each.

# Symmetric Figures

▶ **Learn**

**REFLECT ON IT!** Which letters in this sign have line symmetry? How many lines of symmetry does each letter have?

A figure has **line symmetry** if it can be folded on a line so that the two parts match exactly.

**VOCABULARY**

**line symmetry**

**rotational symmetry**

## Activity

**MATERIALS:** grid paper, pencil, scissors

| STEP 1 | STEP 2 | STEP 3 |
|---|---|---|
| Copy the H on grid paper by shading the squares as shown. Cut out the H. 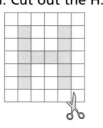 | Fold the H in half so the two halves match exactly. 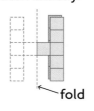 ←fold | Fold the H in half in other ways. If the halves match, then the fold is another line of symmetry.  So, the H has 2 lines of symmetry. Repeat with the other letters. |

The H and O each have 2 lines of symmetry, and the Y, W, and D each have 1 line of symmetry. The L does not have line symmetry.

Another type of symmetry involves turning the figure instead of folding it. A figure has **rotational symmetry** if it can be rotated less than 360° around a central point and still match the original figure.

## Examples

| **A** $\frac{1}{4}$ turn, or 90° | **B** $\frac{1}{3}$ turn, or 120° | **C** $\frac{1}{2}$ turn, or 180° |
|---|---|---|
|  | 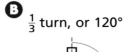 | |

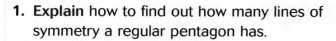

**Technology Link**

**More Practice:**
Harcourt Mega Math,
Ice Station Exploration,
*Polar Planes,*
Levels K & L

1. **Explain** how to find out how many lines of symmetry a regular pentagon has.

**Trace each figure. Draw the lines of symmetry. Tell whether each figure has rotational symmetry. Write *yes* or *no*.**

2.      3.      4.      5.      6.

▶ **Practice and Problem Solving**    (Extra Practice, page 450, Set E)

**Trace each figure. Draw the lines of symmetry. Tell whether each figure has rotational symmetry. Write *yes* or *no*.**

7.          8.          9.

10.          11.          12.

**Each figure has rotational symmetry. Tell the fraction and the angle measure of each turn.**

13.    14.     15.

**Trace each half figure and line of symmetry on grid paper. Then draw the other half of the figure.**

16.      17.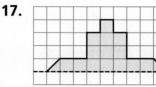

18.  **Write About It** Describe how you could use a mirror to test a figure's line of symmetry.

19. Look again at the Hollywood sign. Which is greater, the fraction of letters in the sign that are consonants or the fraction of letters that are vowels?

┌─ **Getting Ready for FCAT** ──────────────────────────────

20. How many letters in the word FAST have line symmetry?

    **A.** 1        **C.** 3

    **B.** 2        **D.** 4

# FAST

# Problem Solving Strategy
## Find a Pattern

**PROBLEM**  While volunteering at an archaeological dig, Kelly found this piece of painted pottery. She wants to copy the design onto a pot she is making. What should the rest of the design look like?

### UNDERSTAND

- What are you asked to find?

- What information will you use?

- Is there any information you will not use?

### PLAN

- What strategy can you use to solve the problem?

  You can *find a pattern* in the design. Patterns are details that repeat in the same order over and over again. If Kelly can find the pattern, she can repeat it.

### SOLVE

- How can you use the strategy to solve the problem?

  Find the part of the design that repeats.

  So, the repeated pattern of the design is 1 hexagon, 2 triangles, 1 square, 2 triangles. The next hexagon is the beginning of the repeating pattern.

### CHECK

- What shape should Kelly paint next to continue from the broken edge of the pottery's design?

## Problem Solving Practice

**Find a pattern to solve. Describe the pattern.**

1. **What if** there were two hexagons next to each other instead of one hexagon on the pottery's design? What pattern should Kelly repeat on her pot?

2. Pablo painted half of the border below on the kitchen walls. Tony wants to continue the border. Draw the shapes and colors Tony should paint next.

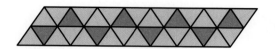

Ronnie painted the bricks along the driveway to his house.

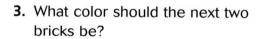

3. What color should the next two bricks be?

   **A** red, green    **C** red, blue

   **B** red, gray    **D** red, red

4. What color will the fiftieth brick in the border be?

   **F** red    **H** gray

   **G** green    **J** blue

**Strategies**

Draw a Diagram or Picture
Make a Model or Act It Out
Make an Organized List
▶ Find a Pattern
Make a Table or Graph
Predict and Test
Work Backward
Solve a Simpler Problem
Write an Equation
Use Logical Reasoning

**Problem Solving**

## Mixed Strategy Practice

**For 5–6, use the figures at the right.**

5. Draw the next figure in the pattern.

6. Write the number that goes with each figure in the pattern. What is the eighth number in the sequence?

7. Ted's quilt is 5 ft $2\frac{1}{2}$ in. wide and 10 ft 2 in. long. He wants to sew cording around the edge. How much cording does he need?

8. Anne spent half of her money on CDs. After she spent half of what was left on stickers, she had $9.50 left. How much did she have to start?

9. The daily temperatures for one week in Atlanta were 78°, 80°, 78°, 81°, 80°, 82°, and 82°. Make a graph to display these data. Explain your choice of graph.

10. Danny, Brenda, Ari, and Laura won the first four prizes in a contest. Danny won second prize. Laura did not win third prize. Ari won fourth prize. What prize did Brenda win?

**FCAT TESTED** SSS/GLEs MA.D.1.2.1.5.1 Describes, extends, creates, predicts, and generalizes numerical and geometric patterns using a variety of models . . . .

**Chapter 20  449**

# Extra Practice

## Set A (pp. 428–431)

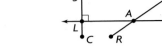

**Use the figure at the right. Name an example of each.**

**1.** point **2.** right angle **3.** ray **4.** parallel lines **5.** line segment

## Set B (pp. 434–437)

**Name each polygon and tell if it is *regular* or *not regular*.**

**1.**  **2.**  **3.**  **4.**

**Find the unknown angle measure.**

**5.**  **6.**  **7.**  **8.**

## Set C (pp. 438–441)

**Measure each central angle.** | **Find the unknown angle measure.**

**1.**  **2.**  **3.**  **4.**

**5.** The pizza restaurant will deliver only within a 3-mile radius. Tasha lives 2 miles from the restaurant. Will it deliver?

## Set D (pp. 442–445)

**Write whether the figures appear to be *similar, congruent, both,* or *neither*.**

**1.** 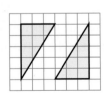 **2.** 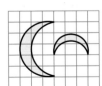 **3.**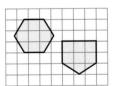

## Set E (pp. 446–447)

**Trace each figure. Draw the lines of symmetry. Tell whether each figure has rotational symmetry. Write *yes* or *no*.**

**1.**  **2.**  **3.**

# Review/Test

##  CHECK VOCABULARY AND CONCEPTS

Choose the best term from the box.

1. If a figure can be rotated less than 360° around a central point and still match the original figure, it has __?__. (p. 446)

2. A closed plane figure with all points the same distance from the center point is a __?__. (p. 438)

3. Figures that have the same size and shape are __?__. (p. 442)

> circle
> congruent
> line symmetry
> rotational symmetry
> perpendicular
> regular polygon
> similar

##  CHECK SKILLS

Draw and label a figure for each. (pp. 428–431)

4. ∠CLS      5. $\overline{SO}$      6. $\overrightarrow{KA}$      7. $\overleftrightarrow{AC}$

Use a protractor to draw each angle. Then write *acute*, *right*, or *obtuse* for each angle. (pp. 432–433)

8. 110°      9. 30°      10. 145°      11. 95°

Name each polygon and tell if it is *regular* or *not regular*. (pp. 434–437)

Find the unknown angle measure. (pp. 434–437)

12.       13.       14. 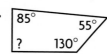      15.

Write whether the figures appear to be *similar, congruent, both,* or *neither*. (pp. 442–445)

16.       17. 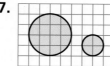      18.

## CHECK PROBLEM SOLVING

Find a pattern to solve. (pp. 448–449)

19. What shape and color should you draw next to continue the design?

20. The school bell rang at 8:30 A.M., 9:15 A.M., 10:00 A.M., and 10:45 A.M. If the pattern continues, what is the next time the school bell will ring?

# Getting Ready for FCAT

## ⭐ GEOMETRY AND SPATIAL SENSE

**1.** Which statement about these figures is true?

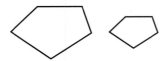

   **A.** They are congruent.

   **B.** They are similar.

   **C.** They are hexagons.

   **D.** They are regular pentagons.

**2.** Which figure contains only acute angles?

   **F.**

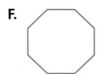

   **G.**

   **H.**

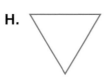

   **I.**

**3. Explain It** A quadrilateral has two right angles and one angle that measures 67°. What is the measure of the fourth angle? Explain how you found your answer.

## ⭐ DATA ANALYSIS AND PROBABILITY

**4.** In which country did the earthquake with the **greatest** magnitude occur?

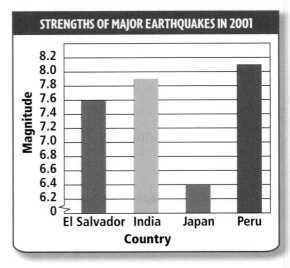

   **A.** El Salvador   **C.** Japan

   **B.** India   **D.** Peru

**5.** Look at the graph above. The strength of earthquakes is measured according to the Richter scale. Each whole number on the scale represents ground vibration 10 times as great as that represented by the next lower whole number. How many times as great was the strength of the earthquake in India than the earthquake in Japan?

   **F.** 1.5   **G.** 15   **H.** 150   **I.** 1,500

**6. Explain It** Patti counted the number of peanuts in four mixed-nut snack packs.

| MIXED-NUT PACKS | | | | |
|---|---|---|---|---|
| **Package** | 1 | 2 | 3 | 4 |
| **Number of Peanuts** | 12 | 15 | 16 | 13 |

Predict the number of peanuts Patti is likely to find in the fifth pack of mixed nuts. Explain your prediction.

**NUMBER SENSE, CONCEPTS, AND OPERATIONS**

**7.** Look at the table below. Which shows the insect speeds, in feet per second, in order from slowest to fastest?

| INSECT SPEED | |
| --- | --- |
| **Insect** | **Speed (in feet per second)** |
| Honeybee | 10.5 |
| Hornet | 19.6 |
| Dragonfly | 26.1 |
| Horsefly | 13.2 |

**A.** 10.5, 13.2, 19.6, 26.1

**B.** 10.5, 13.2, 26.1, 19.6

**C.** 26.1, 13.2, 19.6, 10.5

**D.** 26.1, 19.6, 13.2, 10.5

**8.** Look at the table in Problem 7. How many feet can a dragonfly fly in 6 seconds?

**F.** 156.6 feet

**G.** 117.6 feet

**H.** 79.2 feet

**I.** 63 feet

**9. Explain It** Leslie recorded the number of minutes she spent solving four math problems.

| TIME SOLVING PROBLEMS | | | | |
| --- | --- | --- | --- | --- |
| Problem | 1 | 2 | 3 | 4 |
| Time (in minutes) | $1\frac{1}{2}$ | $2\frac{1}{2}$ | $1\frac{3}{4}$ | 2 |

Leslie has 20 problems to solve in all. ESTIMATE to decide about how long it will take Leslie to solve all the problems. Explain how you found your answer.

 **ALGEBRAIC THINKING**

**TIP** **Decide on a plan.** See item 10. Look at each figure to see how it differs from the figure before it. Then, use the strategy *draw a diagram* to show the fourth figure in the pattern.

**10.** Dorothy drew a pattern with squares.

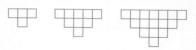

If the pattern continues, how many squares will be in the fourth figure?

**A.** 15      **C.** 25

**B.** 20      **D.** 28

**11.** The goal at Windward Elementary School was to collect 350 pounds of aluminum cans. The first week students collected 20 pounds. Each week they collected 10 pounds more than they had collected the previous week. How long did it take the students to reach their goal?

**F.** 35 weeks      **H.** 7.5 weeks

**G.** 10 weeks      **I.** 7 weeks

**12. Explain It** The sum along each side of this triangle is the same.

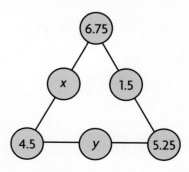

What are the values of *x* and *y*? Explain how you found your answer.

# Classify Plane and Solid Figures

## TYPES OF POLYGONS

| Shape | Name |
|-------|------|
| △ | Triangle |
| ▱ | Quadrilateral |
| ⬠ | Pentagon |
| ⬡ | Hexagon |

**≡FAST FACT • SOCIAL STUDIES**

The Sears Tower is the tallest building in Chicago, Illinois. On a clear day it is possible to see four states from the top of the building: Illinois, Indiana, Wisconsin, and Michigan.

PROBLEM SOLVING   Look at the photograph of the skyline of Chicago. Identify the polygon that is outlined in red. What other polygons can you see?

## CHECK WHAT YOU KNOW

Use this page to help you review and remember
important skills needed for Chapter 21.

### ✓ CLASSIFY ANGLES

Classify the angle. Write *acute*, *right*, or *obtuse*.

1.     2.     3.     4.

### ✓ FACES OF SOLID FIGURES

Name the plane figure that is the shaded face of the solid figure.

5. 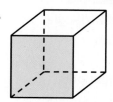    6.     7. 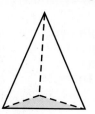    8.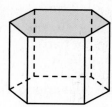

9. 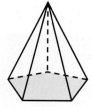    10. 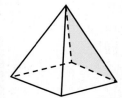    11. 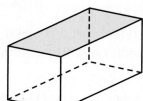    12.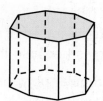

## VOCABULARY POWER

### REVIEW

**congruent** [kən•grōō′ənt] *adjective*
The word *congruent* is from the Latin
word *congruens,* which means "to come
together, correspond, or agree." Use some
of the words in the definition to explain
what it means to say that two triangles are
congruent.

### PREVIEW

| | | |
|---|---|---|
| isosceles triangle | triangular numbers | reflection |
| scalene triangle | trapezoid | rotation |
| equilateral triangle | parallelogram | tessellation |
| hypotenuse | rhombus | polyhedron |
| leg | transformation | prism |
| figurate numbers | translation | base |
| | | pyramid |

ON-LINE

www.harcourtschool.com/mathglossary

# Triangles

## ▶ Learn

**SIDE BY SIDE**  The crystal ball that was dropped in Times Square for New Year's Eve 2002 contained 504 equilateral triangular pieces. Why are the triangles called equilateral?

You can classify triangles by the lengths of their sides.

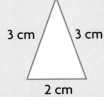

3 cm   3 cm

2 cm

A triangle with exactly two congruent sides is an **isosceles triangle**.

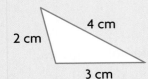

4 cm

2 cm

3 cm

A triangle with no congruent sides is a **scalene triangle**.

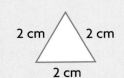

2 cm   2 cm

2 cm

A triangle with all sides congruent is an **equilateral triangle** .

So, the triangles of the crystal ball are called equilateral triangles because they each have three congruent sides.

- A regular polygon has congruent sides and angles. Which triangle is a regular polygon?

You can classify triangles by the measures of their angles.

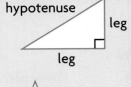

hypotenuse

leg

leg

A triangle that has a right angle is a *right* triangle. The **hypotenuse** is the side opposite the right angle and is the longest side. The other sides are called **legs**.

A triangle that has three acute angles is an *acute* triangle.

A triangle that has one obtuse angle is an *obtuse* triangle.

- Without measuring the angles, how can you tell that the triangles on the crystal ball are acute?

---

## Quick Review

Classify each angle as right, acute, or obtuse.

**1.**

**2.**

**3.**

**4.**

**5.**

## VOCABULARY

**isosceles triangle**
**scalene triangle**
**equilateral triangle**
**hypotenuse**
**leg**
**figurate numbers**
**triangular numbers**

▲ The crystal ball is 6 feet in diameter and contains 600 light bulbs, 96 strobe lights, and 90 pyramid mirrors.

# Draw Triangles

## Activity

**MATERIALS:** ruler, protractor

Draw a triangle with angles measuring 30°, 60°, and 90°. Make the side between the 30° angle and the 60° angle 2 inches long.

**STEP 1**

Use the protractor to draw a 30° angle. Label the vertex *A*.

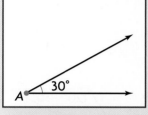

**STEP 2**

Make a dot 2 inches from *A* along one of the rays. Label the point *B*.

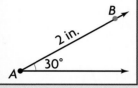

**STEP 3**

Draw a 60° angle with its vertex at *B*.

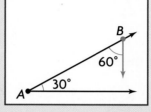

**STEP 4**

Extend the rays until they intersect. Label the point of intersection *C*.

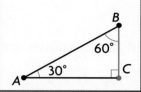

- What is the measure of ∠*C*? What kind of triangle is triangle *ABC*? Explain.

**Technology Link**

More Practice: Harcourt Mega Math Ice Station Exploration, *Polar Planes,* Levels E and F

## ▶ Check

1. **Explain** why the other two angles of a triangle must be acute if one angle is a right angle.

2. Name the legs and the hypotenuse of the right triangle in the Activity above.

**Classify each triangle. Write *isosceles, scalene,* or *equilateral*.**

3.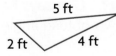
   5 ft, 2 ft, 4 ft

4.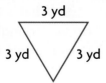
   3 yd, 3 yd, 3 yd

5.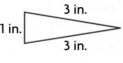
   3 in., 1 in., 3 in.

6.
   8 ft, 6 ft, 4 ft

**Classify each triangle. Write *acute, right,* or *obtuse*.**

7.

8.

9.

10.

11.

12.

13.

**LESSON CONTINUES**

FCAT TESTED ⚑ SSS/GLEs MA.C.1.2.1.5.1 Uses appropriate geometric vocabulary to describe properties and attributes of two- and three-dimensional figures. *also* MA.C.1.2.1.5.2

Chapter 21  **457**

**Classify each triangle. Write *isosceles, scalene,* or *equilateral*.**

**14.**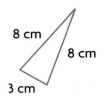
8 cm
8 cm
3 cm

**15.**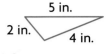
5 in.
2 in.
4 in.

**16.**
3 in. 4 in.
5 in.

**17.**
5 m
5 m 5 m

**Classify each triangle. Write *acute, right,* or *obtuse*.**

**18.**

**19.**

**20.**

**21.**

**Find the unknown angle measure.**

**22.**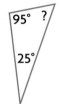
95° ?
25°

**23.**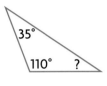
35°
110° ?

**24.**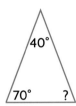
40°
70° ?

**25.**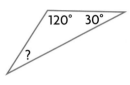
120° 30°
?

**Use a protractor and ruler to draw triangle *ABC* according to the given measurements. Classify the triangle by its sides and by its angles. Then find the measure of the third angle.**

**26.** $\angle A = 60°$
$\angle B = 60°$
$\overline{AB} = 2$ in.

**27.** $\angle C = 90°$
$\angle B = 55°$
$\overline{CB} = 3$ in.

**28.** $\angle A = 65°$
$\angle C = 65°$
$\overline{AC} = 4$ in.

**29.** $\angle C = 50°$
$\angle B = 20°$
$\overline{CB} = 2\frac{1}{2}$ in.

**30.** **? What's the Question?** In a triangle, two angles measure 30° and 60°. The answer is right triangle.

**31.** **? What's the Error?** Dan says he drew a triangle with two obtuse angles. Describe his error.

**32.** Copy this design onto your paper. See how many congruent triangles you can draw within the square array, using only three dots.

• • •
• • •
• • •

**33.** ✎ **Write About It** Describe a relationship shown in this Venn diagram.

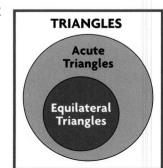

**34.** ☰**FAST FACT** • **SOCIAL STUDIES** The first time a ball was lowered in Times Square to celebrate the new year was in 1907. How many months ago was that?

**35.** Keith drew an equilateral triangle. By drawing one line, how can he divide the triangle into two right triangles?

**36.** Draw a square and one of its diagonals. Classify the triangles by their angles and by their sides.

**37.** Mrs. Rizzo asked her class to draw an isosceles triangle containing an angle with a measure of 70°. Britney drew one triangle. Justin drew two triangles. Who was correct? Explain your answer.

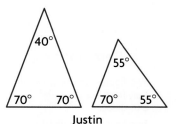

Justin

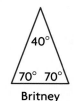

Britney

**38.** Logan is building a fence. Each section is in the shape of a rectangle with a diagonal support piece.

He noticed the support piece formed two triangles. Classify the triangles by their angles and their sides. Then describe a relationship between them.

# Problem Solving · Thinker's Corner

**ALGEBRA** **Figurate numbers** are numbers that can be represented by geometric patterns. The number of dots used to make each of the triangular arrays below shows the first four **triangular numbers**.

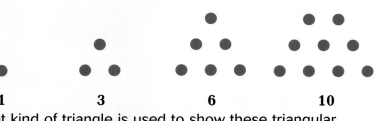

1         3         6         10

**1.** What kind of triangle is used to show these triangular numbers? Explain.

**2.** Draw the pattern of dots for the next three triangular numbers. How many dots did you draw for each triangular number?

**3.** **REASONING** Explain how the number of dots added for each new triangular number is related to the number of dots added to the triangular number just before it.

▲ More than 2,500 years ago, the Greek mathematician Pythagoras studied figurate numbers.

# Quadrilaterals

## Quick Review

Write the number of sides for each polygon.
1. square       2. triangle
3. rectangle    4. pentagon
5. octagon

**VOCABULARY**

trapezoid       parallelogram
rhombus

## ▶ Learn

**FOUR BY FOUR**   The faces of the Jacksonville, Florida, office building shown below are quadrilaterals because they have four sides and four angles. What types of quadrilaterals are suggested in the faces of this building?

Just as there are many types of triangles, there are many types of quadrilaterals.

**Remember**

Two figures are *congruent* if they have the same size and shape.

Two lines are *parallel* if they are in the same plane, never intersect, and are the same distance apart at every point.

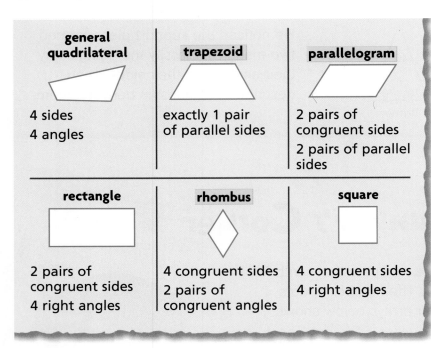

| general quadrilateral | trapezoid | parallelogram |
| --- | --- | --- |
| 4 sides  4 angles | exactly 1 pair of parallel sides | 2 pairs of congruent sides  2 pairs of parallel sides |

| rectangle | rhombus | square |
| --- | --- | --- |
| 2 pairs of congruent sides  4 right angles | 4 congruent sides  2 pairs of congruent angles | 4 congruent sides  4 right angles |

So, the faces of the top section of the building suggest rectangles, and the faces of the lower section suggest trapezoids.

- Besides *quadrilateral* and *rectangle,* what other name can you use to classify the faces of the top section of the building? Explain.

 **MATH IDEA**   You can classify quadrilaterals by the characteristics of their sides and angles.

## ▶ Check

1. **Explain** how a square and a rectangle are alike and how they are different.

Classify each figure in as many ways as possible. Write
*quadrilateral, parallelogram, square, rectangle, rhombus,*
or *trapezoid.*

**2.** **3.** **4.** **5.**

▶ **Practice and Problem Solving**      Extra Practice, page 474, Set B

Classify each figure in as many ways as possible. Write
*quadrilateral, parallelogram, square, rectangle, rhombus,*
or *trapezoid.*

**6.** **7.** **8.** **9.**

Write all of the names for each figure. Then write
the names that do *not* name the figure. Choose from
*trapezoid, parallelogram, rhombus, rectangle,* and *square.*

**10.** **11.** **12.** **13.**

**For 14–17, draw and classify each quadrilateral described.**

**14.** a parallelogram that has all sides congruent

**15.** a parallelogram with 4 right angles

**16.** a figure that is both a rhombus and a rectangle

**17.** a figure that has only 1 pair of parallel sides

**18.** The building on page 460 has 37 stories and is 535 feet tall. To the nearest foot, how tall is each story?

**19. REASONING** Troy says that all parallelograms are rectangles. Do you agree? Explain.

**20.** I have 540 rectangles and trapezoids. I have 120 more trapezoids than rectangles. How many of each do I have?

**21.** Sam earns $6 per hour walking dogs. He worked 4 hours each day for 5 days. He put $\frac{1}{3}$ of his earnings into a savings account. How much did he have to spend?

**Getting Ready for FCAT** THINK SOLVE EXPLAIN

**22.** A quadrilateral has two pairs of congruent sides, two pairs of parallel sides, and two pairs of congruent angles. Name all the possible figures that this quadrilateral can be.

# 3 Transformations and Tessellations

▶ **Learn**

**MOVING ALONG** A movement of a figure without changing the size or shape of the figure is called a rigid **transformation**.

## Examples

A **translation**, or a slide, is the movement of a figure along a straight line.

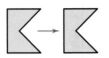

A **reflection**, or a flip, is the movement of a figure by flipping it over a line.

A **rotation**, or a turn, is the movement of a figure by turning it around a point, or vertex.

 90°
clockwise

### Quick Review

Tell the number of sides and angles in each polygon.

1. triangle   2. decagon
3. pentagon   4. octagon
5. quadrilateral

**VOCABULARY**

transformation    translation
reflection    rotation
tessellation

 **Technology Link**

**More Practice: Harcourt Mega Math Ice Station Exploration, *Polar Planes*, Level O**

---

**HANDS ON**

**Activity 1** Follow these steps to show a 90° counterclockwise rotation.

**MATERIALS:** dot paper, tracing paper, ruler

**STEP 1**
Draw this figure on a sheet of dot paper.

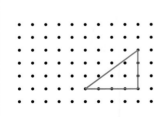

**STEP 2**
Draw a point of rotation. Trace the figure and the point of rotation.

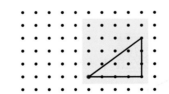

**STEP 3**
Using the point of rotation, rotate the tracing counterclockwise 90°. Draw the figure in its new location on the dot paper.

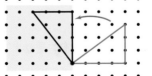

• Draw the triangle in Step 1 on your dot paper. Using the same point of rotation, show a 270° clockwise rotation ($\frac{3}{4}$ turn). Compare this rotation with the rotation in Activity 1.

**462**

## Tessellations

You can make a design by tracing a figure or figures and then translating, reflecting, or rotating the figures. When closed figures are arranged in a repeating pattern to cover a surface, with no gaps or overlaps, the pattern is called a **tessellation**.

### Activity 2

**MATERIALS:** tracing paper, ruler, scissors

Follow these steps to make a tessellation.

**STEP 1**

Trace these two figures and cut out 6 of each.

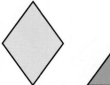

**STEP 2**

Use translations, reflections, or rotations of your figures to make a tessellation.

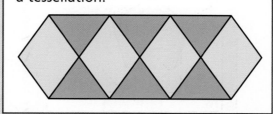

• What transformation or transformations did you use to make your tessellation?

### Check

1. **Explain** how you move a figure to show a translation, to show a reflection, and to show a rotation.

2. **Explain** how you know if a figure can be used to form a tessellation.

**Tell how the first figure was moved. Write *translation, reflection,* or *rotation*. For a rotation, write *clockwise* or *counterclockwise* and *90°, 180°,* or *270°*.**

3.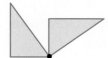

4.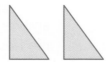

5.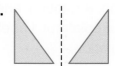

**Trace and cut out several of each figure. Tell if the figure or pair of figures will tessellate. Write *yes* or *no*.**

6.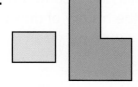

7.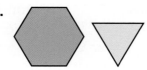

8.

LESSON CONTINUES

FCAT TESTED  SSS/GLEs MA.C.2.2.2.5.2 Knows the effects of a flip, slide, or turn (90°, 180°, 270°) and direction (clockwise or counterclockwise). *also* MA.C.2.2.2.5.1 and MA.C.2.2.2.5.3

Chapter 21  **463**

**Tell how the first figure was moved. Write** *translation, reflection,* **or** *rotation.* **For a rotation, write** *clockwise* **or** *counterclockwise* **and** *90°, 180°,* **or** *270°.*

9.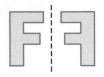

10.

11.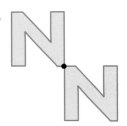

**Trace and cut out several of each figure. Tell if the figure or pair of figures will tessellate. Write** *yes* **or** *no.*

12.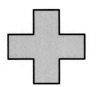

13.

14.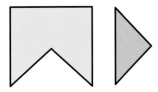

15.

16.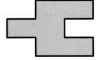

17.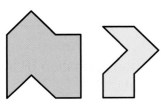

**Tell what moves were made to transform each figure into its next position.**

18.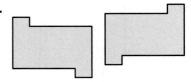

19.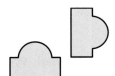

20. Draw a quadrilateral. Then draw a translation, a rotation, and a reflection of the quadrilateral. Label each transformation.

21. **VISUAL THINKING** Shelley's mom wants to cover her kitchen floor with square and regular octagon tiles. Draw what the design might look like.

22. Erica bought oranges that were marked as $0.89 per pound. At the cash register, she was charged $0.99 per pound. Show how you can find how much Erica was overcharged for the oranges.

23. **Vocabulary Power** The root of the word *tessellation* is *tessera,* which means "four." Tessera describes square pieces of stone or glass that are used to form a mosaic. Research the history of mosaic.

**24.** Kay wants to lay floor tile in a kitchen that measures 12 feet by 15 feet and a hallway that measures 4 feet by 15 feet. What is the total area to be covered?

**25.** Leticia has pattern blocks that are equilateral triangles, squares, and hexagons. All blocks have sides that are 1 inch long. Which two of these blocks can be used together for a tessellation?

**Getting Ready for FCAT**

**26.** Which shows the figure reflected over the line and then rotated 90° clockwise?

A.     B.     C.     D.

**27.** Which of the figures will NOT tessellate?

F.     G.     H.     I.

# Problem Solving LINKUP...to Art

**SYMMETRY AND ART** M. C. Escher, one of the world's most famous graphic artists, used tessellations in his work.

1. Trace one of the butterflies in *Symmetry Watercolor 70*. Move your tracing to cover other butterflies in the drawing. What transformations did you use?

2. Look at the point where the blue and yellow butterflies touch wings, shown by a black dot. How many blue butterflies and how many yellow butterflies rotate around this point?

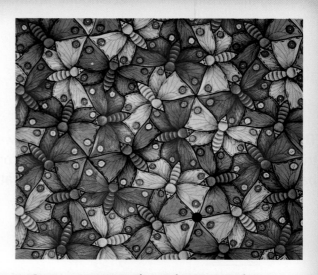

▲ **Symmetry Watercolor 70 by M. C. Escher**

# Solid Figures

▶ **Learn**

**BOX, BALL, OR CAN?** The design of the Rock and Roll Hall of Fame and Museum in Cleveland, Ohio, suggests several solid figures.

A solid figure with flat faces that are polygons is called a **polyhedron**.

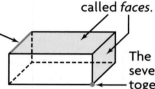

All of the flat surfaces are called *faces*.

The line where two faces come together is an *edge*.

The point where several edges come together is a *vertex*.

The main tower suggests a rectangular prism. A **prism** is a polyhedron that has two congruent polygons as **bases**. All other faces of a prism are rectangles. Polyhedrons are named by the polygons that form their bases.

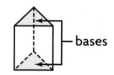

bases

**triangular prism**

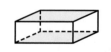

**rectangular prism**

**pentagonal prism**

**hexagonal prism**

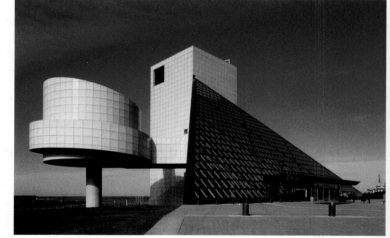

▲ I. M. Pei, the architect of the Rock and Roll Hall of Fame, is known for combining pyramids and other solids in his designs.

The glass structure next to the museum's tower suggests a triangular pyramid. A **pyramid** is a polyhedron with only one base. All other faces are triangles that meet at the same vertex.

base

**triangular pyramid**

**square pyramid**

**pentagonal pyramid**

**hexagonal pyramid**

# Classify Solid Figures

Solids with curved surfaces are *not* polyhedrons.

**cylinder**
A cylinder has 2 flat circular bases and 1 curved surface.

**cone**
A cone has 1 flat circular base and 1 curved surface.

**sphere**
A sphere has no bases and 1 curved surface.

 **MATH IDEA** Solid figures can be classified by the shape and number of their bases, faces, vertices, and edges.

## Examples

Classify the solid figure suggested by each building. If the figure is a polyhedron, tell the number of faces, vertices, and edges it has.

**Ⓐ Flatiron Building New York City, NY**

It has 2 triangular bases.
Faces: **5**
Vertices: **6**
Edges: **9**

**Classify: triangular prism**

**Ⓑ Grande Louvre Paris, France**

It has 1 square base.
Faces: **5**
Vertices: **5**
Edges: **8**

**Classify: square pyramid**

**Ⓒ Renaissance Center Detroit, MI**

It has 2 circular bases. It is not a polyhedron.

**Classify: cylinder**

## ▶ Check

1. **Explain** why a cylinder is *not* a polyhedron.

Classify each solid figure. Write *prism, pyramid, cone, cylinder,* or *sphere.*

**2.**

**3.**

**4.**

**5.**

Classify the solid figure. Then, write the number of faces, vertices, and edges.

**6.**

**7.**

**8.**

**9.**

**LESSON CONTINUES**

FCAT TESTED SSS/GLEs MA.C.1.2.1.5.1 Uses appropriate geometric vocabulary to describe properties and attributes of two- and three-dimensional figures.

Chapter 21  **467**

Classify each solid figure. Write *prism, pyramid, cone, cylinder,* or *sphere.*

**10.**

**11.**

**12.**

**13.**

Classify the solid figure. Then, write the number of faces, vertices, and edges.

**14.**

**15.**

**16.**

**17.**

**Draw and classify each solid figure described.**

**18.** I have a base with 4 congruent sides. My other faces are 4 triangles.

**19.** I have 2 bases that are congruent circles.

**20.** I have 2 congruent triangles for bases and 3 rectangular faces.

**21.** All of my 4 faces are congruent triangles.

**Copy and complete the table of solid figures.**

| | Name of Solid Figure | Number and Name of Bases | Number of Faces | Number of Vertices | Number of Edges |
|---|---|---|---|---|---|
| **22.** | rectangular prism | 2 rectangles | 6 | ■ | ■ |
| **23.** | triangular pyramid | 1 triangle | ■ | ■ | 6 |
| **24.** | pentagonal prism | ■ | 7 | 10 | ■ |
| **25.** | pentagonal pyramid | ■ | ■ | ■ | 10 |

**For 26–28, use the picture at the right of the Octagon House in Camillus, NY.**

**26.** What shape is the floor of the building?

**27.** What kind of angle does each corner of the building form?

**28.** When the Octagon House was built, each of its sides was 17 feet long. What was the perimeter of the house?

**29.** Which faces on a rectangular prism are parallel? Which faces are perpendicular and adjacent?

▼ **Octagon House, Camillus, NY**

**30.** Yoko walked around the perimeter of a rectangular building. The length of the building was 110 ft and the width was 82 ft. How many yards did Yoko walk?

**31.** The Miller family spent 4 days on a camping trip. They spent $\frac{1}{6}$ of the time hiking. How many hours did they spend hiking?

**32.** Leonardo is looking for a new fish tank at the pet store. He likes this one.

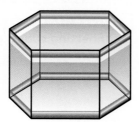

What is the name of this solid figure? Explain how you know.

**33.** Gloria sorted the shapes into two groups.

**Group A**

**Group B**

Describe one characteristic of the shapes in each group.

---

## Problem Solving   Thinker's Corner

**ALGEBRA EXPRESS!** You can write and evaluate expressions to find the number of faces, vertices, and edges for prisms and pyramids.

| Prisms | Pyramids |
|---|---|
| Let $n$ = the number of sides on the base | Let $n$ = the number of sides on the base |
| $n + 2$ = number of faces | $n + 1$ = number of faces |
| $n \times 2$ = number of vertices | $n + 1$ = number of vertices |
| $n \times 3$ = number of edges | $n \times 2$ = number of edges |

**hexagonal prism**

The number of sides on the base is 6.
So, $n = 6$.
number of faces:    $n + 2 = 6 + 2 = 8$
number of vertices: $n \times 2 = 6 \times 2 = 12$
number of edges:    $n \times 3 = 6 \times 3 = 18$

▲ An 18th century mathematician, Leonhard Euler, showed that for both prisms and pyramids, the number of faces plus the number of vertices minus the number of edges is 2.

**Tell how many faces, vertices, and edges each figure has.**

**1.** triangular prism

**2.** hexagonal pyramid

**3.** octagonal prism

# Draw Solid Figures from Different Views

**Quick Review**

Identify the solid that has the base or bases described.
**1.** 2 squares    **2.** 1 circle
**3.** 1 rectangle    **4.** 2 circles
**5.** 2 hexagons

**MATERIALS**
connecting cubes, grid paper

▶ **Explore**

You can use cubes to build a solid figure. Then you can use grid paper to draw the figure from different views.

How does the figure at the right look from the top, from the side, and from the front?

## Activity

Use connecting cubes to build the solid above. Draw three pictures on grid paper to show how the figure looks from the top, from the side, and from the front.

**Top View** | **Side View** | **Front View**

## Try It

Use cubes to build each figure. On grid paper, draw each figure from the top, from the side, and from the front.

**a.** 14 cubes

**b.** 10 cubes

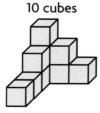

**c.** 10 cubes

**d.** 11 cubes

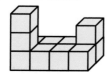

Which squares should I shade to show the front view?

**470**

**Technology Link**

**More Practice:** Harcourt
Mega Math Ice Station
Exploration, *Frozen
Solids,* Level M

You can identify some solids by the way they look from different views.

**Example** Which solid figure is shown by these three views?

**Top View**
The top view shows that the base is a circle and that the top comes to a point.

**Front View**
From the front the figure looks like a triangle.

**Side View**
From the side the figure looks like a triangle.

So, a solid figure with these views is a cone.

• What solid figure has squares in the top, front, and side views?

► **Practice and Problem Solving**

Use centimeter cubes to build each figure. On grid paper, draw each figure from the top, from the side, and from the front.

**1.** 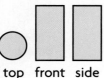   **2.**    **3.** 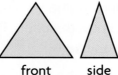   **4.**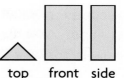

Identify the solid figure that has the given views.

**5.**

top   front   side

**6.**

top

front   side

**7.**

top   front   side

**8.** A side of a square measures 2 cm. A rectangle measures 1.5 cm by 2.1 cm. How much greater is the square's perimeter than the rectangle's?

**9.** Which solids have circles in some of their views?

**Getting Ready for FCAT**

**10.** Which solid figure has the given views?

**A.** triangular pyramid   **C.** cone
**B.** triangular prism   **D.** square pyramid

top

front

side

# Problem Solving Strategy
## Make a Model

**PROBLEM** For a math assignment, Tyler needs to draw the solid figure that has the top, side, and front views shown. How can Tyler determine what the solid figure looks like and find how many cubes he needs?

## UNDERSTAND

- What are you asked to find?
- What information will you use?

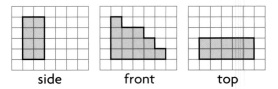

side          front          top

## PLAN

- What strategy can you use to solve the problem?

  You can *make a model* of the figure with cubes.

## SOLVE

- How can you use the strategy to solve the problem?

  Look at the drawings of the views to help you make the model with cubes. Then count the cubes you used.

  So, Tyler can see how the figure looks by observing his model. He used 26 cubes to make the model.

## CHECK

- Look back at the drawings. Does your model match all of the drawings?
- To check the number of cubes, count the cubes in each layer and find the sum.

## Strategies

Draw a Diagram or Picture
**Make a Model or Act It Out**
Make an Organized List
Find a Pattern
Make a Table or Graph
Predict and Test
Work Backward
Solve a Simpler Problem
Write an Equation
Use Logical Reasoning

**Problem Solving**

**Make a model to solve.**

1. **What if** Tyler decided to add to the figure another layer that is the same as the existing bottom layer? How many more cubes would he need?

2. Rachel is designing a tile mosaic for the top of her table. The shape she chooses for the tile must tessellate. Can she use the shape at the right? Explain.

**Sara, Nicole, Dee, Brittney, and Jana are in line to buy lunch. Sara is between Nicole and Dee. Dee is next to Jana, who is first in line.**

3. Who is last in line?

   A Sara
   B Nicole
   C Dee
   D Brittney

4. Suppose Sara leaves the line. Which of the following lists the remaining four students in order from first to last?

   F Jana, Dee, Nicole, Brittney
   G Jana, Nicole, Dee, Brittney
   H Jana, Brittney, Nicole, Dee
   J Jana, Nicole, Brittney, Dee

## Mixed Strategy Practice

5. Kevin spent $20.00 at the mall. He bought a book for $12.50 and two hats that were the same price. How much did he pay for each hat?

6. Ray started at home. He walked 2 blocks north, 3 blocks east, 4 blocks south, and 3 blocks west. How far was Ray from home then?

7. The shelves on the wall are 0.5 meter apart. The bottom shelf is 1.5 meters from the floor. There are 6 shelves.

8. Describe a relationship shown in this Venn diagram.

9. Jenna slept 9 hours, worked 8 hours, exercised 1 hour, read 2 hours, and shopped for 4 hours today. What type of graph should Jenna make to show how she spent her day? Explain.

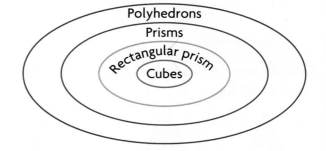

Polyhedrons
Prisms
Rectangular prism
Cubes

# Extra Practice

## Set A (pp. 456–459)

**Classify each triangle by its sides and angles. Write *isosceles, scalene, equilateral, right, acute,* or *obtuse*.**

**1.**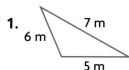

**2.**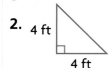

**3.**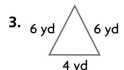

**4.**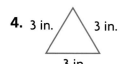

**5.**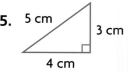

**6.** The measures of two angles of a triangle are 30° and 60°. What is the measure of its third angle? Classify the triangle by its angles.

## Set B (pp. 460–461)

**Classify each figure in as many ways as possible. Write *quadrilateral, parallelogram, square, rectangle, rhombus,* or *trapezoid*.**

**1.**

**2.**

**3.**

**4.**

**5.**

**6.**

**7.** The measures of three angles of a quadrilateral are 60°, 120°, and 60°. What is the measure of the fourth angle? If all of its sides are congruent, what kind of quadrilateral is it?

## Set C (pp. 462–465)

**Tell how the first figure was moved. Write *translation, reflection,* or *rotation*. For a rotation, write *clockwise* or *counterclockwise* and *90°, 180°,* or *270°*.**

**1.**

**2.**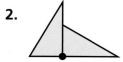

**3.**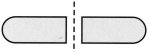

## Set D (pp. 466–469)

**Classify each solid figure. If it is a prism or pyramid, write the number of faces, vertices, and edges.**

**1.**

**2.**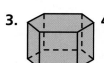

**3.**

**4.**

**5.**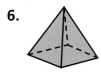

**6.**

# Review/Test

##  CHECK VOCABULARY AND CONCEPTS

**Choose the best term from the box.**

> rhombus
> bases
> prism
> trapezoid

1. Prisms and pyramids are named by the polygons that form their __?__. (p. 466)

2. A quadrilateral with 4 congruent sides and 2 pairs of congruent angles is a __?__. (p. 460)

##  CHECK SKILLS

**Classify each triangle by its sides and angles.** (pp. 456–459)

3.  3 ft  3 ft  2 ft

4.  4 in.  3 in.  5 in.

5.  2 cm  2 cm  2 cm

6.  6 yd  10 yd  8 yd

Classify each figure in as many ways as possible. Write *quadrilateral, parallelogram, square, rectangle, rhombus,* or *trapezoid.*

7.

8.

Tell how the first figure was moved. Write *translation, reflection,* or *rotation.* For a rotation, write *90°, 180°,* or *270°* and *clockwise* or *counterclockwise.* (pp. 462–465)

9.

10.

**Classify each solid figure. If it is a prism or pyramid, write the number of faces, vertices, and edges.** (pp. 466–469)

11.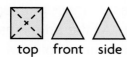

12.

13.

14.

**Identify the solid figure that has the given views.** (pp. 470–471)

15.
top  front  side

16.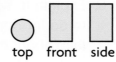
top  front  side

17.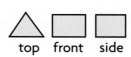
top  front  side

18.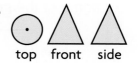
top  front  side

##  CHECK PROBLEM SOLVING

**Joe, Sue, Les, and Barb are in line to buy movie tickets. Bob is in front of Sue and behind Les. Joe is first in line.** (pp. 472–473)

19. Who is in front of Bob?

20. Who is last in line?

# Getting Ready for ⭐FCAT

## ⭐ GEOMETRY AND SPATIAL SENSE

**1.** Casey drew these diagrams of the top view, front view, and side view of a figure he built with blocks.

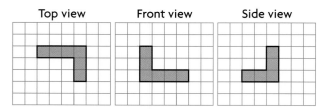

Top view     Front view     Side view

Which figure matches the diagrams?

**A.**      **C.**

**B.**      **D.**

**2.** Which figure is NOT a pyramid?

**F.**      **H.**

**G.**      **I.**

**3. Explain It** Evan drew a rectangle with a diagonal. He marked the measures of some of the angles.

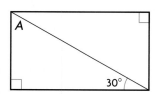

Explain how you can find the measure of angle *A*. Then write the measure of angle *A*.

## ⭐ NUMBER SENSE, CONCEPTS, AND OPERATIONS

**4.** How much longer than the Brooklyn-Battery Tunnel is the St. Gotthard Tunnel?

| TUNNEL LENGTHS | |
|---|---|
| **Tunnel and Location** | **Length (in miles)** |
| St. Gotthard, Switzerland | $10\frac{1}{10}$ |
| Brooklyn-Battery, New York | $1\frac{7}{10}$ |
| Delaware Aqueduct, New York | 85 |

**A.** $8\frac{2}{5}$ miles

**B.** $8\frac{3}{5}$ miles

**C.** $9\frac{3}{5}$ miles

**D.** $11\frac{4}{5}$ miles

**5.** Use the table in Problem 4. Suppose there are 425 equally-spaced lights in the Delaware Aqueduct. How many lights are in each mile?

**F.**       0.5

**G.**       5

**H.**       50

**I.** 36,125

**6. Explain It** Kenya has 24 math problems to do for homework. All the problems take about the same amount of time to solve. She finished 16 problems in $1\frac{1}{2}$ hours. Explain how you can ESTIMATE to decide whether Kenya should be able to finish the remaining problems in less than 40 minutes.

**DATA ANALYSIS AND PROBABILITY**

**7.** On which spinner is the probability of spinning a vowel $\frac{1}{2}$?

**A.**

**C.**

**B.**

**D.**

**8.** Penny rolled a 2 on a number cube labeled 1 to 6. She is going to roll the number cube again. What is the probability that the sum of her two rolls will be less than or equal to 5?

**F.** $\frac{1}{2}$

**G.** $\frac{1}{3}$

**H.** $\frac{1}{5}$

**I.** $\frac{1}{6}$

**9. Explain It** Jerry tried to make a graph to show the data in the table. Find the errors in his graph and explain how he can correct the errors.

| JACKET SALES | | | | |
|---|---|---|---|---|
| Color | Red | Yellow | Blue | Black |
| Number Sold | 3 | 5 | 2 | 4 |

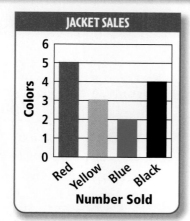

**ALGEBRAIC THINKING**

**10.** What are the next three figures in the pattern?

▲◗▽◖▲◑▽◖▲◗▽

**A.** ◖▲◗

**B.** ◗▼◖

**C.** ◑▼◖

**D.** ◖▲◑

> **TIP** **Understand the problem.** See item 11. The equation states that $n + 9 = 15$. To find the value of $n$, you need to find a number that is 9 less than 15. Then, use the value of $n$ to find the value of the expression $9 \times n$.

**11.** If $n + 9 = 15$, what is the value of $9 \times n$?

**F.** 96

**G.** 54

**H.** 24

**I.** 6

**12.** The table shows how many minutes it takes Heidi to read the pages in her book.

| HEIDI'S READING PATTERN | | | | | | |
|---|---|---|---|---|---|---|
| Number of Minutes | 1 | 2 | 3 | 4 | 5 | 6 |
| Number of Pages Read | 1.5 | 3 | 4.5 | 6 | ■ | ■ |

How many pages can Heidi read in 6 minutes? Explain how the number of pages Heidi reads changes as the number of minutes changes.

# Algebra: Integers

**FAST FACT • SPORTS** At the age of 24, Tiger Woods became the first golfer to be under par in every PGA Tour event for an entire year. In golf, the object of the game is to get the ball into the hole in as few strokes (hits) as possible. The standard number of strokes to get the ball into the hole is called par. A golfer's score is sometimes shown as the number of strokes above (+) or below (−) par.

**PROBLEM SOLVING** Use the tournament scorecard to find the players whose scores were below par.

| Player | Rounds | | | | Total Score | Par |
|---|---|---|---|---|---|---|
| | 1 | 2 | 3 | 4 | | |
| Sergio Garcia | 74 | 69 | 73 | 69 | 285 | −3 |
| Phil Mickelson | 70 | 70 | 69 | 70 | 279 | −9 |
| Loren Roberts | 74 | 72 | 71 | 73 | 290 | +2 |
| Brian Watts | 72 | 74 | 73 | 70 | 289 | +1 |
| Tiger Woods | 66 | 67 | 70 | 67 | 270 | −18 |

TOURNAMENT SCORECARD
82nd PGA CHAMPIONSHIP–LOUISVILLE, KENTUCKY

**Tiger Woods**

# CHECK WHAT YOU KNOW

Use this page to help you review and remember
important skills needed for Chapter 22.

## COMPARE WHOLE NUMBERS

Compare. Use <, >, or = for each ●.

**1.** 112 ● 111　　**2.** 98 ● 99　　**3.** 82 ● 87　　　**4.** 905 ● 950　　**5.** 997 ● 999

**6.** 12 ● 10　　**7.** 56 ● 65　　**8.** 102 ● 120　　**9.** 752 ● 725　　**10.** 425 ● 424

**11.** 81 ● 88　　**12.** 32 ● 320　　**13.** 111 ● 101　　**14.** 323 ● 423　　**15.** 121 ● 120

## READ A THERMOMETER

Write the Fahrenheit temperature reading for each.

**16.**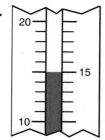

**17.**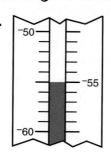

**18.**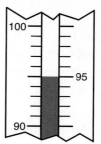

**19.**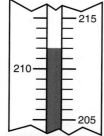

**20.**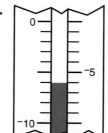

**21.**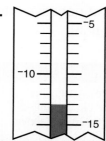

# VOCABULARY POWER

### REVIEW

**number** [num′bər] *noun*

A number can have many names, such
as whole number, even number, or
prime number. Give an example and a
nonexample of a whole number, an even
number, and a prime number. Explain your
choices.

### PREVIEW

integers　　　　　opposites

negative integers　absolute value

positive integers

www.harcourtschool.com/mathglossary

# Understand Integers

▶ **Learn**

**HIGHS AND LOWS**   The highest temperature in the United States, recorded in California, was ⁺134°F. The lowest temperature, recorded in Alaska, was ⁻80°F.

The numbers ⁺134 and ⁻80 are **integers**. You read ⁺134 as "positive one hundred thirty-four" and ⁻80 as "negative eighty."

Just as a thermometer shows temperatures above and below 0°, a number line shows numbers to the right and to the left of 0. Integers can be shown on a number line.

**VOCABULARY**

**integers**
**negative integers**
**positive integers**
**opposites**
**absolute value**

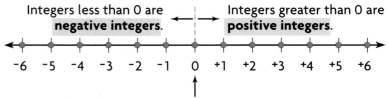

Integers less than 0 are **negative integers**.          Integers greater than 0 are **positive integers**.

⁻6  ⁻5  ⁻4  ⁻3  ⁻2  ⁻1   0   ⁺1  ⁺2  ⁺3  ⁺4  ⁺5  ⁺6

The integer 0 is neither positive nor negative.

Positive and negative integers can be used to represent word situations.

| Situation | Integer |
|---|---|
| Mt. McKinley, Alaska, the highest point in the United States, is 20,320 feet above sea level. | +20,320 |
| Ken deposited $75 in his checking account. | +75 |
| The Lions gained 6 yards for a first down. | +6 |
| Death Valley, California, the lowest point in the United States, is 282 feet below sea level. | -282 |
| Ken withdrew $25 from his checking account. | -25 |
| The Bears lost 5 yards on the last play. | -5 |

The polar bear's body is designed to stay warm when the air is as cold as ⁻49°F. Under its fur, the bear has a layer of blubber 4 inches thick to help keep it warm. ▼

## Opposites and Absolute Values

The opposite of going up 3 steps is going down 3 steps. In both cases the same distance is traveled, 3 steps.

Integers include all whole numbers and their opposites. For every positive integer, there is an opposite, negative integer. Integers that are **opposites** are the same distance from 0 on a number line, but in opposite directions.

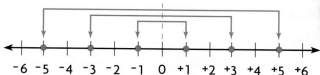

The number line above has these opposites graphed:

$^-1$ and $^+1$        $^-3$ and $^+3$        $^-5$ and $^+5$

**Technology Link**

More Practice:
Harcourt Mega Math
The Number Games,
*Tiny's Think Tank,*
Level V

The **absolute value** of an integer is its distance from 0 on a number line.

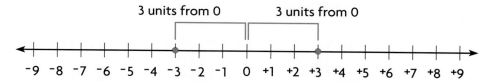

3 units from 0        3 units from 0

**Write:** $|^-3| = 3$   **Read:** The absolute value of negative three is three.

**Write:** $|^+3| = 3$   **Read:** The absolute value of positive three is three.

### Examples

**A** Name the opposite of $^-11$.

$^-11 \rightarrow {}^+11$

**C** Name the opposite of $^+14$.

$^+14 \rightarrow {}^-14$

**B** Use the number line to find $|^-4|$.

$|^-4| = 4$

**D** Use the number line to find $|^+9|$.

$|^+9| = 9$

▶ **Check**

1. **Tell** how many total points you have if you win 10 points on your first turn and then lose 10 points on your second turn. Write the integers that represent what happens on each turn. Explain how these integers are related.

LESSON CONTINUES

**Identify the integers graphed on the number line.**

**2.** 
-4 -3 -2 -1 0 +1 +2 +3 +4

**3.** 
-6 -4 -2 0 +2

**Write an integer to represent each situation.**

**4.** a deposit of $30    **5.** 85 degrees above 0    **6.** a loss of 15 yards

**Write the opposite of each integer.**

**7.** $^+7$    **8.** $^-9$    **9.** $^-2$    **10.** $^+8$    **11.** 0

## Practice and Problem Solving    Extra Practice, page 492, Set A

**Identify the integers graphed on the number line.**

**12.** 
-1 0 +1 +2 +3 +4 +5 +6 +7 +8

**13.** 
-2 0 +2 +4 +6

**Write an integer to represent each situation.**

**14.** three points ahead    **15.** a growth of 8 inches    **16.** 8 feet below sea level

**17.** a gain of 5 pounds    **18.** 15 feet underground    **19.** 4 seconds before liftoff

**Write the opposite of each integer.**

**20.** $^-3$    **21.** $^+4$    **22.** $^+16$    **23.** $^-22$    **24.** $^+41$

**25.** $^+54$    **26.** $^-29$    **27.** $^-73$    **28.** $^+102$    **29.** $^+2,314$

**Write each integer's absolute value.**

**30.** $|^+25|$    **31.** $|^-10|$    **32.** $|^+1,000|$    **33.** $|^-1|$    **34.** $|0|$

**35.** ALGEBRA    What values can $n$ have if $|n| = 6$?

**For 36–37, use the number line to locate each integer.**

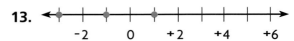

A B C D E F G H I J K
-5 0 +5

**36.** Write the letter for each integer.

   **a.** $^-3$    **b.** $^+4$    **c.** 0    **d.** $^-1$

**37.** Write the letter for the opposite of each integer.

   **a.** $^-2$    **b.** $^+3$    **c.** $^+4$    **d.** $^-3$

**38.** Which of the integers $^-7$, $^+4$, $^-13$, $^-4$, $^+2$, $^-2$, $^+7$, $^+13$ are positive? negative? Name the opposite pairs.

**39.** **REASONING**  If 0 stands for today, which integers stand for yesterday and tomorrow?

**40.** Write About It  Describe a situation that uses positive and negative integers. Then write each integer and explain what each integer means.

**41.** One week, Becka earned $2 on Sunday and $5 on each of the other days of the week. How much did she earn that week?

**42. Vocabulary Power** Many words used in mathematics have meanings outside of math. Write a mathematical and a nonmathematical definition for *opposite*.

**43.** Library books are arranged on the shelves of libraries by call numbers. The call number of a book is shown below.

513.876

Which digit is in the hundredths place of the call number?

**A.** 5  **C.** 7

**B.** 6  **D.** 8

Reviews Florida SSS/GLE MA.A.1.2.1.5.2.

**44.** Which book shown below has a call number that is read as "forty and six hundred fifty-two thousandths"?

Coins for Kids — 40.652
Let's Calculate! — 46.052
Plants for All — 40,652
Chinese Characters — 460.52

**F.** Coins for Kids
**G.** Let's Calculate!
**H.** Plants for All
**I.** Chinese Characters

# Problem Solving LiNKUP . . . to Reading

**STRATEGY • USE CONTEXT** To *use context,* look for words and phrases that help you understand the meanings of words, sentences, paragraphs, and situations. The words below can help you decide if an integer is negative, zero, or positive.

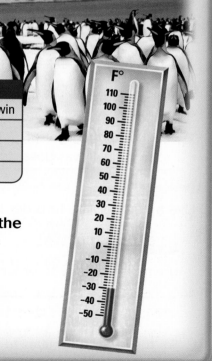

| Negative | Zero | Positive |
|---|---|---|
| withdraw, loss, spend, lose, lost | no change, break even | deposit, profit, earn, gain, win |
| below, below sea level, down | sea level | above, above sea level, up |
| drop, behind | even | rise, ahead |
| before | now | after |

**Write an integer to represent what happens in each situation. Then write the word or phrase that helps you decide whether the integer is positive, negative, or zero.**

**1.** Karen deposited $20 in her savings account on Monday.

**2.** Between ages 16 and 17, Antoine did not change in height.

**3.** When the cold front moved in, the temperature dropped five degrees.

# Compare and Order Integers

▶ **Learn**

**IN THE DEEP**  In 1718, the pirate Blackbeard's flagship, *Queen Anne's Revenge (QAR),* sank at Beaufort Inlet, North Carolina. In 1996, divers discovered a shipwreck believed to be the *QAR.* The ship's cannons were found 21 feet below the water's surface, and its bell was found 20 feet below the surface. Which was closer to the surface, the cannons or the bell?

Use a number line to compare. On a number line, a number to the right is always greater than a number to the left.

## Example 1

### STEP 1

Name the integers that represent each situation.
   cannons 21 feet below the surface: $^-21$
   bell 20 feet below the surface: $^-20$
   water's surface: 0

### STEP 2

Graph the integers $^-21$, $^-20$, and 0 on a number line.

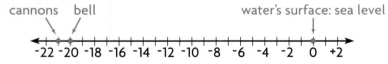

cannons   bell                   water's surface: sea level

To find the integer closer to sea level, or 0, find the greater integer.

$^-20$ is to the right of $^-21$. $^-20 > ^-21$

So, the bell was closer to the surface than the cannons.

▲ **A diver examines an anchor fluke at the QAR site. Excavation is done in 10-foot square units.**

**Technology Link**

More Practice:
Harcourt Mega Math
Fraction Action,
*Number Line Mine,*
Level T

Use a number line to order integers.

## Example 2

Use a number line to order $^+5$, $^-2$, $^-4$, $^+1$, and $^-5$ from least to greatest.

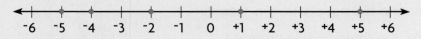

So, the order from least to greatest is $^-5$, $^-4$, $^-2$, $^+1$, and $^+5$.

1. **Explain** why integers are easier to compare when they are graphed on a number line.

**Compare. Write <, >, or = for each ●.**

2. $^+5$ ● $^+4$     3. $^-6$ ● $^-3$     4. $^+2$ ● $^-5$     5. $^-1$ ● $0$     6. $|^-2|$ ● $^-2$

▶ **Practice and Problem Solving**   ( Extra Practice, page 492, Set B )

**Compare. Write <, >, or = for each ●.**

7. $0$ ● $^+1$     8. $^-8$ ● $^-9$     9. $^-2$ ● $^+4$     10. $|^-3|$ ● $^-6$     11. $|^-4|$ ● $^+4$

**Draw a number line to order each set of integers from greatest to least.**

12. $^+1, ^-2, 0, ^-3$     13. $^-4, ^+3, ^-2, ^+1$     14. $^+5, ^-6, ^+7, ^-8$     15. $^-10, ^+10, ^+8, ^-7$

**ALGEBRA**   **Name the integer that is 1 less.**

16. $^+8$        17. $^-4$        18. $^-1$        19. $0$        20. $^+3$

**ALGEBRA**   **Name the integer that is 1 more.**

21. $^-4$        22. $^-1$        23. $^+6$        24. $^-8$        25. $^-10$

**USE DATA**   For 26–27 and 30, use the table.

26. One mile is 5,280 feet. Which ocean is less than 1 mile deep?

27. Mt. Fuji in Japan is 12,388 feet tall. Which ocean's depth is closest to being the opposite of Mt. Fuji's height?

28. **REASONING**   Oarfish live at $^-3,000$ feet. Below $^-2,300$ feet, light cannot reach through water. Do oarfish live in the dark? Explain.

30. ✎ **Write a problem** that uses the table and requires comparing or ordering integers.

| AVERAGE DEPTHS OF OCEANS | |
|---|---|
| Ocean | Depth in feet |
| Atlantic | 12,880 |
| Indian | 13,002 |
| Arctic | 3,953 |
| Pacific | 13,215 |

29. ▤**FAST FACT** • SCIENCE The most valuable shipwreck was found off Key West, Florida. The ship carried 21 tons of gold and 15 tons of silver. Was that more than or less than 50,000 pounds? Explain.

⌐ **Getting Ready for FCAT** ⌐

31. Which shows the weights in order from **greatest** to **least**?

   **A.** D, A, B, C        **C.** D, B, A, C
   **B.** C, A, B, D        **D.** B, A, D, C

| **A** | **B** | **C** | **D** |
| 0.325g | 0.35g | 0.032g | 0.5g |

Reviews Florida SSS/GLE MA.A.I.2.2.5.3.

# Addition and Subtraction of Integers

**MATERIALS**
two-color counters

▶ **Learn**

**UNDER PAR** In golf, *par* is the number of strokes needed to get the ball into a hole. The number of strokes it takes a golfer to do this is compared to par. $^-1$ means 1 stroke less than par or one under par.

In Round 4 of the 2002 Masters Tournament, Tiger Woods was $^-2$ for Holes 1 through 9 and $^+1$ for Holes 10 through 18. So in Round 4, Tiger was $^-2 + {^+1}$.

You can use two-color counters to add integers. Find $^-2 + {^+1}$.

◀ Tiger Woods won his third Masters Tournament in 2002. His final score was 276, which was $^-12$, or 12 strokes under par.

**HANDS ON**

**Activity 1** Find $^-2 + {^+1}$.

**STEP 1**

Use yellow counters to represent positive integers and red counters to represent negative integers.

$= {^-2}$
$= {^+1}$

**STEP 2**

Make as many opposite pairs of one yellow and one red counter as possible. The sum of each opposite pair is 0, so take away each opposite pair.

**STEP 3**

The number and color of unpaired counters represent the sum.

 $= {^-1}$

There is 1 red counter left, so $^-2 + {^+1} = {^-1}$.

So, Tiger was $^-1$ for Round 4.

## Examples

Ⓐ Find $^-3 + {^-2}$.

$= {^-5}$

So, $^-3 + {^-2} = {^-5}$.

Ⓑ Find $^+4 + {^-3}$.

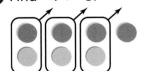 $= {^+1}$

So, $^+4 + {^-3} = {^+1}$.

## Subtract Integers

You can also use two-color counters to subtract integers.

**Activity 2** Find ⁻4 − ⁻1.

| STEP 1 | STEP 2 | STEP 3 |
|---|---|---|
| Make a row of 4 red counters to show ⁻4.  = ⁻4 | To subtract ⁻1, take away 1 red counter. 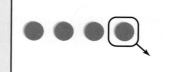 | The number and the color of counters left represent the difference. ●●● = ⁻3  There are 3 red counters left, so ⁻4 − ⁻1 = ⁻3. |

At 10:00 A.M., the temperature in Barrow, AL, was ⁺3°F. By midnight, it had fallen 5 degrees. What was the temperature at midnight?

**Activity 3** Find ⁺3 − ⁺5.

| STEP 1 | STEP 2 | STEP 3 |
|---|---|---|
| Make a row of 3 yellow counters.  = ⁺3 | The value of an opposite pair is 0. In order to have 5 yellow counters to take away, add 2 opposite pairs. The model still shows ⁺3. 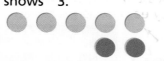 | To subtract ⁺5, take away 5 yellow counters. 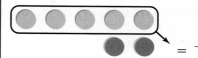 = ⁻2  There are 2 red counters left, so ⁺3 − ⁺5 = ⁻2. |

So, the temperature at midnight was ⁻2°F.

## Examples

**C** Find ⁻4 − ⁺2.
Model ⁻4 using 2 opposite pairs. Then, take away 2 yellow counters.

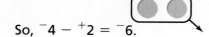

So, ⁻4 − ⁺2 = ⁻6.

**D** Find ⁺6 − ⁻1.
Model ⁺6 using 1 opposite pair. Then, take away 1 red counter.

So, ⁺6 − ⁻1 = ⁺7.

LESSON CONTINUES ▶

1. **Explain** how to make a model of $^+5 - {}^-2$. Tell how you decided the number of opposite pairs to add. Then, find $^+5 - {}^-2$.

**Copy and complete the number sentence.**

2. $5 + {}^-3 = \blacksquare$

3. $^-3 - {}^+4 = \blacksquare$

**Find the sum or difference. You may wish to use counters.**

4. $^+2 + {}^-3$     5. $^+2 - {}^-3$     6. $^-2 - {}^+3$     7. $^+7 + {}^-3$

**Copy and complete the number sentence.**

8. $^-3 + {}^+1 = \blacksquare$

9. $^-6 - {}^-2 = \blacksquare$

**Find the sum or difference. You may wish to use counters.**

10. $^+6 - {}^+3$     11. $^-8 - {}^+3$     12. $^-7 + {}^+5$     13. $^+9 + {}^+4$

14. $^+5 + {}^-2$     15. $^-6 + {}^+5$     16. $^-4 - {}^+9$     17. $^+1 - {}^-8$

18. $^+6 + {}^-7$     19. $0 - {}^+12$     20. $^-5 + {}^-3 + 0$     21. $^+4 + {}^-4 + {}^+4$

**Compare. Write $<$, $>$, or $=$ for each $\blacksquare$.**

22. $^-4 + {}^-5 \ \blacksquare \ {}^-1$     23. $^+7 + {}^-4 \ \blacksquare \ {}^-3$     24. $^+17 + {}^-3 \ \blacksquare \ {}^-20$

**USE DATA For 25–26, use the chart.**

25. Suppose 0 represents even par for a hole. Write an integer for each of the scores listed, and order them from least to greatest.

26. In golf, the lowest score is the best. On the fifth hole, Jenny made an eagle and Paul made a double bogey. Write an integer to represent each player's score. Who won the hole?

27. **?  What's the Question?** There are 6 red counters and 4 yellow counters. The answer is $^-2$.

| GOLF TERMS |
| --- |
| Bogey = 1 stroke over par |
| Double Bogey = 2 strokes over par |
| Birdie = 1 stroke under par |
| Eagle = 2 strokes under par |

**28.** Pontchartrain Park in New Orleans, Louisiana is 5 feet below sea level. Write this elevation as an integer.

**29.** 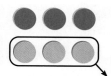 **? What's the Error?** Correct the error in this model of ⁻3 − ⁺3.

**30.** Lance forgot to list some records in his check register.

| Date | Check | Deposit | Balance |
|------|-------|---------|---------|
|      |       |         | $238.61 |
| 5/1  | ▪     |         | $162.98 |
| 5/3  |       | ▪       | $338.43 |
| 5/4  | $179.05 |       | ?       |

What was the amount of the check that Lance wrote on May 1?

**A.** $75.63    **C.** $301.59
**B.** $175.63   **D.** $401.59

**31.** Look at the check register in Problem 30. How much did Lance deposit on May 3?

**F.** $75.45     **H.** $401.42
**G.** $175.45    **I.** $501.42

**32.** Look at the check register in Problem 30. What was the balance on May 4 after Lance wrote the check for $179.05?

**A.** $59.38     **C.** $159.38
**B.** $141.42    **D.** $517.48

Reviews Florida SSS/GLE MA.A.3.2.2.5.1

# Problem Solving **LINKUP** . . . to Science

The inner planets are Mercury, Venus, Earth, and Mars. The outer planets are Jupiter, Saturn, Uranus, Neptune, and Pluto. Scientists measure the surface temperatures of Mercury, Venus, Earth, Mars, and Pluto. Since Jupiter, Saturn, Uranus, and Neptune are gas and have no surface, scientists measure the temperature of the highest layer of clouds.

**USE DATA** Use the tables.

**1.** Which are the coldest and hottest inner planets?

**2.** Which are the coldest and hottest outer planets?

**3.** Order the planets from coldest to hottest.

| TEMPERATURE AT CLOUD TOPS | |
|---------|-------------|
| **Planet** | **Temperature** |
| Jupiter | ⁻160°F |
| Saturn | ⁻220°F |
| Uranus | ⁻323°F |
| Neptune | ⁻330°F |

| AVERAGE SURFACE TEMPERATURE | |
|---------|-------------|
| **Planet** | **Temperature** |
| Mercury | 333°F |
| Venus | 865°F |
| Earth | 45°F |
| Mars | ⁻80°F |
| Pluto | ⁻382°F |

# Problem Solving Strategy
## Draw a Diagram

**Quick Review**

1. $^-2 + {}^+5$
2. $^-8 - {}^+3$   3. $^+10 + {}^-2$
4. $^-4 - {}^+5$   5. $^-6 + {}^+1$

**PROBLEM** Carson parked in the deepest underground parking garage in London, the Aldersgate Car Park. It has 14 floors for 670 cars. After a long day of sightseeing, he returned to the parking garage to find his car. He forgot where he had parked. So, he entered the elevator on the ground floor and took the elevator down 8 floors and looked. Then he went up 2 floors, down 5 floors, and up another 4 floors before he found his car. His car was parked on which floor?

### UNDERSTAND

- What are you asked to find?

- What information will you use?

- Is there any information you will not use?

### PLAN

- What strategy can you use to solve the problem?

  You can *draw a diagram* of the underground floors.

### SOLVE

- How can you use this strategy to solve the problem?

  Draw a vertical number line to represent the parking garage's levels. Start at the ground floor and model Carson's movements.

  So, Carson found his car parked 7 floors underground, or on the $^-7$ floor.

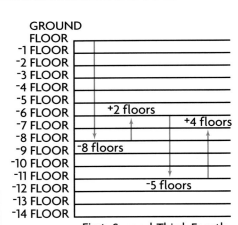

| GROUND FLOOR |
|---|
| -1 FLOOR |
| -2 FLOOR |
| -3 FLOOR |
| -4 FLOOR |
| -5 FLOOR |
| -6 FLOOR |
| -7 FLOOR |
| -8 FLOOR |
| -9 FLOOR |
| -10 FLOOR |
| -11 FLOOR |
| -12 FLOOR |
| -13 FLOOR |
| -14 FLOOR |

+2 floors    +4 floors
-8 floors
-5 floors

First Second Third Fourth
Look Look Look Look

### CHECK

- How can you decide if your answer is correct?

## Problem Solving Practice

### Strategies

▶ **Draw a Diagram or Picture**
Make a Model or Act It Out
Make an Organized List
Find a Pattern
Make a Table or Graph
Predict and Test
Work Backward
Solve a Simpler Problem
Write an Equation
Use Logical Reasoning

**Draw a diagram to solve.**

1. **What if** Carson entered the elevator on the ground floor and took the elevator down 6 floors and looked? Then he went up 3 floors, down 7 floors, and up another 5 floors before he found his car. His car was parked on which floor?

2. At 7:00 A.M., the temperature was ⁻3°F. At 1:00 P.M., the temperature had risen by 11 degrees. By 11:00 P.M., it had dropped 15 degrees. What was the temperature at 11:00 P.M.?

3. A scuba diver descended to 14 feet below sea level. She then ascended 4 feet and swam 10 feet ahead. She then descended 6 feet. At what depth is she now?

4. Starting on their own 40-yard line, the Tigers gained 5 yards on their first play. Then they lost 15 yards in a penalty. What yard line are they on now?

## Mixed Strategy Practice

**USE DATA** For 5–8, use the table. The table shows the same time in each time zone from the West coast to the East coast.

| TIME ZONES IN THE UNITED STATES | | | | | |
|---|---|---|---|---|---|
| Hawaii-Aleutian | Alaska | Pacific | Mountain | Central | Eastern |
| 2 P.M. | 3 P.M. | 4 P.M. | 5 P.M. | 6 P.M. | 7 P.M. |

5. What integer represents the change from Eastern time to Pacific time?

6. Describe the time pattern as you travel west across the time zones.

7. Suppose a pilot left the Mountain time zone at 6 P.M., flew west for 2 hours, and landed in the Pacific time zone. What time did he land?

   **A** 6 P.M.    **B** 7 P.M.    **C** 8 P.M.    **D** 9 P.M.

8. Suppose a pilot left the Pacific time zone at 3 P.M., flew east for 3 hours, and landed in the Central time zone. What time did she land?

   **F** 6 P.M.    **G** 7 P.M.    **H** 8 P.M.    **J** 9 P.M.

9. On May 6, 1992, a U.S. diver went underwater in a module and stayed there for a record 69 days. On what date did he come up?

10. ✎ **Write a problem** using integers that you can solve by drawing a diagram. Draw your diagram.

# Extra Practice

## Set A (pp. 480–483)

**Identify the integers graphed on the number line.**

1.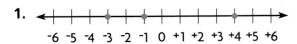

2.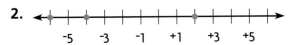

**Write an integer to represent each situation.**

**3.** spend $100   **4.** 75° above 0°   **5.** a loss of $3   **6.** gain 12 yards

**7.** Israel, the hottest place in Asia, recorded a temperature of almost 129°F. That is the opposite of the coldest recorded temperature in Antarctica. How cold has it been in Antarctica?

## Set B (pp. 484–485)

**Compare. Write <, >, or = for each ●.**

**1.** $^+6$ ● $^+3$   **2.** $^-6$ ● $^-3$   **3.** $^+10$ ● $^-12$   **4.** $^-3$ ● $0$   **5.** $^-2$ ● $^-4$

**Order each set of integers from least to greatest.**

**6.** $^+6, ^-1, ^+7, ^-5$   **7.** $^+3, ^-2, 0, ^-4$   **8.** $^-9, ^+8, ^-11, ^+4$   **9.** $^+2, ^-2, ^+1, 0$

**10.** The average temperatures for 3 weeks in Alaska were $^-21$°F, $^-26$°F, and $^-25$°F. Which is the coldest?

## Set C (pp. 486–489)

**Copy and complete the number sentence.**

1.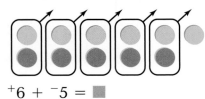

$^+6 + ^-5 = $ ■

2.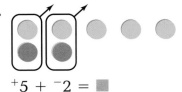

$^+5 + ^-2 = $ ■

3.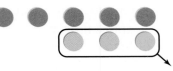

$^-2 - ^+3 = $ ■

4.

$^-6 - ^-5 = $ ■

**Find the sum or difference. You may wish to use counters.**

**5.** $^+3 + ^-4$   **6.** $^-5 + ^+2$   **7.** $^+9 + ^-7$   **8.** $^+6 + ^-6$

**9.** $^+12 - ^+4$   **10.** $^-5 - ^+5$   **11.** $^-10 - 0$   **12.** $^-5 - ^+9$

# Review/Test

## ✅ CHECK VOCABULARY AND CONCEPTS

**Choose the best term from the box.**

1. The distance that an integer is from 0 is the __?__ of the integer. (p. 481)

2. An integer less than 0 is a __?__. (p. 480)

3. Integers that are the same distance from 0 on a number line, but in opposite directions, are called __?__. (p. 481)

4. Whole numbers and their opposites are called __?__. (p. 481)

> absolute value
> integers
> negative integer
> opposites
> positive integer

## ✅ CHECK SKILLS

**Name an integer to represent each situation.** (pp. 480–483)

5. a profit of $50
6. 20 degrees below 0
7. a loss of 10 yards

**Write the opposite of each integer.** (pp. 480–483)

8. $^+14$    9. $^-6$    10. $^-5$    11. $^+22$    12. $^-7$

**Order each set of integers from least to greatest.** (pp. 484–485)

13. $^+2, ^-3, ^+8, ^-8$    14. $^+1, ^-4, 0, ^-5$    15. $^-7, ^+3, ^-6, ^+2$    16. $^+5, ^-5, ^+3, ^+2$

**Find the sum or difference. You may wish to use counters.** (pp. 486–489)

17. $^+3 + ^-2$    18. $^-11 - ^+1$    19. $^-8 + ^-3$    20. $^-4 - ^-11$    21. $^-7 + ^+2$

22. $^+8 + ^-4$    23. $^-9 - ^+4$    24. $^-7 + ^+7$    25. $^-10 - ^+1$    26. $^+9 + ^-10$

27. $^+6 - ^+3$    28. $^-7 + ^+3$    29. $^-6 - ^+2$    30. $^+5 + ^-4$    31. $^-1 - ^-3$

## ✅ CHECK PROBLEM SOLVING

**Draw a diagram to solve.** (pp. 490–491)

32. Tara works in the mail room on the second floor. For her first two deliveries she went up 4 floors and then down 3 floors. Then she went down 4 floors for her last delivery. If the 1st floor is also the ground floor, on what floor was her last delivery?

33. The temperature at 6 A.M. was $^-2$°F. By 10 A.M., it had risen 5°. By 10 P.M., the temperature had dropped 3°. What was the temperature at 10 P.M.?

# Getting Ready for FCAT

 **NUMBER SENSE, CONCEPTS, AND OPERATIONS**

**1.** The diagram shows distances between several locations.

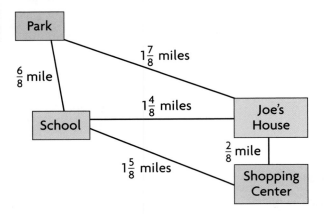

How many miles would Joe walk if he went from his house to school, then to the park, and then straight home from the park?

**A.** $2\frac{17}{24}$ miles  **C.** $4\frac{1}{8}$ miles

**B.** $3\frac{7}{8}$ miles  **D.** $21\frac{7}{8}$ miles

**2.** Look at the diagram above. How much farther is it from Joe's house to the park than from his house to the school?

**F.** $\frac{3}{8}$ mile

**G.** $1\frac{3}{8}$ miles

**H.** $2\frac{3}{8}$ miles

**I.** $3\frac{3}{8}$ miles

**3. Explain It** Joe likes to walk between 3 and 4 miles each evening after dinner. Look at the diagram and suggest a route he could take that begins and ends at his home. Explain how you chose your route.

 **DATA ANALYSIS AND PROBABILITY**

**4.** The table shows the lengths of four of the largest snails.

| LARGEST SNAILS | |
|---|---|
| **Snail** | **Length (in inches)** |
| California Sea Hare | 30 inches |
| Apple | 20 inches |
| Trumpet | 15 inches |
| African Land | 10 inches |

Which graph or table is **most** appropriate to display the snail data?

**A.** bar graph

**B.** frequency table

**C.** line graph

**D.** circle graph

**5.** Look at the table above. Which is the **most** reasonable interval for graphing the snail data?

**F.** 5

**G.** 20

**H.** 50

**I.** 100

**6. Explain It** Fong is drawing a graph that shows how the United States population has changed over the past 50 years. Lena is drawing a graph that shows how her school enrollment has changed over the past 50 years. Explain what type of graph they should each draw, and tell why the scales for the two graphs would be different.

**GEOMETRIC AND SPATIAL SENSE**

**7.** Mia drew two squares. The sides of Square B are 2 times the length of the sides of Square A. How does the area of Square B compare to the area of Square A?

 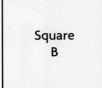

Square A

Square B

**A.** The area of Square B is equal to the area of Square A.

**B.** The area of Square B is 2 times the area of Square A.

**C.** The area of Square B is 3 times the area of Square A.

**D.** The area of Square B is 4 times the area of Square A.

**8.** The letter E is shown below.

E

Which of the following is a reflection of the letter E?

**F.** Ш      **H.** Ǝ

**G.** ш      **I.** Ǝ

> **TIP** **Decide on a plan.** See item 9. Use the strategy *draw a diagram or picture.*

**9. Explain It** Mr. Thomas has a solid figure with 5 faces. He shows the class one face that is a triangle and another face that is a rectangle. What are the possible solid figures that Mr. Thomas has? Explain your answer.

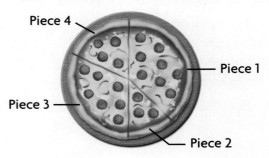 **MEASUREMENT**

**10.** Deana cut a pizza into 4 pieces. She took the piece with the largest acute angle. Which piece did she eat?

Piece 4

Piece 1

Piece 3

Piece 2

**A.** Piece 1

**B.** Piece 2

**C.** Piece 3

**D.** Piece 4

**11.** Erin weighed a bunch of grapes on the scale at the supermarket.

How much do the grapes weigh to the nearest ounce?

**F.** 1 pound 4 ounces

**G.** 1 pound 8 ounces

**H.** 1 pound 14 ounces

**I.** 2 pounds

**12. Explain It** Jason started his homework at 4 P.M. He spent $\frac{1}{2}$ hour doing math problems, $\frac{3}{4}$ hour writing a book report, and $1\frac{1}{4}$ hours finding data for a science report. ESTIMATE to find out if Jason finished his homework before 6 P.M. Explain how you know.

# Geometry and the Coordinate Plane

**≡FAST FACT** • SOCIAL STUDIES When a city is planned, a grid is sometimes used to lay out the streets. The first city in the United States to be laid out in a grid was central Philadelphia, by William Penn in 1682. Every street was laid out at right angles with another except one, Dock Street.

**PROBLEM SOLVING** Use the map grid to find the landmark, Independence Hall. Where is it located?

PHILADELPHIA HISTORIC DISTRICT

Independence Hall, known as the birthplace of the United States, is where the Declaration of Independence and the Constitution of the United States were adopted.

# CHECK WHAT YOU KNOW

Use this page to help you review and remember important skills needed for Chapter 23.

## IDENTIFY POINTS ON A GRID

Use the ordered pairs to name each point on the grid.

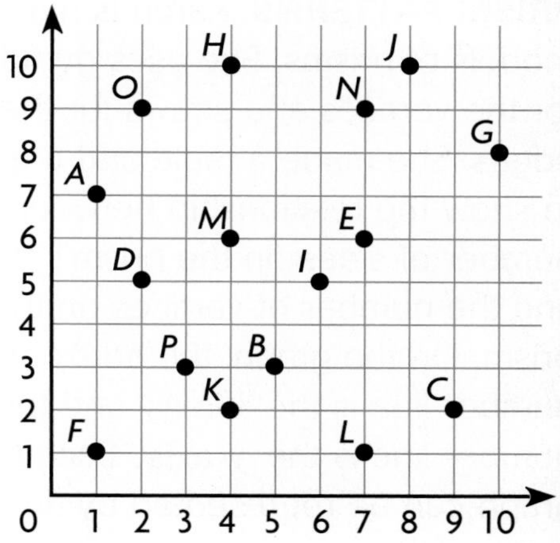


| | | |
|---|---|---|
| **1.** (5,3) | **2.** (1,1) | **3.** (7,6) |
| **4.** (1,7) | **5.** (2,9) | **6.** (7,1) |
| **7.** (6,5) | **8.** (7,9) | **9.** (4,2) |
| **10.** (4,10) | **11.** (4,6) | **12.** (3,3) |
| **13.** (10,8) | **14.** (8,10) | **15.** (9,2) |

## TRANSFORMATIONS

Tell how each figure was moved. Write *translation, reflection,* or *rotation.*

**16.** 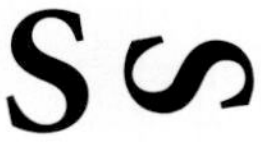

**17.** 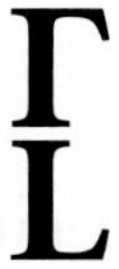

**18.** 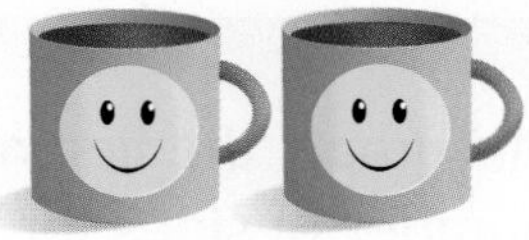

**19.** 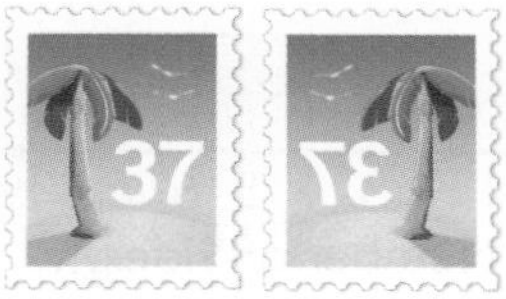


**20.** 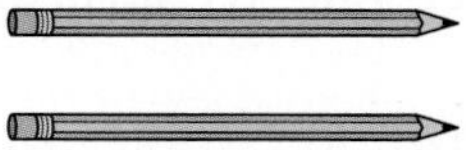

**21.** 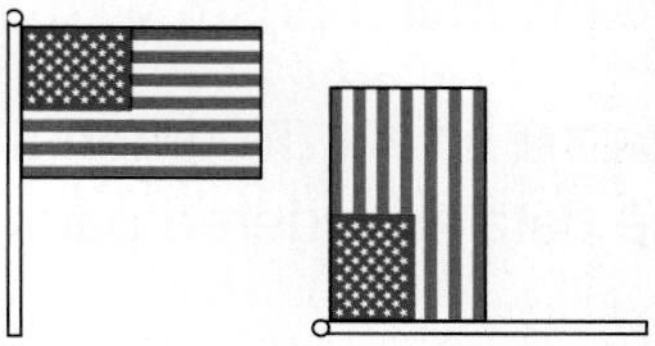

# VOCABULARY POWER

## REVIEW

**ordered pair** [ôr′dərd pâr] *noun*

When things are ordered, they are arranged in a certain way for a reason. Explain how this applies to the numbers in the ordered pair (3,5).

## PREVIEW

*x*-axis
*y*-axis
coordinate plane
origin
coordinates

GO ON-LINE www.harcourtschool.com/mathglossary

# Graph Relationships

 **Learn**

**PRISM PATTERNS** Karen is making models of prisms. She uses gumdrops for the vertices and straws for the edges. She made a table and a graph to show the relationship between the number of sides on the prism's base and the number of vertices on the prism. On the graph, the horizontal number line is the **x-axis** and the vertical number line is the **y-axis**. Each point on the graph can be represented by an ordered pair, (*x,y*).

| Number of Sides on Base, *x* | 3 | 4 | 5 | 6 |
|---|---|---|---|---|
| Number of Vertices, *y* | 6 | 8 | 10 | 12 |

On this graph, the first number in an ordered pair tells the number of sides for the base of the prism. The second number tells the number of vertices in the prism. So, (5,10) means that a prism with 5 sides on its base has 10 vertices.

**MATH IDEA** To graph a relationship shown in a table, write the data as ordered pairs and then graph the ordered pairs.

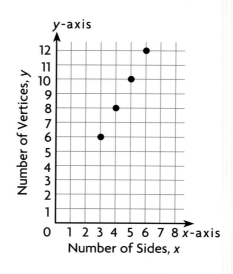

## Example

Graph the relationship shown in the table.

| Number of Sides on Base, *x* | 3 | 4 | 5 | 6 |
|---|---|---|---|---|
| Number of Faces, *y* | 5 | 6 | 7 | 8 |

• Write ordered pairs for the data.

  (3,5), (4,6), (5,7), (6,8)

• Graph the ordered pairs.

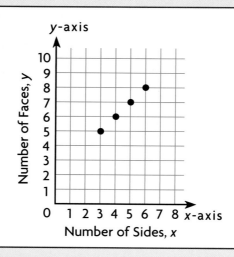

1. **Explain** what the point (5,7) means in the second graph on page 498.

**Write the ordered pairs. Then graph them.**

2.
| Input, *x* | 1 | 2 | 3 | 4 |
|---|---|---|---|---|
| Output, *y* | 3 | 6 | 9 | 12 |

3.
| Input, *x* | 4 | 5 | 6 | 7 |
|---|---|---|---|---|
| Output, *y* | 2 | 3 | 4 | 5 |

▶ **Practice and Problem Solving**  ( Extra Practice, page 508, Set A )

**Write the ordered pairs. Then graph them.**

4.
| Input, *x* | 0 | 1 | 2 | 3 |
|---|---|---|---|---|
| Output, *y* | 3 | 4 | 5 | 6 |

5.
| Input, *x* | 7 | 8 | 9 | 10 |
|---|---|---|---|---|
| Output, *y* | 3 | 4 | 5 | 6 |

6.
| Input, *x* | 1 | 2 | 3 | 4 |
|---|---|---|---|---|
| Output, *y* | 4 | 8 | 12 | 16 |

7.
| Input, *x* | 1 | 2 | 3 | 4 |
|---|---|---|---|---|
| Output, *y* | 2 | 4 | 6 | 8 |

**USE DATA**   For 8–10, use the table.

| Number of Sides on Base, *x* | 3 | 4 | 5 | 6 |
|---|---|---|---|---|
| Number of Vertices on Pyramid, *y* | 4 | 5 | 6 | 7 |

8. Write the ordered pairs. Then graph them. What does (4,5) mean?

9.  **Write About It** What kind of pyramid is represented by the ordered pair (5,6)? Explain.

10. **REASONING**   How can you use your graph to find the number of vertices in an octagonal pyramid?

11. **Vocabulary Power** *Vertices* is the plural form of *vertex*. Write the plural form of *prism, face,* and *axis*.

12. A triangle has a perimeter of 27 cm. One side is 7 cm long and a second side is 9 cm long. Find the length of the third side.

**Getting Ready for FCAT** [THINK SOLVE EXPLAIN]

| Number of Sides on Base, *x* | 3 | 4 | 5 | 6 | 8 |
|---|---|---|---|---|---|
| Number of Edges on Prism, *y* | 9 | 12 | 15 | ■ | ■ |

13. Complete the table about prisms. Explain the relationship of the number of sides on the base of a prism to the number of edges on the prism.

Graph the ordered pairs from the table on a coordinate grid.

# Graph Integers on the Coordinate Plane

▶ **Learn**

**MAPPING HISTORY** Archaeologists record the locations of artifacts and features that they find in a dig site by graphing them on a coordinate plane.

A **coordinate plane** is formed by two intersecting and perpendicular number lines called axes. The point where the two lines intersect is called the **origin**, or (0,0).

The numbers to the left of the origin on the *x*-axis and below the origin on the *y*-axis are negative.

Start at the origin. Move 4 units to the left on the *x*-axis and 2 units up on the *y*-axis. The **coordinates**, or numbers in the ordered pair, are (⁻4,⁺2).

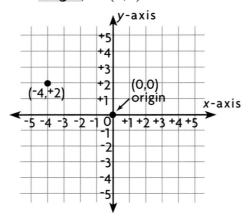

▲ Christopher Wolfe, at the age of 7, co-discovered the oldest horned ceratopsian dinosaur.

**HANDS ON**

## Activity

**MATERIALS:** coordinate plane

- Graph the ordered pair (⁺4,⁻5). Start at the origin. Move **right** 4 units and then **down** 5 units. Plot and label the point, *A*.

- Graph the ordered pair (⁻3,⁻2). Start at the origin. Move **left** 3 units and then **down** 2 units. Plot and label the point, *B*.

- In which direction and how far would you move to graph (⁻4,⁺5)?

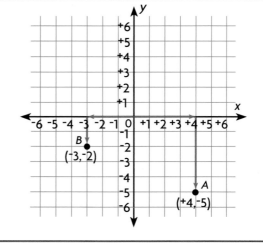

**MATH IDEA** The coordinates of a point tell you how far and in which direction to move first horizontally and then vertically on the coordinate plane.

# Graphing Ordered Pairs

## Examples

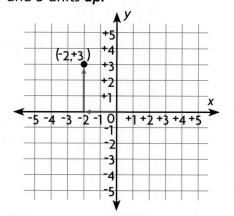

**A** To graph (⁻2,⁺3), start at the origin. Move 2 units to the *left* and 3 units *up.*

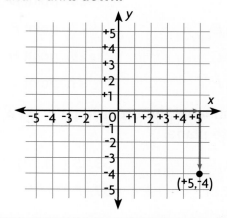

**B** To graph (⁺5,⁻4), start at the origin. Move 5 units to the *right* and 4 units *down.*

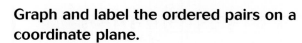

## ▶ Check

**1. Explain** how to graph (⁺4,⁺2) on a coordinate plane.

**For 2–7, identify the ordered pair for each point.**

**2.** point *A*

**3.** point *B*

**4.** point *C*

**5.** point *D*

**6.** point *E*

**7.** point *F*

**Graph and label the ordered pairs on a coordinate plane.**

**8.** *A* (⁻5,⁺8)

**9.** *B* (⁻7,⁻4)

**10.** *C* (⁺4,⁺4)

**11.** *D* (⁺1,⁻2)

**12.** *E* (⁻6,⁺5)

**13.** *F* (⁻2,⁺8)

**14.** *G* (⁺2,⁺6)

**15.** *H* (⁺3,⁻3)

**Name the ordered pair that is described.**

**16.** Start at the origin. Move 2 units to the right and 3 units down.

**17.** Start at the origin. Move 3 units to the left and 6 units up.

**18.** Start at the origin. Move 5 units to the left and 5 units down.

**19.** Start at the origin. Move 1 unit to the right and 3 units up.

**20.** Start at the origin. Move 3 units up.

**21.** Start at the origin. Move 4 units to the left.

**LESSON CONTINUES**

FCAT
TESTED  SSS/GLEs MA.C.3.2.2.5.1  The student knows how to identify, locate, and plot ordered pairs of whole numbers on a graph or on the first quadrant of a coordinate system.

Chapter 23  **501**

**For 22–31, identify the ordered pair for each point.**

22. point A
23. point B
24. point C
25. point D
26. point E
27. point F
28. point G
29. point H
30. point I
31. point J

**Graph and label the ordered pairs on a coordinate plane.**

32. A ($^-$1,$^+$3)
33. B ($^-$3,$^-$7)
34. C ($^+$6,$^+$7)
35. D ($^+$1,$^-$5)
36. E (0,$^+$8)
37. F ($^+$2,$^+$3)
38. G ($^+$9,$^-$2)
39. H ($^-$3,$^+$3)

**For 40–45, name the ordered pair that is described.**

40. Start at the origin. Move 8 units to the left and 7 units up.

41. Start at the origin. Move 3 units to the right and 9 units up.

42. Start at the origin. Move 6 units up.

43. Start at the origin. Move 5 units down.

44. Start at the origin. Move 4 units to the right and 6 units down.

45. Start at the origin. Move 5 units to the left and 6 units down.

**For 46–51, use the archaeology grid.**

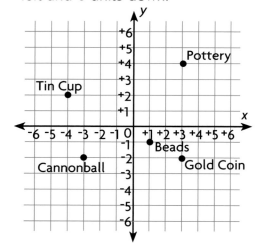

46. Which artifact is 3 units to the right of the origin and 4 units up from the origin?

47. Which two artifacts have negative x-coordinates?

48. Which two artifacts have opposite x-coordinates and the same y-coordinates?

49. What are the coordinates for the gold coin?

50. Write a problem that uses the archaeology grid to solve.

51. **? What's the Error?** Tamara says the location of the beads is ($^-$1,$^+$1). Describe and correct her error.

52. **FAST FACT • SCIENCE** The Triceratops was a dinosaur that was 3 meters high and had a mass of 5,500 kilograms. If the Triceratops was three times as long as it was high, how long was it?

53. **? What's the Question?** Mark placed a coordinate grid over a map of his neighborhood. He labeled his house point *H*. The answer is ($^+$4,$^-$3).

54. The temperature at 6 P.M. was 12°F. It fell 17° during the night, then rose 4° by 6 A.M. What was the temperature at 6 A.M.?

**Technology Link**

More Practice:
Harcourt Mega Math
The Number Games,
*Arachna Graph,* Level H

## Getting Ready for FCAT

**For 55–57, use the map.**

55. Mary, Jake, and Sara went to see a movie. They met at the Grocery Store and walked to the movie. What are the coordinates of the movie theater?

    **A.** (3,6)     **C.** (6,3)

    **B.** (8,5)     **D.** (1,4)

56. Whose house is located at (3,6)?

57. If Sara lives 1 block east of Mary's house and 2 blocks south of the park, what ordered pair can you write to show the location of Sara's house?

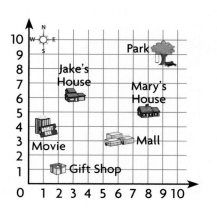

# Problem Solving    LiNKUP . . . to Geometry

You can draw geometric figures by locating and connecting points on the coordinate plane.

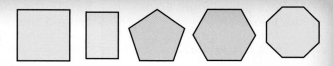

- Look at the coordinate plane at the right. What ordered pair tells the location of the fourth point that would make the figure a square?

**Locate and connect the points in order on a coordinate plane. Then name the geometric figure that you drew.**

1. ($^+$2,$^+$4) ($^+$2,$^+$6) ($^-$3,$^+$6) ($^-$3,$^+$4)

2. ($^+$3,$^+$2) ($^+$3,$^-$4) ($^-$4,$^-$4)

3. (0,$^+$4) ($^+$3,$^+$2) ($^+$3,$^-$5) ($^-$3,$^-$4) ($^-$3,$^+$1)

4. ($^+$4,$^-$2) ($^+$4,$^+$6) ($^-$4,$^+$6) ($^-$4,$^-$2)

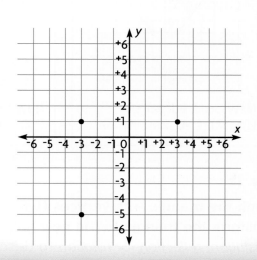

# Transformations on the Coordinate Plane

## Quick Review

How many congruent sides must each quadrilateral have?
1. square
2. rectangle
3. rhombus
4. trapezoid
5. parallelogram

## ▶ Explore

Explore rigid transformations by moving a figure on the coordinate plane. Place the figure so that its vertices can be named by ordered pairs. Then transform it.

**MATERIALS**
coordinate planes, straightedge, scissors, colored pencils

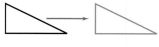 Sliding a figure in a straight line is called a *translation*.

 Flipping a figure over a line is called a *reflection*.

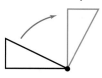 Turning a figure around a point or vertex is called a *rotation*.

## Activity

Graph a triangle with vertices ($^+1$,$^+2$), ($^+4$,$^+2$), and ($^+4$,$^+6$). Trace a copy, color it, and cut it out. Place the tracing over the original triangle on the coordinate plane. Transform the triangle. Name the ordered pairs for the new vertices.

**Reflection**
Reflect the triangle across the *y*-axis.

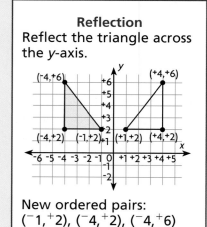

New ordered pairs:
($^-1$,$^+2$), ($^-4$,$^+2$), ($^-4$,$^+6$)

**Rotation**
Rotate the triangle 90° around the origin.

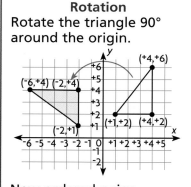

New ordered pairs:
($^-2$,$^+1$), ($^-2$,$^+4$), ($^-6$,$^+4$)

**Translation**
Translate each vertex 2 units left and 1 unit down.

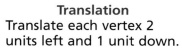
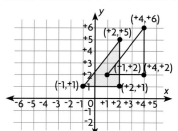

New ordered pairs:
($^-1$,$^+1$), ($^+2$,$^+1$), ($^+2$,$^+5$)

## Try It

Graph the triangle with vertices (1,1), (3,1), and (1,4). Then transform the triangle to the new given vertices. Write *translation*, *reflection*, or *rotation* to describe the move.

**a.** (3,3), (3,1), and (6,3)     **b.** (4,$^-1$), (6,$^-1$), and (4,2)

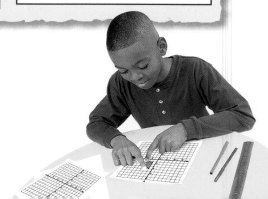

**504**

**SPATIAL THINKING** You can predict the effect of a translation, reflection, or rotation of a given figure.

**Use the triangles on the coordinate plane to make predictions.**

- Predict which figure could result from a translation of Triangle A.

- Predict which figure could result from a reflection of Triangle A.

- Predict which figure could result from a rotation of Triangle B.

- Predict which figure could result from a reflection of Triangle E.

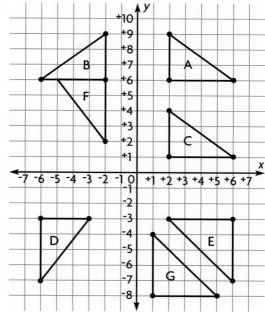

 **MATH IDEA** A rigid transformation, or movement of a figure, does not change its size or shape.

▷ **Practice and Problem Solving**

**Graph a triangle with vertices (2,2), (2,4), and (6,2). Then transform the triangle to the new given vertices. Write *translation, reflection,* or *rotation* to describe the move.**

**1.** (4,0), (4,2), and (8,0)    **2.** (6,6), (8,6), and (6,2)    **3.** (2,2), (2,4), and (⁻2,2)

**For 4–5, graph a triangle with vertices (1,2), (5,2), and (1,4).**

**4.** Translate the triangle 4 spaces to the right and 1 space up. What are the ordered pairs for the vertices of the triangle's new location?

**5.** Look at the coordinate plane above. Predict what two transformations would move Triangle A to Triangle D. Check your predictions.

**Getting Ready for FCAT**

**6.** Alex flipped the figure at the right over the dashed line. Then he rotated it 90° clockwise. Which of the following shows the figure after the flip and 90° clockwise rotation?

**A.**     **B.**     **C.**     **D.**

FCAT TESTED  SSS/GLEs MA.C.2.2.2.5.2 The student knows the effect of a flip, slide, or turn. (90°, 180°, 270°) on a geometric figure. *also* MA.C.2.2.2.5.1

**Chapter 23 505**

# Problem Solving Skill
## Relevant or Irrelevant Information

UNDERSTAND > PLAN > SOLVE > CHECK

**TREASURE HUNT** Jeff found this old map with instructions for finding a buried treasure. Where is the treasure?

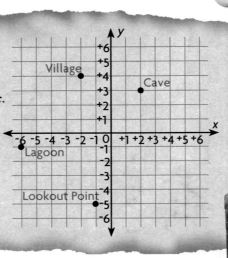

The *x*-coordinate of the treasure is 2 times the cave's *x*-coordinate. The lagoon is southwest of the cave. The lagoon and the treasure have the same *y*-coordinate.

Sometimes a problem contains more information than you need to answer the question. You must decide which information is relevant, or needed, to solve the problem.

| Read each fact and decide whether it is relevant or irrelevant to solving the problem. | • The *x*-coordinate of the treasure is 2 times the cave's *x*-coordinate. | relevant |
| --- | --- | --- |
| | • The lagoon is southwest of the cave. | irrelevant |
| | • The lagoon and the treasure have the same *y*-coordinate. | relevant |
| Use the relevant information to solve the problem. | • Cave: ($^+$2,$^+$3). The treasure's *x*-coordinate is 2 × 2 = 4. | |
| | • Lagoon: ($^-$6,$^-$1). The treasure's *y*-coordinate is $^-$1. | |

So, the coordinates of the treasure are ($^+$4,$^-$1).

## Talk About It

• Which of the locations on the map are irrelevant to finding the treasure?

**Technology Link**

More Practice: Harcourt Mega Math, Ice Station Exploration, *Polar Planes*, Level T

**For 1–2, use the map. Tell the relevant information and solve.**

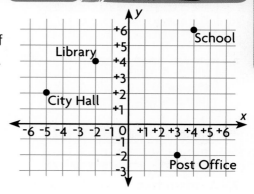

1. The park and the library have the same *x*-coordinate. The library is 5 units left and 6 units up from the post office. The *y*-coordinate of the school is 3 more than the park's *y*-coordinate. Where is the park?

2. The Mall is south of the school and east of City Hall. If you go down 3 units and right 4 units from the library, you will find the Mall. Where is the Mall?

**At 1 P.M., Amy left her house and rode her bike north 3 miles to Jeb's house. Next she rode east 2 miles and then turned south and rode 3 miles to Ann's house, where they had lunch. From there, she rode west back to her house. What shape did her trip make?**

3. Which information is irrelevant to solving the problem?

   **A** Amy rode north to Jeb's house.
   **B** Amy and Ann had lunch at Ann's house.
   **C** Amy rode east and then south from Jeb's house to Ann's house.
   **D** Amy rode west back home.

4. Which question cannot be answered with the given information?

   **F** In what direction did Amy ride to Jeb's house?
   **G** What shape did her trip make?
   **H** How long did it take Amy to get to Ann's house?
   **J** How far is it from Amy's house to Ann's house?

## Mixed Applications

5. The most valuable violin in the world is the Kreutzer, made in Italy in 1727. It was sold at auction for $1,516,000 in England in 1998. How old was the violin when it was sold?

6. Dante received $25.50 for his birthday. He bought a hat that cost $14.85 and a comic book. He has $7.70 left. How much did he spend on the comic book?

7. Kenya has two dogs. The sum of their ages is 7 years, and the difference in their ages is 3 years. How old are her two dogs?

8. **Patterns** Draw the next figure in this sequence.

9. ❓ **What's the Question?** Sue's triangle has vertices (1,2) and (1,5). The answer is (⁻2,⁻2).

10. ✏️ **Write a problem** that includes relevant and irrelevant information. Exchange problems with a partner. Identify the relevant and irrelevant information and solve.

FCAT
TESTED  SSS/GLEs MA.C.3.2.2.5.1 The student knows how to identify, locate, and plot ordered pairs of numbers on a graph or on the first quadrant of a coordinate system.

**Chapter 23  507**

# Extra Practice

## Set A (pp. 498–499)

**Write the ordered pairs. Then graph them.**

**1.**
| Input, x | 0 | 1 | 2 | 3 |
|---|---|---|---|---|
| Output, y | 4 | 5 | 6 | 7 |

**2.**
| Input, x | 5 | 10 | 15 | 20 |
|---|---|---|---|---|
| Output, y | 1 | 2 | 3 | 4 |

**3.**
| Input, x | 1 | 3 | 5 | 7 |
|---|---|---|---|---|
| Output, y | 2 | 4 | 6 | 8 |

**4.**
| Input, x | 0 | 2 | 3 | 6 |
|---|---|---|---|---|
| Output, y | 2 | 3 | 4 | 5 |

**5.**
| Input, x | 3 | 6 | 9 | 12 |
|---|---|---|---|---|
| Output, y | 1 | 2 | 3 | 4 |

**6.**
| Input, x | 4 | 8 | 16 | 24 |
|---|---|---|---|---|
| Output, y | 2 | 4 | 8 | 12 |

**7.** A prism has 3 sides on its base and 6 vertices. What ordered pair can you write to show this relationship? What kind of prism is it?

**8.** The ordered pair for a prism is (4,8). Explain the relationship of the prism's sides on base to its vertices. What kind of prism is it?

## Set B (pp. 500–503)

**For 1–10, identify the ordered pair for each point.**

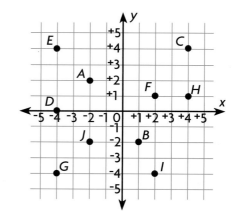

**1.** Point A

**2.** Point B

**3.** Point C

**4.** Point D

**5.** Point E

**6.** Point F

**7.** Point G

**8.** Point H

**9.** Point I

**10.** Point J

**Graph and label the ordered pair on a coordinate plane.**

**11.** A ($^-$1,$^+$3)

**12.** B ($^-$3,$^-$7)

**13.** C ($^+$6,$^+$7)

**14.** D ($^+$1,$^-$5)

**15.** E (0,$^+$8)

**16.** F ($^+$2,$^+$3)

**For 17–20, name the ordered pair that is described.**

**17.** Start at the origin. Move 11 units to the left.

**18.** Start at the origin. Move 7 units to the left and 4 units down.

**19.** Start at the origin. Move 8 units to the right and 1 unit up.

**20.** Start at the origin. Move 6 units to the left and 6 units up.

# Review/Test

## ✔ CHECK VOCABULARY AND CONCEPTS

**Choose the best term from the box.**

> coordinate plane
> *x*-axis
> *y*-axis
> origin

1. The horizontal line on a coordinate plane is the __?__. (p. 498)

2. The point where the *x*-axis and the *y*-axis intersect is the __?__. (p. 500)

3. Two intersecting perpendicular number lines form a __?__. (p. 500)

## ✔ CHECK SKILLS

**USE DATA** For 4–12, identify the ordered pair for each point. (pp. 500–503)

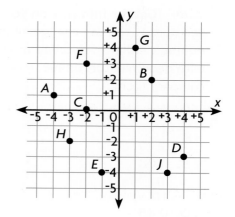

4. point *A*
5. point *B*
6. point *E*
7. point *D*
8. point *C*
9. point *F*
10. point *H*
11. point *G*
12. point *J*

**Graph and label the ordered pairs on a coordinate plane.** (pp. 500–503)

13. *A* ($^-$5,$^+$8)
14. *B* ($^-$7,$^-$4)
15. *C* ($^+$4,$^+$4)
16. *D* ($^+$2,$^-$5)

**Write the ordered pairs. Then graph them.** (pp. 498–499)

17.

| Input, *x* | 2 | 4 | 6 | 8 |
|---|---|---|---|---|
| Output, *y* | 5 | 7 | 9 | 11 |

18.

| Cost of Items, *x* | 1 | 2 | 3 | 4 |
|---|---|---|---|---|
| Amount, *y* | $6 | $12 | $18 | $24 |

## ✔ CHECK PROBLEM SOLVING

**For 19–20, use the grid. Tell the relevant information and solve.** (pp. 506–507)

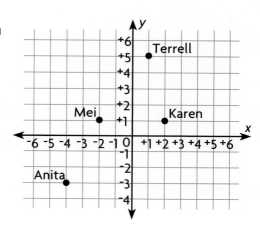

19. Mei and Bobby are on the same *y*-coordinate. Bobby is south of Terrell. Karen's *x*-coordinate is 1 more than Bobby's. Where is Bobby?

20. Sam is between Mei and Terrell. If you go up 6 units and right 3 units from Anita, you will find Sam. Where is Sam?

# Getting Ready for  FCAT

## ⭐ NUMBER SENSE, CONCEPTS, AND OPERATIONS

**1.** Michael wrote these numbers on cards. Which is the second greatest number?

| $\frac{4}{5}$ | 0.08 | $\frac{9}{10}$ | 0.45 |

> **TIP** **Get the information you need.**
> See item 1. You can change all the numbers either to decimals or to fractions with denominators of 100 in order to compare them.

    **A.** $\frac{4}{5}$

    **B.** 0.08

    **C.** $\frac{9}{10}$

    **D.** 0.45

**2.** One carat equals 200 milligrams. The blue Hope diamond equals 45.52 carats. How many milligrams is the blue Hope diamond?

    **F.**    910.4 milligrams

    **G.**   9,104 milligrams

    **H.**  91,040 milligrams

    **I.** 910,400 milligrams

**3. Explain It** Carla sold 9 pairs of sneakers. Three pairs sold for $39.99 each. The other pairs sold for $59.99 each. ESTIMATE to determine whether the average price for the 9 pairs of sneakers was greater than or less than $50.00. Explain how you found your answer.

## ⭐ GEOMETRY AND SPATIAL SENSE

**4.** Donna used a grid to make a map of her neighborhood. What are the coordinates of Donna's house?

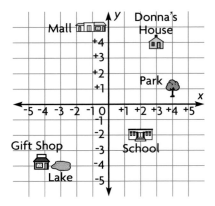

    **A.** $(^+4,^+1)$        **C.** $(^+3,^+4)$

    **B.** $(^-3,^-4)$        **D.** $(^-4,^-4)$

**5.** Use the grid in Problem 4. After school, Donna went to point $(^-1,^+5)$. Where did Donna go?

    **F.** Gift Shop        **H.** Lake

    **G.** Park           **I.** Mall

**6. Explain It** Troy is planning to fence in a pen for his pet rabbit. At first he planned to make a pen like the one shown in the drawing below. Then he decided to increase the length of the shorter side to 6 feet.

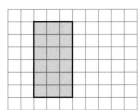

$\vdash\!\!\dashv$ = 1 foot

Explain how to find the perimeter of the pen he has decided to make now. Write the number of feet in the perimeter.

**ALGEBRAIC THINKING**

**7.** The cookies have been baking for 10 minutes. They need to bake for 25 minutes in all. How many more minutes do the cookies need to bake? Suppose $m$ represents the number of minutes the cookies still need to bake. Which equation could be used to solve the problem?

**A.** $10 - m = 25$     **C.** $10 + 25 = m$

**B.** $10 + m = 25$     **D.** $m - 10 = 25$

**8.** The bar graph shows the low temperature in six cities on October 29. For which two cities can the inequality $n < 70$ be used to describe the low temperature, $n$?

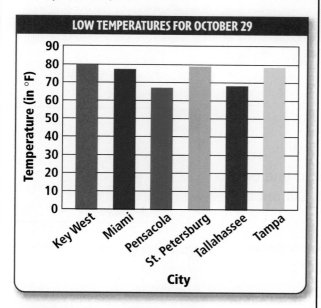

**F.** Key West and Tampa

**G.** Miami and Pensacola

**H.** Pensacola and Tallahassee

**I.** St. Petersburg and Tampa

**9. Explain It** Write a problem that can be modeled with the equation $10 - a = 6$. Tell what $a$ represents, solve the equation, and explain how you solved it.

 **DATA ANALYSIS AND PROBABILITY**

**10.** Which statement best describes what a line graph shows?

**A.** It shows how parts of the data are related to the whole.

**B.** It shows countable data with symbols or pictures.

**C.** It shows how data change over time.

**D.** It shows data compared by category.

**11.** A number cube is labeled 1–6. What is the probability of rolling a 3 or a 4 on the number cube?

**F.** $\frac{1}{6}$

**G.** $\frac{1}{3}$

**H.** $\frac{1}{2}$

**I.** $\frac{2}{3}$

**12. Explain It** Leni tossed a coin and rolled a number cube labeled 1–6.

Explain how Leni can find the possible outcomes for this experiment. How many outcomes are there?

# IT'S IN THE BAG

## Tessellation Puzzle

**PROJECT** Make a puzzle to show a tessellation.

### Materials

- Different color card stock
- Scissors
- Figures blackline

## Directions

1. Cut out the figures from the blackline. *(Picture A)*

2. Choose a figure to make a puzzle. Trace it onto one or two colors of card stock as many times as will fit. Cut out all the figures that you traced. *(Picture B)*

3. Lay your cutout figures together so there are no gaps between pieces. You have made a tessellation puzzle! *(Picture C)*

4. Choose a different figure and make another puzzle. Exchange puzzles with a classmate and put each other's puzzles together.

# Challenge

## Graph an Equation

You can make a table of values to graph an equation on the coordinate plane.

**Example**   Graph the equation $y = 2x + 1$.

### STEP 1

- Make a table of values.
- First, pick values for $x$.
- Use the values for $x$ and the equation to find the values for $y$.
- Write the ordered pairs.

| x | 2x + 1 | y | Ordered Pair (x,y) |
|---|--------|---|--------------------|
| 0 | 2 × (0) + 1 | 1 | (0,1) |
| 1 | 2 × (1) + 1 | 3 | (1,3) |
| 2 | 2 × (2) + 1 | 5 | (2,5) |
| 3 | 2 × (3) + 1 | 7 | (3,7) |

### STEP 2

Make the graph.
- Plot each ordered pair on a coordinate plane.
- Connect the points using a straight line.
- Include arrows on both ends of the line to show that the line continues in both directions.
- Label the line with the equation.

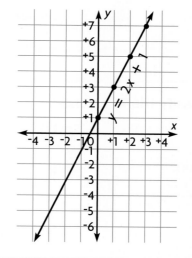

## Try It

**Make a table of values like the one at the right for each equation. Then graph the equation on a coordinate plane.**

**1.** $y = x$   **2.** $y = x + 2$   **3.** $y = x + 4$   **4.** $y = 2x$

| x | y | Ordered Pair |
|---|---|--------------|
| 0 | | |
| 1 | | |
| 2 | | |
| 3 | | |

# Study Guide and Review

## VOCABULARY

Choose the best term from the box.

| absolute value |
| opposite |
| polygon |
| sphere |
| polyhedron |

**1.** The distance of an integer from 0 is the __?__ of the integer. (p. 480)

**2.** A closed plane figure formed by three or more line segments is a(n) __?__. (p. 434)

**3.** A solid figure with faces that are polygons is called a(n) __?__. (p. 466)

## STUDY AND SOLVE

### Chapter 20

**Identify congruent and similar figures.**

Tell whether the figures appear to be similar, congruent, both, or neither.   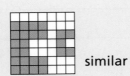   similar

Write *similar, congruent, both,* or *neither* to describe each pair. (pp. 442–445)

**1.**    **2.**

### Chapter 21

**Identify and classify triangles and quadrilaterals.**

Classify the figure in as many ways as possible.

This is a quadrilateral, a parallelogram, and a rectangle.

Classify each figure in as many ways as possible. For 3, write *isosceles, scalene,* or *equilateral* and *right, acute,* or *obtuse.* For 4, write *quadrilateral, parallelogram, square, rectangle, rhombus,* or *trapezoid.* (pp. 456–461)

**3.** 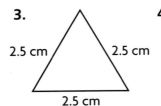   **4.**

2.5 cm   2.5 cm

2.5 cm

**Identify solid figures.**

Identify the solid figure.      This is a cone.

Classify each solid figure. Write *prism, pyramid, cone, cylinder,* or *sphere.* (pp. 466–469)

**5.**    **6.**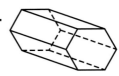

## Chapter 22

**Add and subtract integers.**

Subtract. ⁻3 − ⁺2

Model ⁻3 using two opposite pairs of counters.
Then take away 2 yellow counters.

So, ⁻3 − ⁺2 = ⁻5.

**Find each sum or difference.**

(pp. 486–489)

**7.** ⁺3 + ⁻2          **8.** ⁻4 − ⁺3

**9.** ⁻2 − ⁺5          **10.** ⁻4 + ⁻4

**11.** ⁻2 − ⁺7          **12.** ⁺3 − ⁺6

**13.** ⁺1 + ⁻6          **14.** ⁻8 − ⁺7

## Chapter 23

**Identify ordered pairs on a coordinate plane.**

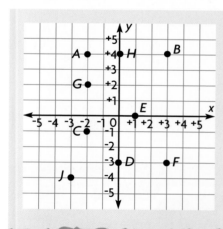

Identify the ordered pair for Point A.

Start at the origin. Move left 2 units and then up 4 units.

So, Point A is at (⁻2,⁺4).

**Use the graph at the left. Identify the ordered pair for each point.** (pp. 500–503)

**15.** Point B          **16.** Point C

**17.** Point D          **18.** Point E

**19.** Point F          **20.** Point G

**21.** Point H          **22.** Point J

## PROBLEM SOLVING PRACTICE

**Solve.** (pp. 448–449, 490–491)

**23.** A scuba diver was 22 ft below the surface of the water when he saw 3 starfish and 4 sea urchins. He then swam up 10 ft and down 7 ft. How far below the surface was he then?

**24.**

What colors are the next three circles in the pattern?

# PERFORMANCE ASSESSMENT

## TASK A • THE WINNING DESIGN

The math club is having a poster contest. The winning design will be used on posters to advertise the Spring Art Fair. These are the rules for the design:

1. The design should fit on a 24-inch by 24-inch poster.

2. Only a ruler, compass, protractor, and pencil may be used to create the design.

3. A circle must be the first figure drawn.

4. There must be some rotational symmetry in the design.

5. There must be similar and congruent figures in the design.

a. Create a design for the poster. Then write descriptions of shapes and sizes in the design so that someone else could make the same design.

b. The rules ask you to show rotational symmetry in your design. What did you draw?

c. Identify the figures in your design that are congruent.

## TASK B • NAMING ORDERED PAIRS

The map shows where some of the furniture in Mrs. Henderson's classroom is located. She has asked her students to draw a new arrangement for the furniture.

a. Write the ordered pairs to show the locations for the corners of the bookshelf, the desk, and the table as they appear on the map.

b. Draw the new location for each piece of furniture on the grid.

c. Give the ordered pairs to show the new locations of the bookshelf, the desk, and the table.

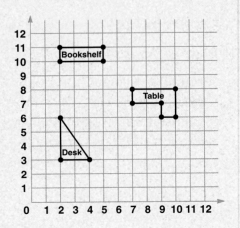

# Technology Linkup

## Congruence and Similarity

You can use the drawing toolbar and *AutoShapes* in a word processing software program to draw congruent and similar figures. The figures in *AutoShapes* include triangles, rectangles, parallelograms, trapezoids, pentagons, and octagons.

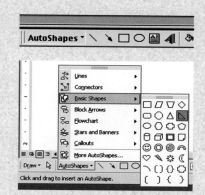

Draw two congruent right triangles.

- Open the drawing toolbar and Click *AutoShapes*. Then click *Basic Shapes* and select the right triangle.

- Go to the place on the page where you want to place the figure and click.

- To change the size or shape of the figure, move the cursor over the dots along the border of the figure until you see a vertical or horizontal arrow. Click and drag vertically to lengthen the figure. Click and drag horizontally to widen the figure.

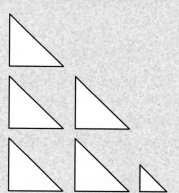

- To draw a congruent figure, place the cursor inside the figure and click. Click *Edit* from the main menu and select *Copy*. This will make a copy of the figure. Then click *Edit* and select *Paste*. A congruent figure will appear slightly offset from the original figure. Click the middle of the new figure and drag it to a new location.

- To draw a similar figure, first draw a figure congruent to the first figure. Move the cursor over one of the dots that appear in the corners until you see the diagonal arrow. Click and drag along the diagonal away from the figure to enlarge the figure, or inside the figure to reduce it.

## Practice and Problem Solving

Use drawing tools. Draw a congruent figure and a similar figure.

**1.** rectangle      **2.** pentagon      **3.** parallelogram

**GO ON-LINE**

**Multimedia Math Glossary** www.harcourtschool.com/mathglossary

**Vocabulary Power** Choose five new vocabulary words from Chapters 20 through 23 that are related. Locate them in the Multimedia Math Glossary. Write five sentences that each contain at least one of these words.

▲ The Art Deco District in Miami consists of the seasonal hotels, the commercial district, and the residential district.

PROBLEM SOLVING IN FLORIDA

Miami Beach

The Colony Hotel is typical of the *Art Deco* style of South Beach. ▼

## MIAMI BEACH ARCHITECTURE

The architectural style known as *Art Deco* comes from machine-produced designs of the early twentieth century. To truly appreciate this architectural style, just take a trip to the Art Deco Historic District in South Beach, Miami. Hundreds of buildings designed and built during the 1930's still remain.

USE DATA For 1–7, use the photograph.

1. What plane figures do you see in the photograph at the right? Describe each figure as completely as you can.

2. The design of the Colony Hotel shows mostly what kind of angle? Explain how you can tell.

3. Describe any lines that are part of the design of the building.

4. Does this building appear to be symmetrical? Support your answer with examples from the photograph.

5. Describe the 3-dimensional figures that were used to build the sign on the hotel.

6. Which parts of the building appear to be congruent? Explain how you know.

7. ✍ Write About It Do you think that the *Art Deco* design is pleasing to the eye? Explain your answer.

# ARCHITECTURAL SITES

The buildings, historic districts, and other structures throughout the greater Miami area offer a wealth of information about America's architectural past. The sites shown on the map below are just a few of the places on the National Park Service's National Register list.

Venetian Pool

Vizcaya

**USE DATA For 1–6, use the map.**

1. Give the whole-number coordinates of the point closest to the Art Deco Historic District.

2. What other location on the map has approximately the same second coordinate as the Venetian Pool?

3. Name two roads that appear to be parallel. Name two others that appear to be perpendicular.

4. Suppose that you are driving from Miami International Airport south on SW 42 Ave. You turn left and go north on Rt 1 to SW 12th Ave. Take SW 12th Ave. to West Flagler St., and then go west on West Flagler St. back to SW 42 Ave. What figure does your path suggest?

5. What places are located nearest the following coordinates:
   **a.** (8,1)   **b.** (3,6)   **c.** (5,6)   **d.** (1,6)

6. **STRETCH YOUR THINKING** Describe a trip that would form an obtuse triangle if you were to drive along a straight path from one site to another.

# Customary and Metric Systems

≡**FAST FACT** • SCIENCE Most of the United States has a *temperate* climate with warm summers and cool-to-cold winters. Florida's climate is *subtropical moist* with warm-to-hot summers and cool winters.

PROBLEM SOLVING   The graph below shows the average July temperatures for five U.S. cities. Which city's average July temperature is higher than 76°F and lower than 85°F?

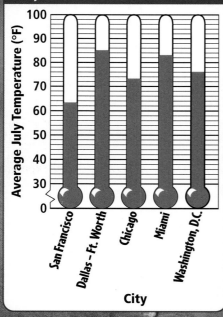

**JULY TEMPERATURES IN FIVE CITIES**

Average July Temperature (°F)

San Francisco · Dallas – Ft. Worth · Chicago · Miami · Washington, D.C.

City

Miami Beach, Florida

# CHECK WHAT YOU KNOW

Use this page to help you review and remember
important skills needed for Chapter 24.

## CUSTOMARY UNITS AND TOOLS

Choose the tool you would use to
measure each.

1. the length of the chalkboard

   a.

   b.

2. the amount of flour needed to
   make a cake

3. the weight of a stapler

   c.

Choose the unit you would use to measure each.

4. length of your foot
   **inches** or **yards**

5. weight of a truck
   **pounds** or **tons**

6. water in a pool
   **quarts** or **gallons**

## METRIC UNITS AND TOOLS

Choose the tool you would use to measure each.

7. the temperature outside

   a.

8. the mass of a bracelet

9. the distance across the classroom

   b.

   c.

Choose the unit you would use to measure each.

10. distance run in a race
    **centimeters** or **kilometers**

11. mass of a big dog
    **grams** or **kilograms**

12. large bottle of soda
    **liters** or **milliliters**

# VOCABULARY POWER

### REVIEW

**unit** [yoo′nət] *noun*

A unit is a quantity used as a measure.
Customary and metric units are *standard
units*. Explain what you think a *nonstandard
unit* might be. Give some examples.

### PREVIEW

| | |
|---|---|
| precision | centimeter (cm) |
| millimeter (mm) | meter (m) |
| kilometer (km) | Celsius (°C) |
| Fahrenheit (°F) | |

www.harcourtschool.com/mathglossary

# Customary Length

## Learn

**CHOICES! CHOICES!** Lengths are often measured in the customary system using *standard units* such as inches, feet, or yards. You can also use *nonstandard units* such as the length of a paper clip or a piece of string.

**HANDS ON**

### Activity 1

Measure and compare lengths using nonstandard units.

- Use a paper clip to measure the width of a table or desk. Record the width of the object in paper clips.
- Use a piece of string to measure the width of the same table or desk. Record the width in string lengths.
- Which unit is longer, a paper clip or a string length?
- Which unit would be more appropriate for measuring the width of a room—paper clips or pieces of string? Explain.

When you measure an object, you need to choose the appropriate unit and tool.

**HANDS ON**

### Activity 2

Estimate and then measure the length of your classroom using an appropriate standard unit and measuring tool.

- Which unit is best for measuring the length of your classroom—inches, feet, yards, or miles? Explain.
- Choose a tool to make the measurement. Why did you choose that tool?
- Measure the length and record the measurement.
- Was your estimate close to the actual measurement?
- Which unit is best for measuring the distance from New Orleans, Louisiana, to Charleston, West Virginia? Explain.

**Quick Review**

Compare. Write $<$ , $>$ , or $=$ for each ⬤.

1. $\frac{2}{16}$ ⬤ $\frac{3}{16}$   2. $\frac{1}{4}$ ⬤ $\frac{4}{16}$

3. $\frac{5}{16}$ ⬤ $\frac{1}{2}$   4. $\frac{8}{16}$ ⬤ $\frac{1}{2}$

5. $\frac{3}{4}$ ⬤ $\frac{15}{16}$

**VOCABULARY**

precision

**MATERIALS**

paper clips, string, customary measuring tools

**CUSTOMARY UNITS OF LENGTH**

12 inches (in.) = 1 foot (ft)

3 feet = 1 yard (yd)

5,280 feet = 1 mile (mi)

1,760 yards = 1 mile

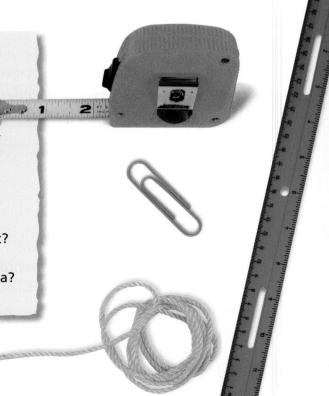

# Precision

The **precision** of a measurement is related to the unit of measure you choose. The smaller the unit, the more precise the measurement will be.

$\frac{1}{8}$-in. mark

?

To the nearest inch, the crayon's length is 4 inches.
A more precise measurement is $3\frac{7}{8}$ inches.

**HANDS ON**

## Activity 3 — Estimate and measure the length of each object.

### STEP 1

Copy the table.

| Object | Estimate (nearest inch) | Measurement (nearest $\frac{1}{4}$ inch) | Measurement (nearest $\frac{1}{8}$ inch) |
|---|---|---|---|
| marker | | | |
| paper clip | | | |
| pencil | | | |

### STEP 2

Estimate the length of each object to the nearest inch. Record your estimate in the table.

### STEP 3

Use a ruler. Measure the length of each object to the nearest $\frac{1}{4}$ inch and to the nearest $\frac{1}{8}$ inch. Record your measurements in the table.

- Why is measuring to the nearest $\frac{1}{8}$ inch more precise than measuring to the nearest $\frac{1}{4}$ inch?
- Carlos said that his desk is 2 feet $1\frac{1}{2}$ inches wide. How many inches wide is his desk?

## ▶ Check

1. **Explain** which unit would be the most appropriate for measuring the width of a postage stamp: inches, feet, yards, or miles.

**Tell the best unit and tool for measuring each.**

2. width of a shoe　　　3. height of the room　　　4. distance from school to your home

**LESSON CONTINUES**

FCAT TESTED  SSS/GLEs MA.B.I.2.2.5.I solves real-world problems involving measurement of the following: length (for example, eighth-inch, kilometer, mile) . . . *also:* MA.B.I.2.I.5.I, MA.B.2.2.2.5.I

Chapter 24　**523**

**Tell which measurement is more precise.**

**5.** 1 foot or 13 inches

**6.** 2 miles or 10,565 feet

**7.** 5 feet or 2 yards

**8.** 34 inches or 1 yard

**9.** $12\frac{1}{4}$ feet or $12\frac{1}{8}$ feet

**10.** $35\frac{3}{8}$ inches or 3 feet

**Estimate the length of the marker in inches. Then measure the length**

**11.** to the nearest inch.

**12.** to the nearest $\frac{1}{2}$ inch.

**13.** to the nearest $\frac{1}{8}$ inch.

**14.** In Exercises 11–13, which measurement is most precise? Explain.

---

▶ **Practice and Problem Solving**     Extra Practice, page 542, Set A

**Tell the best unit and tool for measuring each.**

**15.** length of a pen

**16.** distance from Miami to Orlando

**17.** length of the classroom

**Tell which measurement is more precise.**

**18.** 2 miles or 3,526 yards

**19.** 4 yards or 13 feet

**20.** 26,300 feet or 5 miles

**21.** $5\frac{7}{8}$ feet or 2 yards

**22.** $2\frac{1}{2}$ miles or 13,000 feet

**23.** 1 foot or $11\frac{3}{8}$ inches

**Measure the length of the pencil**

**24.** to the nearest foot.

**25.** to the nearest inch.

**26.** to the nearest $\frac{1}{8}$ inch.

**Estimate the length in inches. Then measure to the nearest $\frac{1}{8}$ inch.**

**27.**

**28.**

**29.** Joel measured the length of his garden in feet and in yards. Which was greater, the number of feet in the measurement or the number of yards? Explain.

**30.** Measure the width of the door to your classroom. Then measure the width of a door at home. Compare the widths and tell which door is wider. How much wider is it?

**31.** ✎ **Write About It** Explain how you would measure your pencil to the nearest $\frac{1}{8}$ inch.

**32.** Trenton's ruler has only $\frac{1}{4}$-inch marks. Explain how he can measure $3\frac{6}{8}$ inches of string.

**33.** On Monday, Tara drove 52.6 mi to Ocala and then 75.8 mi farther to Orlando. On Tuesday, she drove 167.8 mi. To the nearest $\frac{1}{2}$ mile, how much farther did Tara drive on Tuesday than on Monday?

**34.** The sum of Jason's and Elton's ages is 30 years. Jason is 8 years older than Elton. How old is Elton?

## Getting Ready for FCAT

**35.** Mr. Hudson needs a box to hold the new baseball bat he bought for his son's birthday. Which of these measurements best describes the length of an appropriate box for the baseball bat?

**A.** 3 inches

**B.** 3 feet

**C.** 3 yards

**D.** 3 miles

## Problem Solving   LINKUP . . . to Science

Echoes can be used to measure distances. Weather forecasters send sound waves toward weather systems such as tornadoes or hurricanes. They time how long it takes the waves to reach a system, "bounce off" it, and return. This method of measuring distances is called **sonar.**

**Solve.**

**1.** A ship was in a heavy fog. The navigator knew there was an iceberg nearby, and he sounded a horn. Four seconds later he heard an echo returning from the iceberg. Sound travels about 1,100 feet per second in air. About how far was the iceberg from the ship?

**2.** Sound travels about 1 mile per second in water. Suppose a ship's sonar emits a loud sound under water. Four miles away there is a submarine. How long will it be before the echo reaches the ship?

**3.** ✍ **Write a problem** about using echoes to measure distances. Have a classmate solve your problem.

**HANDS ON**

# Metric Length

**Quick Review**

1. $4 \times 100$
2. $500 \times 100$
3. $13 \times 10$
4. $2,000 \div 10$
5. $75 \div 10$

▶ **Explore**

You can use standard metric units to measure length or distance.

A **millimeter (mm)** is a very small unit. It is about the thickness of a spoke on a bicycle wheel.

A **centimeter (cm)** is about the thickness of a bicycle pedal.

A **meter (m)** is about the height of a bicycle.

A **kilometer (km)** is how far you can ride a bicycle in a few minutes.

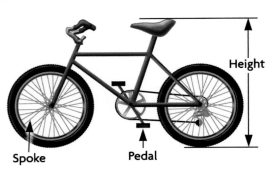

Height

Spoke          Pedal

**VOCABULARY**

**millimeter (m)**
**centimeter (cm)**
**meter (m)**
**kilometer (km)**

**MATERIALS**

metric measuring tools, paper clips

**METRIC UNITS OF LENGTH**

10 millimeters (mm) = 1 centimeter (cm)
100 centimeters = 1 meter (m)
1,000 meters = 1 kilometer (km)

## Activity

Estimate and measure the length of one of your textbooks.

• Make a table to record your estimated length and your measurement.

• Choose an appropriate metric unit for measuring the book.

• Estimate the length of the book in your chosen unit. Record your estimate.

• Choose an appropriate tool for measuring the book. Measure and record the length of the book.

• Which unit and tool did you choose? Explain your choice.

## Try It

**Estimate and measure each. Record your data.**

**a.** length of your desk

**b.** distance from your desk to the door

Is the desktop longer or shorter than a meter?

## Connect

You can find the length or height of something that you cannot reach.

Find the height of the building in the picture.
The height of one floor in the building is 14.5 meters. Count the number of floors in the building. Multiply the number of floors by the height of one floor to find the height of the building.

$$14.5 \times 8 = 116$$

So, the building is about 116 meters tall.

- **What if** the height of one floor in the building were 12.25 meters. Explain how to find the height of the building.

## Practice and Problem Solving

**Write the appropriate metric unit for measuring each.**

**1.** height of your school

**2.** thickness of a book

**3.** distance from New York to Los Angeles

**Estimate and measure each.**

**4.**

**5.**

**6.**

**7.** your height

**8.** width of your pencil

**9.** length of your little finger

**Find the measurement of each.**

**10.** the length of a road 12 blocks long if 1 block is 0.125 km long

**11.** the height of a building 12 stories high if 1 story is 13 m high

**12.** the length of a floor 92 tiles long if 1 tile is 30 cm long

**13.** ✎ **Write About It** Find the height of a building or an object you cannot reach. Draw a picture to explain your method.

**14. GEOMETRY** A rectangular frame has a perimeter of 50.6 cm. If the length is 8.3 cm, what is the width?

**15. NUMBER SENSE** Anne says 0.2 cm is the same as 2 mm. Do you agree? Explain.

## Getting Ready for FCAT

**16.** Caryn measured the length of each crayon to see if it would fit into her school box.

Which is the best estimate of the length of Caryn's crayon?

**A.** 1 meter    **B.** 9 centimeters    **C.** 900 millimeters    **D.** 10 kilometers

FCAT TESTED ✎  SSS/GLEs MA.B.3.2.1.5.2 Solves real-world problems involving estimated measurements, including the following: length to the nearest quarter-inch, centimeter . . . also: MA.B.1.2.2.5.1, MA.B.2.2.1.5.1, MA.B.2.2.2.5.1

Chapter 24    **527**

# Change Linear Units

▷ **Learn**

**CUSTOM TOWELS** Jenna is making personalized beach towels for each member of her family. She needs 30 feet of fabric. Since fabric is sold by the yard, how many yards of fabric does Jenna need?

**Think:** 30 feet = ■ yards

To change smaller units to larger units, divide.

| number ÷ of feet | number of feet in 1 yard | = total yards |
|:---:|:---:|:---:|
| ↓ | ↓ | ↓ |
| 30 ÷ | 3 | = 10 |

So, Jenna needs 10 yards of fabric.

**CUSTOMARY UNITS OF LENGTH**

12 inches (in.) = 1 foot (ft)
3 feet = 1 yard (yd)
5,280 feet = 1 mile (mi)
1,760 yards = 1 mile

**METRIC UNITS OF LENGTH**

10 millimeters (mm) = 1 centimeter (cm)
100 centimeters = 1 meter (m)
1,000 meters = 1 kilometer (km)

## Examples

**Ⓐ How many millimeters are in 230 centimeters?**

**Think:** 230 cm = ■ mm

To change larger units to smaller units, multiply.

| number of cm | × | number of mm in 1 cm | = | number of mm |
|:---:|:---:|:---:|:---:|:---:|
| ↓ | | ↓ | | ↓ |
| 230 | × | 10 | = | 2,300 mm |

There are 2,300 millimeters in 230 centimeters.

**Ⓑ How many feet are in 168 inches?**

**Think:** 168 inches = ■ feet

To change smaller units to larger units, divide.

| number of inches | ÷ | number of inches in 1 foot | = | number of feet |
|:---:|:---:|:---:|:---:|:---:|
| ↓ | | ↓ | | ↓ |
| 168 | ÷ | 12 | = | 14 |

There are 14 feet in 168 inches.

You can also use a calculator to change linear units.

7,200 ft = ■ mi

  ÷  = = 1.3636363

So, 7,200 ft is approximately equal to 1.4 mi.

## Add and Subtract Measurements

You may need to change units to add and subtract measurements.

### Example 1

Jenna needs 5 feet 7 inches of fabric for her mother's towel and 4 feet 6 inches for her little brother's towel. How much fabric does she need for both towels?

Find 5 ft 7 in. + 4 ft 6 in.

| STEP 1 | STEP 2 | STEP 3 |
|---|---|---|
| Add each kind of unit.<br><br>  5 ft   7 in.<br>+4 ft   6 in.<br> 9 ft  13 in. | **Think:** 12 in. = 1 ft<br>Since 13 in. is more than 1 ft, rename 13 in. as 1 ft + 1 in.<br><br>9 ft 13 in. = 9 ft + (1 ft + 1 in.) | Combine like units.<br>9 ft + (1 ft + 1 in.) =<br>(9 ft + 1 ft) + 1 in. = 10 ft 1 in. |

So, she needs 10 feet 1 inch of fabric.

### Example 2

Mary made a towel bar with a piece of wooden dowel that was 1 m long. If she used 48.9 cm of the dowel, how much of it remained?

Find 1 m − 48.9 cm.

| STEP 1 | STEP 2 | STEP 3 |
|---|---|---|
| **Think:** 1 m = 100 cm<br>Use 100 cm for 1 m.<br><br>  100<br>− 48.9 | Place a zero to show an equivalent decimal.<br><br>  100.0<br>− 48.9 | Subtract.<br><br>      9 9<br>  0 10 10  10<br>  100.0<br>− 48.9<br>  51.1 |

So, 51.1 cm of wooden dowel was left.

▷ **Check**

1. **Explain** how you would rename units to subtract 4 feet 6 inches from 7 feet 2 inches.

**Change the unit.**

2. 3 ft = ▇ in.      3. 5 yd = ▇ ft      4. 60 in. = ▇ ft      5. 24 ft = ▇ yd

6. 5 m = ▇ cm      7. 20 mm = ▇ cm      8. 2 km = ▇ m      9. 4,000 m = ▇ km

**Complete.**

10. 4 ft 3 in. = 3 ft ▇ in.      11. 5,360 ft = 1 mi ▇ ft      12. 10 yd 1 ft = 9 yd ▇ ft

**LESSON CONTINUES**

FCAT TESTED ▇ SSS/GLEs MA.B.2.2.1.5.3 Uses multiplication and division to convert units of measure within the customary or metric system. *also:* MA.B.1.2.2.5.1

Chapter 24   **529**

**Change the unit.**

**13.** 24 in. = ■ ft **14.** 30 ft = ■ yd **15.** 13 yd = ■ ft **16.** 8 ft = ■ in.

**17.** 4 mi = ■ yd **18.** 48 in. = ■ ft **19.** 6 m = ■ cm **20.** 50 mm = ■ cm

**21.** 7 km = ■ m **22.** 65 cm = ■ mm **23.** 8 m = ■ cm **24.** 700 cm = ■ m

**25.** 4 yd = ■ in. **26.** 10,560 ft = ■ mi **27.** 3 m = ■ mm **28.** 6,000 m = ■ km

**Complete.**

**29.** 235 cm = ■ m 35 cm **30.** 25 ft 12 in. = ■ yd 2 ft **31.** 3 cm 25 mm = ■ mm

**32.** 7 mi 250 ft = ■ ft **33.** 2 km 50 m = ■ cm **34.** 62 m = 6,150 cm ■ mm

**35.** 2 ft = 1 ft ■ in. **36.** 12 yd 2 ft = 11 yd ■ ft **37.** 3 mi 27 ft = 2 mi ■ ft

**Find the sum or difference.**

**38.** 2 ft 2 in.
+3 ft 7 in.

**39.** 3 yd 2 ft
+8 yd 1 ft

**40.** 7 ft 4 in.
−5 ft 1 in.

**41.** 14 yd
− 5 yd 2 ft

**42.** 15 ft 4 in.
+12 ft 6 in.

**43.** 3 mi 345 ft
+1 mi 39 ft

**44.** 8 ft 6 in.
−3 ft 10 in.

**45.** 12 yd 2 ft 3 in.
− 3 yd 1 ft 11 in.

**46.** 88 cm − 69 cm **47.** 50 km + 6.8 km **48.** 830 mm − 4.6 cm

**49.** 13.4 km − 2.8 km **50.** 10.3 cm + 7.8 cm **51.** 15.6 cm − 6.4 cm

**52.** **? What's the Error?** Jason had 14 yd of string. He used 5 yd 8 in. for a string art project. He said that he had 8 yd 2 in. left. Describe his error and give the correct amount of string that was left.

**53.** **ESTIMATION** Estimate how many yards long your classroom is. Then use a yardstick to check. Record your estimate and the actual measurement.

**54.** **NUMBER SENSE** Describe how you could find the number of centimeters in a kilometer.

**55.** **NUMBER SENSE** Joel says that 40 cm is the same as 0.4 m. Do you agree? Explain your thinking.

**56.** Mr. Gomez had 15 ft of cable. He used 12 ft 6 in. to hook up his television. How long was the remaining piece?

**57.** Grace has 13 feet of fabric. Her pattern calls for $4\frac{1}{4}$ yards of fabric. Does she have enough? Explain.

**58.** Use the diagram on the right. By car, how many kilometers is it from Bill's house to the library following the path shown?

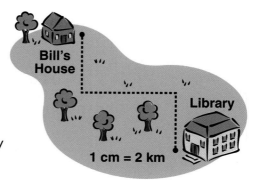

**530**

| ROOM | PERIMETER |
|------|-----------|
| Bedroom | 44 feet 6 inches |
| Living room | 14 yards |
| Den | 31 feet 8 inches |

**59.** Tiffany is installing new molding in her house. The table at the right shows the amounts of molding she needs for some of the rooms. How much molding does she need for the bedroom and living room?

   **A.** 58 feet 6 inches

   **B.** 58 yards 6 inches

   **C.** 76 feet 2 inches

   **D.** 86 feet 6 inches

**60.** How much more molding does Tiffany need for the bedroom than for the den?

   **F.** 13 feet 8 inches

   **G.** 13 feet 2 inches

   **H.** 12 feet 10 inches

   **I.** 12 feet 8 inches

# Problem Solving   THiNKer's CorNer

**RELATING SYSTEMS** You can use the comparisons below to explore the relationship between some customary and metric units of measure.

| One yard is slightly shorter than 1 meter. |
|---|
| One mile is slightly longer than 1.5 kilometers. |
| One gallon is about 3.75 liters. |
| One pound is about 0.5 kilogram. |

If a kilometer is about 6 city blocks long, about how many city blocks long is one mile?

There are about 6 city blocks in 1 kilometer, so 0.5 kilometer is about 3 city blocks. Since a mile is about 1.5 kilometers, one mile is about 6 + 3, or 9 city blocks long.

▲ **Miracle Mile is a popular shopping area in Coral Gables, Florida.**

**1.** Carmen's poodle Tinkerbell weighs 8 kilograms. Does Tinkerbell weigh more than 10 pounds? Explain.

**2.** A football field is 120 yards long, including the end zones. Is a football field shorter or longer than 120 meters?

**3.** Liam's fish tank holds 80 liters of water. Liam's new fish needs to be in a tank that holds at least 30 gallons of water. Does Liam's tank hold enough water? Explain.

**4.** Marlys is running in two 5K, or 5 kilometer, races this month. She is running in a 10K race next month. Will Marlys run more or less than 10 miles in all? Explain.

# Customary Capacity and Weight

## Learn

**ALL SHOOK UP!** Al's Deli uses 1 pint of milk in each milkshake. There are 15 milkshakes ordered. If Al has 8 quarts of milk, does he have enough for all the milkshakes?

**Think:** 8 quarts = ■ pints

To change larger units to smaller units, multiply:

$$
\begin{array}{ccccc}
\text{number of} & \times & \text{number of pints} & = & \text{total} \\
\text{quarts} & & \text{in 1 quart} & & \text{pints} \\
\downarrow & & \downarrow & & \downarrow \\
8 & \times & 2 & = & 16
\end{array}
$$

There are 16 pints in 8 quarts. Since $15 < 16$, there is enough milk for 15 milkshakes.

| CUSTOMARY UNITS OF CAPACITY |
| --- |
| 8 fluid ounces (fl oz) = 1 cup (c) |
| 2 cups = 1 pint (pt) |
| 2 pints = 1 quart (qt) |
| 4 cups = 1 quart |
| 4 quarts = 1 gallon (gal) |

| CUSTOMARY UNITS OF WEIGHT |
| --- |
| 16 ounces (oz) = 1 pound (lb) |
| 2,000 pounds = 1 ton (T) |

## Example

Al uses 2 ounces of cheese for each sandwich. If he makes 40 sandwiches, how many pounds of cheese does he use?

### STEP 1

Find how many ounces of cheese are used in 40 sandwiches.

**Think:** 40 sandwiches = ■ ounces of cheese

$$
\begin{array}{ccccc}
\text{number of} & \times & \text{number of ounces} & = & \text{total} \\
\text{sandwiches} & & \text{in 1 sandwich} & & \text{ounces} \\
\downarrow & & \downarrow & & \downarrow \\
40 & \times & 2 & = & 80
\end{array}
$$

### STEP 2

Find how many pounds are in 80 ounces.

**Think:** 80 ounces = ■ pounds

$$
\begin{array}{ccccc}
\text{number of} & \div & \text{number of ounces} & = & \text{total} \\
\text{ounces} & & \text{in 1 pound} & & \text{pounds} \\
\downarrow & & \downarrow & & \downarrow \\
80 & \div & 16 & = & 5
\end{array}
$$

So, he uses 5 pounds of cheese to make 40 sandwiches.

1. **Explain** how you could find the number of pounds in 160 ounces.

**Change the unit.**

2. 3 gal = ☐ qt

3. 32 c = ☐ qt

4. 4 gal = ☐ c

5. 2 pt = ☐ c

6. 48 oz = ☐ lb

7. 2 lb = ☐ oz

8. 1 T = ☐ oz

9. 8,000 lb = ☐ T

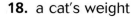

▶ **Practice and Problem Solving** (Extra Practice, page 542, Set C)

**Change the unit.**

10. 10 pt = ☐ qt

11. 5 c = ☐ fl oz

12. 3 gal = ☐ pt

13. 16 fl oz = ☐ pt

14. 2 T = ☐ lb

15. 6 lb = ☐ oz

16. 112 oz = ☐ lb

17. 1.5 T = ☐ lb

**Choose the best tool to measure each.**

18. a cat's weight

19. amount of water in a bathtub

20. amount of juice in a glass

21. outside temperature

A   B   C

D   E   F

22. **What if** Al had 23 milkshake orders and 3 gallons of milk? Would he have enough milk for 1 pint in each milkshake? Explain.

23. Use the Frosty Freeze ad. Toby needs 1 gallon of ice cream for a party. What is the better buy? Explain.

24. **▰FAST FACT • HEALTH** You should not carry a backpack that weighs more than $\frac{1}{5}$ of your weight. Weigh each item in your backpack to the nearest ounce, and find the total weight. Is your backpack under the weight limit? Explain.

25. ▰ **Write About It** Describe three items that are measured by capacity. Describe three items that are measured by weight.

26. Heather used 5 cups of milk from a 1-gallon container. How many cups of milk are left?

 **A.** 11 c   **B.** 5 c   **C.** 4 c   **D.** 3 c

27. Ken's skateboard weighs $5\frac{1}{2}$ lb, and Lucy's skateboard weighs $4\frac{1}{4}$ lb. How many ounces more is Ken's skateboard?

 **F.** 16 oz   **G.** 18 oz   **H.** 20 oz   **I.** 22 oz

# Metric Capacity and Mass

▶ **Learn**

**PUNCH LINE** Ms. Allison needs 4 liters of juice to make fruit punch. The cafeteria sends her 12 metric cups of juice. Is this enough juice to make the punch?

**Think:** 12 metric cups = ■ liters

To change smaller units to larger units, divide.

| number of metric cups | ÷ | number of metric cups in 1 liter | = | total liters |
|:---:|:---:|:---:|:---:|:---:|
| ↓ | | ↓ | | ↓ |
| 12 | ÷ | 4 | = | 3 |

There are 3 liters in 12 metric cups.
Since 3 < 4, Ms. Allison does not have enough juice.

**250 milliliters (mL), or 1 metric cup**  **1 liter**

## Example

Ms. Allison needs to make 50 sandwiches for the fifth grade. If she uses two 1-kilogram jars of peanut butter, how many grams of peanut butter will she use for each sandwich?

### STEP 1

Find how many grams are in 2 kilograms.

**Think:** 2 kilograms = ■ grams

To change larger units to smaller units, multiply.

| number of kilograms | × | number of grams in 1 kilogram | = | total grams |
|:---:|:---:|:---:|:---:|:---:|
| ↓ | | ↓ | | ↓ |
| 2 | × | 1,000 | = | 2,000 |

So, there are 2,000 grams in 2 kilograms.

### STEP 2

To find how many grams will be used for each sandwich, divide 2,000 grams into 50 equal groups.

| number of grams | ÷ | number of sandwiches | = | grams per sandwich |
|:---:|:---:|:---:|:---:|:---:|
| ↓ | | ↓ | | ↓ |
| 2,000 | ÷ | 50 | = | 40 |

So, Ms. Allison will use 40 grams of peanut butter for each sandwich.

> **METRIC UNITS OF CAPACITY**
> 1,000 milliliters (mL) = 1 liter (L)
> 250 milliliters = 1 metric cup
> 4 metric cups = 1 liter
> 1,000 liters = 1 kiloliter (kL)

**A large paper clip is about 1 gram.**  **A large container of peanut butter is about 1 kilogram.**

> **METRIC UNITS OF MASS**
> 1,000 milligrams (mg) = 1 gram (g)
> 1,000 grams = 1 kilogram (kg)

1. **Explain** whether you multiply or divide to find how many milliliters are in 5 liters.

**Technology Link**

More Practice: Harcourt Mega Math The Number Games, *Tiny's Think Tank*, Level Q

**Change the unit.**

2. 4,000 L = ▓ kL        3. 8 metric cups = ▓ L   4. 6 kg = ▓ g        5. 2,000 mg = ▓ g

**Measure each. Explain your method.**

6. mass of a box of crayons                7. capacity of water in a bottle

**Practice and Problem Solving**    ( Extra Practice, page 542, Set D )

**Change the unit.**

8. 1.5 kg = ▓ g            9. 8 kL = ▓ L            10. 5 L = ▓ mL      11. 3 g = ▓ mg

**Measure each. Explain your method.**

12. capacity of water in a sink            13. mass of a straight pin

**Compare. Write <, >, or = for each ●.**

14. 6 L ● 16 metric cups            15. 4,000 mg ● 4 g            16. 5 kg ● 15,000 g

**Choose the best estimate.**

17. the mass of a strawberry is
    a. 6 mg
    b. 6 g
    c. 6 kg

18. the dropper holds
    a. 3 mL
    b. 3 L
    c. 3 kL

19. the mass of a cat is
    a. 6 mg
    b. 6 g
    c. 6 kg

20. the bottle of soda holds
    a. 1 mL
    b. 1 L
    c. 1 kL

21. The 4 members of We-Care Lawn Mowers drank a total of 2 L of water. If they all drank an equal amount of water, how many mL did each member drink?

22. A can of soda holds 355 mL. Which holds more, a 2-L bottle of soda or a 6-pack of soda cans? Explain.

23. **? What's the Question?** Monique had a 1-kg jar of peanut butter for sandwiches. She used 750 g of peanut butter in one week. The answer is 250 g.

24. Sometimes you can use a nonstandard measure, like a *handful*. How many handfuls of sand will fill a small plastic bag?

**Getting Ready for FCAT**

25. Mr. Brown brought 8 liters of soda to the picnic. How many paper cups like the one at the right can he fill?
    A. 24            C. 32
    B. 28            D. 36

**250 milliliters**

FCAT TESTED    SSS/GLEs MA.B.2.2.1.5.3 Uses multiplication and division to convert units of measure within the customary or metric system. *also:* MA.B.1.2.2.5.1, MA.B.1.2.2.5.2, MA.B.3.2.1.5.2, MA.B.4.2.1.5.1

**Chapter 24    535**

# Time and Temperature

**Quick Review**

1. 2 hr = ■ min
2. 3 wk = ■ days
3. 30 mo = ■ yr
4. 1 wk = ■ hr
5. ■ hr = 3,600 sec

▶ **Learn**

**BEAT THE CLOCK**   Naomi wants to run 5 miles in less than $1\frac{3}{4}$ hours. If she starts her run at 10:47 A.M. and runs 5 miles by 12:26 P.M., has she reached her goal?

**VOCABULARY**

**Fahrenheit (°F)**
**Celsius (°C)**

**One Way** Use a clock.

Count forward on the clock from the starting time to the ending time.

**Another Way** Use subtraction.

12 hr 26 min = 11 hr 86 min

```
    11    86
    1̸2 hr 2̸6 min    ← ending time
  − 10 hr 47 min    ← starting time
     1 hr 39 min
```

So, Naomi ran for 1 hr 39 min. Since 1 hr 39 min is less than $1\frac{3}{4}$ hr, or 1 hr 45 min, she has reached her goal.

You can use a calendar to find elapsed time.

## Examples

**A** Count the whole days from 10 P.M. September 16 to 10 P.M. September 18.

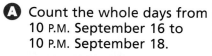

| September | | | | | | |
|---|---|---|---|---|---|---|
| | | | 1 | 2 | 3 | 4 |
| 5 | 6 | 7 | 8 | 9 | 10 | 11 |
| 12 | 13 | 14 | 15 | 16 | 17 | 18 |
| 19 | 20 | 21 | 22 | 23 | 24 | 25 |
| 26 | 27 | 28 | 29 | 30 | | |

2 days

**B** Count the weeks from 2:00 A.M. April 3 to 2:00 A.M. April 24.

| April | | | | | | |
|---|---|---|---|---|---|---|
| | | | | 1 | 2 | 3 |
| 4 | 5 | 6 | 7 | 8 | 9 | 10 |
| 11 | 12 | 13 | 14 | 15 | 16 | 17 |
| 18 | 19 | 20 | 21 | 22 | 23 | 24 |
| 25 | 26 | 27 | 28 | 29 | 30 | |

3 weeks

**UNITS OF TIME**

60 seconds (sec) = 1 minute (min)

60 minutes = 1 hour (hr)

24 hours = 1 day

7 days = 1 week (wk)

about 52 weeks = 1 year (yr)

365 days = 1 year

366 days = 1 leap year

10 years = 1 decade

100 years = 1 century

1,000 years = 1 millennium

# Measuring Temperature

Temperature is measured in degrees **Fahrenheit (°F)** in the customary system and in degrees **Celsius (°C)** in the metric system.

When Naomi began her run, the Fahrenheit thermometer outside her house read 65°F. She ended her run at the library, where a Celsius thermometer read 20°C. By how many degrees Fahrenheit had the temperature changed?

You can find the change by comparing the temperatures on the two thermometers. The Celsius reading of 20°C is about 70°F. From 65°F to 70°F is 5 degrees. So, the temperature changed by 5 degrees Fahrenheit.

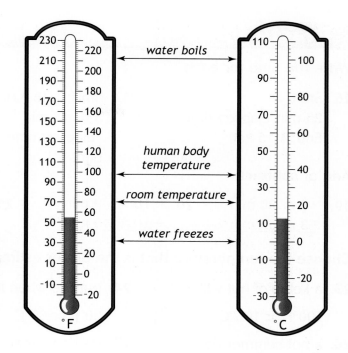

---

▶ **Check**

1. **Explain** how to use a clock to find the elapsed time between 3:00 P.M. Wednesday and 1:00 A.M. Thursday.

2. **Explain** how you know whether 0°F or 0°C is colder.

**Write the time for each.**

3. Start: 4:30 P.M.
   45 min elapsed time
   End: ■

4. Start: ■
   25 min elapsed time
   End: 8:00 P.M.

5. Start: June 11, 9:00 P.M.
   ■ time has elapsed.
   End: June 16, 5:30 A.M.

**Add or subtract.**

6.   5 hr 10 min
   +2 hr 45 min

7.   8 hr 11 min
   −3 hr 24 min

8.   5 hr 15 min
   −3 hr 35 min

9.   1 hr 50 min
   +3 hr 22 min

**Choose the temperature that is the better estimate.**

10. a glass of ice water
    34°F or 34°C

11. a classroom
    23°F or 23°C

12. a bowl of hot stew
    80°F or 80°C

**Use the thermometers above to find the change in temperature.**

13. 25°F to 41°F

14. ⁻5°C to ⁻20°C

15. 45°F to 20°C

**LESSON CONTINUES**

FCAT TESTED    SSS/GLEs MA.B.I.2.2.5.3 uses schedules, calendars, and elapsed time to solve real-world problems. *also:* MA.B.I.2.2.5.I

Chapter 24    **537**

**Write the time for each.**

**16.** Start: ■
25 min elapsed time
End: 4:15 P.M.

**17.** Start: 1:45 A.M.
3 hr 15 min
elapsed time
End: ■

**18.** Start: May 1, 2:00 P.M.
3 days, 6 hr, 10 min
elapsed time
End: ■

**Add or subtract.**

**19.**    8 hr 36 min
       +3 hr 55 min

**20.**    16 hr  9 min
       −10 hr 15 min

**21.**    6 hr 23 min
       −2 hr 47 min

**22.**    24 hr 49 min
       +12 hr 33 min

**Choose the temperature that is the better estimate.**

**23.** a kettle of hot water

100°F or 100°C

**24.** outside when it's snowing

30°F or 30°C

**25.** a good day for a picnic

70°F or 70°C

**26.** a hot summer day

90°F or 90°C

**27.** inside your school

20°F or 20°C

**28.** a winter day in Alaska

5°F or 5°C

**Use the thermometers on page 537 to find the change in temperature.**

**29.** 47°F to 82°F

**30.** ⁻10°C to ⁻44°C

**31.** 13°F to ⁻5°F

**USE DATA For 32–34, use the graph.**

**32.** By how many degrees did the temperature change between the lowest and highest recorded temperatures?

**33.** At what time of day was the temperature 9° colder than it was at 2:00 P.M.?

**34.** Between which two times was the greatest change in temperature?

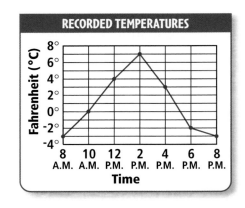

**35.** Hiromi began practicing his tuba at 11:20 A.M. If he needs to practice for 45 minutes, at what time should he stop?

**36.** Leeza began doing her chores at 3:30 P.M. She finished at 4:45 P.M. How many minutes did it take her to finish her chores?

**37.** ✏ **Write About It** Jennifer has a thermometer, a meter stick, a balance, and a measuring cup. Name something she could measure with each tool. Then, describe how she would use the tool to measure.

**38. Vocabulary Power** The Celsius scale is named after Anders Celsius. It has also been called the centigrade scale. Look up the prefix *centi-*, and then explain why centigrade is an appropriate name for this scale.

**538**

**39.** 📓 **Write a problem** about how much time it might take to do your homework or bake cookies. Include beginning and ending times.

**40.** Order these times from shortest to longest length of time. 1 century, 120 minutes, 60 seconds, 10 days, 1 week, 1 hour, 125 years

## Getting Ready for FCAT

**41.** When Dwight finished mowing the lawn, he looked at his watch. If he started mowing at 2:35 P.M., how long did it take him to mow the lawn?

**A.** 15 minutes     **C.** 35 minutes

**B.** 25 minutes     **D.** 40 minutes

**42.** Dwight is leaving for a trip in 15 hours 45 minutes. On what day is he leaving?

**F.** May 1    **G.** May 2    **H.** May 3    **I.** May 4

**Dwight's watch**

## Problem Solving — THINKER'S CORNER

**USING A SCHEDULE** Your aunt will pick you up at 10:30 A.M. for the train trip to City Museum. It takes 20 minutes to drive to the North Conway train station. You must be home by 5:00 P.M. How long can you stay at the museum? Make a table to record your trip.

**Think:**

• You'll get to the train station at 10:50 A.M.

• The next train is at 11:10 A.M.

• To get home in time, take the 3:30 P.M. train.

• You will be at the museum from 11:40 A.M. to 3:30 P.M.

So, you can spend 3 hr 50 min at the museum.

**Find how long can you stay at the museum.**

| Departure | Arrival |
|-----------|---------|
| *N. Conway* | *City Museum* |
| 9:50 A.M. | 10:20 A.M. |
| 11:10 A.M. | 11:40 A.M. |
| 12:30 P.M. | 1:00 P.M. |
| *City Museum* | *N. Conway* |
| 2:00 P.M. | 2:30 P.M. |
| 3:30 P.M. | 4:00 P.M. |
| 4:45 P.M. | 5:15 P.M. |

**1.** Your aunt picks you up at 9:00 A.M. and you must be home by 3:00 P.M.

**2.** Your aunt picks you up at noon and you must be home by 4:30 P.M.

# Problem Solving Skill
## Estimate or Actual Measurement

UNDERSTAND ⟩ PLAN ⟩ SOLVE ⟩ CHECK

**SHELVE IT** Enrique and Angela each have a 15-foot board to use to make shelves to display their miniature car collections.

## Problem 1

Enrique wants to make two 10-in.-long shelves, three 20-in.-long shelves, and two 35-in.-long shelves. Does he have enough wood?

## Problem 2

Angela wants to use all her wood to make six shelves that are all the same length. How many inches long should each shelf be?

Sometimes you need an *actual measurement*. Sometimes an *estimate* will do.

Enrique can estimate by rounding each length up to the nearest foot.

| | | |
|---|---|---|
| 10 in. → 1 ft | two shelves → | 2 ft |
| 20 in. → 2 ft | three shelves → | 6 ft |
| 35 in. → 3 ft | two shelves → | 6 ft |
| | | 14 ft |

Since 14 < 15, Enrique has enough wood.

Angela wants to use the entire 15-foot board, so she needs to know the actual length of each shelf. First, she finds the number of inches in 15 feet. Then, she divides to find the length of each shelf.

Find the number of inches in 15 feet. Multiply. 15 × 12 in. = 180 in.

Find the number of inches in each shelf. Divide. 180 in. ÷ 6 = 30 in.

So, each shelf should be 30 inches long.

## Talk About It

• Why did Enrique round up when estimating the length of the shelves?

• Describe situations that require an actual measurement and those that only require an estimate.

**Decide whether you need an estimate or an actual measurement.**

1. Debbie has 15 meters of wood. She uses 7 meters for a bookcase and 2.5 meters for shelves. How much wood does she have left?

2. Barbara needs 2 quarts of water to fill a pot for soup. How many times will she have to fill an 8-ounce measuring cup to fill the pot?

3. Mario is buying wallpaper border. The wallpaper comes in rolls that are 22 feet long. He needs 58 feet of border. How many rolls should he buy?

4. Tony's party starts in 3 hours. He figures it will take about 1 hour to cook, 40 minutes to clean, and 30 minutes to decorate. Will he have time to shower before his guests arrive?

**Eric is having a barbecue. He needs a $\frac{1}{4}$-lb hamburger patty for each of his 11 guests. He bought four packages of hamburger meat weighing 13 oz, 9 oz, 14.5 oz, and 11.5 oz.**

5. Which question about Eric's barbecue requires an estimate?

   **A** How much hamburger meat does he need for his guests?
   **B** How much meat did he buy?
   **C** About how much meat will be left over?
   **D** Which package of meat is closest to one pound?

6. Which shows how to find the amount of hamburger meat Eric needs?

   **F** $\frac{1}{4} + 11 = 11\frac{1}{4}$
   **G** $13 + 9 + 14.5 + 11.5 = 3$
   **H** $3 \div 11 = 2.72$
   **J** $\frac{1}{4} \times 11 = 2\frac{3}{4}$

## Mixed Applications

**For 7–10, use the items shown at the right.**

7. James has $10 to buy 1 folder, 1 pen and pencil set, and 2 spiral notebooks. Does he have enough money for all the items?

8. Jan buys three markers and an eraser. If she pays with a $20 bill, how much change will she receive?

9. Cindy has $2.50. If she can get only one of each item, which combination of supplies can she afford?

10. Tanya bought a folder and an eraser. The answer is $3.36. What's the question?

PRICE LIST
spiral notebook $0.99
eraser ............ $0.35
package of paper $0.50
folder ............ $1.29
marker ............ $2.99
pen and pencil set $3.35

FCAT TESTED  SSS/GLEs MA.B.3.2.1.5.1 Knows how to determine whether an accurate or an estimated measurement is needed for a solution. *also:* MA.B.3.2.1.5.2

Chapter 24  **541**

Problem Solving

# Extra Practice

## Set A (pp. 522–525)

**Estimate the length in inches. Then measure to the nearest $\frac{1}{8}$ inch.**

1. 

2. 

**Choose the unit and tool to measure each.**

3. width of a door
4. distance from New York to Boston
5. length of the kitchen

## Set B (pp. 528–531)

**Change the unit.**

1. 15 ft = ■ yd
2. 72 in. = ■ ft
3. 100 mm = ■ cm

**Find the sum or difference.**

4. 3.9 cm + 4.8 cm
5. 6.1 cm − 5.2 cm
6. 5 ft 1 in. − 2 ft 9 in.

## Set C (pp. 532–533)

**Change the unit.**

1. 3 gal = ■ c
2. 32 pt = ■ qt
3. 6 T = ■ lb
4. $\frac{1}{2}$ lb = ■ oz
5. Jane bought five 3-lb bags of apples to make apple pies. How many ounces of apples did she buy?
6. The Chungs ordered 500 gallons of juice for their restaurant. How many quarts of juice did they order?

## Set D (pp. 534–535)

**Change the unit.**

1. 1,000 g = ■ kg
2. 3.5 kg = ■ g
3. 1.5 L = ■ mL
4. 1 kL = ■ L
5. Juan bought ten 1-L sodas. How many mL of soda did he buy?
6. Bob ate 10 g of fat at breakfast, 15 g at lunch, and 5 g at dinner. How many mg of fat did he eat?

## Set E (pp. 536–539)

**Write the time for each.**

1. Start: noon<br>6 hr 26 min elapsed time<br>End: ■
2. Start: midnight<br>■ elapsed time<br>End: 11:45 P.M.
3. Start: Jan. 10, 3:05 A.M.<br>6 days 4 hr 16 min elapsed time<br>End: ■
4. It is a warm, sunny day in June. Which would be a better estimate of the temperature, 80°C or 80°F?

# Review/Test

## ✅ CHECK VOCABULARY AND CONCEPTS

**Choose the correct term from the box.**

centimeter
liters
millimeters

1. There are 10 __?__ in 1 centimeter. (p. 526)

2. A __?__ is about the thickness of a bicycle pedal. (p. 526)

## ✅ CHECK SKILLS

**Estimate the length in inches. Then measure to the nearest $\frac{1}{8}$ inch.** (pp. 522–525)

3.

4.

**Choose the appropriate tool to measure each.** (pp. 522–539)

5. a pencil
   ruler or odometer

6. soda in a bottle
   liter or kilometer

7. your height
   paper clip or string

8. your weight
   thermometer or scale

**Change the unit.** (pp. 528–535)

9. 2 mi = ▩ yd

10. 900 yd = ▩ ft

11. 200 cm = ▩ m

12. 20 mm = ▩ cm

13. 5 T = ▩ lb

14. 8 pt = ▩ gal

15. 15 g = ▩ mg

16. 20 metric cups = ▩ L

17. 2.5 kg = ▩ g

**Find the sum or difference.** (pp. 528–531)

18.  8 yd 2 ft
    −5 yd 1 ft

19. 67 m + 29 cm

20.  4 ft 6 in.
    −2 ft 7 in.

21. 3.6 cm − 19 mm

**Write the time for each.** (pp. 536–539)

22. Start: March 18, 10:05 A.M.
    5 days 5 hr 40 min elapsed time
    End: ▩

23. Start: 5:10 A.M.
    ▩ time has elapsed.
    End: 12:49 P.M.

**Decide whether you need an estimate or an actual measurement. Then solve.** (pp. 540–541)

24. Rick needs 16.5 pounds of soil for a science project. If he has one 12-pound bag, how much more soil does he need?

25. Jenna is painting the walls of the game room, which is 22 ft by 18 ft and 9 ft high. A gallon of paint covers about 350 ft². How many gallons of paint should she buy?

# Getting Ready for FCAT

 **MEASUREMENT**

1. A Fahrenheit thermometer inside a greenhouse read 90°F. A Celsius thermometer outside read 20°C. About how much warmer, in degrees Celsius, is the temperature inside the greenhouse than outside?

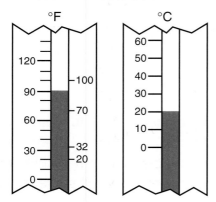

   A. 70°C     C. 30°C

   B. 50°C     D. 10°C

2. The weight of the people and goods in an elevator is 550 pounds. How much more weight can the elevator hold?

   | 1 ton = 2,000 pounds |
   |---|

   F.     450 pounds    H. 2,450 pounds

   G. 1,450 pounds    I. 2,550 pounds

3. **Explain It** Alan's goal is to run a 26.2-mile marathon in less than 5 hours. If he runs at an average rate of 4.8 miles per hour, will he reach his goal? ESTIMATE to solve. Explain your answer.

 **ALGEBRAIC THINKING**

4. Jillian is making a tile pattern. If she continues the pattern, how many tiles will be in the next group?

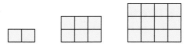

   A. 24

   B. 20

   C. 16

   D. 14

   > **TIP** **Decide on a plan.** See item 5. Use the strategy *draw a diagram* to sketch the diagrams in the answer choices. Then write numbers on the diagrams as you count the places where people will seat.

5. A restaurant is setting up square tables for a party. Which arrangement will seat the **most** people?

   F.       H.

   G.       I.

6. **Explain It** Eric forgot to fill in one of the numbers in this table.

   | Input | 2 | 9 | ■ | 4 |
   |---|---|---|---|---|
   | Output | 12 | 54 | 42 | 24 |

   What is the missing number? Explain how you know.

**DATA ANALYSIS AND PROBABILITY**

**7.** Which mountain is about twice the height of Mt. Rogers?

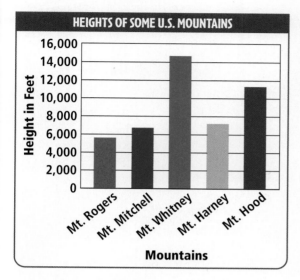

**HEIGHTS OF SOME U.S. MOUNTAINS**

*Height in Feet* — Mt. Rogers, Mt. Mitchell, Mt. Whitney, Mt. Harney, Mt. Hood

**Mountains**

   **A.** Mt. Mitchell

   **B.** Mt. Whitney

   **C.** Mt. Harney

   **D.** Mt. Hood

**8.** This stem-and-leaf plot shows the number of hours that some students watched television for a week.

| Stem | Leaves |
|---|---|
| 0 | 3 8 9 |
| 1 | 0 1 1 2 2 3 5 6 6 7 7 7 7 8 9 |
| 2 | 0 1 3 |

What was the median number of hours of television watched?

   **F.** 15.5       **H.** 16.5

   **G.** 16         **I.** 17

**9. Explain It** Explain how line graphs and bar graphs are similar. How are they different?

 **NUMBER SENSE, CONCEPTS, AND OPERATIONS**

**10.** Four students each wrote a number on a card.

| Sean | Heidi | Frank | Priscilla |
|---|---|---|---|
| 0.09 | $\frac{4}{5}$ | 0.45 | $\frac{3}{4}$ |

Which shows the numbers in order from **least** to **greatest**?

   **A.** $0.45, \frac{3}{4}, \frac{4}{5}, 0.09$

   **B.** $0.45, \frac{3}{4}, 0.09, \frac{4}{5}$

   **C.** $0.09, \frac{4}{5}, 0.45, \frac{3}{4}$

   **D.** $0.09, 0.45, \frac{3}{4}, \frac{4}{5}$

**11.** Four people plan to rent a fishing boat for 2 hours. They will share the cost equally.

**Boat Rentals**

Canoe...............$20 per hour
Fishing Boat.......$30 per hour
Jet Ski .............$50 per $\frac{1}{2}$ hour

How much will each person save if they can find a fifth person to share the cost?

   **F.** $3.00

   **G.** $7.50

   **H.** $12.00

   **I.** $15.00

**12. Explain It** Marie's salary this year is $36,000. She says that if next year she gets a raise of $100 per month, she will earn $48,000. Is her answer reasonable? Explain how you know.

# Perimeter

**FAST FACT • SOCIAL STUDIES** Tryon Palace, in New Bern, North Carolina, was built in 1770. After the Revolutionary War, Tryon Palace was the first state capitol building. In the 1950s, the palace and its gardens were reconstructed and restored to their original conditions.

PROBLEM SOLVING   The diagram below shows the palace with part of its grounds. Find the perimeter of Tryon Palace.

82 ft
Tryon
Palace   59 ft

Use this page to help you review and remember important skills needed for Chapter 25.

 **PERIMETER**

Find the perimeter of each figure.

**1.**

**2.**

**3.**

**4.**

**5.**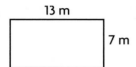
13 m
7 m

**6.**
5 yd
8 yd

**7.**
2 cm
8 cm

**8.**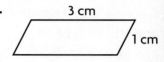
3 cm
1 cm

 **MULTIPLY DECIMALS BY WHOLE NUMBERS**

Find the product.

| | | | |
|---|---|---|---|
| **9.** $\begin{array}{r} 0.5 \\ \times\ 5 \\ \hline \end{array}$ | **10.** $\begin{array}{r} 0.75 \\ \times\ 4 \\ \hline \end{array}$ | **11.** $\begin{array}{r} 0.25 \\ \times\ 8 \\ \hline \end{array}$ | **12.** $\begin{array}{r} 2.6 \\ \times\ 3 \\ \hline \end{array}$ |
| **13.** $\begin{array}{r} 4.8 \\ \times\ 4 \\ \hline \end{array}$ | **14.** $\begin{array}{r} 8.5 \\ \times\ 6 \\ \hline \end{array}$ | **15.** $\begin{array}{r} 0.10 \\ \times\ 10 \\ \hline \end{array}$ | **16.** $\begin{array}{r} 1.5 \\ \times\ 6 \\ \hline \end{array}$ |

# VOCABULARY POWER

**REVIEW**

**polygon** [pä′lē•gän] *noun*

*Polygon* comes from the Greek root words *poly-* and *gonia*, which mean "many" and "angle." Use these meanings to write your own definition of *polygon*.

**PREVIEW**

perimeter

circumference

www.harcourtschool.com/mathglossary

# Estimate Perimeter

**VOCABULARY**

perimeter

**MATERIALS**
metric and customary rulers, string

## ▶ Explore

The map shows that Florida's border touches Alabama, Georgia, the Atlantic Ocean, and the Gulf of Mexico. How can you estimate the perimeter of Florida?

The **perimeter** is the distance around a figure.

One way to estimate the perimeter of Florida is by using a map, a length of string, and a ruler.

1 cm = 42 mi

## Activity

Follow the steps to estimate the perimeter of Florida.

**STEP 1**

On the map, lay a piece of string around the state of Florida. Mark the string where it meets itself.

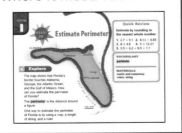

**STEP 2**

Use a ruler to measure the marked section of the string in centimeters.

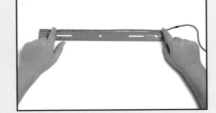

**STEP 3**

Use the map scale. To estimate the perimeter in miles, multiply your measurement in centimeters by 42.

42 × 36 = 1,512

So, the estimated perimeter of Florida is 1,512 miles.

## Talk About It

• What does a map scale tell you?

**548**

## ▶ Connect

You can also use a string to estimate the perimeter of polygons.

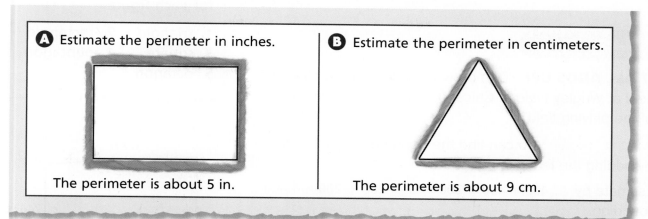

**A** Estimate the perimeter in inches.

The perimeter is about 5 in.

**B** Estimate the perimeter in centimeters.

The perimeter is about 9 cm.

## ▶ Practice and Problem Solving

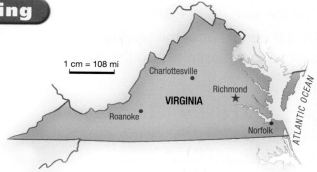

**For 1–2, use the map of Virginia.**

1. Use string and a metric ruler. Estimate the perimeter of the state of Virginia on the map in centimeters.

2. Use the scale. What is an estimated perimeter of Virginia in miles?

**Estimate the perimeter of the polygon in centimeters.**

3.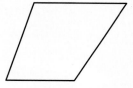

4.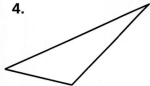

5.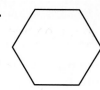

6.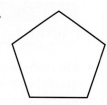

7. On a sheet of paper, trace the outline of your hand with your fingers closed. Then, use string and a ruler to estimate the perimeter in inches.

8. Using string and a ruler, estimate the perimeter of your desktop in inches.

## Getting Ready for FCAT ■ THINK SOLVE EXPLAIN

9. Jamie drew a polygon in his notebook. Explain how Jamie can use a string and a ruler to ESTIMATE its perimeter. Then ESTIMATE its perimeter in centimeters.

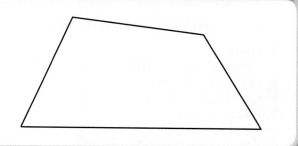

FCAT TESTED  SSS/GLEs MA.B.3.2.1.5.3 Knows how to estimate the area and perimeter of regular and irregular polygons.

Chapter 25  **549**

# Algebra: Find Perimeter

▶ **Learn**

**IT ALL ADDS UP!** Dan drew a diagram of the playing field at Wrigley Field in Chicago. What is the perimeter of the playing field?

**MATH IDEA** You can find the perimeter of any polygon by adding the lengths of its sides.

Estimate by rounding. $400 + 400 + 200 + 0 + 200 + 200 = 1,400$

$$a + b + c + d + e + f = P$$
$$\downarrow \quad \downarrow \quad \downarrow \quad \downarrow \quad \downarrow \quad \downarrow \quad \downarrow$$

Find the sum. $390 + 377 + 246 + 25 + 232 + 155 = 1,425$

So, the perimeter of the playing field is 1,425 ft. The answer is close to the estimate, so the answer is reasonable.

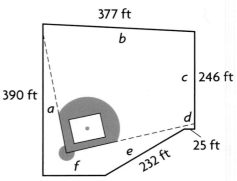

**HANDS ON**

## Activity

**MATERIALS:** metric ruler

- Draw a square, a rectangle, a trapezoid, and a parallelogram. Make a table for your data.

| FIGURE | SIDE 1 | SIDE 2 | SIDE 3 | SIDE 4 | P | FORMULA |
|--------|--------|--------|--------|--------|---|---------|
| Square |        |        |        |        |   |         |

- Measure and record the lengths of the sides of each quadrilateral. Then record each perimeter.

- For each quadrilateral, describe the relationship between the lengths of the sides and the perimeter. Then generate a formula for finding the perimeter and record it.

- Draw and measure another square, rectangle, trapezoid, and parallelogram. Use your formulas to find the perimeters.

▲ Built in 1914, Wrigley Field is an old-fashioned baseball park.

You can use the following formulas to find perimeter.

**Rectangles**
$l$ = length   $w$ = width
$P = (2 \times l) + (2 \times w)$
$P = (2 \times 12) + (2 \times 8)$
$P = 40$
Perimeter: 40 cm

12 cm

8 cm

**Regular Polygons**
$s$ = side
$P = (\text{number of sides}) \times s$
$P = 6 \times s$
$P = 6 \times 2$
$P = 12$
Perimeter: 12 ft

2 ft

## ▶ Check

**1.** Write three formulas you could use to find the perimeter of a square park measuring 150 ft by 150 ft.

**Find the perimeter of each polygon.**

**2.**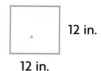
12 in.
12 in.

**3.**
4 cm  5 cm
3 cm

**4.**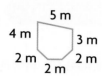
3 ft
6 ft   6 ft
5 ft

**5.**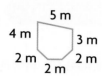
5 m
4 m   3 m
2 m   2 m
2 m

## ▶ Practice and Problem Solving   Extra Practice, page 556, Set A

**Find the perimeter of each polygon.**

**6.**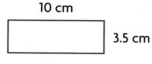
10 cm
3.5 cm

**7.**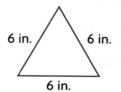
6 in.   6 in.
6 in.

**8.**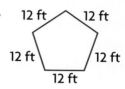
12 ft   12 ft
12 ft   12 ft
12 ft

**9.**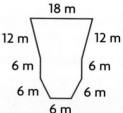
18 m
12 m   12 m
6 m   6 m
6 m   6 m
6 m

**10.**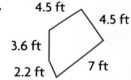
4.5 ft
4.5 ft
3.6 ft
2.2 ft   7 ft

**11.**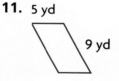
5 yd
9 yd

**12.**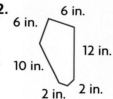
6 in.
6 in.
12 in.
10 in.
2 in.   2 in.

**13.**
$3\frac{1}{2}$ ft
$4\frac{3}{4}$ ft
$2\frac{1}{6}$ ft

**USE DATA** For 14, use the figures.

**14.** Compare the shapes of Figures 1 and 2. Then compare the perimeter of Figure 1 to the total perimeter of A and B in Figure 2. Which perimeter is greater?

**15.**  Write About It The perimeter of a triangle is 30 cm, and two of its sides are 10 cm and 7 cm long. Explain how to find the length of its third side.

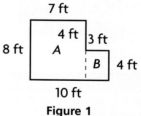
7 ft
4 ft   3 ft
8 ft   A
B   4 ft
10 ft
**Figure 1**

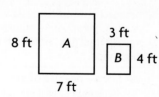
8 ft   A   3 ft
B   4 ft
7 ft
**Figure 2**

## Getting Ready for FCAT

**16.** Dennis put a dog run in his backyard. He used 40 feet of fencing around it. Which dog run did he make?

**A.**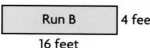
Run A   8 feet
12 feet

**B.**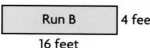
Run B   4 feet
16 feet

**C.**
Run C   4 feet
8 feet

**D.**
Run D   5 feet
11 feet

**FCAT TESTED** SSS/GLEs MA.B.1.2.2.5.2 Solves real-world problems involving perimeter, area, capacity, and volume using concrete, graphic, or pictorial models. also MA.C.3.2.1.5.2

**Chapter 25   551**

# Problem Solving Skill
## Make Generalizations

UNDERSTAND ▶ PLAN ▶ SOLVE ▶ CHECK

**GENERALLY SPEAKING . . .**   The Luxor Hotel in Nevada and the Great Pyramid in Egypt are the same shape. The Great Pyramid is a square pyramid. Each side of its base is 756 feet long. The perimeter of the base of the hotel is 600 feet less than the perimeter of the base of the Great Pyramid. What is the perimeter of the base of the hotel?

Sometimes you need to *make generalizations* to solve a problem. When you generalize, you make a statement that is true about a whole group of similar situations or objects.

### Quick Review

Find the perimeter of each regular polygon.

**1.** 6 cm

**2.** 3 yd

**3.** 4 ft

**4.** 2 cm

**5.** 5 m

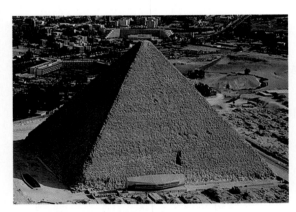

▲ The Great Pyramid in Giza, Egypt

▲ The Luxor Hotel in Nevada

| What You Know | Generalization | Conclusion |
| --- | --- | --- |
| The Great Pyramid is a square pyramid. The Luxor Hotel is the same shape. | Square pyramids have square bases. | The hotel has a square base. |
| Each side of the base of the Great Pyramid is 756 feet long. | The perimeter of a square is 4 × length of one side. | The perimeter of the base of the Great Pyramid is 4 × 756 ft, or 3,024 ft. |
| The perimeter of the base of the hotel is 600 feet less than the perimeter of the base of the Great Pyramid. | To find an amount less than a given amount, you subtract. | The perimeter of the base of the hotel is 3,024 ft − 600 ft, or 2,424 ft. |

So, the perimeter of the base of the hotel is 2,424 feet.

### Talk About It

• What are some generalizations you can make about a building that is the same shape as the model at the right?

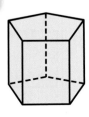

**Make generalizations to solve.**

1. Two brands of juice are packaged in congruent cylinders. The first brand contains 12 ounces of juice in each can. How many ounces are in a 6-pack of the second brand?

2. The Pyramid of Khafre is the second largest pyramid in Giza. It is the same shape as the Great Pyramid. The perimeter of its base is 2,816 feet. How long is each side of its base?

**A plane figure has 4 congruent sides.**

3. The perimeter of the figure is 6 centimeters. What is the length of each side?

   **A** 24 cm     **C** 3 cm
   **B** 12 cm     **D** 1.5 cm

4. One of the angles of the figure has a measure of 110°. What is the shape of the figure?

   **F** rectangle     **H** circle
   **G** square       **J** rhombus

## Mixed Applications

**USE DATA**   For 5–7, use the bar graph.

5. What is the difference in length between the longest leg bone and longest arm bone?

6. **REASONING** This bone's length has a 1 in the tens place and a 9 in the tenths place. It is not the second-longest bone. Which bone is it?

7. What is the range of the data displayed on the graph?

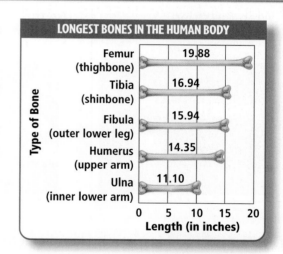

LONGEST BONES IN THE HUMAN BODY

| Type of Bone | Length (in inches) |
|---|---|
| Femur (thighbone) | 19.88 |
| Tibia (shinbone) | 16.94 |
| Fibula (outer lower leg) | 15.94 |
| Humerus (upper arm) | 14.35 |
| Ulna (inner lower arm) | 11.10 |

8. **FAST FACT • SOCIAL STUDIES** About 2,300,000 stone blocks were used to build the Great Pyramid. If each block weighed 2.5 tons, about how much did they weigh in all?

9. **REASONING** Keyshawn's tree house is 5 feet by 7 feet. His circular table has a radius of 3 feet. Will the table fit in his tree house? Explain.

10. I have a circular base. From the side I look like a rectangle. What figure am I?

11. My two parallel bases are congruent. I have 3 other faces. What figure am I?

12. **? What's the Question?** The printer estimated it would cost $0.14 per brochure to print 1,000 one-color brochures. The answer is $140.

13. **Write a problem** using the data in the bar graph above.

# Algebra: Circumference

**Quick Review**

**1.** $1.2 \div 3$    **2.** $2.4 \div 8$
**3.** $3.5 \div 7$    **4.** $0.81 \div 9$
**5.** $0.56 \div 8$

▶ **Explore**

Carla wants to find the distance around a can for a crafts project. The distance around a circular object is its **circumference**.

Find the circumference and diameter of the can. Round your measurements to the nearest tenth of a centimeter.

— diameter

**VOCABULARY**

**circumference**

**MATERIALS**
metric ruler, string, cans

## Activity

| STEP 1 | STEP 2 | STEP 3 |
|---|---|---|
| Wrap the string around a can. | Use the ruler to measure the length of the string. This is the circumference ($C$) of the can. | Trace the base of the can, and measure the diameter ($d$) of the circle. |

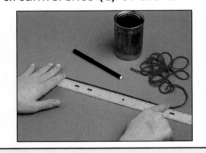
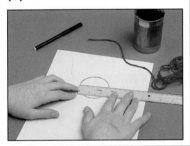

• Divide the circumference by the diameter. How many times as long as the diameter is the circumference?

## Try It

Use three different size cans. Follow the steps above. Copy and complete the table. Round each quotient to the nearest hundredth of a centimeter.

| Circle | Circumference (C) | Diameter (d) | C ÷ d |
|---|---|---|---|
| Example | 15.7 cm | 5 cm | |
| A | | | |
| B | | | |

What do you do next to find the relationship between the circumference and the diameter?

• Use your results to describe the ratio between the circumference and the diameter of a circle.

## ▶ Connect

The ratio of the circumference to the diameter of a circle,
$C : d$, is called pi (π). The approximate decimal value of π is 3.14.

So, when you know the diameter,
use the formula at the right to
find the circumference.

$$C = π × d$$
↑        ↑     ↑
**circumference ≈ 3.14 × diameter**
↑
≈ means "is approximately equal to"

**Examples** Find the circumference to the nearest tenth.

**A**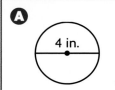
4 in.

$C = π × d$
$C ≈ 3.14 × 4$
$C ≈ 12.56$
The circumference
is about 12.6 in.

**B**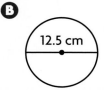
12.5 cm

$C = π × d$
$C ≈ 3.14 × 12.5$
$C ≈ 39.35$
The circumference
is about 39.3 cm.

## ▶ Practice and Problem Solving

For 1–3, complete the table.

| Object | C | d | C ÷ d |
|--------|-----|------|-------|
| **1.** spool | 9.4 cm | 3 cm | ■ |
| **2.** mug | 28.3 cm | ■ | 3.14 |
| **3.** CD | ■ | 12 cm | 3.14 |

**4.** Marta is putting lace trim around a can for her project. The diameter of the can is 7.5 cm. How many centimeters of lace trim does she need?

To the nearest tenth, find the circumference of a circle that has

**5.** a diameter of 10 cm.

**6.** a diameter of 17.8 ft.

**7.** a radius of 6 in.

**8.** The diameter of Bobby's cup is 8 cm. He wants to put two rows of red tape around the cup. How many centimeters of tape does he need?

**9. Vocabulary Power** The Greek word parts *dia-* and *metron* mean "across" and "to measure." What math word comes from the combination of these word parts?

**10.** ❓ **What's the Error?** Madeleine says that to find the circumference of a quarter, you multiply pi by the radius. Is she correct? Explain.

**11. REASONING** The radius of the Earth is about 3,960 miles. About how long is the equator?

## Getting Ready for FCAT

**12.** Which is a true statement about the circumference of the circle shown at the right?

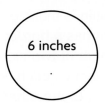
6 inches

**A.** It is less than 6 inches.

**C.** It is about 18 inches.

**B.** It is about 5 inches.

**D.** It is greater than 50 inches.

FCAT TESTED  SSS/GLEs MA.B.1.2.1.5.5 Investigates measures of circumference using concrete materials (for example, uses string or measuring tape to measure the circumference of cans or bottles).

Chapter 25  **555**

# Extra Practice

## Set A (pp. 550–551)

**Measure and find the perimeter of each polygon.**

**1.**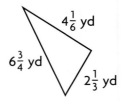

**2.**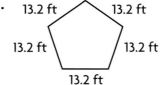

**3.**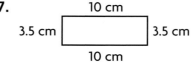

**Find the perimeter of each polygon.**

**4.**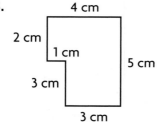
$4\frac{1}{6}$ yd
$6\frac{3}{4}$ yd
$2\frac{1}{3}$ yd

**5.**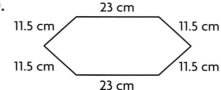
13.2 ft  13.2 ft
13.2 ft  13.2 ft
13.2 ft

**6.** 4.5 in.  3.6 in.
2.1 in.
7.9 in.  2.0 in.

**7.** 10 cm
3.5 cm  3.5 cm
10 cm

**8.** 4 cm
2 cm
1 cm
5 cm
3 cm
3 cm

**9.** 23 cm
11.5 cm  11.5 cm
11.5 cm  11.5 cm
23 cm

**10.** Marcy's bedroom is 18 feet long and 15 feet wide. Her sister's bedroom is 20 feet long and 13 feet wide. Which room has a greater perimeter, Marcy's room or her sister's?

**11.** Ricky's farm is about 275 yards long and 450 yards wide. He needs to fence the farm to protect his crops from the deer. About how much fencing will he need?

**12.** Kaitlin is making a blanket for her dog that has a border of 80 inches. The length of two sides of the border is 25 inches each. What is the length of each of the other two sides?

**13.** Mr. Berry's garden is 15 feet wide by 20 feet long. He will be fencing his garden and has 50 feet of fencing. How many more feet of fencing will he need?

# Review/Test

## ✅ CHECK VOCABULARY AND CONCEPTS

Choose the best term from the box.

1. The distance around a figure is the __?__. (p. 548)

2. The distance around a circle is its __?__. (p. 554)

> base
> circumference
> perimeter

## ✅ CHECK SKILLS

Estimate the perimeter of the polygon in centimeters. (pp. 548–549)

3.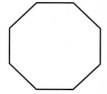

4.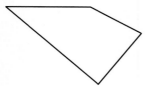

5.

6.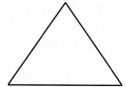

Find the perimeter of each polygon. (pp. 550–551)

7.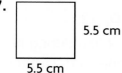
5.5 cm
5.5 cm

8.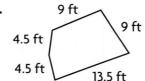
9 ft
9 ft
4.5 ft
4.5 ft
13.5 ft

9.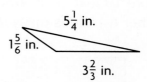
$5\frac{1}{4}$ in.
$1\frac{5}{6}$ in.
$3\frac{2}{3}$ in.

To the nearest tenth, find the circumference of each circle.
Use π = 3.14. (pp. 554–555)

10.
5 cm

11.
4.3 ft

12.
4 yd

13.
12 m

## ✅ CHECK PROBLEM SOLVING

For 14–15, the figure has one right angle and a total of
three angles. (pp. 552–553)

14. The second angle measures 45°. What is the third angle measure?

15. What is the shape of the figure? Can all 3 sides of the figure be the same length?

# Getting Ready for FCAT

## ⭐ MEASUREMENT

**1.** Three of the figures below have the same perimeter. Which figure does NOT have the same perimeter as the others?

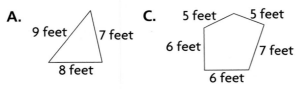

A.
9 feet  7 feet
8 feet

C.
5 feet  5 feet
6 feet  7 feet
6 feet

B.
5 feet
7 feet

D.
4 feet

**2.** A rectangular swimming pool has a perimeter of 96 feet. Two of the sides measure 16 feet each. What do each of the other two sides measure?

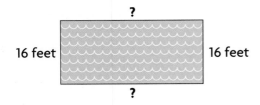

?
16 feet   16 feet
?

Perimeter = distance around a figure

   **F.** 32 feet      **H.** 40 feet

   **G.** 36 feet      **I.** 80 feet

**3. Explain It** A bicycle wheel has a diameter of 25 inches. About how many revolutions will the wheel make if you ride the bike 100 feet? Explain how you found your answer.

25 inches

## ⭐ NUMBER SENSE, CONCEPTS, AND OPERATIONS

**4.** Sara has 312 stamps. She can display 48 stamps on each album page. How many stamps will be left over if she fills 6 pages?

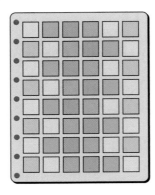

**A.** 36           **C.** 18

**B.** 24           **D.** 12

**5.** Michael used 2 rolls of film during his vacation. Each roll contained 24 photos. He used the flash for 9 of the photos. It costs $0.12 to develop each photo.

Which of the following information is NOT needed to find out how much it will cost to develop Michael's photos?

   **F.** He used the flash for 9 photos.

   **G.** He used 2 rolls of film.

   **H.** Each roll contained 24 photos.

   **I.** It costs $0.12 to develop each photo.

**6. Explain It** The Gazelles played 12 home games in July and 16 home games in August. The total number of people who attended these games was 9,187. ESTIMATE to find the average attendance per game. Explain your answer.

**GEOMETRY AND SPATIAL SENSE**

**7.** Which of these nets can be folded to form a cube?

**A.**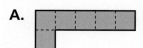

**B.**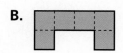

**C.**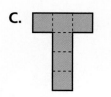

**D.**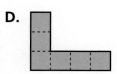

**8.** Which describes how the triangle was moved?

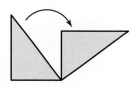

   **F.** reflection

   **G.** translation

   **H.** rotation, 90° clockwise

   **I.** rotation, 90° counterclockwise

**9. Explain It** Jessica used an equilateral triangle and an isosceles triangle to make a wrapping-paper design. Draw the figures she used. Explain how the triangles you drew are alike and how they are different.

 **ALGEBRAIC THINKING**

**10.** Felipe made a pattern by shading some of the squares in the figures below.

Suppose the pattern continues. How many squares should Felipe shade in the next figure?

   **A.** 4         **C.** 30

   **B.** 19        **D.** 32

**11.** For her portable CD player, Eliza bought 32 batteries in 4 packs. Each pack had the same number of batteries. Let $n$ represent the number of batteries in each pack. Which equation could you use to find the number of batteries in each pack?

   **F.** $n + 4 = 32$

   **G.** $4 \times n = 32$

   **H.** $n - 4 = 32$

   **I.** $n \div 4 = 32$

> **TIP** **Check your work.** See item 11. Solve the equation you chose. Does your solution give you a reasonable amount for the number of batteries in each pack?

**12. Explain It** Explain why $n = 3$ is a solution of the inequality $n + 1 \leq 7$, but $n = 7$ is NOT a solution. Then, draw the number line and draw dots to show all the whole numbers greater than 0 that $n$ could represent to make the inequality true.

**≡FAST FACT • SCIENCE**
Central Park, located in the center of Manhattan Island, New York, is home to 275 of the more than 800 species of birds found in the United States.

**PROBLEM SOLVING** The park is shaped like a rectangle that is 2.5 miles by 0.5 mile. What are the perimeter and area of Central Park? How does the area of Central Park compare to the areas of the parks in the graph?

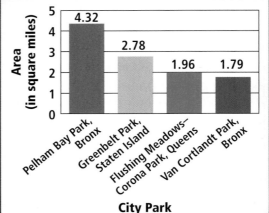

**NEW YORK CITY'S LARGEST PARKS**

Area (in square miles)

| | |
|---|---|
| Pelham Bay Park, Bronx | 4.32 |
| Greenbelt Park, Staten Island | 2.78 |
| Flushing Meadows–Corona Park, Queens | 1.96 |
| Van Cortlandt Park, Bronx | 1.79 |

**City Park**

# CHECK WHAT YOU KNOW

Use this page to help you review and remember
important skills needed for Chapter 26.

## AREA

Find the area of each figure in square units.

1.

2.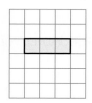

3.

4.

5.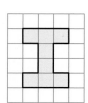

6.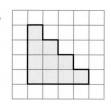

7.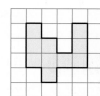

8.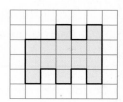

## MULTIPLICATION

Find the product.

9.  $\begin{array}{r} 12 \\ \times\ 5 \\ \hline \end{array}$

10. $\begin{array}{r} 19 \\ \times\ 6 \\ \hline \end{array}$

11. $\begin{array}{r} 29 \\ \times 12 \\ \hline \end{array}$

12. $\begin{array}{r} 35 \\ \times 21 \\ \hline \end{array}$

13. $\begin{array}{r} 1.29 \\ \times\ \ 6 \\ \hline \end{array}$

14. $\begin{array}{r} 2.35 \\ \times\ \ 8 \\ \hline \end{array}$

15. $\begin{array}{r} 4.6 \\ \times 1.5 \\ \hline \end{array}$

16. $\begin{array}{r} 2.8 \\ \times 2.8 \\ \hline \end{array}$

17. $\begin{array}{r} 3.24 \\ \times\ 12 \\ \hline \end{array}$

18. $\begin{array}{r} 4.12 \\ \times\ 1.4 \\ \hline \end{array}$

# VOCABULARY POWER

**REVIEW**

**perimeter** [pə•ri′mə•tər] *noun*

The word *perimeter* comes from the Greek
root words *peri,* meaning "around," and
*metron,* meaning "measure." Explain how
the root words help you understand the
meaning of *perimeter*.

**PREVIEW**

area
base
height

www.harcourtschool.com/mathglossary

# Estimate Area

**Quick Review**

1. 14 + 12    2. 16 + 6
3. 19 + 4    4. 13 + 8.5
5. 9 + 7.5

**VOCABULARY**

area

▶ **Learn**

**BEAR CROSSING** A biologist drew a diagram showing the territory of a black bear in the Appalachian Mountains of Tennessee. How can you use the diagram to estimate the area of the bear's territory?

The **area** of a figure is the number of square units needed to cover it.

**Activity**

**MATERIALS:** grid paper

Copy the diagram of the territory, shown at the right. Each square on the grid is one square mile.

**STEP 1**

Count the number of full squares. There are 8 full squares.

**STEP 2**

Count the number of squares that are half or more than half full. There are 4. Do not count the squares that are less than half full.

**STEP 3**

Add the number of squares you counted.
8 + 4 = 12

So, the area of the bear's territory is about 12 sq mi, or 12 mi².

• Why is your answer an estimate, rather than the actual answer?

**Example** Estimate the area of the figure. Each square on the grid is 1 square yard.

There are 21 full blue squares.

There are 11 almost-full red squares.

There are 7 half-full yellow squares. Combine the half-full squares to make $3\frac{1}{2}$ full squares.

Find the sum of the squares counted.

$$21 + 11 + 3\frac{1}{2} = 35\frac{1}{2}$$

So, the area of the figure is about $35\frac{1}{2}$ yd².

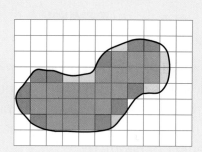

1. **Explain** how to estimate the area of the figure.

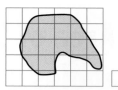

$\square$ = 1 ft$^2$

**Estimate the area of the shaded figure. Each square on the grid is 1 cm$^2$.**

2.

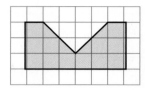

3.

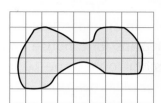

## Practice and Problem Solving (Extra Practice, page 582, Set A)

**Estimate the area of the shaded figure. Each square on the grid is 1 yd$^2$.**

4.

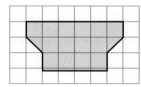

5.

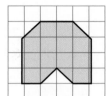

6.

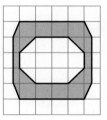

**Estimate the area of the shaded figure. Each square on the grid is 1 cm$^2$.**

7.

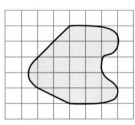

8.

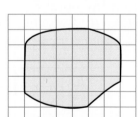

9.

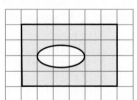

10. In the diagram of Heather's two flower-garden designs, each grid square represents 1 square foot. Estimate the total area of Heather's two gardens.

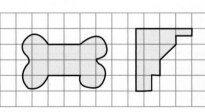

## Getting Ready for FCAT

11. Nick drew a plan for a flower garden. Each square represents 1 square foot. ESTIMATE the area of the garden. Explain how you found your answer.

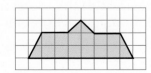

FCAT TESTED SSS/GLEs MA.B.3.2.1.5.3 Knows how to estimate the area and perimeter of regular and irregular polygons.

Chapter 26 **563**

# Algebra: Area of Squares and Rectangles

▷ **Learn**

**MAKING PLANS!** In art class, Holly and Jake are designing floor plans for a house. In her floor plan, Holly designs her room to be 10 feet by 8 feet. In Jake's floor plan, his room is 9 feet by 9 feet. The rooms have the same perimeters. Are the areas the same?

You can make models to find the area of squares and rectangles.

**Activity**

**MATERIALS:** grid paper

Let each square on the grid be 1 square foot.

**STEP 1**

Draw a rectangle 8 squares by 10 squares and shade it. Count the number of shaded grid squares.

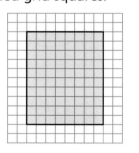

**STEP 2**

Draw a square 9 squares by 9 squares and shade it. Count the number of shaded grid squares.

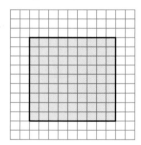

**STEP 3**

Compare the areas of the two rooms.

Area of Holly's room = 80 ft²
Area of Jake's room = 81 ft²
80 ft² < 81 ft²

So, the areas of the rooms are not the same. Jake's room has the greater area.

💻 **Technology Link**

More Practice: Harcourt Mega Math Ice Station Exploration, *Polar Planes,* Level R

• For each figure, look at the relationship between its area and its length and width. Write a formula you could use to find the areas.

# Formulas

You can also use formulas to find the area of rectangles and squares.

**Area of a rectangle = length × width**

$A = l \times w$

$A = 7 \times 3\frac{1}{2}$

$A = 24\frac{1}{2}$

The area is $24\frac{1}{2}$ yd².

7 yd

$3\frac{1}{2}$ yd

**Area of a square = side × side**

$A = s \times s$

$A = 8.2 \times 8.2$

$A = 67.24$

The area is 67.24 cm².

8.2 cm

8.2 cm

- Write a formula for the area of a square by using exponents.

You can find the area of some polygons by separating them into two or more different polygons.

Look at the drawing of Mr. Kelly's farm. It is divided into a square and a rectangle. How does the area of the combined field compare with the sum of the areas of the divided fields?

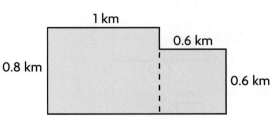

1 km

0.8 km

0.6 km

0.6 km

| COMBINED FIELD | DIVIDED FIELDS | |
| | Rectangle | Square |
| **Area** | **Area** | **Area** |
| $A = (1 \times 0.8) + (0.6 \times 0.6)$ | $A = (1 \times 0.8)$ | $A = (0.6 \times 0.6)$ |
| $A = 0.8 + 0.36 = 1.16$ | $A = 0.8$ | $A = 0.36$ |
| The area is 1.16 km². | The area is 0.8 km². | The area is 0.36 km². |

Sum of the areas: 0.8 km² + 0.36 km² = 1.16 km²

The area of the combined field is equal to the sum of the areas of the divided fields.

- Find the perimeters of the combined field and both of the divided fields. How does the perimeter of the combined field compare to the sum of the perimeters of the divided fields? If the perimeters are different, explain why.

## Check

1. **Explain** how the formula for the area of a rectangle can be used to find the area of a square.

**Find the area of each figure.**

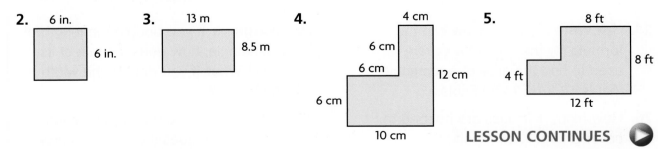

2. 6 in.
6 in.

3. 13 m
8.5 m

4. 4 cm
6 cm
6 cm
6 cm
12 cm
10 cm

5. 8 ft
8 ft
4 ft
12 ft

**LESSON CONTINUES** ▶

FCAT TESTED SSS/GLEs MA.B.1.2.2.5.2 Solves real-world problems involving perimeter, area, capacity, and volume using concrete, graphic, or pictorial models. *also* MA.B.1.2.1.5.2

**Chapter 26 565**

**Find the area of each figure.**

**6.**
12 in.
12 in.

**7.**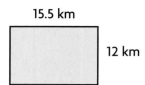
$3\frac{1}{4}$ ft
$2\frac{1}{2}$ ft

**8.**
15.5 km
12 km

**9.**
32 mi
32 mi

**10.**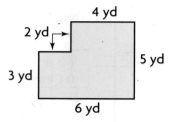
4 yd
2 yd
5 yd
3 yd
6 yd

**11.**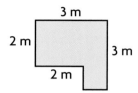
3 m
2 m
3 m
2 m

**12.**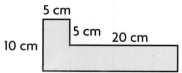
5 cm
5 cm   20 cm
10 cm

**13.**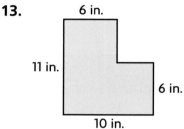
6 in.
11 in.
6 in.
10 in.

**Find each missing measurement.**

**14.** $s = 4\frac{1}{2}$ yd
$A = $ ■

**15.** $s = 3.5$ km
$A = $ ■

**16.** $s = 7$ ft
$A = $ ■

**17.** $s = 1.25$ m
$A = $ ■

**18.** $l = 3.2$ m
$w = 4$ m
$A = $ ■

**19.** $l = $ ■
$w = 7.2$ cm
$A = 28.8$ cm$^2$

**20.** $l = 2\frac{2}{3}$ ft
$w = 4\frac{1}{4}$ ft
$A = $ ■

**21.** $P = 24$ yd
$l = 8$ yd
$w = $ ■
$A = $ ■

**Use a centimeter ruler to measure each figure. Find the area and perimeter.**

**22.**

**23.**

**24.** ✎ **Write About It** How can the formula for the area of a square be used to find the area of a rectangle that is 12 ft by 24 ft? Explain.

**25. REASONING** If you double the length of a rectangle, how does that affect its area? **What if** you double the width and the length?

**26.** How many 1-ft$^2$ tiles are needed to cover a 15 ft × 25 ft patio?

**27. REASONING** If you double the length of a square, how does that affect its area?

**28.** Jan's living room wall is 10 ft wide. She wants to buy 3 bookcases that are each 48 in. wide. Can all of the bookcases be placed against the wall? Explain.

**29.** Pam has a board that is 7 ft long. She needs to cut the board into $1\frac{3}{4}$-ft sections. How many cuts will she have to make?

## Getting Ready for FCAT

**30.** Willie is wallpapering one wall in his bedroom. Each roll of wallpaper covers 25 square feet of wall. How many rolls of wallpaper does he need?

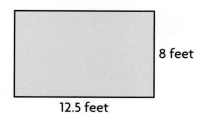

12.5 feet

8 feet

**A.** 4      **C.** 12.5
**B.** 8      **D.** 25

**31.** Mercedes is buying 3 yards of fabric to make curtains. The fabric comes in a width of 45 inches. What is the area of the fabric in square inches?

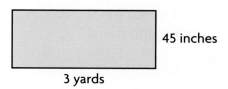

45 inches

3 yards

**F.** 135 square inches
**G.** 405 square inches
**H.** 1,620 square inches
**I.** 4,860 square inches

# Problem Solving Thinker's Corner

**COMPARE THE SQUARES** You can use the strategy *draw a diagram* to compare units of area within the customary system. How many square feet are there in 1 square yard?

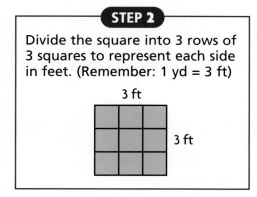

| STEP 1 | STEP 2 | STEP 3 |
| --- | --- | --- |
| Draw a square with sides labeled 1 yard. | Divide the square into 3 rows of 3 squares to represent each side in feet. (Remember: 1 yd = 3 ft) | Count the squares. |

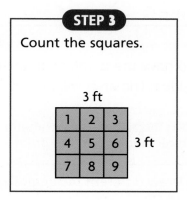

So, there are 9 square feet in 1 square yard.

**1.** Draw a diagram to find the number of square inches in 1 square foot. Explain your thinking.

**2.** How many square centimeters are there in 1 square meter?

**3.** Which measurement gives a better idea about the area of a football field, 8,294,400 in.² or 6,400 yd²? Explain.

**4.** Ken needs to carpet a total of 414 ft² of his house. How many square yards of carpeting are needed?

# Relate Perimeter and Area

▶ **Learn**

**FRAME UP** The students at Park School want to make a rectangular mosaic mural with the greatest possible area. If 16 ft of framing material is used, find the length and width of the mural.

**HANDS ON**

**Activity 1** Make models to find the greatest possible area.

**MATERIALS:** geoboard, string

### STEP 1

Mark a piece of string 16 units long, using the distance between two geoboard pegs as 1 unit. Let each unit be 1 ft. Cut the string slightly longer and tie a 16-unit loop.

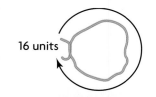

16 units

### STEP 2

Loop the string over geoboard pegs to make rectangles with perimeters of 16 units. Two possible rectangles are shown.

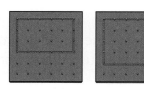

P = 16    P = 16

### STEP 3

Find and record the area of each rectangle. Each square unit represents 1 ft². What is the greatest area you can find?

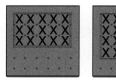

A = 15    A = 16

So, to have the greatest area, the mural should be a square with 4-ft sides. The area will be 4 ft × 4 ft, or 16 ft².

**Example** For a perimeter of 14 cm, find the length and width of the rectangle with the greatest area. Use whole numbers only.

Draw different rectangles with perimeters of 14 cm.

The greatest area is 12 cm². The length is 4 cm and the width is 3 cm.

1 cm 6 cm A = 6    2 cm 5 cm A = 10    3 cm 4 cm A = 12

**MATH IDEA** For a given perimeter, a square has the greatest area of all possible rectangles.

• If you could use the length 3.5 cm in the Example, what would the width be? What shape would the rectangle be?

# The Least Perimeter

Now find the least perimeter of a rectangle with an area of 36 ft².

## Activity 2

**MATERIALS:** square tiles

- Use square tiles to make different rectangles with areas of 36 ft². Let each tile be 1 ft².
- Copy and complete the table with your results. (HINT: To find all of the possible lengths and widths, find all the factors of 36.)
- As the rectangle gets closer to being a square, what happens to its perimeter?

| Length ft | Width ft | Perimeter | Area |
|---|---|---|---|
| 1 | 36 | ■ | 36 ft² |
| 2 | ■ | ■ | 36 ft² |
| 3 | ■ | ■ | 36 ft² |
| ■ | ■ | ■ | 36 ft² |
| ■ | ■ | ■ | 36 ft² |

So, the least perimeter is 24 ft. The rectangle should be a square with sides of 6 ft.

 **MATH IDEA**   For a given area, a square has the least perimeter of all possible rectangles.

## Examples

For the given area, find the length and width of the rectangle with the least perimeter. Use whole numbers only.

**A**  Area: 49 in.²
You can make a square.

7 in.

7 in.   7 in.   $P = 28$

7 in.

The perimeter is 28 in. The length and width are each 7 in.

**B**  Area: 18 cm²

Make a table. Use factors of 18 as lengths and widths.

| LENGTH | WIDTH | PERIMETER | AREA |
|---|---|---|---|
| 18 cm | 1 cm | 38 cm | 18 cm² |
| 9 cm | 2 cm | 22 cm | 18 cm² |
| 6 cm | 3 cm | 18 cm | 18 cm² |

The least perimeter is 18 cm. The length is 6 cm and the width is 3 cm.

## Check

1. **Explain** what happens to the area of a rectangle with a given perimeter as it gets closer to being a square.

**For the given perimeter, find the length and width of the rectangle with the greatest area. Use whole numbers only.**

**2.** 32 cm          **3.** 26 in.          **4.** 18 yd          **5.** 44 m          **6.** 60 cm

LESSON CONTINUES

FCAT TESTED    SSS/GLEs MA.B.1.2.2.5.2 Solves real-world problems involving perimeter, area, capacity, and volume using concrete, graphic, or pictorial models. *also* MA.C.3.2.1.5.1

Chapter 26   **569**

For the given area, find the length and width of the rectangle with the least perimeter. Use whole numbers only.

**7.** 9 m$^2$  **8.** 20 ft$^2$  **9.** 12 cm$^2$  **10.** 64 in.$^2$  **11.** 100 cm$^2$

## Practice and Problem Solving    Extra Practice, page 582, Set C

For the given perimeter, find the length and width of the rectangle with the greatest area. Use whole numbers only.

**12.** 10 cm  **13.** 20 m  **14.** 22 in.  **15.** 42 ft  **16.** 30 yd

For the given area, find the length and width of the rectangle with the least perimeter. Use whole numbers only.

**17.** 8 cm$^2$  **18.** 30 m$^2$  **19.** 40 yd$^2$  **20.** 15 in.$^2$  **21.** 81 ft$^2$

**22.** **ALGEBRA** Copy and complete the table. The perimeter is 8 m. Describe any pattern you see.

| Length (in m) | 0.5 | 1 | 1.5 | 2 | 2.5 | 3 | 3.5 |
|---|---|---|---|---|---|---|---|
| Width (in m) | ▦ | ▦ | ▦ | ▦ | ▦ | ▦ | ▦ |
| Area (in m$^2$) | ▦ | ▦ | ▦ | ▦ | ▦ | ▦ | ▦ |

**23.** **REASONING** If you increase the length of a rectangle with a perimeter of 20 ft, what has to happen to its width to keep the perimeter the same?

**24.** **?** **What's the Error?** Bud says that with a given perimeter, the rectangle with the greatest length has the greatest area. Describe his error.

**25.** Using 48 feet of fencing, what is the greatest area that can be fenced? the least area? (Use whole numbers.)

**26.** Write a problem about a soccer field with dimensions of 110 m by 75 m.

**USE DATA** For 27–28, use the bar graph.

**27.** A pheasant flies 9 miles per hour slower than a common crane. How fast does a pheasant fly?

**28.** How long would it take a mallard to travel 100 mi?

**29.** **FAST FACT • SCIENCE** The eighth fastest bird is the oystercatcher. It can fly 58 km per hour. About how many miles per hour can it fly? (HINT: 1 km is about 0.62 mi.)

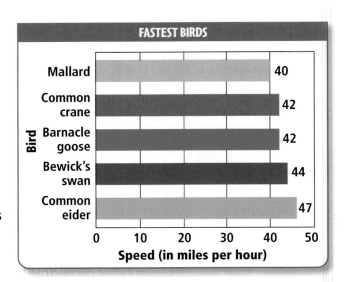

**30.** Emily's dad sells eggs at the Farmer's Market. He had 1,680 eggs. He sold $\frac{2}{5}$ of the eggs on Saturday and $\frac{1}{4}$ of the remainder on Sunday. How many eggs did he sell? How many dozens is that?

**31.** A playground has a perimeter of 100 m. It has the greatest possible area for a playground with that perimeter. What are the length and width of the playground?

**Getting Ready for FCAT**

**32.** Louisa built a dog run for her greyhound that is four times as long as it is wide. She used 100 feet of fencing to enclose the dog run. What is the area of the dog run?

   **A.** 40 square feet

   **B.** 100 square feet

   **C.** 200 square feet

   **D.** 400 square feet

**33.** Mei Ling made a figure with some square tiles. The area of the figure is 375 square inches. What is the perimeter of the figure? Explain how you found your answer.

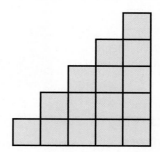

# Problem Solving  Thinker's Corner

You can use grid paper to show how the perimeter and area of a rectangle change when its length and width are doubled or halved.

**Rectangle 1**

**STEP 1** Copy Rectangle 1. Draw a rectangle with sides twice as long as Rectangle 1. Label it Rectangle 2.

**STEP 2** Draw a rectangle with sides half as long as Rectangle 1. Label it Rectangle 3.

**STEP 3** Record the perimeter and area of each rectangle.

  **1.** Compare the perimeters of Rectangle 2 and Rectangle 1. How do the areas compare?

  **2.** Compare the perimeters of Rectangle 3 and Rectangle 1. How do the areas compare?

  **3.** **ALGEBRA** The formula $A = 2l \times 2w$ shows how the area of a rectangle changes when the length and width are doubled. Write a formula to show the change when the length and width are halved.

# Algebra: Area of Triangles

**Quick Review**

1. $\frac{1}{2} \times 10$    2. $\frac{1}{2} \times 16$

3. $\frac{1}{2} \times 24$    4. $\frac{1}{2} \times 2.4$

5. $\frac{1}{2} \times (3 \times 4)$

▶ **Learn**

**SURF THE WIND**

Dion is a windsurfer. He is making a model of his sailboard. The sail will have a base of 5 cm and a height of 10 cm. How much fabric does he need for the sail?

Find the *area* of the triangular sail.

**VOCABULARY**
height    base

The **height** is the length of a line segment perpendicular to the **base** of the triangle.

height

base

## Activity 1

**MATERIALS:** centimeter grid paper

Use grid paper and what you know about the area of a rectangle to find the area of a triangle.

**STEP 1**

Draw and shade a model of the triangular sail on grid paper.

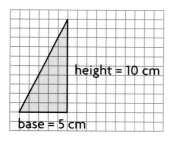

height = 10 cm

base = 5 cm

**STEP 2**

Draw a rectangle around the triangle as shown. Find the area of the rectangle.

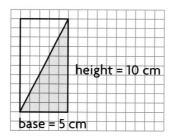

height = 10 cm

base = 5 cm

**Rectangle:**
$A = b$ (base) $\times h$ (height)
$A = 5 \times 10$
$A = 50$

**STEP 3**

Cut out the rectangle. Cut it in half to make two triangles. Notice that they are congruent.

So, the area of the triangle is half the area of the rectangle.

**Triangle:**

$A = \frac{1}{2} \times (b \times h)$

$A = \frac{1}{2} \times 50$

$A = 25$

The area of the triangle is 25 cm².

So, Dion needs 25 cm² of fabric to make the sail.

• How do the base and height of the sail relate to the length and width of the rectangle in Step 2?

**572**

# Other Triangles

## Activity 2

**MATERIALS:** grid paper

Some triangles are not right triangles. Find the area of the triangle below.

**STEP 1**

Draw and shade a model of the triangle inside a rectangle.

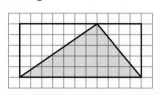

**STEP 2**

Cut out the rectangle and then the shaded triangle.

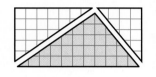

**STEP 3**

The unshaded parts of the rectangle fit exactly over the shaded triangle.

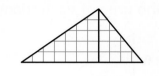

So, the area of the triangle is half the area of the rectangle.

 **MATH IDEA** You can use the formula $A = \frac{1}{2} \times (b \times h)$ to find the area of any triangle.

## Example

**A**

Find the area.

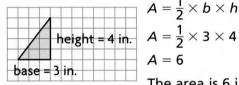

height = 4 in.

base = 3 in.

$A = \frac{1}{2} \times b \times h$

$A = \frac{1}{2} \times 3 \times 4$

$A = 6$

The area is 6 in.$^2$

**B**

Find the area.

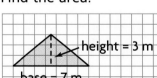

height = 3 m

base = 7 m

$A = \frac{1}{2} \times b \times h$

$A = \frac{1}{2} \times 7 \times 3$

$A = 10.5$

The area is 10.5 m$^2$.

## ▷ Check

1. **Explain** the relationship in Activity 1 between the area of the rectangle and the area of the triangle.

**Find the area of each triangle.**

2.

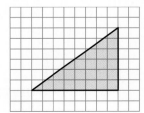

3.

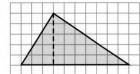

4.

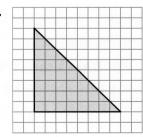

LESSON CONTINUES

FCAT TESTED SSS/GLEs MA.B.I.2.2.5.2 Solves real-world problems involving perimeter, area, capacity, and volume using concrete, graphic, or pictorial models. *also* MA.C.3.2.1.5.2

Chapter 26 **573**

**Find the area of each triangle.**

**5.**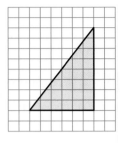

**6.**

**7.**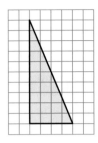

**Find the area of each triangle.**

**8.**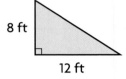

**9.**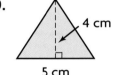

**10.**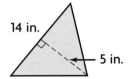

**Using the given measures, draw a right triangle and a triangle that is not a right triangle on grid paper. Then find the area.**

**11.** base *(b)* = 10 cm

height *(h)* = 4 cm

Area *(A)* = ■

**12.** base *(b)* = 6 m

height *(h)* = 6 m

Area *(A)* = ■

**13.** base *(b)* = 7 yd

height *(h)* = 11 yd

Area *(A)* = ■

**ALGEBRA** **Find the missing measurement for the triangle.**

**14.** $b = 2.6$ cm

$h = 4.7$ cm

$A = $ ■

**15.** $b = $ ■

$h = 10$ in.

$A = 40$ in.$^2$

**16.** $b = 5$ ft

$h = $ ■

$A = 15$ ft$^2$

**17.** $b = 3\frac{1}{2}$ yd

$h = 2$ yd

$A = $ ■

**For 18–20, use the diagram of the Bermuda Triangle.**

**18.** What is the perimeter of the Bermuda Triangle?

**19.** What are the base and height of the Bermuda Triangle?

**20.** What is the area of the Bermuda Triangle on the map?

**21.** **? What's the Error?** A triangle has a base of 4 feet and a height of 7 feet. Barbara says its area is 28 ft$^2$. Describe and correct her error.

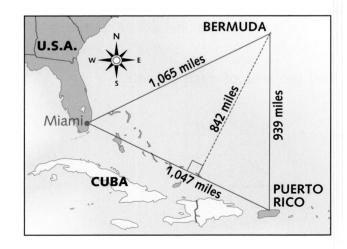

**22.** ✏️ **Write About It** Explain the difference between an inch and a square inch. Draw an example of each.

**23. REASONING** Find the area of the figure.

3 cm
6 cm
6 cm

**24.** Nora painted a triangle on part of her bedroom wall. How many square feet of the wall did she paint?

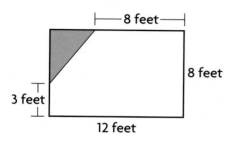

8 feet
8 feet
3 feet
12 feet

**A.** 9 square feet
**B.** 10 square feet
**C.** 12 square feet
**D.** 20 square feet

**25.** José designed a flag for his art class. What is the area of the orange triangle on José's flag?

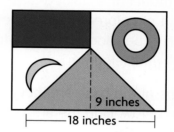

9 inches
18 inches

**F.** 18 square inches
**G.** 27 square inches
**H.** 81 square inches
**I.** 162 square inches

# Problem Solving THINKER'S CORNER 💡

**MATERIALS:** tangram pattern

**VISUAL THINKING** As early as 4,000 years ago, the Chinese were playing with this math puzzle, called a *tangram*. The seven pieces, called *tans*, fit together to make hundreds of different shapes.

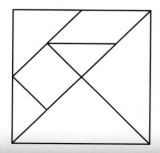

Cut out the tans from your pattern. Arrange them to make these shapes. Use all seven tans to form each shape.

**1.**

**2.**

# Algebra: Area of Parallelograms

▶ **Learn**

**CATCH THE SUN**   Mecha is making a model of a stained-glass window out of colored tissue paper. How much paper does she need for each small parallelogram?

The lengths of the base and height are shown below. Find the area of one parallelogram.

height = 5 cm

base = 11 cm

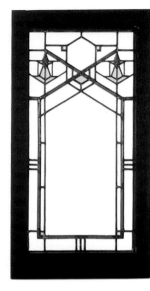

**Remember**

A *parallelogram* is a quadrilateral with parallel and congruent opposite sides.

A *rhombus* is a parallelogram with all sides congruent.

**HANDS ON**

## Activity

**MATERIALS:** centimeter grid paper, scissors

Use grid paper and what you know about the area of a rectangle to find the area of a parallelogram.

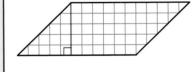
**STEP 1**

Copy the parallelogram and cut it out. Draw a line segment to form a right triangle as shown.

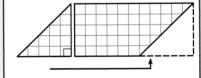
**STEP 2**

Cut out the right triangle on the left, and move it to the right of the parallelogram to form a rectangle.

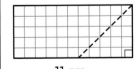
**STEP 3**

The rectangle has the same area as the parallelogram. Count the grid squares to find its area.

5 cm

11 cm

There are 5 rows of 11 squares, or 55 squares.

So, Mecha needs 55 cm² of tissue paper to make each small parallelogram.

• How do the base and height of the parallelogram in Step 1 relate to the length and width of the rectangle in Step 3?

# Use a Formula

 **MATH IDEA**  The area of a parallelogram is equal to the
area of a rectangle with the same base (length) and
height (width).

Area of a rectangle  =  length  ×  width       $A = l \times w$

Area of a parallelogram  =  base  ×  height       $A = b \times h$

## Examples

**A** Find the area.

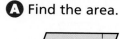

6 cm

9 cm

$A = b \times h$

$A = 9 \times 6$

$A = 54$

The area is 54 cm².

**B** Find the area.

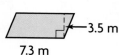

3.5 m

7.3 m

$A = b \times h$

$A = 7.3 \times 3.5$

$A = 25.55$

The area is 25.55 m².

## ▶ Check

**1. Compare** the areas of a rectangle with a length of 6 cm
and a width of 4 cm and a parallelogram with a base
of 6 cm and a height of 4 cm.

**Write the base and the height of each figure.**

**2.**

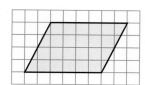

**3.**

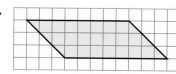

**4.**

**ALGEBRA**   **Find the missing dimension for each parallelogram.**
**Use grid paper if necessary.**

**5.** base *(b)* = ■ cm

height *(h)* = 5 cm

Area *(A)* = 20 cm²

**6.** base *(b)* = 11 ft

height *(h)* = ■ ft

Area *(A)* = 88 ft²

**7.** base *(b)* = ■ in.

height *(h)* = 12 in.

Area *(A)* = 36 in.²

**Find the area of each parallelogram.**

**8.**

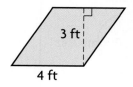

3 ft

4 ft

**9.**

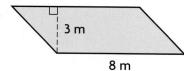

3 m

8 m

**10.**

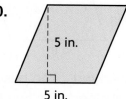

5 in.

5 in.

**LESSON CONTINUES**

**FCAT TESTED**   SSS/GLEs MA.B.1.2.2.5.2 Solves real-world problems involving perimeter, area, capacity, and
volume using concrete, graphic, or pictorial models. *also* MA.C.3.2.1.5.2

**Write the base and the height of each figure.**

11.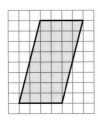

12.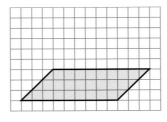

13.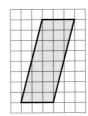

**Find the area of each parallelogram.**

14.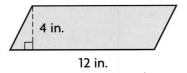
4 in.
12 in.

15.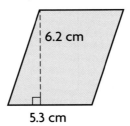
6.2 cm
5.3 cm

16.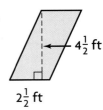
$4\frac{1}{2}$ ft
$2\frac{1}{2}$ ft

17.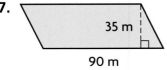
35 m
90 m

18.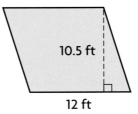
10.5 ft
12 ft

19.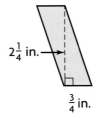
$2\frac{1}{4}$ in.
$\frac{3}{4}$ in.

**Find the missing dimension for each parallelogram.**
**Use grid paper if necessary.**

20. base *(b)* = 3.5 cm

height *(h)* = 8.2 cm

Area *(A)* = ▪

21. base *(b)* = ▪

height *(h)* = 12 in.

Area *(A)* = 24 in.²

22. base *(b)* = 4 ft

height *(h)* = ▪

Area *(A)* = 28 ft²

23. **? What's the Error?** The base of a parallelogram is 7 cm and the height is 6 cm. Tom says the area is 21 cm².

24. **? What's the Question?** The base of a parallelogram is 8 ft. The area is 32 ft². The answer is 4 ft.

25. **REASONING** Can you find the area of this parallelogram with the given measurements? Explain.

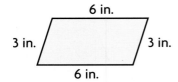
6 in.
3 in.     3 in.
6 in.

26. **Write About It** Describe the relationships shown in this Venn diagram.

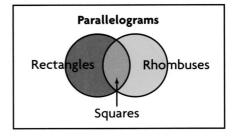
Parallelograms
Rectangles     Rhombuses
Squares

27. **REASONING** The base of a parallelogram is two times its height. If the base is 10 in., what is the area?

**28. Vocabulary Power** A dimension of a figure can be its length, width, or height. A line segment is a figure with one dimension, length. List examples of figures with two and three dimensions. Name the dimensions of each figure.

**29.** Lin's stained-glass model is a rectangle that is 18 in. by 12 in. She divides the model into four congruent triangles. How many square inches of tissue paper does she need for each triangle?

**30.** The parking spaces at the grocery store are parallelograms. What is the area of each parking space?

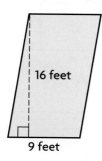

16 feet

9 feet

**A.** 25 square feet
**B.** 50 square feet
**C.** 72 square feet
**D.** 144 square feet

**31.** Mr. Wolf asked his class to find the parallelogram with the greatest area. Which parallelogram should they choose?

**F.**
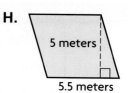
4 meters

6.5 meters

**H.**
5 meters

5.5 meters

**G.**
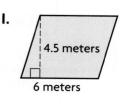

8.5 meters

3 meters

**I.**
4.5 meters

6 meters

# Problem Solving · Thinker's Corner

**DOUBLE IT** You can use the area of a triangle to find the area of a parallelogram.

- Draw this parallelogram on grid paper.

- Cut the parallelogram on a diagonal to form 2 congruent triangles.

**1.** Find the area of one triangle.

**2.** How is the area of the triangle related to the area of the parallelogram?

**3.** Write a formula for the area of a parallelogram.

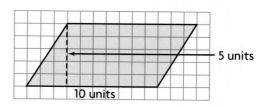

5 units

10 units

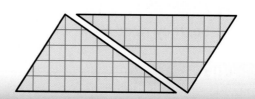

# Problem Solving Strategy
## Solve a Simpler Problem

**PROBLEM**  Mike and Stephanie are designing a flat backdrop for their school play. How many square feet of backdrop will they use to make the house shown at the right?

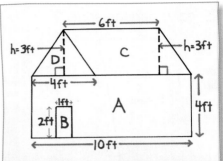

**UNDERSTAND**

- What are you asked to find?
- What information will you use?
- Is there any information you will not use? Explain.

**PLAN**

- What strategy can you use to solve the problem?

  You can *solve a simpler problem* by breaking the diagram of the house into simpler figures.

**SOLVE**

- How can you use the strategy to solve the problem?

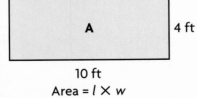

10 ft

Area = $l \times w$

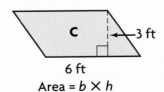

6 ft

Area = $b \times h$

3 ft

**D**

4 ft

Area = $\frac{1}{2} \times b \times h$

| Find the area of each figure in the house. Then add all the areas. | **Area of A** (rectangle) | $10 \times 4$ | $= 40$ |
| --- | --- | --- | --- |
| | **Area of C** (parallelogram) | $6 \times 3$ | $= 18$ |
| | **Area of D** (triangle) | $\frac{1}{2} \times (4 \times 3) =$ | $\underline{+\ 6}$ |
| | | | $64$ |

So, they need 64 ft² of backdrop to make the house.

**CHECK**

- How can you estimate to check your answer?

## Strategies

Draw a Diagram or Picture
Make a Model or Act It Out
Make an Organized List
Find a Pattern
Make a Table or Graph
Predict and Test
Work Backward
**Solve a Simpler Problem**
Write an Equation
Use Logical Reasoning

**Problem Solving**

**Use a simpler problem to solve.**

1. **What if** Mike cuts a 1 ft by 3 ft window from the house? What will the remaining area be?

2. Antoine made this design by wrapping string around nails on a piece of wood. How much string did he use?

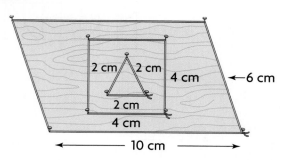

3. The cartons of computer parts are labeled on the top and the front of each carton. How many labels are showing if there are 8 horizontal rows of 3 boxes each?

   **A** 24          **C** 32
   **B** 27          **D** 36

4. What is the area of the figure?

   **F** 28 sq units
   **G** 30 sq units
   **H** 32 sq units
   **J** 36 sq units

## Mixed Strategy Practice

5. Mr. Bell's rectangular garden is 15 ft by 10 ft. Fencing costs $2.50 a foot. How much will he spend to fence in his entire garden?

6. Each can of paint covers 50 ft². How many cans does Vince need to paint a 12 ft by 16 ft backdrop for the play?

7. The diameter of the moon is about 3,500 kilometers. The diameter of the sun is 400 times the diameter of the moon. What is the circumference of the sun? the moon? (Use π = 3.14.)

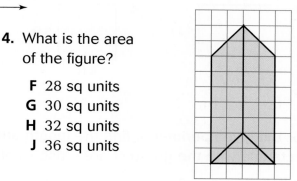

8. Mr. Kelly shopped for art supplies. He bought 3 canvases for $10.98 each, a box of brushes for $6.50, and 8 bottles of paint for $5.69 each. He paid with five $20 bills. How much change did he receive?

9. Two equilateral triangles are put together to form a quadrilateral. Draw a diagram to find what kind of quadrilateral is formed.

10. Describe one way you could break apart a pentagon to find its area.

FCAT TESTED   SSS/GLEs MA.B.1.2.2.5.2 Solves real-world problems involving perimeter, area, capacity, and volume using concrete, graphic, or pictorial models. *also* MA.C.3.2.1.5.2

**Chapter 26   581**

# Extra Practice

## Set A (pp. 562–563)

**Estimate the area of the shaded figure. Each square is 1 cm².**

**1.**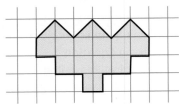

**2.**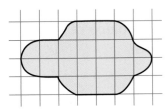

## Set B (pp. 564–567)

**Find the area of each figure.**

**1.**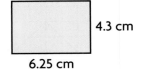

**2.**

**3.**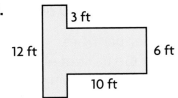

**4.**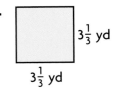

## Set C (pp. 568–571)

**For the given perimeter, find the length and width of the rectangle with the greatest area. Use whole numbers only.**

**1.** 28 m     **2.** 16 yd     **3.** 12 cm     **4.** 8 ft     **5.** 36 in.     **6.** 46 yd

## Set D (pp. 572–575)

**Find the area of each triangle.**

**1.**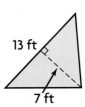

**2.**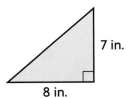

**3.**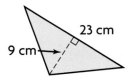

## Set E (pp. 576–579)

**Find the area of each parallelogram.**

**1.**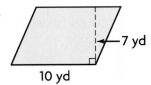

**2.**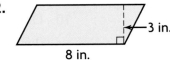

**3.**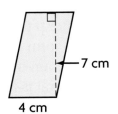

# Review/Test

## ✔ CHECK VOCABULARY AND CONCEPTS

**Choose the best term from the box.**

> area
> base
> height
> perimeter

1. To find the area of a parallelogram, multiply its __?__ by its __?__. (p. 576)

2. The number of square units needed to cover the surface of an object is the __?__. (p. 562)

## ✔ CHECK SKILLS

**Find the area of each figure.** (pp. 564–565)

3.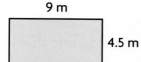
9 m
4.5 m

4.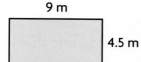
13 yd
13 yd

5.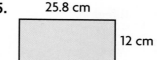
25.8 cm
12 cm

6.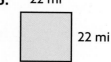
22 mi
22 mi

**For the given area, find the length and width of the rectangle with the least perimeter. Use whole numbers only.** (pp. 568–569)

7. 56 cm$^2$

8. 63 yd$^2$

9. 121 ft$^2$

10. 130 m$^2$

**Find the area of each figure.** (pp. 562–563, 572–579)

11.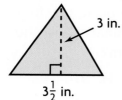
3 in.
$3\frac{1}{2}$ in.

12.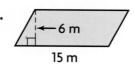
6 m
15 m

13.
= 1 cm$^2$

## ✔ CHECK PROBLEM SOLVING

**Use a simpler problem to solve.** (pp. 580–581)

14. By drawing 1 vertical line and 1 horizontal line, you can divide a sheet of paper into 4 sections. Into how many sections can you divide a sheet of paper by drawing 6 vertical and 6 horizontal lines?

15. Bill's Sign Shop makes road signs in this shape. What is the area of each sign?

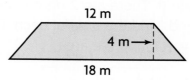
12 m
4 m
18 m

# Getting Ready for FCAT

## ⭐ GEOMETRY AND SPATIAL SENSE

> **TIP** **Decide on a plan.** See item 1. Use the strategy *solve a simpler problem*. Break the deck into a rectangle and a square and find the area of each.

**1.** Mr. Imanis is building a deck on the back of the house. This is the design.

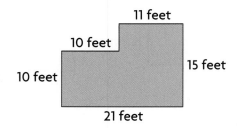

What is the area of the deck?

**A.** 72 square feet

**B.** 265 square feet

**C.** 415 square feet

**D.** 420 square feet

**2.** Look at the diagram above. Mr. Imanis will put up a railing around the deck. To order enough wood for the railing, he needs to know the perimeter of the deck. Which is the perimeter of the deck?

**F.** 36 feet    **H.** 72 feet

**G.** 67 feet    **I.** 82 feet

**3. Explain It** There are 2 right triangles on the grid. Find the area of each. Explain how you found the area.

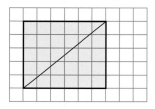

## ⭐ NUMBER SENSE, CONCEPTS, AND OPERATIONS

**4.** Art had 7 quarters, 3 dimes, 2 nickels, and 4 pennies in his pocket. This was the exact amount needed to buy which of the following items?

**A.** 4-pack light bulbs, $1.99

**B.** 6.4-oz toothpaste, $1.89

**C.** 24-exposure film, $2.19

**D.** 5 pens, $2.29

**5.** Matthew's mother sent him to the grocery store to buy these items.

64-oz bottle of apple juice: $1.79
Corn Crispies cereal:  $2.89
Cleanz detergent:  $5.49

If she gave him one bill to pay for the items, which is the smallest bill she could have given him?

**F.** $1     **H.** $10

**G.** $5     **I.** $20

**6. Explain It** Teri collects shells and uses them to decorate frames for mirrors. So far she has used 15 shells on this frame.

ESTIMATE the total number of shells she will need for the whole frame. Explain your estimate.

**ALGEBRAIC THINKING**

**7.** Brian is reading a book that has 35 chapters. He read 2 chapters on Monday, 3 chapters on Tuesday, and 4 chapters on Wednesday. If he continues this reading pattern, on what day of the week will he finish the book?

**A.** Thursday

**B.** Friday

**C.** Saturday

**D.** Sunday

**8.** Martin made a pattern with toothpicks.

If he continues the pattern, how many toothpicks will he need to make 5 triangles?

**F.** 13

**G.** 11

**H.** 9

**I.** 8

**9.** When the bus arrived at the station, 37 people got off the bus and 29 remained on board. Which equation could be used to find $p$, the number of people on the bus before some people got off?

**A.** $37 - 29 = p$

**B.** $37 - p = 29$

**C.** $p - 37 = 29$

**D.** $29 + p = 37$

**10. Explain It** Explain why $x = 8$ is a solution of the inequality $x + 7 \leq 15$, but $x = 9$ is NOT a solution.

 **DATA ANALYSIS AND PROBABILITY**

**11.** The stem-and-leaf plot below gives the number of games won by each of the National Basketball Association teams in the Eastern Conference for 2000–2001.

| Stem | Leaves |
|------|--------|
| 1 | 5 9 |
| 2 | 5 6 |
| 3 | 0 2 6 |
| 4 | 1 3 6 7 8 |
| 5 | 0 2 6 |

2|5 means 25.

Which is the range of the number of games won?

**F.** 41

**H.** 35

**G.** 37

**I.** 31

**12.** Look at the stem-and-leaf plot above. Which is the median number of games won?

**A.** 37.7

**B.** 38.5

**C.** 41

**D.** 42

**13. Explain It** The table shows the number of students who walked to school and the number of students who rode to school for 3 days.

| Day | 1 | 2 | 3 | 4 |
|--------|----|----|----|----|
| Walked | 6 | 3 | 6 | ■ |
| Rode | 20 | 24 | 19 | ■ |

Based on these data, predict the numbers of students who will walk and ride to school on Day 4. Explain how you made your predictions.

# CHAPTER 27 · Surface Area and Volume

**≡FAST FACT · SCIENCE**

The National Aquarium in Baltimore, Maryland, is one of the largest public aquariums in the United States. More than 10,000 marine and freshwater animals are maintained at the aquarium.

**PROBLEM SOLVING** Based on the measurements shown in the table, which tank has the smallest viewing window?

| TANK DIMENSIONS | | | |
|---|---|---|---|
| **Exhibit** | **Length (feet)** | **Width (feet)** | **Depth (feet)** |
| Atlantic Shelf | $8\frac{3}{4}$ | $6\frac{1}{2}$ * | $7\frac{2}{3}$ |
| Seahorse | 3 | $1\frac{1}{2}$ * | $1\frac{1}{2}$ * |
| Pacific Coral Reef | $9\frac{1}{6}$ | $8\frac{3}{4}$ | $7\frac{1}{2}$ |
| *estimated measure | | | |

Use this page to help you review and remember
important skills needed for Chapter 27.

## ✓ FACES, EDGES, AND VERTICES

Copy and complete the following table.

| | | Name of Figure | Number of Faces | Number of Edges | Number of Vertices |
|---|---|---|---|---|---|
| 1. | | Cube | 6 | 12 | 8 |
| 2. | | ? | ■ | ■ | ■ |
| 3. | | ? | ■ | ■ | ■ |
| 4. | | ? | ■ | ■ | ■ |
| 5. | | ? | ■ | ■ | ■ |

## ✓ MULTIPLYING WITH THREE FACTORS

**6.** $4 \times 4 \times 4$   **7.** $(3 \times 5) \times 1$   **8.** $8 \times (5 \times 2)$   **9.** $10 \times 10 \times 10$

**10.** $7 \times (5 \times 4)$   **11.** $2 \times 5 \times 20$   **12.** $(3 \times 3) \times 9$   **13.** $6 \times (2 \times 15)$

**14.** $6 \times (4 \times 2)$   **15.** $3 \times 6 \times 2$   **16.** $7 \times 12 \times 4$   **17.** $(15 \times 3) \times 4$

## VOCABULARY POWER ✓

### REVIEW

**polyhedron** [pol•i•hē′drən] *noun*

*Polyhedron* comes from the Greek root
words *poli,* meaning "many," and *hedros,*
meaning "face." Use this information to
write your own definition of a polyhedron.

### PREVIEW

net
surface area
volume

www.harcourtschool.com/mathglossary

# Nets for Solid Figures

## ▶ Learn

**BOXED IN**  Boxes that contain products you buy in stores are made from patterns, or nets. A **net** is a two-dimensional pattern that can be folded into a three-dimensional polyhedron.

Here is one net for a cube-shaped box. A cube is formed by 6 congruent square faces: 1 for the top, 1 for the bottom, and 4 for the sides.

Top

4 sides

Bottom

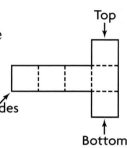

 ## Activity

**MATERIALS:** 1-inch grid paper, scissors, tape

Use the net to make a cube-shaped box.

| **STEP 1** | **STEP 2** | **STEP 3** |
|---|---|---|
| Copy the net onto grid paper and cut it out. | Fold on the dashed lines. | Tape the edges together. Be sure there are no gaps and that none of the sides overlap. |

4 sides  Top →

Bottom →

## Examples

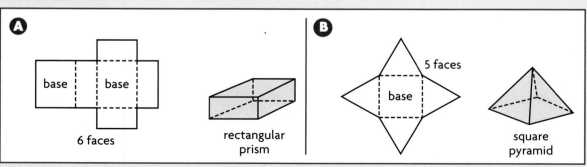

**A**

base   base

6 faces

rectangular prism

**B**

5 faces

base

square pyramid

• How are the faces of a triangular prism and a triangular pyramid different?

1. **Explain** why a cube is a prism.

**Match each solid figure with its net. Write *a, b, c,* or *d*.**

2.     3.     4.     5.

a. 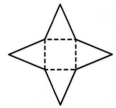    b.     c. 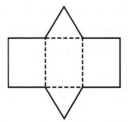    d.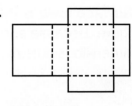

▶ **Practice and Problem Solving**   ( Extra Practice, page 600, Set A )

**Match each solid figure with its net. Write *a, b, c,* or *d*.**

6.     7.     8.     9.

a. 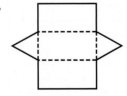    b. 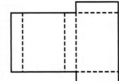    c. 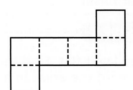    d.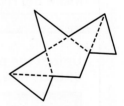

10. Draw two different nets for a cube. Cut out the nets. Fold and tape the nets to form cubes.

11. Brittani had a piece of string $4\frac{1}{9}$ yards long. She cut it into $9\frac{1}{4}$-inch pieces. How many pieces did she get?

12. Find the area of one of the 5-in. × 7-in. bases of a rectangular prism.

13. 📖 **Write About It**   Explain how to make a net for a square pyramid.

┌─ **Getting Ready for FCAT** ─────────────────────

14. Which solid figure can be made from the net?

   A. rectangular pyramid
   B. rectangular prism
   C. cube
   D. triangular prism

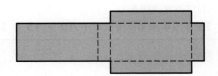

FCAT TESTED   SSS/GLEs MA.C.2.2.1.5.1 Uses manipulatives to solve problems requiring spatial visualization. *also* MA.C.3.2.1

**Chapter 27   589**

# 2 Surface Area

**Quick Review**

1. $9 \times 7$
2. $2 \times (4 \times 5)$
3. $2 \times (3 \times 1.5)$
4. $2 \times (1\frac{1}{2} \times \frac{3}{4})$
5. $2 \times (0.75 \times 4)$

 **Learn**

**WRAPPED UP!** You can use what you know about finding the area of a rectangle to find the surface area of a rectangular prism.

**Surface area** is the sum of the areas of the faces of a solid figure. Because surface area is a measurement of two dimensions, it is expressed in square units.

**VOCABULARY**

surface area

 **Activity**

**MATERIALS:** 1-centimeter grid paper, scissors, tape
To find the surface area of a rectangular prism, use its net.

### STEP 1

Copy the net onto centimeter grid paper. Label the faces *A–F* as shown.

### STEP 2

Cut out the net and fold on the lines to make the rectangular prism.

### STEP 3

Unfold the prism and lay it flat. Find the area of each face, *A–F*. Record the areas in a table.

| Face | Length | Width | Area = $l \times w$ |
|------|--------|-------|---------------------|
| A | 5 cm | 3 cm | 15 cm² |
| B | ■ | ■ | ■ |
| C | ■ | ■ | ■ |
| D | ■ | ■ | ■ |
| E | ■ | ■ | ■ |
| F | ■ | ■ | ■ |

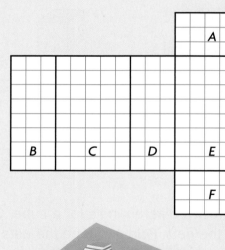

### STEP 4

Add the areas of the faces to find the surface area.
**15 + 24 + 40 + 24 + 40 + 15 = 158**

So, the surface area is 158 cm².

• Which faces have the same area? Why?

# Check

1. **Explain** how you would find the surface area of a cube.

**Use the net to find the area of each face. Then find the surface area of the prism.**

2.

3.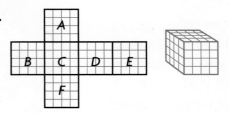

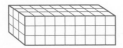

# Practice and Problem Solving — Extra Practice, page 600, Set B

**Use the net to find the area of each face. Then find the surface area of the prism.**

4.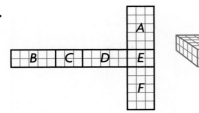

5.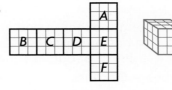

**Find the surface area in cm². You may want to make the net.**

6.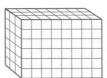

7.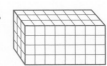

8.

9. What is the surface area of a box 5 feet long, 3 feet wide, and 7 feet high?

10. What is the surface area of a box 11 cm long, 10 cm wide, and 12 cm high?

11. Ellie and Jon each wrapped a package that was a rectangular prism. Ellie's package was 2 ft by 3 ft by 4 ft. Jon's package was 3 ft by 3 ft by 3 ft. Whose package had the greater surface area? Explain how you know.

12. **ESTIMATION** Edward is painting a room that is $11\frac{3}{4}$ ft long, $10\frac{1}{2}$ ft wide, and 10 ft high. He will not paint the ceiling or the floor. If one can of paint covers 350 ft², will 2 cans of paint be enough? Use estimation to explain.

## Getting Ready for FCAT

13. Julie built a prism out of centimeter cubes. What is the area of all of the faces of the prism?

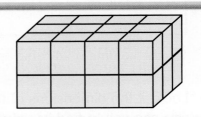

    **A.** 12 square centimeters     **C.** 26 square centimeters

    **B.** 24 square centimeters     **D.** 52 square centimeters

**FCAT TESTED** SSS/GLEs MA.B.1.2.2.5.2 Solves real-world problems involving perimeter, area, capacity, and volume using concrete, graphic, or pictorial models. *also* MA.C.2.2.1.5.1

Chapter 27 **591**

# Algebra: Estimate and Find Volume

▶ **Learn**

**YO-YO FUN** Alex is putting yo-yo boxes into a carton. By thinking about volume, he estimates that 60 yo-yo boxes will fit in the carton.

**Volume** is the amount of space a solid figure occupies. Volume is measured in *cubic units*. You can estimate the volume of a prism by visualizing how many cubes will fill it.

## Quick Review

Find the area of each rectangle in square inches.
1. $l = 3, w = 4$
2. $l = 4, w = 5$
3. $l = 5, w = 5$
4. $l = 3, w = 6$
5. $l = 10, w = 9$

**VOCABULARY**
**volume**

---

About 5 cubes fit along the length and about 3 cubes fit along the width. The bottom layer has about 15 cubes. There are about 4 layers of about 15 cubes each.

4 layers × 15 cubes = 60 cubes

So, about 60 yo-yo boxes will fit in the carton.

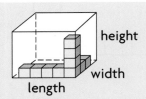

---

You can use cubes to find the volume of a rectangular prism.

**HANDS ON**

## Activity

**MATERIALS:** centimeter cubes

1 cubic centimeter (cm³)

**STEP 1**

**One Dimension**
Make a row of 4 cubes.

This is the length: 4 cm.

**STEP 2**

**Two Dimensions**
Make 2 rows of 4 cubes to make 1 layer.

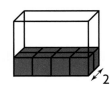

This is the width: 2 cm.
Count the number of cubes in each layer.
8, or 2 × 4

**STEP 3**

**Three Dimensions**
Make 3 layers of 8 cubes to complete the prism.

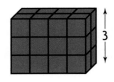

This is the height: 3 cm.
Count the total number of cubes that make the prism.
24, or 3 × 2 × 4

So, the volume is 24 cubic centimeters, or 24 cm³.

- Look at the dimensions of the rectangular prism. Write a formula you can use to find its volume.

# Use a Formula

Instead of counting cubes, you can use a formula to find the volume of a rectangular prism:

**Technology Link**

More Practice: Harcourt Mega Math Ice Station Explorations, *Frozen Solids*, Level J

**Volume = length × width × height, or $V = l \times w \times h$**

## Examples

**A**

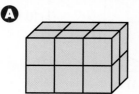

$V = l \times w \times h$
$V = 3 \times 2 \times 2$
$V = 12$

Volume is 12 units³.

**B**

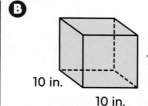

10 in.

10 in.

10 in.

$V = l \times w \times h$
$V = 10 \times 10 \times 10$
$V = 1,000$

Volume is 1,000 in.³

**C**

You can use a calculator to compute volume.

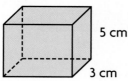

5 cm

3 cm

6 cm

Volume is 90 cm³.

- Explain how to use rounding to estimate the volume of a prism that is 5.8 cm long, 4.2 cm wide, and 1.9 cm high.

If you know the volume of a rectangular prism and two of its dimensions, you can use the formula to find the unknown dimension.

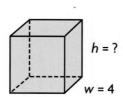

h = ?

w = 4

l = 5

Volume: 120 in.³

$V = l \times w \times h$
$120 = 5 \times 4 \times h$
$120 = 20 \times h$
$\dfrac{120}{20} = h$   The inverse of multiplication is division, so divide.
$6 = h$   The height is 6 in.

## ▶ Check

1. **Explain** how to estimate the volume of a cereal box in cubic inches.

**Find the volume of each rectangular prism.**

2.

3.

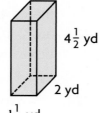

$4\frac{1}{2}$ yd

2 yd

$1\frac{1}{2}$ yd

4.

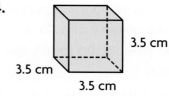

3.5 cm

3.5 cm

3.5 cm

**LESSON CONTINUES**

FCAT TESTED   SSS/GLEs MA.B.1.2.2.5.2 Solves real-world problems involving perimeter, area, capacity, and volume using concrete, graphic, or pictorial models. *also* MA.C.2.2.1.5.1

**Chapter 27** **593**

**Find the volume of each rectangular prism.**

**5.**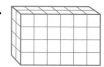

**6.**

**7.**

**8.** 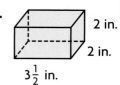 2 in.   2 in.   $3\frac{1}{2}$ in.

**9.** 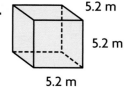 5.2 m   5.2 m   5.2 m

**10.** 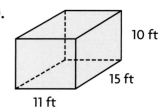 10 ft   15 ft   11 ft

**ALGEBRA**    **Find the unknown dimension.**

**11.** $V = 60$ ft$^3$

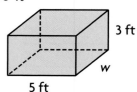 3 ft   $w$   5 ft

**12.** $V = 64$ m$^3$

8 m   2 m   $l$

**13.** $V = 144$ in.$^3$

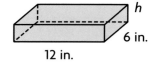 $h$   6 in.   12 in.

**14.** $l = 3$ in.
$w = 2$ in.
$h = 10$ in.
$V = \blacksquare$

**15.** $l = 6$ yd
$w = 4$ yd
$h = \blacksquare$
$V = 48$ yd$^3$

**16.** $l = 12$ ft
$w = \blacksquare$
$h = 2$ ft
$V = 192$ ft$^3$

**17.** $l = \blacksquare$
$w = 7$ m
$h = 5$ m
$V = 350$ m$^3$

**For 18–20, use the drawings.**

**18.** What is the volume of the small refrigerator? the height of the larger one?

**19.** How much area of the floor does each refrigerator cover?

**20.** Alan bought 2 small refrigerators. What is the difference between their combined volume and the volume of 1 large refrigerator?

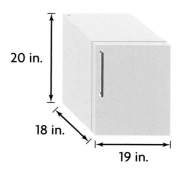 20 in.   18 in.   19 in.

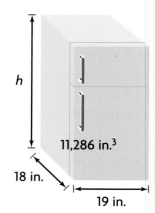 $h$   18 in.   11,286 in.$^3$   19 in.

**21.** **FAST FACT • SCIENCE** The total capacity of your lungs is about the same as the volume of a 10 in. × 6 in. × 5 in. box. What is the total capacity of your lungs?

**22.** Maria is packing boxes into a carton that is 4 in. × 6 in. × 3 in. The boxes are 2 in. × 1 in. × 1 in. How many boxes will fit in the carton?

**23.** A packing crate is $5\frac{1}{4}$ ft × $2\frac{7}{8}$ ft × $2\frac{1}{4}$ ft. Estimate the volume of the crate.

**24.** ✎ **Write a problem** that requires finding volume to solve.

**25. REASONING** Explain the difference between an inch, a square inch, and a cubic inch. Make a model of each.

**26. Vocabulary Power** A dimension of a figure is a measure of either length, width, or height. Draw an example of a one-, a two-, and a three-dimensional figure and explain each choice.

## Getting Ready for FCAT

**27.** Lindsay is filling this carton with small boxes that are cubes. The volume of each small box is 27 cubic inches.

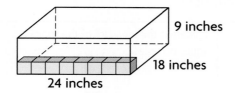

How many small boxes will fit inside the carton?

**A.** 12
**B.** 48
**C.** 100
**D.** 144

**28.** Danny needs a box that has a volume of 36 cubic feet. Which of the following boxes should he use?

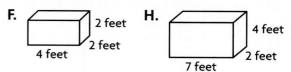
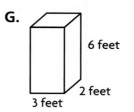
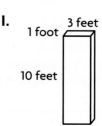

## Problem Solving  Thinker's Corner

**VISUAL THINKING** Look at the models of a cubic inch and a cubic centimeter. You can think about models to help you compare different units of volume.

A cubic inch is larger than a cubic centimeter.

The volume of this marble box is 4 in. × 3 in. × 2 in., or 24 in.$^3$

Is the volume of the box greater than or less than 24 cm$^3$?

Since a cubic inch is greater than a cubic centimeter, 24 in.$^3$ must be greater than 24 cm$^3$.

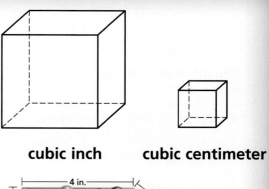

**cubic inch       cubic centimeter**

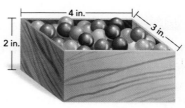

**Choose the greater volume.**

**1.** 12 in.$^3$ or 12 cm$^3$

**2.** 8 yd$^3$ or 8 m$^3$

**3.** 6 ft$^3$ or 6 yd$^3$

# Measure Perimeter, Area, and Volume

## Quick Review

1. 24 in. = ▇ ft
2. 27 ft$^2$ = ▇ yd$^2$
3. 2 yd = ▇ in.
4. 3 m = ▇ cm
5. 35 cm = ▇ m

## ▶ Learn

**ANOTHER DIMENSION**  Geometric figures can be measured in one, two, or three dimensions. The unit you choose depends upon the number of dimensions being used.

| | | |
|---|---|---|
| *Perimeter* is the distance around a figure.  Its measure is in one dimension, *length*. Use linear units, such as in., ft, yd, mi, cm, m, or km. | *Area* is the measure of the flat surface of a figure.  Its measure is in two dimensions, *length* and *width*. Use square units, such as in.$^2$, ft$^2$, yd$^2$, mi$^2$, cm$^2$, m$^2$, or km$^2$. | *Volume* is the measure of the space a figure occupies.  Its measure is in three dimensions, *length*, *width*, and *height*. Use cubic units, such as in.$^3$, ft$^3$, yd$^3$, mi$^3$, cm$^3$, m$^3$, or km$^3$. |

### HANDS ON  Activity

**MATERIALS:** 1-centimeter grid paper, centimeter ruler, centimeter cubes

**STEP 1**

On grid paper, draw a rectangle that is 3 cm by 4 cm. Measure or count to find the perimeter of the rectangle.

The perimeter, measured in linear units, is 14 cm.

**STEP 2**

Shade the squares to show the area of the rectangle.

The area, measured in square units, is 12 cm$^2$.

**STEP 3**

Use centimeter cubes to build a 3-layer prism on the rectangle. Find the volume of the prism.

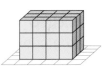

The volume, measured in cubic units, is 36 cm$^3$.

• Explain how the units used to measure perimeter, area, and volume are different.

## ▶ Check

1. **Describe** real-life situations in which you might need to find perimeter, area, and volume.

**Tell the appropriate units for measuring each. Write *linear*, *square*, or *cubic*.**

2. surface area      3. volume      4. perimeter      5. area

**Tell the appropriate units for measuring each. Write** *linear,* *square,* **or** *cubic.*

**6.** fence for a garden

**7.** tile for a floor

**8.** paper to cover a box

**9.** space in a refrigerator

**Write the units you would use to measure each.**

**10.** area of this rectangle

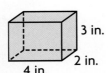

3 ft
6 ft

**11.** volume of this prism

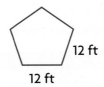

3 in.
2 in.
4 in.

**12.** perimeter of this figure

12 ft
12 ft

**13.** surface area of this figure

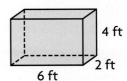

4 ft
2 ft
6 ft

**14.** wood for an 8-in. by 10-in. picture frame

**15.** fabric covering a box, 5 cm × 3 cm × 2 cm

**16.** a 9-ft by 10-ft rug

**17.** space inside a box, 2 ft × 8 ft × 4 ft

**Tom and his dad are making a toy box for Tom's little sister. Use the picture for 18–20.**

**18.** Tom used tape to put two stripes around the toy box. What did he measure to find out how much tape he needed? How much tape did Tom use?

**19.** Tom said his dad's goal was for the toy box to have less than 25 ft³ of space. What should Tom measure to see if they met the goal? How much space does the box have?

2 ft
3 ft
4 ft

**20.** Tom painted the top, bottom, and sides of the outside of the toy box. A can of paint covers 20 ft². How many cans of paint did Tom need to paint the toy box? Explain.

**21.** ⚡ **? What's the Error?** Joe's lunchbox is 10 in. long, 8 in. wide, and 3 in. high. He estimates the volume to be 240 in.² Explain his error.

**Getting Ready for FCAT**

**22.** Joanna wants to buy wallpaper for her bedroom walls. Which is the most appropriate unit for labeling the amount of wallpaper she needs?

**A.** cubic inches

**B.** square feet

**C.** cubic feet

**D.** square miles

FCAT TESTED ► SSS/GLEs MA.B.4.2.1.5.1 Selects an appropriate measurement unit for labeling the solution to real-world problems. *also* MA.B.1.2.2.5.2

Chapter 27 **597**

# Problem Solving Skill
## Use a Formula

> UNDERSTAND ▶ PLAN ▶ SOLVE ▶ CHECK

**Quick Review**

1. $\frac{3}{8} \times 8$
2. $8 \times 6 \times 4$
3. $36 + 40 + 36$
4. $6.3 \times 4.5$
5. Find the value of $n$.
   $15 + (2 \times 5) - n = 5$

**FILL IT UP!** Mr. Lee plans to build a sandbox in his backyard that is 5 feet long, 4 feet wide, and $\frac{1}{2}$ foot high.

Use this table to help you decide which formula to use to solve each problem below.

| RECTANGLE FORMULAS | | |
|---|---|---|
| **Want To Know** | **Find** | **Formula** |
| Distance around an object | Perimeter | $P = (2 \times l) + (2 \times w)$ |
| Number of square units needed to cover a flat surface | Area | $A = l \times w$ |
| Space occupied by a solid figure | Volume | $V = l \times w \times h$ |

 **MATH IDEA** To use a formula to solve a problem, first decide what you want to know. Then put your information in the formula and do the calculations.

## Examples

**A** What length of 6-in. boards will Mr. Lee need to **surround** the sandbox?

He needs to find the *perimeter* of the sandbox.

Use a formula:

$P = (2 \times l) + (2 \times w)$
$P = (2 \times 5) + (2 \times 4)$
$P = 10 + 8 = 18$

He needs 18 feet of 6-in. boards to make the sides of the sandbox.

**B** How much of his yard will the sandbox **cover**?

He needs to find the *area* of the sandbox.

Use a formula:

$A = l \times w$
$A = 5 \times 4$
$A = 20$

The sandbox will cover 20 square feet of his yard.

**C** How much sand will he need to **fill** $\frac{3}{5}$ of the sandbox?

He needs to find $\frac{3}{5}$ of the *volume* of the sandbox.

Use a formula:

$V = l \times w \times h$
$V = 5 \times 4 \times \frac{1}{2}$
$V = 10$

Find $\frac{3}{5}$ of 10:
$\frac{3}{5} \times 10 = 6$

He needs 6 cubic feet of sand to fill $\frac{3}{5}$ of the sandbox.

• If you did not use formulas, how could you answer Examples *A–C*?

**Use a formula to solve.**

1. **What if** Mr. Lee decides to make the sandbox $\frac{3}{4}$ foot deep? How much sand will he need to fill $\frac{3}{5}$ of the sandbox?

2. Rachel's bedroom is 15 ft long and 12 ft wide. She is having wall-to-wall carpet installed. How many square yards of carpet does she need?

3. A playground area that is 66 ft long and 42 ft wide needs to be fenced. How much fencing will be needed?

4. Mrs. Lopez wants to store some boxes of winter clothes in a cabinet with inside dimensions slightly greater than 5 ft by 2 ft by 6 ft. Each box is 1 ft × 2 ft × 2 ft. How many boxes can she fit into the cabinet?

**A regulation American football field is 120 yards long, including the end zones, and $53\frac{1}{3}$ yards wide. Each end zone is 10 yards deep and $53\frac{1}{3}$ yards wide.**

5. What is the perimeter of the field?

   **A** $5,033\frac{1}{3}$ yd²    **C** $346\frac{2}{3}$ yd²

   **B** $5,033\frac{1}{3}$ yd    **D** $346\frac{2}{3}$ yd

6. What is the area of each end zone?

   **F** $306\frac{2}{3}$ yd²    **H** $5,033\frac{1}{3}$ yd

   **G** $533\frac{1}{3}$ yd²    **J** $53,033\frac{2}{3}$ yd²

## Mixed Applications

7. The veterinarian puts bird seed in a bin 15 in. × 5 in. × 6 in. How much bird seed can the bin hold?

8. A bag of fertilizer will cover an area of 100 ft². Will 4 bags be enough to cover a garden 25 ft × 18 ft?

9. Janine's book shelf is $4\frac{2}{3}$ ft tall. Her desk is $\frac{3}{4}$ as high as the book shelf. How high is Janine's desk?

10. 📖 **Write About It** Explain how you know whether to use the perimeter formula or the area formula in a problem.

11. ❓ **What's the Question?** Mr. Lyle needs 66 yd² of ceiling tile for his basement. Each box of tiles contains 30 yd² of tile. The answer is 3 boxes.

12. Mr. Chu is unpacking some books from a box. There are 4 layers of books. Each layer has 3 rows with 3 books in each row. How many books are in the box?

FCAT TESTED   SSS/GLEs MA.C.3.2.1.5.2 Applies the concepts of area, perimeter, and volume to solve real-world and mathematical problems using student-developed formulas.

**Chapter 27**   **599**

# Extra Practice

## Set A (pp. 588–589)

**Match each solid figure with its net. Write *a, b, c,* or *d*.**

1.
2.
3.
4.

a.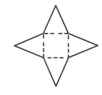
b.
c.
d.

5. Which solid has more faces: a triangular pyramid or a square pyramid? Explain.

## Set B (pp. 590–591)

**Find the surface area in cm².**

1.
2.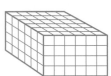
3.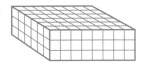

4. How many square inches of paper are needed to cover a box that is 4 inches long, 10 inches wide, and 3 inches high?

## Set C (pp. 592–595)

**Find the unknown measure.**

1. length = 8 ft
   width = 2 ft
   height = 3 ft
   volume = ■

2. length = ■
   width = 10 ft
   height = 10 ft
   volume = 1,000 ft³

3. length = 5.5 in.
   width = 2 in.
   height = 3 in.
   volume = ■

4. Rick's fish tank has 10,640 cm³ of water in it. If the length is 38 cm and the width is 28 cm, what is the height of the water?

## Set D (pp. 596–597)

**Tell the appropriate units for measuring each. Write *linear,* *square,* or *cubic.***

1. room inside a space shuttle
2. fence for a play yard
3. carpet for a room
4. paper to cover a box

# Review/Test

## ✓ CHECK VOCABULARY AND CONCEPTS

Choose the best term from the box.

1. The measure of the space a solid figure occupies is __?__. (p. 592)

2. A two-dimensional pattern for a three-dimensional prism or pyramid is a __?__. (p. 588)

3. The sum of the areas of the faces of a solid figure is the __?__. (p. 590)

| net |
| --- |
| base |
| surface area |
| volume |

Match each solid figure with its net. Write *a, b,* or *c.* (pp. 588–589)

4.

5.

6.

a.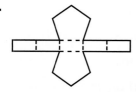

b.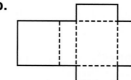

c.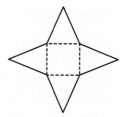

## ✓ CHECK SKILLS

Find the surface area in cm². (pp. 590–591)

7.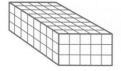

8.

Find the unknown dimension. (pp. 592–595)

9. length = 3 yd
   width = 10 yd
   height = 17 yd
   volume = ■

10. length = 9 ft
    width = ■
    height = 8 ft
    volume = 504 ft³

Tell the appropriate units for measuring each. Write *linear, square,* or *cubic.* (pp. 596–597)

11. wood for a picture frame

12. fabric to cover a triangular prism

13. space in a closet

## ✓ CHECK PROBLEM SOLVING

Solve. (pp. 598–599)

14. The stereo packaging box is 3 ft long and 2.5 ft wide. What is the area of the base of the box?

15. The storage locker is 5 yd long, 3.5 yd high, and 6 yd wide. How much space is in the locker?

# Getting Ready for FCAT

 **MEASUREMENT**

1. The average length of a giraffe's tongue is 53.34 centimeters. What is the average length in millimeters?

   **A.**     5.334 millimeters

   **B.**     533.4 millimeters

   **C.**  5,334 millimeters

   **D.** 53,340 millimeters

   > **TIP** **Decide on a plan.** See item 2. First find the dimensions of the area that includes the pool and the deck.

2. A deck surrounds a rectangular-shaped pool. The pool is 16 feet wide and 32 feet long. The deck is 4 feet wide. What is the area covered by the deck?

   **F.** 208 square feet

   **G.** 256 square feet

   **H.** 448 square feet

   **I.** 512 square feet

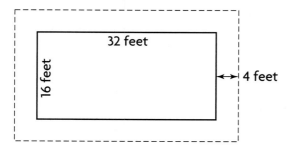

3. **Explain It** Mel has two boxes that are shaped like cubes. Box A has sides with lengths of 1 inch. Box B has sides with lengths of 2 inches. About 5 marbles fit in Box A. About how many marbles will fit in Box B? Explain how you know.

 **GEOMETRY AND SPATIAL SENSE**

4. Which figure can be made from this net?

   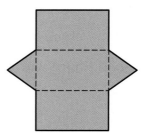

   **A.** triangular pyramid

   **B.** triangular prism

   **C.** square pyramid

   **D.** pentagonal prism

5. This drawing could be the top view of which solid?

   **F.** hexagonal prism

   **G.** triangular prism

   **H.** triangular pyramid

   **I.** square pyramid

6. **Explain It** On a grid, graph the points (1,1), (4,1), (6,4) and (1,4). Connect the points in the order given and then connect (1,4) to (1,1). Classify the figure in as many ways as you can. Explain how you know how to classify the figure.

DATA ANALYSIS AND PROBABILITY

**7.** A post office clerk recorded these weights for some packages.

| PACKAGE WEIGHTS | | | | | | |
|---|---|---|---|---|---|---|
| Package | A | B | C | D | E | F |
| Weight (in ounces) | 5 | 7 | 12 | 17 | 9 | 4 |

What is the mean weight of the packages?

A. 6 ounces

B. 8 ounces

C. 9 ounces

D. 13 ounces

**8.** A builder made a pictograph showing the number of new homes sold from April to June.

| NEW HOME SALES | |
|---|---|
| April | 🏠 🏠 🏠 |
| May | 🏠 🏠 |
| June | 🏠 🏠 🏠 🏠 |

Key: Each 🏠 = 10 homes.

How many more houses were sold in June than in April?

F. 40     H. 20

G. 25     I. 15

**9. Explain It** Before an election for class president, you survey 50 boys and 50 girls in the fifth grade to find out which candidate each group plans to vote for. What kind of graph or plot would you choose to display the data you collect? Explain your choice.

 ALGEBRAIC THINKING

**10.** The table shows how much Noelle earned baby-sitting and how much she saved each month for 4 months.

| NOELLE'S EARNINGS AND SAVINGS | | | | |
|---|---|---|---|---|
|  | Jan | Feb | Mar | Apr |
| Earnings | $114 | $96 | $144 | $156 |
| Savings | $38 | $32 | $48 | $52 |

If $s$ represents Noelle's savings, which expression represents Noelle's earnings?

A. $3 \times s$

B. $s \div 3$

C. $s + 76$

D. $38 + s$

**11.** Ramon's dog is missing. He wants to make photocopies of a flyer to help find his dog. Copies cost $0.07 each for the first 100 copies and $0.04 for each additional copy. Which expression shows the cost for 150 copies of the flyer?

F. $0.07 + (50 \times 0.04)$

G. $150 \times (0.07 + 0.04)$

H. $100 + (50 \times 0.04)$

I. $(100 \times 0.07) + (50 \times 0.04)$

**12. Explain It** Describe this pattern.

1, 2, 2, 4, 8, 32 . . . .

Then write the next number in the pattern.

# IT'S IN THE BAG

## From Net to Solid

**PROJECT** Make a solid figure from a two-dimensional pattern.

### Materials

- Box pattern
- Tagboard or large side of a cereal box
- Scissors
- Markers

### Directions

1. Cut out the pattern. Place the pattern on the tagboard, and trace it. Cut out the tracing. *(Picture A)*

2. On the tagboard, use your scissors to carefully cut a slit down the flap as shown. *(Picture B)*

3. Fold the rectangular flaps in toward the center, joining them at the slits. Then fold in the other flaps and secure them. *(Picture C)*

4. Measure the dimensions of the top, sides, and bottom of your solid figure.

5. Make other patterns for solid figures. Exchange the patterns with your classmates, and make the solid figures. Talk about how the figures are alike and different.

## Area of a Circle

To find the area of a circle, use the formula $A = \pi \times r^2$. The $r$ in the formula represents the length of the radius of the circle. The approximate decimal value of $\pi$ (pi) is 3.14.

To find the area of the circle, replace $r$ with 5 and $\pi$ with 3.14.

$A = \pi \times r^2 \qquad r = 5$

$A \approx 3.14 \times (5)^2$

$A \approx 3.14 \times 25$

$A \approx 78.5 \text{ in.}^2$

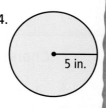

5 in.

The answer is expressed in square units because area is measured in square units.

### Examples

**A**
$A = \pi \times r^2 \qquad r = 7$
$A \approx 3.14 \times (7)^2$
$A \approx 3.14 \times 49$
$A \approx 153.86$
The area is about 154 cm².

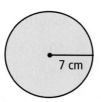
7 cm

**B**
$A = \pi \times r^2 \qquad r = 9$
$A \approx 3.14 \times (9)^2$
$A \approx 3.14 \times 81$
$A \approx 254.34$
The area is about 254 yd².

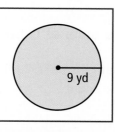
9 yd

## Talk About It

- How do you determine what unit to use to express the area of a circle?

## Try It

**Find the area of the circle with the given radius. Use $\pi = 3.14$.**

**1.** 4 in.

**2.** 6 cm

**3.** 8.5 ft

**4.** 10 mi

**Find the radius of the circle with the given area.**

**5.** 28.26 ft²

**6.** 19.625 m²

**7.** 254.34 in.²

**8.** 379.94 cm²

# Study Guide and Review

## VOCABULARY

**Choose the best term from the box.**

1. The distance around a circle is the __?__. (p. 554)

2. A two-dimensional pattern that can be folded into a three-dimensional prism or pyramid is a __?__. (p. 588)

3. The amount of space a solid figure occupies is its __?__. (p. 592)

> circumference
> net
> volume
> radius
> area

## STUDY AND SOLVE

### Chapter 24

**Change linear units.**

> To change smaller units to larger units, divide.
> 200 cm = ■ m
> 200 ÷ 100 = 2 ← 100 cm = 1 m
> So, 200 cm = 2 m.
> To change larger units to smaller units, multiply.
> 3 ft = ■ in.
> 3 × 12 = 36 ← 1 ft = 12 in.
> So, 3 ft = 36 in.

**Change units of capacity and mass.**

> To change smaller units to larger units, divide.
> 8 qt = ■ gal
> 8 ÷ 4 = 2 ← 4 qt = 1 gal
> So, 8 qt = 2 gal.
> To change larger units to smaller units, multiply.
> 2 kg = ■ g
> 2 × 1,000 = 2,000 ← 1 kg = 1,000 g
> So, 2 kg = 2,000 g.

**Change the unit.** (pp. 528–531)

4. 5 ft = ■ in.

5. 15 yd = ■ ft

6. 6,160 yd = ■ mi

7. 7 m = ■ cm

8. 2.5 km = ■ m

9. 45 mm = ■ cm

**Change the unit.** (pp. 532–535)

10. 7 kL = ■ L

11. 5 qt = ■ pt

12. 64 oz = ■ lb

13. 4 kg = ■ g

14. 300 mL = ■ L

15. 6 qt = ■ gal

### Chapter 25

**Find the perimeter of a polygon.**

> Find the perimeter.
> $P = (2 \times l) + (2 \times w)$
> $P = (2 \times 5.6) + (2 \times 3)$
> $P = 11.2 + 6$
> $P = 17.2$   Perimeter: 17.2 cm
> 3 cm
> 5.6 cm

**Find the perimeter of each polygon.** (pp. 550–551)

16.
$4\frac{1}{2}$ ft
$2\frac{1}{2}$ ft

17.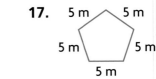
5 m   5 m
5 m   5 m
5 m

## Chapter 26

**Find the area of a polygon.**

Find the area.

$A = l \times w$
$A = 6.4 \times 4.5$
$A = 28.8$

4.5 cm

6.4 cm

So, the area is 28.8 cm².

**Find the area of each figure.** (pp. 564–579)

**18.** 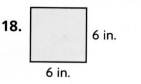 6 in.

6 in.

**19.** 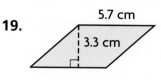 5.7 cm

3.3 cm

**20.** 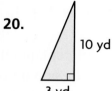 10 yd

3 yd

**21.** 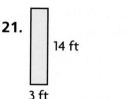 14 ft

3 ft

## Chapter 27

**Find the surface area.**

Surface area is the sum of the areas of the faces of a solid figure.

Find the surface area.

$2 \times (3 \times 4) = 24$
$2 \times (2 \times 3) = 12$
$2 \times (2 \times 4) = 16$
$24 + 12 + 16 = 52$

So, the surface area is 52 units².

**Find the surface area in cm². You may want to make the net.** (pp. 590–591)

**22.**

**23.**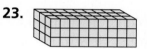

**24.**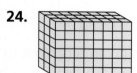

**25.**

**Find the volume of a rectangular prism.**

Find the volume.

$V = l \times w \times h$
$V = 6 \times 2 \times 10$
$V = 120$

10 in.

2 in.

6 in.

So, the volume is 120 in.³

**Find the volume of each rectangular prism.** (pp. 592–597)

**26.** 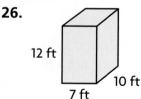 12 ft

10 ft

7 ft

**27.** 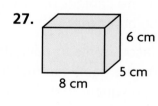 6 cm

5 cm

8 cm

## PROBLEM SOLVING PRACTICE

**Solve.** (pp. 580–581, 598–599)

**28.** The fish market sold 10,000 pounds of salmon on Friday. This was $\frac{2}{5}$ as much as the amount sold on Saturday. How many pounds of salmon were sold on Saturday?

**29.** Marie is using construction paper to cover a box 1 ft long, 3 ft wide, and 2 ft high. How much construction paper does she need?

# PERFORMANCE ASSESSMENT

## TASK A • WOODWORKING

**MATERIALS:** centimeter grid paper

Mr. Leon makes wooden jewelry boxes. On the tops of the boxes, he uses different kinds of wood to create geometric designs with triangles and quadrilaterals.

**a.** Draw a figure that is less than 15 centimeters by 15 centimeters. In the figure, design a box top that includes triangles, rectangles, and parallelograms.

**b.** Use a centimeter ruler to measure the dimensions of the largest triangle and rectangle in your design. Write the dimensions on the diagram. Then find the areas of those figures.

**c.** Mr. Leon charges $0.25 per square centimeter to make his box tops. How much would he charge for the top you designed?

## TASK B • STORAGE CABINET

Jason and his mother are designing a cabinet to store his sports equipment. They want the cabinet to have about 50 cubic feet of space.

**a.** Jason wants the cabinet to be 5 feet wide. Decide what dimensions for the depth and height of the cabinet you would use for a volume of about 50 cubic feet.

**b.** Jason wants to paint the cabinet. He reads on the paint can that the paint will cover 100 square feet. Does he have enough paint to cover the back, sides, and the top of the cabinet?

**c.** Suppose Jason decides to put a wooden ledge around the top of the cabinet. How many feet of trim will he need?

# Technology Linkup

## Finding Volume

The table shows the length, width, and height of different packing boxes. You can use a spreadsheet to find the volume of each box.

| BOX | LENGTH | WIDTH | HEIGHT |
|-----|--------|-------|--------|
| 1 | 24 in. | 18 in. | 6 in. |
| 2 | 12 in. | 12 in. | 12 in. |
| 3 | 36.5 in. | 6.25 in. | 6.25 in. |

You can find the volume of a rectangular prism by using the formula volume = length × width × height, or $V = l \times w \times h$.

- Enter the headings length, width, height, and volume into Columns A1 to D1 in the spreadsheet.
- Enter the data from the table into the appropriate cells.
- Click cell D2. Type = (A2*B2*C2). Then press *Enter*. Multiply cell A2 × cell B2 × cell C2. Use *Fill Down* and enter the formula in cells D3 and D4.

So, the volume of each box is: Box 1: 2,592 in.$^3$; Box 2: 1,728 in.$^3$; Box 3: 1,425.8 in.$^3$

| ◇ | A | B | C | D |
|---|------|------|------|--------|
| 1 | length | width | height | volume |
| 2 | 24 | 18 | 6 | 2592.0 |
| 3 | 12 | 12 | 12 | 1728.0 |
| 4 | 36.5 | 6.25 | 6.25 | 1425.8 |

## Practice and Problem Solving

Use a spreadsheet to solve the following problems.

1. $l$ = 4 in.
   $w$ = 3 in.
   $h$ = ■
   $V$ = 72 in.$^3$

2. $l$ = 7 m
   $w$ = ■
   $h$ = 10 m
   $V$ = 350 m$^3$

3. $l$ = 5 yd
   $w$ = 6 yd
   $h$ = ■
   $V$ = 270 yd$^3$

4. $l$ = ■
   $w$ = 3 ft
   $h$ = 4 ft
   $V$ = 96 ft$^3$

5. $l$ = 4.5 cm
   $w$ = 2.5 cm
   $h$ = 6 cm
   $V$ = ■

6. $l$ = ■
   $w$ = 3 m
   $h$ = $8\frac{1}{2}$ m
   $V$ = 153 m$^3$

7. **REASONING** Explain how the volume changes when 1, 2, and 3 dimensions of a rectangular prism are doubled.

**GO ON-LINE**

**Multimedia Math Glossary** www.harcourtschool.com/mathglossary

**Vocabulary Power** Compare the definitions in the Multimedia Math Glossary of *surface area* and *volume* of a rectangular prism. What dimensions do you need to find each? What units do you use to measure each?

▲ The Hulk has a zero-G roll 110 feet above the ground.

# PROBLEM SOLVING IN FLORIDA

## COASTING ALONG

Some of the most popular attractions in the amusement parks in Florida are the roller coaster rides. The sudden drops, twists, and high speeds make the roller coaster rides in Florida thrilling.

**USE DATA** For 1–3, use the table.

| Roller Coaster | City | Track Length (in ft) | First Drop Height (in ft) | Speed (mph) |
|---|---|---|---|---|
| Kraken | Orlando | 4,177 | 144 | 65 |
| The Hulk | Orlando | 3,700 | 105 | 67 |
| Kumba | Tampa | 3,978 | 135 | 63 |

1. Describe how you can find the number of yards equal to Kraken's track length. Round your answer to the nearest whole number.

2. One of the roller coasters' first drop in height is 1,620 inches. Which roller coaster is it? How can you tell?

3. **REASONING** If this were your very first roller coaster ride, which roller coaster would you choose? How did the table help you make your choice?

4. Kumba has the world's largest vertical loop, in which riders travel a 360-degree loop. The diameter of the loop is 108 feet. Find the distance that riders travel around the loop.

# GOING 'ROUND IN CIRCLES

An exciting and new attraction at the Lowry Park Zoo is the Jungle Carousel. Unlike most carousel rides, this one features riding on jungle animals rather than horses. Many of the carousel animals are replicas of endangered animals, such as the rhino, elephant, gorilla, and the Florida panther.

1. The diameter of the Jungle Carousel is 10 meters. What is the circumference?

2. The Jungle Carousel and its surrounding walkways form a square with one side measuring 12.5 meters. Draw a diagram to show the carousel and the walkway. Find the perimeter and area of this square.

3. **STRETCH YOUR THINKING** To ride the Jungle Carousel at the Lowry Park Zoo, you must be at least 107 centimeters tall. If you are 40 inches tall, could you ride? Explain your answer. (1 in. = 2.54 cm)

4. Sophia bought a box of popcorn at the zoo. The box is shaped like a rectangular prism. If the box is 12 inches high and has a length of 4 inches and a width of 5 inches, what is its volume?

# Ratio

CHAPTER
28

Ratio

≡**FAST FACT** • SPORTS

Ice hockey players use a special stick to drive a puck forward at speeds that can exceed 100 miles per hour. The table lists the results of four ice hockey games.

**PROBLEM SOLVING** What is the ratio of the number of goals the Sharks made to the number of goals the Otters made?

### ICE HOCKEY GAME RESULTS

| Team | Goals | Team | Goals |
|------|-------|------|-------|
| Badgers | 2 | Pelicans | 0 |
| Ducks | 4 | Eagles | 2 |
| Bears | 5 | Penguins | 1 |
| Sharks | 4 | Otters | 3 |

Use this page to help you review and remember important skills needed for Chapter 28.

## PARTS OF A GROUP

Write a fraction for the following.

**1.** 

What fraction of the triangles are red?

**2.** 

What fraction of the circles are blue?

**3.** 

What fraction of the squares are *not* red?

**4.** 

What fraction of the circles are red?

**5.** 

What fraction of the squares are red?

**6.** 

What fraction of the triangles are either red or blue?

## EQUIVALENT FRACTIONS

Write an equivalent fraction for each.

**7.** $\frac{3}{6}$  **8.** $\frac{2}{5}$  **9.** $\frac{50}{100}$  **10.** $\frac{6}{16}$  **11.** $\frac{8}{15}$

## SIMPLEST FORM

Write each fraction in simplest form.

**12.** $\frac{5}{15}$  **13.** $\frac{4}{20}$  **14.** $\frac{14}{63}$  **15.** $\frac{6}{36}$  **16.** $\frac{10}{14}$

**17.** $\frac{8}{12}$  **18.** $\frac{7}{7}$  **19.** $\frac{25}{45}$  **20.** $\frac{11}{44}$  **21.** $\frac{6}{18}$

# VOCABULARY POWER

**REVIEW**

**simplest form** [sim′pləst] *noun*

The root word of *simplest* is *simple,* which means "easy to do, solve, or understand." Write a sentence to explain how this definition can be applied to writing a fraction in simplest form.

**PREVIEW**

ratio   equivalent ratios

proportion  scale drawing

map scale

ON-LINE

www.harcourtschool.com/mathglossary

# Understand Ratios

 **Explore**

A **ratio** is a comparison of two quantities. For example, when you compare the number of red counters to the number of yellow counters, the ratio is 2 to 3.

## Quick Review

Write a fraction for the shaded part.

1.
2.
3.
4.              5.

**VOCABULARY**

**ratio**

_____

**MATERIALS**
two-color counters

## Activity

In a group of 10 students, 4 are boys and 6 are girls. Find the ratio of the number of boys to the number of girls.

### STEP 1

Use the yellow side to represent all 10 students in the group. Each counter represents one student.

### STEP 2

Turn the red side up to represent the number of students who are boys.

The ratio of boys to girls is the same as the ratio of red counters to yellow counters, 4 to 6.

*How many counters do you turn red side up to represent the ratio 4 baseballs to 3 basketballs?*

## Try It

Use two-color counters to represent 4 baseballs and 3 basketballs. Write each ratio.

   **a.** baseballs to basketballs
   **b.** basketballs to all balls
   **c.** baseballs to all balls

▶ **Connect**

You can use a ratio to compare two numbers in *three ways:* whole to part, part to whole, and part to part. Sumi has 6 yellow counters and 3 red counters. Here are three examples of ratios that she can form.

| Compare | Ratio | Type of Ratio |
|---|---|---|
| all counters to yellow counters | 9 to 6 | whole to part |
| red counters to all counters | 3 to 9 | part to whole |
| red counters to yellow counters | 3 to 6 | part to part |

- Which type of ratio has the same meaning as a fraction?

▶ **Practice and Problem Solving**

**Use two-color counters. Write each ratio and name the type of ratio.**

**1.** Tennis is played by 3 out of 7 students.

**2.** There were 2 rainy and 5 sunny days.

**3.** There were 5 dogs and 6 cats in the room.

**Write each ratio.**

**4.**

wheels to skate

**5.**

baseballs to players

**6.**

tires to bicycles

**7.** What is the ratio of vowels to consonants in the word PARALLELOGRAM? What kind of ratio is this?

**8.** Michelle packed 20 more boxes of books than Emily. Lisa packed 20 fewer boxes than Michelle. Emily packed 15 boxes of books. How many boxes of books did Michelle and Lisa pack?

**9.** ⭐ **What's the Error?** Jordan has 3 goldfish, 2 turtles, and 1 snail. He says that the ratio of turtles to the total number of animals is 2 to 5. Find and correct Jordan's error.

**10.** **GEOMETRY** What is the ratio of number of sides of a triangle to number of sides of an octagon?

**Getting Ready for FCAT**

**11.** Which fraction represents the number of red triangles out of the total number of triangles?

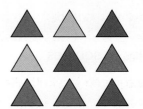

   **A.** $\frac{1}{3}$       **C.** $\frac{4}{9}$

   **B.** $\frac{4}{7}$       **D.** $\frac{5}{9}$

Reviews Florida SSS/GLEs MA.A.1.2.1.5.1

 **Learn**

**READING RATIOS** At the library, 5 out of 8 books Loren checked out are about dogs. The other 3 books are about cats. The ratio of dog books to the total number of books he checked out is part to whole.

**Write:** 5 to 8    5:8    $\frac{5}{8}$

**Read:** "five to eight"

Find other ratios by considering the number of cat books Loren checked out.

**Ⓐ** cat books:all books
3 to 8, 3:8, $\frac{3}{8}$
part to whole

**Ⓑ** all books:cat books
8 to 3, 8:3, $\frac{8}{3}$
whole to part

**Ⓒ** cat books:dog books
3 to 5, 3:5, $\frac{3}{5}$
part to part

**MATH IDEA** You can use ratios to express the relationships between sets. The relationships of part to whole, whole to part, and part to part can be written in three ways.

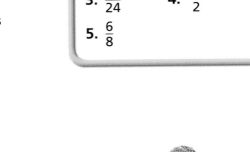

 **Check**

1. **Explain** why the order in which you write a ratio is important.

**Write each ratio in three ways. Then name the type of ratio.**

2. circles to squares

3. all figures to red

4. circles to all figures

5. blue to red

6. all figures to squares

7. green to all figures

**Write each ratio in three ways. Then name the type of ratio. Use the circles, squares, and stars on page 616.**

**8.** squares to stars　　　　**9.** red to green　　　　**10.** stars to all figures

**Write *a* or *b* to show which fraction represents each ratio.**

**11.** 5 to 2　　　　**12.** 5:9　　　　**13.** 8 to 4　　　　**14.** 1:20

　**a.** $\frac{2}{5}$　**b.** $\frac{5}{2}$　　　　**a.** $\frac{9}{5}$　**b.** $\frac{5}{9}$　　　　**a.** $\frac{8}{4}$　**b.** $\frac{4}{8}$　　　　**a.** $\frac{20}{1}$　**b.** $\frac{1}{20}$

**USE DATA** For 15–17, use the circle graph. Write each ratio in three ways.

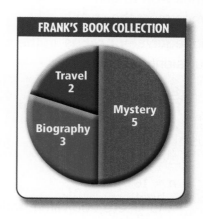

FRANK'S BOOK COLLECTION

Travel 2 · Mystery 5 · Biography 3

**15.** What is the ratio of mystery books to biography books?

**16.** What is the ratio of all books to biography books?

**17.** What is the ratio of travel books to all books?

**USE DATA** For 18–21, use this information: Out of every 60 people in the world, 12 live in China, 10 live in India, and 3 live in the United States. Match each ratio with its comparison.

　**a.** 60:3　　**b.** 10:60　　**c.** 12:10　　**d.** 3:12

**18.** India:world　　　**19.** U.S.:China　　　**20.** world:U.S.　　　**21.** China:India

**22. REASONING** If the ratio of games won to games lost is 3:2, what is the ratio of games won to the total number of games played?

**23.** **ALGEBRA** Find the value of *n*.
$$\frac{5}{7} = \frac{(5 \times n)}{56}$$

**24.** **FAST FACT** • SOCIAL STUDIES The Floating Garden Observatory atop Umeda Sky City in Osaka, Japan, is 54 meters by 54 meters. What is the area in square yards? (HINT: $1\text{m}^2 \approx 1.2 \text{ yd}^2$)

**25.** Write About It Last month 2 out of every 4 dogs adopted were Dalmatians. Explain why you can compare the number of Dalmatians to the total number with the ratio $\frac{1}{2}$.

## Getting Ready for FCAT

**26.** Julie built a prism out of centimeter cubes. If all the cubes in the bottom layer are red, what fraction of the prism is made up of red cubes?

　**A.** $\frac{3}{4}$　　　　**C.** $\frac{1}{2}$

　**B.** $\frac{2}{3}$　　　　**D.** $\frac{1}{3}$

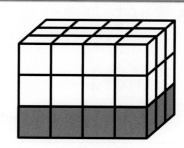

Reviews Florida SSS/GLEs MA.A.1.2.1.5.1

# Ratios and Proportions

▶ **Learn**

**POWER PLAY**   Last year Lisa's ice-hockey team won 8 out of a total of 10 games. This year's team will play 20 games. The players hope to have the same ratio of games won to games played as last year. How many games must they win?

Find **equivalent ratios** in the same way you find equivalent fractions.

$$\frac{8}{10} = \frac{n}{20} \quad \begin{array}{l}\leftarrow \text{games won} \\ \leftarrow \text{games played}\end{array}$$

$$\frac{8 \times \boxed{2}}{10 \times \boxed{2}} = \frac{16}{20} \quad \text{Think: } 10 \times 2 = 20, \text{ so } 8 \times 2 = 16.$$

$$n = 16$$

So, $\frac{8}{10}$ and $\frac{16}{20}$ are equivalent ratios. Lisa's team must win 16 games this year.

**VOCABULARY**

equivalent ratios
proportion

 **MATH IDEA**   To find an equivalent ratio, first express the ratio as a fraction, then multiply or divide the numerator and the denominator by the same number, using a fraction equal to 1.

---

### Example 1 Write an equivalent ratio.

**A** $\frac{3}{5}$

$$\frac{3 \times \boxed{3}}{5 \times \boxed{3}} = \frac{9}{15}$$

So, $\frac{9}{15}$ is equivalent to $\frac{3}{5}$.

**B** 10:24

$$10:24 = \frac{10}{24} \quad \frac{10 \div \boxed{2}}{24 \div \boxed{2}} = \frac{5}{12}, \text{ or } 5:12$$

So, 5:12 is equivalent to 10:24.

### Example 2 Tell whether the ratios are equivalent.

**C** $\frac{20}{16}$ and $\frac{5}{4}$

$$\frac{20 \div \boxed{4}}{16 \div \boxed{4}} = \frac{5}{4}$$

So, $\frac{20}{16}$ and $\frac{5}{4}$ are equivalent ratios.

**D** 3:8 and 5:16

$$3:8 = \frac{3}{8} \qquad 5:16 = \frac{5}{16}$$

$$\frac{3 \times \boxed{2}}{8 \times \boxed{2}} = \frac{6}{16} \qquad \frac{5}{16} < \frac{6}{16}$$

So, 3:8 and 5:16 are NOT equivalent ratios.

# Proportions

Each container of hockey pucks holds 4 game pucks and 10 practice pucks. The ratio of game pucks to practice pucks in one container is $\frac{4}{10}$. Three containers would have 12 game pucks and 30 practice pucks, which is three times as many as are in one container. The two ratios $\frac{4}{10}$ and $\frac{12}{30}$ are equivalent ratios.

A **proportion** is an equation that shows two equivalent ratios.

$$\frac{4}{10} = \frac{12}{30} \leftarrow \text{proportion}$$

## Example 3

Builders use ratios and proportions in reducing and enlarging drawings. This drawing of a hockey rink needs to be reduced to half size. Write a proportion to show the old and new lengths and widths.

The ratio of length to width in units is $\frac{10}{4}$. Divide both 10 and 4 by 2.

$\frac{10 \div 2}{4 \div 2} = \frac{5}{2}$   The new ratio of length to width is $\frac{5}{2}$.

$\frac{10}{4}$ and $\frac{5}{2}$ are equivalent ratios. $\frac{10}{4} = \frac{5}{2}$

So, $\frac{10}{4} = \frac{5}{2}$ is a proportion that shows the old and new lengths and widths.

Original drawing of hockey rink

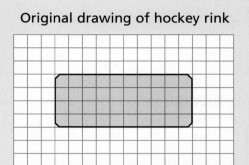

New drawing of hockey rink

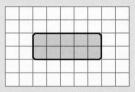

• Suppose that the size of the new drawing is twice the size of the original drawing. Write a proportion to show the old and new lengths and widths.

## ▶ Check

**1. Explain** whether the ratios $\frac{5}{4}$ and $\frac{10}{8}$ form a proportion.

**Write three ratios that are equivalent to the given ratio.**

**2.** 3:1          **3.** $\frac{3}{5}$          **4.** 1 to 4          **5.** 2:7

**Tell whether the ratios are equivalent. Write *yes* or *no*.**

**6.** $\frac{2}{4}$ and $\frac{6}{12}$          **7.** 2:5 and 5:10          **8.** 4 to 12 and 1 to 3

LESSON CONTINUES ▶

**Tell whether the ratios are equivalent. Write *yes* or *no*.**

**9.** $\frac{3}{4}$ and $\frac{12}{20}$

**10.** 5:10 and 1:2

**11.** 1 to 4 and 25 to 100

**12.** 3:9 and 9:27

**13.** 4 to 9 and 6 to 18

**14.** $\frac{5}{8}$ and $\frac{20}{32}$

**Write three ratios that are equivalent to the given ratio.**

**15.** 10 to 1

**16.** $\frac{1}{7}$

**17.** 9 to 3

**18.** 26:36

**19.** $\frac{1}{5}$

**20.** 50:100

**21.** $\frac{2}{2}$

**22.** 100 to 1

**ALGEBRA**  **Find the unknown value.**

**23.** $\frac{4}{5} = \frac{x}{20}$

**24.** $\frac{n}{2} = \frac{21}{14}$

**25.** $\frac{8}{9} = \frac{8}{p}$

**26.** $\frac{9}{h} = \frac{3}{9}$

**27.** $\frac{12}{10} = \frac{y}{5}$

**28.** $\frac{c}{3} = \frac{10}{15}$

**29.** $\frac{36}{8} = \frac{9}{k}$

**30.** $\frac{20}{y} = \frac{4}{3}$

**Tell whether the ratios form a proportion. Write *yes* or *no*.**

**31.** $\frac{2}{4}$ and $\frac{6}{12}$

**32.** $\frac{1}{6}$ and $\frac{3}{15}$

**33.** $\frac{12}{5}$ and $\frac{24}{10}$

**34.** $\frac{12}{15}$ and $\frac{16}{20}$

**35.** $\frac{9}{6}$ and $\frac{15}{9}$

**36.** $\frac{3}{8}$ and $\frac{9}{25}$

**37.** $\frac{20}{15}$ and $\frac{15}{10}$

**38.** $\frac{6}{15}$ and $\frac{4}{10}$

**Copy and complete the ratio table.**

**39.**

| Number of Apples | 3 | ▪ | ▪ | ▪ |
|---|---|---|---|---|
| Cups of Apple Cider | 1 | 3 | 9 | 27 |

**40.**

| Number of Canoes | 1 | 4 | 7 | 10 |
|---|---|---|---|---|
| Number of People | 3 | ▪ | ▪ | ▪ |

**41. REASONING**  During the ice hockey game, 3 of the 20 shots were goals. What is the ratio of shots made to all shots taken and shots made to shots missed? Do these two ratios make a proportion?

**42. NUMBER SENSE**  Find the missing numbers in the pattern of equivalent ratios: $\frac{2}{\blacksquare}, \frac{4}{10}, \frac{8}{\blacksquare}, \frac{\blacksquare}{40}$. Describe the pattern.

**For 43–44, use the ratio of 4 oranges to 1 glass of juice.**

**43.** How many oranges will Bryce need to make 3 glasses of orange juice?

**44.** Write three ratios equivalent to the ratio of oranges to glasses of orange juice.

**45.** Make a drawing of a hockey puck on grid paper that is half the size of the drawing to the right. Write a proportion to show the old and new lengths and widths.

**Hockey Puck, side view**

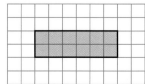

**46.** On average, 2 of every 50 CDs in a shipment were defective. Mrs. Snyder bought 600 of the CDs for her store. How many would she expect to be defective?

**47. Vocabulary Power** A fraction names a part of a whole or part of a group. How is a ratio like a fraction? How is it different?

**Getting Ready for FCAT**

**48.** The pattern at the right is for a tablecloth. Stephanie wants to make a tablecloth that has twice the length and twice the width of the one that can be made with this pattern. She is going to put a ribbon border around the edge of the tablecloth. How much ribbon does she need?

⊢⊣ = 2 inches

- **A.** 125 inches
- **B.** 150 inches
- **C.** 200 inches
- **D.** 225 inches

**49.** If the length and width of the tablecloth pattern at the right are doubled, how will the area change?

- **F.** It will stay the same.
- **G.** It will double.
- **H.** It will be 3 times as great.
- **I.** It will be 4 times as great.

Reviews Florida SSS/GLEs MA.C.3.2.1.5.3

# Problem Solving LINKUP ... to Art

The Greeks experimented with the use of triangles and rectangles in their architecture. The length-to-width or length-to-height ratio of rectangular shapes in some buildings is called a Golden Ratio. A **Golden Ratio** is any ratio equivalent to the value of about 1.6.

**Example** Does Rectangle A show a Golden Ratio?

$\frac{l}{w} = \frac{8}{5}$    Write the length-to-width ratio for the rectangle.

$\frac{8}{5} = 1.6$    Write the equivalent decimal for the ratio.

So, Rectangle A shows a Golden Ratio.

**1.** The Parthenon was constructed around 450 B.C. in Athens, Greece. The front of the Parthenon has a length of 101 feet and a height of 60 feet. Does the front show a Golden Ratio? Explain.

**2.** Measure the length and width of the cover of your math book. Is the ratio of the measures a Golden Ratio?

# 4 Scale Drawings

## Learn

**GO THE DISTANCE!** A **scale drawing** shows a real object smaller than (a reduction) or larger than (an enlargement) the real object. A map is a scale drawing. The ratio that compares the distance on a map to the actual distance is the **map scale**.

### Quick Review

Find *n* to make the ratios equivalent.

1. $\frac{7}{14} = \frac{n}{28}$    2. $\frac{8}{n} = \frac{16}{32}$

3. $\frac{5}{25} = \frac{n}{75}$    4. $\frac{3}{100} = \frac{30}{n}$

5. $\frac{36}{42} = \frac{n}{7}$

### VOCABULARY

scale drawing    map scale

### Example

You can use the scale to compute the distance from Asheboro to Greensboro.

| Read the map scale. | The map shows a scale of 1 cm = 12 km, or $\frac{1 \text{ cm}}{12 \text{ km}}$. |
|---|---|
| Use a centimeter ruler to measure the distance from Asheboro to Greensboro on the map. | The distance is 3.5 cm on the map. |
| Use equivalent ratios to find the actual distance. | $\frac{1}{12} = \frac{3.5}{n}$ <br> $\frac{1 \times 3.5}{12 \times 3.5} = \frac{3.5}{42}$ <br> $n = 42$ |

So, the distance is 42 kilometers.

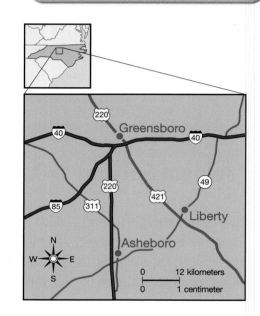

 **MATH IDEA** You can use scale drawings and map scales to determine actual sizes and actual distances.

## Check

1. **Explain** how to find the distance from Liberty to Asheboro.

**Copy and complete the map scale ratio table.**

2.

| Map Distance (inches) | 1 | ■ | 2.6 | ■ | 7.8 |
|---|---|---|---|---|---|
| Actual Distance (miles) | 100 | 150 | ■ | 680 | ■ |

**Copy and complete the ratio table.**

**3.**

| Scale Length (in.) | 1 | ■ | 3.5 | ■ | ■ |
|---|---|---|---|---|---|
| Actual Length (ft) | 10 | 30 | ■ | 50 | 60 |

**4.**

| Scale Distance (cm) | 1 | 3 | ■ | 8 | ■ |
|---|---|---|---|---|---|
| Actual Distance (m) | 7.5 | ■ | 37.5 | ■ | 75 |

**5.**

| Scale Length (in.) | 1 | 2 | 4 | ■ | ■ |
|---|---|---|---|---|---|
| Actual Length (ft) | 12 | ■ | ■ | 60 | 72 |

**6.**

| Scale Distance (cm) | 1 | 2.6 | ■ | 7.6 | ■ |
|---|---|---|---|---|---|
| Actual Distance (m) | 75 | ■ | 375 | ■ | 600 |

**7.**

| Scale Length (in.) | 1 | ■ | 4 | 4.4 | 5 |
|---|---|---|---|---|---|
| Actual Length (ft) | 200 | 500 | ■ | ■ | ■ |

**8.**

| Scale Distance (cm) | 3 | 6 | ■ | 12 | ■ |
|---|---|---|---|---|---|
| Actual Distance (m) | 150 | ■ | 450 | ■ | 750 |

**For 9–11, use the map and map scale to find the distance to the nearest mile.**

**9.** Cincinnati to Columbus

**10.** Toledo to Columbus

**11.** Columbus to Akron

**12.**  **Write a problem** about driving between two cities that are less than 100 miles apart. Use the map of Ohio.

**13.** A rectangular garden is 48 ft long and 42 ft wide. Fencing for the garden costs $12 for each foot. How much will it cost to fence in the garden?

**14.** Choose a scale for this drawing. Then use it to find the actual length and width of the cabin.

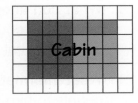

**15.** Maura has a dollhouse with a scale of 1 inch to 1.5 ft. The dimensions of the living room are 10 in. by 12 in. What would be the dimensions of this room in an actual house?

**16.** **REASONING** Joy planned a scale drawing with a scale of 1 in. = 4 ft. She found that her drawing would not fit on her paper. How should she change the ratio to make the drawing fit? Explain.

**Getting Ready for FCAT** THINK SOLVE EXPLAIN

**17.** Ben drew a map of his neighborhood. He made the table at the right to show distances on his map.

Write a rule for the pattern in the table. Copy and complete the table.

**18.** On the map, Ben's house is 8 spaces from the school. Explain how to use the table to find the distance from Ben's house to school.

| Spaces | 1 | 2 | 3 | 4 | 5 | 6 |
|---|---|---|---|---|---|---|
| Miles | 0.5 | 1 | 1.5 | 2 | ■ | ■ |

Reviews Florida SSS/GLEs MA.D.1.2.2.5.2 and MA.D.1.2.2.5.3

# Problem Solving Skill
## Too Much/Too Little Information

### Quick Review

Is the ratio equivalent to $\frac{3}{5}$?

1. $\frac{2}{3}$    2. $\frac{6}{10}$    3. $\frac{9}{15}$

4. $\frac{1}{2}$    5. $\frac{15}{20}$

**CAN YOU SOLVE IT?** Yoko found these people-to-pet ratios on the Internet. For her report she wants to know the ratio of pet dogs in the United States to pet cats.

Sometimes you have too much or too little information to solve a problem. If there is too much, you have to decide what to use. If there is too little, you can't solve the problem.

To decide, read the problem carefully and then ask yourself these questions:

1. **What do I want to know?**
   pet dogs:pet cats

2. **What do I know?**
   people:pet dogs = 30:6
   people:pet cats = 30:7

3. **What information is unnecessary?**
   people-to-bird ratios

4. **What necessary information is missing?**
   none

Since the number of people compared to dogs and cats is the same, you can compare dogs to cats.

So, the ratio of pet dogs to pet cats is 6:7.

## Talk About It

• How can you decide what information is necessary to solve a problem?

U.S. Populations
People to pets
People : cats 30:7
People : dogs 30:6
People : parakeets 300:15
People : parrots 3,000:15

Problem Solving

**USE DATA** For 1–4, use the chart on page 624. Write whether each problem has *too much* or *too little* information. Then solve if possible, or describe the additional information needed.

1. How many people are there in the U.S. for every one pet dog?

2. How many people are there in the U.S. for every one Siamese cat?

3. Which is the more popular pet in the U.S., a parrot or a goldfish?

4. How many pet parakeets are there for every 3,000 people in the U.S.?

Tomás needs to walk the dog, do the dishes, and finish his homework. It will take him 15 minutes to walk the dog, 30 minutes to do the dishes, and 1 hour 10 minutes to finish his homework. Does he have enough time to complete all three tasks?

5. What other information do you need to solve the problem?
   A the name of Tomás's dog
   B how much time Tomás has
   C how many dishes are dirty
   D what homework he needs to do

6. What is the least amount of time Tomás needs to complete all three tasks?
   F 2 hours
   G 1 hour 55 minutes
   H 1 hour 45 minutes
   J 1 hour 35 minutes

## Mixed Applications

**USE DATA** For 7–8, use the table.

7. What is the weight difference between the largest and smallest dogs?

8. Which dog was bigger, the mastiff or the Great Dane?

9. The first year of a dog's life equals 15 "human years." The second year equals 10 human years. Every year thereafter equals 3 human years. Use this formula to find a 6-year-old dog's age in human years.

10. **❓ What's the Question?** An African gray parrot named Prudle was found in 1958. From then until 1977, it learned nearly 1,000 words. The answer is about 50.

11. 📖 **Write a problem** that has too little information to be solved. Then write one that includes information that is not needed to solve the problem.

| WORLD DOG RECORDS | | |
|---|---|---|
| **Record** | **Breed** | **Measurement** |
| Largest | Old English Mastiff | 343 pounds |
| Tallest | Great Dane | 3.5 feet |
| Smallest | Yorkshire Terrier | 4 ounces |

FCAT TESTED ▸ SSS/GLEs MA.A.3.2.3.5.1 Solves real-world problems involving addition, subtraction, multiplication, and division of whole numbers, and addition, subtraction, and multiplication of decimals, fractions, and mixed numbers . . . .

**Chapter 28 625**

# Extra Practice

## Set A (pp. 616–617)

**Write a or b to show which fraction represents the ratio.**

1. 5 to 3
   a. $\frac{3}{5}$  b. $\frac{5}{3}$

2. 4:9
   a. $\frac{4}{9}$  b. $\frac{9}{4}$

3. 5 to 5
   a. $\frac{5}{5}$  b. $\frac{1}{5}$

4. 7:2
   a. $\frac{7}{1}$  b. $\frac{7}{2}$

5. 1 to 6
   a. $\frac{1}{6}$  b. $\frac{6}{1}$

**For 6–8, use the graph.**

6. What is the ratio of guards to forwards in the league?

7. What is the ratio of forwards to the total number of players in the league?

8. If 2 more guards join the league, what will be the ratio of guards to total players in the league?

## Set B (pp. 618–621)

**Tell whether the ratios form a proportion. Write yes or no.**

1. $\frac{8}{12}$ and $\frac{12}{24}$

2. $\frac{6}{6}$ and $\frac{8}{8}$

3. $\frac{2}{4}$ and $\frac{5}{10}$

4. $\frac{7}{6}$ and $\frac{6}{5}$

5. $\frac{3}{5}$ and $\frac{6}{10}$

6. $\frac{4}{8}$ and $\frac{16}{24}$

**Write three ratios that are equivalent to the given ratio.**

7. 1 to 3

8. 4:5

9. $\frac{10}{7}$

10. 1 to 1

11. Twelve members of the drama club acted in the school play, and the remaining 19 members were stagehands. What is the ratio of actors to the total club membership?

12. The science club has 40 members, but only 30 members went on the trip to the aquarium. What is the ratio of members who went on the trip to those who did not?

## Set C (pp. 622–623)

**Copy and complete the map scale ratio table.**

1.

| Scale Length | 1 in. | ▨ in. | 5 in. | ▨ in. |
|---|---|---|---|---|
| Actual Length | 5 mi | 15 mi | ▨ mi | 35 mi |

2.

| Scale Length | 1 cm | 8 cm | ▨ cm | 12 cm |
|---|---|---|---|---|
| Actual Length | 4.5 km | ▨ km | 45 km | ▨ km |

# Review/Test

##  CHECK VOCABULARY AND CONCEPTS

Choose the best term from the box.

> equivalent ratios
> map scale
> ratio
> scale drawing

1. You can use a __?__ to compare two quantities. (p. 614)

2. A ratio that compares the distance on a map to the actual distance is called the __?__. (p. 622)

3. Ratios that describe the same comparison of quantities are called __?__. (p. 618)

##  CHECK SKILLS

For 4–6, use the letters in the word MULTIPLICATION to write each ratio. (pp. 614–615)

4. consonants to total letters    5. consonants to vowels    6. total letters to vowels

Write *a* or *b* to show which fraction represents each ratio. (pp. 616–617)

7. 5 to 1    8. 9 to 5    9. 12:36    10. 25:100    11. 1 to 50

   a. $\frac{1}{5}$  b. $\frac{5}{1}$    a. $\frac{9}{5}$  b. $\frac{5}{9}$    a. $\frac{1}{3}$  b. $\frac{3}{1}$    a. $\frac{4}{1}$  b. $\frac{1}{4}$    a. $\frac{1}{50}$  b. $\frac{50}{1}$

Write three ratios that are equivalent to the given ratio. (pp. 618–621)

12. 6 to 8    13. 3:7    14. 9:5

Tell whether the ratios form a proportion. Write *yes* or *no*. (pp. 618–621)

15. $\frac{3}{21}$ and $\frac{1}{7}$    16. $\frac{4}{6}$ and $\frac{2}{4}$

Copy and complete the map scale ratio table. (pp. 622–623)

17.

| Scale Length (in.) | 1 | 4 | ■ | 8 |
|---|---|---|---|---|
| Actual Length (ft) | 50 | ■ | 300 | ■ |

18.

| Scale Length (cm) | 1 | ■ | 4 | ■ |
|---|---|---|---|---|
| Actual Length (m) | 2.5 | 5 | ■ | 15 |

## ✔ CHECK PROBLEM SOLVING

Write whether each problem has *too much* or *too little* information. Then solve if possible, or describe the additional information needed. (pp. 624–625)

19. At Jerry's Market a gallon of chocolate milk costs $2.15, a half gallon costs $1.20, and a gallon of skim milk costs $1.75. How much will 2 gallons of chocolate milk cost?

20. The music store is having a CD sale. If you buy two CDs, you get one free. How much will three CDs cost?

# Getting Ready for FCAT

 **MEASUREMENT**

1. What is the perimeter of the *Mona Lisa*?

| SIZES OF FAMOUS PAINTINGS | | |
|---|---|---|
| **Title** | **Artist** | **Dimensions (in inches)** |
| *Mona Lisa* | da Vinci | 30 × 21 |
| *Water Lily Pond* | Monet | 35 × 36 |
| *Apples and Oranges* | Cézanne | 29 × 37 |
| *Dancers in Blue* | Degas | 34 × 30 |

A. 51 inches     C. 102 inches

B. 81 inches     D. 630 inches

2. Look at the table in Problem 1. Which painting has the greatest area?

F. *Mona Lisa*

G. *Water Lily Pond*

H. *Apples and Oranges*

I. *Dancers in Blue*

3. **Explain It** Julie wants to buy ribbon to decorate the perimeter of a picture frame. She measured part of the perimeter. ESTIMATE to determine about how many centimeters of ribbon she needs. Explain how you found your estimate.

5.8 centimeters

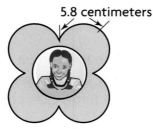

 **NUMBER SENSE, CONCEPTS, AND OPERATIONS**

4. The table shows the countries with the most movie theaters.

| COUNTRIES WITH THE MOST MOVIE THEATERS | |
|---|---|
| **Country** | **Number of Theaters** |
| India | 8,975 |
| United States | 23,662 |
| China | 4,364 |
| Ukraine | 14,960 |

Suppose a film is shown in half of all the theaters in the United States and in half of all the theaters in China. In how many theaters is the film shown?

A.  1,413

B.  2,182

C.  11,831

D.  14,013

5. Look at the table in Problem 4. How many more theaters are there in the United States than in China and Ukraine combined?

F. 42,986

G. 23,662

H.  8,702

I.  4,338

6. **Explain It** Jacob sleeps for about $8\frac{1}{6}$ hours each night. ESTIMATE to determine about how many hours he sleeps in a month. Explain how you found your answer.

**ALGEBRAIC THINKING**

**7.** After 6 students left the debate team to join the yearbook staff, there were 20 students on the team. Which equation can be used to find *n*, the number of people who were on the team before some left?

**A.** $20 + n = 6$

**B.** $20 - 6 = n$

**C.** $6 + n = 20$

**D.** $n - 6 = 20$

> **TIP** **Check your work.** See item 7.
> Express the equation that you chose in words. Check to make sure that the words make sense and match the problem.

**8.** A grocery store is putting up a display of cans. The bottom row has 47 cans, the second row from the bottom has 39 cans, and the third row from the bottom has 31 cans. If this pattern continues, how many cans will be in the sixth row from the bottom?

**F.** 1

**G.** 7

**H.** 8

**I.** 15

**9. Explain It** What are the missing numbers in this pattern of fractions?

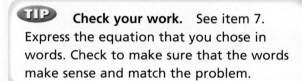
$$\frac{3}{5}, \frac{6}{10}, \frac{9}{15}, \frac{12}{\blacksquare}, \frac{\blacksquare}{25}, \frac{18}{\blacksquare}$$

Explain how the fractions are related.

 **DATA ANALYSIS AND PROBABILITY**

**10.** A jar contains 20 pink, 15 green, 12 blue, and 2 purple jelly beans. Which color jelly bean are you **least likely** to pull from the jar?

**A.** pink

**B.** green

**C.** blue

**D.** purple

**11.** What is the probability that the pointer on the spinner below will land on an odd number?

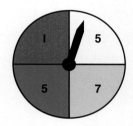

**F.** 0

**G.** $\frac{1}{7}$

**H.** $\frac{1}{5}$

**I.** 1

**12. Explain It** Colleen gathered this data on the high temperature outdoors for five days last week.

| AVERAGE HIGH TEMPERATURE (IN DEGREES F) | | | | |
|------|------|------|------|------|
| Mon | Tue | Wed | Thu | Fri |
| 75 | 82 | 85 | 74 | 75 |

Which type of graph is most appropriate for displaying the data? Explain your choice. Then make a graph of the data.

**≡FAST FACT • SOCIAL STUDIES** The United States government owns 632.7 million acres of land. The National Park System is part of that land. The largest park is Wrangell-St. Elias National Park and Preserve in Alaska. It covers 13,200,000 acres. The smallest park is the Thaddeus Kosciuszko National Memorial in Pennsylvania. It is only 0.02 acre.

**PROBLEM SOLVING** Look at the circle graph. Of the acres that are owned by the government, how many acres are in the National Park System?

**NATIONWIDE ACREAGE**
(Owned and Managed by U.S. Federal Agencies)

Bureau of Land Management
43%

U.S. Forest Service
30%

National Park System
13%

Fish and Wildlife Service
14%

Denali National Park, Alaska

# CHECK WHAT YOU KNOW ✓

Use this page to help you review and remember
important skills needed for Chapter 29.

## ✓ MULTIPLY DECIMALS BY WHOLE NUMBERS

Find the product.

**1.**  $\begin{array}{r} 0.07 \\ \times\quad 5 \\ \hline \end{array}$

**2.**  $\begin{array}{r} 0.29 \\ \times\quad 7 \\ \hline \end{array}$

**3.**  $\begin{array}{r} 0.65 \\ \times\quad 4 \\ \hline \end{array}$

**4.**  $\begin{array}{r} 0.06 \\ \times\quad 3 \\ \hline \end{array}$

**5.**  $\begin{array}{r} \$0.69 \\ \times\quad 8 \\ \hline \end{array}$

**6.**  $\begin{array}{r} \$0.19 \\ \times\quad 5 \\ \hline \end{array}$

**7.**  $\begin{array}{r} \$0.55 \\ \times\quad 9 \\ \hline \end{array}$

**8.**  $\begin{array}{r} \$0.48 \\ \times\quad 2 \\ \hline \end{array}$

## ✓ RELATE FRACTIONS AND DECIMALS

Write a decimal and a fraction for the shaded part.

**9.**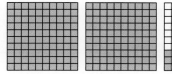

**10.**

**11.**

Write as a decimal.

**12.** $\frac{54}{100}$

**13.** $\frac{36}{100}$

**14.** $\frac{3}{4}$

**15.** $\frac{19}{1,000}$

**16.** $\frac{4}{5}$

Write as a fraction.

**17.** 0.25

**18.** 0.9

**19.** 0.5

**20.** 0.63

**21.** 1.2

# VOCABULARY POWER ✓

**REVIEW**

**ratio** [rā′shē•ō] *noun*

A ratio is the comparison of two numbers.
The word rate is similar in meaning to *ratio*.
A rate is a ratio of two quantities, such as
miles and hours for rate of speed. Name
some ratios or rates that are used in
everyday life.

**PREVIEW**

percent

www.harcourtschool.com/mathglossary

# Understand Percent

 **Explore**

Did you know that fifty percent of the Earth's species live in rain forests? **Percent** means "per hundred." A percent is a ratio of a number to 100. The symbol for percent is %. 1% means "1 out of 100." So, "50% of the Earth's species" means that 50 out of every 100, or $\frac{50}{100}$, species on Earth live in rain forests.

**VOCABULARY**

**percent**

**MATERIALS**
10 × 10 grid paper,
colored pencils

## Activity

Use a grid with 100 squares to model percents.

Out of every 100 known bird species on Earth, 30 live in rain forests. What percent of known bird species live in rain forests?

 **STEP 1**

Let each grid square represent 1 bird species. To show 30 bird species out of 100, shade 30 squares.

**STEP 2**

Write the ratio of shaded squares to the total squares. Then write the percent.

$$\frac{\text{shaded squares}}{\text{total squares}} = \frac{30}{100} = 30\%$$

So, 30% of all known bird species live in rain forests.

• The unshaded squares represent the bird species that do not live in rain forests. What percent of known bird species do not live in rain forests?

## Try It

**Model each ratio on grid paper. Then write the percent.**

a. 42 ducks out of 100 birds

b. 50 lions out of 100 cats

c. 25 puppies out of 100 pets

What model can I make to show 42 ducks out of 100 birds?

Remember, a ratio is a comparison of two numbers. A percent is a special ratio because it always compares a part to 100. Percent is often used with money.

One dollar has 100 parts, or cents. Look at the $10 \times 10$ grid. There is 1 cent, or penny, in each of 100 squares, or a total of $1.00.

1% of $1.00 is 1 penny, or $0.01.

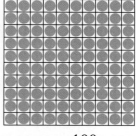

$$100\% = \frac{100}{100} = 1$$

## Talk About It

- What is 50% of $1.00? 10% of $1.00? 76% of $1.00?

- What part of a dollar do you have if you have 0% of it? 100% of it?

- **REASONING** What does 200% of a number mean?

▶ **Practice and Problem Solving**

**Model each ratio on grid paper. Then write the percent.**

**1.** 31 tigers out of 100 animals

**2.** 100 red balls out of 100 balls

**3.** 4 dimes out of $1.00

**4.** 5 blue pens out of 100 pens

**Write a percent to describe the shaded part.**

**5.**

**6.**

**7.**

**8.**

**Choose the more reasonable percent. Write a or b.**

**9.** *"Almost everyone* passed the test," Mrs. Philips said with pride.
   **a.** 95% passed.    **b.** 15% passed.

**10.** *"Very few* children like spicy foods," said the chef.
   **a.** 40% like them.    **b.** 8% like them.

**11. REASONING** A few months ago, Van had 100 days to wait until his birthday. His wait is 98% over. Today is Monday. What day of the week is Van's birthday?

**12. Vocabulary Power** The *cent* in *percent* means "100." Write a list of words that contain *cent*, and explain how their definitions relate to 100.

## Getting Ready for FCAT

**13.** Jeff has the coins shown. What percent of a dollar does Jeff have?

   **A.** 4%       **C.** 45%
   **B.** 40%      **D.** 400%

# 2 Relate Decimals and Percents

▶ **Learn**

**MONEY, MONEY, MONEY!**  A quarter of a dollar can be written as the decimal $0.25.

**MATH IDEA**  You can write a decimal as a percent.

What percent of a dollar is $0.25?

**Write:** 0.25

**Read:** twenty-five hundredths

**Ratio:** 25 out of 100, or $\frac{25}{100}$

**Percent:** 25%

So, $0.25 is 25% of a dollar.

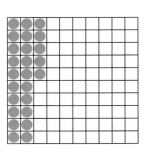

## Examples

**A** Write 0.07 as a percent.

0.07 = 7 out of 100

So, 0.07 is 7%.

**B** Write 90% as a decimal.

90% = 90 out of 100

So, 90% is 0.90, or 0.9.

**C** Write 125% as a decimal.

125% = 125 out of 100

So, 125% is 1.25.

▶ **Check**

1. **Explain** why you can write the decimal in Example B as 0.90 and as 0.9 but you can't write 90% as 9%.

For 2–4, write a decimal and a percent to describe each shaded part of the model.

2. purple squares
3. yellow and blue squares
4. all the shaded squares

The Federal Reserve estimates that $395 million could be saved annually by replacing bills with coins like the Golden Dollar. ▶

**USE DATA** For 5–7, use the circle graph. Write a decimal and a percent to describe each.

HAIR COLORS IN THE U.S.

70% Brown
15% Blond
10% Black
5% Red

5. What part of the population has either brown or black hair?

6. What part of the population does not have red hair?

7. Fifteen hundredths of the population has the same color hair as I do. What color is my hair?

**Write the number as a decimal and a percent.**

8. eighty-one hundredths

9. twelve hundredths

10. thirty-seven hundredths

11. four hundredths

**Write each decimal as a percent.**

12. 0.78    13. 0.99    14. 0.06    15. 0.2    16. 1.2

**Write each percent as a decimal.**

17. 35%    18. 100%    19. 2%    20. 60%    21. 104%

**REASONING** Write the greater number of each pair.

22. 0.5, 5%    23. 0.14, 140%    24. 0.08, 80%    25. 1.9, 19%    26. 2, 2%

27. Out of 100 students in the spelling bee, 23 girls and 28 boys misspelled *aardvark*. What percent of the students spelled the word correctly?

28. **REASONING** Jeb read that 10% of people are left-handed. If he surveys 200 people, about how many left-handers should he expect to find?

29. **≡FAST FACT • SOCIAL STUDIES** In early 2000, a poll found that 75 out of every 100 Americans opposed eliminating the $1 bill and using a $1 coin. What percent was this?

30. Write About It What pattern do you see in the placement of the decimal point when you write a decimal as a percent? a percent as a decimal?

**Getting Ready for FCAT**

31. Lili drew the design at the right. What percent of the squares in Lili's design have Xs?

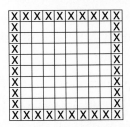

A. 40%
B. 38%
C. 36%
D. 4%

# 3 Fractions, Decimals, and Percents

▶ **Learn**

**DON'T BUG ME!**  There are more beetles on Earth than any other animals. One out of four, or $\frac{1}{4}$, of all animals are beetles. What percent of the animals on Earth are beetles?

You can write a ratio that is in fraction form as a percent.

**One Way**  Write an equivalent fraction with a denominator of 100. Then write the fraction as a percent.

$$\frac{1}{4} = \frac{1 \times 25}{4 \times 25} = \frac{25}{100}$$

$$\frac{25}{100} = 25\%$$

**Another Way**  Divide the numerator by the denominator. Then write the decimal as a percent.

$$\frac{1}{4} \rightarrow 4\overline{)1.00}^{0.25}$$

$$0.25 = 25\%$$

So, 25% of all animals on Earth are beetles.

## Examples

Write each fraction as a percent.

**A**

$$\frac{7}{20} = \frac{7 \times 5}{20 \times 5} = \frac{35}{100}$$

$$\frac{35}{100} = 35\%$$

**B**

$$\frac{4}{5} \rightarrow 5\overline{)4.00}^{0.80}$$

$$0.80 = 80\%$$

**C**

$$\frac{3}{40} \rightarrow 40\overline{)3.000}^{0.075}$$

$$0.075 = 7.5\%$$

• **REASONING**  Which way would you use to write $\frac{1}{8}$ as a percent? Explain your choice.

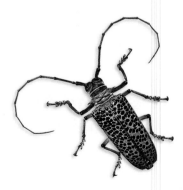

# Percents as Fractions

Scientists estimate that ants make up 10% of the Earth's biomass, the amount of living matter. What fraction of the Earth's biomass are ants?

## Example

You can write a percent as a fraction.

**STEP 1**

Write the percent as a ratio in fraction form. Use the percent as the numerator and 100 as the denominator.

$$10\% = \frac{10}{100}$$

**STEP 2**

Write the fraction in simplest form.

$$\frac{10}{100} = \frac{10 \div 10}{100 \div 10} = \frac{1}{10}$$

So, ants make up $\frac{1}{10}$ of the Earth's biomass.

## More Examples

Write each percent as a fraction in simplest form.

**D** $8\% = \frac{8}{100}$

$$\frac{8}{100} = \frac{8 \div 4}{100 \div 4} = \frac{2}{25}$$

**E** $17\% = \frac{17}{100}$

**F** $155\% = \frac{155}{100}$

$$\frac{155}{100} = \frac{155 \div 5}{100 \div 5} = \frac{31}{20}$$

**MATH IDEA** To show a comparison, you can write a ratio as a fraction, as a decimal, or as a percent.

| Ratio | Fraction | Decimal | Percent |
|-------|----------|---------|---------|
| 25 to 100 | $\frac{25}{100}$, or $\frac{1}{4}$ | 0.25 | 25% |

## Check

1. **Explain** how a fraction, a decimal, and a percent are related. Write $\frac{12}{25}$ as a decimal. Then rewrite your answer as a percent.

**Copy and complete the tables. Write each fraction in simplest form.**

| | Fraction | Decimal | Percent |
|---|----------|---------|---------|
| 2. | $\frac{8}{25}$ | ■ | ■ |
| 4. | ■ | 0.80 | 80% |

| | Fraction | Decimal | Percent |
|---|----------|---------|---------|
| 3. | ■ | 0.04 | ■ |
| 5. | $\frac{147}{100}$ | ■ | 147% |

**LESSON CONTINUES**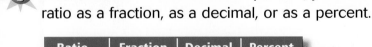

FCAT TESTED  SSS/GLEs MA.A.1.2.4.5.1 Knows that numbers in different forms are equivalent or nonequivalent, using whole numbers, decimals, fractions, mixed numbers, and percents. *also* MA.A.1.2.2.5.3

Chapter 29  **637**

Copy and complete the tables. Write each fraction in simplest form.

| | Fraction | Decimal | Percent |
|---|---|---|---|
| **6.** | ■ | 0.35 | 35% |
| **8.** | ■ | ■ | 20% |
| **10.** | $\frac{1}{20}$ | ■ | ■ |
| **12.** | ■ | 0.60 | 60% |
| **14.** | $\frac{4}{25}$ | ■ | 16% |
| **16.** | $\frac{1}{40}$ | ■ | 2.5% |

| | Fraction | Decimal | Percent |
|---|---|---|---|
| **7.** | $\frac{29}{100}$ | ■ | ■ |
| **9.** | $\frac{3}{50}$ | ■ | ■ |
| **11.** | ■ | 0.11 | ■ |
| **13.** | ■ | 2.0 | ■ |
| **15.** | $\frac{117}{100}$ | ■ | 117% |
| **17.** | $\frac{3}{8}$ | ■ | ■ |

Express the shaded part of each model as a decimal,
a percent, and a fraction in simplest form.

**18.**    **19.**    **20.**    **21.**

**ALGEBRA**  Find the value of each variable. Let *f* represent
a fraction, *d* represent a decimal, and *p* represent a percent.

**22.** $f = 0.20 = 20\%$   **23.** $\frac{1}{4} = d = 25\%$   **24.** $f = 0.4 = 40\%$   **25.** $\frac{1}{2} = d = p$

**26.** $f = 75\% = d$   **27.** $p = \frac{9}{20} = d$   **28.** $f = p = 0.13$   **29.** $d = \frac{9}{10} = p$

Tell whether each fraction or decimal is greater than
100% or between 1% and 100%. Write *greater* or *between*.

**30.** 0.64   **31.** $\frac{24}{50}$   **32.** 2.50   **33.** $\frac{300}{100}$   **34.** $\frac{1}{5}$

**35.** 0.72   **36.** 3.0   **37.** $\frac{35}{50}$   **38.** $\frac{1}{4}$   **39.** $\frac{125}{100}$

**40. NUMBER SENSE**  Ted scored 85% on his
spelling test. Kenya spelled 4 out of 5
words correctly. Rosa scored $\frac{16}{20}$ on the
test. Who got the highest test score?

**41.** At the concert, 100 students performed.
Out of that group, 35% played the flute.
How many students played a different
instrument?

**42.** Sophie misspelled 2 out of 20 words
on her spelling test. What percent of
the words did she spell correctly?

**43.** Zack spent $0.37 for a stamp. Write that
amount as a fraction and a percent of a
dollar.

**44.** ✏ **Write About It** How is writing a percent as a fraction like
writing a decimal as a fraction?

**45.** Mrs. Simms drove 240 miles on Monday and 85% of that distance on Tuesday. How many miles in all did she drive on those two days? Explain your thinking.

**46.** Bill's car uses 0.875 of a tank of gas each week. His car has a 20-gallon tank. Gas costs $1.40 per gallon. How much does he spend each week for gas?

## Getting Ready for FCAT

**47.** Three students got the same grade on a test. One student did not. Who got the different grade?

   **A.** Brett

   **B.** Melissa

   **C.** Eric

   **D.** Lindsay

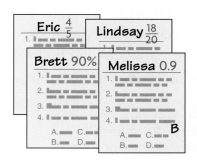

# Problem Solving LiNKUP...to Science

The Earth's outside layer is called the crust, or lithosphere. The name comes from the Greek word *lithos,* meaning "rock." There are different kinds of rocks on the surface, made up of a variety of elements. The graph shows the most common elements in the crust.

The title tells you the subject of the graph.

The whole circle represents the whole crust.

**MAIN COMPONENTS OF THE EARTH'S CRUST**

47% Oxygen

28% Silicon

17% Other Elements

8% Aluminum

Each section of the circle represents one part of the crust. The label for each section names the element that makes up the part of the crust. The size of the section tells you how many parts of the whole it makes up.

**Use the circle graph to solve each problem.**

**1.** Which element composes about $\frac{1}{4}$ of the Earth's crust?

**2.** What fraction of the Earth's crust is composed of aluminum?

**3.** What percent of the Earth's crust is composed of oxygen or silicon?

**4.** The percent of oxygen in Earth's crust is about 2.25 times as great as in the air we breathe. About what percent of the air we breathe is composed of oxygen?

# Compare Fractions, Decimals, and Percents

## Quick Review

**Write as a percent.**

**1.** 0.85    **2.** $\frac{8}{50}$

**3.** $\frac{8}{5}$    **4.** 5.8

**5.** $\frac{5}{8}$

▶ **Learn**

**FIELDER'S CHOICE** Numbers can be written as fractions, decimals, and percents. Whatever their form, they can be compared and ordered.

Compare the fraction $\frac{19}{20}$ with the percent 90%.

**One Way** Write both numbers as fractions with denominators of 100. Then compare the numerators.

$$\frac{19}{20} = \frac{19 \times 5}{20 \times 5} = \frac{95}{100}$$

$$90\% = \frac{90}{100}$$

Since 90 < 95, then 90% < $\frac{19}{20}$.

**Another Way** Write both the fraction and the percent as decimals. Then compare the decimal values.

$$\frac{19}{20} = 19 \div 20 = 0.95$$

$$90\% = \frac{90}{100} = 0.90$$

Since 0.90 < 0.95, then 90% < $\frac{19}{20}$.

## Example

Mike, Marty, and Meg are Florida Marlins fans. Their team has won 24 games and lost 23 games. So, the team's record of wins is just over 50%. The three friends report this record in three different ways.

| | | |
|---|---|---|
| Mike: | 51% | percent |
| Marty: | $\frac{24}{47}$ | fraction |
| Meg: | 0.511 | decimal |

Order these numbers from least to greatest.

Express the percent and the fraction as decimals.

$$51\% = \frac{51}{100} = 0.51 \qquad \frac{24}{47} = 24 \div 47 \approx 0.5106 \qquad \overset{0.5106}{47\overline{)24.0000}}$$

Compare and then order by using the decimal values.

$$0.51 < 0.5106 < 0.511 \qquad \text{So, } 51\% < \frac{24}{47} < 0.511.$$

These same three numbers can be ordered using a number line.

1. **Explain** two different methods for comparing $\frac{7}{20}$ and 36%.

**Compare. Write <, >, or = for each ●.**

2. 20% ● 0.02

3. $\frac{4}{5}$ ● 60%

4. 25% ● $\frac{1}{3}$

5. $\frac{3}{2}$ ● 150%

▶ **Practice and Problem Solving**   Extra Practice, page 648, Set C

**Compare. Write <, >, or = for each ●.**

6. 30% ● 0.30

7. $\frac{3}{10}$ ● 40%

8. 175% ● $\frac{7}{4}$

9. $\frac{6}{10}$ ● 80%

10. 104% ● $\frac{4}{4}$

11. 0.077 ● 77%

12. $\frac{10}{3}$ ● 305%

13. 40% ● $\frac{8}{25}$

14. 1.05 ● 105%

15. 35% ● $\frac{2}{5}$

16. 225% ● 2.025

17. $\frac{5}{8}$ ● 0.625

**Order from least to greatest. You may use a number line.**

18. 65%, 0.59, $\frac{3}{5}$

19. 1.20, 125%, $\frac{3}{4}$

20. 58%, $\frac{5}{8}$, 5.8

21. 3%, 0.003, $\frac{3}{10}$

22. 0.25, $\frac{3}{8}$, 23%

23. $\frac{10}{3}$, 3.20, 325%

24. 16%, 0.6, $\frac{1}{6}$

25. 4.26, $\frac{18}{4}$, 440%

26. **? What's the Error?** 50% of the 120 sixth graders and $\frac{3}{8}$ of the 120 fifth graders walk to school. Bob says the number of students who walk to school is the same for both grades. Find and correct Bob's error.

27. The math test had 25 problems. Beau got 88% of the problems correct, and Sandy got $\frac{23}{25}$ correct. How many more problems did Sandy answer correctly than Beau?

28. **Write About It** Explain how to order $\frac{9}{4}$, 35%, 0.3, and $2\frac{1}{2}$.

29. Kiley wanted to leave 15% of the cost of the meal for the tip. Joe said to leave $\frac{1}{5}$ of the cost and Kim said to leave 0.18 of the cost. Who wants to leave the greatest tip? Explain.

30. **REASONING** Andre has $10 more than Cassie, and Cassie has $5 more than Avery. Altogether they have $50. What percent of the money does Cassie have?

▶ **Getting Ready for FCAT**

31. Gabrielle is playing a card game. She has drawn 3 cards and is trying to put the cards in order from the least number to the greatest number. Which order should she use?

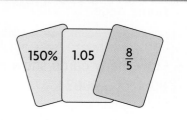

   A. 1.05, $\frac{8}{5}$, 150%

   C. $\frac{8}{5}$, 150%, 1.05

   B. $\frac{8}{5}$, 1.05, 150%

   D. 1.05, 150%, $\frac{8}{5}$

**FCAT TESTED**   SSS/GLEs MA.A.1.2.2.5.3 Compares and orders commonly used fractions, percents, and decimals to thousandths using concrete materials, . . . . also MA.A.1.2.2.5.1

**Chapter 29  641**

# Find a Percent of a Number

 **Learn**

**ZZZZZ . . .** The students in Andrew's science class hope 5,000 people visit their *Sleeptime* home page by the end of the school year. According to the latest tracking report, they have reached 30% of their goal. How many people have visited the home page? What is 30% of 5,000?

**Activity**

Make a model to find 30% of 5,000.
**MATERIALS:** index cards

**STEP 1**

Let each card represent 10% of the number of visitors. Put down 10 cards to represent 100%, or 5,000. Each 10% represents 500 since 10 × 500 = 5,000.

← 5,000 →

| 10% | 10% | 10% | 10% | 10% | 10% | 10% | 10% | 10% | 10% |
|-----|-----|-----|-----|-----|-----|-----|-----|-----|-----|
| 500 | 500 | 500 | 500 | 500 | 500 | 500 | 500 | 500 | 500 |

**STEP 2**

Now separate 3 cards to show 3 × 10%, or 30%.

| 10% | 10% | 10% |   | 10% | 10% | 10% | 10% | 10% | 10% | 10% |
|-----|-----|-----|---|-----|-----|-----|-----|-----|-----|-----|
| 500 | 500 | 500 |   |     |     |     |     |     |     |     |

Since each card represents 500, the 3 cards that make up 30% represent 3 × 500, or 1,500.

So far, 1,500 people have visited the *Sleeptime* home page.

 **Technology Link**

**More Practice:**
Harcourt Mega Math
The Number Games,
*Buggy Bargains,*
Levels Q and R

• How many cards show 50% of 5,000? 80% of 5,000?

## Change the Percent and Multiply

When asleep, the average person dreams about 25% of the time. If you sleep for 9 hours, for how long do you dream?

You can find a percent of a number by changing the percent to a decimal or a fraction and multiplying.

**Example** Find 25% of 9.

**One Way**

| STEP 1 |
|---|
| Change the percent to a decimal. |
| 25% = 0.25 |

| STEP 2 |
|---|
| Multiply the number by the decimal. |
| 0.25 × 9 = 2.25 |
| 25% of 9 equals 2.25. |

**Another Way**

| STEP 1 |
|---|
| Change the percent to a fraction. |
| $25\% = \frac{25}{100}$ |
| $\frac{25}{100} = \frac{25 \div 25}{100 \div 25} = \frac{1}{4}$ |

| STEP 2 |
|---|
| Multiply the number by the fraction. |
| $\frac{1}{4} \times \frac{9}{1} = \frac{9}{4}$, or $2\frac{1}{4}$ |
| 25% of 9 equals $2\frac{1}{4}$. |

So, you dream about 2.25, or $2\frac{1}{4}$, hours on average.

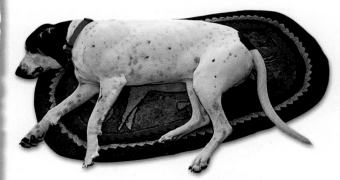

▲ Since everyone dreams for about a quarter of his or her nightly sleep, the total world dream time per night is one million years!

You can also find a percent of a number by using a calculator.

About 12% of people snore. Out of 600 people, how many of them snore?

Find 12% of 600.

          72.

So, about 72 out of 600 people snore.

## ▶ Check

**1. Explain** how to find a percent of a number.

**Find the percent of the number.**

| | | | |
|---|---|---|---|
| **2.** 5% of 80 | **3.** 25% of 64 | **4.** 15% of 120 | **5.** 50% of 92 |
| **6.** 40% of 60 | **7.** 75% of 120 | **8.** 35% of 39 | **9.** 150% of 400 |

**LESSON CONTINUES**

FCAT TESTED    SSS/GLEs MA.A.I.2.3.5.I Translates problem situations into diagrams, models, and numerals using whole numbers, decimals, fractions, mixed numbers, and percents. also MA.A.I.2.4.5.I

Chapter 29  **643**

**Find the percent of the number.**

**10.** 30% of 130

**11.** 15% of 40

**12.** 8% of 44

**13.** 35% of 160

**14.** 90% of 64

**15.** 100% of 15

**16.** 23% of 175

**17.** 200% of 190

**18.** 65% of 100

**19.** 70% of 210

**20.** 40% of 20

**21.** 15% of 60

**22.** 2% of 37

**23.** 60% of 60

**24.** 85% of 42

**25.** 150% of 14

You can find the sales tax for any item you buy by finding a percent of the price. Find the sales tax for each price to the nearest cent.

**26.** price: $25.00
tax rate: 5%

**27.** price: $8.50
tax rate: 4%

**28.** price: $0.99
tax rate: 7%

**29.** price: $198.23
tax rate: 9%

**30.** price: $32.00
tax rate: 7.5%

**31.** price: $1.79
tax rate: 6%

**32.** price: $45.00
tax rate: 8.25%

**33.** price: $79.80
tax rate: 8.5%

**USE DATA**   For 34–37, use the graph.

**34.** On average, how many hours a day does a child sleep?

**35.** On average, how many more hours a day does an infant sleep than an adult over 65?

**36.** On average, how many hours does an adult sleep in a year?

**37.** ✎ **Write a problem** using the information in the graph.

**38.** ❓ **What's the Question?** Karen scored 85% on the test. The test had 20 questions. The answer is 3 questions.

**39.** **REASONING** Eduardo showed Jim 50% of his card collection. If he showed him 25 cards, how many cards does Eduardo have in all?

**40.** **NUMBER SENSE** Tom says that when you find any percent of a number, the answer is always less than the number. Do you agree? Explain.

**41.** On average, a cat sleeps 15.1 hours a day, a dog sleeps 10.6 hours a day, and a guppy sleeps 7.0 hours a day. Order the animals from the smallest percent of the day they sleep to greatest percent they sleep.

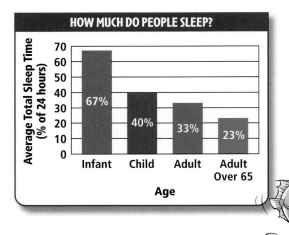

HOW MUCH DO PEOPLE SLEEP?

Average Total Sleep Time (% of 24 hours)

Infant 67% · Child 40% · Adult 33% · Adult Over 65 23%

Age

**42.** Huang is stringing 8-mm beads for a garland. There are about 3.25 beads per inch. How many beads will he need to make a garland 48 inches long?

**43.** Anya won 40% of her 20 games. Linda won 60% of her 15 games. Who won more games?

**44.** 20% of the students in Miss Keddy's fifth grade class are absent today. How many students are absent?

**A.** 6    **B.** 5    **C.** 4    **D.** 3

**45.** 75% of Miss Keddy's class ride the bus. How many students do NOT ride the bus?

**F.** 2    **G.** 3    **H.** 4    **I.** 5

**Miss Keddy's Class List**

| | |
|---|---|
| Avery | Aaron |
| Brittani | Bill |
| Caitlin | Dan |
| Dina | Dante |
| Kim | Enrique |
| Kira | Juan |
| Mia | Marco |
| Nicole | Nate |
| Sophia | Tyler |
| Tori | |
| Yolanda | |

# Problem Solving  Thinker's Corner

**SALE PRICE** Now that you know how to find a percent of a number, you can find the sale price of any item. Follow these steps to find the sale price of a sleeping bag.

Camping Gear Sale

REGULAR PRICE $159.75

Now 30% off

**STEP 1**

Change the percent to a decimal.

30% = 0.30

**STEP 2**

Multiply the regular price by the decimal.

$159.75 × 0.30 = $47.925
$47.93 ← Round to the nearest cent.

**STEP 3**

Subtract the discount from the regular price.

$159.75 − $47.93 = $111.82

So, the sale price is $111.82.

**Find the sale price to the nearest cent.**

**1.** Regular price: $15.00

**2.** Regular price: $17.50

**3.** Regular price: $24.89

20% OFF

Nighty-Night Lullabies

½ OFF

The Dreamer

SAVE 75%

**4.** Describe another way to find the sales price in Exercise 3.

# Problem Solving Strategy
## Make a Graph

**PROBLEM** Sonya surveyed 200 students in her school to find out their favorite type of music. She wants to display her data to show how the votes for each type of music relate to the total number of votes. What is the best way to display her data?

**UNDERSTAND**

- What are you asked to find?
- What information will you use?

**PLAN**

- What strategy can you use to solve the problem?

  You can *make a graph* to display the data, showing the percent of students who prefer each type of music.

**SOLVE**

- What graph would be the best to make?

  Since Sonya wants to show how the parts relate to the whole, a circle graph is best. Divide a circle into ten equal parts. Each part represents 10% of the 200 students. Find the percent of total votes for each type of music.

| Pop Rock | Jazz, Classical, Rap | Country |
|---|---|---|
| $\frac{60}{200} = 30\%$ | $\frac{20}{200} = 10\%$ each | $\frac{80}{200} = 40\%$ |

  Shade the parts to represent each percent. Label and title the graph.

**WHAT TYPE OF MUSIC IS YOUR FAVORITE?**

| Music | Student votes |
|---|---|
| Pop Rock | 60 |
| Jazz | 20 |
| Classical | 20 |
| Rap | 20 |
| Country | 80 |

**CHECK**

- Why is this the best way to display the data?
- What is the sum of the percents that represents the whole, or 200 students?

**WHAT TYPE OF MUSIC IS YOUR FAVORITE?**

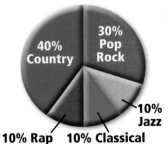

**Strategies**

Draw a Diagram or Picture
Make a Model or Act It Out
Make an Organized List
Find a Pattern
► **Make a Table or Graph**
Predict and Test
Work Backward
Solve a Simpler Problem
Write an Equation
Use Logical Reasoning

**Make a graph to solve.**

1. **What if** 80 of the students liked pop rock, 40 liked country, 20 liked jazz, 40 liked classical, and 20 liked rap? What percent of the vote would pop rock receive? What percent of the vote would all the other types of music receive?

2. Out of $100 for the class trip, Kim spent $\frac{1}{10}$ for food, 20% for museum tickets, $\frac{3}{10}$ for souvenirs, and 40% for the bus ride. Which section of your graph is the largest? How much money does it represent?

**USE DATA** Use the circle graph. Each year people in the United States throw away more than 180 million tons of trash.

3. What fills $\frac{2}{25}$ of the trash?
   **A** paper      **C** yard waste
   **B** plastic    **D** other

4. How much paper goes in the trash in an average month?
   **F** 1 million tons  **H** 6 million tons
   **G** 3 million tons  **J** 72 million tons

**WHAT'S IN THE TRASH?**

40% Paper
18% Yard Waste
11% Other
7% Glass
7% Food Waste
8% Plastic
9% Metal

## Mixed Strategy Practice

**USE DATA** For 5–8, use the table to make a circle graph. There are 50 musicians in the school orchestra.

| WHO PLAYS WHAT INSTRUMENT IN THE SCHOOL ORCHESTRA? | |
|---|---|
| **Section** | **Percent** |
| Strings | 60% |
| Percussion | 10% |
| Brass | 10% |
| Woodwind | 20% |

5. How many musicians play woodwind instruments?

6. How many more musicians play stringed instruments than brass instruments?

7. How many fewer musicians play woodwind instruments than stringed instruments?

8. **What if** there were 100 musicians in the orchestra. How many would play stringed instruments?

9. There are 56 teachers at Sunridge Elementary. Of the teachers, $\frac{1}{4}$ have no pets. Some teachers have one pet, and twice as many teachers have two or more. How many have two or more pets?

10. ✎ **Write About It** Out of 50 students surveyed on favorite national parks, 30 chose Yellowstone, 10 chose Everglades, and 10 Death Valley. Explain how you would display this data.

FCAT TESTED  SSS/GLEs **MA.E.3.2.1.5.3** Creates an appropriate graph to display data, including titles, labels, scales, and intervals. *also* **MA.E.1.2.1.5.5; MA.E.3.2.1.5.1**

Chapter 29 **647**

# Extra Practice

## Set A (pp. 634–635)

**Write the number as a decimal and a percent.**

**1.** six tenths      **2.** two hundredths      **3.** nineteen hundredths

**Write each decimal as a percent.**

**4.** 0.22    **5.** 0.37    **6.** 1.21    **7.** 2.08    **8.** 0.75

**Write each percent as a decimal.**

**9.** 64%    **10.** 25%    **11.** 250%    **12.** 50%    **13.** 10%

## Set B (pp. 636–639)

**For 1–4, copy and complete the tables.**
**Write each fraction in simplest form.**

| | FRACTION | DECIMAL | PERCENT |
|---|---|---|---|
| **1.** | $\frac{3}{5}$ | ▦ | 60% |
| **3.** | ▦ | ▦ | 10% |

| | FRACTION | DECIMAL | PERCENT |
|---|---|---|---|
| **2.** | ▦ | ▦ | 40% |
| **4.** | $\frac{1}{20}$ | ▦ | ▦ |

**5.** Shawn scored 30% of the points. Mike scored 30 points out of 100. Jeff scored $\frac{2}{5}$ of the points. Who scored the most points?

## Set C (pp. 640–641)

**Compare. Write <, >, or = for each ●.**

**1.** 60% ● 0.50    **2.** $\frac{4}{6}$ ● 60%    **3.** $\frac{4}{3}$ ● 135%    **4.** $\frac{7}{10}$ ● 70%

**5.** 95% ● $\frac{9}{10}$    **6.** 0.045 ● 45%    **7.** $\frac{5}{2}$ ● 250%    **8.** 24% ● $\frac{1}{4}$

**Order from least to greatest. You may use a number line.**

**9.** 25%, 0.23, $\frac{1}{5}$    **10.** 0.40, 39%, $\frac{3}{5}$    **11.** 105%, $\frac{6}{5}$, 1.5    **12.** 2%, 0.20, $\frac{1}{10}$

**13.** 0.75, $\frac{4}{5}$, 70%    **14.** $\frac{12}{5}$, 2.50, 205%    **15.** 12%, 0.20, $\frac{11}{100}$    **16.** 3.25, $\frac{14}{4}$, 320%

## Set D (pp. 642–645)

**Find the percent of the number.**

**1.** 10% of 10    **2.** 12% of 75    **3.** 150% of 130    **4.** 70% of 65

**5.** 20% of 50    **6.** 100% of 97    **7.** 25% of 300    **8.** 40% of 80

**9.** Mark got 70% out of 80 questions correct and Richard got 80% out of 70 questions correct. Who got more correct?

**10.** Julie found a quarter, 2 dimes, and 4 pennies in her coat pocket. What percent of a dollar did she find?

# Review/Test

##  CHECK VOCABULARY AND CONCEPTS

Choose the best term from the box.

> decimal
> percent
> product
> ratio

1. You can write a __?__ as a fraction, a decimal, or a percent. (p. 636)

2. A ratio of a number to 100 is a __?__. (p. 632)

3. You can find a percent of a number by changing a percent to a __?__ and multiplying. (p. 643)

**Model each ratio on grid paper. Then write the percent.**
(pp. 632–633)

4. 27 tiles out of 100 tiles

5. 8 bats out of 100 bats

6. 49 balls out of 100 balls

##  CHECK SKILLS

**Write each decimal as a percent.** (pp. 634–635)

7. 0.35

8. 0.75

9. 0.49

10. 1.23

**Copy and complete the tables. Write each fraction in simplest form.** (pp. 636–639)

11.

| Fraction | Decimal | Percent |
|----------|---------|---------|
| ■        | 0.20    | ■       |

12.

| Fraction | Decimal | Percent |
|----------|---------|---------|
| ■        | ■       | 43%     |

**Compare. Write <, >, or = for each ●.** (pp. 640–641)

13. 10% ● 0.01

14. $\frac{3}{4}$ ● 80%

15. 125% ● $1\frac{1}{3}$

16. 2.09 ● 209%

**Order from least to greatest.** (pp. 640–641)

17. 0.25, 24%, $\frac{3}{8}$

18. 60%, $\frac{2}{3}$, 0.62

19. $\frac{5}{2}$, 248%, 2.6

**Find the percent of the number.** (pp. 642–645)

20. 6% of 50

21. 200% of 75

22. 15% of 345

23. 99% of 99

##  CHECK PROBLEM SOLVING

For 24–25, make a circle graph to solve.
120 students were surveyed. (pp. 646–647)

| FAVORITE BEVERAGES | | | | |
|---|---|---|---|---|
| **Beverage** | Water | Milk | Soda | Juice |
| **Student votes** | 12 | 36 | 48 | 24 |

24. What percent of the students liked soda the best?

25. What percent of the students liked milk the best?

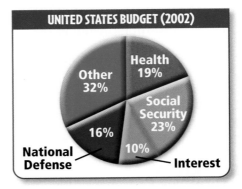

# Getting Ready for FCAT

## NUMBER SENSE, CONCEPTS, AND OPERATIONS

> **TIP** **Get the information you need.**
> See item 1. You need to find what part of the total number of students is studying Italian. Write a fraction to represent this.

1. Brendan made a chart to show the languages that the 24 students in his fifth-grade class are studying.

| LANGUAGE STUDY | |
|---|---|
| **Language** | **Number of Students** |
| Spanish | 12 |
| French | 8 |
| Italian | 4 |

What fraction of the students in his class study Italian?

A. $\frac{1}{6}$     C. $\frac{1}{3}$

B. $\frac{1}{4}$     D. $\frac{1}{2}$

2. About 70% of the students at Jamie's school ride a bus to school. Which of the following is NOT equivalent to 70%?

F. 0.07

G. 0.7

H. $\frac{70}{100}$

I. $\frac{7}{10}$

3. **Explain It** Kelly's lunch bill was $9.89. She wants to leave a 15% tip. ESTIMATE to determine how much she should leave for a tip. Explain how you found your estimate.

## DATA ANALYSIS AND PROBABILITY

4. What percent of the United States budget for 2002 was spent on health and Social Security?

**UNITED STATES BUDGET (2002)**

Other 32%, Health 19%, Social Security 23%, Interest 10%, National Defense 16%

A. 13%     C. 32%

B. 19%     D. 42%

5. Use the circle graph in Problem 4. What percent of the budget is NOT spent on national defense?

F. 84%     H. 70%

G. 75%     I. 67%

6. **Explain It** The table shows the results of a survey of 100 travelers who were asked to name a continent they have visited.

| SURVEY OF TRAVELERS | |
|---|---|
| **Continent** | **Number of Travelers** |
| Africa | 10 |
| Asia | 20 |
| Australia | 10 |
| Europe | 40 |
| South America | 20 |

What type of graph would be best to display this data? Explain your choice and how you would make the graph.

**ALGEBRAIC THINKING**

**7.** Marcy made a pattern with dots.

If the pattern continues, how many dots should she draw below the line if there are 6 dots above the line?

**A.** 6

**B.** 12

**C.** 18

**D.** 24

**8.** A bus stops at the corner of Main Street and First Avenue every 20 minutes.

If the first bus stops at 7:00 A.M., at what time does the seventh bus stop?

**F.** 7:20 A.M.

**G.** 8:40 A.M.

**H.** 9:00 A.M.

**I.** 9:20 A.M.

**9. Explain It** Carlton wrote a pattern of numbers.

3, 6, 4, 7, 5, 8, 6, 9,

What is a rule for the pattern? What could be the next number in the pattern? Explain how you found your rule.

 **MEASUREMENT**

**10.** Which figure has the greatest volume?

**A.**

**B.**

**C.**

**D.**

**11.** The diagram below shows the actual size of a large paper clip. Which of the following best describes the length of this paper clip?

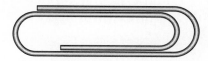

**F.** 5 kilometers

**G.** 5 meters

**H.** 5 centimeters

**I.** 5 millimeters

**12. Explain It** Scott is putting boxes that each hold a baseball into a carton. ESTIMATE to determine how many boxes will fit in the carton. Explain how you found your estimate.

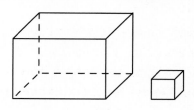

# Probability

**FAST FACT** • SOCIAL STUDIES Pachisi is a game of chance that is the national game of India. The players toss cowrie shells and move pieces around a gameboard according to how the shells land.

**PROBLEM SOLVING** Sometimes winning a game depends on chance, and sometimes it depends on skill and strategy. Look at the games in the photos. Tell whether each is a game of chance or one of skill and strategy.

| | |
|---|---|
| 4000 B.C. | **Babylonian board game played that was ancestor of chess and checkers** |
| 3000 B.C. | **Backgammon played in ancient Sumeria** |
| 2000 B.C. | **Egyptians played game like modern-day checkers** |
| 1000 B.C. | |
| B.C. A.D. | |
| | **Pachisi played in India** |
| A.D. 1000 | **Mah-Jongg first played in China** |
| | **A modern version of Pachisi first played in 1959** |
| A.D. 2000 | **Computer games first played in 1970's** |

# CHECK WHAT YOU KNOW

Use this page to help you review and remember important skills needed for Chapter 30.

## IMPOSSIBLE, CERTAIN, LIKELY, UNLIKELY

Classify each event as *certain, impossible, likely,* or *unlikely.*

1. pulling a red counter from a bag containing only blue counters

2. pulling a yellow marble from a bag of 9 yellow and 2 green marbles

3. becoming warmer in front of a fire

4. going to the planet Jupiter on a family vacation

5. tossing a 3 on a cube labeled 1, 1, 1, 2, 2, 3

6. spinning an odd number on a spinner labeled 1, 3, 5, and 7

7. pulling a blue or red marble from a bag of 3 blue, 5 red, and 2 green marbles

8. spinning an even number on a spinner with equal sections labeled 1, 3, 5, 6, 7, and 9

## PARTS OF A WHOLE

Write a fraction that names the shaded part.

9.        10.        11.

12.       13.        14.

# VOCABULARY POWER

## REVIEW

**unlikely** [un•līk′lē] *adverb*

The prefix *im-* or *un-* can be used to form a new word by adding "not" to the meaning of a word.

*im + possible = impossible,* which means "not possible"

Write a sentence with *likely.* Then write a sentence with *unlikely.*

## PREVIEW

probability
possible outcomes
sample space
theoretical probability
equally likely

experimental probability
tree diagram
arrangement
combination

www.harcourtschool.com/mathglossary

# HANDS ON

# Probability Experiments

## ► Explore

Mark conducted an experiment. He put 5 red, 3 green, and 2 yellow tiles into a bag and pulled samples without looking. He predicted that half of his pulls would be red.

**Probability** is the chance that an event will happen. In Mark's experiment, the events are the colors. The three different events are red, green, yellow.

In his experiment, Mark pulled a tile from the bag 10 times, replacing the tile after each pull. He pulled 6 red tiles in 10 tries. Based on these results, the probability of pulling a red tile would be 6 out of 10.

| COLOR-TILE EXPERIMENT | | | |
|---|---|---|---|
| Event | Yellow | Red | Green |
| Frequency | | | |
| Total | | | |

**Conduct the same experiment as Mark. Place 5 red, 3 green, and 2 yellow tiles in the bag.**

- Make a table like the one shown.
- Pull a tile without looking. Record your pull in the table with a tally mark. Repeat 10 times. Replace the tile after each pull. Total your tally marks in the table.
- Based upon your results, what would you predict for the probability of pulling a red tile? Explain.

## Try It

**Use a bag with 6 blue, 2 red, and 2 yellow tiles.**

a. If you pull 1 tile from the bag, what color do you think it will be?

b. Make a prediction about the probability of pulling a yellow tile.

c. Make your own table. Pull, record, and replace a tile 10 times. How do your results compare with your prediction above?

*If you pull out 1 tile, what color do you think it will be?*

Look back at Mark's experiment. Predict how many times out of 100 he would pull red. Since half of the tiles are red, a good prediction is 50 pulls.

Mark and nine other students recorded their results.

**Technology Link**

**More Practice:** Harcourt Mega Math Fraction Action, *Last Chance Canyon*, Level I

| COLOR-TILE EXPERIMENT (100 Pulls) | | | | | | | | | | | |
|---|---|---|---|---|---|---|---|---|---|---|---|
| Students | A | B | C | D | E | F | G | H | I | J | Total |
| Red Pulls | 4 | 6 | 4 | 7 | 5 | 4 | 6 | 7 | 5 | 4 | 52 |
| Yellow Pulls | 2 | 2 | 3 | 1 | 2 | 2 | 1 | 1 | 3 | 2 | 19 |
| Green Pulls | 4 | 2 | 3 | 2 | 3 | 4 | 3 | 2 | 2 | 4 | 29 |

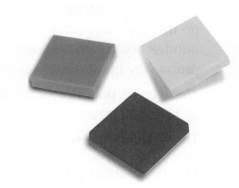

With nine other classmates, make a table for 10 pulls each, and find the totals.

- How do your group's actual results compare to the prediction for pulling red? To the results of other groups?

## ▶ Practice and Problem Solving

1. Justin pulls a marble from a bag of marbles 20 times. He pulls 7 blue marbles. Predict the probability of pulling a blue marble.

2. Kristin pulls a tile from a bag of tiles 15 times. She pulls 10 red tiles. Predict the probability of pulling a tile that is not red.

3. Half of the marbles in Jackson's bag are his favorite color, orange. If he pulls 12 marbles, how many do you predict will be orange?

4. Jonathan has a bag with 25 tiles. Fifteen of the tiles are red. Predict the probability of Jonathan pulling a red tile.

5. **USE DATA** Kyla pulls a tile from a bag 30 different times. Based on these results, what are the chances that neither the most likely nor the least likely color is pulled?

| EVENT | RED | GREEN | YELLOW |
|---|---|---|---|
| Number of pulls | ЖΙΙΙ | ЖΙΙ | Ж Ж Ж |
| Total | 8 | 7 | 15 |

6. Ben is making a sandbox for his brother. He has 12 ft of wood for the sides. He wants the sandbox to have the greatest area possible. What will be the dimensions and area of the sandbox?

## Getting Ready for ★FCAT

7. Leah pulls a marble from a bag 40 different times. Based on the results in her table, what are the chances of pulling a red marble on the next pull?

   **A.** 9 out of 40       **C.** 16 out of 40

   **B.** 15 out of 40      **D.** 17 out of 40

| Marble Color | Number of Pulls |
|---|---|
| Yellow | 15 |
| Red | 16 |
| Blue | 9 |

# Probability Expressed as a Fraction

▶ **Learn**

**SPINNER WINNER!** Ami draws a card and spins the pointer on the spinner below. She wins if the pointer stops on a number that matches what is shown on the card. What is the probability that the pointer stops on a number greater than 5?

There are 8 **possible outcomes**, or results. The **sample space**, or set of all possible outcomes, is 1, 2, 3, 4, 5, 6, 7, 8.

Three outcomes, 6, 7, 8, are greater than 5.

The **theoretical probability** of an event is a comparison of the number of favorable outcomes to the number of possible, equally likely outcomes. **Equally likely** outcomes have the same chance of happening. You can write theoretical probability as a fraction.

$$\frac{\text{Probability}}{\text{of an event}} = \frac{\text{number of favorable outcomes}}{\text{number of possible, equally likely outcomes}}$$

$$\frac{\text{Probability}}{\text{of a win}} = \frac{\text{number of choices greater than 5}}{\text{number of choices on the spinner}} = \frac{3}{8}$$

So, the probability that the pointer stops on a number greater than 5 is $\frac{3}{8}$.

The probability of an event can always be expressed as 0, 1, or a fraction between 0 and 1.

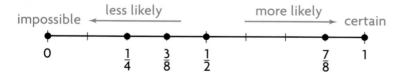

### Quick Review

Write in simplest form.

1. $\frac{10}{12}$     2. $\frac{9}{15}$

3. $\frac{8}{24}$     4. $\frac{14}{18}$

5. $\frac{12}{16}$

### VOCABULARY

**possible outcomes**
**sample space**
**theoretical probability**
**equally likely**

Greater than 5

---

**Examples** Find the probability of each event. Use Ami's spinner.

**A** | 2, 3, 5, or 7

4 out of 8 — Express the probability using words.

$\frac{4}{8}$, or $\frac{1}{2}$ — Express the probability as a fraction.

**B** | an integer

1, 2, 3, 4, 5, 6, 7, 8 — List the integers.

8 out of 8

$\frac{8}{8}$, or 1 — Express the probability using words and as a fraction.

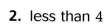

## Check

1. **Explain** how to use this spinner to find the probability that the event is a multiple of 3.

**Use the spinner above to write a fraction for the probability of each event.**

2. less than 4

3. greater than $\frac{1}{2}$

4. factor of 28

5. prime number

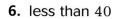

## Practice and Problem Solving   Extra Practice, page 666, Set A

**Use the spinner at the right to write a fraction for the probability of each event.**

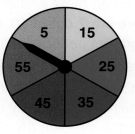

6. less than 40

7. a prime number

8. a factor of 100

9. between 15 and 25

10. a composite number

11. an integer greater than 40

**Write a fraction for the probability of each event with a number cube labeled 1 to 6.**

12. 2 or 3

13. 0 or 1

14. a prime number

15. not 6

16. **Vocabulary Power** In mathematics, an *outcome* is a possible result. Name two ways the word *outcome* is used outside of mathematics.

17. Write the sample space for tossing a number cube labeled 1 to 6.

18. Without looking, Jo pulled a marble from the bag at the right. Using a number line from 0 to 1, order the events *red, yellow or blue, not green, orange* by their probabilities.

19. ✏ **Write a problem** involving probability and a spinner with six equal-size sections. Three sections are red, two sections are blue, and one section is green.

## Getting Ready for FCAT

20. Ken placed six green and four blue marbles into a bag. If he chooses one marble at random, what is the probability of choosing a blue marble?

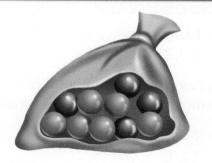

A. $\frac{1}{5}$

C. $\frac{3}{5}$

B. $\frac{2}{5}$

D. $\frac{2}{3}$

FCAT TESTED  SSS/GLEs MA.E.2.2.1.5.3 Calculates the probability of a particular event occurring from a set of all possible outcomes. *also* MA.E.2.2.2.5.2

Chapter 30  **657**

# Probability and Predictions

## ▶ Learn

**FRACTION ACTION** Vicki has a favorite video game. She won 7 of the first 10 games she played. Use a fraction to predict her chances of winning the next game.

Based on these results, Vicki's chances of winning the next game are 7 out of 10, or $\frac{7}{10}$. As she plays more games, she might get better at winning, so this probability may change.

The **experimental probability** of an event can be found by conducting repeated trials. Compare the number of times a certain event actually occurs to the total number of trials, or times you repeat the activity.

$$\text{Experimental probability} = \frac{\text{number of times event occurs}}{\text{total number of trials}}$$

You can use experimental probability to predict future events.

**Quick Review**

Find the product.

**1.** $\frac{1}{2} \times 36$    **2.** $\frac{2}{3} \times 24$

**3.** $\frac{5}{8} \times 40$    **4.** $\frac{3}{5} \times 60$

**5.** $\frac{3}{4} \times 300$

**VOCABULARY**

**experimental probability**

## Example

Vicki's sister, Becky, won 2 of the first 5 video games she played. Based on these results, how many times can Becky expect to win in her next 20 games?

| | |
|---|---|
| $\text{Probability of winning} = \frac{\text{number of wins}}{\text{total number of games}} = \frac{2}{5}$ | Find the experimental probability based on the games already played. |
| $\frac{2}{5} \times \frac{20}{1} = \frac{40}{5}$, or 8. | Multiply by 20, the number of new games to be played. |

So, Becky can expect to win 8 of her next 20 games.

## ▶ Check

1. **Explain** how to predict the number of wins in 100 games if the experimental probability of winning is $\frac{3}{10}$.

**Express the experimental probability as a fraction. Use it to predict the same event in future trials.**

2. 5 wins in 6 games
   12 more games

3. 4 heads in 7 tosses
   14 more tosses

4. 8 red tiles in 12 pulls
   6 more pulls

**Technology Link**

More Practice: Harcourt Mega Math Fraction Action, *Last Chance Canyon,* Level J

The probability of winning is $\frac{9}{20}$. Predict the number of wins.

**5.** in 60 games

**6.** in 100 games

**7.** in 240 games

**8.** in 120 games

**9.** in 180 games

**10.** in 360 games

**Express the experimental probability as a fraction. Use it to predict the same event in future trials.**

**11.** 3 wins in 4 games
8 more games

**12.** 2 heads in 6 tosses
12 more tosses

**13.** 4 red tiles in 5 pulls
25 more pulls

**14.** 3 losses in 6 games
10 more games

**15.** 4 tails in 12 tosses
6 more tosses

**16.** 8 blue tiles in 12 pulls
3 more pulls

**17. USE DATA** Use the coin toss table at the right to find the experimental probability of tossing heads. How does it compare with the theoretical probability of $\frac{1}{2}$?

| COIN TOSS EXPERIMENT ||
|---|---|
| **Outcome** | **Times Tossed** |
| **Heads** | 47 |
| **Tails** | 53 |

**Ken searches through the first 100 letters in a newspaper article and finds 13 e's. Use this information for Exercises 18–20.**

**18.** Find the experimental probability that a randomly chosen letter is an *e*.

**19.** How many *e*'s would you predict in the first 800 letters of this article?

**20. REASONING** The entire newspaper article contains 916 words. Each word has an average of 5 letters. Predict the total number of *e*'s in the entire article.

**21.** Nancy has $23.75 in quarters and Lynn has $5.85 in nickels. Who has more coins? Explain.

**22.** Holly takes $\frac{1}{2}$ hour to walk to school. She spends $\frac{1}{2}$ of that time walking down her street. What part of an hour does Holly spend walking down her street? How many minutes is this?

**23.** **? What's the Question?** In a random survey of 100 students at Holt School, 30 students chose cats as their favorite pet. There are 500 students at Holt School. The answer is 150.

**Getting Ready for FCAT**

**24.** Eve tossed a number cube labeled 1 to 6 and recorded the results in the table. In the next 6 tosses, how many even numbers should she expect to toss?

| NUMBER CUBE EXPERIMENT ||
|---|---|
| **Outcome** | **Times Tossed** |
| Odd | 8 |
| Even | 4 |

**A.** 1

**C.** 4

**B.** 2

**D.** 6

FCAT TESTED  SSS/GLEs MA.E.2.2.2.5.2 Explains and predicts which outcomes are most likely to occur and expresses the probabilities as fractions. *also* MA.E.2.2.1.5.3

Chapter 30  **659**

# Tree Diagrams

▶ **Learn**

**TEXT TYPE** Nadine needs to choose a type font and size for her poster notes. The 3 fonts she has are Courier, Helvetica, and Times. The 4 sizes are 9 point, 10 point, 12 point, and 14 point. How many choices of fonts and sizes combined does she have?

**One Way** You can use a **tree diagram** to organize and show all possible choices or outcomes.

| Fonts | Sizes | Choices |
|---|---|---|
| Courier | 9 pt | Courier font in 9 point |
| | 10 pt | Courier font in 10 point |
| | 12 pt | Courier font in 12 point |
| | 14 pt | Courier font in 14 point |
| Helvetica | 9 pt | Helvetica font in 9 point |
| | 10 pt | Helvetica font in 10 point |
| | 12 pt | Helvetica font in 12 point |
| | 14 pt | Helvetica font in 14 point |
| Times | 9 pt | Times font in 9 point |
| | 10 pt | Times font in 10 point |
| | 12 pt | Times font in 12 point |
| | 14 pt | Times font in 14 point |

Count the number of choices. Nadine has 12 different font-and-size choices.

**Another Way** You can find the number of choices or outcomes by multiplying.

| Number of type fonts | | Number of type sizes | | Number of choices |
|---|---|---|---|---|
| ↓ | | ↓ | | ↓ |
| 3 | × | 4 | = | 12 |

• Would the number of outcomes be different if you listed size first and font second?

 **MATH IDEA** You can use a tree diagram to organize and show a list of all possible choices. You can multiply to find the number of choices.

1. **Explain** how the outcomes would change if Nadine could choose from 5 type fonts but only 3 type sizes.

**For 2–3, make a tree diagram to show the possible choices.**

2. **School Outfits**
   **Pants:** tan, blue, black
   **Shirts:** white, brown, blue

3. **Room Decorating Choices**
   **Paint:** white, blue, pink
   **Borders:** wallpaper, stencils
   **Windows:** blinds, curtains

**Practice and Problem Solving** ( Extra Practice, page 666, Set C )

**For 4–5, make a tree diagram to show the possible choices.**

4. **Summer School Classes**
   **Subject:** art, math, music, computers
   **Session:** first, second

5. **Sandwich Selections**
   **Peanut Butter:** smooth, chunky
   **Jelly:** grape, peach, apricot
   **Bread:** white, whole wheat

6. Ben can buy only one book. His choices are mystery, biography, or science fiction. He can choose hardback or paperback. How many choices does Ben have?

7. Chris has packed 4 shirts and 3 pairs of shorts for his trip. How many more shirt-and-shorts choices will he have if he packs another shirt and another pair of shorts?

8. Milo and Jill are playing a game. Milo chooses one letter from the word COMPUTER and one from MOUSE. How many choices does he have?

9. Jill chooses one letter from the word MATH and one from MUSIC. How many choices does she have? How many do not contain M?

10. For her notes, Nadine can choose single or double spacing and plain, bold, or italic type. How many choices of spacing and type does Nadine have?

11.  **ALGEBRA** The numbers of different choices for shirts and slacks are *x* and *y*. Write an expression to show how many shirt-and-slacks outfits can be made.

**Getting Ready for FCAT** | THINK SOLVE EXPLAIN

12. A make-your-own-sundae bar offers the choices shown. Make a tree diagram to show how many different sundaes can be made when choosing one item from each category.

| SUNDAE BAR | | |
|---|---|---|
| **Ice Cream** | **Syrup** | **Topping** |
| Vanilla | Chocolate | Nuts |
| Chocolate | Butterscotch | Sprinkles |
| Swirl | | |

**FCAT TESTED** SSS/GLEs MA.E.2.2.1.5.2 Represents all possible outcomes for a simple probability situation or event using models such as organized lists, charts, or tree diagrams.

**Chapter 30** **661**

# Arrangements and Combinations

**Quick Review**

Find the product.

1. $1 \times 2 \times 3$
2. $1 \times 2 \times 3 \times 4 \times 5$
3. $1 \times 2 \times 3 \times 4$
4. $1 \times 3 \times 5 \times 7 \times 9$
5. $2 \times 4 \times 6 \times 8$

▶ **Learn**

**BUG BITES** Jon is making a poster for a science report on bugs. He wants to have three pictures in a row, showing a fly, a bee, and a mosquito. How many different arrangements are possible?

In this problem, the order of the pictures is important. An **arrangement** is an ordering of items.

**VOCABULARY**

**arrangement**
**combination**

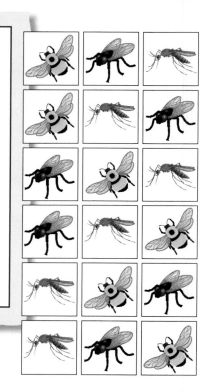

**One Way** Make an organized list of all possible arrangements.

This list is organized in alphabetical order using the first letter of the name of each bug.

> BFM    BMF    FBM    FMB    MBF    MFB

**Another Way** Multiply to find the total number of arrangements.

**Think:** What choices are available for the three positions?

| 3 choices for the first picture | 2 choices remain for the second | 1 choice left for the third |
|:---:|:---:|:---:|

$$3 \quad \times \quad 2 \quad \times \quad 1 \quad = 6$$

So, there are 6 possible arrangements.

A **combination** is a choice in which the order of the items does not matter.

## Example

In his report, Jon has time to talk about only 2 of the bugs. How many combinations of 2 bugs are possible?

Make an organized list of all possible combinations. Do not include pairs that reverse the ones already listed.

bee and fly
bee and mosquito
fly and mosquito

**Think:** The pairs "bee and fly" and "fly and bee" represent the same combination.

So, Jon has 3 possible combinations of 2 bugs.

1. **Explain** how to find the number of arrangements possible if Jonathan puts 4 different pictures in a row instead of 3.

**For 2–3, use the letters L, E, G.**

2. List the 6 two-letter arrangements that are possible.

3. List the 3 combinations, or choices, of two letters that are possible.

▷ **Practice and Problem Solving** ( Extra Practice, page 666, Set D )

**For 4–5, use the digits in 9,631.**

4. List the 12 two-digit arrangements that are possible.

5. List the 6 combinations, or choices, of two digits that are possible.

6. In how many different ways can a penny, nickel, and dime be stacked, face-up, one on top of the other?

7. List the combinations, or choices, of two letters that are possible using the letters in the word METRIC.

**Each card has a different arrangement of the letters in the word BUG. One card is chosen at random. Find the probability of each event.**

8. The letters are in alphabetical order.

9. The letter U is the middle letter.

10. The letters B and G are together.

11. The letter B comes before the letter G.

UGB
BUG   UBG
GBU
BGU
GUB

12. **═FAST FACT • SCIENCE** There are about 248,000 different kinds of plants. About 9 out of every 10 are flowering plants. About how many non-flowering plants are there?

13. **? What's the Error?** June has a bag of 99 blue tiles and 1 red tile. June says that it is certain she will pull a blue tile from the bag. Describe her error and write the correct answer.

**Getting Ready for FCAT**

14. Four students each made a list of the combinations of two letters from the word *MATH*. Which student is correct?

   A. Alana
   B. Bruce
   C. Cody
   D. Diana

| Alana | MA, AT, TH, HM |
|-------|----------------|
| Bruce | MA, MT, MH, AT, AH, TH |
| Cody | MA, MT, MH |
| Diana | MA, MT, MH, AT, AH, HT, MAT, MAH, MTH, ATH |

FCAT TESTED ↘ SSS/GLEs MA.E.2.2.1.5.1 Determines the number of possible combinations of given items and displays them in an organized way. *also* MA.E.2.2.1.5.3

**Chapter 30 663**

# Problem Solving Strategy
## Make an Organized List

**PROBLEM** Selena likes number games. She designed this game using a number cube and a coin.

A player tosses a number cube and a coin. The score is determined by using these rules. If the coin lands heads up, multiply the number by itself. If the coin lands tails up, add the number to itself. A winning result is a score of 10 or more. What is the probability of winning Selena's game?

### UNDERSTAND

• What are you asked to find?

• What information will you use?

### PLAN

• What strategy can you use to solve the problem?

You can *make an organized list* of all the possible outcomes.

### SOLVE

• How can you use the strategy to solve the problem?

You can make a tree diagram to list all the possible outcomes.

There are 12 possible outcomes. Only 5 of these outcomes result in a score of 10 or more. So, the probability of winning is 5 out of 12, or $\frac{5}{12}$.

```
Cube  Coin  Score    Result
 1  < H   1×1=1      loss
    < T   1+1=2      loss
 2  < H   2×2=4      loss
    < T   2+2=4      loss
 3  < H   3×3=9      loss
    < T   3+3=6      loss
 4  < H   4×4=16     win
    < T   4+4=8      loss
 5  < H   5×5=25     win
    < T   5+5=10     win
 6  < H   6×6=36     win
    < T   6+6=12     win
```

### CHECK

• How can you check your answer?

## Strategies

Draw a Diagram or Picture
Make a Model or Act It Out
**Make an Organized List**
Find a Pattern
Make a Table or Graph
Predict and Test
Work Backward
Solve a Simpler Problem
Write an Equation
Use Logical Reasoning

**Problem Solving**

**Make an organized list to solve.**

1. **What if** Selena's rules were changed so that you won if the score was a multiple of 3? How would the probability change? Would you be more or less likely to win?

2. Pauline plays Selena's game with a number cube labeled 2 to 7. What is the probability of winning with this new number cube?

**Marcus is conducting a probability experiment by tossing a coin and taking 1 marble from the bag below. Marcus will replace the marble after each turn.**

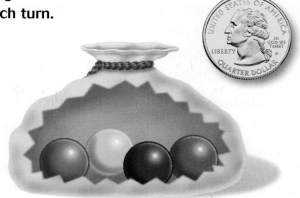

3. How many possible outcomes are there for this experiment?

   **A** 4        **B** 6        **C** 8        **D** 16

4. What is the probability that Marcus will choose a red marble and toss heads?

   **F** $\frac{1}{2}$        **G** $\frac{1}{4}$        **H** $\frac{1}{6}$        **J** $\frac{1}{8}$

## Mixed Strategy Practice

5. After school, Li rode his bike to the library. The ride took 10 minutes. He stayed there for 2 hours and 10 minutes. Riding home took another 35 minutes. If Li got home at 5:15 P.M., at what time did he leave school?

6. Sam stacks 4 cubes, one on top of another, to make a plant stand. He paints the outside of the stand blue, but not the bottom. How many faces of the original cubes are painted?

7. Alexandra has $0.30 more than Barbara. Together they have $4.50. How much money does each girl have?

8. Marshall has 15¢. How many combinations of coins could he have? What are they?

9. The drawing shows 1-square-foot tiles around a fish pond. What is the area that will be tiled?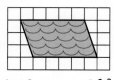

   **Let 1 square = 1 ft²**

10. **REASONING** How many arrangements of the letters in the word FLORIDA start with an F and end with an A? Explain.

FCAT TESTED  SSS/GLEs MA.E.2.2.1.5.2 Represents all possible outcomes for a simple probability situation or event using models such as organized lists, charts, or tree diagrams. *also* MA.E.2.2.1.5.1

**Chapter 30  665**

# Extra Practice

## Set A (pp. 656–657)

**Write the probability of the pointer landing on each color.**

1. green
2. purple or yellow
3. white
4. purple, green, or yellow

5. Mark has a bag of fruit candy. Of the candies, 5 are strawberry, 4 are grape, and 1 is apple. What is the probability that Mark will pick grape?

6. If you toss one coin and roll one number cube, how many outcomes are possible? What is the probability that the result will include heads?

## Set B (pp. 658–659)

**Express the experimental probability as a fraction. Use it to predict the same event in future trials.**

1. 6 wins in 8 games
   4 more games
2. 4 heads in 8 tosses
   6 more tosses
3. 3 red tiles in 5 pulls
   10 more pulls

**The probability of winning is $\frac{2}{5}$. Predict the number of wins.**

4. in 20 games
5. in 75 games
6. in 100 games

## Set C (pp. 660–661)

**For 1–2, make a tree diagram to show the possible choices.**

1. **Lunch Menu**

   **Entree:** sandwich, hot dog, or hamburger
   **Side:** pretzel, apple, or pudding

2. **School Trips**

   **Place:** zoo, museum, or planetarium
   **Day:** Monday, Tuesday, Wednesday, Thursday, or Friday

3. Sarah needs a new television. She can buy one with a 13, 20, or 25 inch screen. She can buy each one with or without a VCR. How many choices does she have?

4. Maurice has to go to the store. He can go through the park or around the park. He can either walk or run. How many choices does he have?

## Set D (pp. 662–663)

**For 1–2, use the letters A, R, and M.**

1. List the 6 two-letter arrangements that are possible.

2. List the 3 two-letter combinations that are possible.

3. Larry is ordering dinner. He has a choice of salad or soup. Then he has a choice of meatloaf, steak, spaghetti, or salmon. How many dinner choices does he have?

4. In how many different ways can Pete, Pat, and Paul stand in a row?

# Review/Test

## ✓ CHECK VOCABULARY AND CONCEPTS

**Choose the best term from the box.**

1. A choice in which the order of the items does not matter is a(n) __?__. (p. 662)

2. You can use a __?__ to show all the possible outcomes of an event. (p. 660)

3. All the results that have an equal chance of happening are __?__. (p. 656)

> equally likely
> possible outcomes
> probability
> tree diagram
> arrangement
> combination

## ✓ CHECK SKILLS

**For 4–6, write a fraction for the probability of each event with a number cube labeled 1 to 6.** (pp. 656–657)

4. a 5
5. either 1 or 6
6. an even number

**The experimental probability of winning is $\frac{2}{3}$. Predict the number of wins.** (pp. 658–659)

7. in 9 games
8. in 18 games
9. in 15 games

**Find the number of choices.** (pp. 660–661)

10. **Music Class Choices**
    **Class:** band, choir, orchestra
    **Teacher:** Mr. Gibson, Ms. Garcia

11. **Pizza Choices** (1 topping)
    **Crust:** thick, thin
    **Toppings:** mushrooms, pepperoni, onions, anchovies

**For 12–13, use the cards shown.** (pp. 662–663)

12. List the 6 different ways the cards can be arranged in a row.

13. List the 3 combinations of 2 cards that can be chosen.

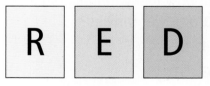

## ✓ CHECK PROBLEM SOLVING

**Solve.** (pp. 664–665)

14. Ben has 25¢, but he does not have any pennies. Find the possible choices of coins he has.

15. Adam tosses 2 coins. What are the possible outcomes? Determine the probability of tossing exactly 2 heads.

# Getting Ready for FCAT

## ⭐ DATA ANALYSIS AND PROBABILITY

**1.** Cards numbered 2, 7, 13, 20, 37, and 52 are placed face down.

| 2 | 7 | 13 | 20 | 37 | 52 |

If you choose one of these cards, which outcome is most likely?

**A.** The number is greater than 20.

**B.** The number is less than 20.

**C.** The number is a one-digit number.

**D.** The number is a two-digit number.

**2.** The line graph shows the number of movies seen by Nan each month.

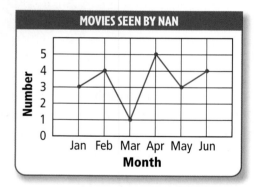

**MOVIES SEEN BY NAN**

In how many months did Nan watch 3 or fewer movies?

**F.** 2

**G.** 3

**H.** 4

**I.** 5

**3. Explain It** Of the 20 equal sections on a spinner, $\frac{1}{2}$ are orange, $\frac{2}{5}$ are blue, and the rest are white. Explain how to find the probability of the pointer landing on white.

## ⭐ GEOMETRY AND SPATIAL SENSE

**4.** Brooke is gift-wrapping a present that is inside the box shown below.

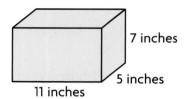

7 inches

5 inches

11 inches

Which is the volume of the box?

**A.** 23 cubic inches

**B.** 77 cubic inches

**C.** 334 cubic inches

**D.** 385 cubic inches

**5.** Peter made this diagram of a top he wants to make for a wooden box.

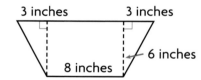

3 inches     3 inches

8 inches     6 inches

What is the area of the figure he drew?

**F.** 48 square inches

**G.** 66 square inches

**H.** 84 square inches

**I.** 144 square inches

**6. Explain It** Which of these figures is NOT a parallelogram? Explain how you know.

**MEASUREMENT**

**7.** Ariana is planning to put a wallpaper border around her bedroom where the walls meet the ceiling. The bedroom ceiling is square and has an area of 144 square feet. How many feet of wallpaper border does Ariana need?

**A.** 12 feet    **C.** 48 feet

**B.** 24 feet    **D.** 144 feet

**8.** Which of the following would be **best** to measure the number of degrees in an angle?

**F.** compass

**G.** ruler

**H.** protractor

**I.** balance scale

**9. Explain It** Jeremy knows that 50 trading cards have a mass of 50 grams. He has a stack of trading cards that has a mass of 0.4 kilogram. ESTIMATE whether there are more than or fewer than 500 cards in his stack. Explain how you know.

 **NUMBER SENSE, CONCEPTS, AND OPERATIONS**

**10.** Four different stores at the mall have the same shirt on sale. If the original price of the shirt at each store is the same, which store is selling the shirt for the **least** price?

**A.**
> **Sale**
> Store A
> Pay **75%** of the regular price.

**C.**
> **Sale**
> Store C
> Pay $\frac{4}{5}$ of the regular price.

**B.**
> **Sale**
> Store B
> Take $\frac{1}{3}$ **off** the regular price.

**D.**
> **Sale**
> Store D
> Take **35% off** the regular price.

**TIP** **Choose the answer.** See item 11. You need to calculate the weight of the water in the aquarium (8.3 × 20). If your answer doesn't match one of the answer choices, check your computation and the placement of the decimal point.

**11.** The aquarium in Mark's room holds 20 gallons of water. If a gallon of water weighs 8.3 pounds, how much does the water in the aquarium weigh?

**F.** 166 pounds    **H.** 160.6 pounds

**G.** 163 pounds    **I.** 28.3 pounds

**12. Explain It** Three bags of apples weigh 3.5 pounds, 2.8 pounds, and 4.7 pounds. Matt says that the apples weigh about 9 pounds in all. Eve says that the apples weigh about 12 pounds in all. Which estimate is closer to the actual weight? Explain how you know.

# IT'S IN THE BAG

## Flying Carpets

**PROJECT** Make a carpet to practice modeling percents.

### Materials

- 10 x 10 piece of 1-cm graph paper
- Construction paper
- Fringe materials (yarn, raffia, ribbon)
- Glue
- Colored pencils
- Scissors
- Hole punch

### Directions

1. Make a design for your carpet. Color the squares on the graph paper using the percents shown:

   50% – purple    10% – red
   10% – yellow    10% – black
   10% – blue      10% – green

2. Cut a piece of construction paper 11 cm × 17 cm. Glue the graph paper in the center of the construction paper. *(Picture A)*

3. Punch the same number of holes along each of the short edges of the construction paper. *(Picture B)*

4. Add fringe materials to the holes along the edges as shown in the photograph. *(Picture C)*

5. Share your "flying carpet" with your classmates to show the percents of color used. Compare the patterns on the carpets.

# Challenge

## Fairness

Number Fun is a two-player game played with a number cube labeled 1 to 6. Each player scores a point when his or her type of number is rolled.

> **Rules**
>
> Player 1 scores 1 point if the number is even.
>
> Player 2 scores 1 point if the number is a multiple of 3.

Is this game fair?

You can use what you know about probability to see if this game is fair. A game is **fair** if each player has the same chance of winning.

### Example

| | |
|---|---|
| Player 1 scores if the number is even. | Player 2 scores if the number is a multiple of 3. |
| Even numbers on the number cube are 2, 4, and 6. | Multiples of 3 on the number cube are 3 and 6. |
| Probability of tossing an even number $= \frac{3}{6}$. | Probability of tossing a multiple of 3 $= \frac{2}{6}$. |

Since $\frac{3}{6} > \frac{2}{6}$, the game is unfair. Player 1's chances of winning are greater than Player 2's.

## Talk About It

• In order for a game to be fair, how should the probabilities of winning compare?

## Try It

**Use the same number cube but different rules. Tell whether the game is *fair* or *unfair*. Explain your answer.**

1. Player 1 wins if the number is even.
   Player 2 wins if the number is odd.

2. Player 1 wins if the number is a multiple of 4.
   Player 2 wins if the number is prime.

# Study Guide and Review

## VOCABULARY

Choose the best term from the box.

1. A comparison of two quantities is a(n) __?__ . (p. 614)

2. The ratio of a number to 100 is a(n) __?__ . (p. 632)

3. The chance that an event will happen is the __?__ . (p. 654)

<table>
<tr><td>probability</td></tr>
<tr><td>ratio</td></tr>
<tr><td>certainty</td></tr>
<tr><td>unlikely</td></tr>
<tr><td>percent</td></tr>
<tr><td>equally likely</td></tr>
</table>

## STUDY AND SOLVE

### Chapter 28

**Write ratios that are equivalent to a given ratio.**

To find equivalent ratios, multiply or divide the numerator and the denominator by the same number.

$$\frac{1 \times 2}{5 \times 2} = \frac{2}{10} \qquad \frac{12 \div 3}{15 \div 3} = \frac{4}{5}$$

So, $\frac{1}{5}$ and $\frac{2}{10}$ are equivalent ratios.

So, $\frac{12}{15}$ and $\frac{4}{5}$ are equivalent ratios.

**Write three ratios that are equivalent to the given ratio.**
(pp. 618–621)

4. $\frac{2}{5}$

5. 10 to 20

6. 3 to 8

7. $\frac{6}{2}$

8. 1:4

9. 7:3

### Chapter 29

**Write a number as a decimal, percent, and fraction.**

twenty-one hundredths

    **decimal:** 0.21

    **percent:** $0.21 \times 100 = 21\%$

    **fraction:** $\frac{21}{100}$

**Write each number as a decimal, percent, and fraction.** (pp. 634–635)

10. sixteen hundredths

11. ninety-one hundredths

12. four tenths

13. two

**Use a percent or decimal to find the percent of a number.**

Find 20% of 70.

$0.20 \times 70 = 14$

So, 20% of 70 = 14.

Change the percent to a decimal and multiply.

**Find the percent of each number.**
(pp. 642–645)

14. 15% of 30

15. 6% of 25

16. 45% of 115

17. 19% of 25

18. 18% of 300

19. 77% of 430

20. 7.5% of 20

21. 300% of 12

# Chapter 30

**Write a probability as a fraction.**

A bag has 3 green, 1 red, and 2 blue marbles. Find the probability of picking a red marble from the bag.

The probability of an event =

$$\frac{\text{number of favorable outcomes}}{\text{total number of possible outcomes}}$$

Probability of red = $\frac{1 \text{ red marble}}{6 \text{ total marbles}} = \frac{1}{6}$

**Write a fraction for the probability of the pointer landing on blue.** (pp. 656–657)

22.   23.

**Write a fraction for the probability of rolling each number on a number cube labeled 1 to 6.** (pp. 656–657)

24. an even number

25. a number less than 5

**Organize possible outcomes or choices.**

For summer vacation, Kerri's family can go to the beach, the mountains, or a theme park. They can travel by plane, train, or automobile. How many different trips can they take?

To find the number of choices, make a tree diagram or multiply the number of locations by the number of ways of travel.

**locations × ways of travel = number of choices**

| ↓ | | ↓ | | ↓ |
| 3 | × | 3 | = | 9 choices |

So, they can take 9 different trips.

**Find the number of choices.**

(pp. 660–661)

26. **Main course:** steak, chicken, fish
    **Dessert:** pie, cake

27. **Shirt:** blue, white, gray, beige
    **Tie:** striped, solid, print

28. Two theaters are each showing a western, a drama, and a comedy at 5:00, 7:00, and 9:00.

## PROBLEM SOLVING PRACTICE

**Solve.** (pp. 664–665)

29. Trey is going to spin the pointer in problem 22 and toss a coin. What is the probability that the pointer will land on blue and the coin will land heads up?

30. Trevor has 3 coins in his pocket. Each is either a nickel or a dime. What are the different amounts of money that he could have with these 3 coins?

# PERFORMANCE ASSESSMENT

## TASK A • SALE TIME

The Sports Shop is having a sale on soccer clothes and equipment.

**a.** Copy and complete the table for the sale items.

| Soccer Item | Regular Price | Percent Off | Discount | Sale Price |
|---|---|---|---|---|
| ball | $12.00 | 40% | $4.80 | $7.20 |
| short | $18.00 | 25% | | |
| knee pads | $10.00 | 40% | | |
| shirt | $15.00 | 25% | | |
| shoes | $45.00 | 40% | | |

**b.** Justin has $50.00. He plans to spend 75% of his money on soccer sale items. Suggest some items he could buy. Tell how much he will spend and how much money he will have left.

**c.** On the last day of the sale, the three soccer balls that were left were sold for 60% off. The regular prices for the balls were $15.00, $22.00, and $30.00. Sara has $10.00. Which soccer balls can she buy? Explain how you know.

## TASK B • PROBABILITY SPINS

Suppose you are designing a spinner like the one below to use in an experiment.

**a.** Use at least 2 different numbers or colors to design your spinner. List the possible outcomes of your spinner. Is each outcome equally likely? Explain.

**b.** Describe a probability experiment using your spinner. Conduct your experiment and record your results in a table.

**c.** Misha designed the spinner at the right.

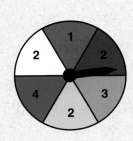

What is the probability of the pointer landing on each number on Misha's spinner? Which has a greater probability using Misha's spinner, the pointer landing on an odd number or on an even number? Explain.

# Technology Linkup

## Use a Calculator to Find Percent

The Warren family went out for dinner. The total bill was $37.45.
Mr. Warren wants to leave a 22% tip. How much will the tip be? What
is the total cost of dinner including the tip?

Use a calculator, such as the TI-15, to solve this problem.

- Since the problem involves money, you want to round to the
  nearest cent. So, press **Fix** **0.01** to set the calculator to round
  numbers to the hundredths place. You will see *Fix* appear at
  the top of the display.

- Put the cost of the dinner into memory.

Fix M
37.45 = 37.45

- Multiply by 22% to find the amount of the tip.

Fix M
37.45 X 22% =
8.24

The tip will be $8.24.

- Use the **MR/MC** key to add the cost for the
  dinner to the tip and find the total cost.

Fix M
8.239 + 37.45
=          45.69

The total cost will be $45.69.

## Practice and Problem Solving

Use a calculator to solve. Remember to clear the memory each
time. On the TI-15, press **MR/MC** twice to reset the memory.

1. Three friends go out for dinner. Their bill is $42.78. They want to
   leave a 17% tip. How much will the tip be? What will be the total
   cost for dinner?

2. **REASONING** Julia and Timothy go out for lunch. Their bill is
   $14.28. They want to leave a 15% tip. How much should each
   person pay if they split the total cost equally? Explain.

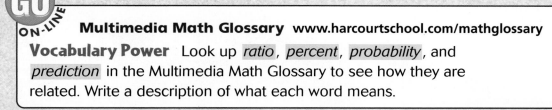

**Multimedia Math Glossary** www.harcourtschool.com/mathglossary
**Vocabulary Power** Look up *ratio*, *percent*, *probability*, and
*prediction* in the Multimedia Math Glossary to see how they are
related. Write a description of what each word means.

# PROBLEM SOLVING IN FLORIDA

Tallahassee
Hobe Sound

## JONATHAN DICKINSON STATE PARK

For those who enjoy hiking in the country, Jonathan Dickinson State Park near Hobe Sound has almost 11,500 acres of pine scrub, pine flatwoods, and cypress swamps. About 20 percent of the park is made up of rare coastal sand pine scrub. You can hike, bike, paddle, or ride a horse on various trails at the park.

**USE DATA** For 1–5, use the paragraph above and the table.

1. Approximately how many acres of the park are made up of rare coastal sand pine scrub? Show how you found your answer.

2. What is the probability that if you choose a trail at random, it will be longer than 2 miles?

| TRAILS AT JONATHAN DICKINSON STATE PARK | | |
|---|---|---|
| **Trail** | **Length** | **Condition** |
| East Loop Trail | 9.4 miles | unpaved |
| Kitching Creek Trail | 5.1 miles | unpaved |
| Multi-Use Trail | 1.5 miles | paved |
| Camp Murphy Off-Road Bicycle Area | 6.1 miles | unpaved |
| Eaglesview Horseback Riding Area | 8 miles | unpaved |

3. The length of the shortest trail is what percent of the length of the longest trail? Round your answer to the nearest whole number. Show how you found your answer.

4. If you can hike at an average rate of $1\frac{1}{2}$ miles per hour, including stopping time, what is the least whole number of hours you should allow for a hike along Kitching Creek Trail? Show how you found your answer.

5. **STRETCH YOUR THINKING** What is the probability that if you choose a trail at random, it will be unpaved and shorter than 6 miles? Explain.

The Loxahatchee River, which runs through the park, is a federally designated wild and scenic river.

## TALLAHASSEE

Tallahassee has been the capital of Florida since 2 years after it was founded in 1822. It could not be decided whether to make Pensacola or St. Augustine the capital. As a compromise Tallahassee was chosen because it is about halfway between those two cities.

Today Tallahassee is a modern city with a modern transportation system. The Tallahassee Transit System is a great way to see the sights of the city.

▲ Tallahassee is an Apalachee Native-American word meaning "old town" or "abandoned fields," which was what the area was called after the Apalachees left.

**USE DATA** For 1–4, use the data in the table.

| TALLAHASSEE TRANSIT SYSTEM | |
|---|---|
| **Pass** | **Cost** |
| Cash Fare | $1.00 |
| Same-Day Unlimited Pass | $2.50 |
| Youth, or Senior Citizen | $0.50 |
| 7-Day Unlimited Pass | $8.00 |
| 31-Day Unlimited Pass | $33.00 |

1. What percent of a same-day unlimited pass is a cash-fare pass?

2. Randall and Carl each bought enough unlimited passes to travel for 28 days. Randall bought only same-day unlimited passes. Carl bought only 7-day unlimited passes.
   a. In one month, Randall bought 28 same-day unlimited passes. How much did he spend, including 7% sales tax?
   b. Carl bought four 7-day unlimited passes. How much did he save compared with what Randall spent, including sales tax?

3. **STRETCH YOUR THINKING** For a passenger who rode every day, which would be a better value during a one-month period, using a 31-day unlimited pass or
   a. using only 7-day unlimited passes? Explain.
   b. using a combination of same-day unlimited passes and 7-day unlimited passes? Explain.

# FCAT HANDBOOK

The tips and the problems on the following pages will help you succeed on FCAT.

## Tips for Success on FCAT . . . . . . . . . . . . . . . . . . . . . . . . . . . . . . . . . . . H2

Before working on the Getting Ready for FCAT problems and before taking FCAT, sharpen your test-taking skills by reviewing these pages. Here you can find tips such as how to get ready for the test, how to understand the directions, and how to keep track of time.

## Getting Ready for FCAT . . . . . . . . . . . . . . . . . . . . . . . . . . . . . . . . . . . . H6

The problems in this section cover the five mathematics strands of the Florida Sunshine State Standards. Use these problems to build your test-taking skills and to prepare for FCAT success.

# Other Resources

## Basic Facts Tests ......................................... H36

Review addition, subtraction, multiplication, and division facts by taking the basic facts tests throughout the year to improve your memorization skills.

## Table of Measures ........................................ H41

All the important measures used in this book are in this table. If you've forgotten exactly how many feet are in a mile, this table will help you.

## Glossary ................................................ H43

This glossary will help you speak and write the language of mathematics. Use the glossary to check the definitions of important terms.

## Index .................................................. H55

Use the index when you want to review a topic. It lists the page numbers where the topic is taught.

## Tips for Success on FCAT

Being a good test-taker is like being a good problem solver. When you answer test questions, you are solving problems. Remember to **UNDERSTAND, PLAN, SOLVE,** and **CHECK**.

### UNDERSTAND

### Read the problem.

- Look for math terms and recall their meanings.
- Each word is important. Missing a word or reading it incorrectly could cause you to get the wrong answer.
- Pay attention to words that are in **bold** type or all CAPITAL letters.
- Reread the problem and think about the question.

**1.** Tony is 10 years younger than Bill. Amber is 5 years older than Tony. Iris is 3 years younger than Amber. Bill is 15 years old. How old is Iris?

**A.** 7      **C.** 13

**B.** 12      **D.** 27

**TIP!** **Understand the problem.**
The critical information is that Bill is 15 years old. List all the given relationships and express them as equations. Use Bill's age to begin solving the equations. Be sure to answer the question asked. The answer is **A**.

### PLAN

### Think about how you can solve the problem.

- Can you solve the problem with the information given?
- Pictures, charts, tables, and graphs may have the information you need.
- Some problems have two steps or more.
- If the path to the solution isn't clear, choose a problem solving strategy and use it to solve the problem.

**2.** A gravel path surrounds a rectangular grass field. The field is 60 feet long and 40 feet wide. The path is 3 feet wide. What is the area covered by the path?

**F.** 300 square feet   **H.** 600 square feet

**G.** 309 square feet   **I.** 636 square feet

**TIP!** **Decide on a plan.**
Using the strategy *draw a diagram* will help you find the dimensions of the larger rectangle so you can find the area. Match the description in the problem and label it. First find the area of the field and the path. Then subtract the area of the field. The answer is **I**.

## Follow your plan, working logically and carefully.

- Estimate your answer. Are any answer choices unreasonable?
- Use reasoning to find the most likely choices.
- Make sure you solved all steps needed to answer the problem.
- Change your plan if it isn't working. Try a different strategy.

**3.** Eduardo needs to find the total weight of a package he is mailing in order to calculate the postage needed. The package contains 15 copies of a document that weighs 2.5 ounces. The mailing envelope weighs 0.25 ounce. What is the total weight of the package?

- **A.** 17.5 ounces
- **B.** 17.75 ounces
- **C.** 37.5 ounces
- **D.** 37.75 ounces

**TIP! Choose the answer.**
You need to calculate the weight of all the copies of the document (15 × 2.5) and then add the weight of the envelope. If your answer doesn't match one of the answer choices, check your computation and the placement of the decimal point. The answer is **D**.

---

**CHECK**

## Take time to catch your mistakes.

- Be sure you answered the question asked.
- Check that your answer fits the information in the problem.
- Check for important words you might have missed.
- Be sure you used all the information you needed.
- Check your computation by using a different method.

**4.** The distance from Todd's home to the soccer field is $\frac{3}{8}$ mile. The distance from Mia's home to the field is $\frac{2}{3}$ as great as Todd's distance. How far is it from Mia's home to the soccer field?

- **F.** $\frac{5}{11}$ mile
- **G.** $\frac{1}{3}$ mile
- **H.** $\frac{7}{24}$ mile
- **I.** $\frac{1}{4}$ mile

**TIP! Check your work.**
Since Mia's distance is $\frac{2}{3}$ of Todd's distance, it must be less than Todd's. To check your multiplication, draw a square. Divide the square into 8 equal columns and 3 equal rows. Shade the amounts given. Count the overlapping parts that are shaded and write the fraction that names that part. The answer is **I**.

# Tips for Multiple Choice

- First solve the problem.
- Find the answer choice that matches your solution.
- If your solution does not match any of the answer choices, check the numbers you used. Then check your computation.
- Once you have identified the correct answer choice, fill in the answer bubble neatly.

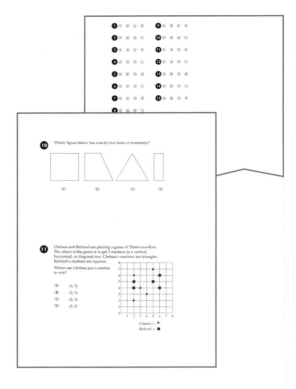

# Tips for Gridded Response

- First solve the problem.
- Carefully write the number from your solution in the spaces above the bubbles.
- Fill in each bubble to match the number above it.
- Blank spaces should not have any marks in the bubbles below them.

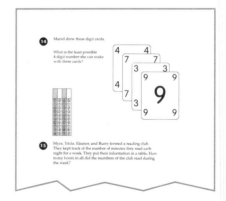

## Tips for Short Response

- Plan to spend about 5 minutes on each short-response item.

- Read the problem carefully and think about what you are asked to do. Explain your answer using numbers, symbols, words, and/or pictures.

- As you write your answer, look back at the problem. Make sure you understand the problem and have answered the question completely.

- Leave time to reread your answer and correct any mistakes.

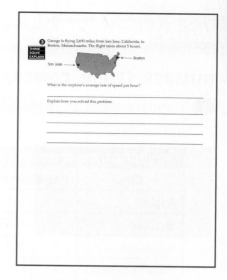

---

## Tips for Extended Response

- Plan to spend between 5 and 15 minutes on each extended-response item.

- Read the problem carefully and think about what you are asked to do. You may be asked to explain your answer with sentences and/or pictures.

- Plan how to organize your response.

- As you write your answer, look back at the problem. Make sure you understand the problem.

- Leave time to reread your answer and correct any mistakes.

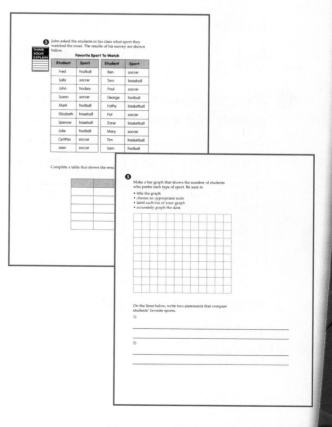

### ✓ NUMBER SENSE, CONCEPTS, AND OPERATIONS

**1** Candace used an almanac to find the populations of some cities in Florida.

| POPULATIONS OF FLORIDA CITIES | |
|---|---|
| **City** | **Population in 2000** |
| Naples | 20,976 |
| St. Cloud | 20,074 |
| Rockledge | 20,170 |
| Royal Palm Beach | 21,523 |

Which of the cities had the **least** population in 2000?

**A.** Naples

**B.** St. Cloud

**C.** Rockledge

**D.** Royal Palm Beach

**2** Juan and Sam ordered a pizza. The picture shows the part of the pizza they did not eat.

Which is NOT another name for the amount of pizza left over?

**F.** 0.25

**G.** $\frac{2}{8}$

**H.** 25%

**I.** 0.14

**3** A car salesperson made a diagram of the models and locations of all the cars on the lot.

| XTE | XTE | XTE | XTE | XTE |
|---|---|---|---|---|
| ST | ST | ST | ST | ST |
| GT | XT | XT | XT | ST |
| GT | GT | GT | GT | GT |

What percent of the cars on the lot are ST's?

**A.** 20%

**B.** 25%

**C.** 30%

**D.** 60%

| Study and Review | |
|---|---|
| Item | Lesson Pages |
| 1 | 10–13 |
| 2 | 640–641 |
| 3 | 636–639 |

**4** In football, a touchdown is worth 6 points and a field goal is worth 3 points. A football team scored 4 touchdowns and 1 field goal during a game. Which expression could be used to find the total number of points that the team scored?

**F.** $(6 + 4) + 3$

**G.** $(6 \times 4) + 3$

**H.** $(6 - 4) + 3$

**I.** $(6 \div 4) + 3$

**5** To solve this problem, you must ESTIMATE.
The section marked on the picture has 24 flowers.

THINK
SOLVE
EXPLAIN

Based on the information above, ESTIMATE the total number of flowers on the trellis. Explain how you made your estimate.

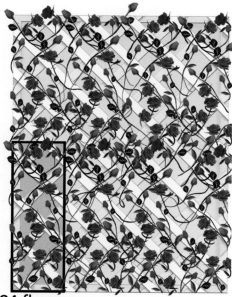

**24 flowers**

**6** The population of the American colonies in 1750, is estimated to have been 1,170,800. Which of the following represents that number in expanded form?

**A.** $(1 \times 10^5) + (1 \times 10^3) + (7 \times 10^2) + (8 \times 10^1)$

**B.** $(1 \times 10^6) + (7 \times 10^3) + (8 \times 10^2)$

**C.** $(1 \times 10^5) + (1 \times 10^4) + (7 \times 10^3) + (8 \times 10^2)$

**D.** $(1 \times 10^6) + (1 \times 10^5) + (7 \times 10^4) + (8 \times 10^2)$

| Study and Review | |
|---|---|
| **Item** | **Lesson Pages** |
| 4 | 246–249 |
| 5 | 148–149 |
| 6 | 296–299 |

## ✅ NUMBER SENSE, CONCEPTS, AND OPERATIONS

**7** Leesa counted all the coins she had saved. She discovered that she could make equal stacks with 3 coins in each stack. Which is Leesa's bag of coins?

**F.**

**28 quarters**

**H.**

**81 pennies**

**G.**

**56 nickels**

**I.**

**65 dimes**

**8** Which number is NOT between 0.1 and 0.2?

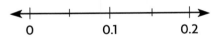

|   |   |   |
|---|---|---|
| 0 | 0.1 | 0.2 |

**A.** 0.19

**B.** 0.12

**C.** 0.102

**D.** 0.02

**9** The students in Mr. Tirone's class made a table showing their hair colors.

| STUDENT HAIR COLOR ||
| Hair Color | Number of Students |
|---|---|
| Black | 7 |
| Brown | 11 |
| Blonde | 5 |
| Red | 2 |

What percent of the students in the class have brown hair?

**F.** 11%

**G.** 44%

**H.** 56%

**I.** 75%

| Study and Review ||
|---|---|
| Item | Lesson Pages |
| 7 | 276–277 |
| 8 | 28–29 |
| 9 | 636–639 |

## NUMBER SENSE, CONCEPTS, AND OPERATIONS

**10** Mia ordered $2\frac{1}{4}$ pounds of cole slaw, $1\frac{3}{4}$ pounds of potato salad, and $1\frac{1}{2}$ pounds of macaroni salad. Which operation would be best to use to find how much more cole slaw she ordered than macaroni salad?

**A.** addition

**B.** multiplication

**C.** subtraction

**D.** division

**11** Sasha is raising money by swimming 75 laps at a swim-a-thon. So far, she has swum the crawl for 19 laps and the backstroke for 6 laps. Which expression can be used to find the number of laps she has left to swim?

**F.** $75 - (19 + 6)$

**G.** $75 - 19 + 6$

**H.** $(19 + 6) - 75$

**I.** $75 - 6 + 19$

**12** Curt did this math problem for homework, but his paper got wet, and one of the digits got smudged.

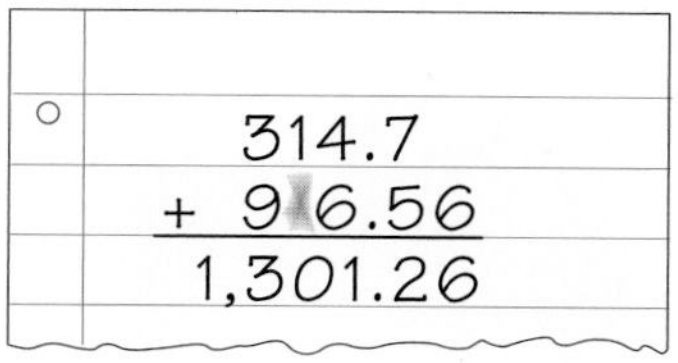

```
    314.7
+  9 6.56
 1,301.26
```

Which is the missing number?

**A.** 6

**B.** 7

**C.** 8

**D.** 9

| Study and Review | |
|---|---|
| Item | Lesson Pages |
| 10 | 236–237 |
| 11 | 64–67 |
| 12 | 48–51 |

## ✔ NUMBER SENSE, CONCEPTS, AND OPERATIONS

**13** The width of your index finger is about 1 centimeter.

THINK
SOLVE
EXPLAIN

ESTIMATE the length of this pencil in centimeters.

**14** Dena picked 4 number cards from a deck.

She wants to make a pair of two-digit numbers that have 3 as the greatest common factor. Which numbers could she use?

**F.** 24 and 78

**H.** 42 and 78

**G.** 48 and 72

**I.** 27 and 48

**15** Janine rides her bicycle for $8\frac{3}{4}$ minutes to get to school. Billie rides his bicycle $1\frac{1}{2}$ times as long to get to school. How long does it take Billie to ride to school?

**A.** $7\frac{1}{4}$ minutes

**B.** $8\frac{3}{8}$ minutes

**C.** $10\frac{1}{4}$ minutes

**D.** $13\frac{1}{8}$ minutes

| Study and Review | |
|---|---|
| **Item** | **Lesson Pages** |
| 13 | 526–527 |
| 14 | 278–281 |
| 15 | 392–393 |

## ✓ MEASUREMENT

**1** While Margarita was hanging up her blouse, she noticed that the sides of the hanger form angles.

What type of angle is formed by the bottom and a side of the hanger?

**A.** acute

**B.** obtuse

**C.** right

**D.** straight

**2** During a trip to a theme park, the Beckers went to the animal show. The show started at 1:45 P.M. and ended at 2:20 P.M. How long was the animal show?

**F.** 15 minutes

**G.** 20 minutes

**H.** 35 minutes

**I.** 45 minutes

**3** Peter is trying to keep rabbits out of his garden. How much fencing does he need to enclose his garden?

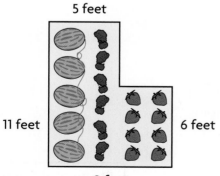

5 feet

11 feet

6 feet

9 feet

**A.** 79 feet

**C.** 30 feet

**B.** 40 feet

**D.** 20 feet

| Study and Review | |
|---|---|
| **Item** | **Lesson Pages** |
| I | 428–431 |
| 2 | 536–539 |
| 3 | 550–551 |

## MEASUREMENT

**4** Hannah's little brother likes to stack blocks. Each block measures 1 unit on each side.

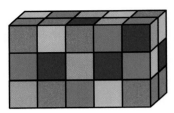

| Volume of a cube = length × width × height |

What is the volume in cubic units of the stack of blocks?

**F.** 10 cubic units  **H.** 20 cubic units

**G.** 15 cubic units  **I.** 30 cubic units

**5** Patrick keeps a comb in his pocket.

What is the length of his comb?

**A.** $4\frac{1}{4}$ inches  **C.** $4\frac{3}{4}$ inches

**B.** $4\frac{1}{2}$ inches  **D.** $4\frac{7}{8}$ inches

**6** Leroy measured his bedroom before buying new carpet. The room is 13 feet long and 12 feet wide. The closet is 5 feet long and 2 feet wide. How much carpet does he need to cover both floors?

| Area = length × width |

**F.** 32 square feet  **H.** 166 square feet

**G.** 64 square feet  **I.** 252 square feet

| Study and Review | |
| --- | --- |
| Item | Lesson Pages |
| 4 | 592–595 |
| 5 | 522–525 |
| 6 | 564–567 |

## ✔ MEASUREMENT

**7** Mario is making a list of his errands. He is planning to buy 3 concert tickets that cost $27.00 each, pick up dry cleaning that will cost $11.00, and rent a movie for $3.95. How much money will he need? Does Mario need an estimate or the exact amount? Explain.

**8** Lorenzo sold 40 cups of lemonade at his lemonade stand.

> 1 cup = 8 ounces

How many ounces of lemonade did he sell?

**A.** 5 ounces

**B.** 80 ounces

**C.** 240 ounces

**D.** 320 ounces

**9** Adam is 5 feet 5 inches tall. Melissa is 4 feet 10 inches tall. How much taller is Adam than Melissa?

**F.** 5 inches

**G.** 7 inches

**H.** 12 inches

**I.** 15 inches

| Study and Review | |
|---|---|
| **Item** | **Lesson Pages** |
| 7 | 540–541 |
| 8 | 532–533 |
| 9 | 528–531 |

### ✓ MEASUREMENT

**10** Alex hit a baseball through Mrs. Clark's window and wants to replace it.

Which of the following is a reasonable measurement for the window?

A. 90 millimeters by 150 millimeters

B. 90 centimeters by 150 centimeters

C. 90 meters by 150 meters

D. 90 kilometers by 150 kilometers

**11** The picture shows a young Madagascar Day gecko.

Which of the following is a reasonable measurement of the length of the gecko?

F. 6 kilometers     H. 6 centimeters

G. 6 meters     I. 6 millimeters

**12** These candles will burn for 5 hours.

The taller candle is new. About how long has the shorter candle been burning?

A. 2 hours     C. 3 hours

B. 2.5 hours     D. 3.5 hours

| Study and Review | |
|---|---|
| **Item** | **Lesson Pages** |
| 10 | 526–527 |
| 11 | 526–527 |
| 12 | 536–539 |

**13** Which of these would you use to measure the outdoor temperature?

**F.**

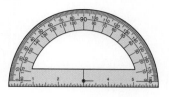

a protractor

**H.**

a measuring cup

**G.**

a tape measure

**I.**

a thermometer

**14** Courtney weighed a box of 100 drinking straws and found that it had a mass of 125 grams.

What number of straws will have a mass of about 1 kilogram?

| 1 kilogram = 1,000 grams |

**A.** 10 straws

**B.** 1,000 straws

**C.** 10,000 straws

**D.** 100,000 straws

| Study and Review | |
|---|---|
| **Item** | **Lesson Pages** |
| 13 | 536–539 |
| 14 | 534–535 |

## MEASUREMENT

**15** Jonathan can walk 1 mile in 20 minutes. Julie can walk 1 mile in 15 minutes. How much farther can Julie walk in 1 hour than Jonathan?

> 1 hour = 60 minutes

**F.** 1 mile

**G.** 2 miles

**H.** 3 miles

**I.** 4 miles

**16** Stacy wanted to know the height of the staircase in her house. She counted 15 steps in the staircase. Each step was 8 inches high. How many feet high was the staircase?

> 1 foot = 12 inches

**A.** 8 feet     **C.** 12 feet

**B.** 10 feet     **D.** 15 feet

**17** Which of these units would be **best** for measuring the mass of an orange?

**F.** gram

**G.** kilogram

**H.** milliliter

**I.** liter

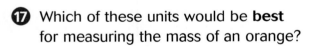

| Study and Review | |
|------|----------------|
| **Item** | **Lesson Pages** |
| 15 | 536–539 |
| 16 | 528–531 |
| 17 | 534–535 |

## ✓ MEASUREMENT

**18** Lisa and Toshi went shopping at the mall. They arrived at 11:15 A.M. and left 3 hours 20 minutes later. What time did they leave the mall?

**A.** 2:15 P.M.

**B.** 2:35 P.M.

**C.** 3:15 P.M.

**D.** 3:35 P.M.

**19** The Green family is taking a trip from Miami to Orlando. This diagram shows the family's progress during the first hour. How many more miles do the Greens have to go?

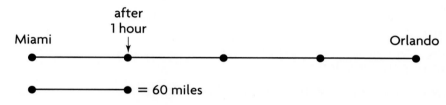

**F.** 60 miles

**G.** 120 miles

**H.** 180 miles

**I.** 240 miles

**20** Shirley baked a pie and cut it into 5 unequal pieces.

Which piece of pie appears to have a right angle?

**A.** piece A

**B.** piece B

**C.** piece C

**D.** piece D

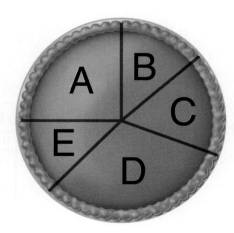

| Study and Review | |
|---|---|
| Item | Lesson Pages |
| 18 | 536–539 |
| 19 | 622–623 |
| 20 | 428–431 |

## ✓ GEOMETRY AND SPATIAL SENSE

**1** Look at the figures.

Figure A          Figure B          Figure C          Figure D

Which figure is a polygon? Explain why this figure is a polygon.

**2** Sofia asked Veronica to draw a geometric figure using these clues.

- It is two-dimensional.
- It is a polygon.
- It has 4 sides.
- It has only one pair of parallel sides.

Use the clues to draw the figure that Veronica drew. What figure did Veronica draw?

**3** Carlos folds this pattern for a three-dimensional figure.

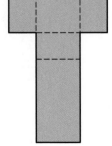

If Carlos folds the pattern into a three-dimensional figure, what figure will he make?

| Study and Review | |
|---|---|
| Item | Lesson Pages |
| 1 | 434–437 |
| 2 | 460–461 |
| 3 | 466–469 |

## GEOMETRY AND SPATIAL SENSE

**4** Brendan took this photograph of the pyramid in front of the Louvre Museum in Paris, France.

What is the name of this solid figure? How many faces, edges, and vertices does this figure have?

**5** Joshua drew a design in a circle.

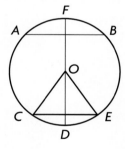

Identify all the parts of a circle that are shown in his design.

**6** Janet wants to find the lines of symmetry in this figure.

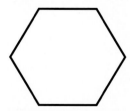

Trace the figure above. Draw the lines of symmetry for the figure. Explain how you know a line drawn on the figure is a line of symmetry.

| Study and Review | |
|---|---|
| **Item** | **Lesson Pages** |
| 4 | 466–469 |
| 5 | 438–441 |
| 6 | 446–447 |

## ✔ GEOMETRY AND SPATIAL SENSE

**7** Diana drew a picture of her apartment building.

Which is NOT true?

**A.** The front of the apartment building has a line of symmetry.

**B.** All the windows on the first floor are congruent.

**C.** All the windows on the second floor are congruent.

**D.** The windows on the first floor are similar to the windows on the second floor.

**8** Which does NOT have a line of symmetry?

**F.** W      **H.** C

**G.** P      **I.** H

**9** What type of movement was used to move the figure from position A to position B?

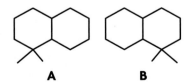

A      B

**A.** rotation

**B.** reflection

**C.** translation

**D.** tessellation

| Study and Review | |
|---|---|
| **Item** | **Lesson Pages** |
| 7 | 442–445 |
| 8 | 446–447 |
| 9 | 462–465 |

## GEOMETRY AND SPATIAL SENSE

**10** Rhosanda is using toothpicks to make congruent equilateral triangles.

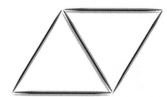

What is the greatest number of congruent equilateral triangles that she can make with **exactly** 11 toothpicks?

**F.** 3 triangles

**G.** 4 triangles

**H.** 5 triangles

**I.** 6 triangles

**11** Ben rotated this figure 90° clockwise.

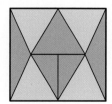

Which drawing shows the figure after the rotation?

**A.**
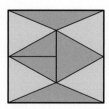

**C.**
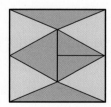

**B.**
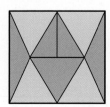

**D.**
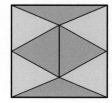

### ✓ GEOMETRY AND SPATIAL SENSE

**⑫** Leanne has four different types of tiles to make a design. She wants the design to be a tessellation. Which design should she use?

**F.**

**G.**

**H.**

**I.**

**⑬** Look at the arrow below.

Which figure below shows the arrow above rotated 180°?

**A.**

**B.**

**C.**

**D.**

| Study and Review | |
|---|---|
| **Item** | **Lesson Pages** |
| 12 | 462–465 |
| 13 | 462–465 |

# GEOMETRY AND SPATIAL SENSE

**14** Jerry built a fence around his swimming pool. He left a walkway around the pool that is 3 feet wide.

THINK
SOLVE
EXPLAIN

20 feet

16 feet

↕ 3 feet

Find the length of fencing Jerry needed to build his fence. Explain how you found the answer.

**15** The Santanas' dining room is 12 feet wide and 12 feet long. They want to buy new carpet that costs $18 per square yard. How much will the new carpet cost?

| 1 square yard = 9 square feet |
|---|

**F.** $216      **H.** $288

**G.** $256      **I.** $2,592

**16** While Melinda was hiking in the woods, she found some items that were left by other hikers.

THINK
SOLVE
EXPLAIN

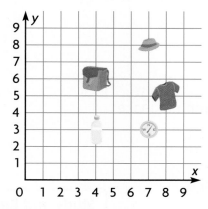

What are the coordinates of the backpack? Explain how you found the coordinates.

| Study and Review | |
|---|---|
| **Item** | **Lesson Pages** |
| 14 | 550–551 |
| 15 | 564–567 |
| 16 | 120–121 |

## GEOMETRY AND SPATIAL SENSE

**17** Jeremy placed some stickers on a coordinate grid.

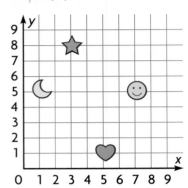

Which sticker did he place at point (5,1)?

A. ☺

B. ☾

C. ★

D. ♥

**18** Corky graphed points *R* and *S* on the coordinate grid below.

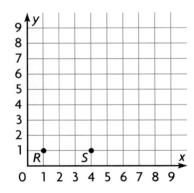

Which of these pairs of coordinates could Corky graph to make a square?

F. (1,6), (6,1)

G. (2,3), (3,3)

H. (1,4), (4,4)

I. (1,3), (4,3)

## ✔ ALGEBRAIC THINKING

**1** Elizabeth is making a design with tiles. She starts with a center tile and 4 'leg' tiles. Then, as shown in the picture, she adds tiles to each leg to make the legs.

 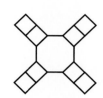 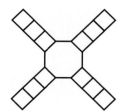

How many tiles will Elizabeth use to make a design that has 5 tiles in each leg?

**A.** 6

**B.** 16

**C.** 20

**D.** 21

**2** Felix made designs by shading squares as shown below.

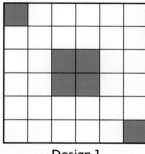 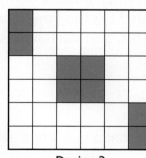 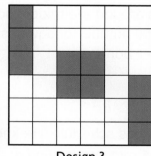

Design 1          Design 2          Design 3

If he continues the pattern, how many squares should he shade in Design 4?

**F.** 8

**G.** 10

**H.** 12

**I.** 14

| Study and Review | |
|---|---|
| **Item** | **Lesson Pages** |
| I | 448–449 |
| 2 | 448–449 |

## ✓ ALGEBRAIC THINKING

**3** Jenny is making a quilt with squares of fabric. She made a border of squares and sewed it around the middle square. Then she made a larger border of squares of a different color and sewed it onto the quilt.

THINK
SOLVE
EXPLAIN

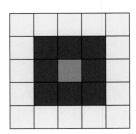

Jenny made a chart to show the total number of squares each time she added a border of a different color to form a larger square.

| Number of different colors around middle square | 1 | 2 | 3 | 4 |
|---|---|---|---|---|
| Number of squares on one side | 3 | 5 | 7 | ■ |
| Total number of squares in quilt | 9 | 25 | ■ | ■ |

How many squares will the quilt contain when it has 4 borders of different colors around the middle square? Explain how Jenny can find the total number of squares in the quilt each time she sews on another border.

**4** Dimetri lost his bus schedule. He knows that a bus stops at the corner every 25 minutes starting at 8:00 A.M. He made a table to figure out what time each of the first five buses will come.

THINK
SOLVE
EXPLAIN

| Bus | Time |
|---|---|
| 1 | 8:00 A.M. |
| 2 | 8:25 A.M. |
| 3 | ■ |
| 4 | ■ |
| 5 | ■ |

At what time will the fifth bus come?

| Study and Review | |
|---|---|
| Item | Lesson Pages |
| 3 | 252–253 |
| 4 | 536–539 |

## ✓ ALGEBRAIC THINKING

**5** Jorge and Tara were running around the track. Tara ran 3 times as many laps as Jorge ran. Let $t$ represent the number of laps that Tara ran. Which expression represents the number of laps that Jorge ran?

**A.** $t + 3$

**B.** $t - 3$

**C.** $3 \times t$

**D.** $t \div 3$

**6** Draw a number line like this on your paper.

THINK
SOLVE
EXPLAIN

Look at the inequality.

$$n \leq 4$$

On the number line, draw dots to show all the whole numbers that $n$ could represent to make the inequality true. Explain how you determined your answer.

**7** Luisa schedules appointments for patients in an optometrist's office. She wrote these inequalities to describe the number of patients, $p$, seen each day last week.

$$p > 25$$

$$p < 32$$

What numbers of patients could $p$ represent?

**F.** 26, 27, 28, 29, 30, 31, 32

**G.** 25, 26, 27, 28, 29, 30, 31

**H.** 26, 27, 28, 29, 30, 31

**I.** 25, 26, 27, 28, 29, 30, 31, 32

| Study and Review | |
|---|---|
| **Item** | **Lesson Pages** |
| 5 | 246–249 |
| 6 | 74–75 |
| 7 | 74–75 |

✓ **ALGEBRAIC THINKING**

**8** Karen has 51 CDs. If Karen had 1 CD fewer, she would have twice the number of CDs that Dorian has. How many CDs does Dorian have?

**A.** 25

**C.** 100

**B.** 26

**D.** 104

**9** The bar graph shows the numbers of home runs scored last year by the 4 best players on a softball team.

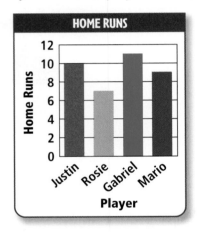

The equation $a + b = 18$ represents the home runs scored by two of the players. Which two players' home runs are represented by $a$ and $b$?

**F.** Rosie and Gabriel

**G.** Justin and Mario

**H.** Justin and Rosie

**I.** Gabriel and Mario

**10** Mr. Sanchez is driving from Pensacola to Tallahassee, a distance of 194 miles. He stopped for gas after driving 125 miles.

Which of the following could be represented by the variable $m$ in the equation $125 + m = 194$?

**A.** the number of gallons of gas he bought

**B.** the number of miles per gallon

**C.** the number of miles he still had to drive

**D.** the number of minutes he stopped

| Study and Review | |
|---|---|
| Item | Lesson Pages |
| 8 | 246–249 |
| 9 | 70–71 |
| 10 | 68–69 |

## ✓ ALGEBRAIC THINKING

**11** John, Glenn, and Chris are brothers. John is 8 years old. Glenn is twice as old as John. Chris is 2 years younger than Glenn. The sum of the brothers' ages is 1 more than the age of their aunt. How old is their aunt?

**F.** 29 years old

**G.** 31 years old

**H.** 37 years old

**I.** 39 years old

**12** Which rule could be used to find the missing number?

| ∈ | Δ |
|---|---|
| 1 | 5 |
| 2 | 6 |
| 4 | 8 |
| 8 | ■ |
| 16 | 20 |

**A.** $∈ \times 2 = Δ$

**B.** $∈ + 3 = Δ$

**C.** $∈ + 4 = Δ$

**D.** $∈ \times 4 = Δ$

**13** Leila is arranging her stickers in her sticker album. She puts 1 sticker in the first row, 2 stickers in the second row, 3 stickers in the third row, and so on. If she has 45 stickers, how many rows of stickers will there be?

**F.** 8

**G.** 9

**H.** 10

**I.** 45

| Study and Review | |
|---|---|
| Item | Lesson Pages |
| 11 | 246–249 |
| 12 | 254–255 |
| 13 | 252–253 |

## DATA ANALYSIS AND PROBABILITY

**1** The fifth-grade classes at Floresta School collected canned goods for a food drive. Each fifth-grade classroom recorded the number of cans collected each day. The results are shown in the table.

| FOOD DRIVE | | | | | |
|---|---|---|---|---|---|
| | **Number of Cans Collected** | | | | |
| **Class** | **M** | **T** | **W** | **Th** | **F** |
| 5-1 | 19 | 23 | 15 | 17 | 21 |
| 5-2 | 14 | 21 | 18 | 24 | 23 |
| 5-3 | 20 | 25 | 21 | 13 | 11 |
| 5-4 | 18 | 19 | 12 | 16 | 20 |
| 5-5 | 25 | 15 | 17 | 12 | 21 |

Using grid paper, make a bar graph showing the total number of cans collected by each class during the week. Be sure to

- write a title.

- label the axes.

- use an appropriate scale.

- accurately graph the data.

Explain how you decided what scale to use for the graph.

Write a question that can be answered by using the information in the bar graph.

| Study and Review | |
|---|---|
| **Item** | **Lesson Pages** |
| 1 | 116–119 |

# DATA ANALYSIS AND PROBABILITY

**2** The fifth-grade students at Everglades School voted for their favorite type of music. The double-bar graph shows the results of the vote.

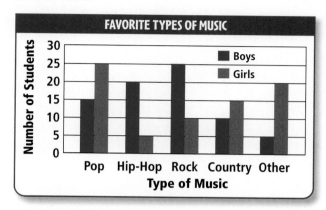

How many more boys voted for pop music than for country music?

**A.** 5

**B.** 10

**C.** 15

**D.** 20

**3** A Florida power company uses various types of fuel to produce electricity. The circle graph shows the percent of the company's electricity that came from each source during the 12 months ending in May 2002.

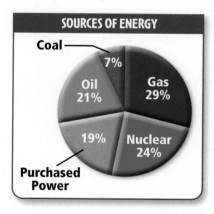

Which statement is NOT supported by the information in the circle graph?

**F.** The power company purchased 19% of the electricity.

**G.** More than one-fourth of the electricity came from nuclear power.

**H.** One-half of the electricity came from gas and oil.

**I.** Coal was the source of energy used least.

| Study and Review | |
|---|---|
| Item | Lesson Pages |
| 2 | 106–109 |
| 3 | 106–109 |

✔ **DATA ANALYSIS AND PROBABILITY**

**4** The manager of a carpet store made a pictograph of the number of carpets sold by each salesperson during the month. However, she forgot to include a key for the pictograph.

**CARPET SALES**

| | |
|---|---|
| **Lucy** | ▪ ▪ ▌ |
| **Dennis** | ▪ ▪ |
| **Meryl** | ▪ ▪ ▪ ▌ |
| **Jeff** | ▪ ▪ |

If 100 carpets were sold in all, which key should be used?

**A.** Key: Each ▪ = 2 carpets.

**B.** Key: Each ▪ = 4 carpets.

**C.** Key: Each ▪ = 5 carpets.

**D.** Key: Each ▪ = 10 carpets.

**5** Ms. Rivera's class recorded the outside temperature at 9:00 A.M. every day for a week.

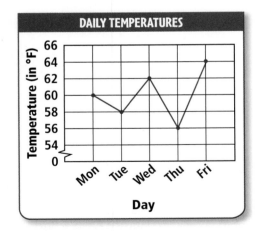

On which days was the recorded temperature above the mean for the week?

**F.** Wed and Fri

**G.** Tue and Thu

**H.** Mon, Tue, and Thu

**I.** Mon, Wed, and Fri

| **Study and Review** | |
|---|---|
| **Item** | **Lesson Pages** |
| 4 | 106–109 |
| 5 | 100–101 |

## DATA ANALYSIS AND PROBABILITY

**6** Mr. Lyon's class researched the number of storms that became Atlantic hurricanes from 1995 to 2001.

| ATLANTIC HURRICANES FROM 1995 TO 2001 ||
| Year | Number of Hurricanes |
| --- | --- |
| 1995 | 11 |
| 1996 | 9 |
| 1997 | 3 |
| 1998 | 10 |
| 1999 | 8 |
| 2000 | 8 |
| 2001 | 9 |

What was the median number of hurricanes from 1995 to 2001?

**A.** 7

**B.** 8

**C.** 9

**D.** 10

**7** A soccer league has 6 teams with 15, 12, 15, 13, 15, and 14 players on them. What is the mode for the number of players on each team?

**F.** 13.5

**G.** 14

**H.** 14.5

**I.** 15

**8** Sean received three trophies at the sports banquet: one for soccer, one for basketball, and one for track.

THINK
SOLVE
EXPLAIN

List all the different ways that Sean can display his trophies on a shelf in his room. How many different ways are there?

| Study and Review ||
| Item | Lesson Pages |
| --- | --- |
| 6 | 102–103 |
| 7 | 102–103 |
| 8 | 662–663 |

### ✓ DATA ANALYSIS AND PROBABILITY

**9** Jordan keeps each pair of socks in his drawer folded together. He has 10 pairs of socks in his drawer.

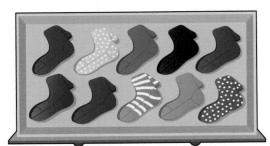

If he randomly pulls a pair of socks from the drawer, what is the probability that they will be blue?

**A.** $\frac{1}{10}$  **C.** $\frac{7}{10}$

**B.** $\frac{3}{10}$  **D.** $\frac{3}{7}$

**10** A bag contains nine strips of paper labeled *A, B, C, D, E, F, G, H,* and *I.* Sonia chooses one strip at random. Which statement **best** describes the outcome?

**F.** The probability of choosing a vowel is $\frac{1}{2}$.

**G.** There is a greater probability of choosing a consonant than of choosing a vowel.

**H.** There is a greater probability of choosing a vowel than of choosing a consonant.

**I.** The probability of choosing a consonant and the probability of choosing a vowel are the same.

**11** The students at Columbia School raised money for new playground equipment. They kept track of how much money was raised by each of the six grades at the school. Which type of graph would be **best** to display the data?

**A.** line graph

**B.** stem-and-leaf plot

**C.** circle graph

**D.** bar graph

| Study and Review | |
|---|---|
| **Item** | **Lesson Pages** |
| 9 | 656–657 |
| 10 | 658–659 |
| 11 | 130–133 |

**DATA ANALYSIS AND PROBABILITY**

**12** Augusto surveyed 12 friends who have pets. He asked them what types of pets they have. The results are shown in the table.

| MY FRIENDS' PETS | | |
|---|---|---|
| **Dogs** | **Cats** | **Other** |
| Andrea | Brice | Colin |
| David | Eduardo | Felipe |
| Jorge | Andrea | Jake |
| Maria | Madelyn | Meredith |
| Sarah | Jake | Andrea |
| | Sarah | |

On your paper, draw a Venn diagram like this one. Complete the Venn diagram by writing the names of the friends who have each type of pet.

Is there a name in the area where all three circles overlap in your Venn diagram? If so, explain what that means.

**13** Camden Hospital kept a record of the number of flu cases each January for 7 years. The data are shown in the line graph.

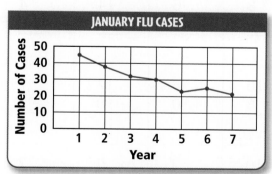

About how many cases of flu should the hospital expect in January of year 8? Explain how you found your answer.

| **Study and Review** | |
|---|---|
| **Item** | **Lesson Pages** |
| 12 | 126–127 |
| 13 | 106–109 |

# ADDITION AND SUBTRACTION FACTS TEST

|   | K | L | M | N | O | P | Q | R |
|---|---|---|---|---|---|---|---|---|
| **A** | 5 +6 | 9 −3 | 8 +6 | 10 − 7 | 18 − 9 | 7 +9 | 11 − 4 | 0 +9 |
| **B** | 12 − 4 | 9 +9 | 14 − 5 | 8 −5 | 9 +4 | 11 − 6 | 5 +3 | 16 − 9 |
| **C** | 6 +5 | 0 +8 | 9 −6 | 4 +4 | 13 − 6 | 3 +6 | 12 − 3 | 7 +4 |
| **D** | 6 +3 | 14 − 6 | 8 +8 | 7 −7 | 13 − 5 | 5 +8 | 9 +7 | 11 − 8 |
| **E** | 4 +6 | 17 − 9 | 10 − 5 | 6 +6 | 8 −4 | 1 +9 | 8 +7 | 12 − 9 |
| **F** | 8 +5 | 4 +7 | 11 − 3 | 3 +7 | 10 − 2 | 9 +0 | 12 − 8 | 7 +2 |
| **G** | 5 +7 | 13 − 4 | 6 +8 | 20 −10 | 8 −0 | 6 +9 | 14 − 7 | 4 +8 |
| **H** | 6 +7 | 11 − 7 | 9 −9 | 9 +8 | 16 − 8 | 8 +10 | 17 −10 | 7 −3 |
| **I** | 13 − 7 | 14 − 9 | 5 +5 | 9 +10 | 10 − 6 | 3 +9 | 9 −7 | 7 +6 |
| **J** | 11 − 2 | 9 +5 | 15 − 7 | 10 +10 | 13 − 9 | 7 +8 | 11 − 5 | 8 +4 |

# MULTIPLICATION FACTS TEST

| | K | L | M | N | O | P | Q | R |
|---|---|---|---|---|---|---|---|---|
| **A** | 4 ×8 | 5 ×4 | 8 ×9 | 6 ×2 | 9 ×5 | 12 × 8 | 3 ×9 | 1 ×5 |
| **B** | 7 ×1 | 6 ×3 | 5 ×3 | 3 ×8 | 5 ×5 | 3 ×3 | 0 ×8 | 8 ×5 |
| **C** | 5 ×7 | 9 ×6 | 6 ×4 | 3 ×4 | 8 ×6 | 7 ×3 | 11 × 7 | 4 ×2 |
| **D** | 3 ×2 | 9 ×8 | 1 ×6 | 7 ×2 | 4 ×6 | 7 ×5 | 12 ×12 | 4 ×7 |
| **E** | 7 ×8 | 2 ×4 | 5 ×9 | 12 ×10 | 7 ×6 | 6 ×9 | 6 ×0 | 4 ×4 |
| **F** | 1 ×9 | 7 ×7 | 12 × 5 | 9 ×3 | 8 ×11 | 6 ×6 | 2 ×9 | 11 ×11 |
| **G** | 3 ×7 | 4 ×3 | 9 ×9 | 7 ×4 | 6 ×10 | 9 ×7 | 2 ×5 | 6 ×8 |
| **H** | 12 × 3 | 11 × 5 | 8 ×3 | 12 × 7 | 10 × 4 | 4 ×5 | 10 ×10 | 9 ×4 |
| **I** | 3 ×5 | 9 ×12 | 12 ×11 | 12 × 6 | 11 ×10 | 8 ×8 | 11 × 3 | 5 ×12 |
| **J** | 7 ×9 | 4 ×12 | 9 ×11 | 3 ×10 | 9 ×10 | 12 × 2 | 8 ×12 | 6 ×12 |

# DIVISION FACTS TEST

| | K | L | M | N | O | P | Q | R |
|---|---|---|---|---|---|---|---|---|
| **A** | $2\overline{)8}$ | $9\overline{)54}$ | $7\overline{)21}$ | $4\overline{)16}$ | $3\overline{)18}$ | $7\overline{)0}$ | $4\overline{)32}$ | $6\overline{)48}$ |
| **B** | $4\overline{)8}$ | $8\overline{)40}$ | $1\overline{)4}$ | $5\overline{)35}$ | $2\overline{)12}$ | $5\overline{)10}$ | $7\overline{)56}$ | $6\overline{)30}$ |
| **C** | $8\overline{)64}$ | $7\overline{)42}$ | $6\overline{)18}$ | $9\overline{)27}$ | $12\overline{)96}$ | $6\overline{)54}$ | $4\overline{)20}$ | $7\overline{)49}$ |
| **D** | $8\overline{)48}$ | $9\overline{)72}$ | $5\overline{)60}$ | $7\overline{)28}$ | $4\overline{)24}$ | $5\overline{)40}$ | $3\overline{)27}$ | $9\overline{)36}$ |
| **E** | $7\overline{)14}$ | $8\overline{)24}$ | $3\overline{)9}$ | $11\overline{)99}$ | $5\overline{)20}$ | $3\overline{)6}$ | $2\overline{)14}$ | $4\overline{)12}$ |
| **F** | $6\overline{)36}$ | $4\overline{)28}$ | $6\overline{)72}$ | $12\overline{)60}$ | $2\overline{)10}$ | $8\overline{)0}$ | $5\overline{)45}$ | $9\overline{)81}$ |
| **G** | $2\overline{)16}$ | $3\overline{)15}$ | $3\overline{)21}$ | $5\overline{)30}$ | $9\overline{)63}$ | $8\overline{)32}$ | $9\overline{)9}$ | $3\overline{)33}$ |
| **H** | $9\overline{)18}$ | $6\overline{)24}$ | $10\overline{)70}$ | $3\overline{)12}$ | $12\overline{)120}$ | $11\overline{)66}$ | $5\overline{)25}$ | $11\overline{)77}$ |
| **I** | $8\overline{)72}$ | $11\overline{)22}$ | $12\overline{)36}$ | $7\overline{)84}$ | $11\overline{)55}$ | $10\overline{)100}$ | $4\overline{)36}$ | $8\overline{)80}$ |
| **J** | $11\overline{)121}$ | $10\overline{)90}$ | $7\overline{)63}$ | $12\overline{)108}$ | $2\overline{)24}$ | $10\overline{)110}$ | $12\overline{)144}$ | $11\overline{)132}$ |

|   | K | L | M | N | O | P | Q | R |
|---|---|---|---|---|---|---|---|---|
| **A** | $2\overline{)18}$ | $\begin{array}{r}8\\ \times4\\ \hline\end{array}$ | $5\overline{)15}$ | $\begin{array}{r}10\\ \times\ 6\\ \hline\end{array}$ | $\begin{array}{r}8\\ \times1\\ \hline\end{array}$ | $3\overline{)24}$ | $6\overline{)12}$ | $\begin{array}{r}5\\ \times8\\ \hline\end{array}$ |
| **B** | $\begin{array}{r}8\\ \times2\\ \hline\end{array}$ | $7\overline{)77}$ | $9\overline{)81}$ | $\begin{array}{r}4\\ \times10\\ \hline\end{array}$ | $\begin{array}{r}7\\ \times12\\ \hline\end{array}$ | $1\overline{)6}$ | $8\overline{)80}$ | $\begin{array}{r}4\\ \times9\\ \hline\end{array}$ |
| **C** | $12\overline{)36}$ | $\begin{array}{r}11\\ \times\ 5\\ \hline\end{array}$ | $\begin{array}{r}7\\ \times7\\ \hline\end{array}$ | $10\overline{)90}$ | $5\overline{)45}$ | $\begin{array}{r}6\\ \times7\\ \hline\end{array}$ | $8\overline{)16}$ | $\begin{array}{r}9\\ \times9\\ \hline\end{array}$ |
| **D** | $\begin{array}{r}10\\ \times\ 2\\ \hline\end{array}$ | $4\overline{)32}$ | $9\overline{)99}$ | $\begin{array}{r}7\\ \times8\\ \hline\end{array}$ | $\begin{array}{r}12\\ \times\ 3\\ \hline\end{array}$ | $9\overline{)108}$ | $11\overline{)88}$ | $\begin{array}{r}12\\ \times\ 4\\ \hline\end{array}$ |
| **E** | $\begin{array}{r}8\\ \times10\\ \hline\end{array}$ | $\begin{array}{r}12\\ \times\ 9\\ \hline\end{array}$ | $12\overline{)84}$ | $2\overline{)20}$ | $\begin{array}{r}9\\ \times0\\ \hline\end{array}$ | $\begin{array}{r}10\\ \times11\\ \hline\end{array}$ | $3\overline{)36}$ | $10\overline{)100}$ |
| **F** | $4\overline{)44}$ | $12\overline{)72}$ | $\begin{array}{r}7\\ \times11\\ \hline\end{array}$ | $\begin{array}{r}12\\ \times\ 6\\ \hline\end{array}$ | $7\overline{)56}$ | $9\overline{)45}$ | $\begin{array}{r}10\\ \times\ 3\\ \hline\end{array}$ | $\begin{array}{r}9\\ \times7\\ \hline\end{array}$ |
| **G** | $12\overline{)144}$ | $6\overline{)60}$ | $\begin{array}{r}9\\ \times2\\ \hline\end{array}$ | $\begin{array}{r}8\\ \times12\\ \hline\end{array}$ | $12\overline{)108}$ | $11\overline{)44}$ | $\begin{array}{r}5\\ \times10\\ \hline\end{array}$ | $7\overline{)84}$ |
| **H** | $\begin{array}{r}6\\ \times5\\ \hline\end{array}$ | $\begin{array}{r}8\\ \times8\\ \hline\end{array}$ | $11\overline{)33}$ | $5\overline{)55}$ | $\begin{array}{r}6\\ \times11\\ \hline\end{array}$ | $\begin{array}{r}12\\ \times\ 5\\ \hline\end{array}$ | $11\overline{)132}$ | $6\overline{)42}$ |
| **I** | $8\overline{)96}$ | $10\overline{)120}$ | $\begin{array}{r}11\\ \times\ 8\\ \hline\end{array}$ | $\begin{array}{r}10\\ \times\ 9\\ \hline\end{array}$ | $5\overline{)60}$ | $\begin{array}{r}11\\ \times\ 4\\ \hline\end{array}$ | $\begin{array}{r}10\\ \times10\\ \hline\end{array}$ | $10\overline{)80}$ |
| **J** | $\begin{array}{r}11\\ \times\ 6\\ \hline\end{array}$ | $\begin{array}{r}12\\ \times11\\ \hline\end{array}$ | $4\overline{)40}$ | $7\overline{)35}$ | $\begin{array}{r}3\\ \times6\\ \hline\end{array}$ | $8\overline{)56}$ | $\begin{array}{r}9\\ \times8\\ \hline\end{array}$ | $\begin{array}{r}12\\ \times12\\ \hline\end{array}$ |

# ADDITION FACTS TEST

| | | | | |
|---|---|---|---|---|
| **1.**<br>□ + 9 = 16 | **2.**<br>7 + □ = 12 | **3.**<br>□ + 8 = 12 | **4.**<br>7 + □ = 10 | **5.**<br>□ + 5 = 13 |
| **6.**<br>□ + 5 = 10 | **7.**<br>6 + □ = 14 | **8.**<br>□ + 9 = 18 | **9.**<br>3 + □ = 9 | **10.**<br>□ + 9 = 13 |
| **11.**<br>□ + 6 = 12 | **12.**<br>7 + □ = 14 | **13.**<br>□ + 9 = 15 | **14.**<br>7 + □ = 11 | **15.**<br>□ + 9 = 17 |
| **16.**<br>□ + 5 = 11 | **17.**<br>2 + □ = 11 | **18.**<br>□ + 0 = 9 | **19.**<br>4 + □ = 14 | **20.**<br>□ + 4 = 12 |
| **21.**<br>□ + 10 = 20 | **22.**<br>3 + □ = 8 | **23.**<br>□ + 3 = 12 | **24.**<br>4 + □ = 10 | **25.**<br>□ + 9 = 14 |
| **26.**<br>□ + 6 = 13 | **27.**<br>5 + □ = 9 | **28.**<br>□ + 8 = 10 | **29.**<br>3 + □ = 15 | **30.**<br>□ + 7 = 9 |

# MULTIPLICATION FACTS TEST

| | | | | |
|---|---|---|---|---|
| **31.**<br>□ × 9 = 81 | **32.**<br>3 × □ = 24 | **33.**<br>□ × 4 = 12 | **34.**<br>5 × □ = 30 | **35.**<br>□ × 7 = 21 |
| **36.**<br>□ × 3 = 15 | **37.**<br>4 × □ = 24 | **38.**<br>□ × 4 = 28 | **39.**<br>5 × □ = 60 | **40.**<br>□ × 3 = 27 |
| **41.**<br>□ × 5 = 25 | **42.**<br>6 × □ = 6 | **43.**<br>□ × 8 = 88 | **44.**<br>5 × □ = 20 | **45.**<br>□ × 2 = 24 |
| **46.**<br>□ × 10 = 60 | **47.**<br>5 × □ = 45 | **48.**<br>□ × 7 = 56 | **49.**<br>9 × □ = 54 | **50.**<br>□ × 5 = 55 |
| **51.**<br>□ × 5 = 35 | **52.**<br>12 × □ = 144 | **53.**<br>□ × 8 = 72 | **54.**<br>4 × □ = 32 | **55.**<br>□ × 8 = 48 |
| **56.**<br>□ × 3 = 36 | **57.**<br>8 × □ = 8 | **58.**<br>□ × 4 = 36 | **59.**<br>9 × □ = 108 | **60.**<br>□ × 10 = 100 |

## METRIC

## CUSTOMARY

### Length

1 centimeter (cm) = 10 millimeters (mm)
1 meter (m) = 1,000 millimeters
1 meter = 100 centimeters (cm)
1 meter = 10 decimeters (dm)
1 kilometer (km) = 1,000 meters

1 foot (ft) = 12 inches (in.)
1 yard (yd) = 3 feet, or 36 inches
1 mile (mi) = 1,760 yards,
   or 5,280 feet

### Capacity

1 liter (L) = 1,000 milliliters (mL)
1 metric cup = 250 milliliters
1 liter = 4 metric cups
1 kiloliter (kL) = 1,000 liters

1 tablespoon (tbsp) = 3 teaspoons (tsp)
1 cup (c) = 8 fluid ounces (fl oz)
1 pint (pt) = 2 cups
1 quart (qt) = 2 pints
1 quart = 4 cups
1 gallon (gal) = 4 quarts

### Mass/Weight

1 gram (g) = 1,000 milligrams (mg)
1 kilogram (kg) = 1,000 grams

1 pound (lb) = 16 ounces (oz)
1 ton (T) = 2,000 pounds

### TIME

1 minute (min) = 60 seconds (sec)
1 hour (hr) = 60 minutes
1 day = 24 hours
1 week (wk) = 7 days
1 year (yr) = 12 months (mo),
   or about 52 weeks
1 year = 365 days
1 leap year = 366 days
1 decade = 10 years
1 century = 100 years
1 millennium = 1,000 years

# TABLE OF MEASURES

## SYMBOLS

| | | | |
|---|---|---|---|
| $=$ | is equal to | % | percent |
| $\neq$ | is not equal to | $\approx$ | is approximately equal to |
| $>$ | is greater than | $\perp$ | is perpendicular to |
| $<$ | is less than | $\parallel$ | is parallel to |
| $\geq$ | is greater than or equal to | $\overleftrightarrow{AB}$ | line $AB$ |
| $\leq$ | is less than or equal to | $\overrightarrow{AB}$ | ray $AB$ |
| $\lvert 4 \rvert$ | the absolute value of 4 | $\overline{AB}$ | line segment $AB$ |
| $2^3$ | the third power of 2 | $\angle ABC$ | angle $ABC$ |
| $10^2$ | ten squared | $\triangle ABC$ | triangle $ABC$ |
| $10^3$ | ten cubed | $\pi$ | pi (about 3.14) |
| $10^4$ | the fourth power of 10 | $\circ$ | degree |
| $(2,3)$ | ordered pair $(x,y)$ | $^{\circ}C$ | degrees Celsius |
| $1:3$ | ratio of 1 to 3 | $^{\circ}F$ | degrees Fahrenheit |

## FORMULAS

### Perimeter

| | |
|---|---|
| Polygon | $P =$ sum of the lengths of the sides |
| Rectangle | $P = (2 \times l) + (2 \times w)$ |
| Square | $P = 4 \times s$ |

### Area

| | |
|---|---|
| Rectangle | $A = l \times w$ |
| Square | $A = s^2$ |
| Parallelogram | $A = b \times h$ |
| Triangle | $A = \frac{1}{2} \times b \times h$ |
| Circle | $A = \pi \times r^2$ |

### Circumference

| | |
|---|---|
| Circle | $C = \pi \times d$ |

### Volume

| | |
|---|---|
| Rectangular prism | $V = l \times w \times h$ |

## Pronunciation Key

| | | | | | | | | | |
|---|---|---|---|---|---|---|---|---|---|
| a | add, map | f | fit, half | n | nice, tin | p | pit, stop | yōō | fuse, few |
| ā | ace, rate | g | go, log | ng | ring, song | r | run, poor | v | vain, eve |
| â(r) | care, air | h | hope, hate | o | odd, hot | s | see, pass | w | win, away |
| ä | palm, father | i | it, give | ō | open, so | sh | sure, rush | y | yet, yearn |
| b | bat, rub | ī | ice, write | ô | order, jaw | t | talk, sit | z | zest, muse |
| ch | check, catch | j | joy, ledge | oi | oil, boy | th | thin, both | zh | vision, |
| d | dog, rod | k | cool, take | ou | pout, now | th | this, bathe | | pleasure |
| e | end, pet | l | look, rule | ŏŏ | took, full | u | up, done | | |
| ē | equal, tree | m | move, seem | ōō | pool, food | û(r) | burn, term | | |

ə   the schwa, an unstressed vowel representing the sound spelled *a* in above, *e* in sicken, *i* in possible, *o* in melon, *u* in circus

Other symbols:
• separates words into syllables
′ indicates stress on a syllable

**absolute value** [ab•sə•lōōt′ val′yōō] The distance of a number from zero on a number line (p. 480)

**acute angle** [ə•kyōōt′ ang′gəl] An angle that has a measure less than a right angle (less than 90°) (p. 428)
*Example:*

### Word History

The Latin word for needle is *acus*. This means "pointed" or "sharp." You will recognize the root in the words acid (sharp taste), acumen (mentally sharp), and *acute*, which describes a sharp or pointed angle.

**acute triangle** [ə•kyōōt′ trī′ang•gəl] A triangle that has three acute angles (p. 456)

**addends** [ad′endz] Numbers that are added in an addition problem (p. 45)

**addition** [ə•dish′en] The process of finding the total number of items when two or more groups of items are joined; the opposite of subtraction

**angle** [ang′gəl] A figure formed by two rays that meet at a common endpoint (p. 428)
*Example:*

**area** [âr′ē•ə] The number of square units needed to cover a surface (p. 562)

**arrangement** [ə′ranj•mənt] An ordering of items (p. 662)

**array** [ə•rā′] An arrangement of objects in rows and columns (p. 300)
*Example:*

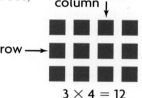

3 × 4 = 12

**Associative Property of Addition** [ə•sō′shē•ə•tiv prä′pər•tē əv ə•di′shən] The property that states that when the grouping of addends is changed, the sum is the same (p. 76)
*Example:* (5 + 8) + 4 = 5 + (8 + 4)

**Associative Property of Multiplication** [ə•sō′shē•ə•tiv prä′pər•tē əv mul•tə•plə•kā′shən] The property that states that the way factors are grouped does not change the product (p. 258)
*Example:* (2 × 3) × 4 = 2 × (3 × 4)

**average** [av′rij] See *mean.* (p. 100)

**axis** [ak′səs] The horizontal or vertical number line used in a graph or coordinate plane (p. 498)

**B**

**bar graph** [bär graf] A graph that uses horizontal or vertical bars to display countable data (p. 106) *Example:*

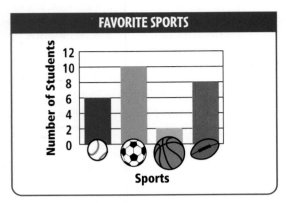

**base** [bās] A number used as a repeated factor (p. 292) *Example:* $8^3 = 8 \times 8 \times 8$. The base is 8.

**base** [bās] A polygon's side or a solid figure's face by which the figure is measured or named (pp. 466, 572) *Examples:*

**benchmark** [bench'märk] A familiar number used as a point of reference (p. 8)

**billion** [bil'yən] One thousand million; written as 1,000,000,000 (p. 4)

**C**

**capacity** [kə•pa'sə•tē] The amount a container can hold (p. 532)

**Celsius (°C)** [səl'sē•us] A metric scale for measuring temperature (p. 536)

**centimeter (cm)** [sən'tə•mē•tər] A unit for measuring length in the metric system; 0.01 meter = 1 centimeter

**central angle** [sen'trəl ang'gəl] The angle formed by two radii of a circle that meet at its center (p. 438)

**certain** [sur'tən] Sure to happen; will always happen (p. 656)

**chord** [kôrd] A line segment with endpoints on a circle (p. 438) *Example:*

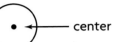

$\overline{AB}$ is a chord.

**circle** [sər'kəl] A closed figure with all points on the figure the same distance from the center point (p. 438) *Example:*

center

**circle graph** [sər'kəl graf] A graph that shows how parts of the data are related to the whole and to each other (p. 106) *Example:*

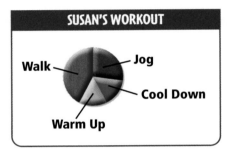

**circumference** [sər•kum'fər•əns] The distance around a circle (p. 554)

**Word History**

One of the oldest words in math is *circumference*. The Latin roots of this word are *circum* (around) and *ferre* (to carry). When you combine these roots, you get "to carry around." Think of a compass whose pencil is carried around a certain distance to trace a circle's perimeter.

**combination** [kam•bə•nā'•shən ] A choice in which the order of items does not matter (p. 662)

**common factor** [kä'mən fak'tər] A number that is a factor of two or more numbers (p. 278)

**common multiple** [kä'mən mul'tə•pəl] A number that is a multiple of two or more numbers (p. 282)

**Commutative Property of Addition** [kə•myoo'tə•tiv prä'pər•tē əv ə•di'shən] The property that states that when the order of two addends is changed, the sum is the same (p. 76) *Example:* $4 + 5 = 5 + 4$

**Commutative Property of Multiplication**
[kə•myōō′tə•tiv prä′pər•tē əv mul•tə•plə•kā′shən] The property that states that when the order of two factors is changed, the product is the same (p. 258)
*Example:* 4 × 5 = 5 × 4

**compass** [kum′pəs] A tool used to construct circles and arcs (p. 438)

**compatible numbers** [kəm•pa′tə•bəl num′bərz] Numbers that are easy to compute mentally (p. 192)

**compensation** [kam•pən•sa′shən] An estimation strategy in which you change one addend to a multiple of ten and then adjust the other addend to keep the balance (p. 76)

**composite number** [käm•pä′zət num′bər] A number having more than two factors (p. 300)
*Example:* 6 is a composite number, since its factors are 1, 2, 3, and 6.

**cone** [kōn] A solid figure that has a flat, circular base and one vertex (p. 466)
*Example:*

**congruent** [kən•grōō′ənt] Having the same size and shape (p. 442)

**coordinate plane** [kō•ôr′də•nət plān] A plane formed by two intersecting and perpendicular number lines called axes (p. 500)
*Example:*

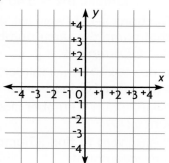

**coordinates** [kō•ôr′də•nəts] The numbers in an ordered pair (p. 500)

**corresponding angles** [kôr•ə•span′ding ang′gəlz] Angles that are in the same position in different figures (p. 442)
*Example:*

∠A and ∠D are corresponding angles.

**corresponding sides** [kôr•ə•span′ding sidz] Sides that are in the same position in different plane figures (p. 442)
*Example:*

$\overline{CA}$ and $\overline{FD}$ are corresponding sides.

**cube** [kyōōb] A solid figure with six congruent square faces (p. 588)
*Example:*

**cubic unit** [kyōō′bik yōō′nət] A unit of volume with dimensions 1 unit × 1 unit × 1 unit (p. 592)

**cumulative frequency** [kyōō′myə•lə•tiv frē′kwən•sē] A running total of data (p. 96)

**cylinder** [si′lən•dər] A solid figure that has two parallel bases that are congruent circles (p. 466)
*Example:*

**D**

**data** [dā′tə] Information collected about people or things, often to draw conclusions about them (p. 96)

**decimal** [de′sə•məl] A number with one or more digits to the right of the decimal point (p. 22)

**decimal point** [de′sə•məl point] A symbol used to separate dollars from cents in money, and the ones place from the tenths place in decimal numbers

**decimal system** [de′sə•məl sis′təm] A system of computation based on the number 10

**decimeter (dm)** [de′sə•mē•tər] A unit of length in the metric system; 10 decimeters = 1 meter

**degree (°)** [di•grē′] A unit for measuring angles or for measuring temperature (pp. 432, 536)

**denominator** [di•nä′mə•nā•tər] The number below the bar in a fraction that tells how many equal parts are in the whole (p. 346)
*Example:* $\frac{3}{4}$ ←denominator

**diameter** [di•am′ə•tər] A line segment that passes through the center of a circle and has its endpoints on the circle (p. 438)
*Example:*

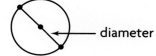

**difference** [dif′ər•əns] The answer to a subtraction problem

**digit** [di′jit] Any one of the ten symbols 0, 1, 2, 3, 4, 5, 6, 7, 8, 9 used to write numbers

**dimension** [də•men′shən] A measure in one direction

**Distributive Property of Multiplication**
[di•strib′yə•tiv prä′pər•tē əv mul•tə•plə•kā′shən] The property that states that multiplying a sum by a number is the same as multiplying each addend in the sum by the number and then adding the products (p. 260)
*Example:* $3 \times (4 + 2) = (3 \times 4) + (3 \times 2)$
$$3 \times 6 = 12 + 6$$
$$18 = 18$$

**dividend** [di′və•dend] The number that is to be divided in a division problem
*Example:* $36 \div 6$; $6\overline{)36}$   The dividend is 36.

**divisible** [də•vi′zi•bəl] A number is divisible by another number if the quotient is a whole number and the remainder is zero. (p. 276)
*Example:* 21 is divisible by 3.

**division** [də•vi′zhən] The process of sharing a number of items to find how many groups can be made or how many items will be in a group; the operation that is the opposite of multiplication

**divisor** [də•vi′zər] The number that divides the dividend
*Example:* $15 \div 3$; $3\overline{)15}$   The divisor is 3.

**double-bar graph** [du′bəl bär graf] A graph used to compare two similar kinds of data (p. 130)
*Example:*

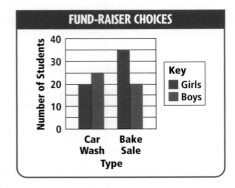

**E**

**edge** [ej] The line made where two or more faces of a solid figure meet (p. 466)
*Example:*

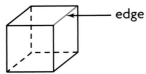

**elapsed time** [i•lapst′ tim] The time that passes between the start of an activity and the end of that activity (p. 536)

**equally likely** [ē′kwəl•lē li′klē] Having the same chance of occurring (p. 656)

**equation** [i•kwā′zhən] An algebraic or numerical sentence that shows that two quantities are equal (p. 68)

**equilateral triangle** [ē•kwə•la′tə•rəl tri′ang•gəl] A triangle with three congruent sides (p. 456)
*Example:*

**equivalent** [ē•kwiv′ə•lənt] Having the same value

**equivalent decimals** [ē•kwiv′ə•lənt de′sə•məlz] Decimals that name the same number or amount (p. 26) *Example:* $0.4 = 0.40 = 0.400$

**equivalent fractions** [ē•kwiv′ə•lənt frak′shənz] Fractions that name the same number or amount (p. 314) *Example:* $\frac{3}{4} = \frac{6}{8}$

**equivalent ratios** [ē•kwiv′ə•lənt rā′shē•ōz] Ratios that make the same comparison (p. 618)

**estimate** [es′tə•mət] *noun* A number close to an exact amount (p. 42)

**estimate** [es′tə•māt] *verb* To find a number that is close to an exact amount

**evaluate** [i•val′yə•wāt] To find the value of a numerical or algebraic expression (p. 246)

**event** [i•vent′] A set of outcomes (p. 578)

**expanded form** [ik•spand′id fôrm] A way to write numbers by showing the value of each digit (p. 2)
*Example:* $832 = 800 + 30 + 2$

**experimental probability** [ik•sper•ə•men′tal prä•ba•bil′ə•tē] The ratio of the number of times the event occurs to the total number of trials or times the activity is performed (p. 658)

**exponent** [ek'spō•nənt] A number that shows how many times the base is used as a factor (p. 292)

*Example:* $10^3 = 10 \times 10 \times 10$;
3 is the exponent.

**expression** [ik•spre'shən] A mathematical phrase or the part of a number sentence that combines numbers, operation signs, and sometimes variables, but doesn't have an equal sign (p. 64)

**face** [fās] A polygon that is a flat surface of a solid figure (p. 466)
*Example:*

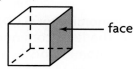
face

**factor** [fak'tər] A number multiplied by another number to find a product

**factor tree** [fak'tər trē] A diagram that shows the prime factors of a number (p. 302)

**Fahrenheit (°F)** [fâr'ən•hīt] A customary scale for measuring temperature (p. 536)

**figurate numbers** [fi'gyə•rət num'bərz] Numbers that can be represented by geometric figures (p. 456)
*Example:*

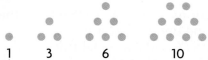

1    3    6    10

**foot (ft)** [foŏt] A unit of length in the customary system; 1 foot = 12 inches

**formula** [fôr'myə•lə] A set of symbols that expresses a mathematical rule (p. 598)
*Example:* $A = l \times w$

**fraction** [frak'shən] A number that names a part of a whole or a part of a group

**frequency table** [frē'kwen•sē tā'bəl] A table that uses numbers to record data about how often something happens (p. 95)

**front-end estimation** [frunt end es•tə•mā'shən] A method of estimating sums or differences by using the value of the front digits of the numbers (p. 42)
*Example:*
$$\begin{array}{r}245 \\ +386 \end{array} \quad \rightarrow \quad \begin{array}{r}200 \\ +300 \\ \hline 500 \end{array}$$

**function** [funk'shən] A relationship between two quantities in which one quantity depends on the other (p. 254)

**function table** [funk'shən tā'bəl] A table that matches each input value with an output value. The output values are determined by the function. (p. 254)

**gallon (gal)** [ga'lən] A customary unit for measuring capacity; 4 quarts = 1 gallon

**gram (g)** [gram] A metric unit for measuring mass; 1,000 grams = 1 kilogram

**greater than (>)** [grā'tər than] A symbol used to compare two numbers, with the greater number given first
*Example:* $6 > 4$

**greatest common factor (GCF)** [grā'təst kä'mən fak'tər] The greatest factor that two or more numbers have in common (p. 278)
*Example:* 6 is the GCF of 18 and 30.

**height** [hīt] The length of a perpendicular from the base to the top of a plane figure or solid figure (p. 572)
*Example:*
height →

**hexagon** [hek'sə•gän] A polygon with six sides and six angles (p. 434)

**histogram** [his'tə•gram] A bar graph that shows the number of times data occur within intervals (p. 128)

**hundredth** [hun'drədth] One of one hundred equal parts (p. 22)
*Examples:* 0.56  fifty-six hundredths
$\frac{45}{100}$  forty-five hundredths

**hypotenuse** [hi•pot′ə•n(y)o͞os] In a right triangle, the side opposite the right angle; the longest side in a right triangle (p. 456)

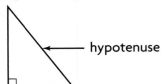
hypotenuse

### Word History

The *hypotenuse* of a right triangle looks like it is a line segment that is s-t-r-e-t-c-h-e-d. The prefix for "under" is *hypo* + the Greek word for "stretch" is *tenuse* (as in tension). So, hypotenuse is the line segment stretched under the right angle of the triangle.

**Identity Property of Addition** [i•den′tə•tē prä′pər•tē əv ə•di′shen] The property that states that when you add zero to a number, the result is that number (p. 76)

**Identity Property of Multiplication** [i•den′tə•tē prä′pər•tē əv mul•te•plə•kā′shen] The property that states that the product of any number and 1 is that number (p. 258)

**impossible** [im•pä′sə•bəl] Not able to happen; can never happen (p. 656)

**inch (in.)** [inch] A customary unit for measuring length or distance; 12 inches = 1 foot

**inequality** [in•i•kwä′lə•tē] A number sentence that shows that two amounts are not equal (p. 74)

**integers** [in′ti•jərz] The set of whole numbers and their opposites (p. 480)

**intersecting lines** [in•tər•sek′ting linz] Lines that cross each other at exactly one point (p. 428)
*Example:*

**interval** [in′tər•vəl] The distance between one number and the next on the scale of a graph (p. 116)

**inverse operations** [in′vərs ä•pə•rā′shənz] Operations that undo each other, like addition and subtraction or multiplication and division (p. 246)

**isosceles triangle** [i•sä′sə•lēz tri′ang•gəl] A triangle with exactly two congruent sides (p. 456)
*Example:*

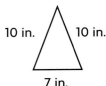
10 in.   10 in.
7 in.

**K**

**kilogram (kg)** [ki′lə•gram] A metric unit that is used to measure mass; 1,000 grams = 1 kilogram

**kiloliter (kL)** [ki′lə•lē•tər] A metric unit that is used to measure capacity; 1,000 liters = 1 kiloliter

**kilometer (km)** [kə•lä′mə•tər] A metric unit that is used to measure length or distance; 1,000 meters = 1 kilometer

**L**

**least common denominator (LCD)** [lēst kä′mən di•nä′mə•nā•tər] The least common multiple of two or more denominators (p. 356)
*Example:* The LCD for $\frac{1}{4}$ and $\frac{5}{6}$ is 12.

**least common multiple (LCM)** [lēst kä′mən mul′tə•pəl] The least number, other than zero, that is a common multiple of two or more numbers (p. 282)

**leg** [leg] In a right triangle, either of the two sides that form the right angle (p. 456)

**less than (<)** [less than] A symbol used to compare two numbers, with the lesser number given first
*Example:* 4 < 6

**like fractions** [lik frak′shənz] Fractions that have the same denominator (p. 346)
*Example:* $\frac{2}{5}$ and $\frac{4}{5}$ are like fractions.

**line** [lin] A straight path in a plane, extending in both directions with no endpoints (p. 428)
*Example:*

**linear unit** [li′nē•ər yo͞o′nət] A measure of length, width, height, or distance (p. 528)

**line graph** [lin graf] A graph that uses a line to show how data change over time (p. 106)

**line plot** [līn plät] A graph that shows frequency of data along a number line (p. 96)
*Example:*

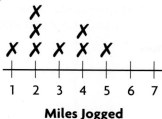

**Miles Jogged**

**line segment** [līn seg′mənt] A part of a line between two endpoints (p. 428)

**line symmetry** [līn si′mə•trē] A figure has line symmetry if a line can separate the figure into two congruent parts (p. 446)

**liter (L)** [lē′tər] A metric unit for measuring capacity; 1 liter = 1,000 milliliters

**map scale** [map skāl] A ratio that compares distance on a map with actual distance (p. 622)

**mass** [mas] The amount of matter in an object

**mean** [mēn] The average of a set of numbers, found by dividing the sum of the set by the number of addends (p. 100)

**median** [mē′dē•ən] The middle number in a set of data that are arranged in order (p. 102)

**meter (m)** [mē′tər] A metric unit for measuring length or distance; 1 meter = 100 centimeters

**mile (mi)** [mīl] A customary unit for measuring length or distance; 5,280 feet = 1 mile

**milligram (mg)** [mil′ə•gram] A metric unit for measuring mass; 1,000 milligrams = 1 gram

**milliliter (mL)** [mi′lə•lē•tər] A metric unit for measuring capacity; 1,000 milliliters = 1 liter

**millimeter (mm)** [mi′lə•mē•tər] A metric unit for measuring length or distance; 1 millimeter = 0.001 meter

**million** [mil′yən] 1,000 thousands; written as 1,000,000 (p. 4)

**mixed number** [mikst num′bər] A number that is made up of a whole number and a fraction (p. 320) *Example:* $1\frac{5}{8}$

**mode** [mōd] The number or numbers that occur most often in a set of data (p. 102)

**multiple** [mul′tə•pəl] The product of a given whole number and another whole number (p. 148)

**multiplication** [mul•tə•plə•kā′shən] A process to find the total number of items made up of equal-sized groups, or to find the total number of items in a given number of groups. It is the opposite operation of division.

**multistep problems** [mul′ti•stəp prä′bləmz] Problems requiring more than one step to solve (p. 378)

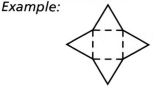

**negative integer** [ne′gə•tiv in′ti•jər] Any integer less than zero (p. 480)
*Examples:* ⁻4, ⁻5, and ⁻6 are negative integers.

**net** [net] A two-dimensional pattern that can be folded into a three-dimensional polyhedron (p. 588)
*Example:*

**number line** [num′bər līn] A line with equally spaced tick marks named by numbers. A number line does not always start at 0. (p. 10)
*Example:*

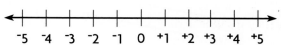

**numerator** [noō′mə•rā•tər] The number above the bar in a fraction that tells how many equal parts of the whole are being considered (p. 314)
*Example:* $\frac{3}{4}$ ←numerator

**obtuse angle** [äb•toōs′ ang′gəl] An angle whose measure is greater than 90° and less than 180° (p. 428)
*Example:*

**obtuse triangle** [äb•toōs′ trī′ang•gəl] A triangle that has one obtuse angle (p. 456)

**octagon** [äk′tə•gän] A polygon with eight sides and eight angles (p. 434)
*Example:*

**opposites** [ä′pə•zəts] Two numbers that are the same distance, but in opposite directions, from zero on a number line (p. 480)

**ordered pair** [ôr′dərd pâr] A pair of numbers used to locate a point on a grid. The first number tells the left-right position and the second number tells the up-down position. (p. 120)

**order of operations** [ôr′dər əv ä•pə•rā′shənz] Rules for performing operations in expressions with more than one operation (p. 250)

**origin** [ôr′ə•jən] The point where the two axes of a coordinate plane intersect, (0,0) (p. 500)

**ounce (oz)** [ouns] A customary unit used to measure weight

**outcome** [out′kum] A possible result of an experiment (p. 654)

**outlier** [out′li•ər] A value separated from the rest of the data (p. 96)

**parallel lines** [par′ə•lel linz] Lines in a plane that do not intersect (p. 428)
*Example:*

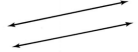

**parallelogram** [pâ•rə•lel′ə•gram] A quadrilateral whose opposite sides are parallel and congruent (p. 460)
*Example:*

**parentheses** [pə•ren′thə•sēz] The symbols used to show which operation or operations in an expression should be done first

**pentagon** [pen′tə•gän] A polygon with five sides and five angles (p. 434)
*Example:*

**percent** [pər•sent′] A ratio of a number to 100 (p. 632)

**perimeter** [pə•rim′ə•tər] The distance around a closed plane figure (p. 548)

**period** [pir′ē•əd] Each group of three digits in a large number (p. 2)

**perpendicular lines** [pər•pen•dik′yə•lər linz] Two lines that intersect to form right angles (p. 428)
*Example:*

**pi (π)** [pī] The ratio of the circumference to the diameter of a circle; an approximate decimal value of pi is 3.14. (p. 494)

**pictograph** [pik′tə•graf] A graph that displays countable data with symbols or pictures (p. 106) *Example:*

| HOW WE GET TO SCHOOL | |
|---|---|
| **Walk** | ✺ ✺ ✺ |
| **Ride a Bike** | ✺ ✺ ✺ ✺ |
| **Ride a Bus** | ✺ ✺ ✺ ✺ ✺ ✺ |
| **Ride in a Car** | ✺ ✺ |

Key: Each ✺ = 10 students

**pint (pt)** [pīnt] A customary unit for measuring capacity; 2 cups = 1 pint

**place value** [plās val′yōo] The value of a place, such as ones or tens, in a number (p. 2)

**plane** [plān] A flat surface that extends without end in all directions (p. 428)
*Example:*

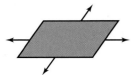

**plane figure** [plān fig′yər] A figure that lies in a plane (p. 434)

**point** [point] An exact location in space, usually represented by a dot (p. 428)

**polygon** [pol′•i•gon] A closed plane figure formed by three or more line segments (p. 434)
*Examples:*

**polyhedron** [pol•i•hē′drən] A solid figure with faces that are polygons (p. 466)
*Examples:*

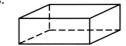

**population** [pä·pyə·lā'shən] The entire group of objects or individuals considered for a survey (p. 96)

**positive integer** [pä'zə·tiv in'ti·jər] Any integer greater than zero (p. 480)

**possible outcomes** [pä'sə·bəl out'kumz] The events that have a chance of happening in an experiment (p. 656)

**pound (lb)** [pound] A customary unit used to measure weight

**precision** [pri·sizh'ən] A property of measurement that is related to the unit of measure used; the smaller the unit of measure used, the more precise the measurement is (p. 522)

**prediction** [pri·dik'shən] A reasonable guess as to the outcome of an event (p. 220)

**prime factorization** [prīm fak·tə·ri·zā'shən] A number written as the product of all its prime factors (p. 302)

**prime number** [prim num'bər] A number that has exactly two factors: 1 and itself (p. 300)
*Examples:* 5, 7, 11, 13, 17, and 19 are prime numbers.

**prioritize** [pri·or'ə·tīz] To put events in order of importance (p. 394)

**prism** [priz'əm] A solid figure that has two congruent, polygon-shaped bases, and other faces that are all rectangles (p. 466)
*Examples:*

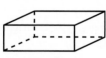 

rectangular prism          triangular prism

**probability** [prä·bə·bil'ə·tē] The likelihood that an event will happen (p. 654)

**product** [prä'dəkt] The answer to a multiplication problem

**proportion** [prə por'shən] An equation that shows that two ratios are equal (p. 618)
*Example:* $\frac{1}{3} = \frac{3}{9}$

**protractor** [prō'trak·tər] A tool used for measuring or drawing angles (p. 432)

**pyramid** [pir'ə·mid] A solid figure with a polygon base and all other faces triangles that meet at a common vertex (p. 466)
*Example:*

**Word History**

A fire is sometimes in the shape of a pyramid, with a point at the top and a wider base. This may be how *pyramid* got its name. The Greek word for fire was *pura*, which may have been combined with the Egyptian word *mer*.

**Q**

**quadrilateral** [kwäd·rə·lat'ə·rəl] A polygon with four sides (p. 460)
*Example:*

**quart (qt)** [kwôrt] A customary unit for measuring capacity; 2 pints = 1 quart

**quotient** [kwō'shənt] The number, not including the remainder, that results from dividing
*Example:* 8 ÷ 4 = 2. The quotient is 2.

**R**

**radius** [rā'dē·əs] A line segment with one endpoint at the center of a circle and the other endpoint on the circle (p. 438)
*Example:*

radius

**random sample** [ran'dəm sam'pəl] A sample in which each subject in the population has an equal chance of being chosen (p. 96)

**range** [rānj] The difference between the greatest number and the least number in a set of data (p. 96)
*Example:* 2, 2, 3, 5, 7, 7, 8, 9
The range is 9 − 2 = 7.

**ratio** [rā'shē·ō] The comparison of two quantities (p. 614)

**ray** [rā] A part of a line; it begins at one endpoint and extends forever in one direction. (p. 428)
*Example:*

**reciprocal** [ri·sip'rə·kəl] One of two numbers whose product is 1 (p. 404)
*Example:* 8 and $\frac{1}{8}$ are reciprocals since $8 \times \frac{1}{8} = 1$.

**rectangle** [rek′tang•gəl] A parallelogram with four right angles (p. 460)
*Example:*

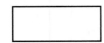

**rectangular prism** [rek•tang′gyə•lər pri′zəm] A solid figure in which all six faces are rectangles (p. 466)
*Example:*

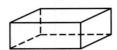

**reflection** [ri•flek′shən] A movement of a figure to a new position by flipping it over a line; a flip (p. 462)
*Example:*

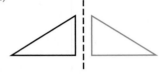

**regular polygon** [re′gyə•lər pä′lē•gän] A polygon in which all sides are congruent and all angles are congruent (p. 434)

**rhombus** [räm′bəs] A parallelogram with four congruent sides (p. 460)
*Example:*

### Word History

*Rhombus* is almost identical to its Greek origin, *rhombos*. The original meaning is "spinning top" or "magic wheel," which is easy to imagine when you look at a rhombus, an equilateral parallelogram.

**right angle** [rīt ang′gəl] A special angle formed by perpendicular lines and equal to 90° (p. 428)
*Example:*

**right triangle** [rīt trī′ang•gəl] A triangle that has a right angle (p. 456)
*Example:*

**rotation** [rō•tā′shən] A movement of a figure to a new position by turning it around a vertex or point of rotation; a turn (p. 462)
*Example:*

**rotational symmetry** [rō•tā′shən•əl si′mə•trē] A property of a figure that, when rotated less than 360° about a central point or a point of rotation, still matches the original figure (p. 446)

**rounding** [round′ing] Replacing a number with one that tells about how many or how much (p. 38)

## S

**sample** [sam′pəl] A part of a population (p. 96)

**sample space** [sam′pəl spās] The set of all possible outcomes (p. 656)

**scale** [skāl] A series of numbers starting at zero and placed at fixed distances on a graph to help label the graph (p. 116)

**scale drawing** [skāl drô′ing] A reduced or enlarged drawing whose shape is the same as an actual object and whose size is determined by the scale (p. 622)

**scalene triangle** [skā′lēn trī′ang•gəl] A triangle with no congruent sides (p. 456)
*Example:*

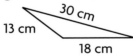

**schedule** [skej′ōō•əl] A table that lists activities or events and the times they happen

**similar** [si′mə•lər] Having the same shape, but not necessarily the same size (p. 442)
*Example:*

**simplest form** [sim′pləst fôrm] A fraction is in simplest form when the numerator and denominator have only 1 as their common factor. (p. 316)

**solid figure** [sä′ləd fig′yər] A three-dimensional figure (p. 466)

**solution** [sə•lōō′shən] A value that, when substituted for the variable, makes an equation true (p. 70)

**sphere** [sfir] A round object whose curved surface is the same distance from the center to all its points (p. 466)
*Example:*

**square** [skwâr] A polygon with four equal sides (p. 460)
*Example:*

**square number** [skwâr num'bər] The product of a number and itself (p. 292)
*Example:* $4^2 = 16$; 16 is a square number.

**square pyramid** [skwâr pir'ə•mid] A solid figure with a square base and with four triangular faces that have a common point (p. 466)
*Example:*

**square unit** [skwâr yoo'nət] A unit of area with dimensions 1 unit × 1 unit (p. 564)

**standard form** [stan'dərd fôrm] A way to write numbers by using the digits 0-9, with each digit having a place value (p. 2)
*Example:* 456 ← standard form

**stem-and-leaf plot** [stem and lēf plot] A table that shows groups of data arranged by place value (p. 104)
*Example:*

| Stem | Leaves | | | |
|------|--------|---|---|---|
| 1 | 1 | 2 | 4 | |
| 2 | 0 | 3 | 4 | 5 |
| 3 | 4 | 5 | 7 | |
| 4 | 0 | 0 | 1 | 2 |

**Number of Tickets Sold**

**subtraction** [səb•trak'shən] The process of finding how many are left when a number of items are taken away from a group of items; the process of finding the difference when two groups are compared; the opposite of addition

**sum** [sum] The answer to an addition problem

**surface area** [sûr'fəs âr'ē•ə] The sum of the areas of all the faces, or surfaces, of a solid figure (p. 590)

**survey** [sûr'vā] A method of gathering information about a group (p. 96)

**ten-thousandth** [ten thou'zəndth] One of ten thousand equal parts (p. 22)
*Example:* 0.5784 = five thousand, seven hundred eighty-four ten-thousandths

**tenth** [tenth] One of ten equal parts (p. 22)
*Example:* 0.7 = seven tenths

**tessellation** [tes•ə•lā'shən] A repeating pattern of closed figures that covers a surface with no gaps and no overlaps (p. 462)
*Example:*

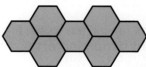

**theoretical probability** [thē•ə•re'ti•kəl prä•bə•bil'ə•tē] A comparison of the number of favorable outcomes to the number of possible equally likely outcomes (p. 656)

**thousandth** [thou'zəndth] One of one thousand equal parts (p. 22)
*Example:* 0.006 = six thousandths

**ton (T)** [tun] A customary unit used to measure weight; 2,000 pounds = 1 ton

**transformation** [trans•fər•mā'shən] A movement of a figure to a new position by a translation, reflection, or rotation (p. 462)

**translation** [trans•lā'shən] A movement of a figure to a new position along a straight line; a slide (p. 462)
*Example:*

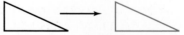

**trapezoid** [tra'pə•zoid] A quadrilateral with exactly one pair of parallel sides (p. 460)
*Example:*

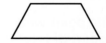

**tree diagram** [trē di'ə•gram] An organized list that shows all possible outcomes for an event (p. 660)

**trend** [trend] A pattern over time, in all or part of a graph, where the data increase, decrease, or stay the same (p. 107)

**triangle** [trī'ang•gəl] A polygon with three sides (p. 434)
*Example:*

**triangular numbers** [trī•ang′gyə•lər num′bərz] Numbers that can be represented by triangular figures (p. 456)
*Example:*

1    3    6    10

**unlike fractions** [un•līk′ frak′shənz] Fractions that have different denominators (p. 348)
*Example:* $\frac{3}{4}$ and $\frac{2}{5}$ are unlike fractions.

**unlikely** [un•līk′lē] Having a less-than-even chance of happening (p. 653)

**variable** [vâr′ē•ə•bəl] A letter or symbol that stands for one or more numbers (p. 64)

**Venn diagram** [ven dī′ə•gram] A diagram that shows relationships among sets of things (p. 126)
*Example:*

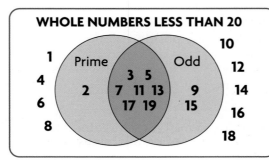

**vertex** [vûr′teks] The point where two or more rays meet; the point of intersection of two sides of a polygon; the point of intersection of three or more edges of a solid figure; the top point of a cone; the plural of vertex is vertices (pp. 428, 466)
*Examples:*

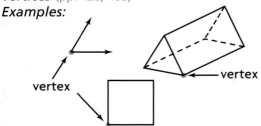

vertex

vertex

vertex

**Word History**

The Latin word *vertere* means to turn and also relates to highest. You can turn a figure around a point or *vertex*.

**volume** [väl′yəm] The measure of the space a solid figure occupies (p. 592)

**whole number** [hōl num′bər] One of the numbers 0, 1, 2, 3, 4, . . . . The set of whole numbers goes on without end.

**word form** [wurd fôrm] A way to write numbers in standard English (p. 2)
*Example:* 4,829 = four thousand, eight hundred twenty-nine

**x-axis** [eks•ak′səs] The horizontal number line on a coordinate plane (p. 498)

**x-coordinate** [eks•kō•ôr′də•nət] The first number in an ordered pair, which tells the distance to move right or left from (0,0)

**y-axis** [wī•ak′səs] The vertical number line on a coordinate plane (p. 498)

**y-coordinate** [wī•kō•ôr′də•nət] The second number in an ordered pair, which tells the distance to move up or down from (0,0) (p. 500)

**Z**

**Zero Property of Multiplication** [zē′rō prä′pər•tē əv mul•tə•plə•kā′shən] The property that states that when you multiply by zero, the product is zero (p. 258)

**Draw Conclusions,** 30–31, 125
**Draw a Diagram strategy,** 126–127, 256–257, 490–491
**Draw a Picture strategy.** *See* Draw a Diagram strategy

## E

**Edges,** 466–468
**Elapsed time,** 536–538
**Equally likely outcomes,** 656–657
**Equations,** 68
    addition, 68–73, 78, 80–81
    division, 245, 247–248
    with exponents, 294, 304
    graphing simple linear, 513
    multiplication, 245, 247–249, 258–259
    solving, 70–72, 244, 247–249, 258–259
    subtraction, 68–72, 80–81
    using mental math to solve, 71–72, 76–79, 258–259
    variables in, 68–76, 80–81, 247–249, 254–255, 258–259
    writing, 62, 68–72, 80–81, 247–249, 254–255, 258–259
**Equilateral triangles,** 456–459
**Equivalent decimals,** 26–27
**Equivalent fractions,** 314–325, 345, 354–355, 374–375
**Equivalent ratios,** 618–620, 622
**Error analysis.** *See* What's the Error?
**Estimate or Actual Measurement,** 540–541
**Estimation**
    to check reasonableness of answer, 46–51, 150–153, 156–157, 197
    clustering, 45
    compatible numbers, 55, 192–193, 196, 210–211
    of decimals, 37, 42–45, 48–51, 55, 170–172, 232
    of differences, 42–44, 46–51, 352–353, 372–373, 376–377
    in division, 190–194, 196–197, 210–211, 216–219, 232
    or exact answer, 540–541
    of fractions, 352–353, 372–373, 376–377
    front-end, 43–44
    of measurements, 8–9, 522–527, 530, 537, 540–541, 548–549
    of mixed numbers, 369–370, 372–373, 376–377
    multiples of ten, 148–149, 156–157
    overestimate, 157
    of products, 8–9, 148–153, 156–157, 170–172
    of sums, 42–51, 54, 352–353, 369–370, 376–377
    underestimate, 157
    use benchmark numbers, 8–9, 352–353
    *See also* Rounding
**Estimation strategies**
    benchmark numbers, 8–9, 352–353
    clustering, 45
    compatible numbers, 55, 192–193, 196, 210–211
    front-end, 43–44
    overestimate, 157
    rounding, 37–45, 148–153, 156–157, 170
    underestimate, 157
**Euclidean algorithm,** 281
**Evaluate Answers for Reasonableness,** 156–157
**Even and odd numbers,** 276–277
**Events.** *See* Probability
**Expanded form**
    of decimals, 21–26
    with exponential notation, 297–299
    of whole numbers, 1–7, 297–299
**Experiments (probability),** 654–655, 658–659, 675
**Explain,** *Opportunities to explain are contained in every exercise set. Some examples are* 5, 40, 49, 98, 107, 149, 193, 213, 228, 255, 350, 373, 657
**Explain It,** 18–19, 34–35, 60–61, 84–85, 112–113, 136–137, 160–161, 224–225, 242–243, 264–265, 288–289, 334–335, 364–365, 382–383, 398–399, 416–417, 452–453, 476–477, 494–495, 510–511, 544–545, 558–559, 584–585, 602–603, 628–629, 650–651, 668–669
**Exponential notation,** 297–299, 303–304
**Exponents,** 292–299

evaluating, 292–296
expressions with, 296–299
of nonnegative integers, 292–299
patterns in, 295–297
in prime factorizations, 303–304
scientific notation, 337
writing, 292–295, 303–304
**Expressions,** 64
    algebraic, 64–67, 246, 248–249, 261
    evaluating, 65–67, 246, 248, 250–251, 261
    with exponents, 296–299
    with variables, 64–67, 246, 248–249, 261
    writing, 64–67, 246, 248–249
**Extra Practice,** 16, 32, 58, 82, 110, 134, 158, 178, 202, 222, 240, 262, 286, 308, 332, 362, 380, 396, 414, 450, 474, 492, 508, 542, 556, 582, 600, 626, 648, 666

## F

**Faces,** 466–468
**Fact families,** 245
**Factor trees,** 302–304
**Factors,** 278–281
    common, 278–281, 314, 336, 392
    finding all, 278–280, 300
    finding prime factors of a number, 302–305
    greatest common, 278–281, 284–285, 316–318, 392–393
    prime, 302–305
    *See also* Multiplication *and* Prime factorization
**Fahrenheit temperature,** 122–124, 537–538
**Fairness,** 671
**Fast Fact,** xxviii, 7, 20, 25, 36, 51, 62, 72, 94, 105, 114, 118, 146, 155, 162, 169, 190, 195, 206, 219, 226, 234, 244, 249, 274, 281, 290, 299, 312, 344, 358, 366, 377, 384, 391, 400, 410, 426, 433, 454, 458, 478, 485, 496, 502, 520, 533, 553, 560, 570, 586, 594, 612, 617, 630, 635, 652, 663
**FCAT Handbook,** H1–H35
**Feet,** 522–524, 528–530, 540–541
**Figurate numbers,** 459
**Figures.** *See* plane figures *and* solid figures
**Find a Pattern strategy,** 448–449
**Finding a rule.** *See* Algebra and Functions
**Flips.** *See* Reflections
**Fluid ounces,** 532–533
**Formulas**
    for area of circles, 605
    for area of rectangles, 564–567, 598–599
    for changing from Celsius to Fahrenheit, 537–538
    deriving
        for area, 564–565, 572, 576–577
        for area of parallelograms, 576–577
        for area of triangles, 572
        for circumference of circles, 554–555
        for volume of rectangular prisms, 592–593
        for perimeter of polygons, 550–551, 598–599
        for surface area of a solid, 590–591
**Fractions**
    adding
        like denominators, 346–347, 423
        unlike denominators, 348–351, 354–361, 423
    change a fraction to a decimal, 238–239, 328–331
    comparing, 313, 322–326, 353
    decimals and, 238–239, 328–331
    decimals, percents, and, 636–641
    denominators, 313, 322–323, 354–359
    dividing, 402–403, 406–410
    equivalent, 314–325, 345, 354–355, 374–375
    estimating, 352–353, 369–370, 372–373, 376–377
    greatest common factor, 317–318, 392–393
    improper, 320–321, 374–375
    least common denominator, 354–359, 368–369, 372, 376
    like, 322–323, 346–347

compare and contrast, 503
congruent, 442–445, 517
measuring and drawing, 428–441, 457–458
perimeter of, 548–551, 596–597
relationship between perimeter and area, 568–571, 596–597
similar, 442–445, 517
symmetry in, 446–447
transforming, 462–465, 504–505
visualize and draw three-dimensional objects from two-dimensional views, 470–471
*See also* Polygons

**Planes,** 428–431

**Plots**
line, 97, 103, 130–132
stem-and-leaf, 104–105, 130

**Points,** 428–431
with ordered pairs, 115, 120–121, 498–507

**Polygons,** 434–437
angles in, 434–437
decagons, 434–437
degrees in, 435–437
hexagons, 434–437
octagons, 434–437
parallelograms, 460–461, 576–579
pentagons, 434–437
quadrilaterals, 434–437, 460–461
rectangles, 460–461, 564–571
regular, 434–437
rhombuses, 460–461
squares, 460–461, 564–571
trapezoids, 460–461
triangles, 434–437, 456–459, 572–575

**Population,** 96–98

**Positive integers,** 480–491

**Possible outcomes,** 656–657

**Pounds,** 532–533

**Powers,** 294
of nonnegative integers, 292–299
of ten, 296–298
of two, 292–293
*See also* Exponents

**Precision,** 523–524

**Predict and Test strategy,** 220–221

**Predictions,** 658–659
of future events, 658

**Prime factorization,** 302–304
exponents in, 303–304
repeated multiplication and, 303

**Prime factors,** 302–305

**Prime numbers,** 300–301, 341

**Prioritizing information,** 394–395

**Prisms,** 466–469
bases of, 466–469
classifying, 466–469
modeling with nets, 588–589
surface area of, 590–591, 596–597
volume of, 592–597, 609

**Probability,** 654–663
arrangements, 662–663
certain events, 656–657
combinations, 662–663
equally likely outcomes, 656–657
experimental, 658–659
experiments, 654–655, 658–659, 675
fairness, 671
impossible events, 656–657
likely events, 656–657
possible outcomes, 654–657
and predictions, 658–659
tree diagrams, 660–661

**Problem solving.** *See* Linkup, Problem Solving in Florida, Problem solving skills, Problem solving strategies, *and* Thinker's Corner

**Problem Solving in Florida,** 92–93, 144–145, 188–189, 272–273, 342–343, 424–425, 518–519, 610–611, 676–677
Anastasia State Recreation Area, 343
Architectural Sites, 519
Butterfly World, 188
Coasting Along, 610
Florida Citrus, 424
Going 'Round in Circles, 611
Hummingbirds, 189
Jonathan Dickinson State Park, 676
Miami Beach Architecture, 518
A Shining Beacon, 92
Ski Flying, 145
Sugarcane, 425
Sunshine Skyway Bridge, 273
Strawberry Festival, 342
Tallahassee, 677
Towers of Light, 93
Wakeboarding, 144
Weedon Island Preserve, 272

**Problem solving skills**
Choose the Operation, 236–237
Draw Conclusions, 30–31, 125
Estimate or Actual Measurement, 540–541
Evaluate Answers for Reasonableness, 156–157
Identify Relationships, 284–285
Interpret the Remainder, 200–201
Make Decisions, 176–177
Make Generalizations, 552–553
Multistep Problems, 378–379
Relevant or Irrelevant Information, 506–507
Sequence and Prioritize Information, 394–395
Too Much/Too Little Information, 624–625
Use a Formula, 598–599
Use a Table, 14–15, 277, 280, 285

**Problem solving strategies**
Compare Strategies, 126–127, 256–257, 490–491
Draw a Diagram/picture, 126–127, 256–257, 490–491
Find a Pattern, 448–449
Make a Graph, 104–105, 646–647
Make a Model, 326–327, 472–473
Make an Organized List, 664–665
Make a Table, 306–307
Predict and Test, 220–221
Solve a Simpler Problem, 412–413, 580–581
Use a Formula, 598–599
Use Logical Reasoning, 56–57
Work Backward, 256–257, 360–361
Write an Equation, 80–81

**Products**
zeros in, 148–149, 174–175

**Projects,** xxiv, 86, 138, 182, 266, 336, 418, 512, 604, 670

**Properties**
Associative Property
of Addition, 76–79
of Multiplication, 258–259
Commutative Property
of Addition, 76–79
of Multiplication, 258–259
Distributive Property, 260–261
Identity Property
of Addition, 76–79
of Multiplication, 258–259
Zero Property, 258–259

**Proportions,** 619–621
enlarging drawings with, 619–620
reducing drawings with, 619–620

**Protractor,** 432–433, 439, 443, 457

**Pyramids**
classifying, 466–469
hexagonal, 466
modeling with nets, 588–589
pentagonal, 466

draw, 470–471
edges of, 466–468
faces of, 466–468
identify, 466–468, 471
prism, 466–469
properties, 466–469
pyramid, 466–469
sphere, 467–469
surface area of, 590–591, 596–597
vertices of, 466–468
visualize and draw two-dimensional views of, 470–471
volume of, 592–597, 609

**Solution,** 74
**Solve a Simpler Problem strategy,** 412–413, 580–581
**Solving equations,** 70–72, 244, 247–249, 258–259
**Sphere,** 467–469
**Spinners,** 656–657
**Spreadsheet,** 91, 143, 609
**Square,** 460–461
**Square number,** 292–294
**Square pyramid,** 466
**Square roots,** 305
**Square units,** 562–567, 596–597
**Standard form**
  of decimals, 22–29
  of whole numbers, 2–6
**Standard units,** *See* Customary units *and* Metric units
**Statistics**
  averages, 100–101
  bar graph, 94, 106, 109, 116–117, 119, 130–132
  circle graph, 107–109, 130–132, 646–647
  line graph, 107–108, 122–125, 130–132
  mean, 100–101, 104–105
  median, 102–105
  mode, 102–105
  pictograph, 51, 106, 108
  range, 98, 104
  survey, 96–98
  *See also* Data
**Stem-and-leaf plots,** 104–105, 130
**Straight angle,** 428–431
**Study Guide and Review,** 88–89, 140–141, 184–185, 268–269, 338–339, 420–421, 514–515, 606–607, 672–673
**Substitution,** 66–68, 246–248
**Subtraction**
  across zeros, 246
  basic facts, H36
  of decimals, 42–44, 48–51, 53–55
  equations, 68–72, 78, 80–81
  estimation and, 42–51, 352–353, 372–373, 376–377
  of integers, 486–489
  of like fractions, 346–347
  mental math, 53–55, 77–78, 82
  of mixed numbers, 372–373, 376–379
  modeling, 346, 348–349, 372, 374–375, 486–488
  of units of measure, 529–530
  of units of time, 536–538
  of unlike fractions, 348–351, 354–361
  of whole numbers, xxvi, 37, 39, 42–44, 46–48, 52–55, 64–66, H36
**Sum.** *See* Addition
**Surface area,** 590–591, 596–597
  using two-dimensional patterns, 590–591
**Surveys,** 96–98, 133
**Symbols**
  angle, 428–430
  degree, 428
  line, 428–430
  line segment, 428–430
  percent, 632–633
  ray, 428–430
**Symmetry**
  line, 446–447
  rotational, 446–447

## T

**Table of Measures,** H41–H42
**Tables and charts**
  analyzing data from, 326–328
  frequency, 95, 97–99, 128–129
  function, 66, 254–255, 498–499
  input/output, 229, 499
  making, 306–307
  organizing data in, 50, 220–221, 306–307
  tally tables, 98, 111, 128, 654–655
  using, 14–15, 101, 105, 116–118, 122–124, 127–129, 248, 378–379
**Tally tables,** 98, 111, 128, 654–655
**Technology**
  Calculators, 52–55, 100, 154–155, 158, 174, 187, 198–199, 218, 238, 271, 293, 316, 341, 356, 372, 392, 423, 528, 593, 609, 643, 675
  Harcourt Mega Math software, 2, 5–8, 13–15, 22, 26, 30, 46, 48, 67, 72, 102, 120, 153, 171, 199, 213, 231, 248, 251, 255, 277, 303, 321, 346, 373, 387, 403, 443, 447, 457, 462, 471, 481, 484, 503, 505, 533, 535, 564, 593, 642, 655, 658
  Multimedia Math Glossary, 1, 21, 35, 63, 91, 95, 115, 143, 145, 161, 187, 191, 205, 227, 245, 271, 275, 291, 313, 341, 345, 367, 385, 401, 423, 427, 455, 479, 495, 517, 521, 547, 561, 587, 609, 613, 631, 653, 675
  using a drawing tool, 517
  using spreadsheets, 91, 143, 609
**Technology Links,** 24, 46, 48, 120, 213, 231, 251, 346, 373, 388, 403, 457, 462, 471, 481, 484, 487, 593, 642, 655
**Technology Linkup,** 91, 143, 187, 271, 341, 423, 517, 609, 675
**Temperature**
  changing from Celsius to Fahrenheit, 537–538
  measuring, 122–124, 537–538
**Ten millions,** 4–7
**Ten-thousandths,** 23–24, 26–27
**Tenths,** 22–31, 255
**Tessellations,** 463–465, 512
**Test-taking strategies.** *See* Tips for Success on FCAT
**Thinker's Corner,** 7, 13, 45, 55, 67, 79, 119, 215, 235, 295, 299, 319, 331, 359, 437, 441, 459, 469, 531, 539, 567, 571, 575, 579, 595, 645
**Thousandths,** 22–29
**Three-dimensional figures**
  attributes, 466–469
  draw, 470–471
  *See also* Solid figures
**Time,** 536–539
  finding elapsed time, 536–538
  leap year, 536
  measuring, 536–539
  sequence, 371
  units of, 536–538
  using a schedule, 539
**Tips for Success on FCAT,** H2–H5
**Tons,** 532–533
**Too Much/Too Little Information,** 624–625
**Transformations,** 462–465, 504–505
**Translations (slides),** 462–465, 504–506
**Trapezoids,** 460–461
**Tree diagrams,** 660–661
**Triangle**
  acute, 456–459
  area of, 572–575
  classifying, 456–459
  degrees in, 435–437
  drawing, 457–458, 517
  equilateral, 456–459
  identify attributes of, 434–437
  isosceles, 456–459
  obtuse, 456–459
  right, 456–459
    hypotenuse, 456–457
    leg, 456–457

# PHOTO CREDITS

iv Gloria H. Chomica/Masterfile; v (t) Todd Warshaw/Allsport USA; v (b) Rod Planck/Dembinsky Photo Associates; viii Duomo Photography; xi Latent Image Photography; xi Tom & Dee Ann McCarthy/The Stock Market; xv (t) Ron Scherl/StageImage; xv (b) Tui De Roy/Bruce Coleman, Inc.; xvi Tony Freeman/PhotoEdit.; xvii NASA; xx Davies & Starr/Stone; xxvii (b) Ron Kimball; 0 Earth Imaging/Stone; 2 David Barnes/Stone; 3 Mark Newman/New England Stock Photo; 4 (t)Leonard McCombe/TimePix; 4 (b) Corbis Digital Stock; 5 NASA; 6 Telegraph Colour Library/FPG International; 8 Mary Eleanor Browning/Photo Researchers; 10 Michael Hubrich/Dembinsky Photo Associates; 13 (t) Telegraph Colour Library/FPG International; 16 W. Metzen/H. Armstrong Roberts; 16 (inset 1) Dr. Dennis Kunkel/Phototake; 16 (inset 2) Grant Heilman/Grant Heilman Photography; 16 (inset 3) Ed Reschke/Peter Arnold Inc.; 16 (inset 4) Larry Lefever/Grant Heilman Photography; 16 (inset 5) E. F. Anderson/Visuals Unlimited; 16 (inset 6) S Lowry/Univ. Ulster/Stone; 16 (inset 7) G. Shih-R. Kessel/Visuals Unlimited; 18 Richard Shiell/Dembinsky Photo Associates; 20 Dennis O'Clair/Stone; 22 Gloria H. Chomica/Masterfile; 23 Shin Yoshino/ Minden Pictures; 24 Mike Powell/Allsport USA; 26 Jeff Foott/Bruce Coleman, Inc.; 27 John Warden/Stone; 30 Stephen J. Krasemann/DRK; 32 Todd Warshaw/Allsport USA; 36 Steve Kaufman/DRK; 38 Al Bello/Allsport Photography; 44 Julia Patriarche/ www.chalkdust.net; 46 Rod Planck/Dembinsky Photo Associates; 48 Julia Patriarche/www. chalkdust.net; 49 Duomo Photography; 53 Index Stock Photography; 55 Duomo Photography; 56 Index Stock Photography; 61 Superstock; 65A-65B Tom Till/Tom Till Photography; 65A Robert Essel/The Stock Market; 65B (t) Cosmo Condina/Stone; 65B (b) Barbara P. Williams/Bruce Coleman Collection; 66 S. Nielsen/Bruce Coleman, Inc.; 68 Carl Roessler/ Bruce Coleman, Inc.; 72 R. Andrew Odum/Peter Arnold, Inc.; 74 Mark J. Thomas/Dembinsky Photo Associates; 75 John Giustina/FPG International; 76 Ken Scott/Dembinsky Photo Associates; 78 Robert E. Daemmrich/Stone; 80 Bill Losh/FPG International; 81 Peter Gridley/FPG International; 84 (inset) Domino arrangement organized by: Scott Suko/Event organized by: EXPO Children's Museum; Gainesville, FL; 84 Henry Blackham/The Stock Market; 86 Photo courtesy of Ralf Laue; 92 AP Photo/Wide World; 97 E.R. Degginger/Dembinsky Photo Associates; 100 Todd Warshaw/Allsport; 106 (b) The Granger Collection; 106 (tl) Corbis; 110 Richard M. Smith/FPG International; 111 Duomo Photography; 114,115 (t) Ron Kimball; 115 (b) Frank Hecker/OKAPIA/Photo Researchers; 118 Stocktrek Corp/The Stock Market; 120 Gerry Ellis/Minden Pictures; 121 Konrad Wothe/Minden Pictures; 122 Tom McHugh/Steinhart Aquarium/Photo Researchers; 123 Robert Torrez/ Stone; 126 Dean Conger/Corbis; 128 Jimmy Rudnick/The Stock Market; 129 Chie Nishio/Omni-Photo Communications; 130 Rafael Macia/ Photo Researchers; 131 Ken Cole/Animals Animals; 137 John K. Gates/Glimpses by Gates; 145A (t) Ty Smedes Nature Photography; 145A (b) Tom Bean Photography; 145B (l) Robert Holmes/Corbis; 145B (r) Marc Muench/Corbis; 146 David Nunuk/Science Photo Library/Photo Researchers; 146 (inset) Stephen Agricola/Stock, Boston; 148 NASA; 150 Art Wolfe/Photo Researchers; 151 David Madison/Bruce Coleman, Inc.; 152 Duomo Photography; 153 Anup Shah/Animals Animals; 154 Richard J. Wainscoat/Peter Arnold, Inc.; 155 Monkmeyer/Rogers; 156 Michael Hubrich/Photo Researchers, Inc.; 157 Spencer Jones/FPG International; 160 Robert A. Tyrrell Photography; 164 M. Lammertink; 166 Robert A. Tyrrell Photography; 167 Rod Planck/Photo Researchers; 168 (fg) E. R. Degginger/Dembinsky Photo Associates; 169 John Mitchell/Photo Researchers; 172 Hans Pfletschinger/Peter Arnold, Inc.; 173 Runk/Schoenberger/Grant Heilman Photography; 182 (c) Rob Tringali Jr./SportsChrome; 183A (t) John Elk III; 183A-183B (both) Randall Hyman; 183B William Iseminger/Cahokia Mounds State Historic Site; 184 Suzanne Murphy-Larronde/Picture Quest; 186 ITAR-TASS/Sovfoto; 187 Philip James (University of Toledo), Steven Lee (University of Colorado) NASA; 188 NASA; 189 NASA; 191 Kazoobie, Inc.; 192 Archive Photos; 193 Ron Scherl/StageImage; 195 (t) Archive Photos; 195 (b) The Granger Collection, New York; 197 Gemma Dickmann; 198 Ed Bock/The Stock Market; 199 Tony Freeman/PhotoEdit; 202 Damian Strohmeyer/Sports Illustrated; 206 (br) Hulton Getty/Liaison International; 207 (c) Corbis; 208 Herb Scharfman/Sports Illustrated/Time; 210 APA/Archive Photos; 212 Associated Press/Wide World Photos; 213 Frank Atura/Asolo Theatre Company; 214 John Cancalosi/DRK; 215 AFP/Corbis; 216 Steinouer Photography; 217 Claudia Parks/ The Stock Market; 220 Wolfgang Kaehler Photography; 222 Tom & Dee Ann McCarthy/The Stock Market; 226 Jay Syverson/CORBIS; 227 Tony Freeman/PhotoEdit; 229 Jose L. Pelaez/The Stock Market; 230 Latent Image Photography; 231 Mark E. Gibson Photograohy; 232 Tony Freeman/PhotoEdit; 233 Mark E. Gibson Photography; 242 Foodpix; 246 Wesley Bocxe/Photo Researchers; 247 Sovfoto/Eastfoto; 251 Index Stock Photography; 255A (t) James M. Mejuto Photography; 255A (b) E.R.Degginger/Color-Pic, Inc.; 255A-255B Joseph Sohm/Corbis; 255B Gail Mooney/Corbis; 256 David Cavagnaro; 258 Bill Aron/Photo Researchers; 265 The Granger Collection, New York; 270 AP Wirephoto/Wide World Photos; 272 Biophoto Associates/Photo Researchers; 274 A. B. Dowsett/Science Photo Library/Photo Researchers; 279 Wolfgang Kaehler Photography; 282 Rosenfeld Images Ltd./Science Photo Library/ Photo Researchers; 286 Myreen Ferguson/PhotoEdit; 301 D. Young-Wolff/PhotoEdit; 305 Hank Morgan/Rainbow/ Picture Quest; 309A-309B W. Metzen/H. Armstrong Roberts, Inc.; 309B (inset) Fred J. Eckert/Eckert Images; 309B Bob Krist/Corbis; 312 Duomo Photography; 313 David Madison; 318 Paul Harris/Stone; 321 S. Nielsen/Bruce Coleman, Inc.; 326 Dave G. Houser/Corbis; 330 Nigel Francis/the Stock Market; 330 (inset) Brian Brake/Photo Researhers; 332 Central Florida Council Boy Scouts of America; 334 (l) Federal Clipart/One Mile Up, Inc.; 334 (r) Federal Clipart/One Mile Up, Inc.; 335 Index Stock Photography; 336 Robert Holmes/Corbis; 337 Mark Greenberg/FPG International; 340 Grant Heilman, Inc.; 342 Scott Barrow, Inc.; 346 Kevin R. Morris/Stone; 350 Ron Scherl/StageImage; 351 Myrleen Ferguson/PhotoEdit; 352 Larry Lefever/Grant Heilman Photography; 353 Carlyn Iverson/Photo Researchers; 360 Larry Evans/Black Star/Harcourt; 364 Tony Freeman/PhotoEdit; 367 Tui De Roy/Bruce Coleman, Inc.; 368 E.R. Degginger/Photo Researchers; 371 Konrad Wothe/Minden Pictures; 372 Marty Snyderman/Waterhouse Stock Photo; 373 F. Stuart Westmorland/Photo Researchers; 377 Index Stock Photography; 381A Jodi Jacobson; 381A-381B Jodi Jacobson; 381B (inset) Jodi Jacobson; 382 Michael Zito/ SportsChrome; 384 Mark J. Thomas/Dembinsky Photo Associates; 387 Johnny Johnson/Animals Animals; 388 Julep Gillman-Bryan, N.C. Division of Archives and History; 389 Karen Kasmauski/Woodfin Camp & Associates; 390 David Cannon/Allsport Photography; 392 Steve Hix/FPG International; 396 Danielle Hayes/Bruce Coleman, Inc.; 398 WORLDSAT International, Inc./Photo Researchers; 399 Lynette Cook/Science Photo Library/Photo Researchers; 404 Lance Nelson/The Stock Market; 408 Hazel & Douglas Wolfe; 412 NASA; 416 Index Stock Imagery; 420 Paraskevas Photography; 420 (inset 1) Alan Schein/The Stock Market; 420 (inset 2) Bob Daemmrich/Stock, Boston; 420 (inset 3) Aneal Vohra/unicorn Stock Photos; 420 (inset 4) Bill Gallery/Stock, Boston; 420 (inset 5) Alan Schein/The Stock Market; 420 (inset 6) Shaun van Steyn/Pictor; 422 J. Messerschmidt/Bruce Coleman, Inc.; 428 L. West/Bruce Coleman, Inc.; 430 (l) Steve Solum/Bruce Coleman, Inc.; 430 (cl) Ken Straiton/The Stock Market; 430 (cr) Jeff Greenberg/PhotoEdit; 430 (r) Alan Schein/The Stock Market; 432 (t) Reuters/HO/Archive Photos; 433 AFP/Corbis; 436 (bg) Richard Dunoff/The Stock Market; 438 Mark Scott/FPG International; 444 Layne Kennedy; 446 Reuters Newsmedia, Inc./Corbis; 449 SEF/Art Resource, NY; 450 Phil Degginger/Bruce Coleman, Inc.; 454 Bill Ross/Corbis; 455 (l) Rafael Macia/Photo Researchers; 455 (c) Fergus O'Brien/FPG International; 455 (r) Vito Palmisano/Panoramic Images; 456 James M. Mejuto; 457 The Granger Collection, NY; 460 (l) Will & Deni McIntyre/Photo Researchers; 460 (r) David Ball/The Stock Market; 469A (t) Kevin R. Morris/Corbis; 469A (b) Kevin R. Morris/Stone; 469B (t) William Strode/Woodfin Camp & Associates; 469B (b) T. Wiewandt/Visions of America; 470 Craig Tuttle/The Stock Market; 474 (c) E.R. Degginger/Bruce Coleman, Inc.; 479 Mark E. Gibson/Dembinsky Photo Associates; 480 Ostentoski & Zoda/Envision; 483 (cr) Barbara Reed/Animals Animals; 484 Bob Daemmrich/The Image Works; 487 Greg Ryan/Sally Beyer; 490 David Ball/The Stock Market; 492 Lee Balterman/FPG International; 500 Jamie Squire/Allsport; 504 Art Resource, New York; 511 John W. Bova/Photo Researchers; 514 Richard T. Nowitz; 529 Comstock; 533 Bill Foley/Bruce Coleman, Inc.; 537A Henry Diltz/Corbis; 537A-537B John Skowronski/Folio; 537B (l) Lynda Richardson/Corbis; 537B (b) Lelia Hendrea/Folio; 538 William R. Sallaz/Duomo Photography; 544 Allsport Photography (USA); 547 Robert Frerck/Woodfin Camp & Associates; 551 (l) Yann Arthus-Bertrand/Corbis; 551 (r) Ron Kimball; 554 Roy Corral/Stone; 560 (tl) Davies & Starr/Stone; 560 (tr) Bruce Coleman, Inc; 560 (bl) Kjell B. Sandved/Bruce Coleman, Inc.; 560 (br) Davies & Starr/Stone; 561 (t) Raymond A. Mendez/Animals Animals; 561 (b) J.C. Carton/Bruce Coleman, Inc.; 563 Richard Reid/Earth Scenes; 565 Jeff Greenberg/PhotoEdit; 568 Carolyn A. McKeone/Photo Researchers; 569 Ron Kimball; 573 Peter Skinner/Photo Researchers; 576 (inset) Doranne Jacobson/International Images; 595A Phillip James Corwin/Corbis; 595A-595B Rich Iwasaki/Stone; 595B Richard Kaylin/Stone; H0 Tom McHugh/Steinhart Aquarium/Photo Researchers; H1 (t) Scott Camazine/Photo Researchers.;

**All other photos by Harcourt Photographers:** Weronica Ankarorn, John Bateman, Victoria Bowen, Ken Kinzie, Ron Kunzman, Alan Maxwell, Sheri O'Neal, Quebecor Digital Imaging, Sonny Senser, Terry Sinclair.

**Chapter Opener Photography Credits by Chapter:** 1 Earth Imaging/Stone; 2 W. Metzen/H. Armstrong Roberts; 3 Zena Holloway/FPG/Getty Images; 4 S. Nielsen/Bruce Coleman, Inc.; 5 Todd Warshaw/Allsport; 6 Transparencies, Inc.; 7 Roger Ressmeyer/Corbis; (inset) Stephen Agricola/Stock, Boston; 8 Robert A. Tyrrell Photography; 9 Suzanne Murphy-Larronde/PictureQuest;10 Apopka Chief; 11 Harrison Shull/shullphoto.com; 12 AP Photo/Chuck Burton; 13 David Cavagnaro; 14 Stocktrek/Corbis; 15 Jeff Greenberg/Photo Edit; 16 Richard T. Nowitz/Corbis; 17 Harrison Shull/shullphoto.com; 18 Kevin R. Morris/Stone; 19 Michael Kevin Daly/Corbis; 20 Mark Richards/Photo Edit. Inc.; (inset) Harcourt; 21 Layne Kennedy Photography; 22 Michael Zito/SportsChrome; 23 Lance Nelson/The Stock Market; 24 502 Alese/MortPechter/The Stock Market; 25 David Forbert/SuperStock; 26 David Ball/The Stock Market; 27 Richard Nowitz; 28 William R. Sallaz/Duomo Photography; 29 Roy Corral/Stone; 30 Harcourt.

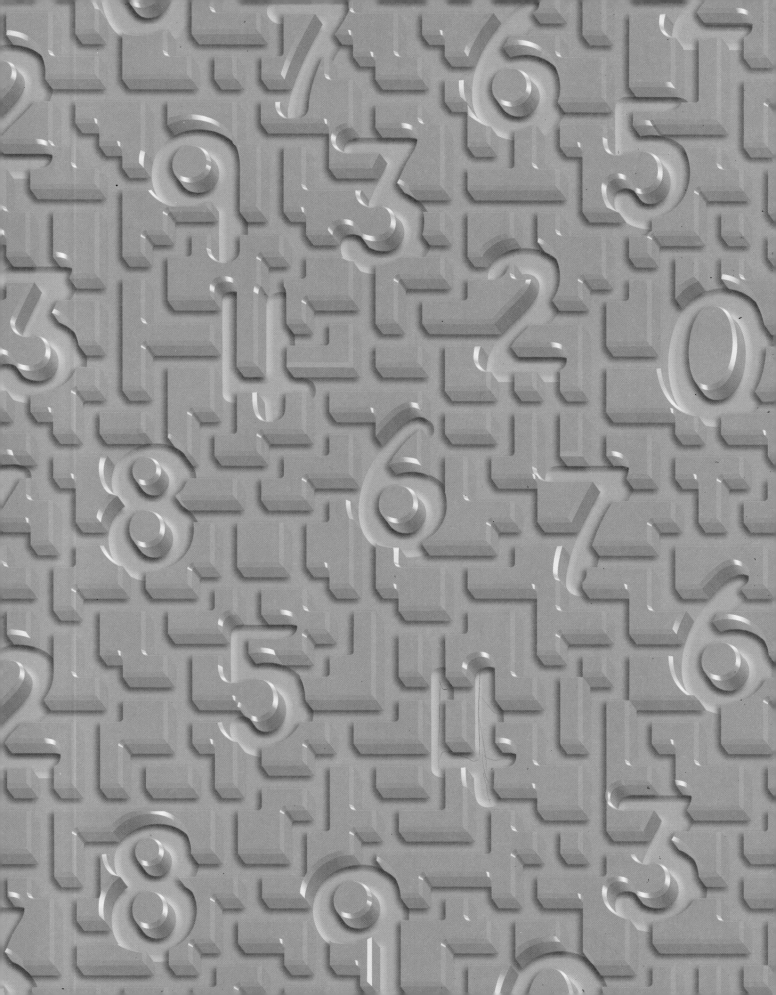